CONTENDING THEORIES OF INTERNATIONAL RELATIONS

Contending Theories of International Relations

A COMPREHENSIVE SURVEY

SECOND EDITION

James E. Dougherty
St. Joseph's University

Robert L. Pfaltzgraff, Jr.
Fletcher School of Law and Diplomacy, Tufts University

HARPER & ROW, PUBLISHERS, New York
Cambridge, Hagerstown, Philadelphia, San Francisco,
London, Mexico City, São Paulo, Sydney

1817

Sponsoring Editor: John L. Michel
Project Editor: Pamela Landau
Senior Production Manager: Kewal K. Sharma
Compositor: American Book–Stratford Press, Inc.

Art Studio: J & R Technical Services
Cover Art: Matthew Jaeger

CONTENDING THEORIES OF INTERNATIONAL RELATIONS:
A Comprehensive Survey
Second Edition

Library of Congress Cataloging in Publication Data

Dougherty, James E
  Contending theories of international relations.
  Includes index.
  1. International relations. I. Pfaltzgraff,
Robert L., joint author. II. Title.
JX1395.D67   1981   327.1′01   80-21038
ISBN 0-06-045215-3

Contents

6. ECONOMIC THEORIES OF IMPERIALISM AND WAR 213

7. MICROCOSMIC THEORIES OF VIOLENT CONFLICT 251

8. MACROCOSMIC THEORIES OF VIOLENT CONFLICT: REVOLUTION AND WAR 301

Preface

During the 1960s, while co-directing the graduate seminar in international relations theories at the University of Pennsylvania, we became aware that students usually felt overwhelmed by the great variety of theoretical approaches that have come to abound in our field. Convinced that at least a preliminary effort should be made to bring order out of confusion, we published *Contending Theories of International Relations* (Philadelphia: J. B. Lippincott, 1971). Instead of emphasizing any one major theoretical perspective, we strove to acquaint students with as broad a range of theories as possible—traditional and behavioral, normative and scientific, qualitative and quantitative. We were more than gratified by the reception given that book by teachers, undergraduate students, and graduate students trying valiantly to master numerous theories of international relations.

This present work is an outgrowth and thorough revision and updating of the earlier book. It reflects on the part of the two authors a total of more than forty years of graduate and undergraduate teaching in the field of international relations, as well as a comparable period of specialized research and writing, along with lectures at universities and research centers and active participation in conferences in the United States and abroad.

This volume represents a comprehensive and unique survey of international relations in which the principal theories (classical and contemporary, traditional and behavioral) are summarized and synthesized, and in which the authors attempt to provide critiques of the various theories as well as to suggest points of intersection whenever possible. We have attempted to examine a wide range of theories systematically and in depth.

About 10 percent of the first edition text has been eliminated or compressed in the present volume. The original version has been expanded by nearly 40 percent to insure adequate coverage of significant new developments in international relations theory since 1971. Among the new topics covered and subjects treated at greater length in this work are: efforts to predict the international future; theories of power, foreign policy, and international equilibrium; ecology and international relations; the controversy over the limits of world economic growth; the causes of war; deterrence and arms control; theories of decision-making; theoretical models for explaining crises and crisis management; integration and interdependence; and theories of imperialism, as well as revisionist theories of the Cold War and their critics. It is our hope that the more than 1400 notes, with bibliographical documentation, will provide valuable research tools.

Because intellectual fashions come and go in academe, we deem it important for students to become acquainted with theories past as well as those present. The analytical insights of penetrating minds in one era can be relevant in another. Thus, although we devote most of our attention to the theorizing of the past three decades (integration, conflict, arms control, man-milieu relationships, systems, decision-making, and games), we do not discard as obsolete the significant explanations of international phenomena of earlier times (such as balance of power, geopolitics, just war, and international organization and disarmament) that may have applicability to the contemporary world or that might have greater utility in the future.

We believe that the development of international relations theory requires an interdisciplinary approach, with inputs from several disciplines—political science, history, economics, geography, psychology, biology, anthropology, sociology, military strategy, communications theory, and other areas. (A half-century ago, A. E. Zimmern, a British pioneer in our field, observed that a student of international relations was one who wanted to know more about a great many different dimensions of human affairs.) We have sought to draw together the ideas of some of the leading figures and to tempt the student to explore some avenues into the rich literature of various academic disciplines which have much light to cast upon the phenomena of international relations. In surveying the various theories, we have attempted to show where different theoretical perspectives may touch, intersect, overlap, converge, and lend themselves to the possibility of theory-building at a higher or more complex (or perhaps simpler) level of synthesis. We are keenly aware that there are many theoretical problems awaiting solution. The field of international relations is a vast and complex one. Given the present state of theorizing, no single theoretical approach promises to provide the answers to problems of theory-building.

ACKNOWLEDGMENTS

The authors are indebted to the following scholars who meticulously read the entire manuscript of the present edition and submitted constructive criticisms along with very helpful comments: Linda Brady, the Department of State; William A. Coplin, Syracuse University; Morton A. Kaplan, University of Chicago; James N. Murray, University of Iowa; and Rudolf Rummel, University of Hawaii. Especially in our ongoing efforts to relate theories of international relations to the complex world of the late twentieth century, we have benefited from participation in the many programs of the Institute for Foreign Policy Analysis, Cambridge, Massachusetts, and Washington, D.C. In particular, these have included an ongoing series of conferences dealing with issues related to deterrence theory and the evolving United States–Soviet strategic-nuclear relationship, as well as problems, both in their theoretical and policy dimensions, related to the principal alliances of the United States and the nature of conflict in the contemporary world. Especially in the preparation of the first edition, more than a decade ago, the authors benefited from professional associations with Professors Emeritus of Political Science at the University of Pennsylvania, Norman D. Palmer and Robert Strausz-Hupé, and the late Hans Kohn of the City University of New York.

Dr. Dougherty has gained much from three European lecture tours, sponsored by the Department of State/U.S. Information Agency (later the International Communications Agency), which brought him into contact with embassy personnel, university scholars, and research centers in Britain, Belgium, Denmark, Norway, Sweden, Netherlands, and the Federal Republic of Germany, and from intensive exchanges with colleagues in a variety of organizational contexts: the International Studies Association; the International Arms Control Symposia held in Ann Arbor and Philadelphia; a dozen Strategy for Peace Conferences at Arden House and Airlie House; annual conferences of the Catholic Association for International Peace; meetings of the International Affairs Committee of the United States Catholic Conference; the Washington Consultations of the Council on Religion and International Affairs; and lectures and discussions at the National War College, the Air University, the Inter-American Defense College, and the Foreign Service Institute, Department of State. Specifically, among the many who have helped to influence his views are Professor William V. O'Brien of Georgetown University; Professor Paul Ramsey of Princeton University; Lt. General Edward L. Rowny (Ret.); Professor Hedley Bull; Jerome Spingarn, formerly of the U.S. Arms Control and Disarmament Agency; the late Thomas E. Murray who was once known as "the conscience of the Atomic Energy Commission"; the late John Courtney Murray, S.J., a magisterial pillar of Woodstock Theological College; the late Donald C. Brennan of the Hudson Institute; and the following friends and colleagues at Saint Joseph's University: Professors Lawrence J. Bell, David Burton, Elwyn Chase, Frank Gerrity, and Terrence Toland, S.J. (formerly President), as well as Edward J. Brady, S.J., now of Bread for the World.

Dr. Pfaltzgraff has received beneficial insights into problems of international relations theory from many colleagues in discussions held under the auspices of the International Security Studies Program, the Fletcher School of Law and Diplomacy; its many colloquia and annual conferences have provided an opportunity for the examination of numerous policy issues set in broader theoretical context. Together, the International Security Studies Program of the Fletcher School and the Institute for Foreign Policy Analysis have furnished a variety of occasions for an examination of issues drawing linkages between international relations theory—in particular conflict theory and strategy—and the international environment of the late twentieth century. Dr. Pfaltzgraff is especially indebted to the Fletcher School of Law and Diplomacy for the numerous opportunities that it has provided, both inside and outside the classroom, for the testing of theoretical approaches to international relations by reference to the real world of policy and diplomacy. He wishes to express special thanks to Dean Emeritus Edmund A. Gullion, and Dean Theodore C. Eliot, as well as to John P. Roche, Academic Dean, and Uri Ra'anan, Chairman of the International Security Studies Program.

Over the past decade Dr. Pfaltzgraff has been benefited by additional opportunities to assess the relationship between international relations theory and the practice of statecraft in a variety of intellectual forums, including those provided by: the Air Command and Staff College and the Air War College, Maxwell Air Force Base; the Air Force Academy; the American Political Science Association; the Cincinnati Council on World Affairs; Claremont Graduate School, Claremont College; the College of Europe (Bruges, Belgium); the Foreign Service Institute, Department of State; the Fourth, Fifth, and Sixth International Arms Control Symposia, Georgetown University; the Institute of International Relations in Today's World; the Institute of International Relations, University of South Carolina; the Institute for Sino-Soviet Studies, George Washington University; the Inter-American Defense College; the International Studies Association; the International Studies Institute, Westminster College; the Konrad-Adenauer Foundation; the National Defense University; the National Strategy Information Center; the Naval War College; the Pacific Forum; the Pittsburgh Council on World Affairs; Southwestern College, Memphis, Tennessee; the U.S. Army War College; the University of Alabama; and the Woodrow Wilson Department of Government and Foreign Affairs, University of Virginia. Furthermore, Dr. Pfaltzgraff has received numerous beneficial insights into international relations theory and its relationship to policy as a result of lectures presented under the auspices of the Department of State and the United States Information Agency (subsequently, the International Communications Agency) in Belgium, Brazil, Britain, Chile, Hong Kong, Japan, Republic of Korea, and Thailand.

Last but not least, the authors express thanks to Karol Kelliher, Stephanie Manganella, Deborah Moore, and Linda Smith for their secretarial assistance. Captain Edgar Kleckley of the Fletcher School of Law and Diplomacy, and Robert C. Herber and Dr. Clifford Kiracofe provided valuable help in the final stages of publication of the manuscript.

James E. Dougherty
Robert L. Pfaltzgraff, Jr.

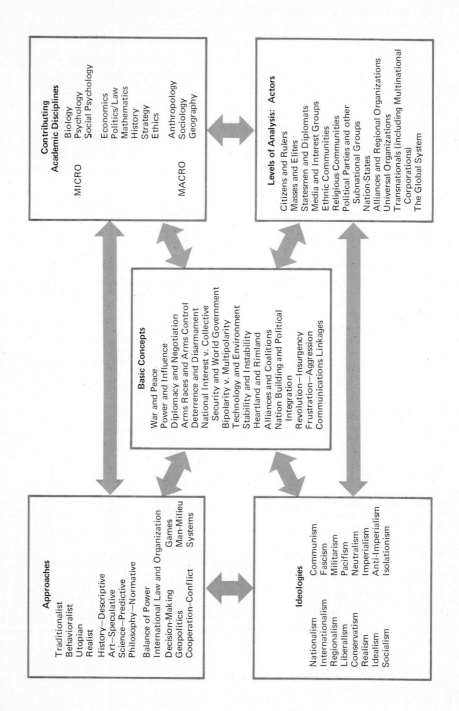

**Contributing
Academic Disciplines**

MICRO
Biology
Psychology
Social Psychology

Economics
Politics/Law
Mathematics
History
Strategy
Ethics

MACRO
Anthropology
Sociology
Geography

Levels of Analysis: Actors

Citizens and Rulers
Masses and Elites
Statesmen and Diplomats
Media and Interest Groups
Ethnic Communities
Religious Communities
Political Parties and other
  Subnational Groups
Nation-States
Alliances and Regional Organizations
Universal Organizations
Transnationals (including Multinational
  Corporations)
The Global System

Basic Concepts

War and Peace
Power and Influence
Diplomacy and Negotiation
Arms Races and Arms Control
Deterrence and Disarmament
National Interest v. Collective
  Security and World Government
Bipolarity v. Multipolarity
Technology and Environment
Stability and Instability
Heartland and Rimland
Alliances and Coalitions
Nation Building and Political
  Integration
Revolution—Insurgency
Frustration—Aggression
Communications Linkages

Approaches

Traditionalist
Behavioralist
Utopian
Realist
History—Descriptive
Art—Speculative
Science—Predictive
Philosophy—Normative

Balance of Power
International Law and Organization
Decision-Making
Geopolitics
Cooperation—Conflict

Games
Man-Milieu
Systems

Ideologies

Nationalism
Internationalism
Regionalism
Liberalism
Conservatism
Realism
Idealism
Socialism

Communism
Fascism
Militarism
Pacifism
Neutralism
Imperialism
Anti-Imperialism
Isolationism

Chapter 1
Theoretical Approaches to
International Relations

Most political scientists and other students of international relations realize that their subject areas are appallingly vast and complex. They are aware also that despite the many nostrums advertised for the world's ills, it is no less difficult to find a permanent solution for conflict and war than a cure for cancer. Understanding either the biological-psychological processes of the human being or the political processes of the international system—in such a way as to control them for rational ends—profoundly challenges humanity's intellect. Yet only through profound understanding can a theory for purposeful action arise. Throughout centuries, and with greater urgency certainly in modern times, people have tried to make sense of the shifting relationships of larger social groupings on the world scene. By surveying the theories that have been advanced, any reader—whether student, policymaker, journalist, or casual observer—may improve his or her understanding of international relations. This book, therefore, is designed to trace for the reader the development of international relations as a field of systematic study as well as to provide an understanding of the many themes that the field has produced.

EARLY APPROACHES TO
INTERNATIONAL RELATIONS THEORY

Efforts at theorizing about the nature of interstate relations are quite old; some in fact go back to ancient times in India, China, and Greece. Although Plato's and Aristotle's reflections on the subject are quite sketchy, the ancient Greek historian Thucydides' *History of the Peloponnesian War* is a classic treatise any student of international relations can still read profitably.[1] Machiavelli's *The Prince*, a harbinger of modern analysis of power and the state system, emphasized a "value-free" science of foreign policymaking and statecraft.[2] Dante's *De Monarchia* became one of the first and most powerful appeals in Western political literature for an international organization capable of enforcing the peace.[3] Other early proponents of a confederation or league of nation-states were Pierre Dubois (French lawyer and political pamphleteer of the late fourteenth and early fifteenth centuries), Emeric Crucé (French monk of the late sixteenth and early seventeenth centuries), the Duc de Sully (minister of France's Henry IV), William Penn, Abbé de Saint Pierre (French publicist and theoretical reformer of the late seventeenth and early eighteenth centuries), Jean-Jacques Rousseau, Jeremy Bentham, and Immanuel Kant.[4]

Yet despite these classical writings no systematic development, comparable to that in internal political theories of the state, occurred in international theory before World War I. Martin Wight has noted that if by "international theory" we mean a "tradition of speculation about relations between states, a tradition imagined as the twin of speculation about the State to which the name 'political theory' is appropriated," it does not exist.[5] Wight suggests that a reason for this situation is that since Grotius (1538–1645), the Dutch jurist and statesman, and Pufendorf (1632–1694), the German jurist and historian, nearly all speculation about the international community fell under the heading of international law. He notes that most writing on interstate relations before this century was contained in the political literature of the peace writers cited above, buried in the works of historians, cloistered in the peripheral reflections of philosophers, or harbored in speeches, despatches, and memoirs of statesmen and diplomats. Wight concludes that in the classical political tradition "international theory, or what there is of it, is scattered, unsystematic, and mostly inaccessible to the layman," as well as being "largely repellent and intractable in form."[6] The only theory which did infuse the thinking of the period—and it was a theory somewhat dearer to practicing diplomats than to academicians—was that of the balance of power. Indeed, it was a collection of what seemed to be common sense axioms rather than a rigorous theory.

The period of European history from 1648 to 1914 was the golden age of diplomacy, the balance of power, alliances, and international law. Nearly all political thought focused on the sovereign nation-state—the origins, functions, and limitations of governmental powers, the rights of individuals within the state, the requirements of order, the imperatives of national self-determination and independence. The economic order was presumed simplistically to be separate from the political. Governments were expected to promote and protect trade, but not to regulate it. Various branches of socialist thought sought to strike out in new directions, but socialists, despite their professed internationalism, did not really produce a coherent international theory. They advanced a theory of imperialism borrowed largely from John A. Hobson (1858–1940), the British economist, and thus derivative from an economic theory indigenous to the capitalist states.[7] Until 1914, international theorists almost uniformly assumed that the structure of international society was unalterable, and that the division of the world into sovereign states was necessary and natural.[8] The study of international relations consisted almost entirely of diplomatic history and international law, rather than of investigation into the processes of the international system.

MODERN APPROACHES TO INTERNATIONAL RELATIONS THEORY

Some impetus to the serious study of international relations in this country came when the United States emerged as a world power. But ambiguities in American foreign policy, combined with the trend toward isolationism during the 1920s and 1930s, hindered the development of international relations as an intellectual discipline. A dichotomy developed between intellectual idealists, who shared Woodrow Wilson's vision of the League of Nations, and politicians who, feeling pressures for a "return to normalcy," blocked United States entry into the world organization. Americans demanded a moral and peaceful world order, but they were unwilling to pay the price. This dichotomy between noble impulses and tendencies toward isolationism was clearly reflected in the Kellogg-Briand Treaty of 1928, which "outlawed" war by moralistic declaration but provided no adequate means of enforcement.[9]

For a decade or more after Versailles, the two most popular approaches to teaching world affairs in American universities included courses in current events and courses in international law and organization. Current events courses were designed more to promote international understanding than to apply social science methodologies to good advantage. Courses in international law emphasized discrepancies between the formal obligations of states (especially League members) and their actual conduct in an era of struggle between powers anxious to preserve the international status quo and those determined to overturn it.[10]

An awareness that the study of international relations must go beyond the study of international law and organization was evident in the writings of scholars in England and the United States during the 1930s. Although Brierly, Eagleton, Fenwick, Hill, Lauterpacht, Moore, Oppenheim, and Potter[11] emphasized an approach to international relations based on law and organization and drew upon legal case materials and international administrative experience, many other writers looked beyond the field of law for more dynamic, comprehensive explanations of forces and events in interstate relations.

After World War I, leading diplomatic historians on both sides of the Atlantic searched for the "causes" or "origins" of the great conflict.[12] Hayes, Kohn, and other historians explored the emotional-ideological content of nationalism, regarded by many as the most potent political force in the modern world despite the advent of universalist ideologies.[13] Specialized writings appeared in a number of areas: on the problems of security, war, and disarmament—Baker, Shotwell, and Wheeler-Bennett;[14] on imperialism—Moon and Priestley;[15] on diplomacy and negotiation—Nicolson;[16] on the balance of power—Friedrich and Vagts;[17] on the geographical aspects of world power (building on the work of Alfred Thayer Mahan and Sir Halford Mackinder)—Fairgrieve and Spykman;[18] on the history of international relations theories—Russell;[19] on economic factors in warfare, the strategic significance of raw materials, and the role of economics in international relations—Angell, Simonds, Emeny, Robbins, Einzig, and Staley.[20] During the interwar period, several textbooks on international relations, in describing the "states system" (as it was then called), tried to bring a knowledge of political, historical, economic, demographic, geographic, and strategic factors to bear upon the effort to understand the actual evolution of foreign policies among the Great Powers. Other important sources of this era include *Foreign Affairs* (the distinguished quarterly journal of the Council on Foreign Relations), *International Conciliation* (published monthly by the Carnegie Endowment for International Peace), the fortnightly *Foreign Policy Reports* (published by the Foreign Policy Association), and the *American Journal of International Law*. A number of partial theories were in the process of being developed, several of which would become elements of more comprehensive efforts toward a synthesis in subsequent decades.

E. H. Carr and the Crisis of World Politics

By the 1930s there was a growing recognition among international relations teachers of the gap between the "utopians" and the "realists." The academic climate after World War I made it conducive for "utopians" and "realists" to concern themselves with the means of preventing another war. Consequently, this task spurred the serious study of international relations. No scholar in that period more trenchantly analyzed the philosophical differences between "utopians" and "realists" than Edward Hallett Carr in his celebrated work,[21] which, although published in 1939, did not have its impact in America until after World War II. Most of the following comparative analysis draws heavily from that work.

Carr saw the utopians, for the most part, as intellectual descendants of eighteenth-century Enlightenment optimism, nineteenth-century liberalism, and twentieth-century Wilsonian idealism. Utopianism is closely associated with a distinctly Anglo-American tendency to assume that statesmen enjoy broad freedom of choice in the making of foreign policy.[22] Marred by a certain self-righteousness, the utopians clung to the belief that the United States had entered World War I as a disinterested, even reluctant, champion of international morality. Emphasizing how people ought to behave in their international relationships rather than how they actually behave, the American Utopians disdained balance of power politics (historically identified with Europe), national armaments, the use of force in international affairs, and the secret treaties of alliance that preceded World War I. Instead, they stressed international legal rights and obligations, the natural harmony of national interests—reminiscent of Adam Smith's "invisible hand"[23]—as a regulator for the preservation of international peace, a heavy reliance upon reason in human affairs, and confidence in the peace-building function of the "world court of public opinion." (The utopians, of course, might argue that the balance of power itself corresponded to the "unseen hand" that had been discredited in their view.)

Realists, on the other hand, stressed power and interest, rather than ideals in international relations. Realism is basically conservative, empirical, prudent, suspicious of idealistic principles, and respectful of the lessons of history. It is more likely to produce a pessimistic rather than an optimistic view of international politics. Realists regarded power as the fundamental concept in the social sciences (such as energy in physics), although they admitted that power relationships are often cloaked in moral and legal terms. Realists viewed theories as rationalizing, rather than shaping, events. They criticized the utopian for preferring visionary goals to scientific analysis.

To the realist, appeals to reason and to public opinion had proven woefully weak supports for keeping the peace in the 1930s; for example, they did not save Manchuria and Ethiopia from aggression. Thus, although the idealist hoped for change that might permit disarmament, the realist continued to worry about national security and the need for military force to support diplomacy.

The argument pitting utopianism and realism is classic. Carr's analysis of this dialectic is still timely: "The inner meaning of the modern international crisis," he contended, "is the collapse of the whole structure of utopianism based on the concept of the harmony of interests."[24] In his view, the international morality of the interwar years merely justified the interests of the dominant English-speaking status quo powers, of the satisfied versus the unsatisfied, of the "haves" versus the "have-nots." Carr, a pragmatist, took utopians *and* realists to task. He saw that whereas the utopians ignore the lessons of history, the realists often read history too pessimistically. Whereas the idealist exaggerates freedom of choice, the realist exaggerates fixed causality and slips into determinism. While the idealist may confuse national self-interest with universal moral principles, the realist runs the risk of cynicism and "fails to provide any ground for purposive and meaningful action"[25]—that is, the realist denies that human thought modifies human action. Purpose precedes observation; the vision of a Plato comes before the analysis of an Aristotle. The vision may even seem totally unrealistic. Carr cites the alchemists who tried to turn lead into gold, noting that when their visionary project failed they began examining "facts" more carefully, thus giving birth to modern science.[26] He concludes that sound political theories contain elements of utopianism and realism, of power as well as moral values.[27]

Interstate Relations and the Political Order

During the 1930s, academicians on both sides of the Atlantic tried to come to grips with the nature and scope of international relations as a field of study within the university. In 1935, Sir Alfred Zimmern, professor of international relations at Oxford University, suggested that "the study of international relations extends from the natural sciences at one end to moral philosophy . . . at the other." He defined the field not as a single subject or discipline but as a "bundle of subjects . . . viewed from a common angle."[28]

Debate on scope, emphasis, and methodology in the discipline of international relations reached a point of intensity before World War II and continues today. Nicholas J. Spykman, among the first to propose a rigorous definition, used the term *interstate relations*, which, however, he did not expect would gain wide acceptance: "International relations are relations between individuals belonging to different states, . . . international behavior is the social behavior of individuals or groups aimed at, . . . or influenced by the existence or behavior of individuals or groups belonging to a different state."[29] Loosely defined, the term *international relations* could encompass many different activities—international communications, business transactions, athletic contests, tourism, scientific conferences, educational exchange programs, and religious missionary activities. The political scientist is interested in such phenomena as world's fairs, Telstar, the Olympic Games, multinational corporations, fluctuations in the pattern of Japan's foreign trade, or the Vatican's relations with Israel and the Arab states—insofar as these have implications for international political relations. The political scientist, as such, cannot learn much from the facts surrounding a single transnational telegram, a periodical subscription, a wedding, or a real estate purchase. Yet significant increases or decreases of these items in the aggregate might have potential political meaning, just as the conclusion of agreements for an international motion picture distribution, a television rerun, a professor and student exchange program, and oceanic ecology might have. Because the policies of governments are so important in all areas of international relations, political scientists generally regard their field as central to international relations. In fact, the study of international relations in a typical American university has usually been organized within the department of political science.[30] Thus a definition of international relations depends on a definition of politics.

One of the most frequently cited of the modern definitions, that of David Easton—that politics is the process whereby societal values are authoritatively allocated[31]—is too limited for our usage. It presupposes the organization of a society under an effective authority for the allocation of values, and hence cannot encompass international politics because there is no effective authority at this level. Political activity aims at policymaking on group goals, procedures, and leadership. The values and interests of the groups shape both the ends and means of politics. As Morton A. Kaplan has suggested, "Politics is the regulation of the system. It involves action manifesting capabilities or 'power'; it may involve restructuring the relationship of the roles in the system or creating or eliminating roles; and it also allocates goods or values."[32] Power is merely a capability of attaining ends, although power may at times become an end in itself. This holds internally, within nations, and externally, in the world at large. However, we must not lose sight of the crucial structural difference between national societies, in which the historical tendency has been toward the centralization of power and values, and international society, in which power and values are decentralized.[33]

Post-World War II Realism

Not surprisingly World War II and its immediate aftermath shifted Western thinking on international relations further away from the idealism of the early League of Nations period toward an older and resurgent realism, from law and organization to the elements of power. There seems to be at least a partial vindication of the Hegelian dialectic (in which history is seen to develop through the clash of opposites) in the fact that war increases people's desire for peace. But when millions engage in military conflict on the scale of World War II, when entire politico-socioeconomic systems of modern nation-states are geared for total war, and when war aims impel scientists and engineers to create new weapons by researching the fundamental mysteries of matter, the postwar generation is likely to regard international politics more than ever as a power struggle. Even idealistically inclined analysts—and there were many who had supported the war effort for reasons of the highest moral idealism—become skeptical of utopian programs and call instead for a merger of international law and organization with effective power to insure international peace, the security of nations, and the equitable settlement of disputes.

Throughout the post-World War II period, the United States' global responsibilities generated within American universities a heightened interest in the study of international relations. War veterans in college showed a keen concern over "foreign affairs." Under the impact of critical international developments, the United States government greatly expanded its operations in the areas of national military security, alliances, and other international organizations, and economic development assistance to foreign countries. All of these operations, of course, increased the need for trained personnel. For the first time, many American businesses became aware of international trade and investment possibilities. Scientists, alarmed at the implications of the new nuclear technology that they had just produced, entered politics as crusading novices, warning of dangers confronting humanity. Civic-minded persons zealously organized councils and associations to educate and exhort in order to make citizens aware of international problems.

Academic scholars in Britain and the United States, the two countries in which the universities had shown most progress in the interwar development of international relations, produced analyses suitable to the postwar reality. Several works published in the late 1940s emphasized the power approach to the study of international relations. One of the more frequently quoted English authors was Martin Wight, who noted that

> What distinguishes modern history from medieval history is the predominance of the idea of power over the idea of right; the very term 'Power' to describe a state in its international aspect is significant; and the view of the man in the street, who is perhaps inclined to take it for granted that foreign politics are inevitably 'power politics,' is not without a shrewd insight.[34]

Another English scholar, Georg Schwarzenberger, analyzed power as a prime factor in international politics. In the absence of genuine international community, he asserted, groups within the international system can be expected to do what they are physically able to do rather than what they are morally exhorted to do. Power, in Schwarzenberger's view, is by no means a wanton, destructive thing. It is a combination of persuasive influence and coercive force, but those who wield power, while maintaining and exhibiting an ability to impose their wills on the noncompliant, normally prefer to achieve their ends merely by posing the threat of effective sanctions, without actually resorting to physical force. Most contemporary political scientists and students of international relations continue to distinguish between power and influence, and to regard power as a type of causation.[35]

To say that international politics is predicated on the concept of power does not necessarily imply the simplistic cynicism that individuals and groups are constantly seeking to maximize their power; that all states are potentially aggressive and expansionist; that the nature of international politics is always "red in tooth and claw." Building up power does not necessarily imply even intending to apply pressure against other states. The pursuit of political power is balanced against other drives of an economic, psychological, social, and cultural nature. People's efforts to attain these nonpolitical wants often impose limits on their ability to pursue political power beyond their national boundaries.[36] Several states use the greater part of their power for self-development and improvement in the quality of their social and cultural life. Some of the lesser states located near larger states focus on power in an inverted manner, seeking security through noninvolvement, isolation, neutrality, appeasement, or the acceptance of a dependent buffer or satellite status.

Even the "Great Powers," who historically have set the competitive tone of international politics, are not perpetually at each other's throats. The history of interstate relations is one of conflict *and* cooperation. The peace among larger rivals may be tense and precarious at times, but rivals may experience periods of relative peace during which their tacit cooperation, although less visible, may be more significant than their public contentiousness. Nevertheless, Great Powers in modern history have either resorted to force or at least threatened the use of force to defend or advance what they considered their basic interests against other states. Perhaps the most fundamental fact of the international system is that both power and values are still decentralized. Certainly an international system—that is, a complex set of variables in interaction—does exist. But it is a society of national political communities and of nonstate actors that try to exert power and to produce effects upon each other. There is, as yet, no international community in which political values are shared sufficiently on a global scale to facilitate the emergence of an orderly set of behavioral expectations with respect to regulation, cooperative relations, adjudication of conflict relations, and the control or elimination of violence.

THE EARLIER TEXTBOOKS AND INTERNATIONAL THEORY

The textbooks in international relations published during the first two decades after World War II generally recognized "power" as a central concept in the field. The text that had the greatest impact on the university teaching of international relations—that of Hans J. Morgenthau—explained nation-state behavior on the basis of national interest (defined in terms of power) as the normal objective pursued by governments when possible.[37] The other important textbooks of that period all devoted on the average at least three chapters to the nature of power and the elements or factors of national power.[38] Typically they provided chapters on subjects that had received attention prior to World War II—international law and morality, international organization and the peaceful settlement of disputes, diplomacy, and the conduct of foreign relations. Most of them also described and analyzed nationalism, imperialism, colonialism, the emergence of the Third World, ideology and propaganda, and the impact of economic and technological factors upon international relations. Some contained chapters on alliances, regional or functional integration, disarmament and arms control, and such specific techniques of foreign policy as intervention, nonalignment, and isolation. Seldom was there an effort to draw precise linkages between the theories examined in one chapter and those examined in another, or to find out whether partial theories could be fitted together into a larger, coherent whole.[39] This is not to suggest that the authors necessarily lacked their own informing theory that might be reconstructed through careful analysis of their writing. But they did not present generalized theory in a systematic manner. Indeed, several of them were probably suspicious of single, overarching theories.

THE DEVELOPMENT OF INTERNATIONAL RELATIONS THEORY

Throughout the period since the late 1940s, there has been a steady development of methodologies and techniques for research, analysis, and teaching in international relations, which have contributed to the growth of theory.[40] Government-supported "think tanks" such as the RAND Corporation, a dozen or so university-centered research institutes, and numerous private organizations, foundations, and conferences, as well as the professional associations, have produced significant effects on trends of thought in the field. The effort toward comprehensive theory-building began with the "Great Debate" between realists and idealists (to be treated in Chapter 3). Originally, most of the members of both of these schools were what we now call *traditionalists*. Those who were interested in rejecting the premises of traditional international politics led the way in the development of behavioral/quantitative methodologies, but they were soon joined by some realists who wished to show that the basic assumptions of a state system founded on the distribution and assessment of power could not be easily set aside.

The early 1960s witnessed a considerable expansion of interest in theoretical analysis,[41] especially in inductive and deductive theory and its validation by means of such methodologies as content analysis and bivariate and multivariate correlations. Insights from the biological, psychological, anthropological, sociological, economic, and other behavioral sciences were borrowed in the effort to explain international politics. There was an emphasis on abstract model-building, as well as a variety of new approaches to the understanding of ecological factors and the individual milieu relationships, regional integration, interaction in the international system, the causes of war, the conditions for deterrence, arms races and arms control, decision-making, games theory and related subjects in foreign policy and international relations. The results of these efforts have been published in numerous books and articles which have appeared in the specialized periodicals of the field—*World Politics, International Organization, International Studies Quarterly, Foreign Policy, The Journal of Conflict Resolution, Orbis, International Security*—as well as in the more general journals in political science and related areas. Much of this literature will be surveyed in the following chapters.

During the past two decades, courses and seminars in international theory have become common in university programs at both graduate and undergraduate levels. Some concentrate on a single favorite theoretical approach or on only a few theories; others are more comprehensive. The authors of this text are convinced that, no matter how esthetically or intellectually satisfying a neat, logically unified theoretical system might be, none at present can adequately explain international reality in all its complexity. The theoretical analyst who makes a significant contribution to the field must choose a coherent intellectual framework within which to work on a specific problem. But there is a remarkable variety of paradigms (or sets of theoretical assumptions) available. Different approaches may be required to account for different types and levels of behavior.[42] The student who wishes to avoid prematurely selecting a single theoretical approach confronts a bewildering amount of material.

THE NATURE, SCOPE, AND FUNCTION OF INTERNATIONAL THEORY

A theory is an intellectual tool that helps us to orient and organize our knowledge, to ask significant questions, and to guide the formulation of priorities in and the design of research; it enables us to apply the methods of scientific inquiry in an orderly way; as it becomes more comprehensive, it enables us to relate knowledge in our own field to that of other fields; and thus it enhances our ability to understand and explain reality in a satisfying way.

Before we can proceed, however, we must have some idea of what the field covers and where its boundaries lie. If any consensus can be said to exist among international relations scholars, it is vague rather than precise. Textbooks and other significant works published over a few decades furnish us with a flexible perspective and thus prevent us from accepting too hastily a neatly phrased, yet intellectually confining, definition. Frederick S. Dunn once warned that the word *scope* is dangerously ambiguous because it implies clearly discernible boundaries as readily identifiable as a surveyor's mark.

> A field of knowledge does not possess a fixed extension in space but is a constantly changing focus of data and methods that happen at the moment to be useful in answering an identifiable set of questions. It presents at any given time different aspects to different observers, depending on their point of view and purpose. The boundaries that supposedly divide one field of knowledge from another are not fixed walls between separate cells of truth but are convenient devices for arranging known facts and methods in manageable segments for instruction and practice. But the foci of interest are constantly shifting and these divisions tend to change with them . . .[43]

• *What Are We Studying?* Although international relations scholars cannot at present agree on what is included in and excluded from the field, students ought to be satisfied in their own minds regarding the phenomena they are investigating. Dunn says that international relations "may be looked upon as the actual relations that take place across national boundaries, or as the body of knowledge which we have of those relations at any given time."[44] This is a fairly standard approach, but is it adequate? It is comprehensive. It does not limit the subject to official relations between states and governments. But returning to a previously raised question, is this delineation too broad, and would it be better to include transnational relations on the basis of their political significance, for example, by focusing upon the influences relationships have among the world's political units? We define international politics as the effort of one state, or other international actor, to influence another state, or other international actor, in some way. An influence relationship may encompass the actual, or threatened, use of military force, or it may be based entirely, or partly, on other inducements. International politics, moreover, like all politics, is the reconciliation of varying perspectives, goals, and interests. Thus international politics includes many but not necessarily all of the transactions or interactions that take place across national frontiers.

When we speak of international relations, we focus upon relations between officially constituted decision-makers, or governments, as well as those at an unofficial, transnational level. Whether the latter are the object of study as international politics, as contrasted with international relations, depends upon the extent to which they in fact represent efforts to influence the official decision-makers for some purpose. In addition to "relations across national boundaries," other phenomena can come within the bounds of international relations, because there are linkages between domestic politics and foreign policy.[45] Thus a transnational relationship may so affect the domestic politics of a state that its official decision-makers are in turn influenced in their foreign policy decisions.

• *What Are the Units of Study? What Is Our Level of Analysis?* At first glance, this seems easy to answer, but it becomes more difficult as we proceed. Even after answering the earlier question concerning the scope of the field in a manner calculated to gather the economic, cultural, and other extrapolitical relations of states, governments, and peoples, one often has a tendency when thinking about "units" and "levels of analysis" to go back to states and government alone. However, even at this purely political level, we encounter problems. The units themselves undergo constant historic changes. Over the short course of a half century from the beginning of World War I to the early 1960s, the political map of the world changed as empires gave way to successor states. Whereas the League of Nations at its peak had scarcely more than 60 members, the United Nations now counts more than 150. Earlier scholars wondered whether they should restrict the scope of the field to relations among sovereign states and exclude colonies, protectorates, trusteeships, and other territories with an extraordinary status. Later they were not sure how to characterize legally the defeated, occupied Powers, the partitioned States, territorially exiguous States (such as the Vatican, San Marino and Liechtenstein), the Commonwealth, intergovernmental organizations (such as the United Nations, the North Atlantic Treaty Organization, the European Economic Community, the Organization of African Unity, and political movements without a territory such as the Palestinian Liberation Organization, or the many revolutionary liberation movements that have operated in Africa)—all entities with which significant numbers of governments have had substantial dealings. During the past decade, considerable attention has been focused on "transnationals," and especially on multinational corporations, as actors on the international scene—important because of their membership and resources, and their consequent ability to intervene in the internal affairs of host countries, as well as to affect interstate relations.[46]

Several other additions or alternatives to organized political communities have been suggested as proper units of study or "actors" in this field. Within nations one might examine the role of such organizations, institutions, and groups as political parties, churches, ethnic minorities, the press, and economic interest groups (labor, farmers, and industries anxious to export or to achieve protection against foreign imports). Arnold Wolfers pointed out that recent decades have witnessed a reaction against the traditional "states-as-sole-actors approach" in which all significant events and changes in the international scene were attributed to the policies of national governments.

> This reaction has taken two distinct forms: one new theory has placed individual human beings in the center of the scene that had previously been reserved to the nation-states; the other emphasized the existence, side by side with the state, of other corporate actors, especially international organizations. . . .
> The 'individuals-as-actors' approach first appeared in the form of what has been called the 'minds-of-men theory of international politics.' It was soon to be followed by the 'decision-making' approach. . . . It was the aim of the new theories to replace the abstract notion of the state with the living realities of human minds, wills, and hearts. But the result, on the whole, was to substitute one set of abstractions for another, because, in politics, it is also an abstraction to examine the individual apart from the corporate bodies by means of which he acts politically.[47]

According to Wolfers, it is wrong to assume that because private individuals in Country A pursue the same goals of personal welfare, happiness and social advancement as private individuals in Country B, it should be a simple matter to eliminate political hostility and promote harmonious relations between the two countries by setting the peaceful interests of individuals against the evil power designs of governments. He found the exclusive minds-of-individuals approach highly misleading because, even though it is true in a sense that international relations take place "in here" (in the minds of citizens) and not just "out there" (in the world), nevertheless "psychological events are not the whole stuff out of which international politics is formed," and thus the psychologist alone, without the political scientist, cannot explain adequately an international reality which proceeds not merely from individuals but also from organized groups of many magnitudes.[48]

This brings us to one of the most crucial and enduring dilemmas in all the social sciences: the relationship between the "macrocosmic" and the "microcosmic," between collective power structures and individual personalities.[49] Stewart E. Perry has attempted to bridge the gap between the two polar levels of international analysis—to integrate psychological data with political concepts—by highlighting the role of the national, "the role played by a person when interacting with others who are not citizens of his own nation."[50] But the nation, too, has been put in some doubt as a result of modern technological developments. In 1957 John H. Herz argued that the territorial nation-state could be the basic unit of the international political system only so long as its "hard shell" defense enabled it to claim impenetrability and thus to afford security and protection to its population. With the advent of nuclear weapons, he said, the territorial state has begun to experience a new permeability "which tends to obliterate the very meaning of unit and unity, power, and power relations, sovereignty and independence."[51] Arnold Toynbee, as a result of his monumental *A Study of History,* suggested (more implicitly than explicitly) that the nation-state does not constitute a viable unit either of historical or political study, and should be replaced by the civilizational area.[52] Morton A. Kaplan offers for our contemplation the whole international system as the most appropriate object of analytical investigation.[53] George Modelski advanced the hypothesis that there are two basic models of social and economic organization—Agraria and Industria—each having distinctive implications for the foreign policy of nations and for international politics as a whole.[54] William H. Riker points to the importance of political coalitions for theory-building purposes.[55] But although there are now innumerable nonstate actors (including terrorist organizations) that come within the purview of the field, and some writers have challenged the validity of the state-centric perspective, few would deny that it is still the states (whether or not we would call them "sovereign" in the traditional sense) that stand in the brighter spotlights on the international stage. The significance of nonstate actors continues to be evaluated largely by reference to their ability to influence, directly or indirectly, the behavior of states.

In any event we face a choice between the microlevel and the macrolevel of analysis; this choice can be not only extremely difficult, but also highly controversial within the discipline. J. David Singer directed attention to the problem in the following trenchant passage:

> In the vernacular of general systems theory, the observer is always confronted with a system, its subsystems, and their respective environments, and while he may choose as his system any cluster of phenomena from the most minute organism to the universe itself, such choice cannot be merely a function of whim or caprice, habit or familiarity. . . . We have, in our texts and elsewhere, roamed up and down the ladder of organizational complexity with remarkable abandon. . . . And though most of us have tended to settle upon the nation as our most comfortable resting place, we have retained our propensity for vertical drift, failing to appreciate the value of a stable point of focus. Whether this lack of concern is a function of the relative infancy of the discipline or the nature of the intellectual traditions from which it springs, it nevertheless remains a significant vari-

able in the general sluggishness which characterizes the development of theory in the study of relations among nations.[56]

• *Should Study and Theory Focus on Contemporary International Reality?* There is an inescapable attractiveness about the present international system for purposes of research. Materials and funding support usually come easier when the subject under study is of relatively contemporary concern, that is, a phenomenon that falls within the time span since World War II. Yet despite the lure of the present, most experienced scholars in international relations realize that if the development of theory is ever to lead to a predictive capability, a knowledge of international relations in the past is essential, because it broadens and strengthens the data base from which projections are to be made.

The argument concerning the value of historical knowledge can only be partially correlated with the argument between "traditionalists" and "behaviorists." Hedley Bull has criticized the latter for "a lack of any sense of inquiry into international politics as a continuing tradition to which they are the latest recruits."[57] But this is not entirely so. Although most behaviorists, given their preferred methodologies, have usually not undertaken research requiring a mastery of historiographical techniques, many have been sensitive to history. Morton Kaplan, for example, opens his principal work with a tribute to history: "There is one respect in which a science of international politics must always be indebted to history. History is the great laboratory within which international action occurs."[58] Kaplan also calls for and has undertaken investigations into the ancient Greek city-state system, the Italian state system of the Renaissance, and the balance-of-power system that dominated Europe during the eighteenth and nineteenth centuries in order to compare typical system behaviors in different eras.[59] (Kaplan's models of the international system have been used in studies discussed in Chapter 4.)

International theorists should be interested in all international systems—past, present, future, and hypothetical.[60] Thus they should not confine their attention exclusively to the existing nation-state system. Indeed, they cannot fully understand what exists unless they have some knowledge of what existed formerly, out of which present reality evolved, and what might exist, toward which the present seems to be moving and by which the present can be evaluated. The history of international relations is *not* an international theory; it *is* the essential raw material with which the theoretician works.[61]

• *What Is the Relationship between Theory and Practice?* Despite their complementarity, basic differences exist between academic social science theory and political-diplomatic practice. There are also differences, perhaps less basic, between general theoretical approaches to international relations and the "policy sciences" that deal with the foreign policy problems of particular states, just as there are differences between the "policy sciences" and the actual conduct of diplomacy. Each of the several levels of knowledge and action has a legitimacy of its own that ought not to be disparaged by one who happens to be operating at another level. In all cases it is useful to keep in mind the distinction between the scholar who seeks to achieve a theoretical understanding of phenomena and to formulate generalizations about political behavior based on a high level of probability and the decision-maker who has to choose a specific course of action in a concrete set of circumstances in which probability analysis may not be helpful.

Long ago Aristotle differentiated between knowing and doing, between the speculative intellect and the practical intellect.[62] David Hume drew a sharp contrast among three classes of knowledge: (1) deductive reasoning which relates to the logical and necessary truths of mathematics and metaphysics; (2) empirical knowledge which pertains to apparently causal relationships that are not really rationally necessary; and (3) value judgments which derive from an accumulation of historical facts as they have affected human emotion and intuition. For Hume, politics and morals must always be inextricably bound with value judgments and hence can be neither deductive nor empirical.[63] To state the problem of theory and practice in Humean terms, we might say that whereas the pure theorist is usually concerned principally with deductive thought processes to generalized formulations, the policymaker has a principal interest in the empirical, inductive knowledge derived from one's own personal experience rather than from any systematic research effort. The policymaker is concerned also with the subtle details of the political values, forces, and preferences operating in a particular situation, so that a decision can be made addressed to this particular situation in all its existential reality rather than to a universal abstraction or probability. Whereas the social theorist wishes to concentrate primarily upon elements common to many situations, the decision-maker invariably wants detailed information about those elements that are unique to the case at hand.

However, lest anyone receive the wrong impression, we stress that the differing emphases of theorist and practitioner do not alter the desirability that each should try to appreciate the modes of knowledge peculiar to the other. Neither can afford to dismiss generalized or particularized knowledge.

The interface between theory and practice leads logically to several corollary questions. Did statesmen of relatively long experience (Talleyrand, Metternich, Canning, Disraeli, Bismarck, Theodore Roosevelt, Wilson, Churchill, Lenin, Stalin, Franklin Roosevelt, and de Gaulle) have an international theory worthy of study? When Metternich engineered the post-Napoleonic restoration of a Europe legitimate and in balance; when Disraeli ordered the purchase of the Khedive's Suez Canal Company shares; when Bismarck concluded the Reinsurance Treaty with Russia; when Wilson presided over the dissolution of the Austro-Hungarian Empire and worked to have the League of Nations made an integral part of the Versailles peace settlement; when de Gaulle arrested the progress of the "federalizers" in the European Economic Community—were these men acting on the basis of a coherent theory of which they were intellectually aware? Or were they acting merely on the basis of pragmatic evaluations in reaction to political pressures of the moment? This is difficult to answer. Some leaders tend more toward theoretical reflections than others.[64]

Metternich and Churchill entertained a balance of power theory, Wilson emphasized the principle of national self-determination, and Lenin and Stalin theorized on the relations of capitalistic imperialism with the colonial areas of the world. But to what extent their decisions responded to situations and to what extent their decisions flowed from theories remain subjects of debate. Some conclusions seem tenable. Most statesmen probably reach most of their important foreign policy decisions through some theoretical reflection, perhaps weighing, even mixing, different theories in their effort to understand, choose, and predict. The theories on which they act may not always be the theories that they articulate publicly. In some cases, they may be able to predict trends and outcomes without the aid of very sophisticated theories. They are likely to think that their own theories, arising out of reflection on their own personal experiences, or out of the accumulated experiences of institutions of which they have long been a part (such as the British Foreign Office or the U.S. Department of State)[65] are more reliable guidelines for policy choices than the more abstract theoretical constructs that have been developed in academic circles and couched, as they often are, in a terminology unfamiliar to policymakers. This discussion leads to the question of whether we are studying and theorizing about foreign policy or international relations, and the implications of this question for the "policy sciences" and for "pure theory."

• *Is the Study of International Relations the Same as the Study of Foreign Policy?* Some writers have assumed that the study of foreign policy and the study of international relations are synonymous, or that too much should not be made of the difference between them.[66] Even when they have not equated their own country's foreign policy with international relations, they identified the latter field with the sum total of the foreign policies of all states (theoretically) or of the states in which they were for all practical purposes interested. It is true that the relations of any two states can provide part of the data input into our empirical study of international relations,[67] although we would not wish to develop a general-ized theory from such a narrow base. But the question is whether, if we consider only two states, we can conclude that their international rela-tions can be fully understood by merely examining their foreign policies regarding each other, and somehow by adding them. We think not.

Even granting that foreign policy decision-makers are compelled to take action-reaction processes into account, to receive "feedback" from abroad in the wake of their decisions, and to modify their policies ac-cordingly,[68] nevertheless "international relations" is not merely the sum of the nations' foreign policies. The concept of "foreign policy" refers to the formulation, implementation, and evaluation of external choices *within* one country, viewed from the perspective of that country. If we consider the whole international system, there must always be something inward about foreign policy, no matter how "internationalist" a coun-try's policies might be. Foreign policy is made inside; international rela-tions take place outside, somewhere between two or more countries. (This is not to deny the significant linkage, referred to previously, be-tween international and domestic politics.) Moreover, whereas foreign policy is something of which policymakers are aware, international rela-tions involve a confluence of forces and the net results of interactive processes to which foreign policymakers may not even be sensitive. In other words, international relations embraces more than the aggregate of national foreign policies; it focuses primarily on the larger interactive process rather than on the way national participants view that process. Still, we quickly add that much of our substantive knowledge about in-ternational relations has always come and will continue to come from studies of national and comparative foreign policies.[69]

• *Is International Relations a Policy Science?* A policy science is a form of theory. But it is not "pure theory," which aims solely at understanding. A policy science aims at action. The policy scientist wishes to understand in order to improve the ability to choose wisely. The problem which the policy scientist wishes to solve is often one society wants solved. The pol-icy scientist's theoretical efforts usually take the form of a particular "if-then" proposition: If we assume that this society wishes to achieve this objective, then the following describes the most effective and available means of doing so under existing circumstances. Policy scientists do not really define the goal, even though they may favor it; they assume some goals as givens and merely provide a technical prescription for the aptest means thereto. (If they allow themselves to become too emotionally at-tached to the attainment of the goal, this might conceivably have an ad-verse effect upon their expert judgment concerning the policy means to be adopted.)[70] Policy scientists are interested in international theory. But instead of playing a creative role in the origination of international theory, some may merely borrow existing pure theory and adapt it (or bend it, as the case may be) for the purpose of achieving certain preselected goals. "To think policy-wise," wrote Lasswell, "is to invent or assess alternative courses of action (or inaction)."[71]

What is, and what should we expect of, a theory of international relations? At the simplest level, a theory—any theory—is a general explanation of certain selected phenomena set forth in a manner satisfactory to someone acquainted with the characteristics of the reality being studied. Even this elementary definition, of course, is fraught with difficulties arising out of the problem of objective and subjective knowledge; a theory might satisfy its expounder and horrify the listener, and yet both may claim to be experts concerning the "characteristics of reality." The authors of this text will refrain from attempting to settle the profound questions of epistemology that have remained unsettled for centuries. We reiterate: Theory is a way of organizing our knowledge so that we can ask questions worth answering, guide our research toward valid answers, and integrate our knowledge with that of related fields. We can now proceed to speak about *theory* as this term is usually employed in physical science and in the social science.[72]

In literature on the philosophy of science the term *theory* has assumed a specific meaning. A theory is defined as a symbolic construction, a series of interrelated hypotheses together with definitions, laws, theorems, and axioms. A theory sets forth a systematic view of phenomena by presenting a series of propositions or hypotheses which specify relations among variables in order to present explanations and make predictions about the phenomena. In the physical sciences a theory may be viewed as a system consisting of the following elements: (1) a set of axioms whose truth is assumed and can be tested only by testing their logical consequences—an axiom cannot be deduced from other statements contained in the system; (2) statements, or theorems, that are deduced from the axioms, or from other theorems and definitions; and (3) definitions of descriptive terms contained in the axioms.[73] A theory is a group of laws which are deductively connected. Some of the laws are premises from which other laws are deduced. Those laws deduced from the axioms are the theorems of the theory. Whether or not a law is an axiom or a theorem depends on its position in a theory.

A theory does not depend necessarily upon empirical referents for validity. It need only state logically deduced relationships among the phenomena with which the theory is concerned.[74] According to Abraham Kaplan, the ability to apply the theory successfully is not a necessary condition for its success, since the failure of application may be traceable to many factors external to the theory itself.[75] But the development of empirical referents makes possible the testing of a theory. Carl Hampel has offered the following analogy:

A scientific theory might therefore be likened to a complex spatial network: Its terms are represented by the knots, while the threads connecting the latter correspond, in part, to the definitions and, in part, to the fundamental and derivative hypotheses contained in the theory. The whole system floats, as it were, above the plane of observation and is anchored to it by rules of interpretation. These might be viewed as strings which are not part of the network but link certain parts of the latter with specific places in the plane of observation. By virtue of those interpretive connectors, the network can function as a scientific theory. From certain observational data, we may ascend, via an interpretive string, to some point in the theoretical network, thence proceed, via definitions and hypotheses, to other points from which another interpretive string permits a descent to the place of observation.[76]

Although students in the social sciences have tried in recent years to develop theories as formally stated as those of the natural sciences, the term *theory* has had several meanings in the social sciences in general and international relations in particular:

1. A deductive system in which propositions are set forth, which purportedly contain internal logical consistency. Although such international systems may be free of direct linkages with the real world, they may be compared with the real world. The systems of Morton H. Kaplan are illustrative of such a conception of theory. (See Chapter 4.)

2. A taxonomy, classificatory scheme, or conceptual framework which provides for the orderly arrangement and examination of data. Data gathered from the real world may be placed in the categories, or slots, provided in the framework. Parsons's social system, Almond and Easton's political systems, and Snyder's decision-making framework are illustrative of such taxonomies. (See Chapters 4 and 11, respectively.)

3. A series of propositions about political behavior inductively derived either from empirical studies or the comparative examination of case materials from the past. The historical comparison made by Deutsch and his associates of the integration of national units in the North Atlantic area represents an effort to develop a series of propositions concerning conditions essential for types of integration. (See Chapter 10.)

4. The development of a series of statements about rational behavior based upon a dominant motive such as power. Such a theory provides a description of the political behavior of rational actors. Such behavioral patterns can then be compared with the real world in one or more historical periods. Morgenthau, for example, holds to such a theory of politics which, "by the very fact of painting a rational picture of the political scene, points to the contrast between what the political scene actually is and what it tends to be, but can never completely become."[77] (See Chapter 3.)

5. A set of norms or values indicating how political actors ought to behave; the study of international relations from the perspective of "ethical desiderata."[78] Traditionally, much of political philosophy consists of such theory. Normative theory establishes sets of standards against which existing conduct can be measured and toward which political behavior ought to aspire. Generally speaking, the potential destructiveness of war in the nuclear age, revolutionary guerrilla conflict, and counterinsurgency, and the economic development gap between the richer and poorer nations have led to an increased emphasis in the United States on ethical factors in the analysis of international relations during the past three decades.

6. A set of proposals of action for the statesman. Such prescriptions are usually (a) assumptions about the international system such as the existence of a balance of power (variously defined) in which political actors supposedly take one or another course of action to achieve a particular kind of goal; or (b) policy recommendations based upon the results of the study of one or several instances of a particular kind of political behavior.

Students in the social sciences have theorized at different levels of observation and analysis. The development of "grand theories" is illustrative of theorizing in which interrelationships among a few or many variables purportedly explain a wide range of phenomena. The attempts of such writers as Parsons and Easton to develop frameworks for the organization of data concerning social and political systems illustrate grand theory in the sense that their taxonomies encompass most, if not all, of political behavior. In international relations the works of realist writers such as Raymond Aron and Hans Morgenthau represent efforts to formulate grand theory.

Other writers have focused upon the development of "middle-range" theories, those designed to explain or study a limited range of political phenomena with a few variables. The study of conditions of political integration, conflict, or the behavior of nations in alliance is illustrative of middle-range theorizing. Here the emphasis is on the development of islands of theory that at some future time may be linked through conceptual bridges into a grand theory of international relations.

According to Quincy Wright, "a general theory of international relations means a comprehensive, coherent, and self-correcting body of knowledge contributing to the understanding, the prediction, the evaluation, and the control of relations among states and of the conditions of the world."[79] Wright elaborates on his definition by arguing that the theory must cover all aspects of the field. It should be expressed in generalized propositions as clear, as accurate, and as few as possible. In other words, the theory should be parsimonious, and not so diffuse and complicated as to be confusing. (Scientists have always been predisposed to equate scientific truth with esthetic beauty, and the latter with intellectual simplicity.) Every part of the general theory should be logically consistent with every other part. The theory should be formulated in a style conducive to continual improvement and updating. Instead of being purely speculative, its theses should be capable of constant verification on the basis of available evidence. It should contribute to an objective understanding of international reality, rather than one distorted by national perspective. It should enable us to predict at least some things, and it should also help us to arrive at value judgments—even if the process or moral valuation may not be entirely consistent with the value-free tradition of the scientific method.[80] Wright himself concedes, and we agree with him, that a theory fulfilling all these ideal requirements would be extremely difficult, and perhaps impossible, to achieve.

Quincy Wright has advanced some ideas which cast light upon the study and theory of international relations. In his major work, A *Study of International Relations,* after admitting that the field of international relations is still "an emerging discipline manifesting little unity from the point of view of method and logic,"[81] he suggests that the field might best be understood if approached through four basic intellectual perspectives. In his opinion, all social reality can be conveniently divided into four categories: (1) the *actual* (what was or what is, known through the method of description); (2) the *possible* (what can be, known through the method of theoretical speculation); (3) the *probable* (what will be, known through the method of prediction); and (4) the *desirable* (what ought to be, known through the method of ethical or valuational or normative reflection). These four categories, says Wright, correspond to history, art, science, and philosophy.[82] The authors find this a categorization worth pondering—one that is useful in all the social sciences.

TRADITIONAL THEORY: BALANCE OF POWER

As an example of a traditional theory, let us consider one of the oldest, most persistent, and most controversial of all theories of international politics—the balance of power. It was recognized at least implicitly in ancient India and in ancient Greece, although it was never formally articulated. David Hume noted that although the term *balance of power* may be modern, "the maxim of preserving the balance of power is founded so much on common sense and obvious reasoning that it is impossible it could altogether have escaped antiquity," concluding that it had been practiced from ancient times to the eighteenth century.[83]

Insofar as it could be called a formal theory of international politics, the modern concept of balance of power was associated with the Newtonian conception of a universe in equilibrium. (Frequently a social science theory has been adapted from a physical science theory or at least influenced by developments of one.) Actually, the notion of equilibrium is basic to many sciences. Chemists speak of a solution in stable equilibrium. Economists perceive a balance of countervailing forces, such as supply and demand. Biologists warn against human activities which disturb the "balance of nature" between organisms and environment. Political writers often analyze the interaction of interest groups or of governmental branches within national society in terms of "checks and balances."[84] Naturally theorists of international social reality employ "balance" as a central organizing concept for the power relations of nation-states and they then assume that the latter are driven, almost by a law of their own nature, to seek their security by some form of power-balancing.

BALANCE OF POWER: PROBLEMS OF DEFINITION

The term *balance of power* has been roundly criticized for causing considerable semantic confusion. Richard Cobden said of it:

> It is not a fallacy, a mistake, an imposture—it is an undescribed, indescribable, incomprehensible nothing; mere words, conveying to the mind not ideas, but sounds like those equally barren syllables which our ancestors put together for the purpose of puzzling themselves about words. . . .[85]

Ernst B. Haas found at least eight distinct meanings for the term: (1) any distribution of power; (2) an equilibrium or balancing process; (3) hegemony or the search for hegemony; (4) stability and peace in a concert of power; (5) instability and war; (6) power politics in general; (7) a universal law of history; and (8) a system and guide to policymakers.[86] "The trouble with the balance of power," says Inis L. Claude, Jr., "is not that it has no meaning, but that it has too many meanings." After noting that the term has been used to connote equilibrium and disequilibrium, or any distribution of power whether balanced or unbalanced, or as both policy and system (either automatic and self-regulating or wholly dependent upon manipulation by shrewd statesmen), Claude concludes that the concept of the balance of power is extremely difficult to analyze and is bound to frustrate students because those who write about it not only fail to provide precise clues as to its meaning but often "slide blissfully from one usage of the term to another and back again, frequently without posting any warning that plural meanings exist."[87]

It is true that the concept of balance of power is riddled with ambiguity. Many statesmen have sought a unilateral superiority rather than an objective bilateral balance with their principal rival. Nevertheless, it is theoretically possible to conceive of the balance of power as a situation or condition, as a universal tendency or law of state behavior, as a guide for statesmanship, and as a mode of system-maintenance characteristic of certain types of international systems. As long as we think in terms of equilibrium rather than of superiority, these four usages need not be inconsistent with each other.

Conceived as a situation or a condition, balance of power implies an objective arrangement in which there is relatively widespread satisfaction with the distribution of power. The universal tendency or law describes a probability—and enables one to predict—that members of a system threatened by the emergence of a "disturber of the balance," that is, a power seemingly bent upon establishing an international hegemony, will form a countervailing coalition. Balance of power as a policy guide prescribes to statesmen who would act "rationally" that they should maintain eternal vigilance and be prepared to organize a countervailing coalition against the disrupter of equilibrium. Balance of power as a system refers to a multinational society in which all essential actors preserve their identity, integrity, and independence through the balancing process.[88]

BALANCE OF POWER: PURPOSES AND FUNCTIONS

Various purposes and functions were attributed to the balance of power in classical theory as expounded by Bolingbroke, Gentz, Metternich, and Castlereagh. It was supposed to (1) prevent the establishment of a universal hegemony; (2) preserve the constituent elements of the system and the system itself; (3) insure stability and mutual security in the international system; and (4) strengthen and prolong the peace by deterring war, that is, by confronting an aggressor with the likelihood that a policy of expansion would meet with the formation of a countercoalition. The traditional methods and techniques of maintaining or restoring the balance were (1) the policy of divide and rule (working to diminish the weight of the heavier side); (2) territorial compensations after a war; (3) creation of buffer states; (4) the formation of alliances; (5) spheres of influence; (6) intervention; (7) diplomatic bargaining; (8) legal and peaceful settlement of disputes; (9) reduction of armaments; (10) armaments competition or races; and (11) war itself.

A review of the list of objectives and methods will show that there were internal inconsistencies in the theory and in the practice, but that they were probably unavoidable, given the historic oscillation between stable and unstable equilibria within the nation-state system. If the balance of power had worked perfectly as all statesmen expected, and if the existing distribution of power had posed no threat to their national security, then the balance of power as situation, law, policy, and system would almost certainly have contributed to the prolongation of peace. But the dynamics of the international political system were conducive neither to serene stability nor to prudent rational decision-making at all times. Moreover, statesmen pursuing only what they considered their own legitimate national interest—a term closely associated with the balance of power system—may have appeared in the eyes of other statesmen as conspiring to overturn the international system and gain predominance. Or conversely, a government embarked upon a hegemonial course might not provoke the formation of a countercoalition until too late to prevent a large-scale war declared to restore the balance. In theory the balance helped preserve the peace and identity of member-states; but in practice balance of power policy sometimes led to war and to the partitioning of "less essential" actors (such as Poland in the 1790s). But keeping the peace and preserving all the lesser members intact were subordinate to the more fundamental aims of preserving the multistate system by observing the maxim expressed by Friedrich Gentz:

> That if the states system of Europe is to exist and be maintained by common exertions, no one of its members must ever become so powerful as to be able to coerce all the rest put together.[89]

Another key concept in the classical theory must be mentioned. Under normal circumstances, with several nations seeking to maximize their power position through the various methods and techniques of balance of power politics, no one nation gains hegemony, and a precarious equilibrium is maintained. But for various reasons the balance might conceivably break down. Perhaps some states will react lethargically to any power trying to upset the balance. At this point an impartial and vigilant "holder of the balance" emerges, which is strong enough to restore the balance swiftly once it is disturbed. Historically, England played this role in the European state system. In a famous memorandum published on January 1, 1907, Sir Eyre Crowe said that it had "become almost an historical truism to identify England's secular policy with the maintenance of this balance by throwing her weight now in this scale and now in that, but ever on the side opposed to the political dictatorship of the strongest single state or group at a given time."[90] Winston Churchill reiterated this as a fundamental tenet of British foreign policy in 1936.[91] Perhaps the theory of the balance of power—as a policy guide to statesmen—is a distinctively British theory, at least in modern times.

CRITIQUES OF BALANCE OF POWER

In recent decades, the balance of power theory has encountered much criticism even from traditional analysts, and for reasons other than the semantic vagueness mentioned earlier. Nicholas J. Spykman held that the theory inadequately explained the practice:

> The truth of the matter is that states are interested only in a balance (imbalance) which is in their favor. Not an equilibrium, but a generous mar-

gin is their objective. There is no real security in being just as strong as a potential enemy; there is security only in being a little stronger. There is no possibility of action if one's strength is fully checked; there is a chance for a positive foreign policy only if there is a margin of force which can be freely used.[92]

Hans J. Morgenthau finds the balance of power deficient on several grounds. It has failed on a number of occasions since the end of the eighteenth century to preserve the independent existence of states. The multistate system precluding a single state from achieving universal dominion has been preserved only at the price of frequent and costly wars. He finds the balance of power (1) *uncertain* because no completely reliable means of measuring, evaluating, and comparing power exist; (2) *unreal* because statesmen try to compensate for its uncertainty by aiming for superiority; and (3) *inadequate* for explaining national restraint during most of the years from 1648 to 1914 because it does not give credit to the restraining influence of the basic intellectual unity and moral consensus then prevailing in Europe.[93]

Charles P. Schleicher has suggested that "peace is most in jeopardy when power is rather evenly balanced and war less likely when there is a preponderant power."[94] (This argument will be developed more fully in Chapter 8.) A. F. K. Organski denies that a "holder of the balance" was ever primarily motivated by a desire to maintain the balance rather than by self-interest, and warns against "elevating the public relations statements of sixteenth-century monarchs and nineteenth-century diplomats to the status of scientific theory."[95] Ernst B. Haas has observed that using the balance of power as a policy guide assumes a high degree of flexibility in national decision-making. The vigilant statesman must engage in a constant power calculus, and must be ready to intervene or enter into coalition almost immediately to preserve the balance—and do this regardless of ideological affinities, economic interests, and domestic political attitudes. Haas has questioned the degree to which policymakers, especially in democratic countries, can enjoy the kind of flexibility that the balance of power theory would seem to demand.[96]

Several writers, including the classical theorists, have insisted that the cultural homogeneity of the European state system from the seventeenth through the nineteenth centuries was an important precondition for the successful operation of the balance of power.[97] All international analysts have recognized that in this century the state system encompasses states with very different cultural backgrounds. Moreover, universalist ideologies now challenge what for a long time has been the most powerful political force on the world scene—nationalism. William G. Carleton observed in 1947 that in modern times nation-centered loyalties have generally proven stronger than internationalist ideologies. But he noted that the rise of ideological conflicts within and between national societies undoubtedly helped complicate the operation of the balance of power. He cautioned that international politics in the latter part of this century may be conducted less along national and more along ideological lines.[98] It is worth noting that virtually no theorists predicted the revived importance of religious factors in international relations as manifested, for example, in the visits of Pope John Paul II to Poland and the United States and in the resurgence of Islam in world politics after the overthrow of the Shah of Iran in 1979.

BALANCE OF POWER: CONTEMPORARY MODELS

Nevertheless, it would be erroneous to suggest that, because the balance of power theory has been buried by an avalanche of criticism, it is dead. Several "modern," "nontraditional," and "scientific" theoreticians have found it attention worthy. Morton A. Kaplan makes it one of his six heuristic models of international systems. He devotes more space to the balance of power system with its essential rules than to any of the other systems.[99] (For a discussion of Kaplan's systems models, see Chapter 4.) Arthur Lee Burns, after studying the problem of the system in stable balance, concludes that "the most stable arrangement would seem to be a world of five or some greater odd number of Powers, independent and of approximately equal strength," since these would not be readily divisible into two equal sides.[100] For simplicity in calculating relationships, and for the certainty and stability which such simplicity would yield, Burns holds that, optimally, the most stable system would be a world of "five roughly equal blocs, each including a family of exchangeable client nations."[101] Several analysts in the field of nuclear deterrence and arms control theory have updated and cast into highly sophisticated forms the categories of balance of power thinking.[102] And although many intellectuals and academicians regard the balance of power theory as a crude, unsophisticated, naively simplistic, or obsolete theory of international politics, large numbers of statesmen, politicians, diplomats, pundits, journalists, and people-in-the-street still regard it as an adequate explanation of what actually happens in the international system and of the basis on which foreign policy ought to be formulated and conducted. The theory retains a charm and a validity for analysts of strategic arms limitations and the triangular relationship of the United States, the Soviet Union, and China.

CAN THERE BE A "SCIENTIFIC" INTERNATIONAL THEORY?

Posing such a question just after discussing the balance of power theory does not imply that the latter was "unscientific." The meaning of "scientific" is relative. The term *science* connotes nothing more than a body of knowledge and a way of discovering new knowledge. Whatever satisfies intelligent human beings in any age as the optimum means of enlarging their intellectual frontiers will pass muster as "scientific."

Genuine scientific progress is usually made when one starts out by accepting that knowledge of the field already generally accepted by scholars. Each individual may wish to reorganize somewhat the existing body of knowledge to enhance one's own working comprehension of it. But the individual must take something as given—something already based upon empirical observation, experience, and human reflection. If learning is social, the individual cannot begin every day to create the universe *de novo*.

Once the investigator has mastered the existing knowledge, and organized it for his or her purposes, the investigator pleads a "meaningful ignorance": "Here is what I know; what do I not know that is worth knowing?" This is a very important question. Once an area has been selected for investigation, the question should be posed as clearly as possible, and it is here that quantification can prove useful,[103] provided that mathematical methods are combined with carefully constructed taxonomic schemes. Achieving a satisfactory merger of appropriate tools of statistical analysis with solid typologies is one of the most difficult aspects of formulating a worthwhile and testable hypothesis in the realm of political reality, where the names we call things and the words we use are of crucial importance. Surveying the field of international relations, or any sector of it, we see many disparate elements and keep sifting them through various permutations in our minds, wondering whether there may be any significant relationships between A and B or between B and C. By a process that we are compelled to call "intuition" until we learn much more about it than we now know, we perceive a possible correlation, hitherto unsuspected or not firmly known, between two or more elements. At this point, we have the ingredients of a hypothesis that can be expressed in measurable referents and which, if validated, would be both explanatory and predictive. (In the strictest scientific sense, what we cannot predict we cannot fully explain,[104] but that is an extremely demanding criterion of explanation in the social sciences.)

From here on, the scientific method becomes more familiar. The hypothesis must be validated through testing. This demands the construction of a verifying experiment or the gathering of data in other ways. In either case every effort must be made to eliminate the influence of the unknown, and to make certain that the evidence sought pertains to the hypothesis and to nothing else. The results of the data-gathering effort are carefully observed, recorded, and analyzed, after which the hypothesis is discarded, modified, reformulated, or confirmed. Findings are published, and others are invited to duplicate this knowledge-discovering adventure, and to confirm or deny. This, very roughly, is what we usually mean by "the scientific method." At every step of the way there is emphasis upon precision of thought and language and upon a distinction between that which is assumed and that which is empirically verifiable.

Application of this scientific method during the past 250 years has produced some very impressive results in the physical sciences in the form of generalized laws. In physics, astrophysics, chemistry, biology, and certain areas of psychology a high degree of predictability has been achieved. But even the "exact" sciences, with all their powerful methodologies, reach limits to what can be known at any given moment. According to Werner Heisenberg's principle of indeterminacy, for example, it is not possible to determine simultaneously both the position and the movement of a particle of matter.[105] In all the sciences, physical and social, we find that our efforts to measure a phenomenon may dislocate or change the thing we are trying to measure.

THE SEARCH FOR RECURRING PATTERNS

Anyone claiming to be a "scientific" theorist—whether "traditional" or future-oriented "behaviorist"—is bound to search for regularities. But we should remember that there are peculiar difficulties confronting all social scientists, and if we keep these in mind we are more likely to make intellectual progress than if we ignore or forget them.

The scientist studying human affairs encounters problems concerning the relation of the observer to the observed to a greater degree than the scientist studying atoms, molecules, or stars. The physical scientist requires certain instruments and techniques that are fairly standardized and that work the same way for all. Physical scientists, no matter how excited they might be about their work, usually avoid that kind of emotional involvement with the observed phenomenon which might influence their perception and their judgment. In the investigation of human society, objective observation is much more likely to be infused with subjective purpose. A physicist or a chemist who happens to be an ardent pacifist in personal outlook is not prone to be swayed by this conviction in the analytic approach to the more fissionable atoms as compared with other atoms. But social scientists who have strong preconceptions about such subjects as war, guerrilla terror, national values, world population and hunger, disarmament, and international organization or the conflict between democracies and dictatorships are much more likely to run into difficulty in their efforts to achieve that complete detachment which the scientific method presupposes. (There is, in the view of the authors, no need for social scientists to apologize for this "human involvement.") Although the method is supposed to be "value-free," the phenomenon being examined is often overladen with value implications which influence the intellectual and psychological set of the observer-analyst. Social scientists hardly agree on which of these two attitudes produces the greater perceptual distortion in the study, let us say, of the problems of war and peace: a purely neutral or nonethical desire to "understand" human aggressiveness for the purpose of explaining it and predicting its manifestations or a moral commitment to study war with a view toward abolishing it in order to make the world a better place. Undoubtedly the effort to build a scientific international theory will continue to be characterized by the interpenetration of these two distinct purposes, both within individual minds and within the field as a whole.[106]

The peculiarities of the observer-observed relationship in the social sciences give rise to additional difficulties. Some of these are well known and frequently cited, such as the inability to conduct controlled experiments in order to isolate the factors being studied. Even the most ruthless totalitarian regime, whatever the efficiency of the technical means of social control at its disposal, would be extremely hard pressed to conduct a strictly controlled scientific experiment with a single nation, not to mention two or more. The point is that in attempting to study any large social aggregates scientifically, the conditions of control for the sake of exactitude must be established primarily through the clarification of one's own thought processes, rather than in the confusing and uncontrollable social universe.

Other problems are less readily recognized. Given the comprehensibility of the field, the sheer mass of pertinent data seems to exceed the bounds of human mastery. Many data are inaccessible and remain so either for a very long time (in governmental archives) or forever (in the minds of individuals who forget or die before they transmit to scholars all they know about what really happened). The scholar and theorist, therefore, often arrive at generalized conclusions from sketchy evidence that might be unreliable on grounds quite apart from its incompleteness.

During the past two decades, scholars have turned to the computer, with its capacity for the statistical manipulation of vast amounts of data, for the building of theories of international relations. "Quantitative international relations," says Harvey Starr, "does not constitute a substantive subfield of international relations, but merely a common methodological approach to the diverse substance that makes up international relations."[107] The use of the computer can greatly speed up the performance of complex statistical analyses and may even suggest correlations that might not otherwise have occurred to scholars. Advanced technologies of information storage and retrieval, as well as of data analysis, have already enhanced our ability to manipulate huge amounts of data. Some writers have suggested that the time has come for the establishment of a global monitoring system for the international measurement of various phenomena.[108] Throughout this book, we shall have occasion to refer to the use of quantitative methods in several areas of theory-building, for example, integration, arms races, and decision-making. Here we discuss just one case to illustrate the utility of the computer in our field—in analyzing the relation between intranational and international conflict.

A CASE STUDY IN QUANTITATIVE METHODOLOGY

In a project designed to find recurrent political patterns within and between nations, Rudolph J. Rummel collected data for 236 variables about 82 nations for one year, in 1955. These data were analyzed through a technique known as factor analysis.[109] In the first phase of the Dimensionality of Nations (DON) Project, three separate analyses were applied to the data: (1) the foreign conflict behavior variables were intercorrelated and factor analyzed separately; (2) the foreign conflict behavior variables were regressed upon dimensions of national characteristics and domestic conflict dimensions (to "regress" means to determine how well data on one variable can be predicted from data on a set of variables); and (3) the foreign conflict and domestic conflict variables were factor analyzed together.

Of the 236 variables, 94 were measures of such aspects of international relations as trade, membership in international organizations, treaties signed, aid given and received, and votes with the United States in the United Nations.

It was found that conflict behavior did not correlate with the degree of a nation's involvement in foreign affairs. Stated differently, nations may be heavily engaged in foreign affairs without necessarily resorting to conflict. In factor analysis of all variables, domestic conflict variables appeared in patterns distinct from foreign conflict variables.

However, these conclusions were based upon a method that does not differentiate among the nations under consideration. Jonathan Wilkenfeld reevaluated Rummel's data using a different method which involved "the rearrangement of the nations under consideration into groups, according to type of nation, in an effort to determine whether type of nation has any bearing on the relationship between internal and external behavior."[110] A group of 74 nations was divided into three groups, based on differences in leadership: personalist (or dictatorial), centrist (centralized government), and polyarchic (representative government, including two or more parties). All possible pairs of domestic conflict behavior dimensions and foreign conflict behavior dimensions were correlated for these groups. Moreover, the possibility of time lags was considered. The results indicated that there is a relationship between internal and external conflict behavior. The nature of the relationship depends upon the type of nation and the dimension of conflict: "As we shift our attention from the personalist, to the centrist, and finally to the polyarchic group, the particular dimensions of conflict behavior which are related change. Indeed, there is no one particular relationship between any pair of internal and external conflict dimensions which holds for all groups equally well. . . . Nations in the international system do not behave solely on the basis of the givens of the international situation. Depending upon the type of nation, we must look beyond the international sphere to the internal situation in the participating nation, to determine that nation's reactions."[111] (The reader is referred to the discussion of the findings of R. J. Rummel and Raymond Tanter concerning the correlation of internal and external conflict in Chapter 8, pp. 304–305.)

Rummel owes a considerable intellectual debt to Quincy Wright, who developed a field theory for the analysis of international relations. Field theory, which had its origins in physics, had been taken over into psychology by Kurt Lewin, who influenced Wright.[112] The field theorist emphasizes the total situation or "life space" of organism-in-environment viewed as a constellation of interdependent factors. Wright, Rummel, and other international field theorists view the behavior of nations in relation to similarities and differences in national attributes—all within the context of a geographic-social field defined by time-space coordinates. Wright's geographic-social field represents a description of the real world, with its distribution of population, resources, agricultural and industrial production, and political and economic power, as well as their changes over time. Wright overlays the geographic-social field with an analytic one consisting of values and capabilities, because he assumes that decision-makers formulate and pursue policies (both foreign and domestic) which relate values to capabilities. By locating each state or other acting unit at a point in these multidimensional fields which reflects its position in respect to each coordinate employed, Wright seeks not only to describe the international field at any moment in history, but also to provide a basis for explaining the past and predicting the future.[113] In the value field, for example, Wright's coordinates define a range of behavior from a narrow to a broad conception of national interest, from the politics of passivity to strategies of foreign intervention.[114]

Field theorists assume that systems of action within each field may move over time to new positions in the field and thus form new relationships with each other. Field theory is essentially a form of spatial analysis in which relative position, accessibility, connectivity, and the direction of movement are studied. R. J. Rummel in particular stresses attribute distance as a central concept, because "nation attribute similarities and differences are field forces creating social space-time motion; attribute distance between nations cause international behavior."[115]

In Rummel's study, the foreign conflict variables were regressed upon other dimensions of national characteristics. The findings were that the magnitude of a nation's characteristics or attributes has little relationship to its foreign conflict behavior. In other words, such factors as the level of economic or technological development, the level of international communications, totalitarianism, power, instability, military capabilities, ideology, or values of any individual nation were not found to correlate importantly with its foreign conflict behavior.

THE ATOMS AND LANGUAGE OF INTERNATIONAL POLITICS

The units we study, whether small groups, socioeconomic classes, institutions, governments, nations, states, intergovernmental entities or cultures, undergo constant change. This fact makes the social sciences much less stable enterprises than the physical sciences, and compounds the difficulty of conducting research such as that described above. Even though theories in the "exact sciences" are always being developed and refined as more knowledge is discovered, the phenomena investigated are stable, enduring, and duplicable. A hydrogen atom is the same in the Soviet Union as in the United States and scientists in both countries have an abundant supply to study. Theorizing about interstate relations might be compared with theorizing about a small container in which several atoms are in motion. No two atoms are alike. Each is unique, having a distinctive atomic weight at any given moment, yet constantly changing positions. Some atoms are quite heavy; some are in the middle range; most are light. The total number of atoms in the container is not fixed. Occasionally a small number of atoms of approximate sizes moves together as if to form a molecule. A light atom spins off from a heavier one. At times a heavier atom may break into a half-dozen or so particles which manifest a long period of weakness and instability after separation. Sometimes several atoms polarize around the two heaviest. The heavier atoms appear to avoid each other, but they may become agitated in their motion when lighter atoms in relatively distant parts of the container collide with each other. Atoms of all weights often engage in intraatomic and interatomic behavior which puzzles scientific observers. Every analogy limps, but this one might furnish a point of departure for initial reflection and discussion concerning the behavior of the "international system."

Finally, we come to the problem of language in which all theory must be couched. Even the exact sciences have not been immune from difficulties in relating language to observation, or verbal symbols to experience. It is inaccurate to say that the exact sciences require quantitative symbols, whereas the social sciences rely on qualitative symbols. Every physical science and every social science require some empirical foundation, and the method is not empirical unless it entails the essential functions of naming and counting. In all the sciences, counting is a very simple thing. An important separator between the physical sciences and the social sciences is the realm of qualitative language or the naming process. No one debates the meaning of such terms as *liquid, vapor, magnetic, electrically charged, sodium chloride,* or *nuclear fission.* But in analyzing the social universe, we constantly face terms such as *democratic, aggressive, revolutionary, illegal, discriminatory,* and *violent.* Not one of these terms is invested with scientific objectivity. Thus although all social scientists can count, and a great many understand the process of statistically correlating dependent and independent variables, or of performing factor analysis, there is reason to believe that the basis of agreement on what is being counted or measured in the field of international relations is very narrow and precarious indeed.

THE CONTROVERSY BETWEEN TRADITIONALISTS AND BEHAVIORISTS

Traditionalists (or advocates of the "classical" way) generally differ from behavioralist quantifiers in their approach to theory. An understanding of the traditionalist-scientist dichotomy, which is largely a product of a split within the field of American political science, will help to cast some light on the differences of perspective that often seem to divide the academic theorist from the practical decision-maker in the realm of foreign policy. This controversy is not the same as the one between idealists and realists, both of whom can choose either traditional or scientific methods to support their arguments, whether liberal or conservative, revolutionary or reactionary. Norman Palmer and others have called attention to the fact that both traditionalists and the scientific quantifiers in this country have tended to accept the assumptions of state-centric realism, but Palmer denies that this is a uniquely "American" approach to the study of international relations.[116]

Hedley Bull calls "classical" that "approach to theorizing that derives from philosophy, history, and law, and that is characterized above all by explicit reliance upon the exercise of judgment and by the assumption that if we confine ourselves to strict standards of verification and proof there is very little of significance that can be said about international relations."[117] Traditionalists are usually skeptical of the effort to predict or to apply probability analysis to human affairs. They will occasionally use quantitative data to illustrate a point which they are trying to make in an otherwise discursive presentation, but they are critical of the proclivity of some contemporary analysts to quantify in order to demonstrate by tortuous statistical analysis a proposition that ought to be obvious to a person of common sense. The traditionalist is typically but not rigidly interested in the single and unique event, case, situation, or problem, which he or she seeks to understand in the subtlety of detail, including relationships with other relevant phenomena. Often the traditionalist will study a few or several cases of a similar nature, drawing appropriate comparisons and contrasts along the way. (Scientists, too, of course, may rely on a small number of case studies to develop, illustrate, or test a general model.) Traditionalists would insist that they are at least as meticulous in gathering, sifting, weighing, and interpreting evidence as any social scientists. They would not deny that they make use of judgment, intuition, and insight in arriving at their conclusions, after having reviewed and digested all the data that they deem relevant and reliable.

The social scientist who studies international relations does not reject in principle the value of the historical-political descriptive method employed by the traditional scholar (although some less competent advocates of the scientific approach may display ignorance of the substance of history, politics, and international relations). But the scientific approach places considerable emphasis upon what it regards as scientifically precise methods. Different social scientists stress different methods or combinations of methods—attitude surveys, content analysis, simulation and gaming, statistical correlations, model-building, and the use of quantitative analysis as well as computers as a basis for achieving precision in measurement.[118] The scientific approach is not to be fully equated with quantitative methodology, but the latter is much more likely to be employed, and certain to be employed on a grander scale, in the scientific than in the traditional approach. Although scientific scholars cannot avoid using personal judgment in the selection of their problems, the formulation of their hypotheses, and the development of their classification scheme, they attempt to go beyond personal judgments and to launch into deductive or inductive methods which are independent of personal bias,[119] and which invoke either logic or mathematics to serve as substitutes for intuitive interpretation.

The traditionalist often criticizes the behavioralist for allegedly being too confident of the ability to generalize, to convert problematic statements into causal propositions, and to use these propositions to predict behavior in an area in which things are not predictable; of attributing to abstract models a congruence with reality that they do not have; of avoiding the substantive issues of international politics because in the zeal for scientific method he or she has perhaps never really mastered those issues in all their complexity; of succumbing to a "fetish for measurement" which ignores crucially important qualitative differences among the quantities being measured.[120]

Behavioralists assert that when they test for statistical correlation between two factors, they are determining whether the relationship between them might have been merely coincidental, and when they engage in multivariate analysis they are trying to find out which of several factors constitutes the most reliable predictor of a particular outcome.[121]

The scientific analyst regards the traditionalist's distrust of precise method, quantification, and verification through statistical testing as irresponsible and arrogant.[122] Traditionalists retort that in their own way they perform a careful "content analysis" of the primary and secondary sources (documentary and otherwise) which they adduce as evidence—speeches, press statements, government reports, diplomatic messages, personal memoirs, newspaper accounts and commentaries, interviews, scholarly studies, and so on—and intuitively select what they deem important and relevant without a systematic counting of words and phrases. The traditionalist remains convinced that the *urstoff* of politics is the qualitative difference—that subtle shade or nuance of meaning that can be communicated in the choice of a single word or phrase but does not lend itself to quantification. To the charge that the scientist glosses over relevant differences between the phenomena being counted, one leading spokesman of the scientific school rejoins as follows:

> In due course the various measurement efforts will show us where we have erred in lumping the unlumpable. But it seems to me that this undue preoccupation, yea obsession, with the unique, the discrete, the noncomparable, is what has largely kept history from developing into a cumulative discipline and has led to so much frivolous debate between the quantifiers and the antiquantifiers.... The fact is that no two events, conditions, or relationships are ever exactly alike; they must always differ in *some* regard, even if it is only in time-space location. The question is whether they are sufficiently similar to permit comparison and combination for the theoretical purposes at hand. To borrow a metaphor of which the anti-quantifiers are fond, there is absolutely nothing wrong with adding apples and oranges if fruit is the subject at hand.[123]

Singer calls attention to one salient difference between the scientific theorizer on the one hand and the traditional scholar (and usually the policymaker) on the other hand. The former prefers to isolate a few variables and analyze a large number of cases to determine the relationships among these variables. The traditionalist, in contrast, will often wish to examine all the variables which could conceivably have a bearing on the outcome of a single case.[124] Whereas the generalizer tends to seek the essential core that links a large number of cases (coups, revolutions, alliance formations, crisis decisions, etc.) and brush aside the "accidental" details which modify every particular instance and impart to it a unique character, both the traditionalist and the practitioner are reluctant to ignore any detail which could impinge upon the case at hand, for only by "feeling" the whole texture of the problem can the traditionalist understand it and the practical decision-maker discover a way of solving or coping with it.

All human beings make choices on the basis of our theories of reality. Those theories may be sophisticated or crude, comprehensive or partial. New theoretical concepts or insights are acquired as we go through life. Frequently the process is an eclectic one. We listen to a lecture on one of the newer approaches or we read about them—games and bargaining theory, simulation techniques, decision-making theory, communications and integration theory, conflict theory, systems theory, and so on—and we incorporate into our thinking whatever appeals to us, discarding the rest as irrelevant for our particular purposes. All academicians do this—traditionalists and behavioralists, proponents of qualitative and quantitative analysis alike. Our various theories, old and new, may peacefully coexist in our minds even when they are not logically consistent with each other. We all succumb to the tendency to add to our mental edifice, like new wings to an older building, without worrying too much about architectural symmetry. As we accumulate new theories in our "collection," storing them for use as needed, we seldom redesign and rebuild the underlying theoretical structure to insure a logical "fit." We must constantly remind ourselves of the requirement to strive for a genuine synthesis of the different modes of knowledge we acquire. Without such an effort, the growth of our knowledge through interdisciplinary studies in the field of international relations may well lead nowhere except to intellectual confusion.

ALTERNATIVE WORLD FUTURES

Before concluding this introductory chapter, it may be useful to look briefly at some of the more recent normative approaches adopted by scholars concerned over the direction in which the international system appears to be heading. During the past decade, two schools of thought in the field of international relations—*peace research* (which pursues a behavioral approach to conflict resolution and war avoidance) and *world order* (which is concerned with problems, of population, growth, resources, environment, poverty, and dehumanization)—have attempted to respond to conditions of rapid change in the global system by focusing upon *alternative world futures*. "Both schools," write Beres and Targ, "are avowedly normative in that they both aim at global transformation along the lines of certain preestablished value hierarchies."[125] Both schools are interdisciplinary in the intellectual tools they employ. Both are interested in going beyond trend analysis, forecasting, and the prediction of things to come (although they make use of these processes), and are determined to give history a shove in the direction of their hearts' desires.

Global design inquiry is at present searching for an appropriate epistemological and methodological foundation. There is some disagreement over the logical priorities and sequences of futuristic research, but most of those involved pursue the following endeavors: (1) articulation of the values that are to guide the research (such as war avoidance and the minimization of violence, economic well-being, social justice, democratic freedom and participation, and environmental balance); (2) description and projection of significant current trends (such as population growth, technological developments, consumption of resources, environmental pollution, and the spread of armaments; (3) design of alternative future world models—an enterprise that calls more for imagination than for reference to present reality (and which, therefore, often invokes the aid of utopian literature and science fiction); (4) selection out of the range of available futures the type or types that appear most desirable; and, finally, (5) development of transitional strategies which will enable humanity, through a mix of individual and collective behavioral changes, to overcome those structures and processes that obstruct the achievement of the preferred future.[126]

Many advocates of the alternative world futures approach regard the nation-state system, military establishments, and some contemporary social elites as "obsolescibles." They criticize the intellectual adherence of the majority of academic specialists in the field of international relations to the concepts of power and deterrence. They object to what they regard as a false dichotomy between "prudent realism" and "utopian idealism." They stress instead the relevance of religious, cultural, and value-change potentialities of human society for alternative world political futures.[127]

Most international political theorists, however, hold that the nation-state is a long-lived, highly adaptable institution, and that the very same technological and economic developments which have allegedly rendered the nation-state obsolete have also enabled it to consolidate its internal strength, making itself more indispensable than ever to its citizens. Hedley Bull, after examining the so-called anarchical setting of international society—anarchical in the sense of lacking a unified government and not in the popular usage sense of being in a state of chaos—concludes that the state system, in spite of all its defects, is remarkably durable. Bull also argues that the present pluralistic system manages to achieve, through the institutions of international law, diplomacy, and the balancing of power in a framework of mutually deterring alliances, a certain order of its own which may not be inferior to, or necessarily more conflict-ridden than, that of a universal political community in which the stakes of political conflict might be raised to that highest possible level of intensity that characterizes civil war.[128] Stanley Hoffmann has written in a similiar vein:

> Among the men who see in national sovereignty the Nemesis of mankind, those who put their hopes in the development of regional superstates are

illogical, those who put their hopes in the establishment of a world state are utopian, those who put their hopes in the growth of functional political communities more inclusive than the nation-state are too optimistic.[129]

Hoffmann argues that national sovereignty has not been superseded, but has been emptied to a considerable extent of its former sting: "there is no supershrew, and yet the shrew has been somewhat tamed"[130], because the number of players has increased, and all of them know much better than before that when they strut upon the world stage, as they are still wont to do, they must do so carefully.

But we are getting ahead of ourselves. We are talking about regionalism, world government, and functionalism without ever having treated these concepts in detail, as we shall in succeeding chapters. Our primary purpose in this introduction has been to show how the study of international relations has evolved in order to set the stage for examining the major theories.

CONCLUSION

To sum up, the essential function of international theory is to enable us to improve our knowledge concerning international reality, whether for the sake of "pure understanding" or for the more active purpose of changing that reality. Theory helps us to order our existing knowledge and to discover new knowledge more efficiently. It provides a framework of thought in which we define research priorities and select the most appropriate available tools for the gathering and analysis of data. Theory directs our attention to significant similarities and differences, and suggests relationships not previously perceived. Done well, theory serves as a proof that the powers of the human mind have been applied to a problem at hand with precision, imagination, and profundity, and this proof inspires others to further efforts for purposes either of agreeing or disagreeing.

There is no one model for theory. Social theorizing occurs at many levels and through many discipline-perspectives, with several experiments at interdisciplinary approaches under way. International theory, which goes beyond "foreign policy" theory, contains components which are descriptive, speculative, predictive, and normative. A single scholar may stress any one of these, but the more highly developed the field of international theory as a whole becomes, the more likely will it involve a synthesis of "what is," "what might be," "what probably will be," and "what ought to be." Good theory may be inductive or deductive; micro or macro; highly specific, midrange, or "grand" in the sense of being as comprehensive as the state of our knowledge at any given time permits. All of these approaches are valid and useful when handled with intelligence and methodological care. But we should remember that theory properly conceived always aims at generalization. It looks, therefore, to the universal and the uniform rather than to the unique, the particular, the discrete. The latter is by no means held in disdain by sound theorists. They respect the singular and they study its subtle complexities, always aware that these may reveal something of value which might deepen their grasp of the larger pattern.[131]

Dare we hope develop an international theory that will enable us to predict or forecast? (Scholars distinguish those two functions.[132]) The question is not easily answered. Certainly up to now the record of social scientists in general and international relations specialists in particular has not, on the whole, been very impressive, whether we have in mind the assignment of precise probabilities to specific events or of probability ranges to contingent events. In the view of the authors, all social science predictions vary from the difficult to the extremely difficult. We think that broad aggregate trends—pertaining to population, scientific research and technological developments, industrial production and GNP, energy consumption levels in various nations, patterns of demand for raw materials, the spread of nuclear power reactors and its implications for arms control, and shifting patterns of trade between various countries or regions of the world—may lend themselves to forecasting under carefully formulated assumptions concerning the significance of increases and decreases. But even in this realm, few aggregate trends operate autonomously and remain unaffected by political decisions of governments, economic decisions of corporate groups and individuals, and scientific-technological breakthroughs. All of these may be highly unpredictable variables. Unique events—such as the occurrence of nuclear war, or the seizure of an embassy by terrorists, or the sudden reversal of alliances by an African or a Middle East country—are virtually impossible to predict according to social science techniques (but they might be predictable by intelligence agencies when they are almost imminent). Even when social scientists speculate that a certain type of specific event is "bound to happen" sooner or later, they seldom can say precisely where or when.

Notes *

1. Thucydides, *The Peloponnesian War*, trans. Rex Warner (Harmondsworth: Penguin Books, 1954). See also William T. Bluhm, *Theories of the Political System: Classics of Political Thought and Modern Political Analysis* (Englewood Cliffs, N.J.: Prentice-Hall, 1965), chap. II; John H. Finley, Jr., *Thucydides* (Cambridge: Harvard University Press, 1942); Charles Norris Cochrane, *Thucydides and the Science of History* (London: Oxford University Press, 1929); Peter J. Fliess,

* *Editor's Note: Harper & Row's policy is to cite the names of publishers in their contemporary form even though the original edition cited by the authors may have been published under a different company name.*

Thucydides and the Politics of Bipolarity (Baton Rouge: Louisiana State University Press, 1966).

2. Niccolo Machiavelli, *The Prince and the Discourses* (New York: Random House [Modern Library], 1940); James Burnham, *The Machiavellians* (New York: John Day, 1943); Herbert Butterfield, *The Statecraft of Machiavelli* (New York: Macmillan, 1956); Friedrich Meinecke, *Machiavellism: The Doctrine of Raison d'État and Its Place in Modern History*, trans. Douglas Scott (New Haven: Yale University Press, 1957).

3. Dante Alighieri, *On World Government*, trans. Herbert W. Schneider, 2nd ed. rev. (New York: Liberal Arts Press, 1957); Etienne Gilson, *Dante and Philosophy*, trans. David Moore (New York: Harper & Row [Torchbooks], 1963), part III.

4. See Daniel S. Cheever and H. Field Haviland, *Organizing for Peace* (Boston: Houghton Mifflin, 1954), chap. 2. For additional reading on the history of international political theory, see F. H. Hinsley, *Power and the Pursuit of Peace: Theory and Practice in the History of Relations Between States* (Cambridge: Cambridge University Press, 1967), pp. 13–149; Frank M. Russell, *Theories of International Relations* (New York: Appleton, 1936), pp. 99–113 and chap. XI; Kenneth N. Waltz, "Political Philosophy and the Study of International Relations," William T. R. Fox, ed., *Theoretical Aspects of International Relations* (Notre Dame: University of Notre Dame Press, 1959).

5. Martin Wight, "Why Is There No International Theory?", *International Relations*, II (April 1960), 35–48, 62.

6. Ibid., pp. 37–38.

7. See in Chapter 6 the section on the Marxist-Leninist theories of imperialism.

8. Martin Wight, op. cit., p. 40.

9. Grayson Kirk, *The Study of International Relations in American Colleges and Universities* (New York: Council on Foreign Relations, 1947), p. 4; Foster Rhea Dulles, *America's Rise to World Power, 1898–1954* (New York: Harper & Row, 1963), pp. 158–161. For an excellent treatment of the dichotomy, see Robert E. Osgood, *Ideals and Self-Interest in America's Foreign Relations* (Chicago: University of Chicago Press, 1953).

10. Kenneth W. Thompson, "The Study of International Politics: A Survey of Trends and Developments," *Review of Politics*, XIV (October 1952), 433–443.

11. James L. Brierly, *The Law of Nations*, 2nd ed. (New York: Oxford University Press, 1936); Clyde Eagleton, *International Government* (New York: Ronald Press, 1932); Charles G. Fenwick, *International Law*, 2nd ed. (New York: Appleton, 1934); Norman L. Hill, *International Administration* (New York: McGraw-Hill, 1931); Hersch Lauterpacht, *The Function of Law in the International Community* (New York: Oxford University Press, 1933); J. B. Moore, *A Digest of International Law* (Washington: Government Printing Office, 1906); Lassa F. L. Oppenheim, *International Law: A Treatise*, 4th ed. (London: Longmans, 1928); Pitman B. Potter, *An Introduction to the Study of International Organization*, 3rd ed. (New York: Appleton, 1928).

12. Sidney B. Fay, *The Origins of the World War*, 2nd ed. (New York: Macmillan, 1930); G. P. Gooch, *History of Modern Europe, 1878–1919* (New York: Holt, Rinehart and Winston, 1923); R. B. Mowat, *European Diplomacy, 1815–1914* (London: Longmans, 1922); Bernadotte E. Schmitt, *The Coming of the War, 1914* (New York: Scribner's, 1930); Raymond J. Sontag, *European Diplomatic History, 1871–1932* (New York: Appleton, 1933); G. P. Gooch and Harold W. Temperley, *British Documents on the Origins of the War, 1898–1914* (London: His Majesty's Stationery Office, 1928). For an historiographical appraisal of the work of American historians, see Warren I. Cohen, *The American Revisionists: The Lessons of Intervention in World War I* (Chicago: University of Chicago Press, 1967).

13. Carlton J.H. Hayes, *Essays on Nationalism* (New York: Macmillan, 1926); Hans Kohn, *A History of Nationalism in the East* (London: George Routledge, 1932), *Nationalism in the Soviet Union* (London: George Routledge, 1933), and *The Idea of Nationalism* (New York: Macmillan, 1944).

14. Philip J. Noel-Baker, *Disarmament* (New York: Harcourt Brace Jovanovich, 1926); James T. Shotwell, *War as an Instrument of National Policy* (New York: Harcourt Brace Jovanovich, 1929); J. W. Wheeler-Bennett, *Disarmament and Security Since Locarno, 1925–1931* (New York: Macmillan, 1932).

15. Parker T. Moon, *Imperialism and World Politics* (New York: Macmillan, 1926); Herbert I. Priestley, *France Overseas: A Study of Modern Imperialism* (New York: Appleton, 1938).

16. Harold Nicolson, *Peacemaking, 1919* (Boston: Houghton Mifflin, 1933), and *Diplomacy* (London: Oxford University Press, 1939).

17. Carl J. Friedrich, *Foreign Policy in the Making: The Search for a New Balance of Power* (New York: Norton, 1938); Alfred Vagts, "The United States and the Balance of Power," *Journal of Politics*, III (November 1941), 401–449.

18. James Fairgrieve, *Geography and World Power* (New York: Dutton, 1921); Nicholas J. Spykman, "Geography and Foreign Policy, I," *American Political Science Review*, XXXII (February 1938), 213–236, and the following two books: *America's Strategy in World Politics* (New York: Harcourt Brace Jovanovich, 1942) and *The Geography of the Peace* (New York: Harcourt Brace Jovanovich, 1944). Spykman also wrote two articles with Abbie A. Rollins, "Geographic Objectives in Foreign Policy I," *American Political Science Review*, XXXIII (June 1939), 391–410, and "Geographic Objectives in Foreign Policy II," ibid. (August 1939), 591–614. The theories of Mahan and Mackinder are treated in Chapter 2. For a discussion of Spykman's theories, see Chapter 3, in this text.

19. Frank M. Russell, *Theories of International Relations* (New York: Appleton, 1936).

20. Norman Angell, *The Great Illusion* (New York: Putnam's, 1933) and *Raw Materials, Population Pressure and War* (New York: National Peace Conference, 1936); Frank H. Simonds, *The ABC of War Debts* (New York: Harper & Row, 1933); Brooks Emeny, *The Strategy of War Materials* (New York: Macmillan, 1936); Lionel Robbins, *Economic Planning and International Order* (New York: Macmillan, 1937); Paul Einzig, *Finance and Politics* (London: Macmillan, 1932) and *The Economics of Rearmament* (London: Routledge and Kegan Paul, 1934); and Eugene Staley, *World Economy in Transition* (New York: Council on Foreign Relations, 1939). Angell's well-known hypothesis concerning the possibility of eliminating war by educating people to its economic futility is discussed in Chapter 5, in this text.

21. *The Twenty-Years' Crisis, 1919–1939: An Introduction to the Study of International Relations* (London: Macmillan, 1939; New York: Harper & Row [Torchbooks], 1964).

22. Arnold Wolfers, "Statesmanship and Moral Choice," *World Politics*, I (January 1949), 175–195, and "Political Theory and International Relations," Arnold Wolfers and Laurence Martin, eds., *The Anglo-American Tradition in Foreign Affairs* (New Haven: Yale University Press, 1956); Kenneth W. Thompson, "The Limits of Principle in International Politics: Necessity and the New Balance of Power," *Journal of Politics*, XX (August 1958), 437–467. George F. Kennan has commented as follows on the American legalistic-moralistic approach to international problems: "Our national genius, our sense of decency, our feeling for compromise and the law, our frankness and honesty—had not these qualities succeeded in producing on this continent a society unparalleled for its lack of strain and violence. . . . ? There was no reason why the outside world, with our assistance, should not similarly compose itself to a life without violence." From *Reali-*

ties of American Foreign Policy, excerpted in David L. Larson, ed., *The Puritan Ethic in United States Foreign Policy* (Princeton: Van Nostrand, 1966), p. 34.

23. Adam Smith and other eighteenth-century economists, following in the individualistic steps of John Locke, taught that people in a competitive system, when they seek their own private gain, are led by an "invisible hand" to promote the interest of the whole society.

24. E. H. Carr, op. cit., p.62; see especially chaps. 1–6. For a fuller exposition of the realist theories, see Chapter 3.

25. Ibid., p. 92.

26. Ibid., pp. 5–6.

27. Ibid., pp. 10, 20–21, 93–94.

28. Alfred Zimmern, "Introductory Report to the Discussions in 1935," Alfred Zimmern, ed., *University Teaching of International Relations,* Report of the Eleventh Session of the International Studies Conference (Paris: International Institute of Intellectual Cooperation, League of Nations, 1939), pp. 7–9. Later, C. A. W. Manning prepared a pamphlet for UNESCO on the university teaching of international relations in which he took a similar position. There is an international relations complex which has to be viewed from a "universalistic angle" and none of the established disciplines as traditionally taught can be relied upon to supply this necessary perspective. See P. D. Marchant, "Theory and Practice in the Study of International Relations," *International Relations,* I (April 1955), 95–102.

29. Nicholas J. Spykman, "Methods of Approach to the Study of International Relations," *Proceedings of the Fifth Conference of Teachers of International Law and Related Subjects* (Washington: Carnegie Endowment for International Peace, 1933), p. 60.

30. Quincy Wright, *The Study of International Relations* (New York: Appleton, 1955), p. 28.

31. David Easton, *The Political System* (New York: Knopf, 1959), pp. 129–131. See also Bruno Leoni, "The Meaning of 'Political' in Political Decisions," *Political Studies,* V (October 1957), 225–239.

32. Morton A. Kaplan, *Macropolitics: Selected Essays on The Philosophy and Science of Politics* (Chicago: Aldine, 1969), p. 68. Kaplan holds that politics occurs within a political system which, "like many other social systems, has recognizable interests which are not identical—though not necessarily opposed and perhaps the complementary—with those of the members of the system and within which there are regularized agencies and methods for making decisions concerning those interests. The rules for decision-making, including the specification of the decision-making roles and the general constitutional rules governing the society, are enacted within the political system." Morton A. Kaplan, *System and Process in International Politics* (New York: Wiley, 1957), pp. 13–14.

33. See Vernon Van Dyke, *Political Science, A Philosophical Analysis* (Stanford: Stanford University Press, 1960), pp. 133–135. On the difference between domestic and international politics, with emphasis on the lack of a common power and the legality of force in the interstate arena, see Raymond Aron, "What Is a Theory of International Relations?" *Journal of International Affairs,* XXI, No. 2 (1967), 190; Stanley Hoffmann, *The State of War* (New York: Praeger, 1965), chap. 2; and Roger D. Masters, "World Politics as a Primitive Political System," *World Politics,* XVI (July 1964), 595–619.

34. Martin Wight, *Power Politics,* "Looking Forward," Pamphlet No. 8 (London: Royal Institute of International Affairs, 1946), p. 11.

35. Georg Schwarzenberger, *Power Politics: A Study of World Society* (New York: Praeger, 1951), pp. 13–14. (The third edition of this work appeared in 1964.) For recent discussions of efforts to clarify the notion of power, see David V. J. Bell,

Power, Influence and Authority (New York: Oxford University Press, 1975); Jack H. Nagel, *The Descriptive Analysis of Power* (New Haven, Conn.: Yale University Press, 1975); and David A. Baldwin, "Power Analysis and World Politics," *World Politics*, XXXI (January 1979), 161–194.

36. Vernon Van Dyke, *International Politics* (New York: Appleton, 1957), p. 10.

37. Hans J. Morgenthau, *Politics Among Nations* (New York: Knopf, 1948, 1954, 1960, 1967).

38. Frederick L. Schuman, op. cit., 4th and 5th eds. (New York: McGraw-Hill, 1948, 1953); Robert Strausz-Hupé and Stefan T. Possony, *International Relations* (New York: McGraw-Hill, 1950, 1954); Norman D. Palmer and Howard C. Perkins, *International Relations* (Boston: Houghton Mifflin, 1953, 1957, 1969); Norman J. Padelford and George A. Lincoln, *The Dynamics of International Politics* (New York: Macmillan, 1962); Ernst B. Haas and Allen S. Whiting, *Dynamics of International Relations* (New York: McGraw-Hill, 1956); Harold and Margaret Sprout, *Foundations of National Power* (Princeton: Van Nostrand, 1945, 1951) and *Foundations of International Politics* (Princeton: Van Nostrand, 1962); Quincy Wright, op. cit.; Charles P. Schleicher, *Introduction to International Relations* (Englewood Cliffs, N.J.: Prentice-Hall, 1954) and *International Relations: Cooperation and Conflict* (Englewood Cliffs, N.J.: Prentice-Hall, 1962); Frederick H. Hartmann, *The Relations of Nations* (New York: Macmillan, 1957, 1962); A. F. K. Organski, *World Politics* (New York: Knopf, 1958); Lennox A. Mills and Charles H. McLaughlin, *World Politics in Transition* (New York: Holt, Rinehart and Winston, 1956); Fred Greene, *Dynamics of International Relations* (New York: Holt, Rinehart and Winston, 1964); W. W. Kulski, *International Politics in a Revolutionary Age* (Philadelphia: Lippincott, 1964, 1967). The reader's attention is called to the following reviews of the earlier international relations texts: Richard C. Snyder, "Toward Greater Order in the Study of International Politics," *World Politics*, VII (April 1955), 461–478; Fred A. Sondermann, "The Study of International Relations: 1956 Version," ibid., IX (October 1957), 102–111; Robert W. Tucker, "The Study of International Politics," ibid., X (July 1958), 639–647; Kenneth E. Boulding, "The Content of International Studies in College: A Review," *The Journal of Conflict Resolution*, VIII (March 1964), 65–71; and Dina A. Zinnes, "An Introduction to the Behavioral Approach: A Review," ibid., XII (June 1968), 258–267. For a content analysis of more recent textbooks and other teaching materials, see James N. Rosenau et al., "Of Syllabi, Texts, Students and Scholarship in International Relations: Some Data and Interpretations on the State of a Burgeoning Field," *World Politics*, XXIX (January 1977), 263–340.

39. Horace V. Harrison, writing in 1964, criticized not only the textbooks but nearly all writing in international theory as being partial, implicit rather than explicit, too narrowly focused, designed to serve particular professional interests, and incapable of providing a guide either to research or to action. He added, however, that some progress toward more general theories had begun since the latter 1950s. See his Introduction to the book he edited, op. cit., pp. 8–9.

40. William T. R. Fox and Annette Baker Fox, "The Teaching of International Relations in the United States," *World Politics*, XIII (July 1961), 339–359: See also Quincy Wright, op. cit., chaps. 3 and 4; Grayson Kirk, op. cit.; Waldemar Gurian, "On the Study of International Relations," *Review of Politics*, VIII (July 1946), 275–282; Frederick L. Schuman, "The Study of International Relations in the United States," *Contemporary Political Science: A Survey of Methods, Research and Training* (Paris: United Nations Educational, Scientific, and Cultural Organization, 1950); Frederick S. Dunn, "The Present Course of International Relations Research," *World Politics*, II (October 1949), 142–146; Kenneth W. Thompson, op. cit.; L. Gray Cowen, "Theory and Practice in the Teaching of International Rela-

tions in the United States," in Geoffrey L. Goodwin, Ed., *The University Teaching of International Relations* (Oxford: Basil Blackwell, 1951); John Gange, *University Research on International Relations* (Washington: American Council on Education, 1958); Richard N. Swift, *World Affairs and the College Curriculum* (Washington: American Council on Education, 1959); Edward W. Weidner, *The World Role of Universities,* The Carnegie Series in American Education (New York: McGraw-Hill, 1962) especially the chapters dealing with student-abroad programs, exchange programs, and international programs of university assistance.

41. The appearance of several anthologies in international theory in the early 1960s attested to a burgeoning interest in the field. See William T. R. Fox, ed., *Theoretical Aspects of International Relations* (Notre Dame: University of Notre Dame Press, 1959); Charles A. McClelland, William C. Olson, and Fred A. Sondermann, eds., *The Theory and Practice of International Relations* (Englewood Cliffs, N.J.: Prentice-Hall, 1960); Stanley Hoffmann, ed., *Contemporary Theory in International Relations* (Englewood Cliffs, N.J.: Prentice-Hall 1960); Ivo D. Duchacek, ed., with the collaboration of Kenneth W. Thompson, *Conflict and Cooperation Among Nations* (New York: Holt, Rinehart and Winston, 1960); Klaus Knorr and Sidney Verba, eds., *The International System: Theoretical Essays* [*World Politics,* XIV [October 1961]] (Princeton: Princeton University Press, 1961); James N. Rosenau, ed., *International Politics and Foreign Policy: A Reader in Research and Theory* (New York: The Free Press, 1961); Horace V. Harrison, ed., *The Role of Theory in International Relations* (Princeton: Van Nostrand, 1964).

42. Michael P. Sullivan, *International Relations: Theories and Evidence* (Englewood Cliffs, N.J.: Prentice-Hall, 1976), x. Cf. also James N. Rosenau, "Assessment in International Studies: Ego Trip or Feedback?" *International Studies Quarterly,* XVIII (September 1974), 339–367.

43. Frederick S. Dunn, "The Scope of International Relations," *World Politics,* I (October 1948), 142.

44. Ibid., p. 143. Stanley Hoffmann warns against excessive preoccupation with the problem of defining scope. A definition, he says, is useful if it merely suggests the proper area of inquiry. It need not pretend to penetrate to the essence of the subject, especially in the social sciences: *Contemporary Theory in International Relations,* op. cit., pp. 4–6. Raymond Aron has similarly noted that, although the definitional difficulty is real, it should not be exaggerated, since every scientific discipline lacks precise limits. More important than knowing where interindividual relations become or cease to be data of international relations, says Aron, is the field's principal focus of interest. For him, this is on interstate relations—the power relations among political units that reserve to themselves the fundamental decisions of peace and war. *Peace and War: A Theory of International Relations,* trans. Richard Howard and Annette Baker Fox (New York: Praeger, 1968), pp. 5–8.

45. For analyses of linkages between domestic political structures and processes on the one hand and foreign policy on the other, see: James Rosenau, *Linkage Politics* (New York: The Free Press, 1969); Henry A. Kissinger, "Domestic Structure and Foreign Policy," in *American Foreign Policy: Three Essays* (New York: Norton, 1969); Wolfram Hanrieder, "Compatability and Consensus: A Proposal for the Conceptual Linkage of External and Internal Dimensions of Foreign Policy," in Hanreider, ed., *Comparative Foreign Policy: Theoretical Essays* (New York: McKay, 1971); and Jonathan Wilkenfeld, ed., *Conflict Behavior and Linkage Politics* (New York: McKay, 1973).

46. The subject of other-than-state actors is fully explored in Richard W. Mansbach, Yale H. Ferguson, and Donald E. Lampert, *The Web of World Politics: Non-State Actors in the Global System* (Englewood Cliffs, N.J.: Prentice-Hall, 1976). On

transnationals and multinational corporations, see also Samuel P. Huntington, "Transnational Organizations in World Politics," *World Politics*, XXV (April 1973); George W. Ball, ed., *Global Companies: The Political Economy of World Business* (Englewood Cliffs, N.J.: Prentice-Hall, 1975); David E. Apter and Louis Wolf Goodman, eds., *The Multinational Corporation and Social Change* (New York: Praeger, 1976); Raymond Vernon, *Storm over the Multinationals: The Real Issues* (Cambridge, Mass.: Harvard University Press, 1977); Louis Turner, *Oil Companies in the International System* (London: Allen and Unwin, 1978).

47. Arnold Wolfers, "The Actors in International Politics," in William T. R. Fox, ed., op. cit., p. 84. A full discussion of decision-making theories is in Chapter 11, and of regional or functional integration with accompanying corporate actors in Chapter 10.

48. Ibid., p. 89.

49. See J. David Singer, "Man and World Politics: The Psychological Interface," *Journal of Social Issues*, XXIV (July 1968), 127–156; Heinz Eulau, *Micro-Macro Political Analysis* (Chicago: Aldine, 1970) and Thomas C. Schelling, *Micromotives and Macrobehavior* (New York: Norton, 1978). See also the discussion on this point in Chapters 5 to 8, especially pp. 185–186 and p. 254, with particular reference to the writings of Herbert C. Kelman and Werner Levi.

50. Stewart E. Perry, "Notes on the Role of the National: A Social-Psychological Concept for the Study of International Relations," *Journal of Conflict Resolution*, I (December 1957), 346–363.

51. John H. Herz, "The Rise and Demise of the Territorial State," *World Politics*, IX (April 1957), 474. Herz later admitted that his earlier deprecation of the role of the state was probably premature and that the same nuclear developments which had rendered the territory of states theoretically vulnerable had also, paradoxically, made all force, even conventional force, "unavailable" in the relations between major powers and their alliance blocs, thus producing trends toward a "new territoriality." See his "The Territorial State Revisited: Reflections on the Future of the Nation-State," James N. Rosenau, ed., op. cit., rev. ed., 1969, pp. 76–89.

52. Toynbee in an earlier period between the wars emphasized the nation-state. This was also his more "idealistic" phase in his theory of international relations. Later he shifted his attention to civilizations and the world religions, as he became more "realistic" in his advocacy of the balance of power. See his "Encounters Between Civilizations," *Harper's*, CXCIV (April 1947), 289–294; and "The International Outlook," *International Affairs*, XXIII (October 1947), 463–476. See also Kenneth W. Thompson, "Toynbee and the Theory of International Politics," *Political Science Quarterly*, LXXXI (September 1956), 365–386.

53. Morton A. Kaplan, op. cit. See also the references to Kaplan's work in Chapter 4.

54. George Modelski, "Agraria and Industria: Two Models of the International System," Knorr and Verba, eds., op. cit.

55. William H. Riker, *The Theory of Political Coalitions* (New Haven: Yale University Press, 1962).

56. J. David Singer, "The Level-of-Analysis Problem in International Relations," Knorr and Verba, eds., op. cit., pp. 77–78.

57. Hedley Bull, "International Theory: The Case for a Classical Approach," *World Politics*, XVIII (April 1966), 375–376.

58. Morton A. Kaplan, *System and Process in International Politics*, op. cit., p. 3. In an article written as a rejoinder to Bull's criticism of the scientific writers, Kaplan accused the traditionalists of using history ineptly, of falling into the trap of "overparticularization and unrelated generalization," and of being unaware that many writers in the modern scientific school regard history as a laboratory for the acquisition of empirical data. See his "The New Great Debate: Traditionalism vs. Science in International Relations," *World Politics*, XIX (October 1966), 15–16.

59. Morton A. Kaplan, "Problems of Theory Building and Theory Confirmation in International Politics," Knorr and Verba, eds., op. cit., p. 23; Morton A. Kaplan, *New Approaches to International Relations* (New York: St. Martin's, 1968), pp. 399–404. See also George Modelski, "Comparative International Systems," *World Politics*, XIV (July 1962), 662–674, in which he reviews Adda B. Bozeman, *Politics and Culture in International History* (Princeton: Princeton University Press, 1960). See also Hoffmann, op. cit., pp. 174–180.
60. Morton A. Kaplan, *System and Process*, chap. 2. See also the reference in the text, p. 23, to Quincy Wright's fourfold approach to all social studies.
61. "The substance of theory is history, composed of unique events and occurrences. An episode in history and politics is in one sense never repeated. It happens as it does only once. . . . In this sense history is beyond the reach of theory. Underlying all theory, however, is the assumption that these same unique events are also more concrete instances of more general propositions. The wholly unique, having nothing in common with anything else, is indescribable. . . ." Kenneth W. Thompson, "Toward a Theory of International Politics," *American Political Science Review*, XLIX (September 1955), 734.
62. *The Ethics of Aristotle*, trans. D. P. Chase (New York: Dutton, 1950), Book VI, p. 147. Hans J. Morgenthau, echoing Aristotle, stressed the difference between "what is worth knowing intellectually and what is useful for practice." "Reflections on the State of Political Science," *Review of Politics*, XVII (October 1955), p. 440.
63. David Hume, *A Treatise of Human Nature*, Part III, "Of Probability and Knowledge," in *The Essential David Hume*, Introduction by Robert P. Wolff (New York: New American Library, 1969), pp. 53–99. See Sheldon S. Wolin, "Hume and Conservatism," *American Political Science Review*, XLVIII (December 1954), 999–1016. Michael Polanyi, too, has treated the difference between the theory of affairs and the practice of affairs. *Personal Knowledge* (Chicago: University of Chicago Press, 1958), pp. 49ff.
64. For insights into the important role played by some leading figures and the significance of their personal theories, see Robert Isaak, *Individuals and World Politics* (Belmont, Calif.: Wadsworth, 1975).
65. For an example of "institutionalized" theory out of the British Foreign Office, the student should read the famous Eyre Crowe memorandum on Anglo-German relations dated January 1, 1907. See G. P. Gooch and Harold V. Temperley, eds., *British Documents on the Origins of the War, 1898–1914* (London: His Majesty's Stationery Office, 1928), III, 402–420. The conventional wisdom regarding the problem-specific (regional or country) needs and interests of foreign policy makers as distinct from basic global research has been questioned by J. Martin Rochester and Michael Segalla, "What Foreign Policy Makers Want from Foreign Policy Researchers," *International Studies Quarterly*, Vol. 22 (September 1978), 435–461.
66. Michael Sullivan, op. cit., p. 3.
67. The concept of international relations need not be restricted to those aspects of reality which affect all the elements of the system simultaneously. Thus we do consider it possible to study the international relations of a region, such as Latin America or the Middle East, so long as the region is recognized as a subsystem of the whole international system. See Leonard Binder, "The Middle East as a Subordinate International System," *World Politics*, X (April 1958), 408–429; and Michael Brecher, "The Subordinate State System of Southern Asia," *World Politics*, XV (January 1963), 213–235.
68. This idea is further elaborated in our discussion of decision-making theories in Chapter 11.
69. The foregoing section owes a great deal to the essay by Fred A. Sondermann, "The Linkage Between Foreign Policy and International Politics," James N. Rosenau, ed., op. cit., pp. 8–17.

70. Daniel Lerner and Harold D. Lasswell, eds., *The Policy Sciences: Recent Developments in Scope and Method* (Stanford: Stanford University Press, 1951). According to William T. R. Fox and Annette Baker Fox, the study of policy problems "is not a threat to objectivity so long as the preferences of the disciplined scholar are permitted to operate only in the selection of the problem and not in the mode of observation and analysis." Op. cit., p. 343. To what extent this can be achieved in practice is another matter.

71. Harold D. Lasswell, "The Scientific Study of International Relations," *The Yearbook of World Affairs 1958*, London Institute of World Affairs (New York: Praeger, 1958), p. 3. See also Philip E. Mosely, "Research on Foreign Policy," in *Research for Public Policy*, Brookings Dedication Lectures (Washington: Brookings Institution, 1961).

72. Anatol Rapoport, "Various Meanings of 'Theory,' " *American Political Science Review*, LII (December 1958), 972. Rapoport illustrates the meaning of theory in an exact science by citing the example of the pendulum. The problem is to explain its motion, and this introduces the notions of "why" and "because." The questions asked flow from what is singled out for observation. The question, "Why does the pendulum move around?", is too vague. "The first task of an exact science, therefore, is to make the questions precise. The question, 'Why does the pendulum move *as it does?*', is more to the point. But the phrase 'as it does' now lays the questioner open to a counterquestion: 'What do you mean, "as it does?" ' This is a challenge to describe how in fact the pendulum does move, and this temporarily turns the attention away from (explanation) toward description." Before we can explain, we must first carefully circumscribe, and thus we face the requirement of exact mathematical measurement of that which we wish to explain. Ibid., p. 974.

73. See Fred N. Kerlinger, *Foundations of Behavioral Research* (New York: Holt, Rinehart and Winston, 1966), p. 11, and Robert Brown, *Explanation in Social Science* (Chicago: Aldine, 1963), p. 174.

74. Gustav Bergmann, *The Philosophy of Science* (Madison: University of Wisconsin Press, 1958), pp. 31–32.

75. Abraham Kaplan, *The Conduct of Inquiry* (San Francisco: Chandler, 1964), p. 319.

76. Carl G. Hempel, *Fundamentals of Concept Formation in Empirical Science* (Chicago: University of Chicago Press, 1952), p. 36.

77. Hans J. Morgenthau, "The Nature and Limits of a Theory of International Relations," William T. R. Fox, ed., op. cit., p. 17.

78. Kenneth W. Thompson, "Toward a Theory of International Politics," *American Political Science Review*, XLIX (September 1955), 740.

79. Quincy Wright, "Development of a General Theory of International Relations," in Horace V. Harrison, ed., op. cit., p. 20.

80. Ibid., pp. 21–23.

81. Quincy Wright, *A Study of International Relations*, op. cit., p. 26.

82. Ibid., p. 11 and chaps. 8, 9, 10, and 11. In addition to these four basic intellectual perspectives, Wright dwells at length on the root disciplines of international relations in chap. 5—international law, diplomatic history, military science, international politics, international organization, international trade, colonial government, and the conduct of foreign relations—and in chap. 6 on "disciplines with a world point of view", such as world history, world geography, the sociology and social psychology of international relations, and studies of population and technology.

83. David Hume, *Essays and Treatises on Several Subjects* (Edinburgh: Bell and Bradfute, and W. Blackwood, 1825), vol. I, pp. 331–339. Reprinted in Arend Lijphart, ed., *World Politics* (Boston: Allyn & Bacon, 1966), pp. 228–234.

84. All these examples are cited in Hans J. Morgenthau, *Politics Among Nations,* op. cit., pp. 161–166.
85. Richard Cobden, *Political Writings,* 2nd ed. (London: William Ridgeway, 1868), I, p. 259.
86. Ernst B. Haas, "The Balance of Power: Prescription, Concept or Propaganda?" *World Politics,* V (July 1953), 442–477.
87. Inis L. Claude, Jr., *Power and International Relations* (New York: Random House, 1962), pp. 13 and 22.
88. This paragraph and the one following constitute a synthesis from several different sources. For fuller treatments of the balance of power, see Inis L. Claude, Jr., op. cit.; Edward V. Gulick, *Europe's Classical Balance of Power* (Ithaca: Cornell University Press, 1955); Sidney B. Fay, "Balance of Power," in *Encyclopedia of the Social Sciences,* vol. II (New York: Macmillan, 1930); Alfred Vagts, "The Balance of Power: Growth of an Idea," *World Politics,* I (October 1948), 82–101; Paul Seabury, ed., *Balance of Power* (San Francisco: Chandler, 1965). See also the chapters on the balance of power in the textbooks by the following authors, all cited previously: Schleicher, Morgenthau, Palmer and Perkins, Hartmann, Organski.
89. Quoted in Edward V. Gulick, op. cit., p. 34.
90. "Memorandum on the Present State of British Relations with France and Germany," in G. P. Gooch and Harold V. Temperly, eds., op. cit., III, 402.
91. Winston S. Churchill, *The Gathering Storm* (Boston: Houghton Mifflin, 1948), pp. 207–210.
92. Nicholas J. Spykman, *American Strategy and World Politics* (New York: Harcourt Brace Jovanovich, 1942), pp. 21–22.
93. Hans Morgenthau, op. cit., chap. 14.
94. Charles P. Schleicher, op. cit., p. 368.
95. A. K. F. Organski, op. cit., pp. 299 and 283.
96. Ernst B. Haas, "The Balance of Power as a Guide to Policy-Making," *Journal of Politics,* XV (August 1953), 370–398.
97. Edward P. Gulick, op. cit., pp. 10–15.
98. William G. Carleton, "Ideology or Balance of Power?", *Yale Review,* XXXVI (June 1947), 590–602.
99. Morton A. Kaplan, *System and Process,* op. cit., pp. 22–36. Particularly important to his theory is the list of six essential rules of the balance of power system on p. 23.
100. Arthur Lee Burns, "From Balance to Deterrence: A Theoretical Analysis," *World Politics,* IX (July 1957), 505. Whereas Burns prefers five as the optimal number required for security, Kaplan says that five is the minimal number required for security, but that security increases with the number of states up to some as-yet-undetermined upper limit. "Traditionalism vs. Science in International Relations," op. cit., p. 10.
101. Arthur Lee Burns, op. cit., p. 508.
102. See Glenn H. Snyder, "Balance of Power in the Missile Age," *Journal of International Affairs,* XIV, No. 1 (1960); John H. Herz, "Balance Systems and Balance Policies in a Nuclear and Bipolar Age," ibid.; and the books and articles cited below in the extended discussion on deterrence and arms control in Chapter 9.
103. For examples of quantitative studies in international relations, see Morton A. Kaplan, ed., *New Approaches to International Relations* (New York: St. Martin's, 1968); Richard L. Merritt and Stein Rokkan, eds., *Comparing Nations: The Use of Quantitative Data in Cross-National Research* (New Haven: Yale University Press, 1966); John E. Mueller, ed., *Approaches to Measurement in International Relations: A Non-Evangelical Survey* (New York: Appleton, 1969); James N. Rosenau, ed., *International Politics and Foreign Policy* (New York: Free Press, 1969); Ru-

dolph J. Rummel et al., *Dimensions of Nations* (Evanston: Northwestern University Press, 1967); Bruce Russett, *International Regions in the International System* (Chicago: Rand McNally, 1967); J. David Singer, *Quantitative International Politics: Insights and Evidence* (New York: Free Press, 1968).

104. Carl G. Hempel and Paul Oppenheim, "Studies in the Logic of Explanation," *Philosophy of Science*, XV (1948), 135–175.

105. Werner Heisenberg, *Physics and Philosophy* (New York: Harper & Row, 1958), pp. 179, 183, 186. It should be pointed out that the principle of indeterminancy is often referred to less accurately by social scientists as "the uncertainty principle."

106. See Quincy Wright, *A Study of International Relations*, chap. 7, "Educational and Research Objectives"; Ladis K. D. Kristof, "Political Laws in International Relations," *Western Political Quarterly*, XI (September 1958), 598–606. Another penetrating discourse on the role of normative theory in contrast to a purely value-free approach to international relations is to be found in Charles A. McClelland, "The Function of Theory in International Relations," *Journal of Conflict Resolution*, IV (September 1960), 311–314.

107. Harvey Starr, "The Quantitative International Relations Scholar as Surfer," *The Journal of Conflict Resolution*, vol. 18 (June 1974), 337.

108. J. David Singer, "Data-making in International Relations," *Behavioral Scientist*, vol. 10, 1969.

109. Developed in mathematics, used first in psychology, later in economics, and more recently in political science, factor analysis is a statistical technique by which a large number of variables can be clustered on the basis of their intercorrelation. Factor analysis enables the researcher to identify patterns among variables. The results of factor analysis, the factors defining the different patterns, are often termed "Dimensions." Hence the use of the word "Dimensionality" in the DON Project. For a detailed discussion of factor analysis, see Harry H. Harmon, *Modern Factor Analysis* (Chicago: University of Chicago Press, 1967); R. J. Rummel, *Applied Factor Analysis* (Evanston: Northwestern University Press, 1970); L. L. Thurstone, *Multiple Factor Analysis* (Chicago: University of Chicago Press, 1965).

110. Jonathan Wilkenfeld, "Domestic and Foreign Conflict Behavior of Nations," *Journal of Peace Research*, I (1968), 57.

111. Ibid., p. 66.

112. Kurt Lewin's contributions in determining the methodological and conceptual prerequisites for a science of human behavior are said to be relevant to all the social sciences. The psychological field theorist sees human behavior as a function not of the internal characteristics of the person, nor of a historical chain of causation, but of the interaction of the person and contemporary events in the environment. He argued, therefore, that the determinants of human behavior should be treated in a single unified field rather than separated into traditional disciplines. According to Lewin, all behavior can be conceived as change occurring in some state of a field in a given unit of time. By focusing on the dynamics of motivation, conflict, and change, he developed a field theory similar in several respects to systems theory. He showed how living systems seek an equilibrium in relation to their environments through recurring processes of goal-setting, tension-arousal, locomotion of the person within the psychological environment or a change in the structure of the perceived environment, and tension reduction. See Kurt Lewin, *Field Theory in Social Science* (New York: Harper & Row, 1951), p. 45; and the article on "Field Theory" by Morton Deutsch in the *International Encyclopedia of the Social Sciences*, David L. Sills, ed. (New York: Macmillan and The Free Press, 1972), vol. 5, pp. 407–417.

113. Quincy Wright, "Development of a General Theory of International Relations," in Horace V. Harrison, ed., *The Role of Theory in International Relations* (Princeton,

N.J.: Van Nostrand, 1964), p. 38 and *The Study of International Relations* (New York: Appleton, 1955), pp. 524–569.

114. For a more complete examination of coordinates in field theory, see Quincy Wright, *The Study of International Relations*, pp. 540–567.
115. R. J. Rummel, "A Status Field Theory of International Relations," *Dimensionality of Nations Project Report No. 50* (Honolulu, 1971), p. 5.
116. See Norman D. Palmer, "The Study of International Relations in the United States: Perspectives of Half a Century," Paper to the International Studies Association, Toronto, March 1979. Cf. also Klaus Knorr and James N. Rosenau, "Tradition and Science in the Study of International Politics," in the book they edited, *Contending Approaches to International Politics* (Princeton: Princeton University Press, 1970), p. 13.
117. Hedley Bull, "International Theory: The Case for a Classical Approach," *World Politics*, XVIII (April 1966), 361. Bull's essay is reprinted in the volume by Knorr and Rosenau, eds., op. cit.; cf. p. 20.
118. Klaus Knorr and James Rosenau, op. cit., p. 14.
119. Ibid., p. 15.
120. All of these and other criticisms are presented by Hedley Bull, op. cit.
121. J. David Singer, "The Incompleat Theorist: Insight Without Evidence," in Knorr and Rosenau, eds., op. cit., pp. 72–73.
122. Klaus Knorr and James Rosenau, "Tradition and Science in the Study of International Politics," ibid., p. 16.
123. J. David Singer, op. cit., p. 77.
124. J. David Singer, in discussing differences between "traditionalists" and "behavioralists," has referred to the N/V ratio in which N stands for the number of cases studied and V the number of variables examined. According to Singer, the typical traditional scholar minimizes the N and maximizes the V, whereas the typical behavioral scientist does just the reverse. He notes that each approach has potential disadvantages. If the analyst investigates for only one or very few variables in the whole universe of political phenomena, he runs the risk of overhomogenizing the various units, and of overlooking significant differences among them. Conversely, the analyst who dwells upon only one or very few cases often lapses into the opposite distortion of exaggerating the uniqueness of each, of assuming that differences are more important than similarities, and of concluding too readily not only that the search for general laws of universal political behavior is futile, but that the correlations which the behaviorist calls "statistically significant" are not really all that significant to the political analyst. Singer himself regards the tendency to overhomogenize less dangerous in terms of scientific method than the tendency to overdifferentiate. J. David Singer, "The Behavioral Science Approach to International Relations: Payoff and Prospects," *SAIS Review* (School of Advanced International Studies of the Johns Hopkins University), X (Summer 1966), 12–20, especially p. 14; and "The Level-of-Analysis Problem in International Relations," in Klaus Knorr and Sidney Verba, eds., op. cit., pp. 81–83.
125. Louis René Beres and Harry R. Targ, eds., *Planning Alternative World Futures* (New York: Praeger, 1975), p. xvi. See also Louis René Beres and Harry R. Targ, *Reordering the Planet: Constructing Alternative World Futures* (Boston: Allyn & Bacon, 1974).
126. See the Introduction in ibid., pp. xv–xxv, and Marvin S. Soroos, "A Methodological Overview of the Process of Designing Alternative Future Worlds," in ibid., pp. 3–27.
127. Richard A. Falk, "Contending Approaches to World Order," *Journal of International Affairs*, vol. 31 (Fall/Winter 1977), 171–175. See also his "Toward a New World Order: Modest Methods and Drastic Visions," in Saul H. Mendlovitz, ed.,

On the Creation of a Just World Order: Preferred Worlds for the 1990s (New York: Free Press, 1975), pp. 211–258.

128. Hedley Bull, *The Anarchical Society: A Study of Order in World Politics* (New York: Columbia University Press, 1977), pp. 233–256. See also Herbert Butterfield and Martin Wight, eds. *Diplomatic Investigations: Essays in the Theory of International Politics* (Cambridge, Mass.: Harvard University Press, 1966), and Stanley Hoffmann, "Obstinate or Obsolete? The Fate of the Nation-State and the Case of Western Europe," in Joseph S. Nye, Jr., *International Regionalism: Readings* (Boston: Little, Brown, 1968), pp. 177–230.

129. Stanley Hoffman, ibid., p. 229.

130. Ibid.

131. Charles A. McClelland, "The Function of Theory in International Relations," *Journal of Conflict Resolution*, IV (September 1960), 303–336; and *Theory and the International System* (New York: Macmillan, 1966), pp. 1–32.

132. No brief discussion can do justice to the abundant literature which has appeared since the early 1960s on forecasting, prediction, and thinking about the future as well as planning for it. The more important general works include: Arthur C. Clarke, *Profiles of the Future* (New York: Harper & Row, 1962); Bertrand de Jouvenel, ed., *Futuribles* (Geneva: Droz Library, 1962); Dennis Gabor, *Inventing the Future* (New York: Knopf, 1964); Daniel Bell, "Twelve Modes of Prediction," *Daedalus*, XCIII (Summer 1964), 845–880; *Toward the Year 2000*, Issue of *Daedalus*, XCVI (Summer 1967); Herman Kahn and Anthony J. Wiener, *The Year 2000* (New York: Macmillan, 1967); Herman Kahn, "The Alternative World Futures Approach," in Morton A. Kaplan, ed., *New Approaches to International Relations* (New York: St. Martin's, 1968), pp. 83–136; Robert Jungk and Johan Galtung, *Mankind 2000* (London: Allen & Unwin, 1968); Richard A. Falk, *A Study of Future Worlds* (New York: The Free Press, 1975). See also the work edited by Louis R. Beres and Harry R. Targ, *Planning for Alternative World Futures* (note 124 above) as well as the books and articles cited in the discussion concerning the debate over "the limits of growth" hypothesis of the Club of Rome in Chapter 2 of this text (pp. 76–79); see also Chapter 8, pp. 340–342. The specific problems of dealing with possibilities and probabilities in the future of international relations are treated in Bruce M. Russett, "The Ecology of Future International Politics," *International Studies Quarterly*, XI (March 1967), 12–31; Raymond Tanter, "Explanation, Prediction and Forecasting in International Politics," in James N. Rosenau et al., eds., *Analysis of International Politics* (New York: The Free Press, 1972), pp. 41–57; Nazli Choucri and Thomas W. Robinson, eds., *Forecasting in International Relations: Theory, Methods, Problems, Prospects* (San Francisco: Freeman, 1978); and John R. Freeman and Brian L. Job, "Scientific Forecasts in International Relations," with comments by Nazli Choucri and a reply by the authors, *International Studies Quarterly*, XXIII (March 1979), 113–154. The book edited by Choucri and Robinson, which contains 28 chapters, is the most comprehensive symposium on the subject yet to appear, and will probably constitute the standard source for several years.

Chapter 2
Environmental Theories

THE ROLE OF ENVIRONMENT IN
INTERNATIONAL RELATIONS

Especially since the 1960s there has been a revival of interest, among scholars and policymakers, in environmental theories of political behavior. Factors such as geography, demography, resource distribution, and technological development are now seen as increasingly important to the study, as well as to the practice, of international politics. Indeed, Harold and Margaret Sprout have suggested that the international political milieu cannot be fully understood without reference to the "whole spectrum of environing factors, human as well as nonhuman, intangible as well as tangible."[1] Still, the current manifestation of interest in the impact of geographical and broader environmental factors upon politics is but the most recent phase of an age-old focus of attention that extends back to the ancient world. Aristotle, for example, believed that people and their environment are inseparable, and that they are affected by both geographical circumstances and political institutions. Location near the sea stimulated commercial activity upon which the city-state was based; temperate climate favorably affected the development of national character, human energy, and intellect.[2] Jean Bodin, too, maintained that climatic circumstances influence national characteristics, even determining the foreign policies of states. According to Bodin, the extremes of northern and temperate climates offer conditions most favorable to building a political system based on law and justice. Northern and mountainous regions were said to be conducive to greater political discipline than southern climes which fail to spark initiative.[3] Montesquieu, as well, pointed to various climatic factors that he felt influenced the political divisions of Western Europe, in contrast to the great plains of Asia and Eastern Europe, and contributed to a spirit of political independence. According to Montesquieu, islands could preserve their freedom more easily than continental countries because they are isolated from foreign influences.[4] Here, Montesquieu had in mind Britain, which had evolved unique political institutions that he greatly admired and had withstood invasion from Continental Europe since 1066.

In American history, Frederick Jackson Turner hypothesized that the existence of the frontier, pushed westward by succeeding generations of settlers until the last decade of the nineteenth century, shaped the American character and intellect—"that practical, inventive turn of mind, quick to find expedients; that masterful grasp of material things, lacking in the artistic but powerful to affect great ends; that restless, nervous energy; the dominant individualism, working for good and evil, and withal that buoyancy and exuberance which comes with freedom— these are the traits of the frontier, or traits called out elsewhere because of the existence of the frontier."[5] The use of Social Darwinian analysis in the late nineteenth century also provided an important intellectual stimulus to environmentally oriented studies of international affairs, insofar as it transferred to the social order a scientific perspective in which the evolutionary development of a species was a function of its ability to adjust to its physical habitat. The concept of the "survival of the fittest" was adapted from living organisms to the state, as exemplified in the geopolitical writings of Friedrich Ratzel, discussed later in this chapter.

The physical habitat encompasses resources and population, as well as the impact of population upon resources, including the availability of food supplies. The notion that there are severe "limits to growth" is central to the thought of Thomas Robert Malthus and to many of the writings on imperialism. Beginning in 1798, with his *Essay on the Principle of Population as it Affects the Future Improvement of Society,* Malthus hypothesized that population growth will always outpace the increase in food supplies. If unchecked, population will rise in geometrical progression, although the means of subsistence will be augmented only in arithmetical progression. As a result, poverty will be the inevitable fate of mankind, unless population growth is checked by war, famine, and disease. J. A. Hobson and Lenin, in their related analyses of imperialism, saw a quest for access to markets and raw materials leading capitalist states to become imperialistic. For Lenin, the ultimate effect of capitalism, as noted in Chapter 6, would be a struggle among capitalist states for the world's remaining markets and raw materials. In a contemporary study, Nazli Choucri and Robert C. North hypothesized that there is an inextricable relationship between population growth and resource demand, and that the more advanced the level of technology, the greater will be the need for resources. A population increase of 1 percent is said to make necessary a 4 percent increase in national income merely to maintain living standards at their existing level.[6] As technology advances, together with population growth, societies seek greater access to resources. As societies attempt to extend their interests outward in light of resource needs, the likelihood of conflict is enhanced. Here, Choucri and North draw linkages among resource factors, domestic growth, and foreign policy. Their hypotheses will be examined in greater detail in Chapter 8, along with the writings of Quincy Wright, who emphasized the relationship between cultural, political, institutional, and technological change and conflict.

Peace is said to be dependent upon an "equilibrium among many forces," and to be jeopardized by a transformation in factors such as demography. Rapid increases in population in the past century have produced cultural interpenetration and have greatly increased communication as what Quincy Wright terms *technological distance* has narrowed, but they have also enlarged the opportunities for friction, and for conflict, among peoples.[7] Wright postulated that the growth in size of states had made it more necessary and more likely that conflicts would be resolved without violence, but it had also made more severe those conflicts that could not be settled by peaceful means.[8]

Thus in the late twentieth century, population, as well as resource and technology factors, the so-called global issues of the present era, have contributed to a burgeoning literature focused upon the implications of population growth for resource scarcity; the implications of resource scarcity for potential conflict; the relationship between resources and geography; and the impact of technology upon resources and geography. Technology has made possible the exploitation of resources in inhospitable environments, such as the seabed. At the same time, technology has created the great need for resources that has contributed to their depletion and raised the specter of resource scarcity. The political significance of one or another geographical location has been influenced decisively by technology and by resource issues. In historic context the importance of the seas, in the writings of Alfred Thayer Mahan, for example, stemmed from the mobility they conferred, by virtue of the ability of the sailing vessel and later the steamship, to move military capabilities most effectively from one point to another. Subsequent changes in technology have enhanced the importance of other geographical elements. In the late twentieth century, the increased dependence of industrialized states upon resource imports, especially energy, once again gave renewed significance to the oceans. As Saul B. Cohen has suggested, "The essence of geopolitical analysis is the relation of international political power to the geographical setting. Geopolitical views vary with the changing geographical setting and with man's interpretation of the nature of this change."[9] According to Raymond Aron, geopolitics encompasses a "geographical schematization of diplomatic-strategic relations with a geographic-economic analysis of resources, with an interpretation of diplomatic attitudes as a result of the way of life and of the environment (sedentary, nomadic, agricultural, seafaring)."[10]

Both "utopians" and "realists" in international relations (examined in Chapters 1 and 3, respectively) discussed man in relation to the environment. But they broadened the notion of "environment" to include the products of human culture as well as the physical features of the earth. Drawing upon the writings of theorists of the Enlightenment, utopian theory claimed that international behavior could be altered by transforming the institutional setting. Schemes for international organization and world government, as well as for establishing norms for international conduct, were designed to alter human behavior by changing the international political environment. In contrast, as the analysis undertaken in Chapter 3 reveals, realists in international relations often held that the geographical location of states conditions, if not determines, political behavior. If the political behavior of national units is in large part the product of environmental circumstances, including geography, in which nations find themselves, the statesman's perennial task is to work within the parameters established by the environment.

Man's relationship with the environment remains a focal point of analysis. Recent studies, exemplified by the writings of Harold and Margaret Sprout, have emphasized multiple factor analysis, embracing a variety of environmental conditions and trends in addition to geography. Moreover, writers who have studied politics as a general systems theory have emphasized environment. Systems, discussed in Chapter 4, may be "open" or "closed." The open systems, both biological and social, by definition are susceptible to, and dependent for their survival on, inputs from their environment. In so-called closed or self-contained systems inputs from an external environment have been eliminated, although environmental factors of great importance have often been incorporated into subsystems.

Buckle and Huntington: Climatic Factors

Many nineteenth- and twentieth-century scholars were as convinced as the classical writers of the importance of climate as a conditioner of political behavior. Henry Thomas Buckle (1821–1862), a British historian, realized that climate, food, and soil depend closely on each other. Climate influenced the kinds of crops grown; the quality of the food depended on the soil. Buckle explained the alleged vigor of the northern laborer as a result of the food supply available in a cold climate. In nations in cold climates, "there is for the most part displayed, even in the infancy of society, a bolder or more adventurous character, than we find among those other nations whose ordinary nutriment, . . . is easily obtained, and indeed is supplied to them, by the bounty of nature, gratuitously and without a struggle." Furthermore, Buckle contended that:

> The food essential to life is scarcer in cold countries than in hot ones; and not only is it scarcer, but more of it is required; so that on both grounds smaller encouragement is given to the growth of that population from whose ranks the labor-market is stocked. To express, therefore, the conclusion in its simplest form, we may say, that there is a strong and constant tendency in hot countries for wages to be low, in cold countries for them to be high.[11]

Civilizations with hot climates, and therefore low wage levels, are said to produce large and depressed working classes, with attendant social and economic consequences. Great inequality in the distribution of wealth, political power, and social influence, according to Buckle, led many ancient civilizations to reach a "certain stage of development and then to decline."

Ellsworth Huntington (1876–1947), the American geographer and explorer, found climate a determinant not only of health, activity, level of food production, and other resource availabilities, but of the migration of peoples and their racial mixtures as well. Only the most physically fit, intelligent, and adventurous survive migration. And only those subject to economic distress due to poor harvest and food shortages attempt to migrate to more desirable climates. To support this view, Huntington cited as an example the desiccation of central Asia at different periods of history which led to the invasion of Europe by the barbarians, the Dorian and Ionian invasions of ancient Greece, and the Mongol incursion into southeast Asia. The Arab migration led by Mohammed and strengthened by religious fervor represented a movement from parched deserts to more fertile lands. Improved economic conditions, stimulated by climatic factors, liberated large parts of a population from the tasks of gathering and producing food, and permitted them to develop new and advanced ideas in the fields of art, literature, science, and political life.

Huntington concluded that most of the world's major civilizations had developed in climates where the annual average temperature neared the optimum necessary for maximum human productivity (65–70° Fahrenheit).[12] Great civilizations within the tropic zones have risen only on temperate plateaus or along cool seacoasts in which the temperature in no season far exceeded the optimum level, for example, the Mayas in Mexico and in Guatemala, and the ancient Javanese and Singhalese.

TOYNBEE: ENVIRONMENTAL CHALLENGE AND RESPONSE

Arnold Toynbee held that civilizations are born in environments that pose difficult challenges.[13] Civilizations are said to grow when a society undergoes a catapulting series of challenges. The challenged civilization develops an *élan vital*, which carries it through equilibrium toward another challenge, thereby inspiring another response. The challenge-response cycle is potentially infinite, although it is retrospective, thus not allowing us to predict the potential response to a challenge. He examined five types of challenging stimuli. Two were physical—hard country, that is, country possessing a harsh climate, terrain, and soil; and new ground, that is, the exploration, opening up, and development of a wilderness into productive land. The three nonphysical stimuli include: (1) those challenges emanating from another state; (2) continuous external pressure against a state; and (3) a stimulus of penalization, that is, if a state loses the use of a particular component, it is likely to respond by increasing correspondingly the efficiency of another component. Toynbee adds that overly severe physical challenge can arrest the development of civilization. The Polynesian, Eskimo, Nomad, Spartan, and Osmanli civilizations were retarded as a result of physical challenges which they could not meet.

The breakdown of civilizations results from the degeneration of the creative minority into a "dominant minority which attempts to retain by force a position that it has ceased to merit." This in turn provokes a "secession of a proletariat which no longer admires and imitates its rulers and revolts against its servitude."[14] Thus the society loses its social cohesiveness. Vertical schisms between geographically segregated communities and horizontal schisms between classes or groups that are geographically contiguous but socially segregated characterize the disintegration of a civilization. The horizontal schism may occur when a dominant minority retains its ruling position by force, but loses its right to that role as a result of its loss of creativity. Toynbee's schema is related to modern, more complex theories of social revolution, treated in Chapter 8.

GEOGRAPHICAL FACTORS OF NATIONAL POWER

With the advent of modern communication-transportation technologies, increased attention was given to geography, focusing upon population/resource distribution, the strategic location of states, and the forward projection of national power. For the most part, those writers concerned with the environment have tended to stress the importance of such factors as determinants, or at least conditioners, of political behavior. Environment not only limits human conduct, but it also provides opportunities. Of particular importance are climatic and geographical factors. Uneven distribution of resources, as well as differences in geographical and climatic endowments, affects the potential power of a state. The size of the country influences the availability of indigenous natural resources; and the climate affects the mobilization of human resources necessary for exploiting these natural resources. Variations in these factors may crucially affect the structure of political systems, even influencing their capacity for survival under stress.

If political behavior is affected by environment, individuals have the capacity to alter political behavior by manipulating the environment. Of particular importance to writers such as Alfred Thayer Mahan (1840–1914), an American naval officer and historian, Sir Halford Mackinder (1861–1947), a British geographer, and Giulio Douhet, an Italian advocate of airpower, as well as the Sprouts is the impact of technological change upon our environment. Technology, it is suggested, does not render environmental factors unimportant or obsolete. Rather, it replaces one set of environmental factors with still another set. Mahan saw naval capabilities as the key to national power; Mackinder considered the technology of land transportation as crucial; Douhet focused upon the technology of airpower as it was altering the conduct of warfare earlier in the twentieth century by extending our capacity for the projection of power far beyond historic confines. The advent of the new technologies of the late twentieth century for the extension of control both on the earth's surface and in inner and outer space has enhanced the interest of scholars and policymakers in geopolitical relationships. Thus, for example, in this age of intercontinental ballistic missiles (ICBMs) analysts engaging in the constant calculus of deterrence consider such geographic factors as a country's size, population distribution, together with weapon deployments and target structures.

Although possessing a limited capacity to change our environment, we remain circumscribed in our behavior by environmental factors. Central to geopolitical theories has been the question of the extent to which environmental factors can be modified to suit human needs. This question is not new. It long separated Anglo-American and French theorizing about geopolitical relationships. A French school of geographical "possibilist" thought, represented by Lucien Febvre and Vidal de la Blache, rejected the determinism of Anglo-American and German environmental theories. Drawing upon the intellectual heritage of the Enlightenment, French students of geography suggested that the natural environment could be modified. In fact, human free will ultimately determines the options available. Environment, geography in particular, is but one of many forces governing the development of human activity.[15] Twentieth-century geopolitical writers fall somewhere between a strictly determinist and a possibilist interpretation. If environment does not determine the boundaries of human conduct, it nevertheless provides an important, if not crucial, conditioning influence. As Ladis K. D. Kristof has suggested, "The modern geopolitician does not look at the world map in order to find out what nature compels us to do but what nature advises us to do, given our preferences."[16]

We turn now to the writings of representative geopolitical theorists from the United States and Europe. Among the Americans, we focus on Mahan and the Sprouts. Mahan concentrated on the impact of naval power upon national political potential. The Sprouts probed the implications of a broad range of environmental factors for political behavior. In addition to Mahan and the Sprouts, a list of the most eminent American students of geopolitical relationships includes such diverse writers as Isaiah Bowman, James Fairgreave, Richard Hartshorne, Stephen B. Jones, George F. Kennan, Owen Lattimore, Homer Lea, General William Mitchell, Ellen Churchill Semple, Alexander P. de Seversky, Nicholas J. Spykman, Robert Strausz-Hupé, Frederick Jackson Turner, Hans A. Weigert, Karl A. Wittfogel, Derwent Whittlesey, and Quincy Wright. Moreover, as noted in Chapter 3, geopolitical relationships have been integral to the realist theory of international relations.

MAHAN, THE SEAS, AND NATIONAL POWER

Mahan wrote during the period of the last great wave of European imperial expansion and the rise of the United States to the status of a world power. His ideas greatly influenced Theodore Roosevelt who, first as Assistant Secretary of the Navy and later as President, contributed decisively to the rise of the United States as a leading naval power. Mahan's analysis of maritime history, particularly the growth of British global influence, led him to conclude that control of the seas, and especially of strategically important narrow waterways, was crucial to great power status.[17] Mahan based his theory on the observation that the rise of the British Empire and the development of Britain as a naval power had occurred simultaneously. The world's principal sea routes had become the Empire's internal communications links. Except for the Panama Canal, Britain controlled all of the world's major waterways and narrow seas or choke points—those bodies of water to which access, or passage through, could be controlled relatively easily from either shore: Dover, Gibraltar, Malta, Alexandria, the Cape of Good Hope, the Straits of Malacca at Singapore, the Suez Canal, and the entrance to the St. Lawrence River.

The ocean commerce of Northern Europe passed either through the narrow Strait of Dover under British guns or around the northern tip of Scotland, where the British navy maintained constant vigil. Britain and the United States enjoyed greater access to the oceans than Germany and Russia. Movement by sea was easier than over land, and the land masses were surrounded by oceans. States with ready access to the oceans had greater potential for major power status than states which were land-locked. Islands had an advantage over states sharing land boundaries with other states. Maritime states formed alliances more for purposes of commerce than of aggression.

In Mahan's analysis, seapower was crucially important to national strength and prosperity. The capacity of a state to achieve such status was dependent upon its geographic position, land configuration, extent of territory, population, national character, and form of government. For example, nations such as Britain or Japan, isolated by water, must maintain large naval forces if they were to be great powers, because for nations with long coastlines, the sea is a frontier and their position relative to other states is a function of their capacity to operate beyond that frontier. Geographical position contributed to Britain's power—with sufficient proximity to Continental Europe to strike potential enemies and adequate distance from Continental Europe to be reasonably safe from invasion. By focusing her seapower in the Northeastern Atlantic and the Channel, Britain could control the world commerce of European powers since there were no rivals to British seapower until the rise after 1890 of German, Japanese, and U.S. naval forces.

Such an option was not open to France, whose naval power had to be divided between two oceans to protect Mediterranean and Atlantic coastlines. In Mahan's analysis the length of the coastline and the quality of harbors were important factors, although the extent of territory may constitute a source of weakness if the land does not have adequate levels of population and natural resources. Mahan held that the size and character of population and an aptitude for commercial pursuits, particularly those of international trade, indicated a capacity in a nation to become a major power. A nation with a large portion of its population skilled in maritime pursuits, especially shipbuilding and trade, had the potential to become a great maritime state. In sum, Mahan correlated national power and mobility over the seas, because, at the time he wrote, transportation over land was primitive in contrast to the relative facility of movement over the oceans.

Mackinder and the Heartland

Like Mahan, Mackinder saw an intimate relationship between geography and technology. If the technology of the earlier era had enhanced the mobility of seapower over landpower, the technology of the early twentieth century gave to landpower the dominant position. The railroad, and subsequently the internal combustion engine and the construction of a modern highway and road network, made rapid transportation within much of the land mass of Eurasia possible. Until then the inner regions of Eurasia had been landlocked. Mackinder noted that Eurasia's river systems drain into none of the major seas of the world. The Arctic freezes much of the northern Eurasian coast. But with the advent of the railroad, the Middle East was becoming as accessible to Germany by land in the early twentieth century as it had been to Britain by sea. Although Britain, as a small island, was what Mackinder termed the legatee of a depreciating estate, the major Eurasian powers sat astride the greatest combination of human and natural resources. Mackinder saw the struggle between the land power and the seapower as a unifying theme of history. The first cycle in the evolution of seapower was completed in the closing of the Mediterranean Sea by the Macedonians. In the next cycle in the evolution of seapower, Mackinder noted that Rome, a land power, had defeated maritime Carthage and once again the Mediterranean had become a "closed sea."[18] In both these cycles in the ancient era—the Macedonian-Greek and the Roman-Carthaginian—a land power had successfully challenged a seapower. In modern times Britain dominated the oceans. In the twentieth century, however, Britain found it difficult, if not impossible, to withstand pressures from land powers. Technology, once favorable to seapower, was said to be tipping the advantage in the early twentieth century to land power.

First, in a famous paper read before the Royal Geographic Society of London in 1904, and later, just after World War I, in his book, *Democratic Ideals and Reality,* Mackinder suggested that the "pivot area" of international politics was that vast expanse of territory stretching from the East European and Siberian plains:

> As we consider this rapid review of the broader currents of history, does not a certain persistence of geographical relationship become evident? Is not the pivot region of the world's politics that vast area of Euro-Asia which is inaccessible to ships, but in antiquity lay open to the horse-riding nomads, and is today about to be covered with a network of railroads?[19]

This area, which coincided with the tsarist Russian Empire, "occupies the central strategical position" and possesses "incalculably great" resources. (This "pivot area" Mackinder called the *Heartland.*) The region, he suggested, was surrounded by the "inner crescent," which includes such countries on the periphery of Eurasia as Germany, Turkey, India, and China. This region in turn is surrounded by the "outer crescent," which includes such countries as Britain, South Africa, and Japan.

Mackinder formulated the famous dictum:

Who rules East Europe commands the Heartland
Who rules the Heartland commands the World Island (Eurasia)
Who rules the World Island commands the World.[20]

Mackinder feared the rise of Germany and later the Soviet Union as mighty land states capable of becoming great naval powers. While emphasizing the growing importance of land power, Mackinder did not deprecate the role of seapower. Seapower was as vital to world power as it had ever been. In the twentieth century, however, broader land bases were necessary for seapower than had been needed in the nineteenth century. The World Island had the potential to become the greatest seapower, even though its Heartland would remain invulnerable to attack by seapower. In the twentieth century the state controlling the Heartland and hence the World Island would become a leading seapower in the same way as Macedonia and Rome, although primarily land powers, had eventually gained control of the seas. In fact, Mackinder correctly foresaw international politics of the first half of the twentieth century as principally a struggle between Germany and Russia for control of the Heartland and adjacent areas on the Eurasian land mass. Such a conception has influenced the thought of other writers, including many of the realist school considered in Chapter 3, who have posited that the state capable of dominating Eurasia would have within its grasp the means to control remaining portions of the world.

Without necessarily referring to Mackinder or stating their assumptions as explicitly, a principal objective of American policymakers has been to prevent the domination of the Eurasian land mass by a hostile power; hence the American interest in alliances with Western Europe and Japan and in security commitments elsewhere on the rimlands of Eurasia, including the Middle East. From this conception derives the American diplomacy, especially evident in the Nixon-Kissinger foreign policy and subsequently, to strengthen links between the United States and the People's Republic of China, and thus to help prevent a reconciliation between the two largest land powers of Eurasia.

During World War II Mackinder revised his theory to include in an Atlantic community a counterpoise to the aggregation of power in Eurasia. Although the Soviet Union would emerge from World War II as the "greatest land power on the globe" and "in the strategically strongest defensive position," the nations of the North Atlantic basin would form a counterpoise, which in fact occurred with the formation of the Atlantic Alliance in 1949 as East-West tensions deepened in the early post-World

War II period.[21] Together, Britain, France, and the United States, Mackinder held, could provide power adequate both to prevent a resurgence of Germany and to balance the Soviet Union. Other writers, such as Nicholas J. Spykman and Stephen B. Jones, suggested that the "rimland" of Eurasia might prove strategically more important than the Heartland if new centers of industrial power and communications were created along the circumference of the Eurasian land mass. The "rimland" hypothesis is a central theoretical foundation of George F. Kennan's famous postwar proposal for a "policy of containment" of the Soviet Union, which became the philosophical basis for the American foreign policy of internationalism beginning with the Truman Doctrine and the Marshall Plan in 1947.[22]

The advent of the airplane, and subsequently the means to penetrate outer space, provided a whole new dimension to geopolitics. Once again, technology had the effect of altering the significance of specific geopolitical relationships. Just as Mahan and Mackinder had based their geopolitical theories on an analysis of the implications, respectively, of technologies facilitating movement over the seas and the land, Giulio Douhet, writing in the 1920s, saw the airplane as conferring unprecedented possibilities for the conduct of warfare against targets previously invulnerable to attack and destruction. As long as human activities were restricted to the earth's surface, they were subject to constraints imposed by the terrain. Although the seas are uniform in character, man's mobility via the oceans is limited by virtue of the coastlines that surround them. No such impediments to mobility exist in the air. Writing with great foresight in 1921, Douhet concluded: "The airplane has complete freedom of action and direction; it can fly to and from any point of the compass in the shortest time—a straight line—by any route deemed expedient. . . . By virtue of this new weapon, the repercussions of war are no longer limited by the farthest artillery range of surface guns, but can be directly felt for hundreds and hundreds of miles over all the lands and seas of nations at war. . . . There will be no distinction any longer between soldiers and civilians."[23] It followed that the wars of the future would differ radically from those of the past, and that control of the air would confer upon states unprecedented mobility of power and the capacity to inflict devastation upon an adversary's military forces and industry.

Writing during World War II, and building upon the writings of Douhet and the ideas of General Billy Mitchell, Alexander de Seversky emphasized the implications of advances in technology for rapid increases in the range of aircraft. This would render unnecessary the aircraft carrier, he predicted, because planes could operate from land bases to attack targets in the enemy's homeland. Thus the unprecedented mobility conferred by manned flight, noted by Douhet, was given even greater emphasis by Alexander de Seversky. Airpower made possible not only greater mobility, but also freed man to an unprecedented extent from dependence on an extensive ground organization, including bases for refueling, as the range of aircraft, and thus their operating radius, grew.[24] Control of airspace became as complex a problem as control of the land and the sea.

GEOPOLITICS: THE POLITICAL SIGNIFICANCE OF SPACE

Friedrich Ratzel (1844–1904), a German geographer, coined the term *Anthropogeographie,* which meant a synthesis of geography, anthropology, and politics. Thus the new discipline of political geography was born in Germany in the nineteenth century. This new discipline was directed to the study of man, the state, and the world as organic units. The state was seen as a living organism that occupies space and that grows, contracts, and eventually dies, although Ratzel himself stopped short of imputing to the state an objective reality, asserting instead that states "are not organisms properly speaking but only aggregate-organisms," the unity of which is forged by "moral and spiritual forces."[25]

Political geographers addressed themselves to the question of man's relationship to nature. They concerned themselves with the implications of climate, topography, and natural resources for civilization. In fact, Ratzel attributed the development of superior civilizations, which he identified principally with Europe, to favorable climatic conditions. He contended that mankind was engaged in an unending struggle for living space, an idea that later was integrated in the form of the term *lebensraum* into the thought of Haushofer and Hitler. A state's land area indicates its power position. States strive to extend their territorial frontiers. The urge to territorial expansion is greatest among strong states. Boundaries therefore are constantly shifting. They form the zones of conflict between states as "dynamic frontiers." In twentieth-century German geopolitical writings and in Spykman's work,[26] boundaries or "dynamic frontiers" are viewed as demarcations of zones in which expansion has temporarily ceased.

Rudolf Kjellen (1864–1922), a Swedish geographer, first used the term *geopolitics* to describe the geopolitical bases of national power. Adhering to an organic theory of the state, he held that states, like animals in Darwinian theory, engage in a relentless struggle for survival. States have boundaries, a capital, and lines of communication, as well as a consciousness and a culture. Though Kjellen wrote metaphysically and imputed to the state the quality of a living organism, he nevertheless concluded that "the life of the state is, ultimately, in the hands of the individual."[27] He considered the emergence of a few great powers as a result of efforts of strong states to expand.

In the interwar period, the followers of Kjellen and Ratzel used geopolitics to develop a framework for German national expansion. Karl Haushofer (1869–1946) founded the German Academy at the University of Munich in 1925, together with the journal *Zeitschrift für Geopolitik.* Both received active support from the Third Reich.[28] Haushofer's influence was considerable in military circles and became the basis for many of Hitler's conceptions of Nazi expansion.

For Haushofer, geopolitics represented the relationship of political phenomena to geography. Geopolitics enabled German leaders to establish national objectives and policies. The purpose of geopolitics, in Haushofer's conception, was to place the systematic study of geography at the disposal of a militarized Reich by relating national power to geographic factors, collecting relevant geographical information, and presenting a propaganda rationale for Nazi expansion and aggression. Thus, for Haushofer and his followers, geopolitics and power politics became synonymous. The geopolitical concepts developed by Haushofer (including *lebensraum* and "dynamic frontiers"), to the extent that they shaped Hitler's view of the world, contributed to the outbreak of World War II. In this respect, they stand in sharp contrast to other types of geopolitical analysis based upon a scientific knowledge of geography and its relationship to technology, resources, and population.

German geopolitical thinking, from Ratzel to Haushofer, expressed the need for great states to enlarge their frontiers, to obtain lebensraum, and to gain self-sufficiency in raw materials, industry, and markets, and to achieve population growth. Extensive geographical space and national power were synonymous. Haushofer drew upon Ratzel's writings on the relationship between space and power. Moreover, Haushofer based his recommendations for achieving lebensraum on Japan's successful imperial expansion in the 1930s. He was indebted to Mackinder's conception that the Heartland was the key to global mastery. Warning of the danger posed by an expansionist Nazi Germany, Robert Strausz-Hupé suggested that geopolitics "represents a revolutionary attempt to measure and to harness the forces which make for expansionism."[29] German geopolitical theorists considered conflict among leading states to be inevitable, and so perhaps it was if nations adopted policies for imperial expansion as espoused by Haushofer and his followers. This conflict would pit a continental European grouping dominated by Germany in alliance with a Pacific grouping led by Japan against an Atlantic grouping under the leadership of Britain and the United States. Thus the world would be divided into various pan regions that themselves would have been formed either in anticipation, or as a result, of war.

Haushofer's organic theory of boundaries contains a second major component of German geopolitical thinking. He proposes in this theory that a state strives to achieve a frontier that contains a zone of sparse settlement—a zone outside the living space, separating the state from neighboring states. Haushofer and his followers considered the world to consist of renovating and decadent states. British "decadence" was exemplified by Britain's inability to halt tendencies in her empire toward self-government. In another war, Haushofer believed, Britain could not be assured of the loyalty and support of the self-governing parts of the British Empire, although he acknowledged that the British Empire would probably constitute a formidable obstacle to the development of new pan regions. Finally, the German geopolitical theorists developed geostrategy as a military science. All relevant information about an opponent was gathered so that "blitzkrieg," a quick and decisive attack, could be mounted.

In brief, German geopolitical writings contained five concepts: (1) autarchy, or national economic self-sufficiency, precluding the need for foreign products; (2) lebensraum, or sufficient land area and natural resources to support the population of a nation; (3) pan regions, or broader geographical areas, to replace narrower national frontiers; (4) the assumption that the land mass of Eurasia-Africa, being the most populous and the largest combination of land power and seapower, has therefore the potential for world domination; and (5) the state has the right to "natural frontiers or boundaries set forth by nature."[30]

THE SPROUTS AND MAN-MILIEU RELATIONSHIPS

Harold and Margaret Sprout have made the greatest contribution in the past generation toward the development of hypotheses for examining man-milieu relationships. Although the Sprouts have long believed in the importance of geography in explaining political behavior,[31] they contend that most, if not all, human activity is affected by the uneven distribution of human and nonhuman resources.[32] The Sprouts rejected unidimensional, geopolitical theories in favor of an "ecological perspective" because it appeared to provide a more integrated, holistic view of the international environment that took account of its physical and nonphysical features. The environment, or milieu, was viewed as a multidimensional system, in which no one factor (such as geography) occupied a preeminent position and in which the perceptions held by political leaders of environmental conditions (the psychomilieu) as well as the conditions themselves were the objects of study and analysis. Such research emphasized the *interrelationship* of geography, demography, technology, and resources, and focused upon the importance of perceptual variables, as well as quantitative factors such as population and territorial size.

The milieu is said to affect human activities in only two respects. First, it can influence human decisions only if human beings perceive factors related to the milieu. Second, such factors can limit individual performance or the outcome of decisions based upon perceptions of the environment.[33] Thus decisions may be taken on the basis of erroneous perceptions of the environment with potentially disastrous consequences. Hence the task confronting the decision-maker—to link the Sprouts' analysis to decision-making theories considered in Chapter 11—is to narrow the gap between the perceived and the real environment.

The Sprouts regard geography as "concerned with the arrangement of things on the face of the earth, and with the association of things that give character to particular places." They believe that geography affects all human and nonhuman, tangible and intangible phenomena that "exhibit areal dimensions and variations upon or in relation to the earth's surface."[34] Every political community has a geographical base. Each political community is set on a territory which is a unique combination of location, size, shape, climate, and natural resources. Thus most transactions among nations entail significant, even crucial, geographical considerations. The Sprouts noted that international statecraft exhibits in all periods "more or less discernible patterns of coercion and submission, influence and deference; patterns reflected in political terms with strong geographic connotations."[35]

Cognitive Behavioralism and the Operational Milieu

Important to the Sprouts is the concept of cognitive behavioralism. This concept assumes that a person consciously responds to the milieu through perception "and in no other way."[36] Erroneous ideas of the milieu may be just as influential as accurate ideas in forming moods, preferences, decisions, and actions. The Sprouts proceed to distinguish, somewhat imprecisely, between the environment as the observer perceives it and the environment as it actually exists. The so-called psychomilieu may be compared to Plato's shadows in the cave—"images or ideas which the individual derives from interaction between what he selectively receives from his milieu, by means of his sensory apparatus, and his scheme of values, conscious memories, and subconsciously stored experience."[37] Failure to perceive the limiting condition may result in severe consequences. Inflated illusions about and misinterpretations of geographic circumstances may have similar unfortunate effects.[38] Popular attitudes, as well as the decisions of statesmen, are based upon geographical conceptions which "depend in no small degree upon the kinds of maps to which they are accustomed," as is noted in greater detail in a later section of this chapter. Therefore an analysis of political behavior must take account of assumptions that political leaders make about their milieu.

The decisional entity, acting within the operational milieu and having a psychomilieu,[39] is an environed organism (an individual or a population) rather than an abstraction (the state). It is this decisional entity which is a principal concern of the social scientist and a particular interest of the student of international relations. Thus the Sprouts object to terms such as the "state's motivation" and the "state's needs." They do not apply psychoecological concepts to social organization for much the same reason that they reject giving human attributes to the national or international system. They attribute these concepts only to human beings. They believe that political discussion on such an abstract level muddies rather than clarifies one's understanding of the workings of international politics.[40]

Although political decisions are based on the statesman's perceptions of the milieu, the results of these decisions are limited by the objective nature of the operational milieu, that is to say, by "the situation as it actually exists and affects the achievements and capabilities of the entity in question (whether a single individual, group, or community as a whole)."[41] In short, the operational milieu exists, even though it may not be fully discernible by the political actor. So far as decision-making is concerned, the Sprouts do not see the milieu as inevitably "conditioning," "drawing," or "compelling" the policymaker and "dictating" his choices.

Thus the ecological perspective provides a framework for the consideration of three types of phenomena: (1) the perceived, or psychomilieu; (2) the actions of individuals or groups; and (3) the outcomes of their actions.[42] The three fundamental concepts of importance to the Sprouts include environment, environed entities, and entity-environmental relationships.[43]

Limitations of Geopolitical Theorizing

The Sprouts emphasize that technology and social change play a large role in environmental relationships. Although technology has obviously not altered the physical layout of lands and seas, it has added new dimensions to the international milieu. Although geopolitical speculation has enriched our understanding of the international system, the most serious defect has been the "almost universal failure of the geopolitical theorists to anticipate and allow for the rate of technological and other changes." An accurate assessment of the tools, skills, and technological innovations available to the interacting communities is crucial to all geopolitical theorizing. The Sprouts adduce the ecological principle that substantial change in one sector of the milieu can be expected to produce "significant, often unsettling, sometimes utterly disruptive consequences in other sectors."[44]

Geography, environed organisms, the psychomilieu, technology, the operational milieu, and beliefs all affect each other. "Substantial changes either in the environment or in the genetic makeups of the organisms involved are likely to start chain reactions that ramify throughout the entire 'web-of-life' within the 'biotic community.' "[45] The interrelatedness of the ecological paradigm has grown increasingly with the mounting complexity of modern society resulting from expanding populations and advanced technology. It is increasingly difficult to "isolate and classify human political events as merely domestic matters or foreign affairs, or as political, sociological, or economic." In fact, the complexity of interrelatedness "within and between national communities, and the increasing irrelevance of the time honored distinction between domestic and international questions, constitute major datum points in the ecological perspective on international politics."[46] The focal point for empirical analysis in the past decade has increasingly been the "linkage" between domestic politics and foreign policy.

In their study of environmental relationships, the Sprouts have drawn four major conclusions. First, the ecological perspective and frame of reference provide a fruitful approach to the analysis of foreign policy and the estimation of a state's capabilities. Second, it is helpful to distinguish analytically between the relation of environmental factors to policy decisions and to the operational results of decisions. In the Sprouts' judgment, much of the confusion clouding the discussion of environmental factors in international politics stems from the failure to make this distinction explicit. Third, the ecological approach is a useful complement to the study of both the foreign policy and the international capabilities of states. The Sprouts' paradigm entails the examination of such limiting conditions as the level of available technology, cognition of essential factors, and the ratio of available resources to commitments.[47] Finally, they see the ecological approach as broadening the study of international politics by integrating into it relevant theories and data from geography, psychology, sociology, and other systems of learning.

CURRENT RESEARCH ON ENVIRONMENTAL FACTORS

Some scholars have focused on the relationship between environment and political behavior. Writing in the mid-1970s, George Liska examined the nature of equilibrium in the international system with specific reference to conflict and geopolitical factors. He concluded that conflict between continental and maritime states has been a recurrent phenomenon in international relations, especially in the European system. "The qualitative disparity between principally land-based and sea-oriented states proved commonly incapable of assimilation by competitive or other interactions. . . . The schism was conspicuously manifest whenever a strong land power staged, and the dominant maritime power resisted to the point of vetoing, a drive for seaborne outreach that would expand the scope of the balance of power and adapt its functioning to overseas extensions of the system's continental core."[48] In an effort to determine the impact of insular status on nations, two other authors have compared the policies of Britain, Ceylon, and Japan.[49] Their analysis revealed that insular polities have a "more active involvement" with other countries than noninsular polities. Insular polities are more limited than noninsular states in the range of foreign policies available to them. These authors found similarities in the foreign policies of Britain and Japan. Both countries attempted to occupy sections of the Eurasian mainland, especially those areas from which invasions might be mounted against them. Both tried to maintain a balance of power among mainland nations by supporting the weaker coalition. Both sought alliances with powers outside the region to strengthen their position with respect to more proximate continental national units.

In assessing the effect of noncontiguity on the integration of political units, Richard Merritt's study of territorially discontiguous polities indicated that centrifugal forces increased with the distance.[50] There was greater communication with neighboring than with physically distant peoples. The noncontiguous polity depends on the external environment to preserve communication links among its physically separated parts. Daily dependence upon communications make noncontiguous polities sensitive to shifts in the international environment which affect communications. Such polities have been concerned with the application of international law to internal waters, territorial and high seas, air rights, and land access, to cite only the modern history of problems experienced by such states as Malaysia, Pakistan, the United Arab Republic (Egypt-Syria), and the now defunct West Indies Federation.

CRITIQUES OF ENVIRONMENTAL THEORIES

Critics of environmental theories, including the Sprouts, take issue with writers who engage in "environmentalistic rhetoric" and assume that attitudes or decisions are "determined" or "influenced" or in some other way causally affected by environmental factors.[51] Although the Sprouts reject environment as a determinant of politics, they conceive as crucial (1) the actor's perception of environmental factors and (2) limitations to human activity posed by the environment.[52]

According to Strausz-Hupé, geographic conditions have been modified by man throughout history: "Geographic conditions determine largely *where* history is made, but it is always man who makes it."[53] Although deriving his own work from the geopolitical concepts in Mackinder's writings, Spykman criticized Mackinder for overestimating the potentialities of the Heartland and underestimating those of the Inner

Crescent. According to Spykman, "If there is to be a slogan for the power politics of the Old World, it must be 'Who controls the Rimland rules Eurasia; who rules Eurasia controls the destinies of the world.' "[54] Spykman also noted that a combination of seapowers had never been aligned against a grouping of land powers. "The historical alignment has always been in terms of some members of the Rimland with Great Britain and Russia together against a dominating Rimland power."[55] In his analysis of the German geopolitical school Strausz-Hupé asserts that "there is, in short, no historical evidence in support of the causal nexus alleged by the advocates of *lebensraum* . . . to exist between population pressure and national growth in space."[56] Historically, national expansion has resulted from conditions other than population pressure. For example, Japanese expansionism in Asia antedated the upsurge in Japan's population. Nor does large space necessarily equate with national power, although "whenever large space was thoroughly organized by a state, small nations . . . were not able to withstand its expansive force."[57] According to Derwent Whittlesey, Haushofer's conception of geopolitics was illogical in that it based the need for lebensraum upon Germany's high birth rates. Since the birth rates of the Slavic territories to the East were even higher, their need for territory should have been greater than that of Germany.[58]

Finally, it is often asserted that technological change has rendered both Mackinder's Heartland concept and Haushofer's geopolitical theory obsolete. In the discussion following Mackinder's presentation of his paper, "The Geographical Pivot of History," to the Royal Geographic Society, Leopold Amery asserted, "Both the sea and the railway are going in the future . . . to be supplemented by the air as a means of locomotion, [and] when we come to that, a great deal of this geographical distribution must lose its importance, and the successful powers will be those who have the greatest industrial basis."[59] According to Strausz-Hupé, "If it [the Heartland] ever was a valid concept (for which there is no convincing evidence), there is no guarantee that modern technology will not invalidate it. It may, indeed, have done so already."[60] The Sprouts criticize the theories of both Mahan and Mackinder as being outmoded as a result of innovations in military technology and "paramilitary and nonmilitary forms of political interaction."[61] Kristof faults geopolitical writers for having "marshaled facts and laws of the physical world to justify political demands and support political opinions. One of the best examples of the hopelessly contradictory arguments to which this may lead is a concept akin in spirit to that of the 'natural boundary,' namely, the concept of the 'harmonic state.' "[62]

If the psychomilieu—the world as it is perceived—is central to the work of writers such as the Sprouts, others have focused specifically upon the effects of alternative types of maps—the visual presentation of spatial and geographical relationships—as they relate to the formation of images about the world. Since World War II, special emphasis has been placed upon the distortion introduced into political analysis by reliance upon Mercator equator-based projections. Such maps failed to present the idea of the earth as a sphere and therefore as having geographical unity and continuity. The Mercator projection provided an erroneous conception of distances, for example, the proximity of the United States to the Soviet Union across the Arctic. By viewing the world as a sphere it becomes evident that, for example, Buenos Aires is farther from the United States than every European capital including Moscow.

The advent of airpower, and its indispensable contribution to the allied victory in World War II, contributed decisively to the alteration in traditional Mercator-type conceptions of geography, for the shortest distance by air between two points lay in a line that followed the contour of the earth. In its place came asymmetrical projections based for the most part upon spherical pole-centered maps. Numerous writers, during World War II, pointed to the need for such alternative maps. The need for such maps became apparent also because as Richard E. Harrison and Hans W. Weigert, writing in the 1940s, pointed out:

> We continued using it (the Mercator projection) when land power and land-based air power became pivotal in the greatest of all world conflicts. In a world war that is mainly being fought in the northern hemisphere this proved to be an almost fatal misjudgment; for the Mercator projection whose center of accuracy is along the equator cannot possibly show the relationship between the power spheres of the contending great Powers.[63]

If maps shape a person's perceptions of the world, they also reflect the shared constructs of geographic and spatial relationships that are prevalent. Maps are drawn and redrawn to take account of "those geographical" factors deemed to be important at a given point in time. As Alan Henrickson has written, "One can regard such things as maps as pure subjective ideographs, or as constructs with only a mathematical relation to objective reality, or even as mere reflections of the material processes of history, in which case they would have no independent determining power.... The global maps that helped to guide and explain the war effort (World War II)—and were thus an essential part of the war's intellectual history—were traces on the human mind, etched there not only by man's experience but by man's imagination."[64] This idea is reflected in the works of Richard Edes Harrison and Robert Strausz-Hupé, who went so far as to suggest that the "psychological isolationism" of the United States resulted from the deficiencies of maps, notably the utilization of two-dimensional (Mercator) projections instead of those representing the earth as a globe.[65]

The changing importance of other geographic relationships has contributed, over the past generation, to the development of additional conceptions of the world etched in maps. Some writers have suggested the emergence of global trends that are leading to a new set of geostrategic, and geopolitical, relationships. Of special importance are resources and the increased vulnerability of oil supplies and vital raw materials to disruption either at their source or in transit from producer to consumer states. The growth of resource-import dependence by industrialized states, together with the increase in vulnerability of such resources to interdiction, has contributed to a revival of interest in geopolitical analysis, but in the present context, the potential for conflict over scarce resources is increasing at a time of diffusion of military technologies to a variety of state and nonstate actors.[66] Such trends take place in context of the emergence of a new maritime regime as a result of the growing importance of resources in the seas and/or the seabed, and changing patterns of Western and Soviet overseas base access—more detrimental to the United States than to the Soviet Union. A "new strategic map" is said to have come into existence, whose "practical effects are to resurrect the importance of geography and resources as a factor in military thinking. . . . Thus knowledge about the whereabouts of food, energy, and universal resources, the location of small islands, patterns of sea and air lines of communication, and the impact of arms transfers on regional power balances may become as necessary tools for strategic analysis as familiarity with the acronyms of nuclear warfare has been in the recent past."[67]

This revival of interest in geopolitical analysis has extended beyond resource issues, per se, to an effort to update concepts drawn from such earlier writers as Mahan and Mackinder to the international system of the late twentieth century. In present context, the Soviet Union represents a vast land power whose traditional Eurasian focus has expanded both into the rimlands and into regions far from Eurasia. The superpower relationship of our age pits the Soviet Union, as the leading land power, against the United States, the principal maritime power. Historically, the internal lines of communication between the Soviet Union and its allies have been in the Eurasian land mass. The links between the United States and its allies on the rimlands of Eurasia lie across the oceans. The growth of Soviet naval power, together with the projection of Soviet influence and capabilities far from Eurasia, poses a threat of growing proportions to the United States and its allies. According to Colin S. Gray: "The strength of geopolitical grand theory is that it places local action, or interaction, within a global framework. . . . Just as those who wish to understand nuclear strategy have no choice other than to master the essential concepts of the nuclear strategist (first strike/second strike, counterforce, and countervalue, and so forth), so those seeking to comprehend the geopolitical realities of international security questions need to master the essential concepts of the geopolitician."[68] In operational terms, geopolitical theorizing, in present context, leads to the conclusion that the United States and its allies must prevent the expansion of Soviet power into the rimlands of Eurasia. For this purpose alliances with West European states and Japan are crucially important.

At the same time, the perpetuation of the deep schism between Peking and Moscow is central, for a reestablishment of a close Sino-Soviet relationship would unify the two largest land powers of Eurasia—the Heartland about which Mackinder wrote. Thus geopolitics, Colin Gray suggests, "is not simply one set of ideas among many competing sets that help to illuminate the structure of policy problems. Rather, it is a meta- or master framework that, without predetermining policy choice, suggests long-term factors and trends in the security objectives of particular, territorially organized security communities."[69]

TECHNOLOGY, POPULATION GROWTH, AND ENVIRONMENTAL ISSUES

Technological changes may have altered the significance of the theorizing of certain of the writers examined in this chapter, although advanced technology has rendered environmental relationships ever more important. As many writers have suggested, modern science and technology have transformed the environment in intended, but also in unintended ways.[70] Science and technology have brought "uninvited guests" in such forms as air pollution, traffic congestion, and resource scarcity. In the twentieth century, the pace of scientific-technological innovation has quickened beyond any historical precedent, and people in all parts of the globe have been drawn into the orbit of modern technology. Whether changes wrought by technology are affecting the environment in ways beyond the means of coping with them remains an unanswered question. What is certain is that inextricable relationships or linkages exist among technology, geography, and international politics.

The pollution of the environment has become an enduring concern for the late twentieth century. As Zbigniew Brzezinski has pointed out, those societies that are most advanced technologically—the United States, Western Europe, and Japan—have spawned the most vocal groups in support of issues related to the "quality of life." This is characteristic of the "technetronic age" into which such societies are said already to have entered, or are on the threshold of entering.[71] Population growth, urbanization, and the chemical wastes of products of industrial civilization—all of which are more prevalent in the most advanced societies in contrast to the less developed—are held to be causing changes in the balance of nature.

The revival of interest in the relationship between population growth and the environment was manifested in the burgeoning "limits of growth" literature, and notably in efforts to forecast future ecological relationships. These include works by Jay W. Forrester and by Donella H. Meadows, Dennis L. Meadows, Jorgen Randers, and William W. Behrens III,[72] all of whom develop controversial models containing forecasts of population growth, resource depletion, food supply, capital investment, and pollution. The projections lead to the basic conclusion, set forth in a report submitted to a group called the Club of Rome, that well before the mid-twenty-first century, mankind will face a multifaceted dilemma: a natural resource shortage that will slow down industrial growth; a decline of world population as a result of pollution; food shortages that in time will limit population. If such trends are to be reversed, it is asserted that there must be controls upon population, capital investment, and pollution to produce a global equilibrium based on stationary population levels and living standards, and lower rates of natural resource depletion. Central to such analysis, as Forrester suggests, is the assumption that population, pollution, living standards, food consumption, and capital investment have grown exponentially throughout history and that such forces, at least in the next century, are not amenable to solutions by emigration, economic growth, territorial expansion, and technology. If the curves are not altered, inflation will curtail investment, which will eventually fall below the rate of depreciation of manufacturing facilities; raw materials shortages of all kinds will become endemic; gradually, the industrial and agricultural base, along with most services, will collapse, the curtailment of food and medical supplies will lead to a ravaging of population due to famine and disease. Growth will then be stopped in one way or the other. The question posed by the study was whether growth would be controlled by rational planning or as the result of the inexorable operation of "natural forces"—with widespread suffering as a consequence.

Such latter day Malthusian analyses and forecasts have themselves given rise to critiques. These include criticisms of assumptions upon which the forecasts are based. For example, improvements in antipollution technology, the development of substitutes for depreciated natural resources, the utilization of technology to extract minerals from inhospitable environments, and increasing rates of productivity in agriculture might alter fundamentally the conclusions contained in the "models of doom." Moreover, such models have been faulted for having been erected on so fragile and incomplete a data base, and for the value biases that perhaps inevitably influence the models themselves and the analysis coming from them.[73] The deficiencies of such models are said to include the insufficient attention paid to the possibilities of scientific and technological breakthroughs, and of the discovery of new sources of raw materials; and the exclusion of important political and social factors (such as governmental decisions and moral values and attitudes).[74] Although there was widespread agreement that, if growth were to continue exponentially, the economic, demographic, and ecological problems facing mankind would become unmanageable, there was considerable disagreement over the imminence of doomsday and the necessity for rapid curtailment of growth. On one side was the argument that mere palliatives would not suffice, and that drastic measures were imperative; from the other side came warnings that too rapid and radical responses, instead of putting society into a stable trajectory, might set off a series of sharp oscillations that would destabilize the global system, and thus speed up rather than head off the movement toward disaster.[75]

Some analysts were of the opinion that the study, by emphasizing the need for population constraints and limitations on the rate of industrialization, was aimed at discouraging the countries of the Third World from expectations of high growth rates in the Decade of Development. (Not a few of those countries were suspicious of the industrialized world's new-found concern over the environmental pollution wrought by factories, autos, pesticides, and other chemical products.) Johan Galtung strongly criticized the Club of Rome report for its failure to differentiate between rich nations and poor nations; and for its insinuation that all societies, regardless of the level of their economic development, would have to curb their future growth.[76]

Carl Kaysen found utility in the M.I.T. study for dramatically focusing attention upon serious problems, but he faulted it for ignoring within the model such crucial factors as technological innovation, economic adjustment mechanisms, and available knowledge concerning population growth and the gap between the industrialized and the developing nations. Perhaps his most telling criticism was the first one, pertaining to the possibilities afforded by scientific innovations:

> Once an exponentially improving technology is admitted into the model, along with exponentially growing population and production, the nature of its outcomes changes sharply. The inevitability of crisis when a limit is reached disappears, since the limits themselves are no longer fixed, but grow exponentially too. Catastrophes need no longer be the rule. . . .[77]

In 1974 the Second Report of the Club of Rome was published. Written by two members of that Club, it sought to take into account some of the criticisms leveled at the First Report, and to refine the original world model (whose average curves were not practically applicable to the heterogeneous conditions of different regions) by dividing the globe into ten regions of political, economic, and environmental coherence. The general tone remained one of urgency: Solutions to the impending global crisis can be developed only in a global context in which the futility of narrow nationalism can be transcended; isolated dimensional approaches, such as diplomatic, economic, or ecological, will not suffice in place of comprehensive, integrated approaches; the prospect of short-term gains must be made to give way to assessment of long-term costs; a new ethic of material resources must be developed, based on minimal use of resources and longevity of product. Finally, the cost of delaying hard decisions allegedly will be "monstrous."[78]

Thus in the late twentieth century, the focus on the milieu in the literature of international relations represents a convergence of several principal interests of scholars and policymakers. These include resource scarcity, population growth, and the relationship of geography to political power. In short, a new set of geopolitical or geostrategic relationships has come into existence largely as a result of the pervasive impact of technology on international relations generally and, specifically, on the foreign policies of states. Because the perception of the milieu, and the impact of the milieu itself, is central to decision-making and to political behavior generally, those concerned with the development of theories of political behavior at the international level have taken renewed interest in environmental relationships. Political systems have been hypothesized to be open systems—susceptible to inputs from, and making outputs to, their environments. Last but not least, the issues of pollution and ecology and of population growth and food supply have led to efforts both to forecast trends and to develop models often neo-Malthusian in nature. The milieu then provides a unique focal point not only for older and contemporary theorizing, but for analytical and normative theory in international relations in the years ahead.

Notes

1. Harold and Margaret Sprout, *The Ecological Perspective on Human Affairs with Special Reference to International Politics* (Princeton: Princeton University Press, 1965), p. 27. The Sprouts set forth the following definitions: Environment may be defined as a generic concept under which are subsumed all external forces and factors to which an organism or aggregate of organisms is actually or potentially responsive. Or environment may be limited to the material and spatial aspects of the surrounding world to the exclusion of the melee of human social relations.
2. Aristotle, *The Politics of Aristotle*, trans. Ernest Barker (Oxford: Clarendon, 1961), pp. 289–311.
3. Jean Bodin, *Six Books of the Commonwealth*, trans. E. J. Tooley (New York: Macmillan, 1955), pp. 145–157.
4. Baron de Montesquieu, *The Spirit of Laws* (Worcester, Mass.: Isaiah Thomas, 1802), I, pp. 154–159; 259–274.
5. Frederick Jackson Turner, "The Significance of the Frontier in American History," in Donald Sheehan, ed., *The Making of American History*, Book II (New York: Dryden, 1950), p. 200.
6. Nazli Choucri, "Population Resources and Technology: Political Implications of the Environmental Crisis," in David A. Kay and Eugene B. Skolnikoff, eds., *World-Eco-Crisis: International Organizations in Response* (Madison: University of

Wisconsin Press, 1972), p. 24. See also the discussion in Chapter 8, pp. 340–342 and Notes 110ff.

7. Quincy Wright, *A Study of War* (Chicago and London: The University of Chicago Press, 1965), p. 1144.
8. Ibid., p. 1285.
9. Saul B. Cohen, *Geography and Politics in a World Divided*, 2nd ed. (New York: Oxford University Press, 1973), p. 29.
10. Raymond Aron, *Peace and War* (Garden City, New York: Doubleday, 1966), p. 191.
11. Henry Thomas Buckle, *History of Civilization in England* (London: Longmans, 1903), I, pp. 39–151.
12. Ellsworth Huntington, *Mainsprings of Civilization* (New York: Wiley, 1945), especially pp. 250–275; and *Civilization and Climate* (New Haven: Yale University Press, 1924), especially pp. 1–29; 387–411.
13. For an examination of Toynbee's challenge-response hypothesis, see *A Study of History,* abridgement of vols. I–IV by D. C. Somervell (London: Oxford University Press, 1956), pp. 60–139. Andrew M. Scott has proposed the challenge-response concept as a central approach to the study of international affairs, closely related to the balance-of-power idea. "Challenge and Response: A Tool for the Analysis of International Affairs," *Review of Politics,* XVIII (1956), 207–226.
14. Ibid., p. 246. Toynbee defines breakdown as the termination of growth.
15. See Harold and Margaret Sprout, *The Ecological Perspective on Human Affairs,* pp. 83–98; Lucien Febvre, *A Geographical Introduction to History* (New York: Knopf, 1925), pp. 358–368; P. W. J. Vidal de la Blache, *Principles of Human Geography,* Emmanuel de Martonne, ed. (New York: Holt, Rinehart and Winston, 1926). O. H. K. Spate, "How Determined Is Possibilism?," *Geographical Studies* IV (1957), 3–8; George Tatham, "Environmentalism and Possibilism," in Griffith Taylor, ed., *Geography in the Twentieth Century* (New York: Philosophical Library, 1951), pp. 128ff, 151ff.
16. Ladis K. D. Kristof, "The Origins and Evolution of Geopolitics," *Journal of Conflict Resolution,* IV (March 1960), 19.
17. Alfred Thayer Mahan, *The Influence of Seapower Upon History, 1660–1783* (Boston: Little, Brown, 1897), especially pp. 281–329. See also Margaret Tuttle Sprout, "Mahan: Evangelist of Sea Power," in Edward Mead Earle, ed., *Makers of Modern Strategy: Military Thought from Machiavelli to Hitler* (Princeton: Princeton University Press, 1943), pp. 415–445; Harold and Margaret Sprout, *The Rise of American Naval Power* (Princeton: Princeton University Press, 1942); William Reitzel, "Mahan on Use of the Sea," and James A. Field, Jr., "The Origins of Maritime Strategy and the Development of Seapower," in B. Mitchell Simpson III, ed., *War, Strategy and Maritime Power* (New Brunswick, N.J.: Rutgers University Press, 1977), pp. 77–107.
18. Halford Mackinder, *Democratic Ideals and Reality* (New York: Norton, 1962), pp. 35–39.
19. Halford Mackinder, "The Geographical Pivot of History," *Geographical Journal,* XXIII (April 1904), 434.
20. Halford Mackinder, op. cit., p. 150. See also Hans W. Weigert, "Mackinder's Heartland," *The American Scholar,* XV (Winter 1945), 43–54.
21. Halford J. Mackinder, "The Round World and the Winning of the Peace," *Foreign Affairs,* XXI (July 1943), 601.
22. See Stephen B. Jones, "Global Strategic Views," *Geographical Review,* XLV (October 1955), 492–508; Nicholas J. Spykman, *The Geography of the Peace* (New York: Harcourt Brace and Company, 1944), p. 43; and George F. Kennan, "The Sources of Soviet Conduct," *Foreign Affairs,* XXV (July 1947), 566–582. Spykman, in discussing the value of the "Heartland's interior lines" with respect to the periphery or

"rimland," suggested that the relations between center and circumference are of one sort if the maritime powers are trying to apply their leverage around the rimland from afar; but these relations are changed if local centers of power and communications are developed around the rimland. Op. cit., p. 40.

23. Giulio Douhet, *The Command of the Air*, trans. Dino Ferrari (New York: Coward-McCann, 1942), pp. 10–11.

24. Alexander P. de Seversky, *Victory Through Air Power* (New York: Simon & Schuster, 1942).

25. Friedrich Ratzel, *Anthropogeographie*, 2nd ed. (Stuttgart: J. Engelhorn, 1899), part I, p. 2. See Kristof, op. cit., p. 22.

26. See, in particular, Nicholas J. Spykman and Abbie A. Rollins, "Geographic Objectives in Foreign Policy I," *American Political Science Review*, XXXIII (June 1939), 391–393.

27. Rudolf Kjellen, *Der Staat als Lebensform*, trans. M. Langfelt (Leipzig: S. Hirzel Verlag, 1917), pp. 218–220. See Kristof, op. cit., p. 22.

28. For a discussion of the development of the Germany Academy, see Donald H. Norton, "Karl Haushofer and the German Academy, 1925–1945," *Central European History*, I (March 1958), 82. According to its rules and regulations, the objectives of the Academy were "to nourish all spiritual expressions of Germandom and to bring together and strengthen the unofficial cultural relations of Germany with areas abroad and of the Germans abroad with the homeland, in the service of the all-German folk-consciousness." Quoted in ibid.

29. Robert Strausz-Hupé, *Geopolitics: The Struggle for Space and Power* (New York: Putnam's, 1942), p. vii. Ladis K. D. Kristof suggests the following definition: "Geopolitics is the study of political phenomena (1) in their spatial relationship and (2) in their relationship with, dependence upon, and influence on earth as well as on all those cultural factors which constitute the subject matter of human geography (anthropogeography) broadly defined. In other words, geopolitics is what the word itself suggests etymologically: geographical politics, that is, politics and not geography—politics geographically interpreted or analyzed for its geographical content." Kristof, op. cit., p. 34.

30. Derwent Whittlesey, "Haushofer: The Geopolitician," in Edward Mead Earle, ed., *Makers of Modern Strategy: Military Thought from Machiavelli to Hitler* (Princeton: Princeton University Press, 1943), pp. 398–406.

31. Harold and Margaret Sprout, *The Ecological Perspective on Human Affairs with Special Reference to International Politics* (Princeton: Princeton University Press, 1965), p. 9.

32. Harold and Margaret Sprout, *An Ecological Paradigm for the Study of International Politics* (Princeton: Center for International Studies, 1968), Monograph No. 30, p. 21.

33. Ibid., p. 11.

34. Ibid., p. 13. The definition is quoted by the Sprouts from Preston E. James et al., *American Geography: Inventory and Prospect* (Syracuse: Syracuse University Press, 1954), p. 4.

35. Harold and Margaret Sprout, *The Ecological Perspective on Human Affairs*, op. cit., p. 15.

36. Ibid., p. 140.

37. Ibid., p. 28.

38. See Harold and Margaret Sprout, *An Ecological Paradigm for the Study of International Politics*, op. cit., pp. 39–41. For the implications of perception in foreign policy decision-making, see Chapter 11.

39. Ibid., p. 11.

40. Ibid., p. 42.

41. Ibid., p. 34.
42. Harold and Margaret Sprout, *The Ecological Perspective on Human Affairs*, op. cit., p. 8.
43. Harold and Margaret Sprout, *An Ecological Paradigm for the Study of International Politics*, op. cit., p. 62.
44. Ibid., p. 55.
45. Ibid., p. 20.
46. Ibid., p. 56.
47. Ibid., p. 64.
48. George Liska, *Quest for Equilibrium: America and the Balance of Power on Land and Sea* (Baltimore and London: Johns Hopkins Press, 1977), p. 4.
49. Robert T. Holt and John E. Turner, "Insular Polities," in James N. Rosenau, ed., *Linkage Politics* (New York: The Free Press, 1969), pp. 199–236.
50. Richard L. Merritt, "Noncontiguity and Political Integration." ibid., pp. 237–272.
51. Harold and Margaret Sprout, *Foundations of International Politics* (Princeton: Van Nostrand, 1962), p. 54. Examples of such rhetoric include: "The mountains of Japan have pushed the Japanese out upon the seas *making* them the greatest seafaring people of Asia." "England, *driven* to the sea by her sparse resources to seek a livelihood and to find homes for her burgeoning population, and sitting athwart the main sea routes of Western Europe, seemed *destined by geography* to command the seas." (Italics are the authors'.)
52. Harold and Margaret Sprout, *The Ecological Perspective on Human Affairs*, op. cit., p. 11.
53. Robert Strausz-Hupé, *Geopolitics*, op. cit., p. 173.
54. Nicholas Spykman, *The Geography of the Peace*, op. cit., p. 43.
55. Ibid., p. 181.
56. Robert Strausz-Hupé, op. cit., pp. 164–165.
57. Ibid., p. 181.
58. Derwent Whittlesey, "Haushofer: The Geo-Politicians," in Edward Mead Earle, ed., *Makers of Modern Strategy: Military Thought from Machiavelli to Hitler* (Princeton: Princeton University Press, 1943), p. 400.
59. *Geographical Journal*, XXIII (April 1904), 441.
60. Robert Strausz-Hupé, op. cit., pp. 189–190. A half century after Leopold Amery made his comment about the airplane, long-range bombers carrying nuclear bombs had become prime symbols of international power, and analysts were still arguing, not quite conclusively, as to whether the advent of airpower and nuclear energy had rendered the Heartland concept obsolete. See W. Gordon East, "How Strong is the Heartland?" *Foreign Affairs*, XXIX (October 1950), 78–93; and Charles Kruszewski, "The Pivot of History," *Foreign Affairs*, XXXII (April 1954), 338–401.
61. Harold and Margaret Sprout, *Foundations of International Politics*, op. cit., pp. 338–339.
62. Ladis Kristof, op. cit., p. 29.
63. Richard E. Harrison and Hans W. Weigert, "World View and Strategy," in Hans W. Weigert and Vilhjalmut Stefansson, eds., *Compass of the World: A Symposium on Political Geography* (New York: Macmillan, 1947), p. 76.
64. Alan K. Henrikson, "The Map as an 'Idea': The Role of Cartographic Imagery During the Second World War," *The American Cartographer*, 2, No. 1 (1975), 46–47.
65. Richard Edes Harrison and Robert Strausz-Hupé, "Maps, Strategy and World Politics," in Harold and Margaret Sprout, eds., *Foundations of National Power* (Princeton: Princeton University Press, 1945), pp. 64–68.
66. See, for example, Geoffrey Kemp, Robert L. Pfaltzgraff, Jr., and Uri Ra'anan, eds., *The Other Arms Race: New Technologies and Non-Nuclear Conflict* (Lexington, Mass.: D. C. Heath, 1975).

67. Geoffrey Kemp, "The New Strategic Map," *Survival,* XIX, No. 2 (March–April, 1977), 52. See by the same author, "Scarcity and Strategy," *Foreign Affairs,* 56, No. 2 (January 1978), 396–414.

68. Colin S. Gray, *The Geopolitics of the Nuclear Era: Heartland, Rimlands and the Technological Revolution* (New York: Crane, Russak, for the National Strategy Information Center, 1977), p. 65.

69. Ibid., p. 11.

70. See, for example, Robert Strausz-Hupé, "Social Values and Politics: The Uninvited Guests," *Review of Politics,* XXX (January 1968), 59–78. Another writer, George F. Kennan, who, like Strausz-Hupé, is examined in the following chapter, has suggested the need for an international organization for the collection, storage, and retrieval and dissemination of information and the coordination of research and operational activities on environmental problems at the international level. See George F. Kennan, "To Prevent a World Wasteland," *Foreign Affairs,* XLVIII (April 1970), 404.

71. Zbigniew Brzezinski, *Between Two Ages: America's Role in the Technetronic Era* (New York: Viking, 1970), p. 14.

72. Joy W. Forrester, *World Dynamics* (Cambridge, Mass.: Wright-Allen, 1971); Donella H. Meadows, Dennis L. Meadows, Jorgen Randers, and William W. Behrens III, *The Limits to Growth* (New York: Universe Books, 1972).

73. See, in particular, H. S. D. Cole, Christopher Freeman, Marie Jahoda, and K. L. R. Pavitt, eds., *Models of Doom:* A Critique of the Limits of Growth (New York: Universe Books, 1973); *Rapid Population Growth: Consequences and Policy Implications* (Baltimore and London: The Johns Hopkins University Press, 1971).

74. See, for example, "Commentary" at the end of the Report in ibid.; "The Limits to Growth: Hard Sell to a Computer View of Doomsday," *Science,* 175 (March 10, 1972), 1088–1092; and Garrett Harden and R. Stephen Berry, "Limits to Growth— Two Views," *Bulletin of the Atomic Scientists,* XXVIII (December 1972), 23–27.

75. John R. Maddox, for example, saw the need for adjustments but not for radical transformation of existing systems in *The Doomsday Syndrome* (New York: McGraw-Hill, 1972).

76. John Galtung, "Limits to Growth and Class Politics," *Journal of Peace Research,* Nos. 1–2 (1973), 101–114.

77. Carl Kaysen, "The Computer That Printed Out W°O°L°F°," *Foreign Affairs,* 50 (July 1972), 664. According to Kaysen, the crucial adjustment mechanism ignored in the model was *price:* "As a resource becomes scarce, the consequent rise in price leads to savings in use, to efforts to increase supply, and to technical innovation to offset the scarcity. Ibid., p. 665. Moreover, he says, in the demographic transition birth rates eventually adjust to death rates, and even though the *absolute* gap between per capita income in the richest and the poorest countries (measured in dollars) is increasing, the *relative* gap between the Third World and the industrialized West is narrowing, and "that is what is relevant to the question of equality." Ibid., p. 666.

78. Mihajlo Mesarovic and Éduard Pestel, *Mankind at the Turning Point: The Second Report to the Club of Rome* (New York: Dutton, 1974).

Chapter 3
Power and Realist Theory

REALIST THEORY VERSUS UTOPIANISM

Realist theory dominated the study of international relations in the United States from the 1940s to the 1960s. Textbooks by realist scholars and their other writings, often policy-oriented, had wide currency both in official and academic circles. Realist theory, like utopianism, is normative and policy-oriented, although its proponents purport to present an analysis based upon a theoretical framework drawn from the history of the international system, especially the era of Europe's classical balance of power. But much of realist theory is a critique of utopianism. Utopianism emphasizes the possibility of transforming the nation-state system through international law and organization, while realism posits that the prospects for affecting changes in the international system are not great. The international system is shaped by numerous forces, many of which are immutable. Unlike utopians, realists assume that there is no essential harmony of interests among nations. Instead, they posit that nation-states often have conflicting national objectives, some of which lead to war.

The capabilities of states are crucial for the outcome of international conflict and for one state's ability to influence another's behavior. But seldom, if ever, is the notion of capabilities, or power, synonymous in realist theory with strictly military force levels. Power has both military and nonmilitary components, and realist theorists have developed frameworks for classifying the elements of national power. Such capabilities include not only military forces, but also levels of technology, population, natural resources, geographical factors, form of government, political leadership, and ideology.

Realist theorists assume that certain largely immutable factors such as geography and the nature of human behavior shape international conduct. In contrast to utopianism, realism holds that human nature is essentially constant, or at least not easily altered. In the utopian framework human behavior was held to be improvable, and perhaps even perfectible. Utopianism is based on the idea that politics can be made to conform to an ethical standard. Norms of behavior, such as those specified in international law and organization, can be established and, later if not sooner, can be made the basis for international behavior. In contrast, the realist posits that there are severe limitations in the extent to which political reform or education can alter human nature. Man is evil, sinful, power-seeking. According to realist theory, human nature is not innately good or perfectible. The task of the statesman lies in the fashioning of political frameworks within which the human propensity to engage in conflict can be minimized. Hence the emphasis placed by realist writers upon regulatory mechanisms such as the balance of power, discussed in greater detail in Chapter 1. Because of the difficulty of achieving peace through international law and organization, or even by means of world government, it is necessary to devise other arrangements for the management of power. The balance of power is said to furnish an important regulatory device to prevent any one nation from achieving hegemony.

Realist writers generally agree that a state's location affects its national capabilities and its foreign policy orientation. Geography is said to shape the options available to states and to impose limitations—often severe—upon the choices open to states in their foreign policies. Because of geography certain states are more vulnerable than others to foreign conquest. Some nations occupy more strategically important geographical positions than others. Access to key waterways and the extent to which the configuration of frontiers expose a state to, or affords protection from, hostile neighbors influence its foreign policy. Geographical location affects the climate and length of the growing season for crops, as well as the ability to mobilize against other nations. Such variables are discussed more fully in Chapter 2. Geographic, demographic, resource, and geopolitical factors are central to realist theory of international relations.

Realists assume, moreover, that moral principles in their abstract formulation cannot be applied to political actions. To what extent, the realist would ask, have statesmen succeeded in achieving their major foreign policy objectives without endangering the state on whose behalf they act? The statesman operates in an international environment—distinguishable from a national environment by the absence of authoritative political institutions, legal systems, and commonly accepted standards of conduct—and the standards of conduct at the international level differ from those governing behavior within a national unit. Although not all realists consider the statesman *qua* statesman as amoral, they nevertheless often place less emphasis upon abstract standards of behavior in international conduct than in utopian theory. The statesman acting on behalf of state interests necessarily embodies a standard of conduct substantially different from that of the individual within a civilized political unit and from that of the individual *qua* individual. The statesman is sworn, by oath of office, to safeguard the political unit from external threat. In a world of nation-states, over whom there is no legally and politically superior authority, the power of the nation-state becomes the ultimate arbiter. The protection of the nation state from its enemies, in an international system containing revolutionary, expansionist, revisionist powers, inevitably leads the statesman to adopt or to countenance policies that would be legally and morally repugnant in behavior among individuals or groups within a civilized state. However, as Robert E. Osgood suggests in his analysis of the relationship between self-interest and ideals:

> It is man's reluctance to face the inevitable moral dilemmas of social existence that robs him of his moral perspective and leads him to an easy identification of his own nation's self-interest with high moral purpose and the welfare of mankind. It is this common conceit that persuades men to view the inevitable moral compromises of international relations as good things in themselves rather than as unfortunate expedients designed to maximize ideal values in a society where partial morality is the best morality attainable.[1]

According to the realists politics is not a function of ethical philosophy. Political theory is derived from political practice and from historical experience. Finally, the realist seeks to reconcile national interest with supranational ideals, although he posits that the former has, or should have, primacy over the latter.

POWER AS A DETERMINANT OF INTERNATIONAL BEHAVIOR

Power is one of the words most frequently used in the study of political science, especially in international relations. The absence of adequate institutions and procedures at the international level for resolving conflict comparable to those in most domestic political systems makes the so-called power element more obvious than at the domestic level. In a textbook first published in 1933, Frederick L. Schuman held that in an international system lacking a common government, each unit "necessarily seeks safety by relying on its own power and viewing with alarm the power of its neighbors."[2] According to Nicholas J. Spykman, "All civilized life rests in the last instance on power." Power is the ability to move men in some desired fashion, through "persuasion, purchase, barter, and coercion."[3] Hans J. Morgenthau even defines international politics, and indeed all politics, as a "struggle for power." Thus power has been conceptualized both as a means and an end. Morgenthau holds that power is "man's control over the minds and actions of other men."[4] Robert Strausz-Hupé maintains that international politics is "dominated by the quest for power," and that "at any given period of known history, there were several states locked in deadly conflict, all desiring the augmentation or preservation of their power."[5] Arnold Wolfers argued that power is "the ability to move others or to get them to do what one wants them to do and not to do what one does not want them to do." Moreover, he deemed it important "to distinguish between power and influence, the first to mean the ability to move others by the threat or infliction of deprivations, the latter to mean the ability to do so through promises or grants of benefits."[6] John Burton, himself clearly not an exponent of the realist school of theory or of *Realpolitik*, suggests that "There is probably no greater common factor in all thinking on international relations than the assumption that States depend for their existence upon power, and achieve their objectives by power, thus making the management of power the main problem to be solved."[7]

As noted elsewhere in this chapter, the power of a state is said to consist of capabilities, some of which are economic in nature, such as levels of industrialization and productivity, gross national product, national income, and income on a per capita basis. In an analysis of the economic dimensions of international politics and the political aspects of international economics, Charles P. Kindleberger assesses power in its intertwined economic and political contexts. He defines power as "strength capable of being used efficiently," that is, "strength *plus* the capacity to use it effectively"[8] in support of some objective. Thus, like several other writers, Kindleberger distinguishes between means and ends, or the use of means for the attainment of ends. Thus strength is a means that exists even in the absence of its use for some goal, whereas power is the use of strength for a particular purpose. According to Kindleberger, "Prestige is the respect which is paid to power. Influence is the capacity to affect the decisions of others. Force is the use of physical means to affect those decisions. Dominance is the condition under which

A affects a significant number of B's decisions without B affecting those of A."[9] Power thus conceptualized is related in Kindleberger's analysis to adaptability and flexibility in a nation's economy. Such is the meaning of efficiency in the use of power. Thus power is dynamic and changing, rather than static in nature. Those states, or other entities, best able to adjust to change are likely to possess power.

According to Klaus Knorr, power, influence and interdependence are inextricably related. Two states can be in conflict over some issues while cooperating on others. "When they cooperate they benefit from the creation of new values, material or nonmaterial. When they are in conflict, they attempt to gain values at each other's expense. In either case, they are interdependent."[10] Power becomes important in conflictual situations whereas influence is central both in circumstances of conflict and in cooperative relationships. Power may be used coercively or noncoercively. "When power is used coercively, an actor (B) is influenced if he adapts his behavior in compliance with, or in anticipation of, another actor's (A) demands, wishes, or proposals." Knorr suggests that the term *power* is used by some writers to identify all influence, whether coercive or noncoercive. He prefers to use the term *power* to designate "only the exercise of coercive influence."[11] Developing a model for the analysis of the utility of military power by one actor (A) against another actor (B), Knorr identifies four basic factors: (1) B's estimate of the costs of complying with A's threat; (2) B's estimate of the costs of defying A's threat; (3) B's bargaining skill relative to A's; and (4) B's propensity to act rationally and to assume risks.[12] Knorr holds that many variables "intervene in determining whether or not a military threat will be effective, and to what extent."[13]

In short, interdependence connotes the ability of one state to influence another in some way. If the interdependence is mutual, each could damage the other, and itself, by severing the relationship that exists between them. Thus the costs and the benefits of exercising power by each party in an interdependent relationship increase as the level of interdependence grows.[14]

Power exists to a certain extent in the eyes of the beholder. The element of perception, of subjective assessment, may be high in calculating the resolve of an adversary to use effectively the power at its disposal. Similar considerations are operative in deterrence theory (see Chapter 9), which in turn is closely related to power as discussed here. The perceptual dimension of power has been studied by the scoring and ranking of 103 nations in terms of power perception. It was concluded that perceived national power is some function of GNP or military expenditures if the state has not been at war recently.[15] Another study developed a multidimensional conception of influence for the comparison of the perceived power of seven nations: China, the Federal Republic of Germany, France, Japan, the Soviet Union, the United Kingdom, and the United States.

The attributes of influence consisted of (1) human resources; (2) economic strength, or wealth; (3) technology; (4) trade; and (5) military strength. States were ranked in accordance with numerical values attached to each attribute by the use of expert judgment. The authors concluded that wealth and military strength, in themselves, are not necessarily sufficient to gain for a nation the status of superpowers, although the development of military capabilities may provide a "convenient and relatively inexpensive way" toward influence, especially for poor states, in a relatively short period of time.[16] Yet another writer asks: "given the highly psychological nature of power relationships, is it ever possible to use available information to measure power?"[17]

Power has often been viewed as an influence relationship—the ability of one actor to induce another to act in some desired fashion, or to refrain from undesired behavior.[18] According to Michael P. Sullivan, "Power may not only be distinguished from sheer capabilities, it can also be differentiated from the use of force. Power can be present in situations where force is not used. Indeed, some argue that such instances are illustrations of ultimate power—when one party influences the other to act without even possessing the supposed necessary capabilities. 'Power,' then, can become *psychological control* over others."[19] The use of power to exert influence over another, it has been suggested, is the employment of power most effectively. In such a conception, it is not the actual use of power, as in a military campaign, but rather the political shadow alleged to be cast by its perceived possession. Thus power becomes the "cutting edge" of diplomacy.

Also viewing power as an influence relationship, K. J. Holsti suggests that power is a multidimensional concept consisting of (1) the acts by which one actor influences another actor; (2) the capabilities utilized for this purpose; and (3) the response elicited. Thus Holsti conceptualizes power as a means to an end, even though some political leaders may seek influence as an end in itself, just as some people may value money not only for what it can buy but for its own sake. In short, Holsti defines power as the "general capacity of a state to control the behavior of others."[20] Stated differently, answers are sought to the following questions: In light of our goals what kind of behavior do we seek to obtain from another actor, or actors, and how can such an actor, or actors, be induced to do what we want? What capabilities are available for use in support of our goal? What is likely to be the response to our effort to influence the behavior of another actor, or actors?[21] In such an analysis of power, the idea of causation is implicit. The possessor of power is said to be conducive to its threatened or actual use to produce a desired result. Those who object to causally based theories of political behavior logically fault power theory that is based on causation.[22] In such a critique, we are brought back to one of the enduring questions of power and political behavior: stated simply, it is to what extent can the intentions of states as political actors be inferred from the capabilities in their possession?

Of special concern has been the estimation and measurement of power. According to Robert J. Lieber, power is said to be the

> . . . currency of the political system in the way that money is the currency of the economy. That is, we cannot eat or dress or shelter ourselves with money, but money permits access to the goods and services with which we can be fed, clothed, and housed. And just as the flows of currency are well suited to quantitative analysis by economists, so too this conception of power should provide the opportunity for quantification."[23]

Karl Deutsch views power as a

> . . . symbol of the ability to change the distribution of results, and particularly the results of people's behavior. In this respect, power can be compared in some ways to money, which is our usual standardized symbol of purchasing power—that is, of our ability to change the distribution of goods and resources.[24]

David A. Baldwin holds that power is situationally specific. Although power is far less fungible than money, some aspects of power are more fungible than others and might be so rank-ordered. If power must be related to the situation in which it is used, or available for use, Baldwin maintains, the categorization of states as "great powers" or "small powers" is inadequate if not misleading, since such terms relate to a generalized, rather than to a specific, situational context, or to a particular issue area.[25] The need exists, it is suggested, for students of international politics to examine the "multiple distributional patterns" of power in a large number of issue areas, while recognizing the limitations of power analysis resulting from the absence of a common denominator of political value for comparing different forms and uses of power.

According to Jeffrey Hart, power can be observed and measured by reference to essentially three approaches: (1) control over resources; (2) control over actors; and (3) control over events and outcomes. The latter approach—events and outcomes—constitutes the most promising focal point for the observation and measurement of power in international relations, even though most analysis of power, as noted elsewhere in this chapter, has been based on control over resources, such as military expenditures, size of military capabilities, population, and level of economic development.[26] It may be inferred that power measured as control over events and outcomes becomes in the final analysis situational. But the measurement of an outcome is related, in turn, to the preferences of actors in a power relationship.

Jack H. Nagel has suggested that the "measurement and observation of preferences will be a fundamental difficulty in the study of power, severely restricting outcomes over which power can be measured.[27] Nagel argues for power analysis based on data that relate preferences causally to explanations of outcomes. He contends that this problem extends to motivation theory in psychology as well as to game theory and decision theory. According to Herbert Simon and Roderick Bell, the essential prerequisite for the measurement of power is a theoretical framework or theory of power.[28] The use of cardinal numbers to measure power implies that the observed or measured units have the same properties as, or are isomorphic to, the cardinal numbers. Thus the problem of power measurement relates more to the deficiencies inherent in existing theory than in the measurement techniques themselves, however formidable they remain.

The problems of quantification of power have proven formidable indeed. The inability of political scientists and others to develop adequate means for the quantification of power accounts, to no small extent, for the lack of theories of international relations based upon quantification as widely accepted as have been the theories of economic behavior, and econometrics in particular. In international relations, power has been considered to be relative—to the goals for which it is being used. As we have already seen, power has been conceptualized to include tangible factors such as military capabilities and intangible elements such as political will. Nevertheless, the measurement of power—actual and potential—however difficult, has been, and remains, a central concern of governments in all parts of the world. It promises to gain in importance as the capabilities of states increase with a diffusion of technologies in the late twentieth century. Power measurement will become more complex as a result of the increased salience of its economic dimensions and as a greater variety of weapons systems of unprecedented accuracy and range become available to a larger number of actors.[29]

Especially in the past generation, numerous indicators of relative military capabilities have been developed. If the strategic-military relationship between the United States and the Soviet Union remains central to international politics in the late twentieth century, the ability to estimate as precisely as possible trends in relative superpower force levels is an issue of concern to scholars and policymakers alike. The complexity inherent in the measurement of this important dimension of power derives from differences, or asymmetries, in strategic-military doctrines, which state strikes first, the accuracy of strategic-nuclear missiles, the size and number of warheads, the ability of one side or the other to defend against a strategic-nuclear attack, that is, to safeguard its retaliatory strategic forces from a disarming strike, and to protect its population, especially those segments most important for postattack recovery.[30] There are numerous conceptual relationships between the analysis of strategic-military force levels and theories of conflict and deterrence, discussed in Chapter 9. In short, the measurement of the military capabilities of states—both at the superpower level and among other states in the process of acquiring unprecedented means of destruction—is both a pressing conceptual problem for the scholar and a practical issue of great importance for the policymaker and for the management of power in the late twentieth century.

Among the concepts in which the capacity for power measurement is implicit is that of parity, which in the strategic-military literature of the 1970s was related to deterrence theory. Parity represented what has been termed *strategic equivalence*, that is, possession by both the United States and the Soviet Union of capabilities that in the aggregate are equal or adequate for the deterrence of strategic warfare, although specific components of such forces might favor one side or the other.

Whether or not parity can be said to exist depends upon the relative capabilities of the states. In the absence of agreed methodologies for power measurement, we cannot conclude definitively that a condition of parity does or does not exist. As George Liska has written, "Parity is, in the last analysis, along with several other key normative and strategic political concepts (such as intervention and the balance of power itself) essentially and fruitfully a metaphysical notion. It is such in both the literal sense, of being above the physical aspect of hardware calculations (if not above the physics of power dynamics), and in the wider sense, of being a concept with a debatable concrete meaning but also with meaningful and objectively self-evident connotations (differing thus favorably from, say, the notion of sufficiency in mere weaponry)."[31]

Efforts have been made to measure power, and especially influence, by reference to communications, by who communicates with whom, by who consults with whom. (Such measures have also been utilized in the study of political integration to be discussed in Chapter 10.) It is hypothesized that the more a person, group, or nation is the recipient rather than the originator of communications, the greater the influence of that entity over others. Steven Brams has hypothesized that two nations have an influence relationship with each other which is symmetrical if the transactions between them are approximately equal.[32] If one nation receives the preponderant number of transactions, especially official level visits, it exercises asymmetrical influence over the other.[33] Such a proposition can be, and has been, tested with the use of international visit data, but without conclusive results. Research utilizing such data forms part of a broader emphasis in the past generation upon events/data analysis considered in Chapter 4.

ANTECEDENTS OF REALISM

Like utopianism in international relations theory, realism has its intellectual roots in the older political philosophy of the West and in the writings of non-Western ancient authors such as Mencius and the Legalists in China and Kautilya in India. In his analysis of interstate relations in the Italian system of the sixteenth century, Machiavelli derived a theory of politics from observing the political practice of his time. Machiavelli's emphasis on the need for the ruler to adopt moral standards different from those of the individual in order to insure the state's survival, his concern with power, his assumption that politics is characterized by a clash of interests, his pessimistic view of human nature—all these clearly place him within the realist framework.[34]

Thomas Hobbes, like Machiavelli, viewed power as crucial in human behavior. Man has a "perpetual and restless desire of power after power that ceaseth only in death."[35] Hobbes believed that "covenants, without the sword, are but words and of no strength to secure a man at all."[36] Without a strong sovereign, chaos and violence follow: "If there be no power erected, or not great enough for our own security; man will and may lawfully rely on his own strength and art for caution against all other men."[37]

Like the modern realists, Hobbes concerned himself with the underlying forces of politics and with the nature of power in political relationships. Although Hobbes believed that a strong sovereign was mandatory for maintaining order within the political system, he saw little prospect for fundamentally changing human behavior or the environment. In his emphasis on strong political institutions for managing power and preventing conflict, Hobbes paradoxically was closer to proponents of world government or, to be more precise, world empire than to realists who stress a balance of power among major political groups. Hobbes regarded the latter condition as analogous to an anarchical state of nature, but he doubted the possibility of establishing a world empire.

Hegel, more than any other political philosopher, elevated the position of the state. Although realist writers are usually by no means Hegelian, Hegel's belief that the state's highest duty is its own preservation is found in realist theory. Hegel reasoned that "since states are related to one another as autonomous entities and so as particular wills on which the validity of treaties depends, and since the particular will of the whole is in content a will for its own welfare it follows that welfare is the highest aim governing the relation of one state to another."[38] Moreover, Hegel held that the state has an "individual totality" that develops according to its own laws. The state has objective reality; that is, it exists apart from its citizens. Hegel held that the state has moral standards different from, and superior to, those of the individual—a theme that is found in many realist writings.

REALISM IN TWENTIETH-CENTURY INTERNATIONAL RELATIONS THEORY

Reinhold Niebuhr

Although many scholars, past and present, have shaped the development of realist international relations theory, the writings of the Protestant theologian Reinhold Niebuhr (1892–1971) have had a major—indeed a unique—impact on realist theory.[39] Crucial to Niebuhr's theory is his biblical concept of man who is tainted by original sin and therefore capable of evil. Man's sinfulness stems from his anxiety. "Anxiety is the inevitable concomitant of the paradox of freedom and finiteness in which man is involved."[40] Man is sinful because he denies his finiteness, pretending to be more than he really is.[41]

Man's effort to usurp God's position "inevitably subordinates other life to its will and thus does injustice to other life." Moreover, humans have a "will-to-live" which leads to a "will-to-power." Since our "will-to-live" transcends a mere will to assure physical survival, we invariably seek security against the perils of nature and history by enhancing our individual and collective power.

> The conflicts between men are thus simple conflicts between competing survival impulses. They are conflicts in which each man or group seeks to guard its power and prestige against the peril of competing expressions of power and pride. Since the very possession of power and prestige always involves some encroachment upon the prestige and power of others, this conflict is by its very nature a more stubborn and difficult one than the mere competition between various survival impulses in nature.[42]

Moral behavior is difficult but possible for the individual: It is extremely difficult or impossible for groups, especially large groups. Discussing the nature of power in groups and nations, Niebuhr asserts that national power is the projection of the individual's "will-to-power." When there are fewer moral restraints upon the individual as a member of a group, or a nation, than upon him as an individual, greater violence results at the group, or national, level. An individual acting as a member of a group loses his identity, becoming instead a member of an anonymous mass.[43] Thus the tendencies toward power become magnified at the group, or national, level. (The hypothesis that individual aggressiveness is eventually displaced to the national level is treated in Chapter 6.)

Charting a course that such intellectual disciples as George F. Kennan, Charles Burton Marshall, and Hans J. Morgenthau would follow,

Niebuhr criticized what he considered historic American attitudes toward foreign policy. In particular, as he saw it, Americans have been unaware of the power motive in international politics because their nation enjoyed a long period of isolation from the power confrontations of other nations. The "irony" of American history is that the Founding Fathers' dreams of the United States developing into a uniquely virtuous nation have been shattered. Instead, the United States entered into a struggle for world power. "Our age is involved in irony because so many dreams of our nation have been so cruelly refuted by history."[44] The "irony" is heightened by the "frantic efforts of some of our idealists to escape this hard reality by dreaming up schemes of an ideal world order which have no relevance to either our present dangers or our urgent duties."[45]

In criticizing proponents of world government, Niebuhr implied that political theory derives from political practice:

> Governments cannot create communities for the simple reason that the authority of government is not primarily the authority of law nor the authority of force, but the authority of the community itself. Laws are obeyed because the community accepts them as corresponding, on the whole, to its conception of justice.[46]

Because the forces of cohesiveness are minimal, the prospects for world government are not promising.

There are elements of free will and determinism in Niebuhr's view of the individual. If we are tainted with original sin and are power-seeking, we have capacities for both good and evil. Although our "will-to-live" may lead us to dominate others, it may also be transformed into a "will-to-self-realization." Paradoxically, the highest form of self-realization is self-giving. Our will-to-live may lead us to choose one form of behavior or another.

Although believing that conflict is inherent in intergroup and international relations, Niebuhr did not agree that the statesman *qua* statesman is amoral. He suggested, instead, that realism must be tempered with morality, that "nations must use their power with the purpose of making it an instrument of justice and a servant of interests broader than their own."[47] Moreover, he criticized those realists who overemphasize the "national interest," because at the national as well as the individual level, "egotism is not the proper cure for an abstract and pretentious idealism."[48] Since each nation interprets justice from its own perspective rather than a competing state's, it becomes difficult to give operational meaning to the rule that statesmen must always frame policies based upon the "national interest." For Niebuhr, the balance of power is the organizational device for achieving a semblance of justice. "Some balance of power is the basis of whatever justice is achieved in human relations. Where the disproportion of power is too great and where an equilibrium of social forces is lacking no mere rational or moral demands can achieve justice."[49]

Perhaps we can better understand Niebuhr if we review the evolution of his outlook during the period between the two world wars. In a sense, Niebuhr reflected the dilemma of American pacifism when faced by Nazism. Although disillusioned by the consequences of World War I, he had never been an absolute religious pacifist. He once distinguished between "absolute pacifism" (espoused by religious perfectionists) and "pragmatic pacifism" (based more upon political preferences than upon the Gospel ethic), and eventually identified himself with the latter.[50] Even so, he admitted that some coercion might be necessary in the domestic social struggle against the status quo. But for a time he refused to justify any type of international armed conflict. In the early 1930s, while chairman of the Fellowship of Reconciliation, he declared that members of that pacifist organization would not fight in an international war.[51]

By 1938, at the time of the Munich settlement, he had broken completely with idealist pacifism:

> We may say that the pacifists are right in their conviction that our civilization stands under the judgment of God; no one can have an easy conscience about the social and political anarchy out of which the horrible tyrannies of our age have risen. But they are wrong in assuming that we have no right or duty to defend a civilization, despite its imperfections, against worse alternatives. . . .
>
> The pacifists rightly recognize that it may be very noble for an individual to sacrifice his life or interests rather than participate in the claims and counterclaims of the struggle for justice. . . . They are wrong in making no distinction between an individual act of self-abnegation and a political policy of submission to injustice, whereby lives and interests other than our own are defrauded or destroyed.[52]

After World War II, Niebuhr continued to maintain that political leaders constantly face moral ambiguities. The United States must contain the expansion of communism and at the same time prevent nuclear war. For all its shortcomings, he held that constitutional democracy is a clearly superior form of political organization to communist oligarchy that, by unscrupulously centralizing absolute power, promotes far greater injustices than those the communists attribute to the free society.[53] But Niebuhr frequently warned Americans against thinking that they were innocent of the power drives that have motivated other peoples of the world. The United States has engaged in its own imperialist ventures, but a democratic nation with a strong sense of international mission is always reluctant to admit to itself that its actions spring from any but the noblest of motives. Niebuhr contended that although the mission of preserving and extending democratic self-government had greater validity than some other forms of national messianism, Americans must abandon their illusion of a special national innocence and righteousness and must resist the temptation to "claim more virtue for the exercise of power than the facts warrant."[54]

Nicholas J. Spykman

Several realist writers support the idea that conflict rather than cooperation is more typical of international relations than of intrastate relations. Nicholas J. Spykman (1893–1943), assumed that the conditions characterizing relations among groups within a state only during crises and breakdowns of central authority are normal for relations among states in the international system. States exist because they are strong or have other states protecting them. In the international system, as in other social groupings, Spykman saw several basic processes operating: cooperation, accommodation, and opposition. To assure their survival, states "must make the preservation or improvement of their power position a principal objective of their foreign policy."[55] Because power is ultimately the ability to wage war, states have always emphasized the building of military establishments.

Spykman's geopolitical and balance of power concepts are crucial to his realism. According to Spykman, expansion follows the line of least resistance. "New territories are conquered, held, assimilated, and serve as a starting point for new advance. There is a correlation between the amount of expansion and ease of movement." The limits to expansion are set by natural barriers such as oceans, rivers, and mountains, as well as a tendency to expand up and down river valleys, to seek access to the sea, and to dominate strategic points near communications routes. At any time in history, the frontiers of states indicate their relative power relationship. The potential for conflict increased, Spykman held, as the world became more densely populated and nations encroached upon each other. A country's geographical location determines its problems.

Drawing upon Mackinder's geopolitical theory, Spykman advanced his conception of the goals which should guide American foreign policy during and after World War II. Because the Western Hemisphere did not contain economic, military, and technological resources capable of withstanding the combined resources of the Eurasian land mass, it was crucial for the United States to preserve a balance of power in Europe and Asia.[56] Writing before United States entry into World War II, Spykman concluded that just as the German-Japanese alliance represented a threat to America's security, other powers, namely, Russia and China, would pose security problems for the United States in the postwar period. "A Russian state from the Urals to the North Sea can be no great improvement over a German state from the North Sea to the Urals."[57] In

Asia, Spykman suggested, the United States may face a "modern, vitalized, and militarized China" which would threaten not only the position of Japan, but also that of the Western powers in Asia. Just as the United States twice came to the aid of Britain so "that the small offshore island might not have to face a single gigantic military state in control of the opposite coast of the mainland," the United States would "have to adopt a similar protective policy toward Japan" to preserve a balance of power in Asia. Moreover, Spykman acknowledged that an "equilibrium of forces inherently unstable, always shifting, always changing" is an "indispensable element of an international order based on independent states.[58]

Implicit in Spykman's thought is the pursuit of limited national objectives. He urged the United States to seek only the removal of the then-existing regimes of Germany and Japan, not to have as an objective their destruction as states, because they must play a major role in restraining other powers which one day will vie for hegemony in the Eurasian land mass. Thus he relates the pursuit of limited national interest to balance of power and geopolitical concepts.

Hans J. Morgenthau

Hans J. Morgenthau (1904–   ), sets forth six principles of realist theory. First, he suggests that political relationships are governed by objective rules deeply rooted in human nature. Since these rules are "impervious to our preferences, men will challenge them only at the risk of failure."[59] If these rules themselves cannot be changed, Morgenthau's determinism holds that society can be improved by first understanding the laws that govern society and then by basing public policy on that knowledge.

In theorizing about international politics it is necessary to employ historical data for examining political acts and their consequences. In systematizing these vast amounts of historical data, the students of politics should place themselves "in the position of a statesman who must meet a certain problem of foreign policy under certain circumstances," and ask themselves "what the rational alternatives are from which a statesman may choose who must meet this problem under these circumstances (presuming always that he acts in a rational manner), and which of these rational alternatives this particular statesman, acting under these circumstances, is likely to choose. It is the testing of this rational hypothesis against the actual facts and their consequences that gives meaning to the facts of international politics."[60]

Second, Morgenthau contends that statesmen "think and act in terms of interest defined as power" and that historical evidence proves this assumption.[61] This concept, central to Morgenthau's realism, gives continuity and unity to the seemingly diverse foreign policies of the widely separated nation-states. Moreover, the concept "interest defined as power" makes possible the evaluation of actions of political leaders at different points in history. To describe Morgenthau's framework in more contemporary language, it is a model of interaction within an international system. Using historical data, Morgenthau compares the real world with the interaction patterns within his model.

In his view, international politics is a process in which national interests are adjusted.

> The concept of the national interest presupposes neither a naturally harmonious, peaceful world nor the inevitability of war as a consequence of the pursuit by all nations of their national interest. Quite to the contrary, it assumes continuous conflict and threat of war to be minimized through the continuous adjustment of conflicting interest by diplomatic action.[62]

Third, Morgenthau acknowledges that the meaning of "interest defined as power" is an unstable one. However, in a world in which sovereign nations vie for power, the foreign policies of all nations must consider survival as their minimum requirement. All nations are compelled to "protect their physical, political, and cultural identity against encroachments by other nations." Thus national interest is identified with national survival. "Taken in isolation, the determination of its content in a concrete situation is relatively simple, for it encompasses the integrity of the nation's territory, of its political institutions, and of its culture."[63] As long as the world is divided into nations, Morgenthau asserts, the "national interest is indeed the last word in world politics." Interest, then, is the essence of politics.

Once its survival is assured, the nation-state may pursue lesser interests. Morgenthau assumes that nations ignore the national interest only at the risk of destruction. Yet in twentieth-century foreign policy formulation, lesser interests have sometimes preceded the national interest.[64] Had Great Britain in 1939–1940 based her policy toward Finland upon legalistic-moralistic considerations, backed with large-scale military aid against Soviet aggression, then Britain's position might have been weakened so as to assure her destruction by Nazi Germany. Britain would have neither restored Finland's independence nor safeguarded her most vital national interest, that of physical survival. Only when the national interest most closely related to national survival has been safeguarded can nations pursue lesser interests.

Fourth, Morgenthau states that "universal moral principles cannot be applied to the actions of states in their abstract, universal formulation, but that they must be filtered through the concrete circumstances of time and place."[65] In pursuit of the national interest, nation-states are governed by a morality which differs from the morality of individuals in their personal relationships. In the actions of statesmen *qua* statesmen, the political consequences of a particular policy become the criteria for judging it. To confuse an individual's morality with a state's morality is to court national disaster. Because the primary official responsibility of statesmen is the survival of the nation-state, their obligations to their citizenry require a different mode of moral judgment from that of the individual.

Fifth, Morgenthau asserts that political realism does not identify the "moral aspirations of a particular nation with the moral laws that govern the universe."[66] In fact, if international politics is placed within a framework of defining interests in terms of power, "we are able to judge other nations as we judge our own."[67] This aspect of Morgenthau's realism bears resemblance to Niebuhr's thought and in turn to Augustinian theology.

Sixth, and finally, Morgenthau stresses the autonomy of the political sphere. Political actions must be judged by political criteria. "The economist asks: 'How does this policy affect the welfare of society, or a segment of it?' The lawyer asks: 'Is this policy in accord with rules of law?' The moralist asks: 'Is this policy in accord with moral principles?' And the political realist asks: 'How does this policy affect the power of the nation?' "[68]

In power struggles, nations follow policies designed to preserve the status quo, to achieve imperialistic expansion, or to gain prestige. In Morgenthau's view, domestic and international politics can be reduced to one of three basic types: "A political policy seeks either to keep power, to increase power, or to demonstrate power."[69]

Although the purpose of a status quo policy is to preserve the existing distribution of power, the nation adopting such a policy does not necessarily act to prevent all international change. Instead, status quo nations seek to thwart change that may produce fundamental shifts in the international distribution of power. Morgenthau cites the Monroe Doctrine as an example of a status quo policy that fulfills his two criteria. First, it was designed to maintain the prevailing power balance in the Western Hemisphere. Second, it expressed the unwillingness of the United States to prevent all change. Instead, the United States would act only against change that threatened the existing distribution of power. Likewise, treaties concluded at the end of wars invariably codify the then prevailing status quo.

Imperialism is the second major alternative available to nations. This is a policy designed to achieve a "reversal of existing power relations between nations."[70] The goals of imperialist powers include local preponderance, continental empire, or world domain. Nations may adopt imperialistic policies as a result of victory, defeat, or the weakness of other states. A state whose leaders expect victory may alter its objectives from the restoration of the status quo to a permanent change in the distribution of power. Moreover, a defeated nation may adopt an imperialistic policy to "turn the scales on the victor, to overthrow the status quo created by his victory, and to change places with him in the hierarchy of power."[71] Finally, the existence of weak states may prove irresistible to a strong state.

To attain imperialistic objectives, states may resort to military force or to cultural and economic means. Military conquest is the oldest and most obvious form of imperialism. Economic imperialism is not as effective a technique as military conquest. If one imperialistic state cannot gain control over another by military means, it may attempt to do so by economic capabilities. Cultural imperialism represents an attempt to influence the human mind "as an instrument for changing the power relations between two nations."[72] (For an examination of theories of imperialism, see Chapter 6.)

According to Morgenthau, states may pursue a policy of prestige. This may be "one of the instrumentalities through which the policies of status quo and of imperialism try to achieve their ends."[73] Its objective is to "impress other nations with the power one's own nation actually possesses, or with the power it believes, or wants the other nations to believe, it possesses."[74] Morgenthau suggests two specific techniques of this policy: diplomacy and the display of force. A policy of prestige succeeds when a nation gains such a reputation for power that the actual use of power becomes unnecessary—the political shadow allegedly cast by military power noted earlier in this chapter.

Morgenthau is concerned not only about the quest for power, but also with the conditions for international peace. His concept of international order is closely related to his concept of national interest. The pursuit of national interests that are not essential to national survival contributes to international conflict. In the twentieth century, especially, nations have substituted global objectives for more limited goals that, in Morgenthau's view, constitute the essence of national interest. Modern nationalism, combined with the messianic ideologies of the twentieth century, has obscured the national interest. In the guise of extending communism or "making the world safe for democracy," nations intervene in the affairs of regions not vital to their security. For example, Morgenthau, like Kennan, opposed American military intervention in South Vietnam because Southeast Asia allegedly lay beyond the most vital interests of the United States, and because the United States would find it impossible, except perhaps with a vast expenditure of resources, to maintain a balance of power in southeast Asia. In contrast, he expressed great concern about Soviet influence in Cuba because of its geographic location in close proximity to the United States.

Even in an international system without ideologically motivated foreign policies, competition between opposing nation-states is likely.

Like many other realists, Morgenthau views the balance of power as the most effective technique for the management of power in an international system based on competitive relationships among states. He defines balance of power as (1) a policy aimed at a certain state of affairs; (2) an actual state of affairs; (3) an approximately equal distribution of power; and (4) any distribution of power. However, it is not the balance of power itself, but the international consensus upon which it is built that preserves international peace. "Before the balance of power could impose its restraints upon the power aspirations of nations through the mechanical interplay of opposing forces, the competing nations had first to restrain themselves by accepting the system of the balance of power as the common framework of their endeavors." Such a consensus "kept in check the limitless desire for power, potentially inherent, as we know, in all imperialisms, and prevented it from becoming a political actuality."[75]

The international consensus which sustained the balance of power before the twentieth century no longer exists. Structural changes in the international system have drastically limited, if not rendered ineffective, the classical balance of power. In Morgenthau's view, the balance of world power through the early 1960s rested with two nations, the United States and the Soviet Union, rather than with several great powers. He contended that allies of one superpower could shift their alignment to the other superpower, but they could not alter significantly the distribution of power because of their weakness relative to either the United States or the Soviet Union. Nor was any third power of sufficient strength as to be capable of intervening on either side and greatly changing the power distribution.

Like the balance of power, diplomacy plays a crucial role in the preservation of peace. In fact, a precondition for the creation of a peaceful world is the development of a new international consensus, in the formation of which diplomacy can contribute to "peace through accommodation."[76] Morgenthau decries the "deprecation of diplomacy" in the twentieth century. The diplomat's role has been diminished by the development of advanced communications, by public disparagement of diplomacy and diplomats, and by the tendency of heads of government to conduct their own negotiations in summit conferences. The rise in importance of international assemblies, the substitution of open diplomacy for secrecy, and the inexperience on the part of the superpowers contributed to the decline of diplomacy during much of the twentieth century. Morgenthau clearly prefers a diplomacy similar to that of the international system before the twentieth century. His views on traditional diplomacy as a means for adjusting national interests resemble those of Sir Harold Nicolson, a leading twentieth-century British diplomatist and theoretician of diplomatic practice.[77]

If it is to be revived as an effective technique for managing power, diplomacy must meet four conditions. (1) Diplomacy must be divested of its crusading spirit. (2) Foreign policy objectives must be defined in terms of national interest and must be supported with adequate power. (3) Nations must view foreign policy from the point of view of other nations. (4) Nations must be willing to compromise on issues that are not vital to them. If diplomacy can be restored to a position of importance, Morgenthau believes, it may not only contribute to "peace through accommodation," but also to the creation of an international consensus upon which more adequate world political institutions can be built.

George F. Kennan

Much like Morgenthau, George F. Kennan (1904–   ) bases his theory of international relations upon historical materials, especially from the eighteenth and nineteenth centuries. However, Morgenthau's model was derived largely from a European context, whereas Kennan's is based for the most part on American diplomacy from 1776 to 1812. Kennan divided United States foreign policy into two periods: he dated the first period from the American Revolution to the mid-nineteenth century; the second period extends from that time to the present.

In the first period, for which Kennan clearly shows preference, the United States evolved basic goals that found expression in such documents as the Declaration of Independence and the Constitution. American statesmen developed a foreign policy designed to achieve their objectives. In defining and shaping the limits of foreign policy, American leaders concluded that:

> The first and obvious answer was: that we ought to protect the physical intactness of our national life from any external or political intrusions—in other words, that we ought to look to the national security. . . . Secondly, one could see to it that insofar as the activities of our citizens in pursuit of their private interests spilled over beyond our borders and into the outside world, the best possible arrangements were made to promote and protect them.[78]

According to Kennan, American goals were fixed, limited, and devoid of pretensions of international benevolence or assumptions of moral superiority or inferiority on the part of one nation or another. Like Morgenthau, he derives his model from historical data of an era when limited, rather than universalist, concepts of the national interest prevailed.

Erroneously, in Kennan's estimation, Americans projected to the international arena assumptions based upon their own national experience. Because they believed that the political and legal framework of the United States had contributed decisively to domestic tranquility, American statesmen focused on the creation of a comparable international order in an effort to minimize the likelihood of conflict.

I see the most serious fault of our past policy formulation to lie in something that I might call the legalistic-moralistic approach to international problems. This approach runs like a red skein through our foreign policy of the past fifty years (1900–1950). It has in it something of the old emphasis on arbitration treaties, something of the Hague Conferences, and schemes for universal disarmament, something of the more ambitious American concepts of international law, something of the Kellogg Pact, something of the idea of a universal 'Article 51,' something of the belief in World Law and World Government. . . . It is the belief that it should be possible to suppress the chaotic and dangerous aspirations of governments by the acceptance of some system of legal rules and restraints.[79]

Moreover, Kennan asserts that American statesmen in this first period frankly and confidently dealt with power realities.[80] Recognizing the importance of power factors in international politics, the United States strove to restrain the European powers in their territorial ambitions in the Western Hemisphere. The United States encouraged movements toward political independence and gave guarantees to new countries which had severed their links with European powers. "All of this involved power considerations. Yet none of it was considered evil or Machiavellian, or cynical. It was simply regarded as a response to the obvious and logical requirements of our situation."[81]

In contrast, Kennan assesses U.S. policy in a later period, when America allegedly lost sight of the power factor and substituted legalistic-moralistic assumptions and objectives for earlier foreign policy goals. If Americans forgot the power factor in the nineteenth century, this was only "natural and inevitable." Geographically separated from Europe, shielded by the British navy from Continental European powers, and preoccupied with domestic development, Americans, especially in the second half of the nineteenth century, cultivated a spirit of romanticism:

We were satisfied, by this time, with our own borders; and we found it pleasant to picture the outside world as one in which other peoples were similarly satisfied with theirs, or ought to be. With everyone thus satisfied, the main problem of world peace, as it appeared to us, was plainly the arrangement of a suitable framework of contractual engagements in which this happy status quo, the final fruit of human progress, could be sealed and perpetuated. If such a framework could be provided, then, it seemed, the ugly conflicts of international politics would cease to threaten world peace.[82]

In addition to criticizing the American assumption of an international harmony of interests, Kennan asserts that Americans lost sight that the rules governing the behavior of individuals is likely to differ drastically from that which exists in relations between states. Governmental behavior at the international level cannot be subjected to the same moral standards that are applied to human behavior:

Moral principles have their place in the heart of the individual in the shaping of his own conduct, whether as a citizen or as a government official. . . . But when the individual's behavior passes through the machinery of political organization and merges with that of millions of other individuals to find its expression in the actions of government, then it undergoes a general transformation, and the same moral concepts are no longer relevant to it. A government is an agent, not a principal; and no more than any other agent may it attempt to be the conscience of its principal.[83]

Nevertheless, even though the use of force in international affairs cannot be completely ruled out, this "does not constitute a reason for being indifferent to the ways in which force is applied—to the moral implications of weapons and their use."[84] Finally, Kennan objects to a concept of international affairs that leads one nation to consider its own purposes moral and those of its opponent immoral. "A war fought in the name of high moral principle finds no end short of some form of total domination."[85] Thus the introduction of moralistic principles leads nations to pursue unlimited national objectives, to choose total war, and to impose laws of unconditional surrender upon defeated opponents. In sum, the pursuit of moralistic principles is incompatible with the pursuit of essentially limited foreign policy objectives.

Like most other writers examined in this chapter, Kennan believes that human nature is "irrational, selfish, obstinate, and tends to violence."[86] It is difficult, if not impossible, to effect basic changes in the individual, and few people will ever "have an abstract devotion to the principles of international legality capable of competing with the impulses from which wars are apt to arise."[87] Moreover, it is by no means certain that governments in their foreign policies express the aspirations of their peoples. "Every government represents only the momentary product of the never-ending competition for political power within the respective national framework. In the most direct sense, therefore, it speaks only for a portion of the nation: for one political faction or coalition of factions."[88] In foreign policy, public opinion cannot play a role similar to its role in national politics, since "international affairs are, after all, a matter of relations between governments and not peoples."[89]

The many and varied causes of international conflict are not easily eliminated by human action. Lack of uniformity in the cultural, political, economic, and social development of nations contributes to conflict. Moreover, Kennan believes that "just as there is no uncomplicated personal relationship between individuals, so . . . there is no international relationship between sovereign states which is without its elements of antagonism, its competitive aspects."[90]

Like Morgenthau, Kennan assigns to diplomacy a major role in the mitigation of international conflict, although he is highly critical of the widespread use of summit diplomacy in the late twentieth century because it leads to imprecision in international discourse and accords; makes difficult the conduct of delicate negotiations in private; raises unwarranted expectations among public opinion; and reduces the effectiveness of professional ambassadors and diplomats whose knowledge, training, and temperament equip them more fully than most democratic political leaders to deal with the complex issues of foreign policy. Through diplomacy, nations have usually been able to adjust differences and to achieve peaceful international change. In fact, Kennan is critical of schemes for world government and international law because

> the function of a system of international relationships is not to inhibit this process of change by imposing a legal straight jacket upon it but rather to facilitate it; to ease its transition, to temper the asperities to which it often leads, to isolate and moderate the conflict to which it gives rise, and to see that these conflicts do not assume forms too unsettling for international life in general.[91]

Moreover, to expect the United Nations to play a major role in the resolution of East-West problems is to impose on it burdens it cannot bear.[92] Even to assume that international organizations can cope effectively with global environmental problems is to assign to them tasks beyond their political competence. Instead, Kennan advocates that "leading industrial and maritime nations who have created such problems and who have the resources to study them should play the principal role in their resolution."[93]

Like most other realist theorists, Kennan bases his realism upon geopolitical concepts. He assumes that military strength on a scale capable of reaching the United States can be mobilized only in a few parts of the world, namely, in "those regions where a major industrial power, enjoying adequate access to raw materials, is combined with large reserves of educated and technically skilled manpower." These geographically important regions include the Atlantic Community, Japan, and the Soviet Union.[94] For Kennan, the relationship between Germany and Russia is crucial to United States security.

Both as a diplomat and a scholar, Kennan has been preoccupied largely with East-West problems. As chairman of the State Department's Policy Planning Staff in the early post-World War II period, he played a major role in the development of United States policy toward the Soviet Union. It was his assumption that the Soviet leaders were influenced in large part by communist ideology. Because of their ideology, the Soviets were in no hurry to administer a coup de grace to the West, since capitalism supposedly contained the seeds of its own destruction. In fact, Lenin's teachings advise caution and flexibility in pursuing foreign policy objectives. The Soviet Union, Kennan reasoned, would press its advantage and would seek to fill any apparent power vacuum. Given their belief in the inevitability of the triumph of communism, together with

Lenin's strategic principles, the Soviets have "no compunction about re-treating in the face of superior force."[95]

The immediate problem confronting the United States was to pre-vent the extension of Soviet power into regions of the world that were threatened in the early post World War II period. In the longer run, the United States faced the difficult problem of effecting change within the Soviet Union. If the Soviet leadership could be induced to abandon its ideology, the Soviet Union might substitute limited foreign policy objec-tives for universalist goals. By a policy of containment, Kennan con-cluded, the United States could respond as effectively as possible to the formidable problems of Soviet-American relations. By denying the Soviet Union foreign policy gains the United States would eventually lead So-viet leaders not only to question and reject their ideology, but to adopt limited foreign policy objectives.

A decade after his formulation of the rationale for containment, Kennan discerned changes within the Soviet Union itself, and in the com-munist states of East Central Europe. In calling for the disengagement of U.S. forces in the Federal Republic of Germany, Kennan reasoned that the Soviet Union would be prepared to agree to a similar withdrawal of forces from East Central European countries. The removal of Soviet troops would contribute to internal liberalization of communist regimes as well as to greater independence from the Soviet Union in foreign pol-icy. Thus Soviet influence in this region would be reduced.[96] Of course, the Soviet Union has intervened with massive military power—in Hun-gary in 1956 and Czechoslovakia in 1968—to prevent unacceptable changes in the status quo in East Central Europe. By the late 1970s, Kennan had concluded that the Soviet Union, despite its vast military build-up and increasing interest in Africa, was essentially a power whose "reactions and purposes are much more defensive than aggressive."[97]

In Kennan's conception of international politics, military power is difficult to measure because of the problems of inferring intentions from capabilities. "All depends on the time, the place, the purpose, and the manner, at which, for which, or in which, these weapons or units are employed. A weapon effective in defense may be relatively ineffective in offense. A weapon effective on the plains may be useless in mountainous territory. A weapon in the hands of a highly trained and motivated unit may have a wholly different value than it has in the hands of a differently trained and motivated one. Mere numerical comparisons do not reflect these variables."[98] Kennan views military power as inappropriate, if not irrelevant, to the major issues confronting the United States in the world of the late twentieth century—the organization of global society; a food-population crisis; and the environmental problem.[99] Here, he has been criticized for having failed in his latest book, *The Cloud of Danger*, ac-cording to Uri Ra'anan, to reflect the voluminous Soviet literature on the nature and utility of military power, including nuclear weapons, and for having embraced "action-reaction" models and "mirror-imaging" concepts in his analysis of the Soviet Union.[100]

Nevertheless, given the importance of the German-Soviet relationship and his belief in the pursuit of limited foreign policy objectives, Kennan, both in his earlier and more recent writings, has seen no great urgency about the problems of less developed areas.[101] As in the case of economic assistance, the United States has had no overriding interest in responding around the world to communist wars of national liberation. In fact, Kennan views disdainfully subsequent efforts to extend the containment doctrine from Europe to other geographic regions. He objects to the universalization of containment to situations and times different from those during which he formulated it, just as he opposed in his writings other efforts to develop and apply abstract principles to all foreign policy problems.[102] The United States, he maintains, is largely unable to effect fundamental change in the Third World because of the "enormity of the problems in relation to our resources" and because of the "necessity of concentrating our resources elsewhere."[103]

Writing in the mid-1970s, Kennan reaffirmed his commitment to a United States foreign policy based upon strictly limited capabilities and goals. "We will not, in other words, be able simultaneously to be all that we have tried, since the recent war, to be to others and all that the developing situation will require us to be to ourselves."[104] His conception of United States national interest in the late twentieth century is narrowly defined—perhaps, according to one reviewer, verging on isolationism.[105] His global conception of the role of the United States was based upon the reduction of external commitments to an indispensable minimum—"the preservation of the political independence and military security of Western Europe, of Japan, and—with the single reservation that it should not involve the dispatch and commitment of American armed forces—of Israel."[106]

Arnold Wolfers

There are, of course, important differences among the realist theorists. Although Arnold Wolfers may, for example, be included in a survey of realist thought, his focus differs from that of other proponents of realism. While acknowledging that central to the study of international relations is the "behavior of states as organized bodies of men," he called for "concentration on human beings upon whose psychological reactions the behavior credited to states ultimately rests."[107] The international behavior of states is the amalgam of conflicting pressures. Moreover, subnational, transnational, and supranational actors intrude into international politics, and must be the object of scholarly analysis.

In their relationships nation-states exhibit various kinds of behavior from amity to enmity, depending upon their international goals. Nations set for themselves differing sets of objectives: (1) "possession" goals, such as national independence, physical survival, and territorial integrity, or (2) "milieu" goals, designed to affect the environment beyond a nation's boundaries. Moreover, Wolfers delineated three basic clusters of foreign policy objectives, namely, those related to (1) national self-extension, (2) national self-preservation, and (3) national self-abnegation, such as international solidarity, lawfulness, or peace. Goals of national self-abnegation transcend, although they do not necessarily conflict with, goals of national self-interest. For example, the United States in 1918 was powerful enough to permit President Wilson to indulge in self-abnegation goals without harm to its vital national interests. A nation's foreign policy thus includes overlapping goals. The pursuit of objectives related to national self-preservation often makes necessary the pursuit of goals of national self-extension. In fact, increasing international interdependence contributes to the pursuit among nations of goals of national self-extension in order to achieve goals of national self-preservation, thus rendering difficult the return to foreign policies based upon limited objectives, as Kennan, Kissinger, and Morgenthau have urged.

According to Wolfers, a nation's foreign policy is the amalgam of many factors. Although a policymaker is guided by his conception of the national interest, this concept holds differing meanings for different peoples. At the minimum, national interest encompasses a nation's territorial integrity, independence, and national survival. Yet the goal of "national survival itself is given a wide variety of interpretations by countries facing different conditions."[108] According to Wolfers, "security is a value some countries prize to a greater extent than others. The level of security sought by states is not always identical. In fact, political leaders are often confronted with a dilemma as to whether a given increment in defense conflicts with other values."[109] Decision-makers are constantly confronted with difficult choices in which they are unable to separate interest from morality. In fact, their calculus of interest is based upon a hierarchy of values, since "the 'necessities' in international politics, and for that matter in all spheres of life, do not push decisions and actions beyond the realm of moral judgment; they rest on moral choices themselves. If a statesman decides that the dangers to the security of his country are so great as to make necessary a course of action that may lead to war, he has placed an exceedingly high value on an increment of national security."[110]

Wolfers viewed the balance of power as a useful concept in describing the contemporary international system. Although the term *balance of power* has been given various meanings, Wolfers used it to mean "an equilibrium or a roughly equal distribution of power between two opponents, the opposite, then, of hegemony or domination."[111] The contemporary balance of power consists of two "hub" states—the United States and the Soviet Union, each of which is at the center of a global alliance. Outside the respective alliances of the two superpowers, neutralist states are able to extract concessions from the United States and the Soviet Union, each of which competes for their favor. For the United States the problem arises of reconciling policies toward allies and the nonaligned since policies toward allies affect policies toward the nonaligned. Wolfers preferred foreign policies that attach priority to relations with allies.

Wolfers concluded that "ideological conflict, concentration of power in the hands of two antagonistic superpowers, and the introduction of nuclear weapons have deepened the gulf between nations and made world unity more remote."[112] Whatever its deficiencies, therefore, the balance of power commends itself as a technique for the management of power. Nation-states have shown little inclination to make use of collective security schemes in the resolution of international conflict. Examination of British and French policy between the two world wars shows that France conceived of the collective security framework of the League of Nations only as a supplement to an alliance system against Germany. For France, the principal security threat lay in a resurgent, armed Germany. In contrast, Britain saw collective security in more abstract terms. Britain envisaged collective security as a commitment against any power that breached the peace.[113]

In Wolfers' estimation, the operation of a collective security system depends on a degree of national self-abnegation that few, if any, powers are prepared to accept. In collective security, nations commit themselves to take action against a breach of the peace in parts of the world where they may have few, if any, interests. Nations may find themselves pledged to participate in collective action against a country with which they may have important trading links and other close relationships. The history of collective security does not provide evidence of the willingness of nations to respond to an outbreak of aggression wherever it occurs. The action of the United States, together with other nations, in Korea cannot be interpreted as an example of collective security. Instead, Wolfers views the Korea conflict of 1950–1953 as an instance in which the United States used the United Nations in support of a major American foreign policy objective in Asia, namely, the prevention of communist expansion. The United Nations identified itself with United States action in Korea. The United States' resort to force against North Korea strengthened the American power position with respect to her major opponent, the Soviet Union, and thus did not depart from older patterns of international politics. In summary, Wolfers rejected collective security in favor of balance of power as the technique for the management of power most in keeping with the contemporary international system. In contending that nation-states engage in a spectrum of international behavior from conflict to collaboration, Wolfers provided insights and hypotheses for further testing in the development of international relations theory.

Henry A. Kissinger

Another scholar who has drawn from history, in this case diplomatic history, is Henry A. Kissinger (1923–   ). Kissinger's theory of international relations is derived from his analysis of early nineteenth-century Europe. In his doctoral dissertation, *A World Restored*, Kissinger wrote:

> The success of physical science depends on the selection of the 'crucial' experiment; that of political science in the field of international affairs, on the selection of the 'crucial' period. I have chosen for my topic the period between 1812 and 1822, partly, I am frank to say, because its problems seem to me analogous to those of our day. But I do not insist on this analogy.[114]

Kissinger's fascination with this period lies in the insights that might be provided into the exercise of power by statesmen such as Castlereagh and Metternich for the development of an international structure that contributed to peace in the century between the Congress of Vienna and the outbreak of World War I. Kissinger studied the nature and quality of political leadership, the impact of domestic political structures upon foreign policy, and the relationship between diplomacy and military policy in stable and revolutionary international systems.

As Stephen R. Graubard has written:

> Kissinger saw choice as fundamental to the whole political process. It was of the greatest consequence to him that a given state opted for a specific policy for one reason rather than another: because its bureaucracy determined that there was only one safe course; because its leaders were anxious to test the adversary's reactions; because domestic opinion demanded a specific policy; because the political leadership was confused and saw the necessity of creating the illusion that it was still capable of action.[115]

Drawing heavily upon the 1815 to 1822 period, Kissinger postulates that peace is achieved not as an end in itself, but instead emerges as the result of a stable, contrasted with a revolutionary, international system. Therefore Kissinger develops two models for the study of international politics: first a stable system; and second, a revolutionary system. He contends that stability has resulted not "from a quest for peace, but from a generally accepted legitimacy.[116] By Kissinger's definition, legitimacy means "no more than an international agreement about the nature of workable arrangements and about the permissible aims and methods of foreign policy."[117] Legitimacy implies an acceptance of the framework of the international order by all major powers. Agreement among major powers upon the framework of international order does not eliminate international conflicts, but it limits their scope. Conflict *within* the framework has been more limited than conflict *about* the framework. Diplomacy, which Kissinger defines as "the adjustment of differences through negotiation," becomes possible only in international systems where "legitimacy obtains."[118] In Kissinger's model the primary objective of national actors is not to preserve peace. In fact, "wherever peace—conceived as the avoidance of war—has been the primary objective of a power or a group of powers, the international system has been at the mercy of the most ruthless member of the international community."[119] In contrast, "whenever the international order has acknowledged that certain principles could not be compromised even for the sake of peace, stability based on an equilibrium of forces was at least conceivable."[120]

An understanding of the characteristics of a revolutionary world order can be derived from Kissinger's model of stability. Any order in which a major power is so dissatisfied that it seeks to transform it is revolutionary. In the generation before 1815, revolutionary France presented a major challenge to the existing order.

> Disputes no longer concerned the adjustment of differences within an accepted framework, but the validity of the framework itself; the political contest had become doctrinal: the balance of power which had operated so intricately throughout the eighteenth century suddenly lost its flexibility and the European equilibrium came to seem an insufficient protection to powers faced by a France which proclaimed the incompatibility of its political maxims with those of the other states.[121]

Tracing the diplomacy of European powers between 1812 and 1822, Kissinger concludes that the restoration of a stable order depends on several factors: (1) the willingness of supporters of legitimacy to negotiate with a revolutionary power while at the same time being prepared to use military power; (2) the ability of supporters of legitimacy to avoid the outbreak of "total" war, since such conflict would threaten the international framework which status quo powers wish to preserve; and (3) the capacity of national units to use limited means to achieve limited objectives. No power is compelled to surrender unconditionally. Powers defeated in limited war are not eliminated from the international system. No power, whether victorious or vanquished, is completely satisfied or completely dissatisfied. Limitations placed upon means and goals make possible the restoration of a balance of power between the victorious and the vanquished.

In other writings Kissinger has applied concepts derived from his study of early nineteenth-century European diplomatic history to the contemporary international system. The problems posed by the great destructive potential of nuclear weapons have been of great concern to him. As in the past, it is necessary for nations to develop limited means to achieve limited objectives. "An all or nothing military policy will . . . play into the hands of the Soviet strategy of ambiguity which seeks to upset the strategic balance by small degrees and which combines political, psychological, and military pressures to induce the greatest degree of uncertainty and hesitation in the mind of the opponent."[122] If United States policymakers are to have a choice other than "the dread alternatives of surrender or suicide,"[123] they must adopt concepts of limited war derived from the experience of nineteenth-century warfare. At that time the objective of warfare "was to create a calculus of risks according to which continued resistance would appear more costly than the peace terms sought to be imposed."[124] A strategy of limited warfare would provide the United States with the means "to establish a reasonable relationship between power and the willingness to use it, between the physical and psychological components of national policy."[125]

Writing in the 1960s, Kissinger contended that if the United States were to avoid the stark alternatives of suicide or surrender, it must have both large-scale conventional forces and tactical nuclear weapons. Kissinger established three requirements for limited war capabilities.

1. The limited war forces must be able to prevent the potential aggressor from creating a fait accompli.
2. They must be of a nature to convince the aggressor that their use, although invoking an increasing risk of all-out war, is not an inevitable prelude to it.
3. They must be coupled with a diplomacy which succeeds in conveying that all-out war is not the sole response to aggression and that there exists a willingness to negotiate a settlement short of unconditional surrender.[126]

If nations are to evolve a limited war strategy, they must develop an understanding of those interests that do not threaten national survival. Decision-makers must possess the ability to restrain public opinion if disagreement arises as to whether national survival is at stake. Given a tacit understanding among nations about the nature of limited objectives, it is possible to fight both conventional conflicts and limited nuclear wars without their escalation to total war.

In the adjustment of differences among nations, Kissinger, like most other realists, assigns an important role to diplomacy. Historically, negotiation was aided by the military capabilities a nation could bring to bear if diplomacy failed. The vast increase in destructive capabilities has contributed to the perpetuation of disputes. "Our age faces the paradoxical problem that because the violence of war has grown out of all proportion to the objectives to be achieved, no issue has been resolved."[127]

Moreover, the reduction in the number of powers of approximately equal strength has increased the difficulty of conducting diplomacy.

> As long as no nation was strong enough to eliminate all the others, shifting coalitions could be used for exerting pressure or marshalling support. They served in a sense as substitutes for physical conflict. In the classical periods of cabinet diplomacy in the eighteenth and nineteenth centuries, a country's diplomatic flexibility and bargaining position depended on its availability as a partner to as many other countries as possible. As a result, no relationship was considered permanent and no conflict was pushed to its ultimate conclusion.[128]

Although wars occurred, nations did not risk national survival and were able instead to use limited means to achieve limited objectives.

Like Morgenthau, Kissinger views with disfavor the injection of ideology into the international system. Ideology not only contributes to the development of unlimited national objectives, but it also eventually creates states whose goal is to overthrow the existing international system. In the absence of agreement among powers about the framework for the system—or its legitimacy—the conduct of diplomacy becomes difficult, even impossible. Hence the emphasis in the Nixon-Ford-Kissinger foreign policy upon the creation of a stable structure for the international system: "All nations, adversaries and friends alike, must have a stake in preserving the international system. They must feel that their principles are being respected and their national interests secured. They must, in short, see positive incentive for keeping the peace, not just the dangers of breaking it."[129]

Such a conception for the late twentieth century drew heavily upon the theoretical framework developed by Kissinger in *A World Restored.* His quest for a stable international system as a policymaker, moreover, drew upon a belief in the need for a "certain equilibrium between potential adversaries," namely, the United States and the Soviet Union. In his memoir, Kissinger wrote: "If history teaches anything it is that there can be no peace without equilibrium and no justice without restraint."[130] But the global system of the 1970s differed substantially from that of the early nineteenth century described by Kissinger in *A World Restored.*

> The classical concept of balance of power included continual maneuvering for marginal advantages over others. In the nuclear era this is not realistic because when both sides possess such enormous power, small additional increments cannot be translated into tangible advantage or even usable political strength. And it is dangerous because attempts to seek tactical gains might lead to confrontation which would be catastrophic.[131]

Nevertheless, the balance of power concept pervaded the foreign policy of the United States in this period: The "opening" to China was a means, in part at least, of exerting leverage upon the Soviet Union to mitigate tensions between Washington and Moscow in the so-called detente diplomacy; "tilting" toward Pakistan in the war with India of 1971; and pressing for a cease-fire and disengagement of forces in the October 1973 war, when Israel was on the verge of destroying what remained of the Egyptian Army. Each of these examples is illustrative of a central element of balance of power theory, as noted in Chapter 1, that is, to support the weaker of two protagonists in order to forestall the ascendancy of the stronger.

As Secretary of State, Kissinger proposed several initiatives designed to enhance the cohesiveness of the Atlantic Alliance, although his conception of a world of several power centers, the emphasis placed upon diplomatic flexibility and surprise, and the perceived need to develop a form of détente diplomacy both with the Soviet Union and the People's Republic of China created formidable problems in the early 1970s for United States alliance relationships—both with Western Europe and Japan. The dilemma was that of maintaining, and strengthening, partnerships with allies, while seeking new bilateral relationships with adversaries, against which the alliances were originally formed. Especially in the aftermath of the October 1973 war, moreover, Kissinger saw the need to develop among the United States, Western Europe, and Japan frameworks for the resolution of such problems as energy supply and other global issues of the late twentieth century. Between 1973 and 1977, the United States took initiatives toward establishing the International Energy Agency, the convening of multilateral trade negotiations, the creation of a dialogue between industrialized and developing countries, between producer and consumer states, and among industrialized states, symbolized in summit meetings of heads of government to discuss important economic issues.

Realist writers, Kissinger included, have often sought to separate domestic politics from foreign policy. The conduct of an effective diplomacy is said to be difficult, if not impossible, if it must be subject, both in its conception and execution, to the continuous scrutiny of public opinion in a democracy such as the United States. Flexibility, characteristic of Kissinger's style of diplomacy, can be achieved in secrecy more easily than in a policy process open to the glare of publicity.

But the relationship between domestic politics and foreign policy has another dimension for realists, and especially for Kissinger. Unlike those who subscribe to Wilsonian idealism or utopianism, Kissinger does not seek to transform domestic political structures in the belief that democratic political systems are a prerequisite for a peaceful world:

> We shall never condone the suppression of fundamental liberties. We shall urge humane principles and use our influence to promote justice.

But the issue comes down to the limits of such efforts. How hard can we press without provoking the Soviet leadership into returning to practices in its foreign policy that increase international tensions? . . . For half a century we have objected to Communist efforts to alter the domestic structure of other countries. For a generation of Cold War we sought to ease the risks produced by competing ideologies. Are we now to come full circle and *insist* on domestic compatibility as a condition of progress?[132]

Here Kissinger's theory of international relations contrasts sharply with the view that a precondition for the development of a stable relationship with the Soviet Union is the transformation of its political system to conform with principles of human rights and political freedom cherished in the West. At most, the easing of tensions between states is a complex process, dependent upon diplomacy, mutual interest, and "a strong military balance and flexible defense posture." In short, foreign policy should be based on national power and interest, rather than abstract moralistic principles or political crusades.[133]

Nevertheless, in Kissinger's theory of international relations the domestic political structure of states is a key element. His stable and revolutionary system models of international politics, noted earlier, are linked to the domestic political structures of the states in either system. Stable international systems are characterized by actors whose domestic political structures are based on compatible notions about the means and goals of foreign policies. By definition, governments with stable domestic political structures do not resort to revolutionary or adventuristic foreign policies to restore, or preserve, domestic cohesion. In contrast, revolutionary systems contain actors whose domestic political structures contrast sharply with each other. Kissinger contends that:

When domestic structures—and the concept of legitimacy on which they are based—differ widely, statesmen can still meet, but their ability to persuade has been reduced for they no longer speak the same language. . . . But when one or more states claims universal applicability for their particular structure, schisms grow deep indeed.[134]

Thus Kissinger, in effect, links his conception of domestic political structure not only to his models of stable and revolutionary systems, but also to the notion of legitimacy set forth in *A World Restored*. Presumably, domestic political structures that are compatible are conducive to the development of consensus, or legitimacy, at the international level. Those eras of stability among states coincide with the presence, at the national level, of compatible political structures based on a modicum of stability.

Robert Strausz-Hupé

Although prescriptions for action by the statesman can be found in most realist writings, the works of Robert Strausz-Hupé, in particular, have emphasized the relationship between power and values, between power and the transformation of the international system. Strausz-Hupé (1903–) has had as a major concern the nature of power as well as its exercise and control. In his study of international relations, he contends: "Power is the staff of orderly government. Without the exercise of power, political order could neither be established nor maintained. Power guards society against anarchy. Yet power spawns tyranny and violence, corrupts the mighty and crushes freedom."[135]

Although international conflict is attributable to several causes, it stems largely from the human "power urge," which is "derived from the more basic urge of self-aggrandizement or self-assertion."[136] The power urge may take any one of several forms: "personal ambition, a quest for prestige and gratification; or simply a desire to profit from other people's work."[137] In the modern world, power is more important than ever. Population growth, the emergence of organizational structures with intermediate layers of power holders, and the growth of the physical force of power—all of these enhance the importance of power. Moreover, the religious and metaphysical limitations which once restrained power-holders have broken down. Deification of the state and development of Darwinian theories have strengthened the power urge. Rapid social change, together with the alienation of people from older collectivities, has produced states of anxiety and anomie, which often stimulate in individuals and groups suicidal tendencies and increase the incidence of war and aggressiveness.[138]

The individual's quest for power has the effect of making the entire society more aggressive. Domestic power struggles spill over into the international system. In international politics, the power urge reveals itself in several kinds of conflict: the attempt of one state to impose its political ideology on another state; psychological differences, especially fear, hatred, or divergent manners or customs; differences in social structure and culture; population pressures; conflicts over economic issues; territorial claims; conflicting security interests; and differences between political systems. As a result, a state may seek one of several kinds of objectives: the redrawing of its own borders; the modification of another state's political, social, and cultural system; an increase in its security by removing possible threats and establishing its own power superiority.

In achieving foreign policy objectives, decision-makers must choose among alternative means. Their choice depends upon their degree of motivation to achieve a particular goal, the time available for its attainment, the cost, the risk, and the extent to which one goal conflicts with other goals. Conflict management has many aspects. Four basic techniques are available for shaping an opponent's behavior: evolution (the gradual transformation of an opponent's intention or his ruling class), revolution from above, revolution from below, and war.

Like several other theorists examined in this chapter, Strausz-Hupé is concerned with geographical location, manpower, and natural resources, as well as scientific and technological proficiency, national psychology, and political institutions as elements of national power. Size and structure of population are vital measurements of national power. A decline in population usually precedes a decline in a nation's international position. Those countries which are most powerful "possess an adequate supply of all 'essential,' 'strategic,' and 'critical' materials or. . . are able, by virtue of their mastery over transportation routes, to import, in time of war, materials inadequately supplied at home."[139] Political, economic, and military organization "transforms these elements of power into world-political realities."[140]

Despite changes in technology, geography remains an important factor in the power equation. As a student of geopolitical relationships, Strausz-Hupé attached particular significance to Sir Halford Mackinder's concept of the Heartland. "If domination of the land-locked plains-lands of European Russia is joined to the domination of East Central Europe between the Baltic, Adriatic, and Aegean, then the condition obtains which Sir Halford Mackinder conceived as the final step to the mastery of Europe."[141] Because the "political unification of the European continent under a single power would profoundly alter the distribution of technological and economic potentials,"[142] the defense of Western Europe remains vital to the security of the United States. According to Strausz-Hupé:

> The issues now confronting us and the foreseeable shape of issues-to-come make the (Atlantic) Alliance not only worth preserving but also worth strengthening, for the solutions of the problems pressing upon the West are bound to exceed the reach of any Western sovereign nation, however wise and powerful.[143]

Conflict can be traced to the conditions which attend the breakdown of political systems. It is possible to trace a series of "systemic" revolutions that have transformed political institutions and practices. According to Strausz-Hupé, the first systemic revolution "started with the Peloponnesian War and reached its climax in the Roman Civil Wars which pitted first Pompey against Caesar and then Caesar's heirs against one another. The revolution . . . was not confined to any one city or country. It rolled over the entire Mediterranean region—the universe of the ancients. When it had run its course of four centuries, the state system had changed from one of many city-states into one of a single universal empire."[144] With the dawn of the modern period with the Renaissance and the Reformation, the feudal system gave way to the nation-state system. This system in turn is in decline. In the twentieth century, the world once again is passing through a systemic revolution. The nation-state is no longer adequate to the demands imposed upon it. Ultimately, the systemic revolution ushers in the development of larger political units, and even possibly the eventual unification of the globe. The struggle between the United States and the Soviet Union is but the contemporary expression of pervasive conflict that encompasses all lands, all peoples, and all levels of society. The systemic revolution obeys a law of the dialectic. Within each period there are forces which contend with and eventually lead to the destruction of the existing system. One system gives way to another system, which in turn contains forces that lead eventually to its transformation. Upon the outcome of the systemic revolution depends the future of political organization in the world.

Although Strausz-Hupé attaches great importance to the power urge as well as to certain environmental factors as conditioners of behavior, he believes that humans can shape their political institutions and relationships. In the outcome of the systemic revolution the peoples of the West, and the United States in particular, can play a role of decisive importance. The Atlantic Alliance is the core of the West's federative power and its mightiest bulwark against the Soviet Union, the primary contender of the United States for shaping the future world order.

Because of the importance that he attaches to the outcome of the systemic revolution, Strausz-Hupé has addressed himself to the nature of communist strategy, as well as the strategic concepts adequate to the challenges facing the West. One of his principal preoccupations has been the study of communist strategic concepts, which call for the use of a variety of techniques, most of them nonmilitary, to achieve foreign policy objectives. Strausz-Hupé has been attracted to the study of the limited means employed by communist states to attain their goals without resorting to all-out conflict. In the systemic revolution, the Soviet Union is engaged in a "protracted conflict."

> The salient characteristics of the doctrine of protracted conflict are: the total objective, the carefully controlled methods and the constant shifting of the battleground, weapons systems and operational tactics for the purpose of confusing the opponent, keeping him off balance and wearing down his resistance. The doctrine of protracted conflict prescribes a strategy for annihilating the opponent over a period of time by limited operations, by feints and maneuvers, psychological manipulations and diverse forms of violence. . . . In Communist theory, various techniques of political warfare and graduated violence are so coordinated as to form a spectrum that reaches all the way from the clandestine distribution of subversive literature to the annihilating blow delivered with every weapon available.[145]

As a student of communist strategy and proponent of a Western strategy adequate to the difficult task of mastering the forces sweeping the international system, Strausz-Hupé is concerned with the means by which people shape their destiny in a revolutionary age. As a scholar and policy scientist, he has urged the development of United States strategic superiority and military flexibility, the strengthening of alliance systems, the integration of Western Europe within an Atlantic community, and the exploitation of communist vulnerabilities. In an age when biological survival has been a dominant concern of many, he has given primacy to the development of a world order emphasizing the values of Western civilization and government responsive through representative institutions to the aspirations of people. In doing so he has attempted to restore a balance of thought between the defense of values and the defense of life. His is a realism tempered by what might be called "Atlantic idealism."

Raymond Aron

Because of his attempt in the monumental work, *Peace and War*, to synthesize much of the past and contemporary writings in international relations, Raymond Aron (1904–   ), noted French social philosopher, does not fall easily into a realist category of international theorists. Aron engages in what he terms a fourfold analysis of international relations: theory, sociology, history, and praxiology. What he calls theory corresponds to "ordering of data, selection of problems, and variables."[146] His conceptualization includes the development of propositions about diplomacy and strategy, the nature of power, notions of equilibrium, and models of multipolar and bipolar international systems, and homogeneous and heterogeneous systems.

In Aron's view, theory provides an enumeration of "effect-phenomena, the determined factors, for which the sociologist is tempted to seek cause-phenomena, the determinants."[147] In the section of his work termed sociology, he is concerned with causality and the determinants of international behavior. In particular, Aron addresses himself to the problems of spatial relationships, population, resources, and the origins of war, as well as what he terms the nation, the civilization, and humanity as collectivities that affect conduct at the international level. Aron's examination of history, his third level of conceptualization, consists of an effort to relate his theory and sociology to the international system since 1945. Finally, to use a term that appears frequently in his work, *praxiology* represents Aron's attempt to formulate both a normative theory (what should the goals of states be?) and a series of prescriptions for international conduct (how should statesmen act to achieve those goals?).

According to Aron, international relations consists of relations among the political units into which the world is divided at any given time, from the Greek city-state to the modern nation-state. Although a science or philosophy of politics would include the study of international relations, the case for the uniqueness of international relations stems from the fact that it deals with "relations between political units, each of which claims the right to take justice into its own hands and to be the sole arbiter of the decision to fight or not to fight."[148]

Because of the existence of several or many autonomous political units, the principal objective of each unit is to insure its safety, and ultimately its survival. Given this preoccupation, the political leader can never develop a fully rational diplomatic-strategic behavior. Nevertheless, Aron seeks to develop a "rational type of theory, proceeding from fundamental concepts (strategy and diplomacy, means and ends, power and force, power, glory, and idea) to systems and types of systems."

In international relations the diplomat-strategist faces the risk of war since he confronts opponents in a situation of "incessant rivalry in which each side reserves the right to resort to the *ultima ratio*, that is, to violence."[149] In Aron's conceptualization relations among nations are often marked by conflict. Essentially, relations among political units consist of the alternatives of war and peace, since every collectivity exists among friends, enemies, neutrals, or indifferent parties. The status of political units is determined by the material or human resources that they can allocate to diplomatic-strategic action. The extent to which political units mobilize such resources depends upon many factors, including, of course, accessibility to them, but also the objectives which political leaders choose to pursue. Aron asserts that political units do not desire power for its own sake, but rather as a means toward achieving some goal, such as peace or glory, or in order to influence the future of the international system. Many kinds of circumstances, such as changes in military or economic technique and the transformation of institutions or ideologies, affect the goals of political leaders. Technological innovations modify previously held spatial concepts, including the strategic value of geographical positions and the economic importance of certain natural and human resources. But Aron acknowledges that political units that have the greatest influence on others are not always those that most consciously attempt to impose themselves on others. Although it is possible, as Aron attempts, to examine or even quantify elements of national power, it is more difficult to assess their effectiveness in attaining the goals set by political leaders.

Moreover, the conduct of nations toward each other is the product not only of their relative power, but also of the ideas and emotions that influence the actions of decision-makers. It is necessary, as Aron himself does in his theory, to provide for geographical relationships, alliances, and military structures. But it is essential as well to assess the relationship between the capabilities of political units and the objectives sought by political leaders.

Here Aron introduces two models of the international system, the so-called homogeneous system and the heterogeneous system. In the homogeneous system "states belong to the same type, obey the same conception of policy." In the heterogeneous system, the "states are organized according to different principles and appeal to contradictory values."[150] In homogeneous systems political leaders are in agreement about the kinds of objectives to be pursued. Conflict occurs within the system, but the continued existence of the system itself is not at stake. Thus Aron suggests that from the end of the Thirty Years' War in 1648 until the French Revolution and again from 1815 until the early twentieth century, the international system was largely homogeneous. Especially since 1945, however, the international system has been heterogeneous, because much of the conflict has been concerned with the system itself, not just the attainment of goals within the system.

Although Aron gives great prominence in his theory to power as a means toward attaining national objectives, he sets forth explicitly a systems framework for the analysis of international politics. An international system, he suggests, is "the ensemble constituted by political units that maintain regular relations with each other and that are capable of being implicated in a generalized war."[151] In addition to homogeneous and heterogeneous systems, it is possible to distinguish bipolar and multipolar systems, depending on whether the majority of political units are grouped around two states of far greater strength, or the system includes several political units relatively similar in strength.

Both the bipolar and multipolar systems contain equilibrating mechanisms. At its highest level of abstraction, equilibrium consists of the tendency, found also in other theories, of a state or combination of states to attempt to restrain any state or coalition that seems capable of achieving preponderance. Although this rule, according to Aron, is applicable to all international systems, it is necessary to construct models according to a configuration of forces in order to elaborate rules for the operation of equilibrium. In the multipolar system the essential rule of equilibrium is that "the state whose forces are increasing must anticipate the dissidence of certain of its allies, who will rejoin the other camp in order to maintain the balance."[152] In the bipolar system, the most general law of equilibrium is that "the goal of chief actors is to avoid finding themselves at the mercy of a rival."[153] The principal goal of each of the chief actors is that of preventing the other from acquiring capabilities superior to its own. The chief actor, the leader of a coalition, seeks simultaneously to prevent the growth of the opposing coalition and to maintain the cohesiveness of its own coalition.

In Aron's theory, there are three types of peace: equilibrium, hegemony, or empire. In any historical period, the forces of the political units are in one of three conditions: (1) they are in balance; (2) they are dominated by those of one of the units; or (3) they are outclassed by the forces of one of the political units. Between peace by equilibrium and peace by empire, Aron places what he terms peace by hegemony. The incontestable superiority of one political unit is acknowledged by other members of the international system. Although the smaller states are unable to change the status quo, the hegemonic state does not attempt to absorb them. Germany, for example, in the period after the Franco-Prussian War of 1870 to 1871, possessed a kind of hegemony in the continent which Bismarck sought to make acceptable to other European states.

If peace is the "more or less lasting suspension of violent modes of rivalry between political units," conflict, in Aron's theory, consists of the dialectics of antagonism—deterrence, persuasion, and subversion.

Deterrence is related both to the material means that a state possesses to prevent action by another political unit and the perception of resolution one state is able to convey to another which threatens it. "Today as yesterday, the essential problem of deterrence is both psychologial and technological. How can the state diplomatically on the defensive convince a state diplomatically on the offensive that it will carry out its threat?"[154] If the credibility of a threat depends upon the perceived intention of the state making a threat to carry it out, the threat becomes less convincing as its execution appears to be contrary to the interests of those who make it. The advent of weapons of mass destruction increases the risk of executing a threat and thus reduces the interests for which the use of force can be credibly threatened. Aron outlines a system, similar to Morton Kaplan's unit veto system, in which each state will be in a position to exterminate all others. Thus, in this model, technology affects the credibility of threats made by political actors. (For theories of deterrence, see Chapter 9.)

What Aron terms persuasion, in his dialectics of antagonism, consists of methods designed to modify behavior in some desired fashion and, indeed, includes the strategy of subversion. What Aron describes as subversion is the use of violence to attain an objective. "Abstractly," he suggests, "the goal of subversion is to withdraw a population from the administrative and moral authority of an established power and to integrate it within other political and military frameworks, sometimes in and by conflict."[155]

According to Aron, conflict, in the most general sense, results whenever two individuals, social groups, or political units covet the same property or seek incompatible goals. Aron holds that the human animal is aggressive, but that humanity does not fight by instinct. War is an expression, but not a necessary expression, of human aggressiveness. Although, given human nature, it is impossible to eliminate all conflict, it is not "proved that these conflicts must be manifested in the phenomenon of war, as we have known it for thousands of years, with organized combatants, utilizing increasingly destructive weapons."[156]

Although Aron's theoretical framework is similar in many respects to those of American realists, he contrasts American realism with the work of earlier European scholars such as the German historian Heinrich von Treitschke (1834–1896). In contrast to Treitschke, "the American authors who are commonly regarded as belonging to the realist school declare that states, animated by a will-to-power, are in permanent rivalry, but that they are not self-congratulatory about the situation and do not regard it as a part of the divine plan. The refusal of states to submit to a common law or arbitration seems to them incontestable, intelligible, but not sublime, for they hold neither war nor the right to draw the sword as sublime."[157] But American realists, according to Aron, are "located on the margin of the idealist situation" since, although they criticize the utopian or idealist conception, the realists unconsciously "follow the example of those whom they oppose." Realists, too, develop a normative theory of international relations.

In the portion of his work entitled praxiology, Aron himself engages in normative theorizing. He believes that the political leader ought to remember that international order is the result of a balancing of forces which support the preservation of the system with those which seek its transformation. If statesmen are unable to calculate correctly such forces, they fail to perform their primary responsibility—the security of the persons and values entrusted to their care. For the statesman immorality, in Aron's conception, is a condition in which the political leader "obeys his heart without concerning himself with the consequences of his acts." Thus Aron suggests, as American realists have held, that the morality of the political leader as a political leader differs from that of the citizen within a political unit.

Aron prefers an international community based on world law and order. Such a community is not possible without what he terms a homogeneity of states and a similarity of constitutional practices. States must reduce their levels of armaments, cease to suspect each other of the worst intentions, abandon the resort to force to resolve disputes, and give respect to the same legal and moral ideas.

REALISM: ITS LIMITATIONS AND CONTRIBUTIONS

No theoretical approach to the study of international relations is without its critics. Realism evoked criticism in part because of the boldness with which its proponents stated assumptions about political behavior, as well as the assumptions themselves and the policy proposals issuing from them.

Although each theorist has his supporters and critics, the following critique relates principally to concepts shared by more than one, but not necessarily by all, of those surveyed in this chapter.

For several reasons, the "national interest" concept has been the object of criticism. According to one critique: "That national interest is a necessary criterion of policy is obvious and unilluminating. No statesman, no publicist, no scholar would seriously argue that foreign policy ought to be conducted in opposition to, or in disregard of, the national interest."[158] Moreover, it is difficult to give operational meaning to the concept of national interest. Statesmen are constrained, or given freedom, by many forces in interpreting the national interest. They are often the captive of their predecessors' policies. They interpret national interest as a result of their cultural training, values, and the data made available to them as decision-makers. According to Stanley Hoffmann,

> [T]he conception of an objective and easily recognizable national interest, the reliable guide and criterion of national policy, is one which makes sense only in a stable period in which the participants play for limited ends, with limited means, and without domestic kibbitzers to disrupt the players' moves. In a period when the survival of states is at stake to a far greater extent than in former times, the most divergent courses of action can be recommended as valid choices for survival. Ordinarily less compelling objectives, such as prestige, or an increment of power in a limited area, or the protection of private citizens abroad, all become tied up with the issue of survival, and the most frequent argument against even attempting to redefine a hierarchy of national objectives so as to separate at least some of them from survival is the familiar fear of a 'chain of events' or a 'row of dominoes.'[159]

Therefore, in the absence of empirically based studies, it is difficult to determine what the "national interest" means at any specific time. (See the further discussion in Chapter 11.)

Realist writers have been criticized for their efforts to draw from the past a series of political concepts for the analysis of the contemporary international system. The pursuit of limited national objectives, the separation of foreign policy from domestic politics, the conduct of secret diplomacy, the use of balance of power as a technique for the management of power, and the pleas for nations to place reduced emphasis on ideology as a conditioner of international conduct have little relevance to the international system today. By urging that nations return to the practices of an earlier period, some realist writers overestimate the extent to which such change in the present international system is possible. If nations obey laws of nature, which the realist purports to have discovered, why is it necessary to urge them, as realists do, to return to practices supposedly based upon such laws?[160] Although history provides many examples of international behavior which substantiate realist theory, histori-

cal data offer deviant cases. In calling upon statesmen to alter their behavior, the realist becomes normative in theoretical orientation and fails
to provide an adequate explanation as to why political leaders sometimes
do not adhere to realist tenets in foreign policy.

In emphasizing power as the principal motivation for political behavior, realists have made themselves the object of criticism. Critics have
suggested that realist writers, for the most part, have not clearly conceptualized power. There are formidable problems of measuring power, as
noted earlier in this chapter. There is no common unit into which power
is converted for measurement in realist writings. Moreover, power must
be related to the objective for which it is to be used. The amount and
type of power vary with national goals. In addition, realists have been
criticized for allegedly having placed too much emphasis on power, to
the relative exclusion of other important variables. In Hoffmann's view,
"it is impossible to subsume under one word variables as different as:
power as a condition of policy and power as a criterion of policy; power
as a potential and power in use; power as a sum of resources and power
as a set of processes."[161]

The criticism, which Ernst Haas and Inis L. Claude, Jr., have
directed against the realists' use of the term *balance of power* as being
fraught with too many meanings, has been discussed in Chapter 1.

Despite its critics, realism ranks as the most important attempt thus
far to isolate and focus on a key variable in political behavior, namely
power, and to develop a theory of international relations. To a far
greater extent than their predecessors, realist students of international
relations attempted to construct theory from historical data. In addition
to their efforts to determine how national actors in fact behaved, realists
developed a body of normative theory with prescriptions addressed particularly to policymakers. Having isolated what they considered to be
the important determinants of political behavior in the past, they compared contemporary international politics with a model based on their
study of history. The problems to which realist thought has addressed itself—of the interaction and behavior of human beings as decision-
makers, the nature of power, the foreign policy goals, the techniques for
measuring and managing power, the impact of environmental factors
upon political behavior, and the purposes and practices which ought to
guide political leaders—are central both to the study of international
politics and to the practice of statecraft.

Other approaches are addressed to similar problems. Social-psychological theories of international behavior have focused on the study of
power. In systems theory the study of demand-response relationships encompasses the efforts of one national unit to influence one or more other
national units in either conflictual or collaborative situations. The study
of decision-making is essentially an examination of the interpretation in a

given instance of the national interest. The decision-making system, like all social systems, is "open," that is, it is subject to a variety of inputs from its environment. Hence, environment, or political ecology, becomes important not only to the realist, but also to the student of systems theory as a potential conditioner of political behavior. In summary, in addition to its contribution to international relations theory, realism provides a large number of propositions about political behavior which can be subjected to further examination with the use of other frameworks and methodologies. Nevertheless, academicians and policy analysts have felt compelled to search for theory beyond realism. One result has been the adaptation in political science generally, and international relations specifically, of the concept of "system." To this we now turn.

Notes

1. Robert E. Osgood, *Ideals and Self-Interest in America's Foreign Relations* (Chicago: University of Chicago Press, 1953), p. 22.
2. See Frederick L. Schuman, *International Politics*, 4th ed. (New York: McGraw-Hill, 1969), p. 271; Klaus Knorr, *The War Potential of Nations* (Princeton: Princeton University Press, 1956). For an analysis of the various components of national power, see Klaus Knorr, *Power and Wealth: Military Power and Potential* (Lexington, Mass.: D. C. Heath, 1970).
3. Nicholas J. Spykman, *America's Strategy in World Politics* (New York: Harcourt Brace Jovanovich, 1942), p. 11.
4. Hans J. Morgenthau, *Politics Among Nations*, 4th ed. (New York: Knopf, 1967), pp. 25–26.
5. Robert Strausz-Hupé and Stefan T. Possony, *International Relations* (New York: McGraw-Hill, 1954), pp. 5–6.
6. Arnold Wolfers, *Discord and Collaboration* (Baltimore: Johns Hopkins Press, 1962), p. 103.
7. J. W. Burton, *International Relations: A General Theory* (Cambridge University Press, 1967), p. 46.
8. Charles P. Kindleberger, *Power and Money: The Politics of International Economics and the Economics of International Politics* (New York: Basic Books, 1970), pp. 56, 65.
9. Ibid., p. 56.
10. Klaus Knorr, *The Power of Nations: The Political Economy of International Relations* (New York: Basic Books, 1975), p. 3. See also by the same author, *Power and Wealth: Military Power and Potential* (Lexington, Mass.: D. C. Heath, 1970). *On the Uses of Military Power in the Nuclear Age* (Princeton: Princeton University Press, 1966).
11. Klaus Knorr, *The Power of Nations: The Political Economy of International Relations*, op. cit., p. 4.
12. Ibid.
13. Ibid., p. 10.
14. David A. Baldwin, "Power Analysis and World Politics: New Trends versus Old Tendencies," *World Politics*, XXXI, No. 2 (January 1979), 177. See also Oran R. Young, "Interdependencies in World Politics," *International Journal* (Autumn 1969), 726–750.
15. Norman Z. Alcock and Alan G. Newcombe, "The Perception of National Power," *Journal of Conflict Resolution*, XIV, No. 3 (September 1970), 342.

16. Thomas L. Saaty and Mohamad W. Khowja, "A Measure of World Influence," *Journal of Peace Science*, 2, No. 1 (Spring 1976), 44–45.

17. Jeffrey Hart, "Three Approaches to the Measurement of Power in International Relations," *International Organization*, 30, No. 2 (Spring 1976), 293.

18. See, for example, K. J. Holsti, "The Concept of Power in the Study of International Relations," *Background*, 7 (February 1964), 182.

19. Michael P. Sullivan, *International Relations: Theories and Evidence* (Englewood Cliffs, N.J.: Prentice-Hall, 1976), p. 160.

20. K. J. Holsti, *International Politics: A Framework for Analysis* (Englewood Cliffs, N.J.: Prentice-Hall, 1967), p. 193.

21. Ibid., pp. 194–195.

22. See, for example, Jack H. Nagel, *The Descriptive Analysis of Power* (New Haven and London: Yale University Press, 1975), p. 11; Robert A. Dahl, "Cause and Effect in the Study of Politics," in Daniel Lerner, ed., *Cause and Effect* (New York: The Free Press, 1965); Daniel Lerner, "Power," *International Encyclopedia of the Social Sciences* (New York: The Free Press, 1968).

23. Robert J. Lieber, *Theory and World Politics* (Cambridge, Mass.: Winthrop, 1972), p. 93.

24. Karl W. Deutsch, *The Analysis of International Relations*, 2nd. ed. (Englewood Cliffs, N.J.: Prentice-Hall, 1978), pp. 45–46.

25. David A. Baldwin, "Power Analysis and World Politics: New Trends versus Old Tendencies," *World Politics*, XXXI, No. 2 (January 1979), 161–194.

26. Jeffrey Hart, "Three Approaches to the Measurement of Power in International Relations," *International Organization*, vol. 30, No. 2 (Spring 1976), 289 and 303.

27. Jack H. Nagel, *The Descriptive Analysis of Power* (New Haven and London: Yale University Press, 1975), p. 122.

28. Herbert Simon, "Notes on the Observation and Measurement of Power," and Roderick Bell, "Political Power: The Problem of Measurement," in Roderick Bell, David V. Edwards, and R. Harrison Wagner, eds., *Political Power; A Reader in Theory and Research* (New York: The Free Press, 1969), pp. 26–27; 73–78.

29. See, for example, Geoffrey Kemp, Robert L. Pfaltzgraff, Jr., and Uri Ra'anan, eds., *The Other Arms Race: New Technologies for Non-Nuclear Conflict* (Lexington, Mass.: D. C. Heath, 1974).

30. There have been numerous efforts to measure the respective force levels of the United States and the Soviet Union. They include John M. Collins, *America and Soviet Military Trends Since the Cuban Missile Crisis* (Washington: The Center for Strategic and International Studies, Georgetown University, 1978); Ray S. Cline, *World Power Assessment* (Boulder, Col.: Westview Press, 1977); *The Military Balance* (London: International Institute for Strategic Studies, published annually); *Jane's Ships*, and *Jane's Missile Systems* (London: *Jane's Yearbooks,* published annually); *Strategic Survey* (London: International Institute for Strategic Studies, published annually).

31. George Liska, *Quest for Equilibrium: America and the Balance of Power on Land and Sea* (Baltimore and London: Johns Hopkins University Press, 1977), p. 212.

32. Klaus Knorr, *The Power of Nations: The Political Economy of International Relations* (New York: Basic Books, 1975), p. 11. See also by the same author, *Power and Wealth: Military Power and Potential* (Lexington, Mass.: D.C. Heath, 1970); *On the Uses of Military Power in the Nuclear Age* (Princeton: Princeton University Press, 1966). Wayne H. Ferris, *The Power Capabilities of Nation-States: International Conflict and War* (Lexington, Mass.: D. C. Heath, 1973).

33. Ibid., p. 267.

34. Niccolo Machiavelli, *The Prince and the Discourses* (New York: Random House [Modern Library], 1950), pp. 52–53.

35. Thomas Hobbes, *Leviathan,* ed. and Introduction Michael Oakeshott (Oxford: Basil Blackwell, 1946), p. 64.

36. Ibid., p. 109.

37. Ibid.

38. G. W. F. Hegel, *Philosophy of Right* (Oxford: Clarendon, 1942), p. 264; Friederich Meinecke, *Machiavellism: The Doctrine of Raison d'Etat and Its Place in Modern History* (New York: Praeger, 1965), p. 360.

39. In discussing the realist intellectual debt to Niebuhr, Kennan referred to him as "the father of us all." See Kenneth W. Thompson, *Political Realism and the Crisis of World Politics: An American Approach to Foreign Policy* (Princeton: Princeton University Press, 1960), pp. 23–25.

40. Harry K. Davis and Robert C. Good, eds., *Reinhold Niebuhr on Politics: His Political Philosophy and Its Application to Our Age as Expressed in His Writings* (New York: Scribner's, 1960), p. 75.

41. "In the Christian view, then, for man to understand himself truly means to begin with a faith that he is understood from beyond himself, that he is known and loved of God and must find himself in terms of obedience to the divine will. This relation of the divine to the human will makes it possible for man to relate himself to God without pretending to be God and to accept his distance from God as a created thing, without believing that the evil of his nature is caused by this finiteness." Davis and Good, eds., op. cit., p. 74. See also Reinhold Niebuhr, *Christianity and Power Politics* (New York: Scribner's, 1940), p. 64; and his *Christian Realism and Political Problems* (New York: Scribner's, 1953).

42. Harry K. Davis and Robert C. Good, eds., op. cit., p. 77.

43. Reinhold Niebuhr, *Moral Man and Immoral Society* (New York: Scribner's, 1947), pp. xi–xii.

44. Reinhold Niebuhr, *The Irony of American History* (New York: Scribner's 1952), p. 2. See also Gabriel Fackre, *The Promise of Reinhold Niebuhr* (Philadelphia: Lippincott, 1970), pp. 60–64; Charles Burton Marshall, *The Limits of Foreign Policy* (New York: Holt, Rinehart and Winston, 1954).

45. Ibid., p. 40.

46. Reinhold Niebuhr, "The Illusion of World Government," *Bulletin of the Atomic Scientists,* V (October 1949), p. 290. See also Charles Burton Marshall, op. cit., p. 122. "Legitimate government, let us remember, must rest on a tradition of kingship or aristocracy, or on a popular consensus. . . . Thus proposals to solve all the problems by the magic of world government are invariably hazy on the most serious underlying question of government—how to make it legitimate."

47. Reinhold Niebuhr, *The Irony of American History,* op. cit., p. 40.

48. Ibid., p. 148.

49. Davis and Good, eds., op. cit., p. 65.

50. John C. Bennett, "Reinhold Niebuhr's Social Ethics," in Charles W. Kegley and Robert W. Bretall, eds., *Reinhold Niebuhr* (New York: Macmillan, 1956), p. 64; and Reinhold Niebuhr, "A Critique of Pacifism," *Atlantic Monthly,* CXXXIX (May 1927), 637–641.

51. Reinhold Niebuhr, "Why I Leave the F.O.R.," *The Christian Century* (January 3, 1934), 17–19.

52. Reinhold Niebuhr, "The Christian Faith and the World Crisis," *Christianity and Crisis,* I (February 10, 1941), 4.

53. Reinhold Niebuhr, *Christian Realism and Political Problems,* op. cit., p. 36; and Reinhold Niebuhr, "Coexistence or Total War," *The Christian Century,* LXXI (August 18, 1954), 972–974.

54. Reinhold Niebuhr, *The Irony of American History,* op. cit., p. 35; Reinhold Niebuhr and Alan Heimert, *A Nation So Conceived* (New York: Scribner's, 1963), pp.

129–139, 144 (where the above quotation appears); and Reinhold Niebuhr, "American Hegemony and the Prospects for Peace," *Annals of the American Academy of Political and Social Science,* CCCXLII (July 1962), 156.

55. Nicholas J. Spykman, op. cit., p. 7; Nicholas J. Spykman and Abbie A. Rollins, "Geography and Foreign Policy," *American Political Science Review,* XXXIII (June 1939), 392.

56. "The Old World is two and one-half times as large as the New World and contains seven times the population. It is true that, at present, industrial productivity is almost equally divided, but in terms of self-sufficiency, the Eurasian Continent with the related continents of Africa and Australia is in a much stronger position. If the land masses of the Old World can be brought under the control of a few states and so organized that large unbalanced forces are available for pressure across the ocean fronts, the Americas will be politically and strategically encircled." Spykman, op. cit., pp. 447–448.

57. Ibid., p. 460.

58. Ibid., p. 472. The view that the balance of power in Asia, as well as in Europe, is an essential ingredient of the national interest of the United States was subsequently advanced by Walt W. Rostow in *The United States in the World Arena* (New York: Harper & Row, 1960), Appendix A, pp. 543–550.

59. Hans J. Morgenthau, *Politics Among Nations,* 5th ed. rev. (New York: Knopf, 1978), p. 4.

60. Ibid., p. 5.

61. Ibid.

62. Hans J. Morgenthau, "Another 'Great Debate': The National Interest of the United States," *American Political Science Review,* LXVI (December 1952), 961–998.

63. Ibid. See also Hans J. Morgenthau, *In Defense of the National Interest* (New York: Knopf, 1951); Charles A. Beard, *The Idea of the National Interest* (New York: Macmillan, 1934). The idea of the national interest as a basis for decision-making is examined in Chapter 11.

64. Hans Morgenthau, *Politics Among Nations,* op. cit., pp. 11–14.

65. Ibid., p. 10.

66. Ibid., p. 11.

67. Ibid.

68. Ibid., p. 12.

69. Ibid., p. 36.

70. Ibid., p. 43.

71. Ibid., p. 58.

72. Ibid., p. 64. For a survey of other meanings of "imperialism" and theoretical controversies concerning its nature, see Chapter 6.

73. Ibid., p. 77.

74. Ibid., p. 78.

75. Ibid., pp. 226–227.

76. Ibid., p. 529.

77. See, for example, Harold Nicolson, *Evolution of Diplomatic Method* (New York: Macmillan, 1962); *The Congress of Vienna* (London: Constable, 1946); Morgenthau, *Politics Among Nations,* op. cit., pp. 540–548.

78. George F. Kennan, *Realities of American Foreign Policy* (New York: Norton, 1966), p. 11.

79. George F. Kennan, *American Diplomacy, 1900–1950* (New York: Mentor Books, 1957), pp. 93–94. See also Charles Burton Marshall, op. cit., p. 56: ". . . [o]ur national experience has been such as to root in our minds an excess of confidence in

the political efficacy of documents—in the capability of statesmen to resolve the future by agreement on the written word."

80. George F. Kennan, *Realities of American Foreign Policy*, op. cit., p. 13.
81. Ibid., p. 14.
82. Ibid., p. 16.
83. Ibid., p. 48.
84. George F. Kennan, "World Problems in Christian Perspective," *Theology Today*, XVI (July 1959), pp. 155–172.
85. George F. Kennan, *American Diplomacy*, op. cit., p. 87.
86. George F. Kennan, *Realities of American Foreign Policy*, op. cit., p. 48.
87. Ibid., p. 36.
88. George F. Kennan, "History and Diplomacy as Viewed by a Diplomatist," *Review of Politics*, XVIII (April 1956), 173.
89. George F. Kennan, "World Problems in Christian Perspective," op. cit., p. 156.
90. George F. Kennan, *Russia and the West under Lenin and Stalin* (New York: New American Library, 1960), p. 367.
91. George F. Kennan, *American Diplomacy, 1900–1950*, op. cit., p. 96.
92. George F. Kennan, *Russia, the Atom and the West* (New York: Harper & Row, 1958), p. 27.
93. George F. Kennan, *The Cloud of Danger: Current Realities of American Foreign Policy* (Boston: Little, Brown, 1977), p. 34.
94. George F. Kennan, *Realities of Foreign Policy*, op. cit., pp. 63–64.
95. George F. Kennan, "X," "The Sources of Soviet Conduct," *Foreign Affairs*, XXV (July 1947), 514. Charles Burton Marshall was in substantial agreement when he wrote: "The best hopes lie in creating the circumstances for a heightening of the dilemma within the Soviet framework, eventually to move it along the course of accommodation and thereby toward its own transformation." op. cit., p. 97.
96. George F. Kennan, *Russia, the Atom, and the West*, op. cit., pp. 41–45.
97. Ibid., p. 200. The aging Soviet leadership is "not given to rash or adventuristic policies. It commands, and is deeply involved with, a structure of power, and particularly a higher bureaucracy" (pp. 199–200) that would not easily conflict with the United States.
98. George F. Kennan, *The Cloud of Danger: Current Realities of American Foreign Policy*, op. cit., pp. 159–160.
99. Ibid., p. 27.
100. Uri Ra'anan, "Elder Statesman's Primer," *Strategic Review* (Winter 1978), 80–81.
101. George F. Kennan, *Russia, the Atom, and the West*, op. cit., pp. 66–71.
102. George F. Kennan, *Memoirs, 1935–1950* (Boston: Little, Brown, 1967), p. 367.
103. Ibid., p. 230.
104. George F. Kennan, *The Cloud of Danger: Current Realities of American Foreign Policy*, op. cit., p. 25.
105. See Richard Rovere, "Containers," *The New Yorker* (August 8, 1977), pp. 70–73.
106. George F. Kennan, *The Cloud of Danger: Current Realities of American Foreign Policy*, op. cit., p. 229.
107. Leon N. Lindberg, "Political Integration as a Multidimensional Phenomenon Requiring Multivariate Analysis," in Leon N. Lindberg and Stuart A. Scheingold, eds., *Regional Integration Theory and Research* (Cambridge, Mass.: Harvard University Press, 1971), p. 46.
108. Ibid., p. 48.
109. Ibid., p. 49.
110. Ibid.
111. Ibid., p. 118.

112. Ibid., p. 131.
113. Arnold Wolfers, *Britain and France Between the Two Wars* (Hamden, Conn.: Archon Books, 1963), pp. 11–19, 201–222.
114. Henry A. Kissinger, *A World Restored—Europe After Napoleon: The Politics of Conservatism in a Revolutionary Age* (New York: Grosset and Dunlap, 1964).
115. Stephen R. Graubard, *Kissinger: Portrait of a Mind* (New York: Norton, 1974), p. 11. Graubard points out that Kissinger's doctoral dissertation "could not have been written in many other universities in America, not because the others lacked a library of the distinction of Harvard's, but because they had neither the tradition nor the self-assurance that permitted them to let many of their students run free.... In a more conventionally organized department, questions might have been raised about the appropriateness of the subject Kissinger chose for his dissertation or about the research procedures that he intended to employ. Neither question was even bruited in the Government Department, which, then in the early 1950s was a loose confederation of several disparate disciplines, presided over by men who did not much interfere with what their colleagues consented to." p. 15.
116. Henry A. Kissinger, op. cit., p. 1.
117. Ibid., p. 2.
118. Ibid., p. 1.
119. Ibid.
120. Ibid., p. 4.
121. Henry A. Kissinger, *Nuclear Weapons and Foreign Policy* (New York: Harper & Row, for the Council on Foreign Relations, 1957), p. 16.
122. Henry A. Kissinger, *The Necessity for Choice* (New York: Harper & Row, 1961), p. 63.
123. Henry A. Kissinger, *Nuclear Weapons and Foreign Policy*, op. cit., p. 89.
124. Ibid., p. 84.
125. Henry A. Kissinger, *The Necessity for Choice*, op. cit., p. 65.
126. Ibid., p. 170.
127. Ibid., p. 171.
128. *U.S. Foreign Policy for the 1970s: Shaping a Durable Peace.* A report to the Congress by President Nixon, President of the United States, May 3, 1973 (Washington: U.S. Government Printing Office, 1973), pp. 232–233. For an assessment of Kissinger as policymaker, see Sayom Brown, *The Crises of Power: Foreign Policy in the Kissinger Years* (New York: Columbia University Press, 1979), esp. pp. 107–153.
129. Henry A. Kissinger, *White House Years* (Boston: Little Brown and Company, 1979), p. 55.
130. Ibid., p. 232.
131. "The Nature of the National Dialogue," Address to the Pacem in Terris III Conference, Washington, October 8, 1973. Reprinted in Henry A. Kissinger, *American Foreign Policy*, 3rd ed. (New York: Norton, 1977), p. 126.
132. Ibid., p. 125.
133. Peter W. Dickson, *Kissinger and the Meaning of History* (Cambridge: Cambridge University Press, 1978), p. 20.
134. Henry A. Kissinger, "Domestic Structure and Foreign Policy," in *American Foreign Policy*, 3rd ed. (New York: Norton, 1977), p. 12.
135. Robert Strausz-Hupé, *Power and Community* (New York: Praeger, 1956), p. 3.
136. Robert Strausz-Hupé and Stefan T. Possony, *International Relations*, op. cit., p. 11.
137. Ibid.
138. Ibid., p. 18.

139. Robert Strausz-Hupé, *The Balance of Tomorrow* (New York: Putnam's, 1945), p. 119.

140. Ibid., p. 173.

141. Ibid., p. 262.

142. Ibid., p. 234.

143. Robert Strausz-Hupé, "The Decline of the West? The Challenge," *The Atlantic Community Quarterly*, vol. 15, No. 2 (Summer 1977), 175.

144. Robert Strausz-Hupé, William R. Kintner, James E. Dougherty, and Alvin J. Cottrell, *Protracted Conflict* (New York: Harper & Row, 1959), pp. 8–9.

145. Ibid., p. 2.

146. Raymond Aron, *Peace and War* (New York: Doubleday, 1966), p. 2. For contrasting analyses of Aron's writings on international relations, see Stanley Hoffmann, *The State of War: Essays in the Theory and Practice of International Relations* (New York: Praeger, 1965), pp. 22–53; Klaus Knorr and James N. Rosenau, eds., *Contending Approaches to International Politics* (Princeton: Princeton University Press, 1969), pp. 129–143. For an examination of Aron as an intellectual, see Milton Viorst, "Talk with 'a Reasonable Man,'" *New York Times Magazine* (April 5, 1970), p. 341.

147. Ibid., p. 178.

148. Ibid., p. 8.

149. Ibid., p. 16.

150. Ibid., p. 100.

151. Ibid., p. 94.

152. Ibid., p. 128.

153. Ibid., p. 36.

154. Ibid., p. 405.

155. Ibid., pp. 166–167.

156. Ibid., p. 366.

157. Ibid., p. 592.

158. Thomas I. Cook and Malcolm Moos, "The American Idea of International Interest," *American Political Science Review*, XLVII (March 1953), p. 28.

159. Stanley Hoffmann, *Contemporary Theory in International Relations* (Englewood Cliffs, N.J.: Prentice-Hall, 1960), p. 33.

160. Cecil V. Crabb, *American Foreign Policy in the Nuclear Age* (New York: Harper & Row, 1965), pp. 458–459.

161. Hoffman, op. cit., p. 32.

Chapter 4
Systemic Theories of Politics and International Relations

DEFINITION, NATURE, AND APPROACHES TO SYSTEMS THEORY

System is probably the most widely used term today in political science and international relations literature. *System* describes (1) a theoretical framework for the coding of data about political phenomena; (2) an integrated set of relationships based on a hypothetical set of political variables—for example, an international system involving world government; (3) a set of relationships among political variables in an international system alleged to have existed—for example, the international system of the 1950s; and (4) any set of variables in interaction.

Systems analysis describes a variety of techniques, such as cost-effectiveness studies, which are designed to allow rational choice in decisions regarding the allocation of resources. But in the literature of political science, "system analysis" has often been used interchangeably with "systems theory" insofar as it is employed to describe conceptual frameworks and methodologies for understanding the operation of political systems. As Robert J. Lieber has suggested, ". . . systems analysis is really a set of techniques for systematic analysis that facilitates the organizing of data, but which possesses no ideal theoretical goals. By contrast, general systems theory subsumes an integrated set of concepts, hypotheses, and propositions, which (theoretically) are widely applicable across the spectrum of human knowledge."[1] We define systems theory, or general systems theory, as a series of statements about relationships among independent and dependent variables in which changes in one or more variables are accompanied, or followed, by changes in other variables or combinations of variables. As Anatol Rapoport has defined it, "A whole which functions as a whole by virtue of the interdependence of its parts is called a *system*, and the method which aims at discovering how this is brought about in the widest variety of systems has been called general systems theory."[2] John Burton has written that the concept of system connotes "relationships between units. The units of a system are of the same 'set,' by which is meant that they have features in common that enable a particular relationship."[3] The human nervous system, a car motor, the Hilton Hotel chain, an Apollo spacecraft, the Federal Reserve System, a fishtank in a marine ecology experimental project, and the "balance of power"—all of these are *systems.*

A system can be described in its successive states. It may be loosely or tightly organized. It may be stable or unstable. A stable system requires an input of relatively considerable power to upset it; an unstable system is more precarious and its balance more easily disturbed. Every system seeks to establish, maintain, and return after disturbance to some sort of equilibrium. The equilibrium itself may be stable or unstable. A stable equilibrium is capable of absorbing new components and processing a variety of inputs while continuing to function normally, adjusting to changes, and correcting its behavior by making appropriate reactions to "negative feedback" (i.e., information that it is deviating from course).

Smaller systems (or subsystems) may exist within larger systems. According to John Burton, "Whereas the subsystem is a system in itself that can be isolated (though in isolation its functional relevance will not always be apparent) a system level refers to a complex of relationships comprising all units at that level. Systems have different features at different levels."[4] Every system has boundaries which distinguish it from its operating environment. Every system is, in some sense, a communications net which permits the flow of information leading to a self-adjusting process. Every system has inputs and outputs; an output of a system may reenter that system as an input, or what is termed *feedback.*

Closely related to systems theory has been the term *interdependence,* used to characterize relationships in a global international system. In such a conception, the emergence for the first time in history of a truly global system calls forth the need for a "geocentric," rather than an "ethnocentric," approach to the study of international relations.[5]

J. David Singer suggests that, "By a social system, then, I mean nothing more than an aggregation of human beings (plus their physical milieu) who are sufficiently interdependent to share a common fate . . . or to have actions of some of them usually affecting the lines of many of them."[6] Quoting approvingly Singer's definition of system, Ernest Haas holds that systems are simply "taxonomies devised by the researcher to permit the specification of hypothesized nonrandom events and trends in the hope of gradually mapping reality. If everyone used the construct in this sense, we would have no problem."[7]

According to Robert O. Keohane and Joseph S. Nye, interdependence always carries with it costs, "since interdependence restricts autonomy, but it is impossible to specify a priori whether the benefits of a relationship will exceed the costs. This will depend on the values of the actors as well as on the nature of the relationship."[8] The same authors conceptualize interdependence as having two dimensions: sensitivity and vulnerability. "Sensitivity involves degrees of responsiveness within a policy framework—how quickly do changes in one country bring costly changes in another, and how great are the costly effects."[9] They suggest that "vulnerability can be defined as an actor's liability to suffer costs imposed by external events even after policies have been altered."[10] Interdependence, with its sensitivity and vulnerability dimensions, can be social, political, economic, military, or ideological in nature, as Keohane and Nye demonstrate in their analysis.

Also widely used in international relations studies—and especially in systems theory—is the term *interaction*. The greater the level of interdependence, the greater the amount of interaction. Systems are hypothesized patterns of interaction. As the level of interdependence and the amount of interaction grow, the complexity of the system increases. Interdependence and interaction in turn—like systems theory itself—are closely linked to integration theory, which is discussed in Chapter 10. Interaction consists not only of the demands and responses—the actions—of nation-states, international organizations, and other nonstate actors, but also the transactions across national boundaries, including trade, tourism, investment, technology transfer, and the flow of ideas more broadly.

Examining the international system of the late twentieth century, Andrew M. Scott characterizes interaction in the following way:

> Hundreds of actors are pouring actions into the international arena at the same time, and those actions are being variously deflected and aggregated and combined with one another. . . . In an undirected aggregative process, the behavior of individual actors is purposive, but the process as a whole knows no purpose and is under no overall direction. . . . A process that is only partly under control does not become quiescent because the control

element has ceased to be adequate, but rather, continues to function and produces results only some of which are intended.[11]

In short, problems, or inputs, in the international system are multiplying faster than solutions can be found, thus leading to systems overload. Patterns of interdependence and interaction grow more complex as a result of the pervasive impact of technology upon the international system. Under such conditions, it is hypothesized, the "structural requisites," that is, those needs that must be satisfied for a system to function effectively, become more numerous.[12]

Interdependence and interaction provide focal points for many writers in explaining systems transformation. The formation in the late twentieth century of a global international system for the first time in history, in place of the Eurocentric system that endured from the Treaty of Westphalia in 1648 until World War II, is related to the global diffusion of technology. Edward L. Morse refers to the twofold effects of modernization as "the emergence of certain forms of interdependence among a large set of states and the transnational nature of the international system."[13] Here, interdependence is defined as "the outcome of specified actions of two or more parties (in our case, of governments) when the outcomes of these actions are mutually contingent." Morse sets forth a series of propositions about interdependence within the international system. For example, the greater the degree of interdependence, the greater the likelihood of crisis. "Interdependence does not only breed crises and various forms of linkage, it also increases the potential for any single party to manipulate a crisis for its own domestic or foreign political ends."[14]

Other writers have sought to define interdependence and to ascertain the extent to which levels of interdependence are rising or declining, especially in the late twentieth century. According to Hayward Alker, a "synthetic, multifaceted definition of interdependence is possible." Interdependence is a "social relationship among two or more cross-state actors observable in terms of actual or anticipated interactions among them."[15] Richard Rosecrance and Arthur Stein view interdependence, in the most general sense, as consisting of "a relationship of interests such that if one nation's position changes, other states will be affected by that change" or, in an economic sense, "interdependence is present when there is an increased national 'sensitivity' to external economic developments."[16] They take issue with the conclusion of Karl Deutsch and his associates (see Chapter 10) that levels of transactions, especially trade, at the international level, relative to those within states, have been declining in much of the twentieth century. The growth in the service sector, most pronounced in highly industrialized states, has been underestimated in GNP calculations for earlier periods, especially the previous century. The authors note a paradox in the contemporary international system: "The vertical integration of nationalist processes has moved to a new peak. The horizontal interaction of transnational processes is higher than at any point since World War I.[17]

Although in the past generation systems theory has had a major influence upon the study of politics, the idea of systems was not unknown to earlier political writers. For example, Thomas Hobbes, in Chapter 22 of his *Leviathan,* writes of systems.[18] Modern students of politics have adapted the concept of systems from the physical sciences and the social sciences on which systems theory has had a major impact.

One of the most important exponents of general systems theory (GST) is Ludwig von Bertalanffy, who was for a long time professor of theoretical biology at the University of Alberta, Canada, whose work in this field dates from the 1920s. He suggests that the ever-increasing specialization within modern science begets fragmentation among disciplines: "The physicist, the biologist, the psychologist and the social scientist are, so to speak, encapsulated in a private universe, and it is difficult to get a word from one cocoon to the other."[19] The growth of disciplines and greater academic specialization threaten to fragment the scientific community into isolated enclaves unable to communicate with each other. General systems theory represents a response to this problem. Rapoport suggests that systems theory has the potential of reestablishing approaches that emphasize the functional relationship between parts and whole without sacrificing scientific rigor. The analogies established or conjectured in systems theory are not mere metaphors. According to Rapoport, they are rooted in actual correspondences between systems or theories of systems.[20] Bertalanffy discerns similar viewpoints and conceptions in various fields.

Disciplines such as physics and chemistry study phenomena in dynamic interaction. In biology there are problems of an organismic nature. In such seemingly diverse disciplines, it is essential, according to Bertalanffy, to "study not only isolated parts and processes, but the essential problems are the organizing relations that result from dynamic interaction and make the behavior of parts different when studied in isolation or within the whole."[21]

In short, Bertalanffy, like Rapoport, sees structural similarities or isomorphism[22] in the principles which govern the behavior of intrinsically dissimilar entities. This is because they are in certain respects "systems," that is, "complexes of elements standing in interaction." Because of such similarities, general systems theory offers a "useful tool *providing,* on the one hand, models that can be used in, and transferred to, different fields, and *safeguarding,* on the other hand, from vague analogies which have often marred the progress in these fields."[23] According to Peter

Nettl, general systems theory "is an attempt to explore structural iso-morphisms and homeomorphisms between systems."[24]

As Jerone Stephens has noted, the value of systems theory, in the strictest sense, lies in the extent to which isomorphisms, or structural identities, among political phenomena and between social, physical, and biological systems can be found. "In international relations, as well as in political science, no isomorphisms have been established, and the changes that have been made in GST since its inception have not been any more beneficial in helping us find isomorphic relations than the origi-nal formulation was."[25] Therefore the value of systems theory has de-rived from the conceptualization it is said to provide for assessing the ca-pacity of alternative structures to fulfill various functions. Such struc-tures, many writers have observed, may include nonstate actors such as alliances, multinational enterprise, religous organizations, and other groups that, in their membership and outreach, transcend state fron-tiers.[26]

Kenneth Boulding

From his work in economics and general systems theory, Kenneth Boulding has attempted to classify systems according to levels of in-creasing complexity: mechanical, homeostatic, biological, equivalent to higher animals, and human.[27] The process of gathering, selecting, and using information essential to preservation is far more complex in the human system than in a simple system. A thermostat, for example, reacts only to changes in temperature, and ignores other data. The simpler the system, the fewer the data essential for survival. In contrast to simple systems, humans have a capacity for self-knowledge, which makes possi-ble the selection of information on the basis of a particular cognitive structure, or "image." The image can make possible the restructuring of the information, or stimulus, into something fundamentally different from the information itself. The resulting human behavior is a response not to a specific stimulus, but to a knowledge structure effecting a com-prehensive view of the environment. Difficulties in the prediction of sys-tem behavior arise to account for the intervention of the image between stimulus and response. To a far greater extent than simple systems, com-plex systems have a potential for collapse because the image has screened out information essential for survival.

Social and political systems are structured from the images of par-ticipant human actors. Boulding gives the term *folk knowledge* to the collective images of the members of political systems. The decisions of political leaders conform to the dictates of folk knowledge, screening out conflicting information. The information-gathering apparatus of both national and international systems usually serves to confirm both the images of the leading decision-makers and also the folk knowledge of the system. Boulding is convinced that the elimination of the influence of folk knowledge in decision-making would have as great an effect on international behavior as removing medieval notions about cosmology had on developing modern science. Boulding considers the idea of image a crucial concept in understanding systems and in studying such political phenomena as conflict and decision-making. Thus, general systems theory contributes to conceptualization at a level "between the highly generalized constructions of pure mathematics and the specific theories of the specialized disciplines."[28]

Talcott Parsons

In sociology, Talcott Parsons was the foremost student of systems theory. Parsons postulates the existence of an actor oriented toward attaining anticipated goals by means of a normatively regulated expenditure of energy.[29] Since the relationships between actors and their situation have a recurrent character or system, all action occurs in systems. Although Parsons recognizes that there can be action between an individual and an object, he is more concerned with action in a societal context, or with what he calls an "action system." Parson's action system places persons in the role of subjects and in the role of objects. Subject (alter) and object (ego) interact in a system. If actors gain satisfaction, they develop a vested interest in the preservation and functioning of the system. Mutual acceptance of the system by the actors creates an equilibrating mechanism in the system.

At any given time, a person is a member of several action systems such as one's family, one's employer, and one's nation-state. Three subsystems comprise the Parsonian system: (1) the personality system, (2) the social system, and (3) the cultural system. These subsystems are interconnected within the "action system" so that each affects the other. In summary, Parsons conceives of society as an interlocking network of action systems. A change in one subsystem affects the other subsystems and the whole action system.

It is possible, Parsons suggests, to distinguish and study the actions which persons, or actors, perform as members of a specific system of action. Action is based on the choices among alternative courses that actors believe to be open to them. In Parsons' view, action is "a set of oriented processes," in which there are two major "vectors," the motivational orientations and the value-orientations. Supposedly, the course of action that actors adopt is based on a previous learning experience as well as on their expectations about the behavior of the persons with whom they are interacting. According to Parsons, interaction makes the development of culture possible at the human level, and provides culture with a signifi-cant determinant of patterns of action in a social system.[30]

Parsons proposed a set of five dichotomous pattern variables as con-stituting the basic dilemmas that actors face in all social action. These variables describe the alternatives available to actors confronted with problematic situations. The pattern variables are grouped as follows: (1) universalism-particularism; (2) ascription-achievement; (3) self-orienta-tion-collectivity-orientation; (4) affectivity-affective neutrality; and (5) specificity-diffuseness. The universalism-particularism dichotomy distin-guishes between judging objects in a general frame of reference and judging them in a particular scheme. Whereas the impartial dispensation of justice under law is universalistic, kinship behavior is particularistic. The ascription-achievement dichotomy refers to values governing hu-man advancement in social and political systems—whether, for exam-ple, birth and wealth count for more than intellectual ability and educa-tion. The self-orientation-collectivity-orientation dichotomy categorizes action as taken on behalf of the unit initiating action or as initiated on behalf of other units. Businesses, for example, tend to be self-oriented, whereas governments are collectivity-oriented. The affectivity-affective neutrality variable indicates an individual's sensitivity or insensitivity to emotional stimuli. The specificity-diffuseness variable distinguishes be-tween those relationships which are diffuse and all-encompassing, such as a marriage, and those which are specific and highly structured, such as interaction between a sales clerk and customer. Although diffuseness characterizes traditional societies, specificity of function is a mark of modernized societies.

Parson's pattern variables provide a framework for describing re-curring and contrasting patterns in the norms of social systems. Many au-thors deem the Parsonian pattern variables as useful in examining social and political systems. For example, Parsons suggests that a bureaucracy is built on universalistic and achievement norms, and that the contrac-tual relationships among business corporations are based on norms of specificity. Such variables may be used either in a discussion of interna-tional relations or of political parties at the national or local level in the United States.

In his theory, Parsons attaches great importance to equilibrium as a means of measuring fluctuations in the ability of a social system to cope with problems that affect its structure.[31] Systems theory assumes the in-terdependence of parts in determinate relationships, which impose order upon the components of the system. Although equating order with equi-librium, Parsons asserts that equilibrium is not necessarily equated with "static self-maintenance or a stable equilibrium. It may be an ordered process of change—a process following a determinate pattern rather than random variability relative to the starting point. This is called a moving equilibrium and is well exemplified in growth."[32] Social systems are characterized by a multiple equilibrium process, since social systems have many subsystems, each of which must remain in equilibrium if the larger system is to maintain equilibrium.

Parsons is concerned with how social systems endure stress, how they enhance their position, how they disintegrate. If societal equilibrium and ultimately the social system itself are to be maintained, four functional prerequisites must be performed: (1) *pattern maintenance*—the ability of a system to insure the reproduction of its own basic patterns, its values and norms; (2) *adaptation* to the environment and to changes in the environment; (3) *goal attainment*—the capacity of the system to achieve whatever goals the system has accepted or set for itself; and (4) *integration* of the different functions and subsystems into a cohesive, coordinated whole. In Parsons' social system, families and households are the subsystems which serve the function of pattern maintenance. Adaptation occurs in the economy and in areas of scientific and technological change. The polity—the government in particular—performs the function of goal attainment. The cultural subsystems, which include mass communications, religion, and education, fulfill the integrative function. Parsons' functional prerequisites have been adapted, in varying forms, to the study of politics, which is itself one of his subsystems; and they have influenced those international systems writers who are considered in this chapter.[33] Although Parsons briefly addresses himself to the concept of international systems, he sees in the international system patterns of interaction similar to those within the action system at the domestic level. The major problem for the international system, as well as for the domestic system, is that of maintaining the equilibrium which is important if a system is to manage its inner tensions.[34]

The existence of a bipolar international system increases the difficulty of maintaining equilibrium. According to Parsons, the formulation of common values which cut across national boundaries is essential to international order. Although the international system is deficient in such values, the importance attached to economic development and national independence in many parts of the world over the past generation represents their emergence, at least in rudimentary form, as consensus-building forces at the global level. Parsons sees the need for the development of procedural consensus—agreement among participants in international politics about the institutions and procedures for the settlement of problems and differences. He also calls for the differentiation of interests among peoples in a pluralistic fashion so that they will cut across the historic lines of partisan differentiation. In domestic political and social systems, peoples achieve greater unity as a result of the fact that they have cross-cutting cleavages, that is, some Catholics are Republicans, whereas others are Democrats, and some Protestants are Democrats and others are

Republicans. Such pluralistic differentiation at the international level would enhance the prospects for international stability. Central to his writings is the problem of building a social and political community.[35] Parsons' action system has influenced the thought of students of integration at the international level, as discussed in Chapter 10.

David Easton and Others

Several political scientists have developed, adapted, and employed systems theory. These scholars have concerned themselves with the "political system," which has been defined by Gabriel Almond as "that system of interactions to be found in all independent societies which performs the functions of integration and adaptation (both internally and vis-à-vis other societies) by means of the employment, or the threat of employment, of more or less legitimate physical compulsion."[36] Karl Deutsch, who also adheres to the functional prerequisites of Parsons, holds that a system is characterized by transactions and communications. He is concerned with the extent to which political systems are equipped with adequate facilities for collecting external and internal information as well as for transmitting this information to the points of decision-making. Those political systems which survive stress can receive, screen, transmit, and evaluate information.[37] According to David Easton, systems theory is based on the idea of political life as a boundary-maintaining set of interactions imbedded in and surrounded by other social systems which constantly influence it.[38] According to Easton, political interactions can be distinguished from other kinds of interactions by the fact that they are oriented principally toward the "authoritative allocation of values for a society."[39]

Herbert Spiro holds that a political system can exist wherever people either cooperate or engage in conflict to solve common problems. A political system is a community that is processing its issues. A problem has entered the political system when members of the community have recognized it and begun to disagree about it. A problem leaves the political system after a solution has been recognized.[40] Spiro's conception of system is illustrative of an effort, symbolized by systems theory, to transcend the traditional divisions within political science as a discipline. At the international level or in a subnational unit, a political system may be conceptualized as a "community processing its issues."

Scholars such as Almond, Deutsch, Easton, and Spiro share an interest in functions performed by the political system—in the means by which the system converts inputs into outputs. Easton, in particular, has been identified with what is termed input-output analysis. In his scheme, the principal inputs into the political system are demands and supports, whereas the major outputs are the decisions allocating system benefits.

Almond addresses himself to the question of how political systems engage in political socialization, interest articulation and aggregation, and political communication. Such factors represent means for making demands on the political system; therefore they are input functions. Almond is concerned particularly with political output functions involving rule making, rule application, and rule adjudication. His output functions, in the case of the American political system, correspond to the executive, legislative, and judicial branches.

Deutsch suggests that political systems might be categorized according to their ability to respond effectively to demands upon them.[41] All political systems might be divided into four categories: (1) self-destroying systems, which are likely to break down even in relatively favorable environments; (2) nonviable systems, which are not likely to survive under the range of difficulties found in most environments; (3) viable systems, which are likely to survive over a limited range of environmental conditions; and (4) self-enhancing systems, which are able to increase their probability of survival in a growing variety of environments.

Easton is concerned as well with the capacity of political systems to adapt to their environments. Demands arise either in the environment outside the system or within the system itself. Supports include those resources (e.g., the loyalty, participation, and law-obedience of citizens) which enhance the political system's ability to respond to the demands upon it. In Easton's model, outputs consist of decisions or policies.

The system represents an effort to cut across the boundaries separating seemingly discrete disciplines. Easton, for example, maintains that at the international level, no less than at the national level, it is possible to find sets of relationships through which values are authoritatively allocated. Unlike certain other systems, however, the international system lacks universal, or even strongly held, feelings of legitimacy; nevertheless, its members make demands with the expectation that they will be converted into outputs. According to Easton, authorities in this case are much "less centralized than in most modern systems, less continuous in their operation and more contingent on events, as in the case of primitive systems. But, nonetheless, historically the great powers and, more recently, various kinds of international organizations, such as the League of Nations and the United Nations, have been successful, intermittently, in resolving differences that were not privately negotiated and in having them accepted as authoritative."[42] Employing his system model, Easton suggests the possibility of studying and categorizing political systems, at both the national and international levels, according to their capacity for authoritatively allocating values. In Spiro's framework, the political process consists essentially of four phases: (1) the formulation of issues arising from problems; (2) the deliberation of issues; (3) the resolution of issues; and (4) the solution of the problem that provoked the issue.[43] Although all political systems perform these functions, they vary widely, depending on the political style of the actors. In turn, political style is derived from four basic goals toward which political systems are more or less deliberately directed: stability, flexibility, efficiency, and effectiveness.[44] The effective political system achieves an equilibrium among these goals. Spiro views problems as constituting the inputs, and solutions as the outputs of political systems.

Systems theory, the work of Gabriel Almond in particular, and comparative studies of political systems all share a basic concern with structural-functional analysis that attempts to examine the performance of certain kinds of functions within such seemingly different entities as a biological organism or a political system. Contemporary scholars who employ structural-functional analysis are indebted to the early twentieth-century work of anthropologists Bronislaw Malinowski (1884–1942) and A. R. Radcliffe-Brown (1881–1955). Subsequently, Robert K. Merton developed a framework for structural-functional analysis in the field of sociology.[45] Proponents of structural-functional analysis assume that it is possible, first, to specify a pattern of behavior which satisfies a *functional requirement* of the system and, second, to identify *functional equivalents* in several different structural units. Structural-functional analysis contains as concepts structural and functional requisites. A *functional requisite* is a generalized condition, given the level of generalization of the definition and the unit's general setting.[46] A structural requisite is a pattern or observable uniformity of action necessary for the continued existence of the system.[47] Moreover, an effort is made to distinguish between functions (or what Levy calls eufunctions) and dysfunctions. According to Merton, "eufunctions are those observed consequences which make for the adaptation or adjustment of the system."[48] Thus structural-functional analysis may enable the researcher to avoid the pitfall of associating particular functions with particular structures and, for this reason, may prove useful in comparative research and analysis.

Both the Parsonian functional prerequisites and the functions set forth by Almond and Easton can be located and described within a given political system. Such functions relate to the system's goals, to the system's maintaining an equilibrium, and to the system's ability to interact with and adapt to changes within the environment. Structural-functional analysis provides, at the minimum, a classificatory scheme for examining political phenomena.[49]

Systems concepts have been applied to studies in international integration, foreign policy decision-making, and conflict. Systems theory has been used at several analytical levels of immediate interest to the student of international politics: (1) the development of models of international systems in which patterns of interaction are specified; (2) the study of the processes by which decision-makers in one national unit, interacting with each other and responding to inputs from the domestic and international environment, formulate foreign policy, although, as Raymond Tanter, has suggested, "International systems approaches may imply interaction models, whereas foreign policy approaches may suggest decision-making models";[50] (3) the study of interaction between a national political system and its domestic subsystems, such as public opinion, interest groups, and culture, in order to analyze patterns of interaction; (4) the study of external "linkage groups," that is, other political systems, actors, or structures in the international system with which the national system under examination has direct relations; and (5) the examination of the interaction between external "linkage groups"[51] and those internal groups most responsive to external events, such as foreign affairs elites, the military, and business people engaged in world trade.

These analytic foci are by no means mutually exclusive: An understanding of decision-making processes and systems at the national level is essential to an understanding of interaction between the national units of the international system. To focus on national decision-making is to study a subsystem of the international system; the international system has as a focal point the investigation of interaction among the foreign policies of a series of national units. In this chapter we are concerned in particular with those theorists who concentrate on the international system and its regional subsystems. In subsequent chapters on decision-making and integration theory, we shall examine other applications of systems theory.

THE NATURE OF SYSTEMS AT
THE INTERNATIONAL LEVEL

In the study of international relations, Morton A. Kaplan suggests the existence of a system of action which he defines as "a set of variables so related, in contradistinction to its environment, that describable behavioral regularities characterize the internal relationships of the set of individual variables to combinations of external variables."[52] According to another student of international relations, Charles A. McClelland, systems theory is a technique for developing an understanding of relationships among nation-states:

> The strategy, first of all, of conceiving of many kinds of phenomena in terms of working relations among their parts, and then labeling them *systems* according to a definition of what part of the problem is most relevant, is the key to the approach. Then, the procedures of bypassing many complexities in order to investigate relationships between input and output, of systematically moving to different levels of analysis by recognizing the link of subsystems to systems, of being alert to 'boundary phenomena'

and the ranges of normal operations of subsystems and systems, and of taking into account both 'parameters' and 'perturbations' in the environments of systems are other major parts of the general systems apparatus.[53]

In McClelland's work, systems theory is simply a framework for an event/interaction model or a technique for identifying, measuring, and examining interaction within a system and its subsystems. Systems theory provides for the examination of linkages, or recurrent sequences of behavior that originate in one system and are reacted to in another. If such sequences can be isolated and examined, it may be possible to gain theoretical insights into the nature of the interdependence of national and international systems.

George Modelski defines an international system as a social system having structural and functional requirements. International systems consist of a set of objects, together with the relationships between these objects and between their attributes. International systems contain patterns of action and interaction between collectivities and between individuals acting on their behalf.[54] Richard N. Rosecrance concludes that a system is comprised of disturbance inputs, a regulator which undergoes changes as a result of the disturbing influence, and environmental constraints which translate the state of the disturbance and the state of the regulator into stable or unstable outcomes.[55]

The systems approach has had many adherents because supposedly it furnishes a framework for organizing data, integrating variables, and introducing materials from other disciplines. Kaplan has suggested that systems theory permits the integration of variables from different disciplines.[56] Rosecrance believes that systems theory helps link "general organizing concepts" with "detailed empirical investigation." In his work the concept of system provides a framework for the study of the history of a particular period and enhances the prospects for the development of a "theoretical approach which aims at a degree of comprehensiveness."[57] Dissatisfied with past approaches to the study of international relations, McClelland favors a systems approach because there is a need "to gather the specialized parts of knowledge into a coherent whole."[58] Other writers, especially in the 1970s, have suggested that, by virtue of the inherent complexity of global politics, there does not exist an entity known as an international system. Instead, there are "multiple issue-based systems." International politics is hypothesized as consisting of "many distinctive and overlapping systems that differ from each other in terms of their structural properties and in terms of the purposes of the individuals and groups that constitute them. If we allow that these multiple systems can overlap and/or become linked, then it becomes apparent that there is more than a single relevant global system as well as many that are less than global in domain."[59]

Such a conception of international systems is said to provide the basis for identifying and mapping the patterns of behavior. Areas of overlap among systems, and especially between foreign and domestic policies, patterns of interaction and interdependence, the extent to which issue areas encompass state and nonstate actors—all constitute topics for empirical study.

Writers on international systems develop what are termed *concrete* or *physical systems* and *analytic systems*. A concrete system describes a pattern of interaction among human actors which supposedly exists, or existed, in the *real* world. In contrast, an analytic system is a heuristic device for the analysis of possible future systems, for comparison between some existing systems and a kind of ideal or analytical system.[60] Kaplan's systems are models in the same sense in which a theory of molecular structure could be translated into a model which, if a correct model, would relate to the observable real world. They are theoretical models which can be applied to real systems, but which in principle can also be expressed in purely logical form. Modelski's models, Agraria and Industria, are analytic systems. Rosecrance's international systems derived from the analysis of historical data are concrete systems.

Just as there are similarities in their definitions of systems, those writers discussed in this chapter whose work has dealt primarily with the international level have common elements in their respective international systems frameworks. First, each has an interest in those factors that contribute to stability or instability in the international system. Second, there is a common concern with what are the adaptive controls by which the system remains in equilibrium or "steady-state." Such preoccupation in the study of political and social systems is analogous to the interest of biologists in homeostasis in living organisms. Third, there is a shared interest in assessing the impact upon the system of the existence of units with a greater or lesser ability to mobilize resources and to utilize advanced technology. Fourth, there is a consensus among writers that domestic forces within the national political units exert a major effect on the international system. Fifth, they are concerned, as part of their interest in the nature of stability, with the capacity of the international system to contain and deal effectively with disturbances within it. This leads the writers to share an interest in the role of national and supranational actors as regulators of the system. They are in accord that the international system is characterized by change, rather than by static qualities.

All are concerned with the role of elites, resources, regulators, and environment as factors that enhance or detract from stability in the system. Moreover, the flow of information is crucial in the systems framework of each writer. In fact, systems theory owes much to principles of cybernetics developed by Norbert Wiener and applied by scholars such as Karl W. Deutsch to the study of politics (see Chapter 10). Interaction among the units of a system occurs as a result of a communications process. Communications are crucial to the preservation of the system. Modelski refers to information as the international culture and communication which comprise all contacts among states from diplomacy to the everyday routine communication among states. According to Rosecrance, communication among the elites of the national units takes place within the regulator mechanism. Moreover, Kaplan, Rosecrance, and Modelski all attach importance to the role of elites. According to Rosecrance, feelings of insecurity among the elites contribute to instability in the international system. In his work, Modelski gives emphasis to the composition of the elite, that is, a singular authority in Agraria or a pluralistic authority in Industria, with the latter forming a stabilizing factor in the system. In Kaplan's model, the elites determine whether or not the government of the actor state will be directive (authoritarian) or nondirective (democratic). In Kaplan's models, the nature of the governments of national units is of considerable importance to the stability of the international system. In contrast, McClelland does not address himself specifically to the question of an elite, although he does discuss domestic forces that affect the international system.

Each attaches importance to the ability of actors to mobilize resources and advanced technology. In Rosecrance's model, the availability of disposable resources to the elite is a dynamic determinant in the international system; that is, it will affect the stability of the system, since insecure elites will not be able to resist using resources that can be easily mobilized. In Modelski's models of Agraria and Industria, which, respectively, are international systems based on agricultural and industrialized national units, the ability to mobilize resources by the elites has implications for the structure of the system. Because of the vast amount of resources available to the elites of Industria, it is essential to the stability of the system that the ruling elites be pluralistic in nature and hence subject to democratic control and that they use available resources for purposes other than the destruction of neighboring states. In Kaplan's models of the international system, resources and the states' ability to use resources to attain goals are considered as capability variables. According to McClelland, the specialization of functions leads to an increase in the volume of communications, and makes necessary a highly trained elite.

McClelland and, to a lesser extent, Kaplan deal with the impact of domestic groups on the international system. Kaplan addressed himself to domestic subsystems especially in his hierarchical international and universal international systems. However, Rosecrance and Modelski are concerned with the effect of such domestic forces as nationalism upon the international system. In fact, Rosecrance contends that elites who feel insecure in their domestic political systems are likely to contribute to international instability. Such elites are prone to take aggressive action against other states in order to strengthen their domestic position.

The capacity of the system to contain and cope with disturbance is of concern to each writer. One of Rosecrance's principal interests is the capacity of the system to contain disturbance, in part through the regulator mechanism. Kaplan's concern with this problem is illustrated by his interest in transformation rules, that is, rules that specify the conditions under which an international system having certain characteristics (e.g., tight bipolar) changes to an international system having other characteristics (e.g., loose bipolar). McClelland writes of the international system as being subject to manipulation and exposed to disturbances. His emphasis on an "open and adaptive" system, as well as the communication of information, suggests a concern with the system's ability to change in order to cope with disturbance.

In short, writers who use systems theory are concerned in varying degrees with several categories of questions, concepts, and data: (1) the internal organization and interaction patterns of complexes of elements hypothesized or observed to exist as a system; (2) the relationship and boundaries between a system and its environment and, in particular, the nature and impact of inputs from and outputs to the environment; (3) the functions performed by systems, the structures for the performance of such functions, and their effect upon the stability of the system; (4) the homeostatic mechanisms available to the system for the maintenance of steady-state or equilibrium; (5) the classification of systems as open or closed, or as organismic or nonorganismic systems; and (6) the structuring of hierarchical levels of systems, the location of subsystems within systems, the patterns of interaction among subsystems themselves, and between subsystems and the system itself.

This last category may be restated as the problem of level of analysis, including international subsystems, or "subordinate state systems" to which students of international relations have addressed themselves at considerable length over the past generation.[61] (Reference has previously been made to the level-of-analysis problem in Chapter 1.) Several scholars have attempted to specify patterns of interaction within models and within actual political units in the North Atlantic area, the Middle East, and Asia. Regions have been treated as subsystems of the international system, and efforts have been made to link integration theory to general systems theory. Research on international subsystems has had several focal points: (1) an attempt to specify as precisely as possible patterns of interaction among units in one international subsystem; (2) an effort to compare two or more international subsystems; and (3) studies of relationships between a subsystem and the international system.[62]

Charles A. McClelland and Events Data Analysis

Charles A. McClelland has attempted to link systems theory explicitly to the problem of delineating levels of analysis for the study of international relations, and in doing so has provided the basis for a growing literature focused on events/data interaction—the recording and analysis of data about a variety of relationships among states, including trade patterns, levels of foreign aid, diplomatic exchanges, and communications flows. *Events data* are defined as "single action events of nonroutine, extraordinary, or newsworthy character that in some clear sense are directed across national boundaries and have in most instances a specific foreign target." Visits of heads of state, diplomatic warnings, and participation in international conferences provide examples of such nonroutine single action events. Such data, used either separately or in conjunction with transaction data, may yield a more precise understanding of patterns of interaction among states in carefully defined circumstances. For example, does a shift in foreign policy by Country A toward Country B lead each country to alter its foreign policy toward Country C? If so, what types of transactions and events precede, accompany, or follow such changes?

McClelland's model of the international system is an expanded version of two interacting states. The international system is multidimensional in character. In order to understand McClelland's systems framework, it is necessary to imagine nations of the world having a wide range of official and unofficial contacts with each other—demand-response relationships, in which an action by one nation elicits a response from another, in turn calling forth a response from the nation that initiated the action. According to McClelland, conditions and events in the international system result from sources generated within nations, and from subsystems within the national unit such as public opinion, interest groups, and political parties. Therefore McClelland's model includes not only interaction at the international level, but also interaction between the national unit and its subsystems. He suggests that a nation's "international behavior is a two-way activity of taking from and giving to the international environment. All the giving and taking, when considered together and for all the national actors, is called the international system."[63] A systems framework, McClelland contends, provides an orderly procedure for shifting perspective from one level to another in the study of international politics.

Although the international system is multidimensional, the most promising prospect for theory-building is said to lie in the focus of attention upon one level of analysis at a time. McClelland concentrates on interaction between the national units, rather than interaction between the national unit and its domestic subsystems. He is concerned only with interaction observable outside the "black-boxes" that constitute the national units, with their complex and obscure decision-making processes. In McClelland's scheme, transactions between the national units are recorded and analyzed. Both routine and nonroutine activity between nations may be studied, since the "performance of the participants—the interaction sequences—are reliable indicators of active traits of participating actors. . . . Our basic assumption is that the kind of social organization developed in a nation-state fundamentally conditions its crisis behavior."[64]

In McClelland's own work the "acute international crisis," as a subsystem of the international system, is the object of examination by interaction analysis. He asks the following research questions: Is it possible to detect a "change of state" in the activities of a system in the transition from a noncrisis to a crisis period? Is a designated subsystem that is part of a more general system of action responsive to major disturbances in the general system? McClelland offers three propositions for examination: (1) that acute international crises are "short burst" affairs and are marked by an unusual volume and intensity of events; (2) that the general trend in acute international crises will be toward "routinizing" crisis behavior, that is, dealing with problems by means of increasingly "standard" techniques; and (3) that participants will be reluctant to allow the level of violence to increase beyond that present at the onset of the crisis.

In McClelland's scheme the significant variation in the flow of action within the system is of central interest. McClelland suggests that "information concerning conditions created at a certain moment by the effects of interaction and by factors of the environment is returned to the participating actors. The latter are presumed to receive and process such 'output' information and to feed the processed results (as inputs) into the next phase of participation in the particular and relevant 'system of action.' "[65] In acute international crises, sequences of action can be traced since the time span and the focus of inquiry are narrowed. Because there is little delay between demand and response, sequences of action can be examined and patterns ascertained. The objective of the study of acute international crises is to identify patterns of interaction for purposes of comparison in several crises. Thus McClelland has coded events and traced the sequences of action in crises, focusing in the Berlin crisis on interferences, harassments, and delays on access routes, as well as the responses to these actions: arrests and detainment of personnel, disputes between governing authorities, and decrees, decisions, and regulations affecting Western freedom of movement within the city.[66]

Since the early 1960s, numerous efforts have been made to collect and utilize events data in the study of international interaction. As McClelland notes, a major portion of events data studies has been focused on crisis behavior, not unlike the emphasis in his own research.

(Definitions of "crisis" and a discussion of crisis behavior will be found in Chapter 11.) McClelland suggests that anticrisis early warning systems may be developed from "current intelligence analyses in the policy community and event monitoring and indexing from the flow of the news by the academic community."[67] Thus he sees the need, and the prospect, for theory and research utilizing events data that would serve the interests of both the scholar and the policymaker. The objects of study have been hypotheses about the structure, patterns, and performance of the international system and its subsystems; political behavior in alignments and under conditions of nonalignment; negotiating behavior; the causes, outcomes, and dynamics of crisis and conflict, and relationships between domestic political variables and foreign policy. The results of such analyses are, for the most part, inconclusive. To be sure, the extensive testing of hypotheses has been illustrative of a continuing and broadening effort to validate theoretical frameworks. But differing and often incomplete data sources, as well as statistical techniques, have hampered the development of cumulative knowledge. Sophia Peterson has concluded that, in the area of conflict, in which the greatest research effort has been concentrated: "Four factors have received the most emphasis: previous foreign conflict, domestic conflict, political structure, and power. Of these, findings have been more or less consistently pointing in the direction of the importance of previous foreign conflict and domestic conflict. The findings on power and political structure are contradictory as are the findings on several of the other factors."[68]

Richard N. Rosecrance

Although students of international relations have traditionally turned to historical materials for the construction and validation of theories, their work has been faulted often for its noncomparability or for the failure to develop adequate criteria for the selection of data. Proponents of systemic theories of politics, such as Rosecrance and Kaplan, have made use of historical materials in an effort to construct and validate models of international behavior. Rosecrance bases his systems analysis on the study of nine historical systems.[69] He divides European history between 1740 and 1960 into nine periods or systems, each of which is demarcated by significant changes in diplomatic techniques and objectives. Rosecrance discerns the existence of recurring phenomena in the nine international systems periods, from which he develops two models. Concerned with the conditions for international stability, he selects as his basic elements: disturbance input, the regulator mechanism which reacts to the disturbance, the environmental restraints which influence the range of possible outcomes, and finally the outcomes themselves. Disturbance input includes such forces as ideologies, domestic insecurity, disparities between nations in resources, and conflicting national interests. The regulator mechanism consists of capabilities such as the Concert of Europe, the United Nations, or an informal consensus that, it is often pointed out by historians, the major European nations shared in the eighteenth century. The third element, the presence of environmental restraints, limits the range of possible outcomes. He judges systems to be equilibrial or disequilibrial, depending upon whether the regulator or the disturbance was stronger. From these elements, Rosecrance develops and examines four basic determinants for each of his nine systems: elite direction (attitudes), degree of elite control, resources available to the controlling elites, and the capacity of the system to contain disturbances. Given his choice of determinants, it is evident that Rosecrance attaches considerable importance to the domestic sources of international behavior.

Among his domestic determinants Rosecrance emphasizes the elites of national units. First, was the elite satisfied with its position domestically or did it feel threatened by events in the international system? Second, the control or security of the elite within the society which it commanded was a determinant in each of Rosecrance's international systems. Did the elites perceive a weakening in their internal position? Third, emphasis is placed upon the availability of disposable resources to the elite and its ability to mobilize them. Finally, Rosecrance views the system's capacity to mitigate and contain disturbances as a determinant of equilibrium.[70]

From Rosecrance's work, it is possible to construct essentially two models of the international system. The first is a model with characteristics of stability. A stable system is based on a comparison of systems I, Eighteenth Century, 1740–1789; III, Concert of Europe, 1814–1822; IV, Truncated Concert, 1822–1848; VI, Bismarckian Concert, 1871–1890; and IX, Postwar, 1945–1960. In these systems the amount of disturbance was at a minimum and the regulator, be it Concert, League, or informal consensus, was able to cope with actor disturbance. The elites were satisfied with the status quo, both within their own respective national units and in the international system in general. In their political views they were not strongly influenced by ideology except, perhaps, in system IX (1945–1960). Even in this system, however, the elites were willing for the most part to resolve problems by means short of war. Because of feelings of relative security, the elites were not tempted to mobilize resources or to use whatever means at their disposal to effect changes in the system. Although a state may have been willing to mobilize resources to improve its position with respect to another state, it was not prepared to disrupt the entire system. In a stable system the environmental restraints were usually sufficient to ease whatever disturbance occurred. Territorial ambitions, if they existed, were either transferred to colonial or imperial areas, usually outside Europe, or could be otherwise satisfied without affecting the vital interests of other states. Since a bipolar system characterized three of the four unstable periods, it may be inferred that multipolarity, or perhaps tripolarity is characteristic of a stable system, that is one in which there is an emphasis upon diplomacy and other conventional methods of negotiation and the goals of national units are limited. Although a state would not undertake to improve its own position at a cost of disrupting the entire system, it might attempt to do so at the expense of only one or two states, but even then not if it was necessary to inflict major losses upon other states.

The characteristics of an unstable system may be derived from a comparison of systems II, Revolutionary Imperium (1789–1814); V, Shattered Concert (1848–1871); VII, Imperialist Nationalism (1890–1918); and VIII, Totalitarian Militarism (1918–1945). In these systems, actor disturbance was high relative to the ability of the regulator to cope with it and the variety of means at the disposal of the regulator was minimal. The elites were dissatisfied with the status quo and harbored feelings of insecurity. They sought to improve their own internal and external positions with respect to the international system and other actors. Elites were able to mobilize resources through appeals to nationalism and ideology. Because of their feelings of insecurity, governing elites often could not resist the urge to resort to such appeals. Environmental constraints failed to play a role in restricting disturbances.

Rosecrance suggests that it is impossible to predict future events on the basis of a limited number of variables and that those variables with which he was concerned in this study may not be crucial in future international systems. His major conclusion is that there is a correlation between international instability and the domestic insecurity of elites[71]—a subject that will be treated further under macrocosmic theories of the causes of war. His work is notable for his effort both to develop and apply a systems framework to the analysis of materials which for the most part have been the preserve of the historian.

George Modelski

Other writers have set forth international system models whose parameters and patterns of interaction are carefully specified. George Modelski has developed two models designed to make possible a comparative analysis of international systems. The models represent, respectively, international systems at each end of a spectrum extending from agrarian to industrial societies. These models draw upon and combine elements of international systems from the past and present, and provide a framework in which processes of change or intermediate systems may be studied in relation to the extremes of the spectrum. In Modelski's view, Agraria corresponds to the 21 civilizations studied by Arnold Toynbee, whereas Industria has no comparable historical counterpart. Modelski's two models are "conceptual devices or constructs which draw upon and combine properties of international systems but do not in themselves necessarily represent any concrete international system."[72] Therefore an international system in the real world is likely to embody some of the characteristics of both models.

Industria, as an international system, has a large population. Its resources are more easily mobilized than those of Agraria. Society is largely homogeneous with politically conscious citizens and elites who are specialists. Because a person's position depends upon skill and achievement rather than ascriptive values, Industria is a meritocracy. In Industria, world organizations and improved communications networks provide information and contribute to the development of a world culture.[73] In Industria, power is based upon industrial organization. In contrast to Agraria, in Industria the political community is coexistent with the population. There is a level of integration of the masses of people into a common political form which is lacking in Agraria. An industrial society cannot tolerate recourse to war, as Agraria did, as a means of settling grievances because the destructive capabilities of Industria are such that war might result in the total destruction of the society. Because of the vast amount of destructive power at its disposal, bargaining, subtle coercion, and maneuvers, rather than recourse to war, must be used in pursuit of national goals.

Morton A. Kaplan

Of all writers Morton A. Kaplan has made the greatest effort to specify rules and patterns of interaction within models of alternative international systems. According to Kaplan, the classic statement of systems theory is to be found in the work of W. Ross Ashby on the human brain.[74] Although Ashby is concerned with the human brain and Kaplan with international politics, both are preoccupied in their respective fields with a system as a set of interrelated variables, distinguishable from its environment, and with the manner in which the set of variables maintains itself under the impact of disturbances from the environment.

Accordingly, Kaplan has constructed six models of hypothetical international systems which provide a theoretical framework within which hypotheses can be, and have been, generated and tested.[75] Within each model he has developed five sets of variables: essential rules, transformation rules, actor classificatory variables, capability variables, and information variables. The so-called essential rules are essential because they describe the behavior necessary to maintain equilibrium in the system.[76] The transformation rules specify the changes that take place as inputs other than those necessary for equilibrium to enter the system. The actor classificatory variables set forth the structural characteristics of actors. Capability variables indicate armament levels, technologies, and other elements of power available to actors. Information variables refer to the levels of communication within the system. The rules, to be specified in greater detail in a later examination of each of his models, refer to the kinds of actors, their capabilities, motivations, and goal orientations, their style of political behavior, and the structural characteristics of each of Kaplan's six systems—the balance of power, loose bipolar, tight bipolar, universal, hierarchical, and unit veto—which can be ranged along a scale of integrative activity. The unit veto system is least integrated and the hierarchical system most integrated.

In Kaplan's models, changes in the system are the result of changes in the value of the parameters or constants. He acknowledges that few, if any, existing international systems conform fully with any of his models of hypothetical systems. Nevertheless, he is prepared, so long as the theory set forth in the model explains behavior when "suitable adjustments are made for the parameters of the system," to continue to employ that model. The system has changed when a different theory, or systems model, is needed to account for its behavior. Thus the utility of Kaplan's models lies in the extent to which they permit the student to compare behavior within any given existing international system with one or another of the six models. Moreover, by specifying rules for system change, a step-level function (i.e., a system response to a disturbance input of such a nature as to transform the system itself), Kaplan claims to have built into his models a means of understanding how international systems are transformed.

Kaplan's balance of power system resembles the international system that realist writers such as Morgenthau describe.[77] It is distinguished by an international social system, but lacks a political subsystem, because it does not have regularized agencies and methods for making decisions concerning interests beyond those of the component national units. The balance of power system, like the European state system of the nineteenth century, has five major powers, or "essential actors," whose presence is crucial to the operation of the system.

> The balance of power system in its ideal form is a system in which any combination of actors within alliances is possible so long as no alliance gains a marked preponderance in capabilities. The system tends to be maintained by the fact that even should any nation desire to become predominant itself, it must, to protect its own interests, act to prevent any other nation from accomplishing such an objective. Like Adam Smith's "unseen hand" of competition, the international system is policed informally by self-interest, without the necessity of a political subsystem.[78]

The modal behavior of units is bound in Kaplan's rules for the balance of power system: (1) actors increase their capabilities, but negotiate with each other rather than fight; (2) actors fight rather than pass up an opportunity to increase their capabilities; (3) actors stop fighting rather than eliminate another essential actor; (4) actors oppose any coalition or single actor who threatens to assume a position of predominance within the system; (5) actors seek to constrain those actors who subscribe to supranational organizational principles; and (6) actors permit defeated or constrained essential actors to reenter the system as acceptable role partners, or bring a previously unessential actor within the essential actor category.[79]

The second of Kaplan's models, the loose bipolar, resembles in many respects the international system of the post-World War II period. This model includes major bloc actors (such as NATO and the Warsaw Pact); a leading national actor within each bloc (such as the United States and the Soviet Union); nonbloc national actors (such as India); and universal actors (such as the United Nations).

In its operation, the loose bipolar system reflects the internal organization of bloc actors. If both blocs are hierarchical, their membership becomes rigid, and only uncommitted states, by aligning themselves with one bloc or the other, change the existing alignments. If the blocs are not hierarchically organized, the loose bipolar system resembles the balance of power system, although there are fewer shifts in alignment.

Kaplan posits several rules for the loose bipolar system, including (1) blocs subscribing to directive hierarchical or mixed hierarchical integrating principles eliminate the rival bloc, negotiate rather than fight, fight minor wars rather than major wars, and fight major wars rather than fail to eliminate the rival bloc; (2) bloc actors increase their capabilities in relation to those of the opposing bloc; (3) bloc actors subscribing to nonhierarchical or nondirective hierarchical organizational principles negotiate rather than fight to increase capabilities, but refrain from initiating major wars for this purpose; (4) bloc actors engage in a major war rather than permit the rival bloc to gain preponderant strength; (5) bloc members subordinate the objectives of universal actors to the objectives of their bloc; and (6) universal actors reduce the incompatibility between blocs and mobilize nonbloc member national actors against cases of major deviation, such as resorting to force, by a bloc actor. (Kaplan does not specifically postulate a multipolar or multibloc world; this would fit logically into his balance of power system.)

The tight bipolar system, which is Kaplan's third model, is similar, in many respects, to the loose bipolar system, but it has important differences. The tight bipolar system has fewer types of actors. All actors must be aligned with one of the rival blocs; there is no room for neutrals. The structure of the blocs affects the stability of the system. If both bloc actors are nonhierarchically organized, the system will tend to be transformed to a loose bipolar system. The system is stable if both bloc actors are hierarchically organized. Within the system, integrating mechanisms are weak or nonexistent. In this model the rules are the same as the bloc-directed rules of the loose bipolar system.

The universal-international system, the fourth of Kaplan's models, could conceivably develop as a result of the extension of the functions of the universal actor found in the loose bipolar system. The universal-international system differs from other models thus far discussed in that it has as a subsystem a political system that can allocate prestige and rewards both to national actors and individuals according to their "specific achievements rather than because of special qualities they possess, such as race." The universal-international system possesses integrating mechanisms that perform judicial, political, economic, and administrative functions. It has the following rules: (1) all national actors attempt to increase their rewards and access to facilities; (2) all national actors attempt to increase the resources and productive base of the international system; (3) when rules (1) and (2) conflict, rule (1) is to be subordinated to (2), and if rule (1) threatens minimal standards of any national actor, it is subordinated to considerations involving the ascriptive base of the total society; (4) all actors use peaceful methods to obtain their objectives; and (5) individuals who have functions in organs of the international system make decisions in accordance with requirements of the international system.

In the universal-international system, value structures of the national actors are such that the international system is able to coordinate and integrate them. The international system possesses facilities and resources superior to those of any national actor system and is able to give hope of improvement to underdeveloped national actors. However, this system may be subject to a long period of instability, because it is unlikely initially to have succeeded in integrating the domestic values of the various national actors within a common system. There is the prospect that national actors may wish to change the system to hierarchical, bipolar, or balance of power systems because they may not wish to make the necessary changes in their political and social structures or prove unable to make the sacrifices necessary for this type of system to function effectively.[80]

Kaplan's fifth model, the hierarchical international system, may be either nondirective or directive.[81] It will operate directly upon individuals, since national actors will be territorial subdivisions of the international system, rather than independent political systems. Interest groups, rather than national units, are the primary actors. The system will be solidary, linking rewards and access to facilities to the system's criteria. If the hierarchical system is imposed by force upon a bipolar or universal system, it is likely to be a directive rather than a nondirective system. If the hierarchical system is formed as a result of world conquest by a national actor, rewards will be allocated according to ascriptive criteria such as the qualities of the actors, including race and color. If the system is formed under other conditions, rewards may be based upon achievement criteria, as in the case of the universal system. The hierarchical international system is characterized by great stability. Channels of communication facilitate central control, and render almost impossible any attempts by local regions to revolt or secede. Whatever minor changes are made in the distribution of rewards will be functional, rather than territorial. Since there will be no outside political system capable of aiding a localized revolt, once a hierarchical system is established it will become almost impossible to displace it.[82]

In Kaplan's sixth system, the unit veto, there are no universal actors. It is, Kaplan suggests, a Hobbesian system, in which "the interests of all were opposed—were, in fact, at war—but in which each actor responded to the negative golden rule of natural law by not doing to others what he would not have them do to him."[83] The only condition under which the unit veto system is possible is if all actors have weapons capable of destroying any other actor. Essentially, this system is one arising from complete, universal nuclear proliferation. Even if one actor attacks and destroys another actor, in so doing it may assure its own destruction. So long as national units are prepared to retaliate in case of attack, and their ability to do so forms a credible deterrent to attack by another national unit, the system is stabilized. There is a "stand off" in which the existing state of affairs is preserved. However, the system will be changed if any actor is successfully blackmailed. In this case the number of national units will be reduced. If one member successfully blackmails all other national units, the unit veto system will become a hierarchical system.

Kaplan readily admits that his six systems by no means exhaust the possibilities for useful model building for analytical purposes in international politics. Instead, they represent a spectrum from more loosely to more tightly organized international system models. Moreover, in his scheme national actors are classified according to structural categories: directive or nondirective systems, which in turn may be system dominant or subsystem dominant.

In each of his models Kaplan is concerned with (1) the organizational focus of decisions, including the nature of actors' objectives and the instruments available to attain them; (2) the allocation of rewards, including the extent to which they are allocated by the system or by the subsystem; (3) the alignment preferences of actors; (4) the scope and direction of political activity; and (5) the flexibility or adaptability of units in their behavior.

There have been limited efforts to use historical materials for the testing of propositions drawn from models of international systems. In one research endeavor, Kaplan's models were tested for formal logical consistency with the use of mathematical tools and the computer.[84] They were then compared with historical materials, such as the Chinese warlord system of the early twentieth century and the Italian city-state system of the fourteenth and fifteenth centuries. The author of a study of the Chinese warlord system found that this was "basically a 'balance of power' system operating under many unfavorable parameters." Moreover, this was a "balance of power system in which the actors either deliberately or unwittingly violated many of the essential behavioral rules that are necessary for the stability of such a system."[85] Among the conclusions of a study of the Italian city-state system were that, by and large, essential rules contained in the "balance of power" model were not violated; essential and even nonessential actors were preserved; the territorial capabilities of actors did not change greatly; equilibrium became both less static and less stable, and inevitably the system disintegrated.[86]

Utilizing an approach similar to events data, but drawing upon diplomatic history, rather than current events, Patrick J. McGowan and Robert M. Rood examined the rate of alliance formation in the period between 1814 and 1914 in order to test hypotheses drawn from Kaplan's balance of power model. Specifically, they hypothesized that "in a balance of power international system, a decline in the systemic rate of alliance formation precedes system changing events, such as general war."[87] They tested hypotheses concerning the formation of alliances as a stochastic process. "That is, in a balance of power system alliances occur from time to time, and these events over time are subject to probability laws because the past behavior of the alliance process has no influence on future behavior."[88] There was a tendency, in the nineteenth century European balance of power system, for alliances to be formed "quickly upon one another or with a lag of about three and one-half years." They note that "a clear cut decline in systems flexibility occurred after 1909, and that this period immediately preceded an event (World War I) that destroyed the European balance of power, perhaps forever."[89] They conclude that the data analyzed strongly supported Kaplan's balance of power model. The subject of how alliances relate to the amount of war in the international system is taken up in the following section and in Chapter 8.

Thus Kaplan's models, although less complex than the international system of the real world, are designed to facilitate comparison with the real world to contribute to a meaningful ordering of data, and to build theory at the macrolevel. Only two of them—the balance of power and the loose bipolar—can be clearly discerned in history. However the case can be made that a third model (the unit veto system) is partially validated in the contemporary role of the nuclear powers, while a fourth model (the universal-international system) exists in normative theory and in the aspirations of those scholars and practitioners, past and present, who seek to create such a global system.

THEORIES OF BIPOLARITY, MULTIPOLARITY, AND INTERNATIONAL STABILITY

The relationship between the distribution of power and the incidence of war has been the object of theorizing both in traditional and contemporary writings. Although Kaplan, in his models, has focused on "essential rules" for the operation of several international systems, other scholars, including Karl W. Deutsch, J. David Singer, Kenneth N. Waltz, and Richard N. Rosecrance, have theorized about the implications of multipolarity and bipolarity for the frequency and intensity of war. Deutsch and Singer contend that "as the system moves away from bipolarity toward multipolarity, the frequency of war should be expected to diminish."[90] They assume that coalitions of blocs of nations reduce the freedom of alliance members to interact with outside countries. The greater the number of actors who are not alliance members, the greater the number of possible partners for interaction in the international system. Although alliance membership minimizes both the range and intensity of conflict among those countries which are alliance members, the range and intensity of conflicts with actors outside the alliance are increased.

Although interaction among nations is as likely to be competitive as it is to be cooperative, the more limited the possibility for interaction, the greater the potential for instability. Deutsch and Singer assume that the international system is but a special case of the pluralism model, namely, that "one of the greatest threats to the stability of any impersonal social system is the shortage of alternative partners." Interaction with a great number of nations produces cross-cutting loyalties which induce hostility between any single dyad of nations.

Another hypothesis in support of a correlation between the number of actors and war is based on the "degree of attention that any nation in the system may allocate to all of the other nations or to possible coalitions of nations."[91] The greater the number of dyadic relationships, the less the amount of attention that an actor can give to any one dyadic relationship. If some minimal percentage of a nation's external attention is needed for "behavior tending toward armed conflict, and the increase in the number of independent actors diminishes the share that any nation can allocate to any other single actor, such an increase is likely to have a stabilizing effect upon the system."[92] Multipolarity is said to reduce the prospects for an arms race, since a country is likely to respond only to that part of the increase in armaments spending of a rival power that appears to be directed toward it.

SYSTEM STRUCTURE AND STABILITY

Although there is, as we have seen, little agreement among writers on this subject, some contend that a multipolar world is likely to be less stable than a bipolar system. With fewer important actors and greater certainty in military and political relationships, the prospects for misunderstandings and conflict are said to be less under conditions of bipolarity than in a multipolar world. Stanley Hoffmann, for example, sees the existence of the five uneven power centers, as hypothesized to exist in the early 1970s, to be not only undesirable, but also dangerous since the "balance of uncertainty" is increased and might lead to an arms race.[93] Another writer, Ronald Yalem, saw an emerging tripolar world (United States, Soviet Union, and China), in which there was likely to be a tendency for two powers to coalesce against the third. Because of the tripling of the number of bilateral interactions in comparison with the more simple interaction pattern in a bipolar world, and the additional patterns of potential conflict, there is a greater possibility for conflict in a tripolar world. Stability in such a system depends upon each state's preventing the emergence of a bipolar alignment against itself. Each must resist the temptation to form bipolar alignments against the third major power. "Without any 'balancer' of power to affect the inherent tendency of two of the principals to combine against the third, or a strong supranational actor to regulate tripolarity, the system is likely to be susceptible to continual instability."[94]

Empirical studies by Singer and Melvin Small yielded conclusions not fully in support of the hypothesis about bipolarity-multipolarity and the outbreak of war. Analyzing historical data for the period 1815 to 1945 for possible correlations between alliance aggregation and the onset of war, Singer and Small tested the following hypotheses: (1) the greater the number of alliance commitments in the system, the more war the system will experience; and (2) the closer the system is to bipolarity, the more war it will experience.[95]

For the entire period under examination, the hypothesis about alliance aggregation and the outbreak of war was not confirmed. In the nineteenth century, alliance aggregation and occurrence of war correlated inversely, whereas in the twentieth century the variables covaried. In addition, the authors discovered that regardless of "whether we measure amount of war by numbers of wars, the nation-months involved, or battle deaths incurred, alliance aggregation and bipolarity predict strongly away from war in the nineteenth century and even more strongly toward it in the twentieth."[96] In short, for the period 1815 to 1899, the evidence presented by Singer and Small failed to support the theory about bipolarity and conflict presented earlier by Deutsch and Singer.

Although such a study using aggregate data can show the existence of correlations, it cannot, as Singer and Small acknowledge, establish a causal relationship. Conceivably, a third variable, such as the perception of national decision-makers, is the causal factor which affects the other two variables. For example, leaders may "step up their alliance-building activities as they perceive the probability of war to be rising."[97]

Another study tested hypotheses about the balance of power for a much shorter period—1870 to 1881. Drawing upon international events data, specifically a coded compilation of significant diplomatic events drawn from diplomatic histories and coded, Brian Healy and Arthur Stein found that the alliances of the period—the Three Emperors' League of 1873 and the Dual Alliance of 1879— did not lead to an increase in cooperation among allies and an increase in conflict between allies and other states. In the case of the Three Emperors' League, Germany was the object of sharply increased hostility by one of her allies, Russia, and even by Austria. The authors conclude that there was a decrease in cooperation between members of the Three Emperors' League and outside states, although this decrease was less than that which occurred within the League itself. Similarly, the period following the formation of the Dual Alliance of 1879 between Germany and Austria was marked by a deterioration in relations between the two signatories, together with an improvement in relations with Russia, against which the Dual Alliance was directed.

These findings point to a modification of the Singer-Small hypothesis, as well as the proposition advanced by Arthur Lee Burns and others, that the alignment of two or more states with each other heightens the opposition of others and enhances the risk of war. Moreover, the formation of the Three Emperors League was followed by a decline in interactions among allies, from which Healy and Stein conclude that interactions between members of the League and outside states probably increased. But the findings of this study supported the proposition that there was a tendency toward equilibrium in this international system based on a multipolar balance of power, with the inference that "unbalanced relationships are more likely to be unstable than are balanced relationships," and "the tension caused by the unbalanced relationship induces a change in interaction behavior."[98]

There is little agreement among scholars about the relationship between multipolarity-bipolarity and international stability. In marked contrast to Deutsch and Singer, Kenneth Waltz argues that a bipolar international system, with its inherent disparity between the superpowers and the lesser states, is more stabilizing than a multipolar system. Having the capacity to inflict and control violence, the superpowers are "able both to moderate other's use of violence and to absorb possibly destabilizing changes that emanate from uses of violence that they do not or cannot control."[99] Both superpowers, following their instinct for self-preservation, continually seek to maintain a balance of power based upon a wide range of capabilities, including military and technological strength. Military power is most effective when it deters an attack. Hence Waltz sees utility in the maintenance of strength by each of two competing superpowers in a bipolar system, since states "supreme in their power have to use force less often."[100] According to Waltz, "Bipolarity is expressed as the reciprocal control of the two strongest states by each other out of their mutual antagonism . . . each is very sensitive to the gains of the other."[101]

Offering an alternative system, Richard N. Rosecrance is critical of both the Deutsch-Singer and Waltz models, respectively, of multipolarity and bipolarity, and argues instead for bimultipolarity. Criticizing Waltz's formulation of bipolarity, Rosecrance contends that a bipolar world in which the two superpowers are intensely and vitally interested in the outcome of all major international issues is essentially a zero sum game. Hence the motivation for expansion and the potential for conflict between the bloc leaders are said to be greater in a bipolar system than in a multipolar world.[102]

Although the intensity of conflict may be lower in a multipolar world than in a bipolar system, Rosecrance suggests that the frequency of conflict will be greater because of a greater diversity of interests and demands. "If a multipolar order limits the consequences of conflict, it can scarcely diminish their number. If a bipolar system involves a serious conflict between the two poles, it at least reduces or eliminates conflict elsewhere in the system."[103] Another criticism is that, while reducing the significance of any change in the power balance, multipolarity increases the uncertainty as to what the consequences will be. Thus it makes policy making complex and the achievement of stable results difficult.

The alternative system proposed by Rosecrance combines the positive features of bipolarity and multipolarity without their attendant liabilities. In bimultipolarity, "the two major states would act as regulators for conflict in the external areas; but multipolar states would act as mediators and buffers for conflict between the bipolar powers. In neither case would conflict be eliminated, but it might be held in check."[104] The bipolar nations, and in particular the superpowers, would seek to restrain each other from attaining predominance while acting together from a mutual interest in minimizing conflict or challenge in the multipolar region of the globe. The multipolar states, although having rivalries stemming from a diversity of national perspectives and interests, would have a common interest in resisting the ambitions of the bipolar powers. Therefore the probability of war would be lower in a bimultipolar system than in either a strictly bipolar or multipolar system. He concludes that the increase of multipolarity would enhance the prospects for détente between the superpowers, and thus for collaboration between them on the resolution of problems of a multipolar nature.

As an alternative to each of the foregoing models, Oran R. Young suggests the need for a model that emphasizes "the growing interpenetration of the global or systemwide axes of international politics on the one hand and several newly emerging but widely divergent regional areas or subsystems on the other hand."[105] Critical of the bipolar and multipolar models for their focus on essentially structural problems to the neglect of the dynamics of international systems, Young develops a "discontinuities model" which encompasses the concurrent influence of global and regional power processes in patterns that are strongly marked by elements of both congruence and discontinuity.[106] Young uses the concepts of congruence and discontinuity to refer to the degree to which "patterns of political interests and relationships of power are similar or dissimilar as between the global area and various regional areas and as between the different regional areas themselves."[107] Young's conception of "discontinuities" is similar to the model of a world of "multiple issue-systems" noted earlier.[108] The crisscrossing, overlap, and linkage phenomena entail acute boundary identification problems: Where does system X end and system Y begin?

No final answer can be given to such questions because system boundaries, like systems themselves, are imposed by analysts for particular research purposes and are constantly changing. Some actors, including the superpowers, and certain issues, such as communism, nationalism, and economic development, are relevant throughout the international system. Yet the regional subsystems of the international system have unique features and patterns of interaction. Young proposes a model in which the existence of discontinuities is emphasized. The discontinuities model is designed to generate useful insights about the variety and complexity of interpenetration among subsystems, the tradeoffs, and the possibilities for manipulation across subsystems, the problems of incompatibility of the actors with systemwide interests, and the relationships between various subsystems and the global patterns of international politics.

REGIONAL SUBSYSTEMS IN
THE INTERNATIONAL SYSTEM

As part of the systems perspective in international relations theory, the interest of scholars in delineating subsystems has increased substantially in the past decade. It has been noted elsewhere in this chapter and in Chapter 10 that systems theory and integration theory have been closely associated in the literature of international relations theory. Because much of the theorizing about integration has been focused on the regional level, it follows that integration studies and the regional subsystem have also been linked in the writings of scholars, especially since the early 1960s. As Michael Banks noted in 1969, "A number of attempts have been made to approach regional subsystems from the traditionally ideographic standpoint of area studies, but in a way which employs at least some of the more cogent of the systems' insights into the patterns of world politics."[109] According to Louis Cantori and Steven Spiegel[110] the regional subsystem consists of ". . . one state, or of two or more proximate and interacting states which have some common ethnic, linguistic, cultural, social, and historical bonds, and whose sense of identity is sometimes increased by the actions and attitudes of states external to the system." The systems are delineated by four "pattern variables": (1) the nature and level of cohesion, or the "degree of similarity or complementarity in the properties of the political entities being considered and the degree of interaction between these units"; (2) the nature of communications within the region; (3) the level of power in the subsystem—with power defined as the "present and potential ability and the willingness of one nation to alter the internal decision-making processes of other countries in accordance with its own policies"; and (4) the structure of relations within the region.[111] In order to take account of overlap between subsystems and boundary diffuseness in regional membership, it is necessary, as the authors suggest, to divide each subsystem into first, a core sector, or principal focus of international politics within a given region; second, a peripheral sector, including states that play a role in the political affairs of the region, but which are separated from the core as a result of social, political, economic, organizational, or other factors; and third, an intrusive system, which takes account of external powers whose participation in the subsystem is important.

Another scholar, William R. Thompson, has reviewed and synthesized the literature of international subsystems. According to Thompson, the attributes set forth in the burgeoning literature of international subsystems include: proximity of actors to each other; patterns of relations or interactions exhibiting regularity; intrarelatedness, with a change in one part of the subsystem affecting other parts; internal and external recognition as distinctive units of power that are relatively inferior to those of the dominant system; the effects of change in the dominant system being greater upon the subsystem than vice versa; a certain (unspecified) degree of shared linguistic, cultural, historical, social, or ethnic bonds; a relatively high level of integration, including perhaps explicit institutional relations; intrasystem actions that are predominant over external influences; distinctive military forces, a form of regional equilibrium, and a common level of development.[112] Thus one can say that the level of consensus on the attributes of a subsystem is low.

Thompson concludes that: "Strictly speaking, regional subsystems need not be geographical regions per se. Rather, the subsystems consist of the interactions of national elites, not the physical entities of political units, of which interactions are observed to have more or less regional boundaries. In this sense, it should only be necessary to employ the minimal regional criterion—namely, general proximity."[113] From his analysis, the author infers that the "necessary and sufficient conditions for a regional subsystem include: regularity and intensity of interactions so that a change in one part affects other parts; the actors are generally proximate; there is internal and external recognition of the subsystem as distinctive; and there are at least two, and probably more, actors in the subsystems."[114]

Utilizing such criteria, it is possible to identify many subsystems, although their boundaries may differ, for different purposes. From an institutional perspective, we may identify the European Economic Community as a subsystem. From a geographic and cultural perspective, we may view Western Europe as yet another subsystem. The existence of a state such as Great Britain, France, or Germany within each of these subsystems provides a series of inputs from the international environment into its foreign policy. Elsewhere in the world, we could develop a series of regional subsystems that help to shape the foreign policies of the states which are core or peripheral members, or which are located outside the subsystem.

CRITIQUES OF SYSTEMS THEORY

Although systems theory has become one of the major approaches to the study of politics, it has also been the object of major criticism. According to Harold and Margaret Sprout, some systems theorists (of whom they cite McClelland as an example) "explicitly introduce the 'organismic' concept (reminiscent of Hegelian doctrine) into their discussions of the state and the international system." Although they acknowledge that "most systems theorists would stop far short of claiming that social and biological structures and functions are isomorphic in any but a purely metaphysical sense," the Sprouts question "whether one derives clearer and richer insights into the operations of political organizations by endowing them even metaphorically with pseudobiological structures and pseudopsychological functions."[115] The Sprouts caution against the reification of abstractions.

Another critic, Stanley Hoffmann, contends that systems theory does not provide a framework for achieving predictability. By combining the ideal of a deductive science with the desire to achieve predictability, Hoffmann claims that systems theorists become tautological.

> If one builds a model of the behavior of certain groups (for instance, nations) based on a set of hypotheses about the variables which are supposed

to determine the behavior of the groups, if, further, some of these hypotheses are highly questionable, and if, finally, the model rests on the assumption that these groups are interchangeable, then the 'predictions' about the groups' behavior will be a mere restatement in the future tense of the original hypotheses, and thus comprise a totally arbitrary set of propositions about the groups concerned. Such is the danger of 'formal models of imaginary worlds, not generalizations about the real world.' It is the triumph of form over substance.[116]

In Hoffmann's critique is the contention that systems theorists use inappropriate techniques borrowed from other disciplines such as sociology, economics, cybernetics, biology, and astronomy. At the same time, Hoffmann faults models which posit specific patterns of interaction, such as those of Kaplan and Modelski, for being deficient in empirical referents.

> The construction of purely abstract hypotheses based on a small number of axioms, from which a number of propositions are deduced, either is a strange form of parlor game, too remote from reality to be 'testable,' or else rests on postulates about the behavior of the included variables, which are either too arbitrary or too general: the choice is between perversion and platitude.[117]

Hoffmann contends that systems models, because they aim at a high level of generalization and use tools from other disciplines, do not "capture the stuff of politics." The emphasis of many systems models on communications theory reduces individuals and societies to communications systems, to the relative neglect of the substance of the messages that these networks carry. Stated differently, the measurement of the *quantity* of transactions, or interactions, without reference to the *qualitative* dimension, is inadequate. What the transactions, or interactions, contain is likely to be as important, and probably more important, than their number. Moreover, the tendency to reduce a theory to as few hypotheses as possible "and to prefer a single hypothesis to a complex one, because such simplicity makes a theory easier to use even though it might imply sheer formalism and the tendency to reduce politics to what it is not, entails a loss of such vital elements as institutions, culture, and the action of individuals as autonomous variables rather than social atoms."[118]

In response to Hoffmann's critique, it may be suggested that proponents of systems theory, because they have been preoccupied with the development of macrotheory, have not concerned themselves with many substantive problems, the study of institutions, or the "stuff of politics." However, this is not to conclude that systems theorists necessarily hold that such studies have no place in the field of international relations. For the quantitative study of politics, systems theory has presented problems of operationalization. It is often difficult to develop operational indicators for verifying concepts contained in systems theory, although events data studies have represented an important effort since the 1960s to validate propositions about interaction between and among states, as discussed earlier in this chapter. Moreover, there is disagreement about the extent to which, in the relative absence of empirical studies using hypotheses from systems theory, it is possible to develop criteria of significance in order to judge isomorphic relationships.

Other writers such as Jerone Stephens and George Modelski, both cited earlier in this chapter, are critical of systems theory. Stephens calls for research on the requisites that international systems must fulfill and the ranges within which they can be fulfilled without transforming the system. He maintains that international relations scholars must avoid a further proliferation of works that merely advocate systems theory and systems analysis in favor of empirical studies of the requisites of international systems. "We have had enough heuristic formulations already to last most students of politics a lifetime, and it is now time to ask for results of this heuristic deluge, and, if none are forthcoming, to move on to other ways of studying politics."[119] Similarly, George Modelski believes that systems theory has been "devoid of significant insights" in international relations. "System is a concept of high generality and what is true of all systems, while relevant to world politics, is usually not specific enough to add greatly to our appreciation of that narrowly circumscribed field. What is more, for some practitioners of what has come to be known as systems theory, the mere utterance and frequent repetition of the magic term *system* has become a ritual act of special potency, expected to confer upon the utterer instant admission not only to the circle of the initiated, but also to a sesame of political wisdom." Modelski concludes "that the usefulness of a specific systems approach to international relations may now be approaching its end, despite the fact that the influence expected by it will undoubtedly prove to have been a lasting one."[120] In the same vein, Steven J. Brams has stated: "Verbal formulations abound of the functions systems perform, but notably lacking in most of these systems paradigms is what empirical referents the concepts employed have that would allow propositions linking them to be tested empirically."[121]

Because of its emphasis upon notions of stability, equilibrium, steady-state, and pattern maintenance, systems theory has been criticized for its alleged ideological bias in favor of the status quo, although equilibrium theory does not necessarily connote a bias against change. This criticism has been leveled against structural-functionalism in particular, although in response Robert K. Merton has argued that its proponents could be accused of having a bias in favor of change because of the essentially mechanistic nature of structural-functional analysis and its susceptibility, therefore, to social engineering.[122]

Systemic studies have been faulted for having failed allegedly either to specify or to clarify adequately their epistemological bases. Without such preliminary investigation, writers on systems theory have turned at an early stage of their work to substantive statements about power and stability without having set forth definitions or clearly specified variables. According to Oran Young, such a tendency to dispense with preliminaries "leads to obscurity with regard to conceptual choices" and to ambiguities and confusion within the works of single writers.[123] For example, there is confusion about the distinction between concrete and analytical constructs, the relevance of concepts such as environment, and the use of organismic analogies. There is disagreement among students of systems theory about deductive and inductive studies, quantitative techniques for the manipulation of data, and the relative merits of comparative analyses and historical studies.[124] Thus the problems of definition, scope, and method which divide proponents of systems theory resemble those which beset the study of international relations and political science. Because of such discord among students of systems theory, its contribution to the methodological and conceptual advances of international relations is uncertain. But undoubtedly systems theory will continue to attract interest until more adequate and promising approaches are found for the development of macrolevel theory.

Notes

1. Robert J. Lieber, *Theory and World Politics* (Cambridge: Winthrop, 1972), p. 123. See also Oran R. Young, *Systems of Political Science* (Englewood Cliffs, N.J.: Prentice-Hall, 1968), p. 19; Michael Banks, "Systems Analysis and the Study of Regions," *International Studies Quarterly*, 13, No. 4 (December 1969), 345–350.
2. Anatol Rapoport, "Foreword," Walter Buckley, ed., in *Modern Systems Research for the Behavioral Scientists* (Chicago: Aldine, 1968), p. xvii. (Italics added in text.) See also James E. Dougherty, "The Study of the Global System," in James N. Rosenau, Kenneth W. Thompson, and Gavin Boyd, eds., *World Politics: An Introduction* (New York: The Free Press, 1976), pp. 597–623.
3. J. W. Burton, *Systems, States, Diplomacy and Rules* (Cambridge: Cambridge University Press, 1968), p. 6.
4. Ibid., p. 14.
5. See George Modelski, "The Promise of Geocentric Politics," *World Politics*, XXII, No. 4 (July 1970), 633. According to Modelski: "The mounting problems of the earth as a whole no longer are amenable to attack with the ethnocentric conceptual equipment inherited from the nineteenth century. Although this holds true for all the social sciences and although they all need a reorientation in the direction of geocentricity, nowhere is the need more compelling than it is in political science, still basically the science of the state, and in international relations, still under the spell of the conventional diplomatic wisdom of Metternich and Bismarck," p. 635.
6. J. David Singer, *A General Systems Taxonomy for Political Science* (New York: General Learning Press, 1971), p. 9.
7. Ernest B. Haas, "On Systems and International Regimes." *World Politics*, XXVII, No. 2 (January 1975), p. 150.

8. Robert O. Keohane and Joseph S. Nye, *Power and Interdependence: World Politics in Transition* (Boston: Little, Brown, 1977), pp. 9–10.
9. Ibid., p. 12.
10. Ibid., p. 13.
11. Andrew M. Scott, "The Logic of International Interaction," *International Studies Quarterly,* 21, No. 3 (September 1977).
12. According to Scott, they consist of environmental and resource requisites, system flow requisites (materials, people, energy, technology, information), trained personnel and their services; and control and guidance requisites. "The Logic of International Interaction," *International Studies Quarterly,* 21, No. 3 (September 1977), 445.
13. Edward W. Morse, *Modernization and the Transformation of International Relations* (New York: The Free Press, 1976), p. 14.
14. Ibid., p. 130.
15. Hayward R. Alker, Jr., "A Methodology for Design Research on Interdependence Alternatives," *International Organization,* 31, No. 1 (Winter 1977), 31.
16. Richard Rosecrance and Arthur Stein, "Interdependence: Myth or Reality?", *World Politics,* XXVI, No. 1 (October 1973), 2.
17. Ibid., p. 21.
18. Hobbes defines systems as follows: "By systems I understand any numbers of men joined in one interest or one business of which some are regular and some irregular." Thomas Hobbes, *Leviathan,* Introduction by Michael Oakeshott (Oxford: Basil Blackwell, 1946), p. 146.
19. Ludwig von Bertalanffy, "General Systems Theory," in *General Systems,* I (1956), pp. 1–10; reprinted in J. David Singer, ed., *Human Behavior and International Politics: Contributions from the Social-Psychological Sciences* (Chicago: Rand McNally, 1965), p. 21. See also Roy R. Grinker, ed., *Toward a Unified Theory of Human Behavior* (New York: Basic Books, 1956).
20. Anatol Rapoport, op. cit., p. xxi.
21. J. David Singer, op. cit., p. 21. Bertalanffy has suggested that a "system" implies any arrangement or combination of parts or elements in a whole which may apply to a cell, a human being, or a society. "General Systems Theory: A New Approach to Unity of Science," *Human Biology,* XXIII (1951), 302–304.
22. Isomorphism may be defined as "a one-to-one correspondence between objects in different systems which preserves the relationship between the objects." A. Hall and R. Fagen, "Definition of a System," *General Systems,* I (1956), 18.
23. Ibid., p. 22. (Italics in original.)
24. Peter Nettl, "The Concept of Systems in Political Science," *Political Studies,* 14 (September 1966), 305–338.
25. Jerone Stephens, "An Appraisal of Some System Approaches in the Study of International Systems," *International Studies Quarterly,* 16, No. 3 (September 1972), 328.
26. See, for example, Andrew M. Scott, *The Functioning of the International System* (New York: Macmillan, 1967), p. 27.
27. Kenneth E. Boulding, *The Image: Knowledge in Life and Society* (Ann Arbor: University of Michigan Press, 1956), p. 8; "Political Implications of General Systems Research," *General Systems Yearbook,* VI (1961), 1–7. For a treatment of image theory and international conflict, see Chapter 7, pp. 282–284.
28. Kenneth E. Boulding, *Beyond Economics* (Ann Arbor: University of Michigan Press, 1968), p. 83.
29. Talcott Parsons and Edward A. Shils, eds., *Toward a General Theory of Action* (New York: Harper & Row [Torchbooks]), p. 53.
30. Parsons defines a social system as a "system of interaction of a plurality of actors,

in which the action is oriented by rules which are complexes of complementary expectations concerning roles and sanctions. *As a system,* it has determinate internal organization and determinate patterns of structural change. It has, furthermore, as a system, a variety of mechanisms of adaptation to changes in the external environment. These mechanisms function to create one of the important properties of a system, namely, a tendency to maintain boundaries. A total social system which, for practical purposes, may be treated as self-sufficient—which, in other words, contains within approximately the boundaries defined by membership all the functional mechanisms required for its maintenance as a system—is here called a *society.*" (Italics in original.) Parsons and Shils, ibid., pp. 195–196.

31. Talcott Parsons, "An Outline of the Social System," in Talcott Parsons, Edward A. Shils, Kaspar Naegele, and Jesse R. Pitts, eds., in *Theories of Society* (New York: The Free Press, 1961), p. 37.
32. Talcott Parsons and J. Edward Shils, *Toward a General Theory of Action,* op. cit., p. 107. Parsons defines "process" as "any mode in which a given state of a system or a part of a system changes into another state," *The Social System,* op. cit., p. 201.
33. According to Parsons, the traditional focus of political science has been on such concrete phenomena as government and constitutions rather than on conceptual schemes such as system. Classical political theory has consisted primarily of the normative and philosophical problems of government instead of empirical analysis of its processes and determinants. Parsons ackowledges that government, which is "one of the most strategically important processes and foci of differentiated structures within social systems," forms therefore one of the most crucial disciplines of the social sciences. But Parsons calls for a shift in focus of the study of political science from the concrete phenomena of government to a more sharply theoretical and empirical emphasis. Ibid., p. 29.
34. Talcott Parsons, "Order and Community in the International Social System," in James N. Rosenau, ed., *International Politics and Foreign Policy* (New York: The Free Press 1961), pp. 120–121. For the implications of Parsons' work for sociological theories of conflict, see Chapter 8 Note 1, pp. 355–356.
35. Talcott Parsons, *Sociological Theory and Modern Society* (New York: The Free Press, 1967), pp. 467–488.
36. Gabriel Almond, "Introduction," Gabriel Almond and James S. Coleman, eds., *The Politics of the Developing Areas* (Princeton: Princeton University Press, 1960), p. 7. See also Gabriel A. Almond and G. Bingham Powell, Jr., *Comparative Politics: A Developmental Approach* (Boston: Little, Brown, 1966), especially chap. 2.
37. Karl W. Deutsch, *The Nerves of Government* (New York: The Free Press, 1964), pp. 250-254.
38. David Easton, *A Framework for Political Analysis* (Englewood Cliffs, N.J.: Prentice-Hall, 1965), p. 25.
39. Ibid., p. 50.
40. Herbert J. Spiro, *World Politics: The Global System* (Homewood, Ill.: Dorsey, 1966), p. 51. See also the review article by George Modelski, "The Promise of Geocentric Politics," *World Politics,* 22, No. 4 (July 1970), 617–635.
41. Karl W. Deutsch, op. cit., pp. 248–249.
42. David Easton, *A Systems Analysis of Political Life* (New York: Wiley 1965), pp. 284–285, 484–488. See also N. B. Nicholson and P. A. Reynolds, "General Systems, the International System and the Eastonian Analysis," *Political Studies,* XV, No. 1 (1967), 12–31.
43. Herbert J. Spiro, op. cit., p. 51.
44. Ibid.

45. See Robert K. Merton, *Social Theory and Social Structure* (New York: The Free Press, 1957).
46. Marion J. Levy, Jr., "Functional Analysis," *International Encyclopedia of Social Sciences* (New York: Macmillan and The Free Press, 1968), VI, 23.
47. Ibid.
48. Robert K. Merton, op. cit., p. 51. In addition, Merton distinguishes between manifest and latent functions. Manifest are those whose patterns produce consequences which are both intended and recognized by the participants. Latent functions consist of patterns whose results are unintended and unrecognized by participants.
49. See A. James Gregor, "Political Science and the Uses of Functional Analysis," *American Political Science Review*, LXII (June 1968), 434–435. Even though the point is not central to international theory, the student should be aware of the important distinction drawn in recent years by scholars of comparative politics between static or equilibrium models of the system with dynamic or developmental models. See Gabriel A. Almond, "A Developmental Approach to Political Systems," *World Politics*, XVII (January 1965), 183–214.
50. Raymond Tanter, "International Systems and Foreign Policy Approaches: Implications for Conflict Modeling and Management," in Raymond Tanter and Richard A. Ullman, eds., *Theory and Policy in International Relations* (Princeton: Princeton University Press, 1972), p. 8.
51. James Rosenau has defined "linkage" as "any recurrent sequence of behavior that originates in one system and is reacted to in another." James N. Rosenau, "Toward the Study of National-International Linkages," in James N. Rosenau, ed., *Linkage Politics* (New York: The Free Press, 1969), p. 45.
52. Morton A. Kaplan, *System and Process in International Politics* (New York: Wiley, 1962), p. 4.
53. Charles A. McClelland, "System Theory and Human Conflict," in Elton B. McNeil, ed., *The Nature of Human Conflict* (Englewood Cliffs, N.J.: Prentice-Hall, 1965), p. 258.
54. George Modelski, "Agraria and Industria: Two Models of the International Systems," in Klaus Knorr and Sidney Verba, eds., *The International System: Theoretical Essays* (Princeton: Princeton University Press, 1961), pp. 121–122.
55. Richard N. Rosecrance, *Action and Reaction in World Politics* (Boston: Little, Brown, 1963), pp. 220–221.
56. Morton A. Kaplan, op. cit., p. xii.
57. Richard Rosecrance, op. cit., p. 267.
58. Charles A. McClelland, "Systems History in International Relations: Some Perspectives for Empirical Research and Theory," *General Systems, Yearbook of the Society for General Systems Research*, III (1958), 221–247.
59. Donald E. Lampert, Lawrence S. Falkowski, and Richard W. Mansbach, "Is There an International System?", *International Studies Quarterly*, 22, No. 1 (March 1978), 146.
60. According to Oran Young, "membership (i.e., concrete) systems are those whose basic components are human beings and that can therefore be thought of as collections of individuals. Analytic systems, on the other hand, are abstractions that focus on selected elements of human behavior. In this context we may distinguish a wide range of types of analytic systems such as political, economic, or religious systems." *Systems of Political Science* (Englewood Cliffs, N.J.: Prentice Hall, 1968), pp. 37–38.
    Haas writes: "Systems theories can be divided into deterministic and heuristic constructs. Determinists see the components as relatively unchangeable and arrange them in an eternal preprogrammed dance; the rules of the dance may be unknown to the actors and are specified by the theorist. The recurrent patterns dis-

covered by him constitute a superlogic which predicts the future state of the system. Deterministic systems are 'concrete' in the sense that their designers believe them to be real; such systems *are* the reality out there. Certainty about them facilitates prescription. Heuristic constructs follow the Durkheim-Weber pattern. They are analytic rather than concrete because they do not profess to represent the real world faithfully and accurately, but select for intensive investigation certain features deliberately isolated by the theorist was presumptively crucial in explaining a variety of events or trends." Ernst B. Haas, "On Systems and International Regimes," *World Politics*, XXVII, No. 2 (January 1975), 151–152.

61. See J. David Singer, "The Level-of-Analysis Problem in International Relations," in Klaus Knorr and Sidney Verba, eds., *The International System: Theoretical Essays* (Princeton: Princeton University Press, 1961), pp. 77–92. See *International Studies Quarterly* (special issue on international subsystems), XIII (December 1969).

62. For studies on international subsystems, see Michael Brecher, *The States of Asia: A Political Analysis* (New York: Oxford University Press, 1963), pp. 88–111; Leon N. Lindberg, "The European Community as a Political System" *Journal of Common Market Studies*, V (June 1967), 348–387; Karl Kaiser, "The U.S. and EEC in the Atlantic System: The Problem of Theory," in ibid., pp. 388–425; Stanley Hoffmann, "Discord in Community: The North Atlantic Area as a Partial International System;" in Francis O. Wilcox and H. Field Haviland, Jr., eds., *The Atlantic Community: Progress and Prospects* (New York: Praeger, 1963), pp. 3–31; see *International Studies Quarterly* (special issue on international subsystems), XIII (December 1969).

63. Charles A. McClelland, *Theory and the International System* (New York: Macmillan, 1966), p. 90.

64. Charles A. McClelland, "The Acute International Crisis," in Knorr and Verba, eds., op. cit., p.194.

65. Charles A. McClelland, "The Acute International Crisis," in ibid., p. 194. McClelland's analysis suggests the possibility that in an acute international crisis the intensification of communication which accompanies such a phenomenon might give rise to a condition of "system overload."

66. Charles A. McClelland, "Access to Berlin: The Quantity and Variety of Events, 1948–1963," in J. David Singer, ed., *Quantitative International Politics: Insights and Evidence* (New York: The Free Press, 1968), pp. 160–161.

67. Charles A. McClelland, "The Anticipation of International Crises: Prospects for Theory and Research" *International Studies Quarterly*, 21, No. 1 (March 1977), 35. Other contributions to this special issue on "International Crisis: Progress and Prospects for Applied Forecasting and Management," Robert A. Young, ed., include: Stephen J. Andriole and Robert A. Young, "Toward the Development of an Integrated Crisis Warning System," pp. 107–151; Thomas G. Belden, "Indications, Warning, and Crisis Operations," pp. 181–199; and Richard W. Parker, "An Examination of Basic and Applied International Crisis Research," pp. 225–247. For other studies utilizing events data, see Charles A. McClelland and G. D. Hoggard, "Conflict Patterns in the Interactions Among Nations," in J. N. Rosenau, ed., *International Politics and Foreign Policy* (New York: The Free Press, 1969), p. 713. See also Edward Azar, Richard Brody, and Charles A. McClelland, *International Events Interaction: Some Research Considerations* (Beverly Hills, Calif.: Sage Professional Papers, 1972); Edward E. Azar, *Probe for Peace: Small-State Hostilities* (Minneapolis: Burgess, 1973), especially pp. 45–73; Charles A. McClelland, "Access to Berlin: The Quantity and Variety of Events, 1948–1963," in J. David Singer, ed., *Quantitative International Politics* (New York: The Free Press, 1968), pp. 159–186. See also Jonathan Wilkenfeld, ed., *Conflict Behavior and Linkage*

Politics (New York: McKay, 1973); Edward Azar, "Analysis of International Events," *Peace Research Reviews*, 4, No. 1 (1970); Charles F. Hermann, "What Is a Foreign Policy Event?", pp. 295–321, in Wolfram R. Hanrieder, ed., *Comparative Foreign Policy*; P. M. Burgess and R. W. Lawton, *Indicators of International Behavior: An Assessment of Events Data Research*, Sage Professional Paper in International Studies 02–010 (Beverly Hills, Calif. and London: Sage Publications, 1972); Charles W. Kegley, Jr., G. A. Raymond, R. M. Rood, and R. A. Skinner, eds., *International Events and the Comparative Analysis of Foreign Policy* (Columbia: University of South Carolina Press, 1975); and James N. Rosenau, ed., *In Search of Global Patterns* (New York: The Free Press, 1976).

68. The findings of such research conducted between 1961 and 1972 are summarized succinctly by Sophia Peterson; "Research on Research: Events Dates Studies, 1961–1972, pp. 263–309, in Patrick J. McGowan ed., *Sage International Yearbook of Foreign Policy Studies*, vol. 3 (Beverly Hills, Calif.: Sage Publications, 1975). This volume together with volumes 1 and 2 in the same series, also edited by Patrick McGowan, contain numerous other chapters reporting on research using events data.

69. Richard Rosecrance lists past international systems as follows: (1) Eighteenth Century, 1740–1789; (2) Revolutionary Imperium, 1789–1814; (3) Concert of Europe, 1814–1822; (4) Truncated Concert; 1822–1848; (5) Shattered Concert, 1848–1871; (6) Bismarckian Concert, 1871–1890; (7) Imperialist Nationalism, 1890–1918; (8) Totalitarian Militarism, 1918–1945; (9) Postwar, 1945–1960.

70. Richard Rosecrance, op. cit., pp. 280–296.

71. Ibid., p. 304.

72. "Agraria and Industria: Two Models of the International System," In Knorr and Verba, eds., op. cit., p. 124. For an effort to develop a similar typology in the field of public administration, see Fred W. Riggs, "Agraria and Industria: Toward a Typology of Comparative Administration," in William J. Siffin, ed., *Toward the Comparative Study of Public Administration* (Bloomington: Indiana University Press, 1957), pp. 23–116.

73. George Modelski, op. cit., pp. 138–139.

74. W. Ross Ashby, *Design for a Brain* (New York: Wiley, 1952). Kaplan makes this assertion in "Systems Theory," James C. Charlesworth, ed., *Contemporary Political Analysis* (New York: The Free Press, 1967), p. 150.

75. According to Kaplan, "The conception that underlies *System and Process* is fairly simple. If the number, type, and behavior of nations differ over time, and if their military capabilities, their economic assets, and their information also vary over time, then there is some likely interconnection between these elements such that different structural and behavioral systems can be discerned to operate at different periods of history. This conception may turn out to be incorrect, but it does not seem an unreasonable basis for an investigation of the subject matter. To conduct such an investigation requires systematic hypotheses concerning the nature of the connections of the variables. Only after these are made can past history be examined in a way that illuminates the hypotheses. Otherwise the investigator has no criteria on the basis of which he can pick and choose from among the infinite reservoir of facts available to him. These initial hypotheses indicate the areas of facts which have the greatest importance for this type of investigation; presumably if the hypotheses are wrong, this will become reasonably evident in the course of attempting to use them." Morton A. Kaplan, "The New Great Debate: Traditionalism vs. Science in International Relations," *World Politics*, XX (October 1967), 8.

76. According to Kaplan, "The models are not equilibrium models in the Parsonian sense. Thus they are not static but respond to change, when it is within specified limits, by maintaining or restoring system equilibrium. Equilibrium does not have

an explanatory function within such systems. Rather it is the equilibrium that is to be explained; and the model itself constitutes the explanation by indicating the mechanisms that restore or maintain equilibrium." Morton A. Kaplan, "The Systems Approach to International Politics," in Morton A. Kaplan, ed., *New Approaches to International Relations* (New York: St. Martin's, 1968), p. 388.

77. Hans J. Morgenthau, *Politics Among Nations*, 5th ed. rev., (New York: Knopf, 1978), pp. 173–228.

78. Morton A. Kaplan, "Some Problems of International Systems Research," in *International Political Communities: An Anthology* (Garden City, L.I.: Doubleday, 1966), p. 478.

79. Morton A. Kaplan, *System and Process in International Politics*, op. cit., pp. 22–23.

80. Ibid., pp. 45–58.

81. According to Kaplan, "The nondirective international system functions according to political rules generally operative in democracies. The directive hierarchical system is authoritarian in character." Ibid., p. 48.

82. Ibid., pp. 49-50.

83. Ibid., p. 50.

84. See Donald L. Reinken, "Computer Explorations of the 'Balance of Power': A Progress Report," in Morton A. Kaplan, ed., *New Approaches to International Relations*, op. cit., pp. 459–481.

85. Hsi-Sheng Chi, "The Chinese Warlord System as an International System." Ibid., p. 424.

86. Winfried Franke, "The Italian City-State System as an International System." Ibid., p. 449.

87. Patrick J. McGowan and Robert M. Rood "Alliance Behavior in Balance of Power Systems: Applying a Poisson Model to Nineteenth Century Europe," *American Political Science Review* LXIX, No. 3 (September 1975), 862. The authors note that Poisson sampling, as utilized in their study, "consists of observing the process over a predetermined amount of time, length, or other dimensions, and counting the number of events which occur. . . ." Quoted from Howard Raiffa and Robert Schlaifer, *Applied Statistical Decision Theory* (Cambridge: M.I.T. Press, 1961), p. 283.

88. Ibid., p. 861.

89. Ibid., p. 869.

90. Karl W. Deutsch and J. David Singer, "Multipolar Power Systems and International Stability," *World Politics*, XVI (April 1964), 390. For an earlier theoretical analysis of multipolarity and international stability, see Arthur Lee Burns, "From Balance to Deterrence: A Theoretical Analysis," *World Politics*, IX (July 1957), 494–529. Burns examines several propositions, including the following: The closer the alliance between any two or more Powers, the greater the increase of opposition or "pressure" (other things being equal) between any one of the two and any third Power or group of Powers; other things being equal, considerations of long-run security determine an optimum degree of short-run security; any system embodying the balance of power has some intrinsic tendency to diminish the number of its constituent Powers or blocs, and no intrinsic tendency to increase that number; a deterrent state or system will emerge from a power-balancing system whenever the development of military technology makes (1) the physical destruction of all of an opponent's forces impossible and (2) the physical destruction of the economy very easy.

91. Karl Deutsch and J. David Singer, op. cit., p.392.

92. Ibid., p. 400.

93. Stanley Hoffmann, "Weighing the Balance of Power," *Foreign Affairs*, 59 (July 1972), 618–643.

94. Ronald Yalem, "Tripolarity and the International System," ORBIS (Winter 1972), 1055.

95. International wars (in which at least one participant on each side is an independent and sovereign member of the international system) with total battle-connected deaths of more than 1000 were included in the data. To "operationalize" the dependent variable, the duration and magnitude of each war were measured by "the nation-months-of-war measure; the sum of the months which all nations individually experienced as participants in the war." Furthermore, a distinction was made between major and minor powers, and their wars and nation-months calculated separately.

    To operationalize and quantify this independent variable, namely, "the extent to which alliance commitments reduced the interaction opportunities" two dimensions were considered: (1) the nature of the obligation (whether it was a defense pact, neutrality pact, or entente); and (2) the nature of the signatories' power status (whether it was between two major, two minor, or one major and one minor power).

    After the alliances were discovered and classified, the data on each type of alliance for each year were converted into a percentage figure as follows: (1) percent of all in any alliance; (2) percent of all in defense pact; (3) percent of majors in any alliance; (4) percent of majors in defense pact; and (5) percent of majors in any alliance with minor. J. David Singer and Melvin Small, "Alliance Aggregation and the Onset of War," in J. David Singer, ed., *Quantitative International Politics* (New York: The Free Press, 1968), pp. 247–286.

96. Ibid., p. 283.

97. Ibid., p. 284.

98. Brian Healy and Arthur Stein, "The Balance of Power in International History: Theory and Reality," *The Journal of Conflict Resolution*, XVII, No. 1 (March 1973), 57.

99. Kenneth N. Waltz, "International Structure, National Force, and the Balance of World Power," *Journal of International Affairs*, XXI, No. 2 (1967), 229.

100. Ibid., p. 223.

101. Ibid., p. 230.

102. Richard N. Rosecrance, "Bipolarity, Multipolarity, and the Future," *Journal of Conflict Resolution*, X (September 1966), p. 318.

103. Ibid., p. 319.

104. Ibid., p. 322.

105. Oran R. Young, "Political Discontinuities in the International System," *World Politics*, XX (April 1968), p. 369.

106. Ibid., p. 370.

107. Ibid.

108. Donald E. Lampert, Lawrence S. Falkowski, and Richard W. Mansbach, "Is There an International System?", *International Studies Quarterly*, 22, No. 1 (March 1978), 150.

109. Michael Banks, "Systems Analysis and the Study of Regions," *International Studies Quarterly*, 13, No. 4 (December 1969), 357. Other early efforts to study regional subsystems include: Mario Barrera and Ernst B. Haas, "The Operationalization of Some Variables Related to Regional Integration" *International Organization*, 23, No. 1 (Winter 1969), 150–160; Joseph S. Nye, Jr., ed., *International Regionalism: Readings* (Boston: Little, Brown, 1968); Stanley Hoffman, "Discord in Community: The North Atlantic Area as a Partial International System," *International Or-*

ganization, 17, No. 3 (Summer 1963), 521–549; Michael Brecher, "International Relations and Asian Studies: The Subordinate State System of Southern Asia," *World Politics,* 15, No. 2 (January 1963), 213–235; Larry W. Bowman, "The Subordinate State System of Southern Africa," *International Studies Quarterly,* 12, No. 3 (September 1968), 231–261; Michael Brecher, "The Middle East Subordinate System and Its Impact on Israel's Foreign Policy," *International Studies Quarterly,* 13, No. 2 (June 1969), 117–139; John H. Sigler, "News Flow in the North African International Subsystem"; Thomas W. Robinson, "Systems Theory and the Communist System"; Donald C. Hellmann, "The Emergence of an East Asian International Subsystem," *International Studies Quarterly,* 13, No. 4 (December 1969), Special Issue on International Subsystems, prepared by Peter Berton; Leonard Binder, "The Middle East as a Subordinate International System," *World Politics,* X (1958), 408–429; Michael Brecher, "The Subordinate State System of Southern Asia," *World Politics,* XV (1963), 213–235. See also Michael Banks, "Systems Analysis and the Study of Regions," *International Studies Quarterly,* 13 (1969), 335–360; Karl Kaiser, "The Interaction of Regional Subsystems: Some Preliminary Notes on Recurrent Patterns and the Role of Superpowers," *World Politics,* XXI (1968), 84–107; and Kathryn D. Baols, "The Concept 'Subordinate International System': A Critique," in Richard A. Falk and Saul H. Mendlovitz, eds., *Regional Politics and World Order* (San Francisco: Freeman, 1973).

110. Louis J. Cantori and Steven L. Spiegel, *The International Politics of Regions: A Comparative Approach* (Englewood Cliffs, N.J.: Prentice-Hall, 1970), p. 607.

111. Louis J. Cantori and Steven L. Spiegel, ibid., p. 7–20.

112. William R. Thompson, "The Regional Subsystem: A Conceptual Explication and a Propositional Inventory," *International Studies Quarterly,* 17, No. 1 (March 1973), 93. This article contains an extensive list of propositions about regional subsystem behavior drawn from the literature of the past generation.

113. Ibid.

114. Ibid., p. 101.

115. Harold and Margaret Sprout, *The Ecological Perspective on Human Affairs with Special Reference to International Politics* (Princeton: Princeton University Press, 1965), p. 208; Harold and Margaret Sprout, *An Ecological Paradigm for the Study of International Politics,* Research Monograph No. 30, Center of International Studies (Princeton University Press, 1968), pp. 2–10.

116. Stanley Hoffmann, "Theory as a Set of Questions," in Stanley Hoffmann, ed., *Contemporary Theory in International Relations,* op. cit., p. 44. The quotation in this excerpt is from Ralph Dahrendorf, "Out of Utopia: Toward a Reorientation of Sociological Analysis," *American Journal of Sociology,* LXIX (September 1958), 120.

117. Stanley Hoffmann, "International Relations: The Long Road to Theory," in James N. Rosenau, ed., *International Politics and Foreign Policy* (New York: The Free Press, 1961), p. 426.

118. Ibid., p. 48.

119. Jerone Stephens "An Appraisal of Some System Approaches in the Study of International Systems" *International Studies Quarterly* 16, No. 3 (September 1972), 348.

120. George Modelski, "The Promise of Geocentric Politics," *World Politics,* 22, No. 4 (July 1970), 631; *Principles of World Politics* (New York: The Free Press, 1972), p. 8.

121. Steven J. Brams, "The Search for Structural Order in the International System: Some Models and Preliminary Results," *International Studies Quarterly,* 13, No. 3 (September 1969), 278.

122. See Robert K. Merton, *Social Theory and Social Structure,* op. cit., pp. 37–42.
123. Oran B. Young, *A Systemic Approach to International Politics,* Research Monograph No. 33, Center of International Studies (Princeton: Princeton University Press, 1968), p. 1.
124. Ibid., pp. 2–3.

Chapter 5
The Older Theories of Conflict

PREREQUISITES OF A GENERAL THEORY OF CONFLICT

Regardless of differences in perspective between realists and idealists, or between advocates of systems, integration, decision-making, games, and other analytical theories, all students of international relations recognize the problem of war as a central one. War is one form of social conflict; we now turn our attention in this chapter and the following three chapters to examining the nature of conflict and attitudes toward it, especially on the international level.

No single general theory of conflict exists which is acceptable to social scientists in the several disciplines, much less to authorities in other scientific fields from which analogous concepts might be borrowed. The student of human conflict can gain insights into the phenomenon from a wide variety of intellectual disciplines. If a comprehensive general theory should ever be developed, it would require inputs from biology, psychology, social psychology, sociology, anthropology, history, political science, geography, economics, communications theory and organization theory, games theory and simulation theory, strategic theory and decision-making theory, integration theory and systems theory—as well as ethical philosophy and religious-theological reflection.

Until recently, authorities in each of these fields have tended to approach the phenomenon of conflict within the confines of their own discipline. Each field has adhered to its own ways of perceiving, defining, classifying, correlating, measuring, and evaluating social phenomena. Within the past two decades, the pattern has changed remarkably. Interdisciplinary approaches have been developed. Social scientists have borrowed insights, methodologies, and analogies (hopefully isomorphic) from related fields—and sometimes from fields still difficult to relate. Nevertheless, most students agree that synthesizing is a long and difficult process. There is considerably less agreement that the social sciences will achieve an esthethically and scientifically unified general theory capable of *explaining* "why men fight."

The term *conflict* usually refers to a condition in which one identifiable group of human beings (whether tribal, ethnic, linguistic, cultural, religious, socioeconomic, political, or other) is engaged in conscious opposition to one or more other identifiable human groups because these groups are pursuing what are or appear to be incompatible goals. Lewis A. Coser defines conflict as a "struggle over values and claims to scarce status, power, and resources in which the aims of the opponents are to neutralize, injure, or eliminate their rivals."[1] Conflict is an interaction involving humans; it does not include the struggle of individuals against their physical environment. Conflict implies more than mere competition. People may compete with each other for something that is in shortage without being fully aware of their competitors' existence, or without seeking to prevent the competitors from achieving their objectives. Competition shades off into conflict when the parties try to enhance their own position by reducing that of others, try to thwart others from gaining their own ends, and try to put their competitors "out of business" or even to destroy them. Conflict may be violent or nonviolent (i.e., in terms of physical force), dominant or recessive, controllable or uncontrollable, resolvable or insoluble under various sets of circumstances. Conflict is distinct from "tensions" insofar as tensions usually imply latent hostility, fear, suspicion, the perceived divergence of interests, and perhaps the desire to dominate or gain revenge; however, tensions do not necessarily extend beyond attitudes and perceptions to encompass actual overt opposition and mutual efforts to thwart one another. They often precede and always accompany the outbreak of conflict, but they are not the same as conflict, and are not always incompatible with cooperation. The "causes" of tension, however, are probably closely related to the "causes" of conflict. Moreover, if tensions become powerful enough, they themselves may become a contributory or preliminary "cause" of the occurrence of conflict insofar as they affect the decision-making process.

What Coser provides above is a sociological definition. He is interested in conflict between groups. Other analysts insist that the term must embrace not only intergroup but interpersonal and intrapersonal phenomena. Society would not have to be concerned about conflict within the individual if it were not for the plausible assumption that there is a significant relationship between conflicts within the inner structure of the individual and conflicts in the external social order. No theory of conflict can ignore this relationship. This is not to suggest that all internal conflicts can be explained only in terms of external forces, or that all external conflicts can be explained only in terms of inner psychic forces. The internal and the external can never be completely separated. Neither can the one ever be reduced completely to the other and derived solely from it. Psychological states alone cannot explain social behavior, and social conditions alone cannot explain individual behavior.

Conflict is a universally ubiquitous and permanently recurring phenomenon within and between societies. It is not necessarily continuous or uniformly intense. Many societies experience periods of relative peace, both internal and external. Quite probably, however, a certain amount of low-level, muted, almost invisible conflict goes on constantly in all societies, even those apparently most peaceful. (Individual criminal behavior can be considered a form of conflict.) Conflict, as we said above, need not issue in violent behavior—it may be carried on by subtle political, economic, psychological, and social means. Politics itself is a process for resolving conflicts. Whether or not large-scale, excessively violent, organized international warfare can ever be eliminated from human affairs, as such once "natural" institutions as slavery and human sacrifice were, is a subject worthy of study and debate.[2]

Perhaps the most that can be realistically hoped for at the present time is that the most destructive forms of organized international violence (such as nuclear war and such conventional wars as might escalate to the nuclear level) can be deterred indefinitely as a result of intelligent policies of mutual restraint on the part of governments until effective methods of international arms limitation emerge. But it is too much to expect that all social conflict can ever be abolished, or even that political violence at all levels can be permanently ruled out. H. L. Nieburg has argued that violence is a natural form of political behavior; that the threat of inflicting pain by resorting to violence will always be a useful means of political bargaining within domestic and international society; that the threat of resorting to force demonstrates the seriousness with which the dissatisfied party sets forth its demands against the satisfied, the establishment, the defender of the status quo in order to confront the latter starkly with the alternatives of making adjustments or risking dangerous escalation of violence.[3] Many social scientists, including several identified with the peace movement, recognize that total elimination of conflict from the human situation is not only impossible but undesirable.[4]

MICRO- AND MACROTHEORIES OF CONFLICT

Most social sciences can be roughly divided into two groups, depending upon whether they adopt the "macro" or the "micro" approach to the study of the human universe. Do we seek the origins of conflict in the nature of human beings or in their institutions? Generally speaking, psychologists, social psychologists, biologists, games theorists, and decision-making theorists take as their point of departure the behavior of individuals, and from this they draw inferences to the behavior of the species. Moreover, sociologists, anthropologists, geographers, organization and communication theorists, political scientists and international relations analysts, and systems theorists typically examine conflict at the level of groups, collectivities, social institutions, social classes, large political movements, religious or ethnic entities, nation-states, coalitions, and cultural systems. Some scholars—economists, for example—might divide their efforts between the macro- and microdimensions. One historian might prefer to study the clash of nation-states, while another might prefer to concentrate on the unique factors in the personality, background, and crisis behavior of an individual statesman that prompted the statesman to opt for war or peace in a specific set of circumstances.

Historically, the intellectual chasm between the macro- and the microperspectives of human conflict was nowhere better illustrated than in the earlier polarity of psychology and sociology. The former analyzed conflict from a knowledge of the individual, the latter from a knowledge of collective behavior. Psychologists tended to approach human problems as arising from the inner psychic structure of the individual, from where they assumed that complexes, tensions, and other disorders were projected into the external social situation. Conversely, sociologists were disposed to bring their analysis of all human problems at the level of social structures and institutions, and to trace the effects of disorders at that level back to the psychic life of individuals. The sharpness of the cleavage as it was perceived around the turn of the century is reflected in Emile Durkheim's statement that "every time that a social phenomenon is directly explained as a psychic phenomenon, one may be sure that the explanation is false."[5] The long-standing antipathy of Freudian analysis toward the Marxian dialectic (so severe that for several decades Freudian psychology was completely taboo in the Soviet Union) provides a well-known if somewhat extreme example of the divergent perspectives of the two fields.[6]

In the twentieth century, especially in the past two decades, the distance between the two fields has narrowed. Psychologists have recognized the importance of institutions, groups, and the total cultural environment in the shaping of the individual's psychic life. For their part, sociologists have paid increasing attention to the role of psychic factors in social processes. Social psychologists, in particular, have sought to bridge the gap between the two parent disciplines. But it would be going too far to conclude that the gap has yet been fully bridged, for social psychologists still contend that they are more interested in individual than in collective behavior. Nevertheless, increasing numbers of social scientists are becoming convinced that it is impossible to construct an adequate theory of conflict without fusing the macro- and the microdimensions into a coherent whole.[7] In recent years, as Michael Haas has noted, social scientists, armed with statistical methods and aided by computers, have begun for the first time to study international conflict systematically and to accumulate a definitive body of scientific knowledge about the subject. But theory on international conflict, he concludes, remains at a primitive level partly because "most empirical researchers have been bulldozing exhibitionistically without attempting to put the subject in order analytically."[8]

INTERPERSONAL CONFLICT AND INTERNATIONAL CONFLICT

Social psychologists are more hesitant today than were their predecessors two or three decades ago to extrapolate the explanations of complex social behavior—particularly at the level of international relations—from their knowledge of individual psychic behavior. In the past, some psychologists who were concerned with the problem of conflict assumed too readily that the explanation of group aggression is a mere corollary of the explanation of individual aggression. They took the Platonic notion that the state is the individual "writ large" and converted this into a pseudoscientific analogy under which society came to be uncritically regarded as the psychological organism "writ large." Social psychologists are now much less confident in this respect. J. K. Zawodny has noted that "while there is a remarkable massing of data, particularly for individual behavior, scientists are justifiably cautious against inferring applicable parallels between patterns of behavior in an individual, a group, and a nation."[9] Stephen Withey and Daniel Katz have warned against the attempt to "explain the functioning of social systems by a simple reduction of a macroscopic process."[10] Herbert C. Kelman has also pointed out that many earlier writings on war and peace by psychologists and psychiatrists were not germane to the interactions of nation-states. Kelman holds that the earlier writers tended to overemphasize individual aggressive impulses. They took it for granted that the behavior of states is merely the aggregate of individual behaviors, ignoring the fact that individuals differ widely in their roles, interests, and ability to influence final decisions. The behavior of such a large collectivity as a nation, according to Kelman, cannot be considered a direct reflection of the motives and personal feelings of either its citizens or its leaders.

Kelman suggests that there can be no such thing as an autonomous psychological theory of war and international relations, but only a general theory of these phenomena in which the findings of psychology play their part. Although in war many individuals engage in aggressive behavior, they do not necessarily act from aggressive motives. For strategic reasons leaders may behave aggressively, and the population of a state may manifest such behavior in order to conform socially. Kelman acknowledges that from the findings of psychology valuable insights about international relations can be gained. However, only by analyzing international relations, not by automatically applying psychological findings about the individual, can we identify those points at which such application is relevant. Kelman defines war as a societal and intersocietal action conducted within a national and international political context. Of crucial importance in the study of international relations is the process by which nations develop their national policies and decide upon war. In part, such an explanation includes the motivations and perceptions of individuals as policymakers and relevant publics playing various roles as part of a larger society. But Kelman cautions that psychological analysis is useful to the study of aggressive behavior in an international context only if we know where and how such individuals fit into the larger political and social framework of the nation and the international system as well as the constraints under which they operate.[11]

Most specialists in the fields of political science and international relations would heartily endorse Kelman's conclusion, which is pertinent not only to the problem of ternational war, but also to all forms of large-scale social conflict that have engrossed many American scholars in the past two decades—such as revolutions, coups, insurgencies, civil disorders, and organized political terrorism. Psychological factors alone might go a long way toward explaining instances of anomic violence (i.e., apparently spontaneous and irrational outbursts by either a crowd or an individual), but even in these cases social scientists are now more wary of the "fallacy of the single factor." At more complex levels of politicized conflict, where violence reflects to a much greater degree planning, organization, management, and perhaps even institutionalization, the need for circumspection in the explanation of phenomena by reference to purely psychological factors becomes commensurately greater.

CONFLICT AND SOCIAL INTEGRATION

Social scientists are divided on the question whether social conflict should be regarded as something rational, constructive, and socially functional or something irrational, pathological, and socially dysfunctional. Most Western psychologists and social psychologists in modern times, for example, seem inclined to regard all violent forms of politicized aggression as irrational and undesirable. Virtually all law-oriented thinkers and most ethical philsophers would agree with them.[12] By way of contrast, most modern sociologists and anthropologists both in Europe and America (with the notable exception of the Parsonian school) have been willing to attribute a constructive purpose to conflict, insofar as it helps to establish group boundaries, strengthens group consciousness and sense of self-identity, and contributes toward social integration, community-building, and economic development.[13]

Many economists and political scientists would undoubtedly regard violent conflict as irrational, whereas others would judge it "good" or "bad" depending upon the context in which it arises, the economic issues or political values at stake, the costs incurred, and the net economic or political outcome for the contesting groups, the nation, and the international system. Games theorists, strategists, and decision-making analysts might emphasize the rational elements involved in wishing and planning for a "win" or the accomplishment of an objective through the waging of conflict, but they would readily concede that irrational forces and erroneous perceptions can influence significantly the calculations of "players" who opt for war or revolution.

VARIETIES OF CONFLICT

Several other salient questions occur at the outset of our inquiry. Should we study the phenomenon of conflict in terms of conscious motivations? Do people really fight about what they say they are fighting about? Or must we go beyond stated reasons, regard them with suspicion as mere self-rationalizations, and try to penetrate to the "real," that is, unconscious, murky, and sordid impulses which drive people to aggressive behavior? Is this a false dichotomy? Probably. If we look carefully, we shall see that microscientists are more inclined to probe beneath the surface into the unconscious, the innate, the "instinctive" (to use an obsolete term), whereas macroscientists are somewhat more willing to lend credence to conscious motivations, for these motivations pertain to thought, language, and communications patterns, which, in contrast to internal psychic forces, are products of society. Given humanity's nature as a symbolic animal, words are crucial links between the unconscious and the conscious, between macro and micro.

International war is one form of social conflict—undoubtedly the most important single form in terms of its potential consequences for the individual in the nuclear age. But there are many other forms of social conflict: civil war, revolution, coup, guerrilla insurgency, political assassination, sabotage, terror, riots, demonstrations, strikes and strikebreaking, threats, displays of force, formal protests, economic sanctions and reprisals, psychological warfare, propaganda, legislative lobbying for contrary purposes, tavern brawls, labor-management disputes, flareups at collegiate sports events, divorce contests and legal wrangling over the custody of children, student seizure of university buildings, intrafamily fights, and felonious assault or homicide.

A crucial question that arises frequently in the social sciences regardless of the phenomenon under investigation is: Are we dealing with the *one* or the *many*? Can we understand war as a separate conflict phenomenon in isolation, or must we study it as one highly organized manifestation, at a specific social-structural level, of a general phenomenon? Social scientists are far from agreement as to whether human conflict can be satisfactorily explained as a continuum in which violent outbursts differ only by such accidents as the nature of the parties, the size, the duration, the intensity, the nature of the issues and the objectives sought, the processes and modes of conflict, and the weapons employed, but not in their underlying "causes," or whether human conflict is an indefinite series of discrete phenomena, each of which, despite a superficial external resemblance to the others, requires its own unique theoretical explanation.

Is it possible to explain the Arab-Israeli wars of recent decades, or the quarter-century-long conflict in Vietnam, or the Bangladesh War of 1971, or the Sino-Soviet border clashes along the Amur-Ussuri Rivers according to the same general theory of conflict that we would use to explain food and language riots in India, or civil wars in Spain, Nigeria, and Lebanon, or political-religious strife in Northern Ireland, or the 1968 outburst by students and workers in France, or the insurgencies in Malaya, Algeria, Oman, and Angola? Do conflicts differ substantially by type? If so, how many types are there? Such a question cannot be answered satisfactorily partly because it was only during the decade of the 1960s that American social scientists in any substantial numbers became seriously interested in applying quantitative methodologies to the study of such phenomena as "internal war," "low-level" violence, and "civil strife."[14] Social scientists have not yet come forth with a generally accepted taxonomy for distinguishing, classifying, and arranging coherently various types of conflict. Many proposals have been offered. But at the present time we still lack universal cross-cultural classifications. What we cannot classify, we cannot count, measure, or correlate. The problems of data-gathering are very serious, more serious than social scientists who study the phenomenon of conflict on an international scale usually care to admit.[15]

As to the question of whether each form of conflict is unique and whether all forms of conflict can be incorporated into a unified explanatory scheme, the authors maintain an open mind. They would admit that in some respects there does seem to be a universal phenomenon of conflict. Certainly the history of human beings up to the present time would indicate that conflict in one form or another is a permanent and ubiquitous phenomenon in the social universe—an apparently inescapable aspect of the human condition. Most social scientists, insofar as they weigh empirical evidence, are likely to predict the indefinite continuation of conflict in myriad modes. The authors see merit not only in Charles Lockhart's observation that conflict structures vary greatly and that conflicts with different structures follow distinctive dynamics as they develop, but also in Kenneth Boulding's contention that it is important to examine both the similarities and the differences in the various types of conflict, if social scientists are eventually to derive a general theory of conflict from diverse sources and disciplines.[16]

THE OLDER THEORIES OF WAR, ITS CAUSES AND ITS LAWS

There is available to the student in almost every university and college library a considerable body of literature pertaining to the older theories of war and its causes. Most of these theories we would now call "prescientific," even though some of them were based upon "empirical evidence" drawn from history and human experience. Several of the earlier theories contain perceptive insights that continue to merit our attention as part of our cultural heritage. They enable us to see how the problem of war was looked upon in other historical epochs, and why it was not always regarded as the greatest of evils; they reflect conscious motivations for and rationalizations of war, which at the level of human decision-making can be "causal;" they provide philosophical, religious, political, and psychological arguments for and against war, both in general and in specific circumstances. Whereas modern social scientists often approach the study of conflict through statistical methods and abstract models, earlier thinkers usually analyzed the phenomenon of war at a more "natural" level of immediate human observation and reflection.

In virtually all the ancient religious-ethical civilizations, the problem of war was approached not only as one of political-military strategy, but also as one of spiritual and moral dimensions. It was assumed that human beings enjoyed freedom of choice, that they were responsible for their decisions in a moral universe of rational causality created by God,[17] and that the causes of war lay deep in the wills of individuals whose motives were good or bad. War was seen to result from a moral deficiency in humankind. The path to intellectual comprehension of the problem of war lay through the conscience or practical intellect of the individual decision-maker, who was often advised by religious prophets and ethical teachers to avoid excessive reliance on force of arms and to seek the ways of peace rather than war when possible. But war was generally taken to be an inescapable fact of life that rulers could not ignore and that they might be obliged to undertake at times for the common good.

In ancient China, the theories ranged from Mo-Ti's doctrine of universal love, with which the waging of war was deemed incompatible, to the Realists (including the authors of *The Book of Lord Shang*), who in a more Machiavellian vein stressed the strategic approach to power, foreign policy, and war.[18] A similarly broad spectrum of views is to be found in ancient India, but it is worth noting that the Buddhist doctrine of *ahimsa* (harmlessness toward all living things), famous in modern times as one of the sources from which Gandhi derived the creed of nonviolent resistance, was not originally taken to forbid the waging of war.[19] In Islam, the Prophet Muhammad preached the holy war (*jihad*) as a sacred duty and a guarantee of salvation, and for several centuries Moslem theorists, accepting the reality that Arab rulers were for the most part a war-minded group, assumed that the world is divided into the *dar al-Islam* (the peaceful abode of the true believers and those who submitted to their tolerant rule) and the *dar al-harb* (the territory of war).

Inasmuch as Islam was a universalist system of belief, the two territories were always theoretically at war with each other, for war was the ultimate device for incorporating recalcitrant peoples into the peaceful territory of Islam. The *jihad*, therefore, was a form of *bellum justum* ("just war"), not entirely unlike that of medieval Christian writers. The concept of the *jihad* as a permanent state of war against the non-Moslem world has become obsolete in modern times. Today writers stress that the term refers not only to international war, but also to the spiritual struggle for perfection within the heart of individuals.[20] Mahatma Gandhi declared that he was able to perceive the origins of the doctrine of nonviolence and love for all living things not only in the sacred Hindu writings and the Bible, but also in the Koran.[21]

The predominant historical attitudes toward war which are found in Western culture are a product of several different sources, including the Judaeo-Christian religious tradition, Greek philosophy, Roman legalism, European feudalism, Enlightenment pacifism, and modern scientism, humanitarianism, and other ideologies. The ancient Jewish scriptures reflect the paradox of human yearning for a peaceful existence amidst the constant recurrence of war. Surrounded by hostile peoples, the Israelites relied heavily upon a combination of religious prophetism and military organization for nation-building, defense, and territorial expansion. The God of Israel often appeared as a Warrior-God. Joshua, Gideon, Saul, and David fought wars for His honor and glory, to demonstrate His power as well as His special relationship to the Chosen People.[22]

War and Christianity

The early Christians were divided in their attitude toward the use of military force by the State. During the first three centuries of the Church's history, when Christianity was regarded as an alien and subversive creed within the Roman Empire, there was a strong tendency toward pacifism, and many believed that the Christian both as private person and as a citizen should respond to injury by turning the other cheek, regardless of the consequences for the State. Pacifism, however, did not become the orthodox Christian doctrine. The dominant view among the Fathers of the Church was that political authority was divinely instituted for the benefit of the individual, and that when force was used justly it was a good, not an evil. People are enjoined to turn the other cheek when their own rights are violated, because they seek a salvation beyond history, but the State, which must safeguard the temporal social good here and now, may have to resort to force at times. Saint Ambrose and Saint Augustine, writing after Christians in the West had begun to assume responsibility for the social order, "baptized" the ancient Roman doctrine of the "just war" as a "sad necessity in the eyes of men of principle."[23]

Scholastic philosophers in the Middle Ages considerably refined the "just war" doctrine. The decision to initiate violent hostilities could not be taken by a private individual, but only by public authority. But rulers were enjoined against resorting to war unless they were morally certain that their cause was just, that is, that their juridical rights had been violated by a neighboring ruler. Even then, they were exhorted to exhaust all peaceful means of settling the dispute before initiating the use of force, and this usually meant arbitration. Furthermore, there had to be a reasonable prospect that the resort to force would be more productive of good than of evil and would restore the order of justice. The war had to be waged throughout with a right moral intention, and had to be conducted by means that were not intrinsically immoral, for what begins as a just war could become unjust in its prosecution. These were the common teachings of such medieval writers as Antoninus of Florence and St. Thomas Aquinas.[24]

Throughout the Middle Ages, the Church attempted to impose ethical controls upon the conduct of war by specifying times when fighting could not be carried on, sites where battle was prohibited, types of weapons that could not legitimately be employed, and classes of persons that were either exempted from the obligation of military service or immune as targets of military action. This effort to "soften" the cruelty of warfare was by no means new in Western culture. The ancient Greeks and Romans had been familiar with such agreed rules of war as those forbidding wanton destruction of populations, the burning of cities, and the severance of water supplies. Many circumstances of medieval European culture, including the nature of feudalism, prevailing economic conditions, and the crude state of the military sciences actually reinforced the moral efforts of the Church to mitigate the harshness of warfare during the medieval period.[25]

In the period of transition from medieval to modern Europe, three outstanding exceptions to the dominant theory and practice of morally limited warfare can be perceived. These were invariably expressions of ideological conflict which ran counter to the distinctive tendencies of medieval culture: (1) the Crusades of the twelfth and thirteenth centuries, fought against an alien and infidel civilization; (2) the wars of the fourteenth and fifteenth centuries, especially between the French and English, in which the forces of national feeling made themselves felt for the first time on a large scale; and (3) the religious wars which followed the Reformation. In all of these cases, war ceased to be a rational instrument of monarchical policy for the defense of juridical rights. The concept of war as a small-scale affair of skirmish and maneuver lost its primacy when large numbers of nonprofessional (i.e., nonchivalric) warriors, both volunteers and mercenaries, became enmeshed with cultural, national, or religious antipathies. When a cherished set of values or a way of life was thought to hinge upon the outcome of an encounter, war became an all-consuming psychological and moral experience. Hence the battles of Antioch, Crecy, Poitiers, Agincourt, and Magdeburg were bitter and bloody in the extreme.

The Philosophical Theories of the Nation-State Period

During the classical period of the balance of power which was ushered in by the Peace of Westphalia in 1648, the concept of limited war regained currency in Europe. At the beginning of the modern nation-state period in the sixteenth and seventeenth centuries, the traditional Western doctrine of the "just war" was reaffirmed by scholastic theologians and philosophers, such as Victoria and Suarez, as well as by the earliest systematic expounders of international law—Grotius, Ayala, Vattel, Gentilis, and others. For these writers, the just war emerged as a substitute juridical proceeding—a sort of lawsuit in defense of the legal rights of the state, prosecuted by force in the absence of an effective international judicial superior capable of vindicating the order of justice. Virtually all the classical European writers on international war insisted upon the necessity of sparing the lives of the innocent in war. The slaying of the guiltless could never be directly intended; at best, it was permitted as incidental to the legitimate operations of a just war.[26]

In the latter half of the seventeenth century, after the violence of the religious wars had subsided, the pendulum swung back again toward more moderate forms of warfare. From then on through most of the eighteenth century, wars were less ideological and more instrumental in the traditional sense. Professor John U. Nef suggests a number of factors which influenced this development: a growing distaste for violence; a raising of the comfort level among the European bourgeoisie; the improvement of manners, customs, and laws by an aristocracy that now admired gentility, agility, and subtlety more than prowess in battle; the pursuit of commerce; and the growth of the fine arts, combined with zealous efforts to apply reason to social affairs. All these factors, Nef concludes, helped to weaken the will for organized fighting.[27]

Down to the time of the French Revolution, the nations of Europe were not willing to pursue objectives which required inflicting a great deal of destruction upon the enemy. This period witnessed the emergence of economic motivations for conflict, but, although it is true that colonial and commercial rivalries were added to dynastic feuds as causes of international disputes, the rise of the bourgeoisie helped buttress pacifist rather than militarist sentiments, for the bourgeoisie desired more than anything else an orderly international community in which conditions of trade would be predictable. The very fact that the leading commercial nations of Western Europe were also developing naval power helped to soften the effects of warfare in the eighteenth century insofar as naval forces could carry on hostile engagements without directly involving land populations. Such land warfare as did take place was usually characterized by adroit maneuver, surprise, march and countermarch, and rapier thrusts at the enemy's supply lines, as exemplified in the campaigns of Turenne, Frederick the Great, and Marlborough. War, in the century of "drawing room culture," was not entirely unrelated to the game of chess or the minuet. The prevailing sense of restraint probably led to a slowdown in the innovation rate of military technology. Encounters between armies in the field were often looked upon as mere adjuncts to the diplomatic process, designed to strengthen or weaken the bargaining positions of envoys during prolonged negotiations.

THE ORIGINS OF MODERN PACIFISM

Meanwhile, the post-Renaissance and Enlightenment periods had witnessed the rise in Europe of a school of pacifist thought which rejected the medieval moral-legal doctrine of war. The pacifist writers—Erasmus, More, Comenius, Crucé, Fénelon, Penn, Voltaire, Rousseau, and

Bentham—took their stand either on Stoic and early Christian radical positions or on the newer European ideals of cosmopolitanism, humanitarianism, and bourgeois internationalism. Practically all of them exhibited a pronounced skepticism in their attitudes toward war and the military profession. It was particularly fashionable to compare unfavorably the destructive life of the soldier with the useful life of the merchant. The abolition of force from international politics came to be looked upon as the noblest objective of statesmen. The quest for human happiness unmarred by any trace of the tragic became for European intellectuals the great goal of life.[28]

The *philosophes* were not agreed among themselves as to whether happiness was to be achieved through the application of scientific and technical reason or through people's return to nature and rediscovery of their original simplicity. But rationalists and romantics alike were convinced that society was about to break the shackles of traditional authority and superstition, dispel the historic curses of ignorance, disease, and war, and embark—in the vision of Condorcet—upon the absolutely indefinite perfectibility of humanity; which knows no other limit than the duration of the globe upon which nature has placed us.[29] "The people, being more enlightened," wrote Condorcet, "will learn by degrees to regard war as the most dreadful of all calamities, the most terrible of all crimes."[30] The era was marked by a bitter cynicism concerning the concept of the "just war," which was regarded as mere propaganda calculated to cloak the aggressive urges of ambitious kings. No one at the time denounced the stupidity and incongruities of war with more scathing sarcasm than Voltaire, who poked fun at the two kings, each of whom had *Te Deums* sung in his own camp after the battle.[31] There was an anticipation, reflected in the writings of Montesquieu and others, that the transition from monarchical to republican institutions would be accompanied by a shift from the spirit of war and aggrandizement to that of peace and moderation. The period abounded in projects for abolishing war and establishing perpetual peace.[32]

The hopes of the Enlightenment writers proved ill-founded in the latter part of the eighteenth century. The emergence of liberal nationalist ideologies, sparked by the French Revolution and the Napoleonic aftermath, led once again to an intensification of warfare. Citizen armies, backed by a steadily growing industrial base, fought ferociously for nationalist ideals. Napoleon upset the European balance of power. The conservative reaction of 1815, based on the principle of a return to monarchical legitimacy, restored the classical idea of the balance of power—a Newtonian notion of an international universe in equilibrium—to a central place in the thinking of European statesmen.[33] This restoration helped to minimize the harsh effects of a developing war technology for another hundred years. The era of the Concert of Powers, of which the

Pax Britannica was an important feature, was marked by astute diplomacy and chessboard military moves rather than by violent conflict. Throughout the nineteenth century, Europe experienced no conflict so bloody as the American Civil War, which was in many respects an ideological war fought for absolute objectives.

The latter part of the nineteenth century witnessed the spread of universal conscription in Europe, the mass production of new automatic weapons, armaments races, the creation of alliances, increasing colonial and commercial rivalries among the Powers, and the growth of a popular press which could be converted into a powerful instrument for stirring belligerent sentiments. The rise of modern war industry had an ambiguous significance. On the one hand, it served to make war more frightful and more unprofitable, and hence less readily undertaken. On the other hand, it served to make it much more likely that war, when it did come, would be total in nature, absorbing all available energies. The closely packed battle, in which mass is multiplied by velocity, became the central feature of modern European military thought.[34] For the first time in history, governments were coming into possession of constantly expanding means of waging absolute war for unlimited objectives.

Throughout the nineteenth century, the pacifist movement slowly extended its influence in England and the United States. Jonathan Dymond, an English Quaker, argued that war, like the slave trade, would begin to disappear when people would refuse to acquiesce in it any longer and begin to question its necessity. Dymond denied that the patriotic warrior celebrated in song and story for having laid down his life for his country deserves such praise. The officer, he said, enters the army in order to obtain an income, the private because he prefers a life of idleness to industry. Both fight because it is their business, or because their reputation is at stake, or because they are compelled to do so. Dymond anticipated the contentions of the socialists and the later exponents of the "devil theory of war" by insinuating that the industrialists who profit from war combine forces with the professional military for the purpose of promoting war. He declared that the Christian Scriptures require the individual to refrain from violence under all circumstances. All distinctions between just and unjust war, between defensive and aggressive war he dismissed as being in vain. War must be either absolutely forbidden or else permitted to run its unlimited course.[35] Dymond is one of the early voices of that modern movement of uncompromising pacifism which seeks not only to give religious advice to the conscience of the individual, but also to exert an influence upon the policy of states—or at least those states in which the climate of opinion is sufficiently liberal to permit the propagation of the pacifist doctrine.

The aversion of modern intellectual pacifists to war cannot be explained purely in terms of religious and humanitarian factors. Since the nineteenth century, economic considerations, either liberal or socialist in their foundation, have entered into the thinking of most pacifists on the subject of war and peace. From Richard Cobden down to very recent times, many liberal pacifists have been convinced that there exists an intrinsic and mutually causal relationship between free trade and peace, and that the abolition of trade barriers is the only means of effecting permanent peace.

Sir Norman Angell and War as an Anachronism

The liberal view that war represents the greatest threat to the economic health of modern industrial civilization reached its culmination in the writings of Norman Angell, an English publicist who achieved prominence in the 1920s and 1930s. Shortly before World War I, Angell argued that warfare in the industrial age had become an anachronism. The economic futility of military power, he declared, had been amply demonstrated by recent history, which showed that even when victory in war seems at first glance to bring with it substantial economic gains, such appearances are deceptive. Nearly everyone thought that the Germans had reaped an advantage from the huge indemnity which France was forced to pay after being defeated in the Franco-Prussian War of 1870 to 1871, but, Angell argued, the indemnity actually induced an inflation which hurt the German economy. No nation, he went on to say, can genuinely improve its economic position either through war or through those imperialistic operations which involve costly preparations for military defense. Angell was convinced that "the factors which really do constitute prosperity have not the remotest connection with military or naval power, all our political jargon notwithstanding."[36]

In the final analysis, Angell was a rationalist who believed that war could be eliminated through the growth and progressive application of human reason to international affairs. The modern technical state could no longer expect to profit from waging war, but could only anticipate the disintegration of its own society and the virtue of its individual members. Once people become convinced that war has lost its meaning except as a form of mutual suicide, thought Angell, disarmament and peace would be possible. He was confident that peace was primarily a matter of educating the publics of democratic societies, and he chose to couch his homilies in terms of the economic self-interest of an interdependent European community, rather than in terms of traditional religious morality. But he had no doubt that once human beings fully realized the irrelevance of military force for the attainment, promotion, and preservation of prosperity, or socioeconomic well-being, then political wars would cease as religious wars did in the West a long time ago.[37] It is worth noting the parallel between the thought of Norman Angell and that of contemporary strategic theorists (to be surveyed in Chapter 9), several of whom, coming from a background of economic analysis, concluded that nuclear war makes no sense, that no gain could be worth its cost, that it is unwinnable, and that nuclear weapons can have no use except a deterrent one.

BELLICIST THEORIES

Modern Western theories of conflict and war, including those of utopian pacifism, cannot be understood without some reference to the appearance, following the French Revolution, of a militarist school of thought within the West. Bellicism, as this school might be called, developed at least partly in conscious reaction to idealistic pacifism. Perhaps it would be more accurate to say that the two tendencies in Western thought fed upon each other as polar opposites. Western culture has never lacked thinkers who stressed conflict and tension over cooperation and harmony in social reality.

Most Western theorists of military strategy from the period of the French Revolution until the latter 1950s (when the emphasis shifted from conventional and nuclear strategies to the study of guerrilla warfare and counterinsurgency) showed a distinct preference for direct over indirect strategies for the bludgeoning attack of the massed army over the graceful rapier thrust, for the frontal assault and the quick decision over the more patient strategy of maneuver, encirclement, attrition, and negotiation. Karl von Clausewitz expressed, more vividly than any other writer up to his time, the concept of absolute war pushed to its utmost bounds. The chief object of military strategy, he wrote, is to break the enemy's will to resist. He denied that there is any chance of disarming and defeating the enemy without a good deal of bloodshed. "If bloody slaughter is a horrible spectacle, then it should only be a reason for treating war with more respect, but not for making the sword we bear blunter and blunter by degrees from feelings of humanity, until once again someone steps in with a sword that is sharp, and hews away the arms from our body."[38]

More important than Clausewitz were the nineteenth-century philosophers, Hegel, Nietzsche, Treitschke, and Bernhardi. These writers, carrying to extremes ideas which had been adumbrated by Machiavelli, Hobbes, and Bacon, seemed at times to exalt power and war as ends in themselves. Hegel, for whom reality was the dialectical clash of ideas, regarded the nation-state as the concretization of the absolute in history, "the march of God in the world." On the subject of war, he has perhaps been misunderstood. He did not glorify war and its brutality, but since he valued the nation so highly he accepted war as a phenomenon which could contribute to national unity. Hegel left himself open either to misunderstanding or to justifiable criticism when he said that through war "the ethical health of nations is maintained . . . just as the motion of the winds keeps the sea from the foulness which a constant calm would produce."[39]

The harshest nineteenth-century critic of the values which underlay not only the Western Christian civilization of his day, but even those of pure original Christianity was Friedrich Nietzsche. Emphasizing as he did the "will-to-power" as the basic determinant of human behavior, Nietzsche looked upon the Christian ethos, marked by self-denial, resignation, humility, respect for weakness, and the renunciation of power, as the foe of the truly creative impulses in a person—a religion of failure which inhibits the full development of "Superman."[40] Even more than Hegel, war for Nietzsche plays an indispensable role in the renewal of civilizations. In the following passage, published in 1878, the German philosopher—undoubtedly one of the most important of all nineteenth-century thinkers—seemed to adumbrate in a very stark way the theory of the "moral equivalent of war" which William James would express more optimistically in 1912;

> For the present, we know of no other means whereby the rough energy of the camp, the deep impersonal hatred, the cold-bloodedness of murder with a good conscience, the general ardor of the system in the destruction of the enemy, the proud indifference to great losses, to one's own existence and that of one's friends, the hollow earthlike convulsion of the soul, can be as forcibly and certainly communicated to enervated nations as is done by every great war. . . . Culture can by no means dispense with passions, vices and malignities. When the Romans, after having become Imperial, had grown rather tired of war, they attempted to gain new strength by gladiatorial combats and Christian persecutions. The English of today, who appear on the whole to have also renounced war, adopt other means in order to generate anew those vanishing forces; namely, the dangerous exploring expeditions, sea voyages, and mountaineerings, nominally undertaken for scientific purposes, but in reality to bring home surplus strength from adventures and dangers of all kinds. Many other such substitutes for war will be discovered, but perhaps precisely thereby it will become more and more obvious that such a highly cultivated and therefore necessarily enfeebled humanity as that of modern Europe not only needs wars, but the greatest and most terrible wars—consequently occasional relapses into barbarism—lest, by the means of culture, it should lose its culture and its very existence.[41]

Lesser minds than Nietzsche's followed in his tracks. The German historian Treitschke, who spoke for the Prussian military caste, drew his inspiration from such figures as Machiavelli and Bismarck. Convinced that the independent sovereign nation-state is the highest political achievement of which the individual is capable, he rejected as intolerable the concept of a genuine universal political community. War is frequently the only means available to the state to protect its independence, and thus the ability and readiness to wage war must be preserved in a carefully honed condition. The state ought to be oversensitive in matters of national honor, so that the instinct of political self-preservation can be developed to the highest possible degree. Whenever the flag is insulted, there must be an immediate demand for full satisfaction, and if this is not forthcoming, "war must follow, however small the occasion may seem."[42] There is nothing reprehensible in this, for in Treitschke's eyes war itself was majestic and sublime.[43] Above all, a state should not neglect its military strength in order to promote the idealistic aspirations of mankind, for if it does this "it repudiates its own nature and perishes."[44]

The ideas voiced by Clausewitz, Hegel, Nietzsche, and Treitschke were echoed by several philosophers of military history in Europe and in the United States. General Friedrich von Bernhardi, strongly influenced by the Darwinian concept of "survival of the fittest" (which he understood only superficially), correlated war with human progress, holding that "those intellectual and moral factors which insure superiority in war are also those which render possible a general progressive development [among nations]."[45] The geopolitical writings of Kjellen and Ratzel, as well as the twentieth-century German students of geopolitics represented by Haushofer, were indebted intellectually to Darwinian concepts. (See Chapter 2 in which the geopolitical theories are discussed.)

Alfred Thayer Mahan also saw history as a Darwinian struggle in which fitness is measured in terms of military strength. The habits of military discipline, he thought, are necessary underpinnings of an orderly civilian structure. He viewed the nations of the world as economic corporations locked in a fierce survival competition for resources and markets. Unlike the Marxists, however, he attributed this not merely to the impulses of competition, but rather to human nature and the fact that the supply of economic goods is finite. Contradictions of national self-interest, along with wide and irreducible discrepancies of power, opportunity, and determination, produce the conditions of permanent conflict and render it unrealistic to expect violence to be eliminated from international affairs. Mahan deemed futile all efforts to substitute law for force, since all law depends upon force for its efficacy. Finally, Mahan defended the institution of war against the accusation that it was immoral and un-Christian. He argued that war is the means whereby nation-states carry out the mandates of their citizens' consciences. A state should go to war only when it is convinced of rightfulness, but once it has committed its conscience, there is no choice but war (not even arbitration), for "the material evils of war are less than the moral evil of compliance with wrong."[46]

BELLICISTS AND PACIFISTS POLARIZE

As the nineteenth century gave way to the twentieth, the intellectual polarization of Western pacifists and bellicists became complete. The bellicists and their doctrines may be classified as follows. (1) Realistic positivism, represented by such turn-of-the-century Italian writers as Vilfredo Pareto (1848–1923) and Gaetano Mosca (1858–1941). Pareto, an economist and sociologist, and Mosca, a political scientist, both expounded the concepts of rule by the elite, the importance of coercive instruments in the maintenance of social unity and order, and the inevitable recurrence of revolution. Mosca was not as antihumanitarian and antidemocratic as Pareto, but he shared Pareto's prejudice against pacifism, fearing that if war should be eliminated nations would grow soft and disintegrate.[47] (2) Social Darwinists and nationalists with proclivities toward social Darwinism, such as the sociologists William Graham Sumner and Ernst Haeckel and the jurist Oliver Wendell Holmes.[48] (3) Certain pessimistic philosophers of history, including Oswald Spengler (1880–1936) and Bendetto Croce (1866–1952). Spengler, a German historian, was particularly fascinated by the will-to-power, the virility of barbarians, the subjugation of weaker peoples, and the law of the jungle, while he suffered from a special dread of a world-wide revolution of the colored people against the whites.[49] Croce, an Italian philosopher and statesman, although a critic of the excesses of militarism, regarded war as a necessary tragedy of the human condition, indispensable to human progress, and the dream of perpetual peace as fatuous. (4) The forerunners and cryptorepresentatives of racist theory and/or fascism, as well as the actual archetypes of those ideologies. Writers in these categories included Houston Stewart Chamberlain, Arthur de Gobineau, Giovanni Gentile, Alfredo Rocco, Georges Sorel, Gabriel d'Annunzio, and Benito Mussolini.[50] It would be unfair to insinuate that all the foregoing schools of thought should be linked with the fascists, or even that all fascists were or are racists, but all exalted, in varying degrees, the role of force and virile action in social processes. The individuals mentioned above are more appropriately treated in works on political theory or intellectual (and antiintellectual) history, but the serious students of international relations cannot afford to ignore the impact they had on the thinking of their time, nor should they overlook the "causative" role of conscious ideas and persisting attitudes in decision-making and social conflict.

ANARCHISM AND THE MARXIST SOCIALISTS

Finally, there were the anarchists and the Marxian socialists. These two movements of an extremist nature, antithetical in many respects, produced contrary offshoots, some theoretical and some practical. Both movements helped dialectically to strengthen the theory of pacifism and the practice of politicized violence as an instrument either of abolishing the state or of promoting class revolution as a prelude to establishing a cooperative or a socialist order. The Marxist-socialist theory of imperialism and war will be examined in the next chapter. Here a brief word about anarchism is in order, because it is often misunderstood by the public at large and because it constitutes a more significant component of the contemporary mind, especially the youthful mind in the West, than is generally recognized.

Anarchism is the doctrine that opposes political authority in all its forms. Anarchists view life as a moral drama in which the individual is arrayed against the state and all the oppressive instruments of coercion which they associate with government—bureaucracies, courts, police, and the military, as well as the institutions of private property and religion. They seek liberation from these and all forms of external constraint upon human freedom. Firmly convinced of humanity's innate goodness and reasonableness, a benign anarchist who follows Kropotkin believes that the basic law of society is not conflict but mutual aid and cooperation. According to Irving Louis Horowitz, the anarchist, in addition to being antipolitical, is also antitechnological and antieconomic.[51] Thus anarchists are essentially foes of capitalist and socialist alike: If the former keeps government merely to protect their bourgeois interests and manage their affairs, the latter would replace capitalist tyranny with socialist tyranny—the "dictatorship of the proletariat."

Some branches of anarchism—notably collectivist, communist, syndicalist, and conspiratorial—openly espoused the use of violence both in theory and as a tactical necessity. Sergei Nechaev (1847–1882), a disciple of Mikhail Bakunin (1814–1876), a Russian revolutionary agitator, adopted a creed of "propaganda by deed" and "universal pan destruction." He advocated the nihilistic tactic of assassination for its effects of psychological terror and the demolition of existing institutions.[52] Enrico Malatesta (1850–1932), an Italian journalist, regarded well-planned violence as an apt means of educating the working classes as to the meaning of the revolutionary struggle.[53] Similarly, the French journalist Georges Sorel (1847–1922) perceived value in proletarian acts of violence which serve to delineate the separation of classes. Such violence, he maintained, helps to develop the consciousness of the working class and keeps the middle class in a chronic state of fear, always ready to capitulate to the demands made upon it rather than run the risk of defending its position by resort to force.[54]

Not all anarchists have been advocates of violence. Individualist anarchists in America, such as Henry David Thoreau (1817–1862) and Benjamin R. Tucker (1854–1939), eschewed violence as unrespectable. They preferred to emphasize nonviolent civil disobedience. The two most influential pacifist anarchists of modern times—Mahatma Gandhi (1869–1948) and Leo Tolstoi (1828–1910)—radically opposed a pure religious ethic to a person's willingness to submit to the State, which they excoriated for brutalizing the masses and converting military heroism into a virtue. Deeming it imperative that the law of force be superseded by the law of love, yet finding this impossible within the framework of the existing nation-state system, they insisted that the latter must give way to a universal society.[55]

Anarchism has sometimes been quite trenchant in its moral criticism of existing institutions, but it has not made a significant contribution toward a scientific understanding of the sources of human conflict. Where one finds in anarchist writings a keen insight into group sociology (e.g., in Sorel's awareness of the group-integrating function of externally directed violence), this usually reflects a borrowing from more dispassionate social scientists (e.g., Sorel was strongly influenced by Durkheim). In recent decades, the chief appeal of anarchist theories in the United States, which have a long history in this country, has been to intellectuals, artists, black militants, students, youth and others identified with the "counterculture," and, especially in the late 1960s, the protest against the Vietnam War. On the international plane, anarchist thought has been reflected in an increasing incidence of acts of terrorism—highjacking, bombings, guerrilla raids, kidnapping, assassination, the taking of hostages, and other violent deeds designed nihilistically to transform society by delivering random, indiscriminate blows regardless of the guilt or innocence of those targeted, thus producing widespread insecurity and senseless shocks which shake society to its foundations. "Propaganda by deed" remains the preferred strategy of nihilists who, like Verloc in Joseph Conrad's novel, *The Secret Agent*, ask what response can be made

> ... to an act of destructive ferocity so absurd as to be incomprehensible, inexplicable, almost unthinkable; in fact, mad? Madness alone is truly terrifying, inasmuch as you cannot placate it either by threats, persuasion, or bribes.[56]

Since the terrorizer is an enemy of mind and civilized order, he or she does not present an ideal subject for rational analysis and theory.

THE "JUST WAR" THEORY IN THE NUCLEAR AGE

Since considerable attention was devoted earlier in this chapter to the "just war" doctrine as a set of normative constraints limiting the way a state may act in pursuit of its "necessities" (survival, independence, the preservation of its common good, and the defense of its rights), reference should be made here to the revival of the debate over the ethics of warfare in the twentieth century.

   Several writers have argued that in view of the destructive power of modern military technology, especially nuclear weapons, the conditions of the "just war"—specifically the requirement that the amount of force employed must be proportionate to the political objectives sought—can no longer be validated. According to the "nuclear pacifist" school, even though it may have been theoretically possible to justify the use of force by states in earlier historical periods, nuclear war is potentially fraught with such monstrous consequences that it cannot be deemed politically or morally justifiable under any circumstances. Moreover, the fact that political leaders in all states and at all times have invoked the justice of their cause when they went to war, combined with the fact that history furnishes scant evidence of religious leaders in any nation questioning or denying the justice of their government's policies during wartime, has contributed to a growing skepticism toward the "just war" theory even in respect to nonnuclear war. Finally, the inhumanity of modern warfare has prompted increasing numbers of theologians and ethicians to ask whether the waging of war can ever be made compatible with the imperatives of the Christian conscience.[57]

   Typical contemporary pacifists are appalled by what they regard as the stupidity, futility, or immorality of nuclear war. They allege that such conflict threatens not only mutual extinction for the nations engaging in a large-scale nuclear exchange, but also grave dangers of widespread radioactive fallout and genetic mutations for the rest of humanity. The pacifist is usually skeptical of all theories of nuclear deterrence and of the decision-makers' presumed rationality on which deterrence is supposed to be based. Pacifists abhor the international competition in armaments (or "arms race"), which in their view, even if it does not lead inevitably to war, supposedly piles up an "overkill" capability, produces an international climate of neurotic fear, wastes vast amounts of economic and scientific-technological resources which could otherwise be channeled into other uses, and generally dehumanizes individuals, stifling their impulse to love others. Some writers, after contemplating the tragic situation into which the nations have drifted, advocate unilateral disarmament and nonviolent resistance as the only ways of breaking through the vicious circle. Erich Fromm, Mulford Q. Sibley, and Gordon Zahn have seen nonviolent resistance less as a form of helpless passivity than as a psychic or spiritual "soul" force capable of effecting a significant attitude change or "conversion" on the part of the aggressor.[58]

   Even in the nuclear age with all its potential horrors, the mode of rational analysis embodied in the "just war" tradition has not lacked advocates. Without denying that the theory has often been abused in history, its modern proponents generally take the position that past distortions, while they should make us wary of the self-rationalizing tendency of nations, do not warrant our discarding an intellectual type of ethical analysis which seeks to chart a middle course between the extremes of pacifism and bellicism. Theorists in this group have included John Courtney Murray, Paul Ramsey, Robert E. Osgood, Richard A. Falk, William V. O'Brien, Michael Walzer, and others.[59]

The "just war" writers are convinced that, no matter how far efforts in this area may fall short of an ideal model of moral action, it is still better for people to engage in this kind of evaluation than to try to achieve a sense of inner purification by washing their hands of advanced weapons technology, thereby allowing it to develop according to its own dialectic. That nuclear power exists is a fundamental fact of contemporary political reality which cannot be conjured away by pious rhetoric or wishful thinking. This massive power, wrote the Jesuit theologian John Courtney Murray in 1959, demands a master strategic concept based upon a high sense of moral and political direction.

> This sense of direction cannot be found in technology; of itself, technology tends toward the exploitation of scientific possibilities simply because they are possibilities. . . . It is the function of morality to command the use of power, to forbid it, to limit it; or, more in general, to define the ends for which power may or must be used and to judge the circumstances of its use.[60]

The general consensus of the "just war" writers can be summed up in the following propositions.

1. In the absence of effective international peacekeeping institutions, the moral right of states to resort to war under certain circumstances cannot be denied.

2. Although aggressive war (which was permitted under the traditional doctrine to punish offenses and to restore justice) is no longer considered a lawful means available to states for the vindication of violated rights, there still exists the right to wage defensive war against aggression and to give aid to another party who is a victim of aggression.[61]

3. Modern military technology cannot be allowed to render entirely meaningless the traditional distinction between "combatant forces" and "innocents" even in strategic war. (This issue arose in the somewhat inconclusive strategic debate during the 1960s over "counterforce" versus "countercity" or "countervalue" strategies, and during the 1970s over "selective targeting" and "limited nuclear options.")

4. The "just war" theorist denies that in war the end justifies the means and that once a war starts a government may employ any and every instrument at its disposal in an unlimited quest for victory. Even when the state has the moral right to wage war (*ius ad bellum*), there is an obligation to adhere to the law governing the means used in war (*ius in bello*).[62]

5. Although there is reason to hope that deterrence will succeed

and nuclear war will not occur, the "just war" writers insist that a posture of massive deterrence through the threat of massive retaliation against urban centers is not sufficient. There is a heavy moral obligation upon political leaders to assure an operational readiness, in case deterrence fails, to wage war (including nuclear war) in a limited and discriminating rather than an all-out manner. Ramsey argues that "traditional and acceptable moral teachings concerning legitimate military targets require the avoidance of civilian damage as much as possible even while accepting this as in some measure an unavoidable indirect effect."[63]

6. Thus, the just war theorists insist, nuclear weapons cannot be held intrinsically evil (*malum in se*). According to Ramsey, their strictly controlled use against primarily military targets, under conditions calculated to avoid escalation to uncontrollable levels, is morally conceivable, especially where this seems necessary to contain aggression quickly and bring about early negotiations. But he contends that their indiscriminate use against whole cities cannot be morally justified—not even in retaliation.[64]

The debate over war and morality will go on indefinitely. Pacifists of various persuasions, absolutist, or relativist, will argue that it is either logically absurd or ethically monstrous to analyze warfare in terms of "rationality" or "justice." Other theorists will contend that in a global system which lacks an effective global peacekeeping authority, that is, an international force organized in support of international justice, independent national governments and other political entities are likely to be disposed from time to time to resort to the use of force, and that the world will be better off if those who advise governments—regardless of whether they are pacifists or "just war theorists"—can have recourse to an intellectually credible code of rational, moral, civilized behavior which enjoins decision-makers, in an age of intrinsically inhumane technological possibilities, to observe humane limits in their strategizing. Despite frequent assertions that the "just war" doctrine has become obsolete in a nuclear era of unlimited destructive capability, there have been numerous instances of limited conventional and unconventional warfare, as well as of efforts to develop new systems of advanced weapons technology, to which the traditional analysis of the conditions required for the moral justification of deterrence and force remains quite relevant and—what is more—still applied with remarkable frequency in the public political debate.[65]

Perhaps no student of the "just war" has dealt more intricately than Michael Walzer with the paradox confronted by strategists and moralists in the nuclear age. The human mind seems unable to devise a coherent conceptual framework—political policy, strategic doctrine, and operational military plan—which neatly combines effective deterrence with workable defense, and which is widely acceptable on grounds of rationality, credibility, and morality. Walzer reminds us that superpower governments are deterred from risking even conventional war, not to mention limited nuclear war, by the specter of ultimate horror—the danger that it might escalate to an uncontrollable nuclear exchange. In an era of plentiful nuclear stockpiles, he says, *any imaginable strategy* is likely to deter a "central war" between the giants. Once we understood what the strategists of deterrence were saying, it became unnecessary to adopt any particular strategy for fighting a nuclear war.[66] (Many strategic theorists, of course, would deny this.) It was deemed sufficient merely to pose the ultimate nuclear threat. Deterrence is frightening in principle when we stop to ponder the ultimate, but in actuality deterrence is easy to live with because it has been a bloodless strategy. It causes no pain or injury to its hostages, unless they stop to think it through, which not many people do. Walzer puts distance between himself and most just war theorists when he propounds the view that all nuclear war is immoral.[67]

Notes

1. Lewis A. Coser, *The Functions of Social Conflict* (New York: The Free Press, 1956), p. 3.
2. Cf. Jerome D. Frank, "Human Nature and Nonviolent Resistance," in Quincy Wright et al., eds., *Preventing World War III: Some Proposals* (New York: Simon & Schuster, 1962), p. 193; John G. Stoessinger, *Why Nations Go to War* (New York: St. Martin's, 1974), p. 218.
3. H. L. Nieburg, *Political Violence* (New York: St. Martin's, 1969).
4. Seymour Martin Lipset has noted that both Tocqueville and Marx emphasized the necessity for conflict among social units, and Lipset defines the "existence of a moderate state of conflict" as "another way of defining a legitimate democracy." *Political Man: The Social Bases of Politics* (Garden City, L.I.: Doubleday-Anchor, 1963), pp. 7 and 71. "Conflict is an essential aspect of growth, one that we can neither fully control nor prevent, nor should we wish to do so." H. L. Nieburg, op. cit., pp. 16–17. "Human existence without conflict is unthinkable. Conflict gives life much of its meaning, so that its elimination, even if attainable, would not be desirable." Jerome D. Frank, "Human Nature and Nonviolent Resistance," op. cit., p. 193. Kenneth Boulding has suggested that "in a given situation there may be too much or too little conflict, or an optimal amount which lends to life a certain dramatic interest." *Conflict and Defense* (New York: Harper & Row, 1962), pp. 305–307.
5. Quoted in Abram Kardiner and Edward Preble, *They Studied Man* (New York: New American Library [Mentor Books], 1963), p. 102. Elsewhere Durkheim wrote: "Social facts do not differ from psychological facts in quality only: *They have a different substratum;* they evolve in a different milieu; they depend on different conditions. . . . The mentality of groups is not the same as that of individuals; it has its own laws." S. A. Solvay and J. K. Mueller, *The Rules of Sociological Method*, 2nd ed., trans. G. E. G. Catlin, ed. (New York: The Free Press, 1938), p. xix.
6. See Reuben Osborn, *Freud and Marx* (London: Victor Gollancz, 1937), and *Marxism and Psycho-Analysis* (London: Barrie and Rockliff, 1965).
7. See, for example, the collection of essays from various social science disciplines in Elton B. McNeil, ed., *The Nature of Human Conflict* (Englewood Cliffs, N.J.: Prentice-Hall, 1965); also J. David Singer, "Man and World Politics: The Psycho-Cultural Interface," *Journal of Social Issues*, XXIV (July 1968), 127–156.

8. Michael Haas, *International Conflict* (New York: Bobbs-Merrill, 1974), p. 4.

9. J. K. Zawodny, *Man and International Relations* (San Francisco: Chandler, 1967), Vol. I, p. 2.

10. Stephen Withey and Daniel Katz, "The Social Psychology of Human Conflict," in Elton B. McNeil, ed., *The Nature of Human Conflict* (Englewood Cliffs, N.J.: Prentice-Hall, 1965), p. 65.

11. Herbert C. Kelman, "Social-Psychological Approaches to the Study of International Relations," in Herbert C. Kelman, ed., *International Behavior: A Social-Psychological Analysis* (New York: Holt, Rinehart and Winston, 1965), pp. 5–6. See also the references to the work of Werner Levi in the following chapter.

12. By way of exception, however, it should be noted that Western moralists are under increasing pressure to distinguish between justifiable and unjustifiable violence, including revolutionary terror. For the debate about revolutionary violence and the "theology of liberation," see the October 1968 issue of *Worldview*, devoted to "Revolution and Violence," and also the following works: Guenter Levy, *Religion and Revolution* (New York: Oxford University Press, 1974); Thomas M. McFadden, ed., *Liberation, Revolution and Freedom* (New York: Seabury, 1975); and Jacques Ellul, *False Presence of the Kingdom* (New York: Seabury, 1972).

13. See M. Jane Stroup, "Problems of Research on Social Conflict in the Area of International Relations," *Journal of Conflict Resolution*, IX (September 1965), 413–417. See also Coser, op. cit., pp. 15–38; Jessie Bernard, "Parties and Issues in Conflict," *Journal of Conflict Resolution*, I (June 1957), 111–121; and Raymond W. Mack and Richard C. Snyder, "The Analysis of Social Conflict—Toward an Overview and Synthesis," ibid., I (June 1957), 212–248. For the argument that Talcott Parson's "structural-functional" approach, relegating conflict to the realm of the abnormal, deviant, and pathological, renders itself incapable of explaining social change and conflict, see Ralf Dahrendorf, "Toward a Theory of Social Conflict," *Journal of Conflict Resolution*, II (June 1958), 170–183. According to Dahrendorf, Parsons was more interested in the maintenance of social structures and order than in change. The Parsonians focused attention upon problems of adjustment rather than of change. For them, social conflict was essentially disruptive and dysfunctional. Dahrendorf in his sociology stresses change rather than persisting configurations; conflict rather than integration; constraint rather than consensus. He presents his postulates not to overturn the Parsonian view, but rather to complement it with an organic model of different emphases. He believes that neither model alone, but only the two taken synthetically, can exhaust social reality and supply us with a complete theory of society in its changing as well as in its enduring aspects. For the earlier views of the German sociologist Georg Simmel, see Nicholas J. Spykman, *The Social Theory of Georg Simmel* (New York: Atherton, 1966), especially pp. 3–127; Lewis A. Coser, ed., *Georg Simmel* (Englewood Cliffs, N.J.: Prentice-Hall, 1965), especially pp. 1–77. See also "Conflict," trans. Kurt H. Wolff, in *Conflict and the Web of Group Affiliations* (New York: The Free Press, 1955), p. 13. Simmel wrote: "Just as the universe needs 'love and hate,' that is, attractive and repulsive forces, in order to have any form at all, so society, too, in order to attain a determinate shape, needs some quantitative ratio of harmony and disharmony, of association and competition, of favorable and unfavorable tendencies." Ibid., p. 15. "A certain amount of discord, inner divergence and outer controversy is organically tied up with the very elements that ultimately hold the group together . . ." (pp. 17–18). Even in relatively hopeless situations, the opportunity to offer opposition can help to render the unbearable bearable: "Opposition gives us inner satisfaction, distraction and relief, just as do humility and patience under different psychological conditions" (p. 19). See also R. C. North et al., "The Integrative Functions of Conflict," *Journal of Conflict Resolution*, IV (September 1960), 355–374; and Lewis A.

Coser, "Some Social Functions of Violence," *Annals of the American Academy of Political and Social Science*, CCCLXIV (March 1966), 8–18.

14. See the editor's Introduction in Harry Eckstein, ed., *Internal War: Problems and Approaches* (New York: The Free Press, 1964), p. 1; and Ted Robert Gurr, "Psychological Factors in Civil Violence," *World Politics*, XX (January 1968), 245–246. See also the references to the studies of conflict behavior within and between nations by Rudolph Rummel, Raymond Tanter, and Ted Robert Gurr in Chapter 7, p. 304–305.

15. See Jessie Bernard, "Parties and Issues in Conflict," *Journal of Conflict Resolution*, I (June 1957), 111–121; Raymond W. Mack and Richard C. Snyder, "The Analysis of Social Conflict—Toward an Overview and Synthesis," ibid., XII (December 1968), 412–460.

16. Charles Lockhart, "Problems in the Management and Resolution of International Conflicts," *World Politics*, XXIX (April 1977), 370; and Kenneth E. Boulding, *Conflict and Defense: A General Theory* (New York: Harper & Row, 1962), p. 2.

17. See Daniel Lerner, "On Cause and Effect," Introduction by Daniel Lerner, ed., *Cause and Effect* (New York: The Free Press, 1965), especially pp. 1–5.

18. See the excellent chapter on "Ancient China," in Frank M. Russell, *Theories of International Relations* (New York: Appleton, 1936); Mousheng Lin, *Men and Ideas: An Informal History of Chinese Political Thought* (New York: John Day, 1942); Arthur Waley, *Three Ways of Thought in Ancient China* (London: Allen and Unwin, 1939 [Anchor edition, 1956]); H. G. Creel, *Chinese Thought from Confucius to Mao Tse-tung* (New York: New American Library, 1960), especially pp. 51–53, 113–121, and 129–130; and Ch'u Chai and Winberg Chai, eds., *The Humanist Way in Ancient China: Essential Works of Confucianism* (New York: Bantam, 1965).

19. In other words, *ahimsa* promoted vegetarianism long before it promoted pacifism in India. For further discussion of historic Indian attitudes toward war, see D. Mackenzie Brown, *The White Umbrella: Indian Political Thought from Manu to Gandhi* (Berkeley: University of California Press, 1953), especially part one; U. N. Goshal, *A History of Hindu Political Theories* (London: Oxford University Press, 1923); A. L. Basham, "Some Fundamentals of Hindu Statecraft," in Joel Laurus, ed., *Comparative World Politics: Readings in Western and Pre-Modern Non-Western International Relations* (Belmont, Calif.: Wadsworth, 1964), especially pp. 47–52; and the chapter on "Ancient India," in Frank M. Russell, op. cit.; Norman D. Palmer, "Indian and Western Political Thought: Coalescence or Clash?", *American Political Science Review*, XLIX (September 1955), 747–761; George Modelski, "Kautilya: Foreign Policy and International System in the Ancient Hindu World," ibid., LVIII (September 1964), 549–560.

20. Hamilton A. R. Gibb, *Mohammedanism: An Historical Survey* (New York: New American Library, 1955), pp. 57–58. Majid Khadduri has written two very fine expositions of the subject: *War and Peace in the Law of Islam* (Baltimore, Md.: Johns Hopkins Press, 1955) and "The Islamic Theory of International Relations and Its Contemporary Relevance," in J. Harris Proctor, ed., *Islam and International Relations* (New York: Praeger, 1965), pp. 24–39.

21. D. Mackenzie Brown, op. cit., p. 143.

22. See Joshua, chap. 1:5–9, 23: 2–6; Judges, chap. 6:6–18; Samuel, chaps. 13–18. See also Max Seligsohn, "War-Biblical Data," in Isadore Singer, ed., *The Jewish Encyclopedia* (New York: Funk and Wagnalls, 1905), pp. 464–465; and Y. Yarden, "Warfare in the Second Millenium B.C.E.)," in Benjamin Manzar, ed., *The History of the Jewish People* (New Brunswick, N.J.: Rutgers University Press, 1970).

23. See Franziskus Stratmann, *War and Christianity Today* (Westminster, Md.: Newman Press, 1956); Roland H. Bainton, *Christian Attitudes Toward War and Peace* (Nashville: Abingdon Press, 1960), chaps. 4–6; see Cecil John Cadoux, *The Early*

Church and the World (Edinburgh: T. & T. Clark, 1925), especially pp. 51–57; Franziskus Stratmann, *The Church and War* (New York: Sheed and Ward, 1928); Joan D. Tooke, "The Development of the Christian Attitude to War before Aquinas," in *The Just War in Aquinas and Grotius*, chap. I (London: Society for the Propagation of Christian Knowledge, 1965), pp. 1–20; and James E. Dougherty, "The Catholic Church, War and Nuclear Weapons," *ORBIS*, IX (Winter 1966), especially pp. 845–850.

24. See Frank M. Russell, *Theories of International Relations* (New York: Appleton, 1936), pp. 91–97; Quincy Wright, *A Study of War* (Chicago: University of Chicago Press, 1942), Vol. I, p. 198; Coleman Phillipson, *The International Law and Custom of Ancient Greece and Rome* (New York: Macmillan, 1911), Vol. II, pp. 5–8; Bede Jarrett, *Social Theories of the Middle Ages, 1200–1500* (Westminster, Md.: Newman Press, 1942), pp. 201–202. The most thorough exposition of the medieval doctrine of the "just war" is to be found in Joan D. Tooke, op. cit.

25. Since medieval society exalted cavalry over infantry, only a limited number of full-fledged warriors was available. Given the low level of the armor-making arts, the fully equipped mounted knight represented a considerable investment. Monarchs lacked the financial and organizational resources to raise and maintain large professional armies. Europe, with population sparse and agricultural methods poor, was usually preoccupied with basic problems of survival. Furthermore, the intricate feudal network of land-loyalty relationships gave rise to many conflicts of fealty among vassals and lords. In a society of delicately balanced bargaining relationships, wars were frequent but they were waged on a small scale for strictly limited objectives. See Henri Pirenne, *Economic and Social History of Medieval Europe* (New York: Harcourt Brace Jovanovich, 1937); Joseph R. Strayer and Rushton Coulborn, *Feudalism in History* (Princeton: Princeton University Press, 1956); F. L. Ganshof, *Feudalism* (London: Longmans, 1952); and Richard A. Preston, Sydney F. Wise, and Herman O. Werner, *Men in Arms: A History of Warfare and Its Interrelationships with Western Society* (New York: Praeger, 1962), chaps. 6 and 7. For an account of the rules of warfare laid down by the Church during the twelfth century under the "Truce of God" and the "Peace of God," see Arthur Nussbaum, *A Concise History of the Law of Nations* (New York: Macmillan, 1954), p. 18.

26. See Francisco de Victoria, *De Indis et De Iure Belli Relectiones*, trans. John P. Bate (Washington: Carnegie Endowment for International Peace, 1917); Francisco Suarez, *De Triplici Virtute Theologica*, Disp. VIII, "De Bello," in *Selections from Three Works* (Oxford: Clarendon, 1925); Balthazar Ayala, *Three Books on the Law of War, the Duties Connected with War and Military Discipline* (Washington: Carnegie Institute, 1912); Emerich Vattel, *Le Droit des Gens* (Washington: Carnegie Institute, 1916); and Albericus Gentilis, *De Iure Belli*, trans. John C. Rolfe (Oxford: Clarendon, 1933). All of these works are in the Classics of International Law Series, edited by James Brown Scott.

27. John U. Nef, *War and Human Progress* (Cambridge: Harvard University Press, 1950), pp. 250–259; Richard A. Preston, et al., *Men in Arms*, Chapter 9.

28. Paul Hazard, *European Thought in the Eighteenth Century*, trans. J. Lewis May (New York: World, 1963), p. 18.

29. Kingsley Martin, *French Liberal Thought in the Eighteenth Century*, 2nd ed. (New York: New York University Press, 1954), chap. XI.

30. *Outlines of an Historical View of the Progress of the Human Mind, 1794*. Excerpts from an English translation of 1802 in Hans Kohn, *Making of the Modern French Mind* (Princeton: Van Nostrand [Anvil Books], 1955), pp. 97–98.

31. *Candide*, chap. 3, in Edmund Fuller, ed., *Voltaire: A Laurel Reader* (New York: Dell, 1959), pp. 13–14.

32. William Penn wrote an *Essay Toward the Present and Future Peace of Europe;*

Abbé de St. Pierre, *A Project for Making Peace Perpetual in Europe;* Jean-Jacques Rousseau, *A Lasting Peace Through the Federation of Europe;* Immanuel Kant, *Perpetual Peace;* and Jeremy Bentham, *Plan for a Universal and Perpetual Peace.*

33. An analysis of the balance of power as a theory was presented in Chapter 1. On this see Henry A. Kissinger, *A World Restored—Europe After Napoleon: The Politics of Conservatism in a Revolutionary Age* (New York: Grosset and Dunlap [Universal Library], 1964).

34. R. A. Preston et al., *Men in Arms:* chap. 12.

35. Jonathan Dymond, *An Inquiry into the Accordancy of War with the Principles of Christianity and an Examination of the Philosophical Reasoning by Which It Is Defended,* 3rd ed. (Philadelphia: Brown, 1834).

36. Norman Angell, *The Great Illusion: A Study of the Relation of Military Power to National Advantage* (New York: Putnam's, 1910), p. 71. One of the arguments employed by Angell to prove that economic prosperity can be separated from military capability was that the national bonds of small nonmilitary states were sought after by investors as more secure than bonds of the larger military powers. In rebuttal to Angell, Professor J. H. Jones of the University of Glasgow pointed out that it was the military expenditures of the larger powers which created the conditions of international stability and security on which smaller nations depended, in *The Economics of War and Conquest* (London: King and Son, 1915), p. 25. For a skeptical critique of the view that railways, steamships, and international commerce promote friendship among nations and were responsible for long periods of peace in nineteenth century Europe, see Geoffrey Blainey, *The Causes of War* (New York: Macmillan-Free Press, 1973), esp. Chap. 2, "Paradise Is a Bazaar."

37. Norman Angell, ibid., p. 335.

38. Karl von Clausewitz, *On War,* trans. O. J. Mathhijs Jolles (New York: Random House [Modern Library], 1943), p. 210.

39. G. W. F. Hegel, *Philosophy of Right and Law,* par. 324, in Carl J. Friedrich, ed., *The Philosophy of Hegel* (New York: Random House [The Modern Library], 1953), p. 322.

40. "What is good? All that enhances the feeling of power, the Will-to-Power, and power itself in man. What is bad? All that proceeds from weakness. What is happiness? The feeling that power is increasing—that resistance has been overcome. Not contentment, but more power; not peace at any price, but war; not virtue, but efficiency. . . . The weak and the botched shall perish: first principle of our humanity. And they ought even to be helped to perish. What is more harmful than any vice? Practical sympathy with all the botched and the weak—Christianity." From *The Twilight of the Idols* (1888), in Geoffrey Clive, ed., *The Philosophy of Nietzsche* (New York: New American Library, 1965), p. 427.

41. *Human, All Too Human,* vol. I (1878). Ibid. pp. 372–373. According to William James, peaceful activities involving a challenge to strenuous exertion and sacrifice could serve as a substitute for war in providing the "social vitamins" generated by war. The philosopher-psychologist recognized that war and the military life met certain deeprooted needs of societies and summoned forth human efforts of heroic proportions. He did not think it possible to attenuate the proclivity to war until these same energies could be redirected—for example, by training young men to fight not other human beings but such natural forces as diseases, floods, poverty, and ignorance. If the nation is not to evolve into a society of mollycoddles, youth must be conscripted to hardship tasks to "get the childishness knocked out of them." See William James, "The Moral Equivalent of War," in his *Memories and Studies* (London: Longmans, 1912); and *A Moral Equivalent for War* (New York: Carnegie Endowment for International Peace, 1926). Later, Aldous Huxley was to popularize the hypothesis that many people find an exhilaration in war because their peace-

time pursuits are humiliating, boring, and frustrating. War brings with it a state of chronic enthusiasm, and "life during wartime takes on significance and purposeful-ness, so that even the most intrinsically boring job is enobled as 'war work.'" Pros-perity is artificially induced; newspapers are filled with interesting news; and the rules of sexual morality are relaxed in wartime. But Huxley, writing just before World War II, conceded that the conditions of modern war have become so ap-palling that not only the civilians on the home front, but "even the most naturally adventurous and combative human beings will soon come to hate and fear the pro-cess of fighting." *Ends and Means* (New York: Harper & Row, 1937). Excerpted in Robert A. Goldwin et al., eds., *Readings in World Politics* (New York: Oxford Uni-versity Press, 1959), pp. 13–14.

42. Heinrich von Treitschke, *Politics* (New York: Macmillan, 1916), II, 595.

43. "We have learned to perceive the moral majesty of war through the very processes which to the superficial observer seem brutal and inhuman. The greatness of war is just what at first sight seems to be its horror—that for the sake of their country men will overcome the natural feelings of humanity, that they will slaughter their fel-lowmen who have done them no injury, nay whom they perhaps respect as chival-rous foes. Man will not only sacrifice his life, but the natural and justified instincts of his soul; . . . here we have the sublimity of war." Ibid., pp. 395–396.

44. Ibid., p. 24.

45. Quoted in Russell, op. cit., p. 245.

46. Alfred Thayer Mahan, *Armaments and Arbitration* (1912), p. 31. Quoted in Charles D. Tarlton, "The Styles of American International Thought: Mahan, Bryan, and Lippmann," *World Politics*, XVII (July 1965), 590. The foregoing summary of Mahan is based largely upon Tarlton's analysis. For an analysis of Mahan's work on the relationship between seapower and national power, see Chapter 2.

47. Vilfredo Pareto, *The Mind and Society*, trans. A. Bongiorno and A. Livingston (New York: Harcourt Brace Jovanovich, 1935), vol. IV, pp. 2170–2175 and 2179–2220; Gaetano Mosca, *The Ruling Class*, trans. H. D. Kahn (New York: McGraw-Hill, 1939). For interesting and valuable assessments of both Pareto and Mosca, see parts III and VI of James Burnham, *The Machiavellians: Defenders of Freedom* (New York: John Day, 1943).

48. Holmes glorified war as a romantic adventure and as a necessary corrective for the irresponsible and sybaritic tendencies of modern youth. See Edward McNall Burns, *Ideas in Conflict: The Political Theories of the Contemporary World* (New York: Norton, 1960), p. 54.

49. Oswald Spengler, *The Decline of the West*, trans. Charles F. Atkinson (New York: Knopf, 1926–1928), 2 vols.; and *The Hour of Decision*, trans. Charles F. Atkinson (New York: Knopf, 1934).

50. See A. James Gregor, *The Fascist Persuasion in Radical Politics* (Princeton: Prince-ton University Press, 1974); Anthony James Joes, *Fascism in the Contemporary World: Ideology, Evolution, Resurgence* (Boulder, Colo.: Westview, 1978), Chap. 3; H. S. Harris, *The Social Philosophy of Giovanni Gentile* (Urbana, Ill.: University of Illinois Press, 1960).

51. Irving Louis Horowitz, ed., *The Anarchists* (New York: Dell, 1964), from the edi-tor's Introduction, p. 22.

52. See the excerpt from Thomas G. Masaryk in ibid., pp. 469–473.

53. Irving Louis Horowitz, op. cit., pp. 44–55.

54. Georges Sorel, *Reflections on Violence* (New York: Macmillan, 1961), pp. 77–79, 115. See his chap. 2, "Violence and the Decadence of the Middle Classes." See also part IV, "Sorel: A Note on Myth and Violence," in Burnham, op. cit.; and William Y. Elliott, *The Pragmatic Revolt in Politics: Syndicalism, Fascism and the Constitu-tional State* (New York: Howard Fertig, 1968), pp. 111–141.

55. Irving Louis Horowitz, op. cit., pp. 53–54; Francis W. Coker, *Recent Political Thought* (New York: Appleton, 1934), Chap. VII, esp. pp. 223–225.

56. Quoted in Daniel Bell, *The Cultural Contradictions of Capitalism* (New York: Basic Books, 1976), p. 6. Contemporary terrorists often select at random, for kidnapping or murder, "typical" members of the group or class they seek to terrorize (e.g., business personnel, diplomats, air travelers, or restaurant diners). See Edward Hyams, *Terrorists and Terrorism* (New York: St. Martin's, 1974); Paul Wilkinson, *Political Terrorism* (New York: Wiley, 1974); and J. Bowyer Bell, "Trends on Terror: The Analysis of Political Violence, *World Politics*, XXIX (April 1977), 476–488.

57. For a representative sample of the voluminous literature reflecting these attitudes, see Roland H. Bainton, *Christian Attitudes Toward War and Peace* (Nashville: Abingdon Press, 1960); Franziskus Stratmann, op. cit.; John C. Bennett, ed., *Nuclear Weapons and the Conflict of Conscience* (New York: Scribner's, 1962); Gordon Zahn, *An Alternative to War* (New York: Council on Religion and International Affairs, 1963); Walter Stein, ed., *Nuclear Weapons and Christian Conscience* (London: Merlin, 1961); James Finn, ed., *Peace, the Churches and the Bomb* (New York: Council on Religion and International Affairs, 1965); and Donald A. Wells, *The War Myth* (New York: Pegasus, 1967).

58. See Erich Fromm, "The Case for Unilateral Disarmament," in Donald G. Brennan, ed., *Arms Control, Disarmament and National Security* (New York: Braziller, 1961), pp. 187–197; Mulford Q. Sibley, "Unilateral Disarmament," in Robert A. Goldwin, ed., *America Armed* (Chicago: Rand McNally, 1961), pp. 112–140; Gordon Zahn, op. cit.

59. See John Courtney Murray, *Morality and Modern War* (New York: Church Peace Union, 1959) and republished as "Theology and Modern War" in *Theological Studies*, XX (March 1959), 40–61; Paul Ramsey, *War and the Christian Conscience* (Durham, N.C.: Duke University Press, 1961) and *The Limits of Nuclear War* (New York: Council on Religion and International Affairs, 1963); Robert E. Osgood, "The Uses of Military Power in the Cold War," in Robert A. Goldwin, ed., *America Armed*, op. cit., pp. 1–21; Richard A. Falk, *Law, Morality and War in the Contemporary World*, Princeton Studies in World Politics No. 5 (New York: Praeger, 1963); Robert W. Tucker, *The Just War* (Baltimore: Johns Hopkins Press, 1960) and *Just War and Vatican II: A Critique* (New York: Council on Religion and International Affairs, 1966); William V. O'Brien, *Nuclear War, Deterrence and Morality* (Westminster, Md.: Newman Press, 1967); Michael Walzer, *Just and Unjust Wars* (New York: Basic Books, 1977).

60. Murray, op. cit., p. 61.

61. O'Brien, op. cit., pp. 34–41.

62. Ibid., pp. 23–26 and chap. 5, "Morality and Nuclear Weapons Systems."

63. Ramsey, *The Limits of Nuclear War*, op. cit., p. 10.

64. This point was made by Pope Pius XII in 1954. See O'Brien, op. cit., pp. 34 and 45. It was reiterated by the Second Vatican Council.

65. See Ralph B. Potter, *War and Moral Discourse* (Richmond, Va.: John Knox Press, 1969); Robert Ginsberg, ed., *The Critique of War* (Chicago: Regnery, 1969); Richard A. Wasserstrom, *War and Morality* (Belmont, Calif.: Wadsworth, 1970); Morton A. Kaplan, ed., *Strategic Thinking and Its Moral Implications* (Chicago: University of Chicago Center for Policy Study, 1973); and James T. Johnson, "The Cruise Missile and the Neutron Bomb: Some Moral Reflections," *Worldview*, 20 (December 1977); and Michael Walzer, op. cit.

66. Michael Walzer, op. cit., p. 278.

67. Ibid., p. 274.

Chapter 6
Economic Theories of Imperialism and War

In the study of the essential conditions for world peace and the causes of international conflict, economic factors have held a position of considerable importance. Implicit, if not explicit, in many theories of international relations is the assumption that rising living standards and national economic growth contribute to peace among nations. In modern liberal thought, writers such as Adam Smith, John Stuart Mill, and Richard Cobden considered free trade to be a guarantor of peace. Free trade would create a division of labor based on international specialization in an international economy in which nations were so interdependent as to make virtually impossible the resort to war. The growth of individual and national prosperity would divert public attention from military ventures because of their potentially disruptive effects on economic growth and prosperity. In marked contrast to the proponents of free trade based upon economic competition, other writers have argued that free competition is a principal determinant of international conflict.

There is a widespread disposition to explain all international political relations by reference, more often gratuitously asserted than scientifically demonstrated, to forces associated with the quest for economic gain

213

or advantage. The most significant trends in world politics and the most significant decisions of governments are said to be traceable to such economic forces as complex, powerful multinational corporations engaged in the procurement, processing, and marketing of a vast range of raw materials, semifinished products, and manufactured or assembled goods; the ruthless competition (or sinister collusion) of European Community, Japanese and American manufacturing, agricultural, labor, trading, and banking-financial interests; the divergence of economic interests between the industrialized countries of the North and the less developed countries of the South, with the richer exploiting the poorer; and the systemic rivalry between free market economies and centrally directed socialist economies.

All of these, no doubt, represent powerful forces that allegedly influence the course of international politics, and especially matters of tariffs, trade, aid, investment, monetary, and related policies. Central to economic theories of imperialism and war is the assumption (rejected by the authors) that all international issues—insurgencies, revolutions, imperialism, wars, alliances, arms races, disarmament and arms control, hunger and malnutrition, concern for the environment, social and political development in the Third World, the effort to develop a regime for the oceans, and all other important questions of international politics, diplomacy, law, and organization—are reducible to issues of economic gain rather than political power.

The strength of such an assumption, dubious as it may be, lies in the considerable influence of the philosophical system propounded originally by Karl Marx and Friedrich Engels, as well as of the political pronouncements, whether consistent or contradictory, of their numerous socialist and communist descendants, principally Lenin, Stalin, Mao, Khrushchev, Castro, Brezhnev, and others. Generations of academic and journalistic theoreticians, as well as would-be political practitioners, who never lived under a communist or a socialist regime, have expounded an essentially Marxist analysis of the world. Large numbers of otherwise bourgeois teachers, students, politicians, and writers, and even business people have adopted an economic interpretation of history based at least in part on Marxian analysis.[1] In nearly all Third World countries, elites take for granted the validity of Lenin's notion of imperialism, and this powerfully influences their attitude toward the West. The main elements of the Marxist theory date back to 1848. Yet the theory has shown a remarkable survivability into the final quarter of a century that has often proved brutally critical of abstractions inherited from the past. The Marxist analysis of international relations, especially of imperialism and war, of social conflict and revolution, has survived more as faith than science. But survive it does, even though battered intellectually from all sides. Let us examine the Marxist theory.

THE MARXIST THEORY

Marxism is an admixture of metaphysics (dialectical materialism), theory of history (economic determinism), economic and sociological science, political ideology, theory and strategy of revolution, social ethics, and an eschatalogical moral theology which looks toward a secular salvation: the advent of a classless social order of perfect justice in which conflict ceases and the psychology of a "new man" is generated. If Newton contributed toward an explanation of international conflict in terms of mechanistic equilibrium in the "Golden Age" of the balance of power, if Hegel to the personification of nations and the philosophy of national sentiment and clashes, if Darwin to a conception of international politics based on the notion of biological struggle from which the fittest survive, and if Freud to the concept of social conflict as a result of the projection outward of dark psychological forces from the inner depths of humanity, then Marx more than any other individual strengthened the idea that conflict arises inevitably out of the life-and-death struggle of socioeconomic classes. Capitalism is the bondage from which people strive to be liberated, and this will be accomplished through the knowledge of the inexorable dialectical laws of historical-social development. Up to now, class conflict has been the motor of social change. Once class conflict comes to an end with the establishment of communism, social change will occur only as a result of rational planning, debate, and decision-making.

Karl Marx (1818–1883), born in the Rhineland, spent much of his adult life in England, where he observed at first hand the acceleration of the Industrial Revolution during the nineteenth century. He perceived the emergence of an urban working class and a widening gap between the rich and the poor. Marx evolved a theory of history based on dialectical materialism, in which the system of economic production determines the institutional and ideological structures of society.[2] The one who controls the economic system controls the political system. Marx and Engel's study of history and of nineteenth-century Britain led them to conclude that each period of history contains clashing forces, or a dialectic, from which a new order emerges. "In ancient Rome, we have patricians, knights, plebeians, slaves; in the Middle Ages, feudal lords, vassals, guild-masters, journeymen, apprentices, serfs; in almost all of these classes, again, subordinate gradations."[3]

All history is the history of class struggle between a ruling group and an opposing group, from which comes a new economic, political, and social system. Marx's "model" for the study of society and its transformation contains a thesis (ruling group) and an antithesis (opposing group) which clash and produce a synthesis (new economic, political, and social system).

Before the emergence of capitalism, ownership of land had been the basis of political power. The feudal system was challenged by a growing commercial class, a bourgeoisie, whose economic strength derived from trade and manufacturing and who lived in towns and cities, rather than on landed estates. From this clash of opposing forces emerged a new synthesis, capitalism. The bourgeoisie has concentrated population in large cities, centralized the means of production, and gathered wealth in a few hands. Formerly, independent or loosely connected provinces that once had their separate legal systems, economic interests, and governments have been organized into one nation with a central government and customs tariff.

Like the systems which preceded it, capitalism contains the seeds of its own destruction. Marx foresaw that the growing impoverishment of the working class, or proletariat, would lead to a revolution to overthrow the ruling capitalist class. The lower strata of the middle class are absorbed into the proletariat, since they do not have the capital to compete on the scale of their larger counterparts, and their specialized skills become worthless as a result of new methods of production. As the ranks of the proletariat are increased, the struggle with the bourgeoisie grows in intensity. Initially the struggle is conducted by individual workers, and then by the laborers in one factory against individual members of the exploiting capitalist class. Marx envisaged a series of clashes of increasing intensity between the proletariat and the bourgeoisie until the eruption of a revolution finally resulting in the overthrow of the bourgeoisie.

The founder of scientific socialism developed in elaborate detail his doctrine of surplus value. Stated briefly, the socially useful labor which produces a commodity is considered to be the only measure of its worth. Capitalists themselves produce nothing. Instead, they live like parasites from the labor of the producing class. The capitalist pays the laborer a subsistence wage and keeps the rest. According to Marx, the vast mass of the population is reduced to wage slavery in a capitalist society. The proletariat produces goods and services for which it receives little or no return. In a capitalist system, the bourgeoisie, which controls the means of production, exploits the worker and widens the gap, or surplus value, between the price paid workers for their labor and the price obtained by the bourgeoisie in the marketplace for the goods or services produced by the proletariat.[4]

The coming clash between the capitalist, bourgeois class (thesis) and the proletariat (antithesis) would lead to a socialist order. There would be a period of extensive government controls over production and distribution until the last vestiges of capitalism were removed. Finally, Marx foresaw the withering away of the state with the development of a communist economic, political, and socialist order.

Thus the Marxist views all political phenomena, including imperialism and war, as projections of underlying economic forces. Here all forms of consciousness are subordinated to the economic. Religious, humanitarian, political, cultural and military-strategic motives for any kind of power relationship between a stronger and a weaker community are explained by the Marxist as rationalizations designed to disguise the economic substructure. This has been essentially true throughout history, Marx held, but it becomes more apparent in the case of capitalism. In a passage written avowedly for polemicist purposes rather than to display social science objectivity, Marx and Engels declared:

> The bourgeoisie . . . has left no other bond between man and man than naked self-interest, than callous cash payment. It has drowned the most heavenly ecstacies of religious fervor, of chivalrous enthusiasm, of philistine sentimentalism, in the icy water of egotistical calculation. . . . The bourgeoisie has stripped of its halo every occupation hitherto honored and looked up to with reverent awe. It has converted the physician, the lawyer, the priest, the poet, the man of science, into its paid wage-laborers.[5]

Marx had a vision of peace—the peace of the self-alienated man restored to himself, as a result of the "negation of the negation"—the revolutionary self-appropriation by the proletariat, taking that which rightfully belongs to itself.[6] Thus for Marx, no less than for Saint Augustine, human beings wage war for the sake of peace, and some must fight and suffer and even die for the sake of others and of improving the quality of human life. But there is a notable difference between the "just war" theory of the Christian and that of the Marxist. In the Christian theory, there is in every organized political community an existing human common good which deserves to be defended if violated or attacked by a foreign aggressor. The Marxist "just war" doctrine is waged for the sake of future as-yet-nonexistent individuals; existing political, economic, and social structures (viewed by Christians and others as worth defending because they embody the accumulated values of society despite their imperfections) are seen only as part of the alienation and exploitation of man by man; since for the Marxist their very existence constitutes a violation of justice, those structures must be destroyed and replaced by something better—from within if possible, from outside if necessary.

Marx does not project an image throughout his writings of a man bent upon violent revolution. Especially in his earlier years, he may have preferred or hoped that the inevitable victory of socialism could be achieved through a nonviolent working out of the dialectic. But as he grew older, Marx's youthful philosophical idealism gave way to the thought modes of a frustrated, impatient, professional revolutionary. John Plamenatz has put well the case for avoiding extremes in interpreting Marx—insisting either that Marx was pathologically bent upon violence or that he abhorred violence as a pacifist might:

Logically, violence, the shedding of blood, is no essential part of revolution as Marx and Engels conceived it. True, they thought there would be violence when the proletariat took over power, in most countries if not in all. They even at times, I suspect, took pleasure in the thought that there would be.

They were not very gentle persons; nor did they believe, as certain other socialists and communists of their day did, that violence is wrong or that it corrupts those who use it. But all this takes nothing away from the point I am making: revolution, as Marx and Engels conceived of it, does not necessarily involve violence.[7]

It was Lenin, coming out of a tradition of Russian revolutionary conspiratorial activity which had become a mirror image of the Tsarist oppressiveness it fought, who more than anyone else imparted to twentieth-century Marxist communism its predilection for violence and terror. Lenin was reacting in part against the Revisionism of such German Marxists as Karl Kautsky (1854–1938) and Edward Bernstein (1850–1932), who realized that some of Marx's predictions had gone awry, and that the achievement of socialism might be a long, gradual process utilizing education, psychological intimidation, and the ballot box. Lenin insisted that the appeal of violence was inherent in the makeup of the true revolutionary, and that the bourgeois state cannot be replaced by the proletarian state through a withering away but, as a general rule, only through a violent revolution.

Although Marx fully appreciated the worldwide scope of capitalist operations for acquiring raw materials and marketing manufactures, he himself did not elaborate a theory of imperialism. This task was left to his twentieth-century intellectual heirs—Rudolph Hilferding (1877–1941), a German Social Democrat; Rosa Luxembourg (1870–1919), a German Socialist agitator; and Lenin, whose views will be examined presently.

HOBSON ON IMPERIALISM

Curiously enough, most of the clues to the communist theory of imperialism in this century were provided by the English economist, John A. Hobson (1858–1940). Hobson, an Oxford graduate, was a journalist, essayist, and university lecturer who had been influenced toward liberalism by John Stuart Mill and toward the science of society by Herbert Spencer. Attracted to idealist, humanitarian, and ethical causes of social reform, he became a self-designated religious and economic heretic, and gravitated toward a Fabian-type socialism as he grew increasingly disenchanted with "mechanized capitalism." During the Boer War he went to South Africa as a correspondent for *The Manchester Guardian.* Already a critic of capitalism, his coverage of that conflict, which he saw as a concoction of diamond monopolists and other economic exploiters, moved

him further in the direction of an anticapitalist, antimilitarist polemic
that was not free of anti-Semitic overtones. Perhaps he was merely ap-
pealing to an anti-Semitism that was then on the rise in Western Europe,
just as he was to socialist and pacifist thought trends. In any event it is
not too much to say that Hobson practically invented the modern theory
of imperialism, and did a great deal to create an intellectual-moral revulsion against it in the English-speaking world.[8] (Liberal opinion in the
United States was already manifesting a guilt feeling over Cuba and Pacific expansionism in the wake of the Spanish-American War.)[9]

More than 60 years later, two scholars would conclude that "the
worldwide misinterpretation of the Boer War as a capitalist plot . . . became the basis of all subsequent theory of imperialism."[10] The very word
imperialism that had hitherto been invoked proudly to imply what Britain had contributed toward the civilizing of the parts of the world which
she had once or still controlled—the rule of law, parliamentary institutions, a rational administration of civil servants with some sense of public
responsibility (hitherto a rather rare phenomenon in many regions), and
a conviction of the worth and rights of human beings (even rarer)—became in Britain "a recognized symbol of a strong moral revulsion on the
part of a minority with Liberal, Radical, and Labour learnings, or with
strong religious scruples."[11]

Hobson argued that imperialism results from maladjustments within
the capitalist system, in which a wealthy minority oversaves while an impoverished or "bare subsistence" majority lacks the purchasing power to
consume all the fruits of modern industry. Capitalist societies are thus
faced with the critical dilemma of overproduction and underconsump-
tion. If capitalists are willing to redistribute their surplus wealth in the
form of domestic welfare measures, there would be no serious structural
problem. But the capitalists seek instead to reinvest their surplus capital
in profit-making ventures abroad. The result is imperialism, "the endeavor of the great controllers of industry to broaden the channel for the
flow of their surplus wealth by seeking foreign markets and foreign investments to take off the goods and capital they cannot sell or use at
home."[12]

Hobson was aware that there were noneconomic factors at work in
late nineteenth-century European expansion abroad—forces of a political, military, psychological, and religious-philanthropic character. He
insisted, however, that the essential ingredient in imperialism is finance
capitalism, which galvanizes and organizes the other forces into a coherent whole:

> Finance capitalism manipulates the patriotic forces which politicians,
> soldiers, philanthropists and traders generate; the enthusiasm for expan-
> sion which issues from these sources, though strong and genuine, is irregu-
> lar and blind; the financial interest has those qualities of concentration

and clearsighted calculation which are needed to set imperialism at work.[13]

In Hobson's view, imperialism in the case of Britain had not been necessary to relieve population pressure, for Britain was not overpopulated and its growth rate at the turn of the century was declining toward a stationary level. Furthermore, he noted Englishmen did not seem at all anxious to resettle in most areas of the Empire acquired after 1870.[14]

Hobson condemned late nineteenth-century imperialism as irrational and as bad business policy for the nation as a whole, even though it was rational and profitable for certain groups—bourses, speculative miners, engineers, the shipbuilding and armaments industries, the export industries, contractors to the military services, and the aristocratic classes that sent their sons to be officers in the army, navy, and colonial service.[15] Although the economic activities of these classes comprised but a small fraction of Britain's total enterprise, the groups benefiting from imperialism were well organized for advancing their interests through political channels. Imperialism, said Hobson, involves enormous risks and costs to the nation compared to its relatively meager results in the form of increased trade, and hence the rationale for it must be sought in the advantages it brings to special groups within the society. "To a larger extent every year Great Britain is becoming a nation living upon tribute from abroad, and the classes who enjoy this tribute have an ever-increasing incentive to employ the public policy, the public purse, and the public force to extend the field of their private investments. . . ."[16] E. M. Winslow (1896–1966), evaluating the significance of Hobson's study, concluded: "No other book has been so influential in spreading the doctrine of economic imperialism."[17] Lenin would later clearly acknowledge his indebtedness to Hobson's work.

Hobson anticipated the later Leninist attack upon capitalist profiteering as a major factor in the causation of international war. Policies of aggressive imperialism and war lead to vast arms budgets, public debts, and the fluctuation of the values of securities from which the skilled financier benefits most. "There is not a war, a revolution, an anarchist assassination, or any other public shock, which is not gainful to these men; they are harpies who suck their gains from every new forced expenditure, and every sudden disturbance of public credit."[18] To be sure, Hobson is not saying here that the capitalists are responsible for the wars from which they profit. Almost certainly he would not contend that capitalists lurked behind every anarchist assassin. But the unmistakable thrust of his reasoning—which would be made more explicit by Lenin— was that if the behavior of capitalists is primarily motivated by the desire to gain profits, and if certain segments of capitalist society can profit from imperialistic wars, then these elements can be expected to bend every effort to bring about war when the circumstances call for it. In the last passage quoted, the tone of Hobson's moral indignation becomes less scholarly and more ideological, not unlike that which runs through the writings of Marx and his followers.

Lenin: Imperialism and International Conflict

Rosa Luxembourg (1870–1919), a German Socialist agitator, closely followed Hobson's analysis, while Hilferding sought to refine it by attributing the export of capital to the operation of cartel and monopoly systems which limit domestic investment possibilities. The best known theorist of imperialism in modern times, of course, was Lenin. The architect of the Bolshevik Revolution was neither the scholar nor the original thinker that Hobson was. In addition to borrowing ideas from Hobson, Lenin relied upon Hilferding's analysis of the role of monopoly capitalism:

> Imperialism is capitalism in the stage of development in which the dominance of monopolies and finance capital has established itself; in which the export of capital has acquired pronounced importance; in which the division of the world among the international thrusts has begun; in which the division of all territories of the globe among the great capitalist powers has been completed.[19]

Monopoly capitalism, which he equated with imperialism, Lenin derived from four factors: (1) the concentration of production in combines, cartels, syndicates, and trusts; (2) the competitive quest for sources of raw materials; (3) the development of banking oligarchies; and (4) the transformation of the "old" colonial policy into a struggle for spheres of economic interest in which the richer and the more powerful nations exploit the weaker ones. Thus Lenin took strong exception to Karl Kautsky's thesis that imperialism was merely the "preferred policy" of capitalist states; for Lenin it was inevitable. Moreover, in the Leninist interpretation the receipt of monopoly profits by the capitalists of certain industries enables them to corrupt the workers in those industries, who for the sake of a higher standard of living ally themselves with the bourgeoisie against their fellow workers of the exploited, imperialized countries.

Since finance capitalism is the source of imperialism, it also becomes for the Marxists the principal source of international wars in the capitalist era, or at least the only source in which the Marxists are interested. If there are other sources of conflict, Marxists prefer not to call much attention to them. Hobson, who was a liberal rather than a Marxist, had conceded that there are "primitive instincts" in the human race which played a part in nineteenth-century imperialism—the instinct for the control of land, the "nomadic habit" which survives as love of travel, the "spirit of adventure," the sporting and hunting instincts, and the "lust of struggle," which in the age of spectator sports is transformed into gambling on the outcome of athletic games and into jingoism in war.[20] But Hobson circumvented the theoretical difficulty implicit in the plurality of factors merely by accusing the dominant classes in capitalistic societies of advancing their own interests by playing upon the primitive instincts of the race and channeling them into imperialistic ventures. Lenin, too, recognized that there had been imperialism in the world before the highest stage of capitalism had been reached; but he was not interested in the analysis of imperialism as a general phenomenon of all ages apart from reference to socioeconomic systems and especially capitalism.

Lenin's contribution to communism was twofold. First, he imparted an organizational theory in which the Communist Party became the "vanguard of the proletariat" to hasten the coming of the revolution which Marx had foreseen as inevitable. Second, drawing heavily upon the work of Hobson described above, Lenin developed a theory of imperialism which ranks as the principal communist theory of international relations in an international system consisting of capitalist states.[21]

Looking back upon the history of Europe in the decades after Marx published his *Communist Manifesto*, Lenin concluded that the proletariat would not revolt spontaneously, as Marx had believed, against the ruling bourgeoisie. In his famous tract entitled *What Is to Be Done?*, Lenin held that a strong, tightly knit, highly motivated party of professional revolutionaries was essential to the success of the revolution against the capitalist order. To Lenin, the Communist Party, the "vanguard of the proletariat," was the most class-conscious, devoted, and self-sacrificing part of the proletariat.[22] Lenin held that the Party must be centralized or hierarchical. It must be based on "democratic centralism"—that is, the Party must provide for discussion and debate of issues before a decision was taken, while adopting iron-clad discipline in executing policy after a decision had been made.

Lenin saw imperialism as a special, advanced stage of capitalism. In capitalist systems, competition is eventually replaced by capitalist monopolies.[23] Imperialism is the monopoly stage of capitalism. The need to export capital arises from diminishing investment opportunities in capitalist countries themselves. The export of capital to achieve a higher rate of investment return hastens the development of capitalism elsewhere in the world. The countries that are the principal exporters of capital are able to obtain economic advantages based on the exploitation of peoples abroad. Moreover, the greater the development of capitalism, the greater the need for raw materials and markets, and hence the greater the scramble for colonies. The establishment of political control over overseas territories is designed to provide a dependable source of raw materials and cheap labor and to guarantee markets for the industrial combines of advanced capitalist countries.

Lenin held that imperialist policies would enable capitalist powers to stave off the inevitable revolution, since conditions of the domestic proletariat would be ameliorated by the exploitation of the working class in colonial territories. A portion of the proletariat in advanced capitalist countries even finds it possible to rise to the ranks of the bourgeoisie.

Writing in the spring of 1916, nearly two years after the outbreak of World War I, Lenin viewed the history of the previous generation as a struggle between the advanced capitalist powers for the control of colonies and markets. Capitalist countries have formed alliances for the exploitation of the underdeveloped areas. Especially in East Asia and Africa, the imperialist powers have claimed territories and spheres of influence. But such alliances are only "breathing spells" between wars, since the capitalist powers find it necessary to fight for control of limited overseas markets and raw materials. Because of the ultimate dependence of capitalist economic systems upon such markets and natural resources, international conflict is endemic in a world of capitalist states. The elimination of capitalist states, Lenin concluded, was the essential precondition to abolishing international conflict. Lenin's theory posits, in effect, a relationship between the structure of a country's domestic political and economic system and its foreign policy. Capitalist states, by virtue of their political and economic systems, were said to enhance the likelihood of conflict. For this reason the building of a peaceful world order had as an indispensable prerequisite, in Lenin's theory, the destruction of the system of capitalist states.

For Lenin, capitalism had developed at its own pace in each country, earlier in Holland, England, and France, later in Germany and the United States, later still in Japan and Russia. But as it developed, monopolistic capital engaged in a feverishly competitive search for new markets, sources of raw materials, and cheap labor. Lenin was of the opinion that by this time the cartels had virtually completed the process of parceling out the territories of the world for exploitation. Because the planet has already been divided up, further expansion by some capitalists can occur only at the expense of other capitalists, and thus capitalistic imperialism provokes international wars.[24] Stalin, remembering the Allied intervention in Russia at the end of World War I, regarded the capitalist West with suspicion and hostility, and spoke often of those outside plotting aggression against the Soviet Union. But in his famous "last thesis," issued on the eve of the 1952 meeting of the Communist Party of the Soviet Union, Stalin argued that the "frightful clashes" that Lenin had predicted between the capitalist and socialist camps were no longer inevitable, because such war would jeopardize the very existence of capitalism. Stalin then went on to declare that contradictions within the capitalist systems made the recurrence of war among capitalist states inevitable.[25] This was a rather unusual prophecy to utter at a time when, just a few years after the onset of the Cold War, the "capitalist world" appeared to be more unified than before World War II as a result of the formation of the Atlantic Alliance in 1949. It was less wide of the mark in the 1970s, when many Europeans complained that United States policy in the Middle East jeopardized the uninterrupted flow of oil from that region to Europe and placed heavy strains on NATO's cohesiveness.

LENIN, STALIN, AND WAR

Orthodox Leninist-Stalinist reasoning led inescapably to the conclusion that modern war is a function of capitalist imperialism; that if war should occur between the two systems it would be as a result of capitalist aggression and it would lead to the destruction of capitalism and the universal triumph of socialism; and that in an all-socialist world, once the dangers of "capitalist encirclement" had been eliminated, war would disappear. Stalin declared: "In order to destroy the inevitability of wars, it is necessary to destroy imperialism."[26] Stalin, of course, was not necessarily implying that the socialist camp must someday try to destroy the imperialist camp by carrying out an aggressive military attack across national boundaries. Stalin was, if anything, a cautious, conservative strategist; he certainly was not calling for a socialist holy war against a technologically superior Western state system. Both he and his successor, Khrushchev, propounded the thesis that "capitalist encirclement" must eventually give way to "socialist encirclement." Khurshchev is rather widely thought to have had a better appreciation than did Stalin of the implications of nuclear weapons technology for the "inevitability of war" problem, inasmuch as he formerly recognized that general nuclear war could very well destroy not only capitalist society but communist society as well. Thus, while pursuing limited-risk arms control agreements with the capitalist West in order to render more manageable the strategic-military environment as reflected in international armaments competition, while at the same time continuing to develop Soviet military capabilities, both strategic and tactical, Khrushchev and his successors (Kosygin and Brezhnev) lent support to "wars of national liberation" in the Third World—forms of warfare considered both "just" in terms of socialist ideology and "safe" from the standpoint of strategic analysis in an era of mutual nuclear deterrence.[27] Nevertheless, whatever subtle modifications may have been made in recent decades by Communist leaders who have had to grapple with the realities of the international strategic environment, there has been no significant modification of the Leninist theory of imperialism.

CRITICS OF THE ECONOMIC THEORIES OF IMPERIALISM

Modern critics of the economic theories of imperialism have taken strong exception to the conclusions of Hobson, Lenin, and their followers on grounds of both semantics and economic-political analysis. Generally speaking, the semantic attack has taken the shape of an accusation that the followers of Lenin have been so obsessed by an ideological aversion to finance capitalism as to confuse a particular historical manifestation of the imperialistic impulse with a much more comprehensive sociological-political phenomenon—what St. Augustine called the *animus dominandi*—which has assumed many different shapes throughout history. The analytic critics usually argue that the theorists of economic imperialism err in subordinating politics to economics; that their theory fails to explain what it purports to explain; and that the assumptions on which their theoretical edifice rests depend much more upon an inflammatory rhetoric than upon scientifically convincing evidence.

Within recent decades, the most important critic of the Hobson-Leninist theory of imperialism as a terminological perversion for narrow polemical and ideological purposes has been Hans J. Morgenthau (who certainly can also be numbered among the leading analytical critics of that theory and whose theory of international relations is examined in Chapter 3). Morgenthau lamented the application of the term *imperialism* to any foreign policy which the user of the term found objectionable, and he urged the post-World War II generation of university students to accept an objective, ethically neutral definition of imperialism as "a policy that aims at the overthrow of the status quo, at a reversal of the power relations between two or more nations."[28] He denied that every increase in the international power of a nation is necessarily imperialistic. Moreover, he warned against the disposition to regard every foreign policy which aims conservatively at the maintenance of an already existing empire as imperialistic when the term should be properly reserved for the dynamic process of changing the international status quo by acquiring an empire.[29] The economic interpretation of imperialism, contends Morgenthau, errs in the attempt to build a universal law of history upon the limited experience of a few isolated cases. Such a theory, in his view, ignores the problem of precapitalist imperialism (including the ancient empires of Egypt, Assyria, Persia, and Rome; Arab imperialism of the seventh and eighth centuries; the European Christian imperialism of the Crusades; and the personal empires of such men as Alexander the Great, Napoleon, and Hitler).[30] Moreover, Morgenthau contended that the theory fails to provide a convincing explanation even of capitalist-age imperialism in the *belle epoque* of imperialism—1870 to 1914.

At this point, it will be useful to move from Morgenthau's semantic critique (which represented a noble but on the whole a futile effort) and to consider in a systematic way the political-economic analytical arguments against the Hobson-Lenin interpretation, in which the Morgenthau refutation is joined with that of several other prominent theorists, including the French political sociologist Raymond Aron, the Austrian economist Joseph A. Schumpeter (1883–1950), who taught at Harvard University for two decades prior to his death, the American diplomatic historian William L. Langer (1896–1978), and the American economist Jacob Viner (1892–1970), as well as with the findings of more recent scholars who have uncovered several anomalies in the Hobson-Lenin hypothesis.[31]

1. The followers of Marx, Hobson, and Lenin confuse a particular historical manifestation of the imperialistic impulse with a much more comprehensive, multifaceted political-sociological phenomenon which has assumed many different shapes throughout history. The "turn of the century" economic theory of imperialism is a distortion insofar as it rigidly subordinates international politics to international economics. Those who are well-versed in the modern history of international politics have little difficulty demonstrating that the political impulse is usually stronger than the economic, and that economic interests are frequently only a rationalization for a nation's will-to-power. Jacob Viner argued that in most cases

> The capitalist, instead of pushing his government into an imperialistic enterprise in pursuit of his own financial gain, was pushed, or dragged, or cajoled, or lured into it by his government, in order that, in its relations with the outside world and with its own people, this government might be able to point to an apparently real and legitimate economic stake in the territory involved which required military protection.[32]

2. Schumpeter insisted that imperialism cannot be reduced to the mere pursuit of economic interest when history is repleted with examples of societies "that seek expansion for the sake of expanding, war for the sake of fighting, victory for the sake of winning, dominion for the sake of ruling."[33] Wars are not fought in order to realize immediate utilitarian advantages, even if these are the professed purpose. Imperialism rather is "the objectless disposition on the part of a state to unlimited forcible expansion."[34] Like nationalism, it is irrational and unconscious, a calling into play of instincts from the dim past. Imperialism, in short, is an atavism in the social culture. If one wants to trace it to economic roots, it should be attributed to *past* rather than present relations of production. Undoubtedly it is the ruling classes in any state who take the decisions for war, but it is not the business bourgeoisie who comprise the principal foreign policy decision-makers in the modern world; it is the

vestigial aristocratic classes of an earlier regime who still fill the important governmental, diplomatic, and military posts.[35]

3. Notwithstanding the "devil theory" of war, which traces the causality of war to munitions-makers and others who stand to reap financial gain from its outbreak, capitalists as a whole are not given to bellicosity. Since war involves the irrational and the unpredictable, whereas capitalism thrives best on rational foresight and planning in a stable international environment, most capitalists are partisans of peace rather than of war.[36] Competitive enterprise in the capitalist system, according to Schumpeter, absorbs tremendous amounts of human energy in purely economic pursuits, leaving little excess to be worked off in war and even less tendency to welcome war as a diversion from unpleasant activities or from boredom.[37] Capitalist society creates the sociological basis for a substantial popular opposition to war and armaments, as well as to socially entrenched professional armies. Before the age of capitalism, pacifist principles had been taken seriously only by a few obscure religious sects. Modern pacifism as a significant political movement emerges only in capitalist society in which organized parties produce peace leaders, peace slogans, and peace programs, along with a popular aversion to imperialism and popular support for arbitration of disputes, disarmament, and international organization. In this respect Schumpeter was in basic agreement with Norman Angell and even with Karl Marx and Friedrich Engels, who had noted that national differences and antagonisms between peoples were daily vanishing, owing to the development of the bourgeoisie, to freedom of commerce, to the world market and to uniformity in the modes of production.

4. The fundamental assumptions of the economic theory of imperialism are wrong. "Hobson's theory has not stood the test of critical examination. The examples given by him for the fateful influence of capital investments overseas—South African mines and Chinese concessions—proved of ephemeral significance."[38] The effort to produce a universal theory on the basis of such scant evidence leads to several glaring anomalies in regard to what it leaves unexplained. According to that theory, the most advanced capitalist nations should have been the most expansionist and colonialist in the era of the highest development of monopolies and finance capitalism. Yet actually Europe's acquisition of colonial territories in the late nineteenth and early twentieth centuries was less extensive than in the period from the sixteenth to the eighteenth centuries. North and South America involved genuine colonization; European imperialism in Asia and later in Africa did not, except for relatively small areas. The logical corollary of the Lenin-Hobson theory is that less capitalist states should be less imperialist and colonialist. Yet Portugal, backward among capitalist countries, was a leading colonial power. In con-

trast, Sweden and Switzerland, two states profoundly imbued with the capitalist spirit, exhibited no instinct whatever for imperial-colonial ventures.[39] (One might interpose the objection that Switzerland could not take to the seas. But that introduces a geographical factor, which capitalists ought to be clever enough to circumvent by working out arrangements with fellow capitalists in maritime countries. In any event, Swedish entrepreneurs should have had even more than economic motives for seeking territorial adjuncts in warmer climes.)

Schumpeter points to the United States, a developing country in the first half of the nineteenth century and a rapidly rising capitalist power after the American Civil War (1861–1865). According to the theory, the United States should have tried to seize its two resource-rich but militarily weak neighbors—Mexico and Canada—but it did not do so.[40] (The United States, or at least some decision-makers, may have been aiming at territorial expansion in the 1812 attack on Canada and the 1848 attack on Mexico, but those episodes both fell within the precapitalist phase of American history.) Finally, the theory ignores the role of Western capital in making Japan an independent power of formidable proportions by the early twentieth century and of the United States postwar policy of rebuilding Western Europe's and Japan's ability to compete in world markets.

5. We can now examine the economic bases on which the Hobson-Lenin theory rests. First, it can be noted, in refutation of Hobson's underconsumption-oversavings hypothesis, that the export of surplus capital was not absolutely essential for growth; as Revisionist Marxists such as Karl Kautsky and Eduard Bernstein realized, the capitalists were not playing Marx's "iron law of wages" game to bring about the increasing "immiseration" of the workers; actually the workers' standard of living was on the rise, and domestic purchasing power was increasing in real terms as a consequence of trade union activity and the enfranchisement of larger numbers of people.[41] Second, during the period from 1870 to 1914, more capital moved into England than out of it, and three-quarters of the capital exported from Britain did not come from monopoly companies, but consisted of loans to governments and government-guaranteed public utilities.[42]

Third, the colonies were not as important in the trade and investment patterns of the capitalist countries as the theory indicated. No more than 10 percent of France's overseas investments prior to 1914 were directed to the Empire.[43] Apart from India (which had been brought under imperial control long before *la belle epoque*), the colonies, especially those in Africa, were not a source of much profit to Britain. Aron writes: "The two nations which during the half century before the First World War conquered the largest territories, France and Great

Britain, were also the nations which, economically, least needed to acquire new possessions."[44] Most of the capital exported from the advanced capitalist countries during that period went to other industrially advanced countries, or else to countries like Russia which were just beginning to develop industrially—and which France was anxious to build up for political-strategic reasons against Germany. It cannot be denied that there was a mad scramble for African colonies in the late nineteenth century, but the capitalist imperialist powers did not carry on the conquests for purposes of investment and trade promotion. Both the capital and the trade were directed elsewhere, as always, according to the laws of comparative advantage and as dictated by prices and returns.

6. Lenin's contention that imperialism as he defined it is the principal cause of war in the capitalistic era has not stood up well under the scrutiny of scholars. Morgenthau and Aron, among others, insist that most of the major wars since 1870 have not been fought primarily for economic motives. The Boer War in South Africa and the Chaco War between Bolivia and Paraguay (1932–1935) were, but not the Franco-German War, the Spanish-American War, the Russo-Japanese War, the Turco-Italian War, certainly not the two World Wars, the Arab-Israeli Wars, the Korean War, the Indo-Chinese War, the Indo-Pakistani Wars over Kashmir and Bangladesh, or the Vietnam War (even though leftist critics of the war in the West sometimes tried unconvincingly to reduce the Southeast Asian conflict to a capitalist-imperialist plot, mainly because the United States was identified as the leader of the capitalist-imperialist system).[45]

In the background of World War I, Aron assigns a central place to Anglo-German rivalry, especially the naval arms race, but he denies that this had much to do with capitalism. The British were aware that Germany represented a threat to their prosperity, but they also knew that each country was the best customer of the other's goods. If capitalist imperialism had been the main motive for England's going to war in 1914, then she should have arrayed herself against her major competitor since the turn of the century—the United States.[46] That such a course of action was unthinkable should serve to cast some doubt upon the explanatory power of the Leninist theory. Coming to more recent times, no one has ever bothered to try making a case for economic imperialism as the cause of the Korean War; such a task must strike even the most single-minded Marxist as futile. Kenneth Boulding wrote that any economic benefits the United States might have hoped to derive from the Vietnam War would hardly be worth the cost of waging that war for one day.[47] In the Arab-Israeli conflict since 1948, anyone who wishes to prove that American policy has been based upon considerations of economic imperialism is hard-pressed to explain why the United States has supported Israel even at the risk of alienating the oil-producing Arab states. One can only conclude that the Leninist theory lacks explanatory power in many areas of modern international relations.

To sum up, the Hobson-Leninist theory of imperialism is an analytic tool which has attracted the allegiance of many intellectuals probably more for its anticapitalist ideological content than for any validity it might possess as a result of careful empirical research. Nearly all analysts agree that the theory has a partial validity. It furnishes an adequate interpretation of a few instances of modern imperialism and would have a wider applicability if it did not, merely to "save the appearances" for Marxism, focus excessively upon economic factors to the exclusion of political, psychological, and cultural determinants of human social action. The theory fails to come to grips with the question of whether modern imperialism is to be explained primarily by economic factors unique to the capitalist system or by a greater variety of factors more relevant to the universal phenomenon of social group expansionism in all historic periods. Nor does it face up to the question of whether violent conflict can really be adequately understood as a result of a capitalist imperialism which emanates from societies of strong pacifist inclinations. Granted that some capitalists undoubtedly profit from the waging of wars, this does not prove that they cause or originate wars, or that capitalists at a given time are more bellicose than pacifists, or that the small group who might have an interest in precipitating war actually possesses the power to galvanize the primitive impulses of enough people within the society to determine the choice for war. It could happen occasionally, but serious students of international relations are not likely to accept such a simplistic solution for all modern wars. Nor are they likely to believe that an all-socialist world would be entirely nonimperialistic and peaceful. Resource-scarce industrialized states, whether communist or capitalist, will always be dependent upon overseas suppliers and upon markets outside their own boundaries, and they will use such bargaining levers as they have available. Hence Lenin's focus upon the links between political and economic systems may have obfuscated at least one other variable of central importance—the level of industrialization and its relationship to the need for raw materials.

LENINIST THEORY AND POSTWAR INTERNATIONAL PROBLEMS

The history of international relations since World War II has not dealt too kindly with the Leninist theory of imperialism. That theory is hard-pressed to explain Soviet Communist imperialism in Eastern Europe. Stalin's last thesis concerning the inevitability of war within the capitalist camp has not been verified to the satisfaction of most observers. On the one hand, to be sure, the West has had its internal disagreements (e.g., the allies over Suez, the Greek-Turkish dispute over Cyprus, and French policy toward NATO under de Gaulle), but none of these has been the internecine struggle which Stalin seemed to predict, nor can it be demonstrated that economic factors predominated in any of them. On the other hand, the communist state system itself has known some serious conflicts. Soviet troops suppressed a workers' revolt in East Germany in 1953, crushed the Hungarian uprising in 1956, and, with the Warsaw Pact allies, invaded Czechoslovakia in 1968. North Korea attacked South Korea in 1950 and was later joined in the aggression by Communist China. China launched a major military attack against Tibet in 1950 and against India in 1962, and by 1969 was engaged in hostilities with the Soviet Union along the Amur-Issurri Rivers.

At the time of the Hungarian uprising, Khrushchev declared that the Soviet Union was putting down a counterrevolution. In 1961, he pledged the Soviet Union to support "wars of national liberation" in the developing world. In 1968, after the Soviet military move against Czechoslovakia, party leader Leonid Brezhnev announced the doctrine that the Soviet Union had the right to intervene for the defense of communism in any country of the socialist camp, with or without an invitation. While Marxists offer a theoretical explanation of the Soviet interventions in Eastern Europe and in such national liberation wars as Vietnam in terms of the struggle between the forces of socialism and the forces of capitalism, it is much more difficult to do this for the Sino-Indian War and impossible to do it for the Sino-Soviet conflict, or the wars in Southeast Asia in which four Communist states were parties in the late 1970s, or the Soviet invasion of Afghanistan in 1979.

MODERN MARXISTS AND THE THIRD WORLD

Contemporary Marxist writers who adhere, however vaguely, to the Leninist theory of imperialism often charge that Western colonialism suppressed the economic, social, and political development of the countries that now comprise the Third World and that the West is still to blame for the poverty of those countries. Khrushchev had contended in 1960 that the economic advances made by some Western countries were due to the underdevelopment of Asia, Africa, and Latin America.[48] Western governments have been faulted for having failed during the era of colonial rule to introduce central economic planning in their territories and to promote the growth of indigenous industry with protective tariffs. André Gunder Frank has denied that underdevelopment is attributable to the survival of archaic institutions and capital shortages in regions isolated from the mainstream of world history. "On the contrary, underdevelopment was and still is generated by the very same historical process which also generated economic development: the development of capitalism itself."[49]

Marxists generally accuse the West—or "the world capitalist system"—of keeping the poor countries in a position of subordination, dependence, or bondage by limiting investments to the extractive (raw materials) industries and by Westernizing, subjugating, and bribing the new elites who have an interest in modernizing their societies. Before the period of decolonization, the Marxists predicted that once the colonial territories had gained political independence they would become masters of their own economic destiny, and thus the capitalists would fight to the end to prevent them from achieving self-government, because that would spell the collapse of the capitalist system.

Most of Europe's colonies had gained their independence by the 1960s. The Western capitalists had not fought effectively to hold them. The British and the Belgians, if not the French, the Dutch, and the Portuguese, seemed almost eager at times to get rid of their empires as if they were millstones around their necks.[50] Conflict did indeed attend the independence of some imperial possessions—Algeria, Indonesia, Cyprus, and Congo, Kenya, India, and Pakistan (due, in the latter cases, to historic religious divisions in the subcontinent)—yet more than two score colonial territories in Asia and Africa achieved status as independent states with relatively little or no violence. Furthermore, since the standard of living of the masses in the Western capitalist states had been alleged by the Marxists to be artificially high because it had long been based on the exploitation of native populations, disimperialism should have led to a perceptible decline in the West's standard of living, but this did not occur. To the contrary, the formation of the European Economic Community or Common Market ushered in a period of unprecedented economic growth and prosperity during the decade of decolonization. Western political and business leaders were increasingly convinced that, regardless of how important trade with and the investment in the overseas territories might once have been, economic transactions among the advanced industrial countries were considerably more important for the continued growth of the free "mixed enterprise" system of the democratic social welfare states of the West and Japan.

In the face of international political and economic developments within the last quarter of a century, Communists and other Marxists have been compelled to modify their theories of imperialism and conflict in several compensatory ways. Despite the steady movement of Asia and Africa toward political decolonization, Nikita Khrushchev frequently warned that the Western nations would "halt the disintegration of the colonial system of imperialism and strangle the national liberation movements of the peoples for freedom and independence."[51] The West, said Khrushchev, was desperately seeking new forms for keeping the peoples of economically underdeveloped countries in a state of permanent dependence. If any politically independent government in the Third World entered into a military assistance pact with a Western nation for defense against external attack or internal guerrilla subversion, this was simply a case, in Khrushchev's eyes, of fastening another control upon nominally independent states and propping up their "corrupt regimes" under the pretext of saving them from communism.[52] Khrushchev singled out the European Economic Community as an instrument of "neocolonialism" against which the new states had to be particularly on their guard. There was no doubt that official communist theory, while conceding that some economic development was now taking place in the Third World, still regarded the newly independent countries as part of the world subject to exploitation by the capitalist monopolies. Whereas the native populations had been previously oppressed by foreign capitalists and their colonial governments, they were now opposed by foreign capitalists and their local allies—the national bourgeoisie, which found itself in the contradictory position of being itself an exploiting class, and thus dependent on international finance capital in the struggle against socialism, while seeking to gain its own independence against foreign capitalistic imperialism.[53] This aspect of the theory receives some validation in the oil-producing countries of the Third World.

Following independence, development in Third World countries continued pretty much as before. It did not spurt ahead dramatically. This historic reality of the process of decolonization and its aftermath necessitated further modification of the Marxist-Leninist theory. Political independence for the former colonies was portrayed as a sham, because it led to no significant improvement in their economic status. The poor countries, say the Marxists, are still locked into the capitalist system and are being impoverished by its "iron law of prices," much as Marx used to deplore the increasing "immiseration" of the workers in capitalist countries as a result of the operation of the "iron law of wages." (In Marxist theory, all laws are iron laws.) This new situation explains the failure of the prediction that the capitalists would fight tenaciously to hold on to their colonies: The capitalists knew that they would have no difficulty continuing their economic domination.

According to Thomas E. Weisskopf, several factors at work within the world capitalist system reinforce the subordination of the poor to the rich countries. Rising elites in the poor countries are persuaded to emulate the consumption patterns of the bourgeoisie in the rich countries and to create a demand for the importation of Western goods. The "brain drain" of scientists, engineers, managers, and other educated professionals from poor to rich countries, as well as the importation of production techniques from the West, increases the dependence of the less developed countries (LDCs) on the industrialized regions. Weisskopf notes that it is in the interest of foreign private enterprise to perpetuate the conditions which make foreign capital and aid indispensable:

> Thus the incentives are structured in such a way that it is usually not in the interest of a foreign firm to impart to a domestic counterpart the knowledge of the skills or the advantages upon which its commercial success is based. Under such circumstances, domestic enterprise remains in a subordinate position and an important part of the indigenous capitalist class remains dependent upon foreign capitalists.[54]

Weisskopf also criticizes Western capitalists for creating a labor aristocracy in the poor countries by paying a smaller number of skilled workers higher wages rather than paying a larger number of unskilled workers lower wages. Most non-Marxist Western economists would argue, of course, that the former practice—whether carried out by capitalists or socialists—might contribute more to the development of a modernized economy. He concludes that "capitalist institutions in the poor countries—linked to and strengthened by the expanding world capitalist system—place important constraints upon the mobilization and utilization of resources for economic growth."[55]

As we indicated previously, the Marxists have generally held that the affluence of Western society has not been due to human energy, scientific inventiveness, technological proficiency, managerial and organizational efficiency, economies of scale, and a climate of political freedom in which economic decisions, while subject to public policy regulations, can be taken without excessive constraints imposed by bureaucratic central planners. Instead, they have explained that affluence is attributable in large measure to the exploitation by European and American capitalism of the peoples of Asia, Africa, and Latin America—an exploitation in which even the "bourgeois workers" of the West participated. To offset the paradox of the continued rise in the West's standard of living when it should have declined after the loss of empire, Marxists laid increasing emphasis on the argument that the Western economies were being artificially stimulated by the "arms race" and the fomenting of war hysteria for enriching a handful of monopolists.[56]

Presumably the intrusion of Soviet military power into Eastern Europe at the end of World War II, the invasion of South Korea by communist North Korea in 1950, the Soviet suppression of the Hungarian uprising in 1956, Khrushchev's boasts about Soviet missile power in the late 1950s, the Cuba Missile Crisis of 1962, the rise in the incidence of communist-supported "wars of national liberation" and guerrilla insurgencies throughout the Third World, and various Berlin crises, the invasion of Czechoslovakia by the Warsaw Pact in 1968, and the subsequent steady buildup of Soviet strategic and European theater capabilities—

none of these, so far as the Marxists were concerned, had anything to do with the formation and growth of NATO and with continuing Western concern about strategic deterrence and local defense. Rather, it was primarily a matter of the economic interests of Western capitalists eager for defense contracts. Thus neo-Marxists blame Western imperialism not only for the poverty of the Third World, but also for the world's failure to make progress toward genuine disarmament.

The notion that colonial exploitation has been replaced by the "arms race" does not stand up too well under serious scrutiny. The United States, which had a very meager overseas empire compared to the European nations, would undoubtedly have become the principal military defender of Western civilization after World War II regardless of developments in the colonial world. The Western European nations, which renounced rather enormous colonial holdings, have consistently allocated a much lower percentage of their gross national product to defense than has the United States, and the case could be made that the Western European standard of living has risen more rapidly than that of the United States during the past two decades.

A brief word is in order about the neo-Marxist economic explanation of the lack of progress in disarmament. Even though it is reasonable to expect that the cancellation of military contracts following upon a disarmament agreement would have an adverse multiplier effect upon prices, employment, public spending, and confidence in the health of a capitalist nation's economy, two important points must be made in this connection: (1) in terms of pure economics, the problem of disarmament is a soluble one; and (2) the primary obstacles to disarmament, far from being economic as the Marxists allege, are really technical, strategic, and political. The arms problem in the age of the nuclear missile can hardly be adequately explained by the old "devil theory" of war. It is not an aberration imposed upon the contemporary international system by the profiteering of certain industrialists (the "munitions-makers") or the innate aggressiveness of certain militarists. It is rather an intrinsic part of the system, deeply rooted in the essential characteristics of modern science and technology, of the decision-making and diplomatic processes of governments, of the global ideological-sociopolitical competition, and of a world structure in which nation-states seem driven to seek their security by engaging in some form of power balancing. This at least is as plausible an explanation of the arms race as that furnished by the Marxists. (The obstacles to disarmament will be examined more fully in Chapter 9.)

Among Marxist theorists in the post-World War II period who have sought to link imperialism closely with American foreign policy Harry Magdoff is one of the leading writers. Magdoff takes issue with those who contend that political aims and national security, rather than economic imperialism, have been the prime motivators of United States foreign policy. Such people, says Magdoff, rely on the argument that foreign trade and investment make up such a small part of the GNP of the United States (less than 5 percent in the case of total exports) that economic factors could not possibly determine American foreign policy. Magdoff denies that the size of ratios is by itself an adequate indicator of what motivates foreign policy. He further argues that the stake of American business abroad is many times larger than the volume of merchandise exports. He estimates that the size of the foreign market for all United States firms (domestic and those owned abroad) comes to about two-fifths of the domestic output of all farms, factories, and mines. He sees foreign economic activity as of growing importance to this country and its national security policy, usually justified in political-military terms, as designed to protect the economic interest of giant corporations abroad:

> The widespread military bases, the far-flung military activities, and the accompanying complex of expenditures at home and abroad serve many purposes of special interest to the business community: (1) protecting present and potential sources of raw materials; (2) safeguarding foreign markets and foreign investments; (3) conserving commercial sea and air routes; (4) preserving spheres of influence where United States business gets a competitive edge for investment and trade; (5) creating new foreign customers and investment opportunities via foreign military and economic aid; and, more generally, (6) maintaining the structure of world capitalist markets not only directly for the United States but also for its junior partners among the industrialized nations. . . .[57]

Magdoff, like all Marxists, expresses indignation over the fact that the United States invests primarily in extractive industries in Third World countries, thus insuring sources of raw material supplies to domestic monopolies on the most favorable terms. He implicitly assumes that dependence on primary product exports prevents real development.[58] This Marxist argument, by dint of constant repetition, has exerted an influence upon the thinking of non-Marxist analysts in the West, especially those who have sought to show that the contemporary pattern of international exchange relations based upon a world division of labor in which the less developed countries supply the basic raw materials for the industrially advanced countries to process leads to dynamic growth at one pole of the world economy and to stagnation and impoverishment at the other.

The Norwegian theorist, Johan Galtung, is an eminent proponent of this point of view. Galtung sees trade relationships between the European Community and Third World countries as characterized by a threefold structural dominance—the already-mentioned vertical division of labor plus two additional means of perpetuating the exploitative status quo: (1) "fragmentation" (or the relative absence of horizontal economic relationships among the developing countries); and (2) "penetration" (which involves the growth, previously alluded to, of economic, educational, cultural, and other relationships between local rising elites in Third World countries and the former metropolitan powers).[59] Galtung faults the European Community for "permitting" the Associated States of Africa to produce only such processed goods as will no longer be competitive with European Community exports. Even by granting "Associated" status and selective tariff preferences to certain African states, he declares, the European Community gives them a privileged position vis-à-vis the rest of the Third World, and thus fragments the "Group of 77" in UNCTAD (The United Nations Conference on Trade and Development).[60] Galtung is not a Marxist, but in his structural theory of imperialism he employs several of the same categories of thought as the Marxists and exhibits hardly less suspicion of Western capitalistic enterprise.

CRITIQUE OF THE NEO-MARXISTS

Marxists and others who blame the West for the poverty of the LDCs are roundly criticized for grossly oversimplifying the situation. No matter how much good may be done, it is always easy (and usually true) to say that more should have been done. But to blame the European governments for failing to carry out a higher degree of development in their empires when they held the responsibility, says P. T. Bauer, is to "overstate the potentialities of state power as an instrument of economic progress."[61] Actually, Bauer insists, colonial status was not incompatible with economic development. Whereas there had been virtually no economic growth in Africa before the Europeans arrived, between 1890 and 1960 West African trade (particularly for the Gold Coast and Nigeria) increased by a factor of 100 or more. According to Bauer,

> It is highly probable that over the last century or so the establishment of colonial rule in Africa and Asia has promoted, and not retarded, material progress. With relatively little coercion, or even interference in the lives of the great majority of the people, the colonial governments established law and order, safeguarded private property and contractual relations, organized basic transport and health services, and introduced some modern financial and legal institutions. The resulting environment also promoted the establishment or extension of external contacts, which in turn encouraged the inflow of external resources, notably administrative, commercial, and technical skills, as well as capital. . . . It is unlikely (though this cannot be proved conclusively) that in the absence of colonial rule, the social, political, and economic environment in colonial Africa and Asia would have been more congenial to material progress.[62]

Bauer makes the telling observation that the African states not subject to Western imperialism—Liberia and Ethiopia—are today more backward than their neighbors which had been colonized.[63]

Even in those cases in which the relationship between Western capital and the colonial country was exploitative because of a great disparity in development levels and economic power, the total relationship between the West and the colonial peoples was far from being onesidedly exploitative. With Western domination came literacy and education, hospitals, hygiene, and sanitary methods, and at least a rudimentary knowledge of science and technology. The political impact of the West upon the colonial lands was in some respects greater than the economic. The concepts of "independence," "self-determination," "freedom," and "sovereign equality" which the peoples of Asia and Africa employed with great effect after World War II to express their political aspirations were, as Hans Kohn pointed out, borrowed from the Western political vocabulary by native leaders who had received their university education in Western countries.[64]

Other non-Marxist analysts have argued persuasively that there is no necessary relationship between poverty and the reliance of Third World countries upon extractive and agricultural industries. Posing a serious challenge to the fundamental assumptions of this particular "iron law" thesis are the anomalies of Australia and New Zealand. Taking issue with Galtung, Andrew Mack writes:

> The economic exchange relationships which link Australia and New Zealand with the rich industrialised countries are precisely those which Galtung claims not only characterise Third World/EC relationships but which are also the root cause of the former's underdevelopment. Both countries depend on the export of primary commodities . . . characterised by nonexistent or very low degrees of processing. On the other hand, both countries depend on imports which are typically highly processed. . . . In other words, both countries lie at the lower end of the vertical division of international labour. . . . Yet both countries have experienced steady economic growth *and* a significant degree of domestic industrialisation. This is indeed an anomaly which Galtung's theory cannot explain.[65]

Marxist theorists generally ignore the fact that under the laws of comparative economic advantage it makes sense for many countries to export primary products in order to earn foreign exchange with which to import needed development technology. The "fragmentation" of the Third World reflects a reality that those countries depend (and will for a long time to come) more upon the industrially advanced countries than upon each other for trade and development. Moreover, it is difficult to imagine economic relationships which would not lead to some form of "penetration" of elites and changes in social incentives and lifestyles.

Marxist analysts are at their best when it comes to depicting in lurid terms what capitalists do. Whatever they do, especially when they act like capitalists, constitutes unjust exploitation. Hobson understood quite well that investment, like trade, follows not the flag but the basic laws of economics. If it pays United States capitalists to circumvent the external tariff of the Common Market by investing in the formation of advanced technology firms in the European Community, United States investors will move in that direction, provoking outcries of American imperialism. If profits in the Third World are to be earned in the extractive industries, that is where investment capital will flow. Ever since the days of Adam Smith, capitalists have insisted that they operate according to the only incentive system which is capable of creating new wealth at a dynamic rate. During the last century, free-market economists have usually adopted the plausible position that Marxist socialists are much more interested in the equal distribution of existing wealth than in the creation of new means of producing additional wealth in the future. The Marxists, let it be repeated, have achieved high levels of eloquence in condemning everything the capitalists have done (and some of those things deserved condemnation). But the Marxists have compiled a much less impressive record in spelling out precisely what Western capitalists ought to have done in the Third World for economic development and did not do, since everything that capitalists do is by definition exploitative. Whether the elites of the LDCs will continue to find a credible alternative economic model in what the Marxists have to offer (i.e., state planning and control for indigenous rather than foreign-assisted "imperialist" development) remains to be seen.

All Marxist analysis has a "holier-than-thou" quality to it. Lurking within it is the implication that a socialist system, by very definition, excludes the possibility of exploitation. The Marxists accuse the capitalist nations of giving foreign aid purely for the purpose of gaining political or other advantages. (Many politicians in the West would not only admit this, but they would insist upon it.) The underlying insinuation is that socialist governments are somehow disposed to give economic aid to foreign countries for purely altruistic reasons. Yet serious students of international relations will realize that it takes a great deal of naiveté to believe that Soviet aid for the construction of a steel mill in India, or for the paving of the streets of Kabul, Afghanistan, or for the building of the Aswan Dam in Egypt was given for any other reason than the expectation, well founded or not, of some future political advantage to be derived therefrom. In fact, the point can be made that since Western capitalists possess a much broader intellectual conception of their "global interests" than do the rather myopic bureaucratic central planners in Moscow, Third World development might proceed along a broader spectrum if carried out in cooperation with the West rather than with the East.

ORTHODOX AND REVISIONIST VIEWS OF
THE COLD WAR

It is appropriate at this point to examine a controversy that raged throughout the decade of the 1960s among students of United States foreign policy between the advocates of "orthodox" and "Revisionist" interpretations concerning the origins of the Cold War. By raising the subject in the midst of a discussion of Marxist theories of international relations, the authors do not wish to suggest that there was any simplistic disjunction between an orthodox school that favored a capitalist interpretation and a Revisionist school exposing a neo-Marxist one. The actual controversy, in the view of cautious scholars, was too complex and subtle for such facile categorizations. In fact, there has been considerable debate over the extent to which various explanations as to how the Cold War between the United States and the Soviet Union began, and who was responsible for it, were influenced by the assumptions of neo-Marxism, of political realism, or of traditional Anglo-American liberalism—tinged with a moralistic utopianism which postulates harmony among states as the normal condition of international relations and which seeks to fix blame for the occurrence of conflict upon evil individuals with sinister designs.

For a decade and a half after World War II ended, one view of postwar history—later dubbed "the orthodox"—held unquestioned sway in American and Western European universities and among elites on both sides of the Atlantic. According to this view, which could not be called merely "anti-Communist," the Soviet Union was impelled in its foreign policy by two mutually reinforcing tendencies toward expansion—a Communist ideology avowedly bent on the destruction of the Western capitalist system, imposed upon a much older Russian tradition of universal messianism, and a Tsarist policy of constantly probing for areas into which influence might be extended. During the interwar period, the Soviet Union had not disguised its hostility to the Western capitalist-democratic states; during the war, it had been a somewhat difficult ally, scarcely grateful in the eyes of the West for aid received, or at least delayed, as in the case of Stalin's call for a second front. The policy elites responsible for formulating United States policy during and after the war—the so-called Establishment—were never entirely comfortable at being allied with Josef Stalin, and they were not eager to extend what had been a wartime necessity into the postwar period, once it became apparent that the Stalinist system, which had pushed Russian military power to unprecedented westward frontiers in Central Europe, was replacing wartime collaboration with a revived intransigence. Soviet suppression of non-Communist forces in Eastern Europe (especially in Poland), Moscow's reparations policy toward Germany and its decision to

impose the Berlin blockade, the 1948 coup in Czechoslovakia, Stalin's refusal to allow the satellite countries of Eastern Europe to participate in
the Marshall Plan for regional economic recovery, and the creation of
the militantly anti-Western Cominform—these and similar developments left little doubt in the minds of orthodox Western historians that,
although the Cold War may have been the inevitable result of the sudden intrusion into the Central European power vacuum of two diametrically opposite political-economic systems, if blame had to be assigned for
the onset of the Cold War the greater portion must be borne by Stalin's
government. The policymakers who played such an important part in
shaping postwar United States foreign policy—President Truman, General George C. Marshall, John McCloy, Dean Acheson, Robert Lovett,
Loy Henderson, Averill Harriman, and others—looked upon the policy
of "containment" spelled out by George F. Kennan (and discussed in
Chapter 3) as the only prudent policy for the United States to pursue in
the face of Soviet expansionism. Regarding the economic recovery of
Western Europe insufficient to guarantee political stability and military
security in a region whose future was so inextricably linked to that of
their own country, they saw the formation of the North Atlantic Treaty
Organization as a logical extension of the national interest. Most of the
early chroniclers of the Cold War, despite minor differences of interpretation among themselves, substantially agreed with them.[66]

In contrast Revisionists looked upon orthodox historians as proponents of a foreign policy perspective akin to the official position of the
United States government. The pioneer Revisionist was William Appleman Williams, who held that at the beginning of this century the United
States had devised an open door policy toward China instituted to solve
the internal contradictions of its own capitalistic system (overproduction
and depression) and subsequently tried to globalize this policy because of
a dogmatic belief that domestic well-being depends upon "sustained
ever-increasing economic expansion."[67]

The Revisionists in general stressed the long history of Western opposition to the Bolshevik Revolution, the allied intervention in Russia,
United States nonrecognition policy until 1933, the West's apparent
hopes in 1941 that the Nazi and Communist dictatorships would destroy
each other, and the length of time that had elapsed before the Anglo-
American second front was opened in 1944. D. F. Fleming, a Wilsonian
rather than a New Left historian, looked for the origins of the Cold War
in personalities. Fleming contended that President Truman had reversed
President Roosevelt's policy of trying to understand and get along with
the Russians, particularly with Stalin.[68]

The Truman Administration was accused by Revisionists of failing
to recognize the primacy of Soviet interests in Eastern Europe, of terminating wartime lend-lease agreements with the Soviet Union prema-

turely, and laying down conditions that made it impossible for the USSR to participate in the Marshall Plan. Gar Alperowitz emphasized the eagerness of President Truman to employ the atomic bomb militarily in the closing weeks of the war against Japan and thereafter to deny the Soviet Union (which had remained neutral in the war against Japan) a role in the Far East settlement, diplomatically to influence Soviet policy and behavior in Eastern Europe.[69]

Cold War history as seen by the Revisionists had been placed at least on an equal par with orthodox interpretations in many American universities by the 1970s. Nevertheless Revisionist theories concerning the origins of the Cold War have themselves come in for serious criticism from scholars. Although admitting that some orthodox writers have overstated the liberal case and ignored economic motivations in postwar United States foreign policy, these critics have charged the Revisionists with making their history too polemical and simplistic, for example, by trying to reduce the complexity of European politics in the late 1940s to a naive dichotomy of Left versus Right. Moreover, say the critics, the Revisionists for the most part consistently manifest an ideological bias against the American political system and its economic institutions; they marshal their evidence in a highly selective manner and quote materials out of context in support for their thesis while discarding the kinds of evidence normally cited by impartial scholars to present a more balanced explanation of events; and they dismiss the problem of accuracy in the handling of sources as irrelevant to the larger and more basic historiographical issue of assumptions about the nature of American political-economic institutions and the kinds of policies to which they inevitably must lead, that is, in the eyes of the Revisionists.[70]

James L. Richardson, after reviewing three major Revisionists (Kolko, Alperowitz, and Horowitz), concludes that they violate Karl Popper's methodological rule that one should seek to falsify rather than verify hypotheses:

> It is possible to find confirming evidence for most hypotheses; a hypothesis is not seriously tested until it has withstood attempts to disprove it. The style of the revisionist histories leaves an overwhelming impression that this has not been attempted. Rather, there is an amassing of favorable evidence, and a neglect of awkward evidence or alternative hypotheses. . . . Not infrequently plausibility is achieved only by limiting the discussion to an artificial time period; consideration of subsequent events would expose difficulties for the interpretation. Most striking of all, there is the loss of a sense of the distinction between intended and unintended consequences.[71]

Generally speaking, Revisionism in its more extreme form involves the proposition that the Cold War could have been avoided if only the Western capitalist system had not been so insistent on pursuing its own interests (e.g., by working for the economic recovery and military security of Western Europe), even though Revisionists seldom if ever fault the Soviet Union for employing all available levers in the pursuit of its own interest. Revisionists are more reluctant than orthodox historians to attribute the failure of the United States and the USSR to establish significant economic relations between themselves at the end of the war, as well as the political-economic-military division of Germany and Europe, to the fact that the two principal victorious powers were each determined to pursue objectives that were consistent with their own values and that were incompatible with each other, and that the incompatibility of their value systems was bound to become more salient once the common wartime enemy had been defeated, leaving the leaders of two rival social systems confronting each other directly in the power vacuum of Europe.

Several orthodox historians, in their analysis of the United States decision-making process during the 1945 to 1949 period, typically cited multiple causes of the Cold War, including some of the explanatory factors used by the Revisionists to buttress their own case. Furthermore, the Revisionists have often been in substantial disagreement among themselves on important points. Gabriel Kolko, for example, in sharp contrast with Gar Alperowitz, took the position that military rather than diplomatic considerations were uppermost in the American decision to employ atomic weapons against Japan. But regardless of congruences between orthodox and Revisionist historians, and of incongruities among the latter, there can be little doubt that the Revisionists as a group were bent more single-mindedly upon assigning primary blame for the Cold War to the Americans rather than to the Soviets. It was perhaps this tendency that made some Revisionists who sought to prove discontinuity in the United States policy during the transition from Roosevelt to Truman (such as D. F. Fleming) appear Marxist when they are not. But those who, like Kolko and Horowitz, argued a priori that the American capitalist system was by historical necessity responsible for the onset of the Cold War were, whether they realized it or not, propounding an essentially Marxist-Leninist interpretation of international relations.

IMPERIALISM AS POLITICAL SLOGAN

"Imperialism" has remained the principal slogan or shibboleth of world politics in the second half of the twentieth century. The Leninist theory has often been called narrowly Eurocentric, but the term has taken on a universal applicability since World War II. All of the leading powers have employed it to describe the policies of their rivals. For Stalin, imperialism stood for the conduct of any power unfriendly to communist policy.[72] He condemned the Marshall Plan as a plot of capitalist imperialism and branded the defector Tito as a tool of the imperialists. Arab nationalists railed against British and American-Zionist imperialism in the Middle East.[73] It was inevitable that the activities of United States oil companies in the Middle East and fruit companies in Latin America should be labeled prime examples of imperialism, and that trade agreements between the European Community and its Associated States of Africa and Asia should be characterized as instruments of neo-imperialism. The Indonesian leader Sukarno and other Third World neutralists, in the late 1950s, scored the West for having subjugated all the peoples living along the "imperialist highway" from the Atlantic Ocean to the Indian Ocean and the South China Sea.[74] Until the late 1960s, when the Soviet Union replaced the United States as Peking's principal enemy, Mao Tse-Tung, adhering to a hard Stalinist line, made imperialism the main slogan in China's propaganda war against the United States.

Lenin, Stalin, and Mao all effectively used "imperialism" to arouse Third World resentment against the West for political-strategic reasons. Most Western theorists of international relations, as well as political leaders, regarded the Soviet domination of Eastern Europe as imperialism, even though Third World intellectuals were not greatly exercised over the Soviet suppression of the Hungarian uprising in 1956. Kenneth E. Boulding wrote:

> It is quite impossible to explain modern imperialism in economic terms. The only possible exception to this, paradoxically enough, is the socialist imperialism exercised by the Soviet Union on Eastern Europe and especially on East Germany after the Second World War. The Soviet Union probably extracted more goods from East Germany in the ten years after the Second World War than Britain did in two hundred years from India, and this was pure tribute.[75]

The neutralists of the Third World, for three decades after World War II, seemed to take it for granted, as many had earlier, that imperialists are people who come in ships from distant lands. Those who could impose their dominance simply by marching armies across borders were for a long time excluded from the definition of "imperialists." It was the People's Republic of China, which itself had engaged in some imperialistic adventures against India and Tibet, that began to accuse the Soviet Union of imperialism in a manner credible to leftist elites in the Third World. While trying to replace the Soviet Union as the leader of the forces of world revolution, Mao first accused Soviet leaders of Revisionism, bourgeoisification, and betrayal of the revolution through arms control collusion with capitalist imperialists. Later the Chinese leaders condemned capitalist and socialist imperialism in one breath. Later still, they began to indicate that they regarded the socialist imperialism of the Soviet Union as a greater threat than the capitalist imperialism of the United States, and acted as if they would welcome a tacit alliance with the enemy farther away against the enemy nearer. At the same time, they encouraged the strengthening of NATO, urged Europe to unite, and warned the West not to take a Soviet-promoted détente too seriously. In July 1978, the foreign ministers of more than 100 nonaligned states, meeting in Belgrade, hinted for the first time that they were becoming more worried about Soviet expansion, especially in Africa, than they were about a waning Western imperialism.[76] The Latvians, Estonians, Lithuanians, Poles, Czechs, Hungarians, Rumanians, Bulgarians, East Germans, Turks, Iranians, Afghanis, Ukrainians, Tartars, Uzbeks, Kazakhs, and others would—if they were all given the opportunity— probably have a good deal to say about the historic Russian imperialistic urge which the Bolsheviks inherited in 1917 and which the Soviet leaders have often acted out since then.

Nevertheless, despite its many theoretical deficiencies and failures of prediction and practice—for example, several countries organized along Marxist communist lines have found it harder to feed themselves than they did before—Marxism continues to exercise a worldwide appeal as a vehicle for the expression of criticism, resentment, and protest against the complexities and frustrations of contemporary social reality.[77] According to Adam B. Ulam, the Hobson-Leninist theory of imperialism, "because of its simplicity, because of its psychological appeal and because of the undoubted depredations and brutalities that accompanied the process of colonization," retains its influence by enabling the disadvantaged of the world to express their rage and to disturb the conscience of a guilt-ridden West.[78]

In the final analysis, the Leninist theory of imperialism does a disservice to the developing nations of the non-Western world. The simplistic, polemical urge to blame all or most of those countries' troubles on the exploitation of a few capitalistic states, as Anthony James Joes has noted, diverts the attention of planners who take the ideological explanation seriously from examining carefully the obstacles posed to modernization by indigenous political, cultural, economic, and geographic factors. The theory is also self-serving to some Third World leaders, says Joes, for "it exculpates dogmatic theorists, incompetent windbags, epauleted megalomaniacs, and 'village tyrants' from all responsibility for the deplorable condition of their suffering countrymen even after two decades—or two centuries or two millenia—of political independence."[79]

Notes

1. These included Karl Kautsky and Eduard Bernstein (Germany); G. D. H. Cole, R. H. Tawney, Sidney and Beatrice Webb, Harold J. Laski, and Clement Attlee (England); Jules Guesde, Jean Jaurès, and Leon Blum (France); and Daniel DeLeon, Harry W. Laidler, Norman Thomas, Morris Hillquit, and Herbert Marcuse

(United States). One could also list several Christian socialists, utopian socialists, anarchists, recent Revisionist historians, and advocates of a variety of New Left causes.

2. For a detailed examination of this concept, see Gustav A. Wetter, *Dialectical Materialism: A Historical and Systematic Survey of Philosophy in the Soviet Union* (New York: Praeger, 1963).

3. Karl Marx and Friedrich Engels, *Manifesto of the Communist Party* (New York: International Publishers, 1932), p. 9.

4. See Karl Marx, *Capital: A Critique of Political Economy* (New York: Random House [Modern Library], n.d.), especially chaps. 1, 7, 9, 11, 12, 16, 18, and 24 for Marx's most extensive treatment of the concept of surplus value.

5. Karl Marx and Friedrich Engels, *Manifesto of the Communist Party*, op. cit., p. 11.

6. See Robert C. Tucker, *The Marxian Revolutionary Idea* (New York: Norton, 1970) and *Philosophy and Myth in Karl Marx* (Cambridge: Cambridge University Press, 1972).

7. John Plamenatz, *Man and Society: Political and Social Theory*, vol. II, *Bentham Through Marx* (New York: McGraw-Hill, 1963), p. 310. Hannah Arendt notes in a similar vein that Marx was aware of the role of violence in history, but deemed it less important than the contradictions inherent in the old society in bringing about the latter's end in *On Violence* (New York: Harcourt Brace Jovanovich, 1969), p. 11.

8. See Philip Siegelman's Introduction to J. A. Hobson, *Imperialism: A Study* (Ann Arbor: University of Michigan Press, 1965). Hobson's work was originally published in London by George Allen and Unwin in 1902. Subsequent references will be to the 1965 edition.

9. Foster Rhea Dulles, *America's Rise to World Power, 1898–1954* (New York: Harper & Row, 1954), chaps. 2 and 3.

10. Richard Koebner and Helmut Dan Schmidt, *Imperialism: The Story and Significance of a Political Word, 1840–1960* (New York: Cambridge University Press, 1964), p. 249. For a discussion of the anti-Semitic theme in Hobson's thought, see pp. 226–228. George Lichtheim notes that the American Founding Fathers, both Federalists and Republicans, had no qualms about calling the federal union an empire, and that in nineteenth-century England both Liberals and Tories employed the term *imperialism* for its popular appeal. *Imperialism* (New York: Praeger, 1971), chaps. 4, 5, and 6. For a thorough analysis of British "imperialism of free trade," see William Roger Louis, ed., *Imperialism: The Robinson and Gallagher Controversy* (New York: New Viewpoints, 1976).

11. Richard Koebner and Helmut Dan Schmidt, ibid., p. 233.

12. J. A. Hobson, *Imperialism: A Study* (Ann Arbor: University of Michigan Press, 1965), p. 85.

13. Ibid., p. 59.

14. Ibid., pp. 41–45. Later, Italy and Germany employed the argument concerning population pressure to justify their quest for colonies in Africa prior to World War I, and the Japanese did likewise in their Manchurian venture in the early 1930s. But in all the cases where the *lebensraum* argument was employed, subsequent movement of population to the conquered areas proved negligible. See N. Peffer, "The Fallacy of Conquest," in *International Conciliation* (New York: Carnegie Endowment for International Peace, No. 318, 1938).

15. J. A. Hobson, op. cit., pp. 46–51.

16. Ibid., pp. 53–54.

17. E. M. Winslow, *The Pattern of Imperialism* (New York: Columbia University Press, 1948), p. 106.

18. J. A. Hobson, op. cit., p. 58.

19. V. I. Lenin, *Imperialism: The Highest Stage of Capitalism* (New York: International Publishers, 1939), p. 89. See the section, "Imperialism and Capitalism," by Alec

Nove, "Lenin as Economist," in Leonard Schapiro and Peter Reddaway, eds., *Lenin: The Man, the Theorist, the Leader* (New York: Praeger, 1969), pp. 198–203.

20. "Jingoism is merely the lust of the spectator, unpurged by any personal effort, risk, or sacrifice, gloating in the perils, pains, and slaughter of fellow-men whom he does not know, but whose destruction he desires in a blind and artificially stimulated passion of hatred and revenge. . . . The arduous and weary monotony of the march, the long periods of waiting, the hard privations, the terrible tedium of a prolonged campaign play no part in his imagination; the redeeming factors of war, the fine sense of comradeship which common personal peril educates, the fruits of discipline and self-restraint, the respect for the personality of enemies whose courage he must admit and whom he comes to realize as fellow-beings—all those moderating elements in actual war are eliminated from the passion of the Jingo. It is precisely for these reasons that some friends of peace maintain that the two most potent checks of militarism and of war are the obligation of the entire body of citizens to undergo military service and the experience of an invasion." Hobson, op. cit., p. 215.

21. For the complete works of Lenin, see V. I. Lenin, *Collected Works* (Moscow: Foreign Languages Publishing House, 1963), 44 vols. For biographical accounts of Lenin's life, see Louis Fischer, *The Life of Lenin* (New York: Harper & Row [Colophon Books], 1965); Robert Payne, *The Life and Death of Lenin* (New York: Simon & Schuster, 1946); Stefan T. Possony, *Lenin: The Compulsive Revolutionary* (Chicago: Regnery, 1964); Christopher Hill, *Lenin and the Russian Revolution* (London: English Universities Press, 1961); Bertram D. Wolfe, *Three Who Made a Revolution* (Boston: Beacon, 1955).

22. See V. I. Lenin, *Collected Works*, (1961) vol. V, pp. 425–529.

23. V. I. Lenin, *Imperialism: The Highest Stage of Capitalism*, op. cit., pp. 16–30.

24. Lenin, *Collected Works*, op. cit., vol. XIX, pp. 87 and 104.

25. Bernard Taurer, "Stalin's Last Thesis," *Foreign Affairs*, XXXI (April 1953), 374.

26. Bernard Taurer, ibid., p. 378.

27. See Herbert S. Dinerstein, *War and the Soviet Union* (New York: Praeger, 1959), pp. 68–69, 80–81; Frederick C. Barghoorn, *Soviet Foreign Propaganda* (Princeton: Princeton University Press, 1964), pp. 92–93; Frederic S. Burin, "The Communist Doctrine of the Inevitability of War," *American Political Science Review*, LVII (June 1963), 352–354; Walter C. Clemens, Jr., "Ideology in Soviet Disarmament Policy," *Journal of Conflict Resolution*, VIII (March 1964), 17–20.

28. Hans J. Morgenthau, *Politics Among Nations: The Struggle for Power and Peace*, 4th ed. (New York: Knopf, 1966), p. 42. This definition has been carried in all six editions of the book since 1948.

29. Ibid.

30. Ibid., p. 47. Cf. Raymond Aron, *Peace and War: A Theory of International Relations*, trans. Richard Howard and Annette Baker Fox (New York: Praeger, 1968), p. 259.

31. Raymond Aron, *The Century of Total War* (Boston: Beacon, 1955), chap. III, "The Leninist Myth of Imperialism," especially p. 59; Morgenthau, *Politics Among Nations*, op. cit., pp. 47–50; William L. Langer, "A Critique of Imperialism," *Foreign Affairs*, XIV (October 1935), 102–115.

32. Jacob Viner, "International Relations Between State-Controlled Economies," in *Readings in the Theory of International Trade*, American Economic Association (Philadelphia: Blakiston, 1949), vol. IV, pp. 437–458.

33. Joseph A. Schumpeter, *Imperialism and Social Classes*, trans. Heinz Norden, Paul M. Sweezy, ed. (Oxford: Basil Blackwell, 1951), p. 5.

34. Ibid., p. 6.

35. Hans J. Morgenthau, op. cit., pp. 48–49.

36. Ibid., pp. 84–85. Kenneth E. Boulding has reiterated Schumpeter's view that imperialism was a form of social lag and, from an economic standpoint, unprofitable to the point of being a fraud. "Reflections on Imperialism," in David Mermelstein, ed., *Economics: Mainstream Readings and Radical Critiques*, 2nd ed. (New York: Random House, 1970), p. 201.

37. Joseph A. Schumpeter, op. cit., pp. 89–96. Schumpeter's own analysis of imperialism did not go unchallenged. He was faulted for defining imperialism as both "objectless" and "forcible," the expression of a warrior-class social structure which fights for no other reason but that it is geared for fighting. He therefore excluded from the meaning of imperialism whatever is not a warrior-class social structure. Murray Greene, "Schumpeter's Imperialism—A Critical Note," *Social Research* (An International Quarterly of Political and Social Science), XIX (December 1952), 453–463. Greene took issue with Schumpeter's thesis that capitalism, because it is nationalistic, is antithetical to imperialism, militarism, and armaments.

38. Richard Koebner and Helmut Dan Schmidt, op. cit., p. 255.

39. Hans J. Morgenthau, op. cit., p. 47.

40. Joseph A. Schumpeter, op. cit., p. 57.

41. Andrew Mack, "Theories of Imperialism: The European Perspective," *The Journal of Conflict Resolution*, 18 (September 1974), 518.

42. Ibid., where Mack cites as authorities two Marxist critiques of the Leninist theory: Michael Barratt Brown, "A Critique of Marxist Theories of Imperialism," and Harry Magdoff, "Imperialism Without Colonies," in Roger Owen and Bob Sutcliffe, eds., *Studies in the Theory of Imperialism* (London: Longman, 1973).

43. Raymond Aron, *Peace and War: A Theory of International Relations*, op. cit., p. 261. See also Langer, op. cit., p. 105 and Lichtheim, op. cit., p. 77.

44. Ibid., pp. 262–263.

45. Hans J. Morgenthau, op. cit., pp. 46–47; Aron, *A Century of Total War*, op. cit., pp. 59–62. Referring to the Spanish-American War, Eugene Staley wrote: "The causes of this war, and of the expansionism exhibited in connection with it, have been laid at the door of private investment interests—on the whole, erroneously. Their role was slight compared with that of the interests of the 'yellow' press and of other internal influences in American life which made for chauvinism." *War and the Private Investor* (Chicago: University of Chicago Press, 1935), p. 433. Most diplomatic historians who studied the origins of World War I, including Sidney Bradshaw Fay, G. P. Gooch, A. J. P. Taylor, Bernadotte E. Schmitt, Nicholas Mansergh, and Raymond Sontag, have listed imperialistic rivalry (in its political more than its economic aspects) as *one* of the background causes of that war, but not as important as the interaction of the European alliance systems and nationalisms in a framework dominated by balance of power thinking, security apprehensions generated by militarism and armaments competition, and the condition of international anarchy, that is, the absence of organization adequate to insure peaceful settlement of disputes.

46. Raymond Aron, *The Century of Total War*, op. cit., p. 65; *Peace and War*, op. cit., p. 267. One additional anomaly might be mentioned. Canada took part in the Boer War, World Wars I and II, and the Korean War, not because her capitalistic interests were at stake in those wars but because she was part of a "political empire" (the British Empire/Commonwealth and the U.S. NATO alliance) in which the empire leader took the decision for war and Canada followed out of a sense of political loyalty. Gernot Kohler, "Imperialism as a Level of Analysis in Correlates-of-War Research," *The Journal of Conflict Resolution*, 19 (March 1975), 48.

47. Kenneth E. Boulding, "Reflections on Imperialism," op. cit., p. 202.

48. *The New York Times*, February 12, 1960.

49. André Gunder Frank, "The Development of Underdevelopment," in Robert I.

Rhodes, ed., *Imperialism and Underdevelopment: A Reader* (New York: Monthly Review Press, 1970), p. 9.

50. Kenneth E. Boulding, op. cit., p. 201.
51. Nikita S. Khrushchev, *For Victory in Peaceful Competition with Capitalism* (New York: Dutton, 1960), p. 33; see also pp. 628–629.
52. Ibid., pp. 750–751.
53. G. Mirsky, "Whither the Newly Independent Countries?" *International Affairs* (Moscow), XII (December 1962), 2, 23–27.
54. Thomas E. Weisskopf, "Capitalism, Underdevelopment and the Future of the Poor Countries," in David Mermelstein, ed., op. cit., p. 218.
55. Ibid., p. 223.
56. Nikita S. Khrushchev, op. cit., p. 135.
57. Harry Magdoff, "The American Empire and the U.S. Economy," chap. 5 in *The Age of Imperialism* (New York: Monthly Review Press, 1969). Reprinted in Robert I. Rhodes, op. cit., pp. 18–44; see especially pp. 18–28.
58. Ibid., pp. 28–29.
59. Johan Galtung, *The European Community: A Superpower in the Making* (London: Allen and Unwin, 1973).
60. Speaking of Europe as the economic center, Galtung writes: "Fragmentation means that whereas the center is well coordinated, even unified in the European Community, the periphery, the developing countries, are split in many ways." Ibid., p. 76. To illustrate his point, he notes that in the early 1970s a telephone call from the Central African Republic to Kenya still had to be routed through Paris and London. Economists who study the underdeveloped lands typically point out that the foreign trade of countries within the African, Arab, and Latin American regions is largely extraregional; usually less than 10 percent is intraregional.
61. P. T. Bauer, "The Economics of Resentment: Colonialism and Underdevelopment," *The Journal of Contemporary History*, vol. 4, (1969), p. 59.
62. Ibid., p. 56.
63. Ibid.
64. Hans Kohn, "Reflections on Colonialism," in Robert Strausz-Hupé and Harry W. Hazard, eds., *The Idea of Colonialism* (New York: Praeger, 1958), pp. 6–14.
65. Andrew Mack, "Theories of Imperialism," op. cit., p. 526.
66. Among the writers who viewed the Cold War more or less in these terms were the following: James F. Byrnes, *Speaking Frankly* (New York: Harper & Row, 1947); George F. Kennan, "The Sources of Soviet Conduct," *Foreign Affairs*, XXV (July 1947) and *Realities of American Foreign Policy* (Princeton: Princeton University Press, 1954); Hans J. Morgenthau, *In Defense of the National Interest* (New York: Knopf, 1951); Harry S. Truman, *Memoirs*, 2 vols. (Garden City, L.I.: Doubleday, 1955, 1956); Eric F. Goldman, *The Crucial Decade—And After, America: 1945–1960* (New York: Knopf, 1956); Walt W. Rostow, *The United States in the World Arena* (New York: Harper & Row, 1960); John Spanier, *American Foreign Policy Since World War II* (New York: Praeger, 1960); Norman A. Graebner, *Cold War Diplomacy* (Princeton: Van Nostrand, 1962); William G. Carleton, *Revolution in American Foreign Policy* (New York: Random House, 1963); Louis B. Halle, *The Cold War as History* (New York: Harper & Row, 1967); Dean G. Acheson, *Present at the Creation* (New York: Norton, 1969). John Lukacs, who is usually considered a critic of most "orthodox" and semiofficial versions of the origins of the U.S.-Soviet postwar split, did not doubt that the United States pursued as its supreme strategic interest the conversion of the Pacific, the Atlantic, and the Mediterranean into American-dominated lakes. Nevertheless he reached the conclusion that "Stalin, not Truman, was the principal architect of the iron curtain and the cold war." *A New History of the Cold War* (Garden City, L.I.: Doubleday-Anchor Books, 1966),

p. 63. For an excellent account of the postwar division of Germany and the alignment of West Germany with NATO, see James L. Richardson, *Germany and the Atlantic Alliance* (Cambridge, Mass.: Harvard University Press, 1966), chaps. 1 and 2.

67. William Appleman Williams, *The Tragedy of American Diplomacy* (New York: Dell, 1962), p. 11; a similar thesis was advanced by Gabriel Kolko who perceived United States wartime policy as one of penetrating the entire globe to promote an "integrated world capitalism," in *The Politics of War* (New York: Random House, 1968).

68. D. F. Fleming, *The Cold War and Its Origins*, vol. 1, 1917–1950 (New York: Doubleday, 1961) pp. 266–267. Undoubtedly there were important differences between Franklin Roosevelt, who preferred to promote American interests by asserting idealistic principles, and President Truman, who was willing to use military aid and threats in support of national diplomacy. See Bruce R. Kuniholm, *The Origins of the Cold War in the Near East* (Princeton, N.J.: Princeton University Press, 1980). See also David Horowitz, *The Free World Colossus* (New York: Hill and Wang, 1965).

69. Gar Alperowitz, *Atomic Diplomacy: Hiroshima and Potsdam* (New York: Simon & Shuster, 1965), pp. 229–242.

70. Robert W. Tucker, *The Radical Left and American Foreign Policy*, (Baltimore, Md.: Johns Hopkins Press, 1971); J. L. Richardson "Cold War Revisionism: A Critique," *World Politics*, XXIV (January 1972), 579–612, John L. Gaddis, op. cit.; Robert James Maddox, *The New Left and the Origin of the Cold War* (Princeton: Princeton University Press, 1973), pp. 10–11, 159–164; and Daniel Yergin, *Shattered Peace: A History of the Cold War and the National Security State* (Boston: Houghton Mifflin, 1977).

71. J. L. Richardson, "Cold War Revisionism," op. cit., p. 608.

72. Richard Schmidt and Helmut Dan Koebner, op. cit., p. 316.

73. Ibid., p. 318.

74. Ibid., pp. 321–322.

75. Kenneth E. Boulding, "Reflections on Imperialism," op. cit., p. 202.

76. *The New York Times*, July 31, 1978.

77. Robert G. Wesson, *Why Marxism? The Continuing Success of a Failed Theory* (New York: Basic Books, 1976).

78. Adam B. Ulam, *The Bolsheviks* (New York: Macmillan, 1965), p. 311. See also P. T. Bauer, op. cit., pp. 57–58.

79. Anthony James Joes, *Fascism in the Contemporary World: Ideology, Evolution, Resurgence* (Boulder, Colo.: Westview, 1978), p. 103.

Chapter 7
Microcosmic Theories of Violent Conflict

HUMAN MOTIVATIONS AND CONFLICT

Many theories discussed in Chapters 5 and 6 pertained to a person's conscious motivations, ethical evaluations, and attitudes concerning conflict. Most of those earlier theories, whether derived from religious belief, philosophical reflection, or political experience, are what we call "pre-scientific." However, it would be wrong to imply that people in earlier times were content with superficial or mythical explanations. When Thucydides said that men go to war for reasons of honor, fear, and interest; when the Christian fathers taught that war results from a deep-rooted disorder in human nature that they called "original sin"; when Hume wrote that nations go to war in order to preserve a balance of power, or to prevent one monarch from establishing international hegemony; when some nineteenth-century writers defended or extolled war as a catalyst against social stagnation; when Lenin and his followers traced the outbreak of wars to the profit seeking of the imperialists—all of these were trying to go beyond purely conscious motivations and to probe the underlying reasons for human conflict. Some of them found their reasons in the "dark forces" that lurk within the individual psyche or soul; some found them in the characteristics of the larger social system, or certain aspects of it. Some even implied that thinkers were ill-advised to look for the causes of war when they should be looking for the causes of peace. This was the thrust of William James' argument that we could expect war to recur until we had discovered some moral-psychological equivalent of it. (See Note 47 in Chapter 5.)

Kenneth N. Waltz, in his significant work, *Man, the State and War,* distinguished three images of international relations in terms of which we usually try to analyze the causes of war. According to the first image, war is traceable to human nature and behavior.[1] Partisans of the second image seek the explanation of war in the internal structure of the state, and this group includes both liberals (who believe that democracies are more peaceful than dictatorships) and Marxist-Leninists (who believe that capitalist states foment war while socialism leads to peace—as we saw in the previous chapter.)[2] The third image postulates the causes of war in the condition known to the classical political theorists (including Kant, Spinoza and Rousseau) as "international anarchy," that is, the absence of those instruments of law and organization which would be efficacious for peacekeeping. In other words, a deficiency in the state system makes it necessary for each state to pursue its own interests and ambitions, and act as judge in its own case when it becomes involved in disputes with another state, thereby making the recurrence of conflicts, including occasional wars, inevitable and giving rise to "the expectation of war" as a normal feature of the state system.[3] The political causes of war which flow logically from the third image will be dealt with in Chapter 8. In the present chapter, we shall be concerned primarily with the "first image" theories of conflict—those pertaining to human nature and behavior.

If the human race is ever to come to grips with the problem of war, at least by reducing it to manageable, subcatastrophic proportions, presumably the greater our knowledge of the problem the better off we shall be. No problem can be solved without an understanding of its underlying causes—or those necessary and sufficient conditions that are likely to give rise to it.[4] The historian is interested in the specific and unique events that lead to the outbreak of a particular war. The theorist of international relations cannot ignore the concrete circumstances in which wars occur; these have to be taken into account in the theory. But the theorist seeks to go beyond specific wars in an effort to explain the more general phenomenon of *war* itself, that is, large-scale fighting or other acts of violence and destruction involving the organized military forces of different states. The causality of international war may be, and probably is, related at least in part to the causality of other forms of violent political conflict, such as civil war, revolution, and guerrilla insurgency;

but international war is a specific phenomenon, different from the others, and therefore requires at some point a specific explanation of its own, just as each of the others does.

Waltz, in his treatment of first image theorists, noted that both optimists and pessimists, Utopians and Realists, agree in diagnosing the basic cause of war as human nature and behavior, but disagree in their answers to the question of whether that nature and behavior can be made to undergo a sufficient change to resolve the problem of war.[4] In this chapter, we shall examine the views of modern behavioral scientists concerning human nature and its conflict-related behavior. There is no reason at present to think that either the traditionalists or the behavioral scientists will ever be able to isolate a single dominating causal factor adequate for explaining all violent conflict. Human life is much too diverse and complex to permit that. A more reasonable presumption on which to proceed is that all forms of violence—whether individual or social—share a few common explanatory factors, related to what we refer to here as human nature. Forms of individual aggression and violent behavior can be expected to have more in common with each other than with large-scale societal violence, and vice versa. But this is not to suggest that microcosmic and macrocosmic theories of human aggression, violence, and war can be entirely separated from each other. International war cannot be adequately explained solely by reference to biological and psychological explanations of individual aggressiveness, nor can the latter phenomenon be comprehended purely "internally," without reference to social factors. As in all fields, so in international relations micro and macroapproaches must be appropriately blended.

Modern Studies of Motivations and War

In the twentieth century, social scientists have turned increasingly toward motives, reasons, and causal factors which may be operative both in individual human beings and in social collectivities even though people are not immediately aware of them and do not become consciously aware of them except as a result of scientific observation and methodical analysis. Why do individuals behave aggressively? Why do states wage wars? The two questions are related, but they are not the same. The former pertains to the inner springs of action within individual human beings, the latter to the decision-making processes of national governments. Violent revolution constitutes yet another phenomenon, different from individual aggressiveness, which is rooted in the biological-psychological characteristics of human beings, and from the waging of international war, which is a highly politicized and institutionalized form of learned social behavior. Revolution itself, insofar as it requires organization, leadership, ideology and doctrine, propaganda, planning, strategy, tactics, communications, recruits and supplies, and very often a diplomacy for the acquisition of foreign support, assumes a highly politicized character with the passage of time. Thus an understanding of it requires more of a *macrocosmic* (i.e., political-sociological) than a *microcosmic* (individual psychological) analysis.

Psychological and social psychological factors alone might go much further in helping to explain instances of anomic[5] violence, such as a food or language riot in India, the flareup of a group of students around the goalpost at the end of a hard-fought football game, or a racial disorder at a public beach. But even in these cases social psychologists would be wary of "the fallacy of the single factor," and social scientists would argue that some instances of apparently anomic violence might involve an element of political organization and can be adequately comprehended only when placed in their total sociological and political context. In all cases of social violence it is probably wise to assume the presence of multiple explanatory factors which should be analyzed as complementary rather than as mutually exclusive alternatives.

The phenomenon of international war is the most complex and difficult of all to explain. It is impossible to describe the causes of war purely in terms of individual psychology as if it were a case of psychic tensions within individuals mounting to the breaking point and then spilling over into large-scale conflict. Feelings of hostility might indeed be widespread within a nation vis-à-vis another nation and yet war might be averted by astute statemanship. Conversely, government can lead a people into a war for which there is no enthusiastic support. Professor Werner Levi made several trenchant points on this subject:

> When for instance will certain natural traits or psychological drives find outlets in war, and when in something more peaceful?. . . . What these explanations fail to do is to indicate how these human factors are translated into violent conflict involving all citizens, regardless of their individual nature, and performed through a highly complex machinery constructed over a period of years for just such purpose.
>
> There is always the missing link in these fascinating speculations about the psychological causes of war between the fundamental nature of man and the outbreak of war. . . . Usually, the psychological factors and human traits can be classified as conditions of war more correctly than as causes.[6]

BIOLOGICAL AND PSYCHOLOGICAL THEORIES

Neither the microcosm alone, neither individual nor collectivity alone, neither the biological-psychological approach nor the sociological-anthropological-political approach alone can furnish a completely adequate conceptual framework for understanding human conflict. Conflict has an inside and an outside dimension. It arises out of the internal states of individuals acting singly or in groups, and also out of external conditions and social structures. At all levels of analysis, larger organized aggregates of human beings affect smaller aggregates and individuals, and vice versa. Individuals and groups are in constant interaction. Which is more important—the larger or the smaller? To this question, scientists from the many disciplines interested in conflict will probably never be able to agree on an answer. The only available solution to this dilemma is to regard social situations and individual inner processes as an organic whole.

Peter A. Corning has noted that without an understanding of the evolutionary and genetic aspects of behavior, we cannot fully comprehend the inner principles by which human life is organized, and that social scientists must attend increasingly to the interaction between the organism and the environment. It makes sense to begin with the biological foundations of behavior. Within recent years, a controversial new field has made its appearance in academe—sociobiology. Sociobiologists study the genetic roots of social behavior in insects, animals, and human beings, and seek to bridge the gap between the genetic inheritance of individuals on the one hand and social processes and institutions on the other. It is still too early to predict how the new discipline will fare. There can be little doubt, however, that some of its fundamental insights are either quite old in the social sciences or else are closely related to many of the findings which have appeared in the literature of biologists and ethologists during the last two decades and which will be discussed in succeeding pages.[7]

No one denies that there must be a relationship between the biological structure/mechanisms/processes of living beings and their behavior. All living organisms have certain fundamental species-specific biological requirements. Those of the members of human society are the most complex of all. "These needs include a reasonably pure atmosphere, numerous nutritional requirements, fresh water, sleep, ... shelter and clothing (or, more generally, maintenance of body temperature), health care, including sanitation, physical security, procreation, and the nurture and training of the young."[8] Over the world as a whole, the greater part of all economic activity is devoted to meeting basic biological needs. Among humans, biological needs quickly shade off into higher psychological needs that are often even more difficult to satisfy—sense of belonging, self-esteem and prestige, self-actualization, and so forth.[9] Much of the political and economic competition and conflict among human societies is traceable to the fact that the demand for things required to satisfy biological *and* psychological needs always exceeds the supply.[10] But this does not mean that any theory arising from a Darwinian evolutionary model of the natural selection process necessarily leads to the conclusion that nature is "red in tooth and claw" and that violent aggression and war are inescapable among human societies. Several biologists have insisted that fitness for survival dictates cooperation and mutual aid at least as often as aggressive conflict.[11]

INSTINCT THEORIES OF AGGRESSION

The key microcosmic concept developed by biologists and psychologists for the explanation of conflict is *aggression*. The term is not as easy to define as it might appear to be. Just as political scientists, international lawyers, and diplomats have experienced difficulty for several decades in their efforts to agree on the meaning of international aggression, so the biologists and psychologists have argued among themselves over what constitutes individual aggressive behavior. Normally, our first impulse is to think of aggression as a form of violent behavior directed toward injuring a human object or injuring, damaging, or destroying a nonhuman object. Some writers have distinguished between *hostile aggression*, the aim of which is to inflict injury, and *instrumental aggression*, the purpose of which is to secure extraneous rewards beyond the victim's suffering. This distinction has been criticized as misleading by Albert Bandura, who argues that most acts of hostile aggression serve ends other than the mere production of injury, and hence are instrumental.[12] Bandura defines aggression as behavior that results in personal injury (either psychological or physical) or in destruction of property, but he insists on the importance of the "social labeling process," that is, on social judgments that determine which injurious or destructive acts are to be called "aggressive." We accuse neither the surgeon who makes a painful incision nor the bulldozer operator who razes a condemned building of committing aggression.[13]

Within recent decades, many biologists, psychologists, and social psychologists have been preoccupied with aggression studies. While investigating the relationship between organism and environment (a continuation of the old "nature-nurture" controversy), biologists and psychologists have often crossed paths in the areas of "instinctive" behavior, innate behavior, and aggressive or fighting behavior. It is primarily to these two fields that philosophers and social scientists interested in solving or controlling the problem of war look for an answer to the question: Do human beings carry within their genetic or psychic structures an ineradicable "instinct" or predisposition for aggression? In view of the way in which the debate about instinctive behavior has developed in this century, it will be useful to examine first the positions taken by certain psychologists.

Generally, psychologists have long agreed that aggression is to be understood in some sort of stimulus-response framework. A basic issue that arose in their field early in this century was whether aggressive tendencies are innate, instinctual, and ever-present in humans, or whether they appear only as a result of externally produced frustration. The earlier psychologists were closer to the biologists in postulating an aggressive instinct. Their theories were gradually replaced by the frustration-aggression and social learning hypotheses. However, a brief review of the older theory, and why psychologists came to reject it, may be instructive in view of its revival in the more recent writings of certain animal behaviorists, notably Konrad Lorenz.

Among the leading figures identified with the instinct theories of aggression during the early decades of the century were William James (1842–1910) and William McDougall (1871–1938). McDougall, the leading British psychologist of his day, considered instinct as a psychophysical process inherited by all members of a species; it was not learned, but could be modified by learning. (An instinct differs from the other unlearned form of behavior, the reflex, in that the reflex involves a virtually automatic neuromuscular reaction to an external stimulus, such as the patellar reflex or a kick when the mallet strikes the tendon over the knee; instinct involves some sort of cognition and is a more complex sequence.) McDougall took issue with the psychoanalysts who considered the aggressive impulse as ever-present in humans and constantly seeking release. McDougall insisted that the "instinct of pugnacity," as he called it (one of the 11 which he identified), became operative only when instigated by a frustrating condition.[14] He did not look upon human aggressiveness as a built-in impulse constantly seeking release. Thus he placed himself midway between the pure "instinctivists" and the "frustration-aggression" school which is to be treated presently, seeking his understanding of aggression in neither the organism nor the environment alone, but in their interaction.

The most famous and most controversial of the "instinct" theories was that of the "death instinct," put forth by Sigmund Freud. Originally, Freud was inclined to the view that aggression results from frustration, especially the frustration of the sexual impulses.[15] But after World War I, Freud postulated the existence in the human being of a fundamental *eros*, or life instinct, and a fundamental *thanatos*, or death instinct. In no other way was the Austrian psychoanalyst able to explain why millions of men went to their death on the battlefield between 1914 and 1918.[16] For Freud, all instincts were directed toward the reduction or elimination of tension, stimulation, and excitation. The motivation of pleasure-seeking activity is to attain an unstimulated condition—a sort of Oriental Nirvana or absence of all desire. Death involves the removal of all excitation. Hence all living things aspire to "the quiescence of the inorganic world."[17] But people go on living despite the death instinct, because the life instinct channels the annihilative drive away from the self toward others. Aggressive behavior thus provides an outlet for destructive energies that might otherwise lead to suicide. According to this hypothesis, the recurrence of war and conflict becomes a necessary periodic release by which groups preserve themselves through diverting their self-destructive tendencies to outsiders. This, in brief, is the psychoanalytic foundation for Freud's view, which he exchanged in correspondence with Albert Einstein; that is, a person carries within "an active instinct for hatred and aggression."[18] Hence Sigmund Freud and Emile Durkheim would appear to be not too far from agreement on the proposition that society harbors a certain amount of destructive energy which, if not diverted externally, manifests itself internally against either the individual or the group.

Most contemporary psychologists reject Freud's hypothesis of the death wish as the basis for aggression theory. Professor Leonard Berkowitz called it "scientifically unwarranted."[19] He cited two principal grounds on which it is deemed deficient—one from positivist logic and one from modern experimental science. He maintained that Freudian theory is unacceptable because of its teleological character. In other words, the theory attributes the cause of present behavior to a future condition, that is, the reduction or removal of excitation. "Claiming that some mysterious force—calling it an instinct, compulsion, or drive does not help—seeking to attain a future state in some unknown fashion produces certain behaviors is only the application of 'word magic.' "[20]

As for the experimental evidence, Berkowitz argued that research performed with animals (principally cats, rats, and mice) negates the validity of the notion that all behavior is aimed at tension-reduction, inasmuch as "organisms frequently go out of their way to obtain additional stimulation from their external environment."[21] This is an interesting observation insofar as it casts a different light on the question of why human beings willingly risk the dangers that often accompany conflict and violence. However, it is cited here primarily as an argument *contra* Freud's death wish. One might wonder whether the evidence concerning the desire of living organisms, at least at times, for an increase of tension and stimulation completely invalidates the Freudian hypothesis, or merely introduces greater complexity into it, by suggesting dialectically that the increased excitation is an unconscious step toward the cessation of all stimuli. This latter interpretation, however, would still be open to the logical positivist objection summarized above. It should be remembered that Freud never adduced any compelling body of evidence in support of his hypothesis. Hence there is no scientific need to disprove it. Yet Freud's position in the field of psychoanalysis is so dominant, and his influence on modern Western thought so pervasive, that psychologists sometimes seem anxious to discredit this particular aspect of his theory not only because of its scientific weakness but also because of the rather pessimistic connotations that it has for society.[22]

ANIMAL BEHAVIOR STUDIES

Before making the transition from instinct to frustration theories, we must look at some of the results of animal research behavior. Human behavior and animal behavior are dissimilar; in some respects, though, they may be analogous, and a comparison of basic similarities and subtle differences can be an aid to understanding and can serve to make us wary of oversimplifying by adopting single-factor explanations. From a knowledge of animal behavior we cannot directly infer anything about human behavior. "Work on one species," according to Elton B. McNeil, "can serve as a model only for the formation of *hypotheses* about other species."[23] Thus, although an examination of animal studies can furnish no direct proof as to the way human beings act, it can suggest fruitful areas for future research. The advantage of animal investigation is that it admits of a freedom of experimentation that would be impossible in the case of humans, and it permits the scientist to observe several generations of a species within a short time. The principal caveat to remember, of course, is that humans are vastly more complex than even the most highly developed animals, and that the computing organism of the human nervous system lends itself to individual learning and adaptation, whereas this is much more limited in the lower organisms. Simplicity makes it easier to isolate a factor for study, but harder to apply its implications to humans.

In animals the causes of aggressive behavior are relatively few. They fight over food, females, and territory; they fight to protect the young; they exhibit hostility when strange members of their own species are introduced into their midst, when others make off with objects toward which they have become "possessive," and when their expectations have been first aroused and then frustrated. Researchers have found that there is a relationship between aggressiveness and the production of the male hormone (even though in a few species the female is more aggressive than the male); that within a species, some breeds may be more aggressive than others; that the so-called instinctive targets of aggression (such as the mouse for the cat) appear to be more a matter of learning than of hereditary instinct; that fighting within a species may produce intricate patterns of submission and dominance; that an animal will fight rather than be deprived of status; that repeated success in fighting can make an animal more aggressive; and that various forms of electrical, chemical, and surgical interventions into the brain can produce predictable alterations in animal aggressiveness.[24] Studies have also indicated that the same principles of learning on which the stimulation of conflict behavior is based may be applied in reverse, as it were, to control and reduce the aggressive urge.[25]

Berkowitz, in an effort to cast doubt upon the notion of instinctive aggressiveness, writes that:

> Man presumably possesses an aggressive instinct because of his biological heritage and his membership in the animal kingdom. . . . It certainly is unreasonable phylogenetically to maintain that human beings would have these biological tendencies if the other animals did not. This being the case, the advocate of the instinctive aggression doctrine is hard-pressed to defend himself against the essentially negative evidence provided by biologists and psychologists.[26]

John Paul Scott, an experimental biologist who has based his study of individual aggression and its causes on animal research, denies that there is any physiological evidence pointing to a spontaneous "instinct for fighting" within the body. There is no need for the organism to fight, apart from happenings in the external environment. "There is, however, an internal physiological mechanism which has only to be stimulated to produce fighting."[27] As Scott sees it, aggression is the result of a learning process in which the motivation for fighting is increased by success; the longer success continues, the stronger the motivation becomes. He favors a multifactor theory of aggression, based on a complex network of physiological causes which eventually are traced to external stimulation. If the stimulation is sufficiently high, it may activate unconscious motor centers for fighting which, in the absence of the stimulus, are usually repressed as a result of training. Scott therefore roots the aggressive impulse in physiological processes, but demands a stimulus from the environment and rejects the concept of self-activation.

Generally speaking, biologists have been less reluctant than psychologists to speak of "instinct"—not so much as an explanation of an inherited pattern of behavior (through genetic transmission) as a short-handed description of those behavior differences which are determined by the interaction of heredity and environment.[28] A growing number of biologists now definitely prefer the term *innate behavior* over the older term *instinct*.

Within the past decade, one of the most rapidly advancing branches of biological science has been *ethology*—the study of animal behavior in all its aspects, with particular emphasis on the four basic animal drives of reproduction, hunger, fear, and aggression. It is quite possible that the findings of ethologists will eventually induce psychologists to wonder whether they dismissed the concept of instinct too quickly and too finally, instead of refining it and relating it to data from other disciplines.

Lorenz: Intraspecific Aggression

In recent years new light has been cast upon the nature of aggression by Konrad Lorenz of the Max Planck Institute of Behavioral Physiology.

Lorenz believes that the "fixed motor patterns" of animal behavior follow Mendel's law of inherited characteristics; yet he recognizes that there is a subtle relationship between the two factors of evolutionary adaptation—innate behavior and learning in the environment. From studies of aggression in certain species of fish, dogs, birds, rats, deer, and farmyard animals, Lorenz concludes that aggression is something very different from the destructive principle expressed in the Freudian hypothesis of *thanatos*. According to Lorenz, "aggression, the effects of which are frequently equated with those of the death wish, is an instinct like any other and in natural conditions it helps just as much as any other to insure the survival of the individual and the species."[29]

Lorenz found that aggression, as he defines it, occurs primarily among members of the same species, not between members of different species. When an animal of one species kills an animal of another species for food, this is not aggression; in killing the prey, the food gatherer exhibits none of the characteristics of genuinely aggressive behavior. The typical aggressive instinct, according to Lorenz, is not *inter*specific but *intra*specific, and can best be illustrated by the tenacity with which a fish, an animal, or a bird will defend its territory against members of its own species. Aggression is seen as serving a species-preserving function in the Darwinian sense, because it prevents the members of a species from excessive bunching together and spaces them out over the available habitat:

> The danger of too dense a population of an animal species settling in one part of the available biotope and exhausting all its sources of nutrition and so starving can be obviated by a mutual repulsion acting on the animals of the same species, effecting their regular spacing out, in much the same manner as electrical charges are regularly distributed all over the surface of a spherical conductor. This, in plain terms, is the most important survival value of intraspecific aggression.[30]

Lorenz notes that among animals who hold sway over a particular territorial space, the readiness to offer combat to an intruder is greatest at the center of the individual's territory—the part of the habitat with which it is most familiar. Lorenz contends that "even the slightest decrease in aggression toward the neighboring fellow member of the species must be paid for with loss of territory and . . . of sources of food for the expected progeny."[31]

Here we have a concept which Robert Ardrey has popularized—probably too simplistically and misleadingly, especially in its application to humans—as "the territorial imperative." Ardrey interprets the available evidence to mean that humans, no less than lions, wolves, tigers, eagles, robins, mockingbirds, ring-tailed lemurs, herring gulls, callicebus monkeys, and many other species, are territorial creatures. He is convinced that the territorial drive so often manifested by members of the human species—the fierce attachment both to private property and to the national patrimony—is an innate behavior pattern of an ancient biological order "placed in our nature by the selective necessities of our evolutionary history."[32] Yet paradoxically, the sexual and family bond must overcome the tendency toward repulsion that is at the very heart of an individual's territory, where intraspecific aggression ought to be strongest. Lorenz describes the intimate relationship between bond behavior and aggressiveness in the following passages on the Cichlid species of fish:

> It is a nerve-wracking experience to see the prospective mates in a state of real fury with each other. Again and again they are close to starting a vicious fight, again and again the ominous flareup of the aggressive drive is only just inhibited and murder sidestepped by a hair. . . . At first nervously submissive, the female gradually loses her fear of the male, and with it every inhibition against showing aggressive behavior. . . . As may be expected, the male gets furious, . . . then rushes at his mate, and for fractions of a second it looks as if he will ram her—and then the thing happens which prompted me to write this book: the male does not waste time replying to the threatening of the female; he is far too excited for that, he actually launches a furious attack which, however, is not directed at his mate but, passing her by narrowly, finds its goal in another member of his species.[33]

According to Lorenz, nonaggressive species do not form love bonds, while all species that exhibit bond behavior are highly aggressive. Some birds and animals are bonded only during the mating and rearing seasons, at which times they are aggressive. Bonding therefore protects the partners against each other and insures the safe rearing of the young, but it increases the aggressiveness of the male against the territorial neighbor. Lorenz concluded that analogous processes play a significant role in the family and social life of many higher animals and of the human species.[34]

Besides helping to keep the species spread over the widest area, the aggressive urge as manifested in the rival fight, usually between males, contributes to the selection of the fittest for reproduction. But the aim of aggression, says Lorenz, is to ward off the intruder, or to take possession of the female, or to protect the brood. Its object is never to exterminate fellow members of the species. Among several species one can verify a phenomenon which Lorenz terms the *ritualization of aggression,* by which he means a fixed motor pattern involving a ceremonialized series of inciting or menacing gestures by one individual to ward off an interloping member of the same species. This form of aggressive expression seems to be nature's design to achieve the positive species-preserving purpose of the aggressive instinct without resort to actual violence.[35]

In summary, Lorenz makes aggression out to be a benign instinct among animals. He points out that several animal species have developed some remarkable aggression-inhibiting mechanisms or appease-ment gestures. This is especially true among animals that are hunters of large prey and that are gregarious. The wolf, for example, is armed with such an array of powerful weapons that he had to develop strong aggres-sion inhibitors (such as baring his neck to the fangs of a victorious foe, thus giving the latter pause); otherwise the species might have destroyed itself.[36] Lorenz and other scientists hope that humans will manage to rit-ualize and control their aggressive impulses as well as some of the lower orders of animals have done. But weak creatures (e.g., doves, hares, chimpanzees, and humans) that normally lack the power to kill a foe of their own size and that can rely upon flight or other forms of evasion have not been under much pressure to develop inhibitions against killing their own kind. Lorenz gives this description of a human being's plight:

> In human evolution, no inhibitory mechanisms preventing sudden man-slaughter were necessary, because quick killing was impossible anyhow; the potential victim had plenty of opportunity to elicit the pity of the ag-gressor by submissive gestures and appeasing attitudes. No selection pressure arose in the prehistory of mankind to breed inhibitory mecha-nisms preventing the killing of conspecifics until, all of a sudden, the in-vention of artificial weapons upset the equilibrium of killing potential and social inhibitions.[37]

Lorenz's studies might well prompt the psychologists to revive their interest in the discarded instinct theories, but his concept of the aggres-sive impulse should not be confused with that of the Freudians or others who subscribe to the notion of a self-stimulating urge to destroy. For Lorenz, the purpose of the instinct is to warn outsiders to keep their dis-tance; it apparently comes into play only when the proper stimulus is applied, although it has been construed by some as a spontaneously operating urge.[38] The older instinct school, however, might be inclined to argue that Lorenz's hypothesis, if valid, really lends support to the the-ory of a modified aggressive instinct in every species—less destructive and more positive than Freud's, but nevertheless constantly operative for all practical purposes, because it can be activated by any member of the species outside of the individual's immediate biological unit.

Lorenz does not insist, as some writers do, that humans are uniquely vicious as killers of their own kind. We know that rats, ants, hyenas, and certain monkeys can be lethally aggressive against members of their own species. New male lions, when taking over a pride, are also quite likely to kill whatever cubs are already there in order to stimulate the reproduc-tive processes of the females.[39] But Lorenz exhorts human beings to ac-quire a proper humility and to conquer the pride which prevents them from acknowledging their evolutionary origins and the natural causation of human behavior.[40] He has no doubt that humans represent the highest achievement of evolution, and that they are essentially more advanced and complex than all other primates, but he warns that the very faculties of conceptual thought and verbal speech which elevate them to a uniquely high level above all other creatures also pose the danger of extinction to humanity.[41]

Lorenz puts little faith in the power of reason alone (as some strategists who analyze deterrence at the societal level appear to do) to overcome the aggressive instinct in individuals. Nevertheless, he strikes a note of cautious optimism. Even though humans cannot develop aggression-inhibitors through biological evolution in time to save themselves (since this process might take hundreds of thousands of years), they are capable—by combining their rational calculus of the consequences of nuclear war, the dynamics of the instinctive drives of species preservation, compassion for the species, culturally ritualized behavior patterns, and the controlling self-disciplining force of responsible politics and morality—of developing aggression-inhibitors in the form of sociopolitical structures within a relatively short time, once the major powers become genuinely convinced that large-scale nulcear war would be a mutually suicidal enterprise. Human beings may be "naked apes," as Desmond Morris called them,[42] but they possess a *culture*, and that makes a great deal of difference. It means that when the cultural environment affecting human behavior changes, the acquired characteristic can be directly transmitted to the next generation.[43]

Lorenz's Critics

Lorenz and those who accept his explanation of biologically grounded aggressivity have drawn fire from analysts for whom "nurture" is more important than "nature" as a determinant of behavior. Erich Fromm strongly criticized the theory of such "instinctivists" as Lorenz, as well as the contentions of those anthropologists who ostensibly support the instinctive aggression school, holding that humans through the first million years have been hunters accustomed to the pleasure of killing, and that a streak of destructive cruelty had consequently become ingrained into their basic structure as a result of the selective process. Against such a view, Fromm cited the findings of Ruth Benedict and Margaret Mead, who insisted that cultures characterized by peacefulness and cooperation, like that of the Zunis, are just as "natural" as the hostile, cruel cultures of other peoples. Fromm scored what he perceived to be a political bias in the theories of all instinctivists, including Lorenz: "To stress the innate character of aggression corresponded to conservative or reactionary attitudes. If aggression was innate, there was little hope for lasting peace and radical democracy." Fromm's complaint was that the theory of an aggressive instinct serves to absolve human beings of a sense of responsibility for their self-destructive belligerent behavior.[44] (Perhaps it should be pointed out, however, that relatively few societies in history have been as peaceful and cooperative as the Zuni Indians.)

Orthodox Freudians, who continue to stress either the death instinct or sexual frustrations in early childhood as decisive determinants of human behavior, reject Lorenz's theories. Behavioral psychologist B. F. Skinner and anthropologist M. F. Ashley Montagu admit that there is such a thing as instinct in human beings, but they staunchly insist that it is not an important component of human behavior—not nearly as important as conditioning and learning. Both Lorenz and Skinner may use the term *imprinting* to refer to messages encoded in the creature's genetic system, but they interpret the term quite differently. Lorenz sees the internal organism as the principal source of imprinting; Skinner looks to the external environment, and clearly deprecates the significance of mental and psychic states as source springs of human behavior. Skinner relies upon a stimulus-response paradigm in which the behavior of the individual organism is elicited solely as a result of consequences in the environment that provide reinforcement to the organism, whether physiological, psychic, or cognitive.[45] Social learning theorist Albert Bandura cites those who fault Lorenz for weak scholarship, for errors of fact and questionable interpretations in his generalizations concerning animal behavior, and for failing to differentiate inborn patterns of behavior from those arising out of experimental learning.[46] Fellow ethologists have criticized Lorenz not only for erroneously applying the result of his animal studies to humans, but also for reaching wrong conclusions about animals in general because his expertise is limited (of necessity) to only a few species.[47]

Before we return from the biological to the psychological explanations of aggression and conflict (including frustration-aggression, social learning, and other theories), some brief mention should be made of other factors that appear to be closely related to human aggressive behavior and toward an understanding of which the biologists can contribute insights. First, there is reason to believe that, since food intake is so important to the proper functioning of the organism, prolonged hunger or chronic malnutrition is likely to affect the operations of the brain and other organs, which in turn may have a significant effect upon the judgment, energy, and other characteristics of human beings. Second, it has been suggested that violent criminal behavior may be associated with the presence of one or more extra male chromosomes (although this finding has been controverted as based only on a biased sample) and also with "spontaneous firings" of brain cells "which correlate with subjective feelings of rage and a high incidence of uncontrollable violent behavior . . . such as fire-setting, aggressive sexual behavior, and murder."[48] Third, studies performed on animals and observations of humans in prisons and concentration camps have led to the conclusion that conditions of over-crowding may produce restlessness, hyperirritability, continuous fighting, and interference with all normal behavior patterns.[49] Fourth, it has been plausibly argued that an international crisis can be a stress-inducing stimulus for political leaders and decision-makers (even though some may feel a "sense of elation" in the midst of crisis pressures), and that their performance under stress may be significantly affected by such factors as health, age, fatigue (especially sleep deprivation), circadian and diurnal rhythms, and the intake of tranquillizing drugs or other medication.[50] These few examples serve to illustrate the variety of ways in which biological factors may have a bearing, beyond the aggressive instinct itself, upon human conflict behavior and political decision-making related to that behavior.

FRUSTRATION-AGGRESSION THEORY

Within recent decades, most psychological authorities have been inclined to trace the source of aggression to some form of frustration. The psychological concept of frustration and its effects deserves particularly close examination because of a widespread assumption that the high conflict potential of the developing areas is a function of frustration caused by economic deprivation.[51] Not infrequently, theorists of social revolution, in describing the attitudes which prevail in a prerevolutionary situation, relate such phenomena as "alienation" and "anomie" to a condition of "general frustration."[52] Rarely do those who explain the unrest in the developing regions by reference to "rising expectations" and economic frustrations present any careful analysis of the psychological processes involved, but they seem to take for granted some kind of undifferentiated frustration-aggression theory.

The Dollard-Doob Hypothesis

The frustration-aggression theory is a relatively old one. McDougall, Freud, and others had suggested it at one time or another. But this theory received its classic expression in the work of John Dollard and his colleagues at Yale shortly before the outbreak of World War II. The Yale group took "as its point of departure the assumption that *aggression is always a consequence of frustration.*" More specifically they took it for granted that "the occurrence of aggressive behavior always presupposes the existence of frustration and, contrariwise, that the existence of frustration always leads to some form of aggression."[53] Frustration they defined as "an interference with the occurrence of an instigated-goal response to its proper time in the behavior sequence."[54] Whenever a barrier is interposed between persons and their desired goals, an extra amount of energy is mobilized. Such energy mobilization, said Ross Stagner, "if continued and unsuccessful, tends to flow over into generalized destructive behavior."[55] Abraham Maslow, however, pointed out a difference between mere deprivation that is unimportant to the organism and a threat to the personality or life-goal of the individual; only the latter, he said, causes aggression.[56]

According to the Dollard study, the strength of the instigation to aggression can be expected to vary with (1) the strength of instigation to the frustrated response; (2) the degree of interference with the frustrated response; and (3) the number of frustrated response-sequences.[57] Aggression occurs only if goal-directed activity is thwarted, not in cases of unperceived deprivation. Moreover, the Yale group pointed out that not every frustrating situation produces some overt aggression. Acts of aggression can be inhibited, especially when their commission would lead to punishment or other undesirable consequences. The anticipation of punishment reduces overt aggression, and the greater the certainty and amount of punishment anticipated for an aggressive act, the less likely is that act to occur.[58]

The individual experiences an impulse to attack whatever barrier stands in the way of goal-directed behavior. The immediate barrier-target, however, may be physically, psychologically or socially immune to attack: The persons who interpose themselves may be stronger, vested with an aura of authority, sacred in character, capable of retaliating with a socially approved punishment, or in some other way rendered invulnerable for all practical purposes. The Dollard group focused primarily on the threat of punishment. The expectation of punishment interferes with the act of aggression and thus gives rise to further frustration, which will intensify the pressure either for direct aggression against the interfering agent or for other indirect forms of aggression.[59] There may occur a displacement of aggression, in which case the individual directs hostility toward someone or something not responsible for the original frustration. Alternatively, the individual who is both frustrated and inhibited may alter not the *object* but the *form* of aggression (e.g., by imagining or wishing injury to someone instead of actually harming the interfering agent). Another form which indirect aggression may take is self-aggression or *regression*, in which individuals castigate themselves, injure themselves, or, in the most extreme cases, commit suicide.[60] Dollard and his colleagues point to the "greater tendency for inhibited direct aggression to be turned against the self when it is inhibited by the self than when it is inhibited by an external agent." But they add that self-aggression is not the preferred type of expression.[61] Finally, it is assumed that any act of aggression (either direct or vicarious, e.g., fantasized physical assault) leads to catharsis, that is, a release of aggressive energy or tension and a reduction in the instigation to aggression.[62] These, in brief, are the essential psychological principles which comprise the Dollard-Doob theory.

Modifications of the Dollard-Doob Hypothesis

The Dollard-Doob hypothesis has undergone several modifications and refinements at the hands of other psychologists and social psychologists since the early 1940s. The crucial question is not whether frustration always leads to some form of aggression; it is conceded that it may be worked off in other ways and that a more accurate statement of the Dollard thesis is "that frustration produces instigation to different types of responses, one of which may be aggression."[63] Rather the crucial question is whether all aggression is traceable to frustration. Several authorities, including Durbin and Bowlby, Karl Menninger, and J. P. Seward, have criticized the frustration-aggression hypothesis on the grounds that there are other causes of aggression besides frustration;[64] and the studies of animal behavior made by Scott and Fredericson, as well as by Lorenz, also point to other causes such as dominance strivings, the sight of a strange animal of the same species, resentment at the intrusion of strangers, disputes over the possession of objects, pain, and interference with comfort. But the psychologists who subscribe to the Dollard hypothesis usually end up broadening the notion of frustration to encompass all these other aggression-arousing factors, or by attempting to reduce all these factors to forms of frustration.[65] Experimental studies have led to the conclusion that while thwarting goal-directed behavior may heighten aggressiveness, it sometimes exerts no significant influence in comparison with social-learning factors to be discussed later.[66]

Even at the level of individual psychology, before we pass on to the realm of social psychology, several difficulties arise in connection with the frustration-aggression hypothesis. These difficulties do not necessarily vitiate the theory, but they certainly complicate it. First, psychologists are not agreed as to whether the frustration-aggression nexus is a simple and virtually automatic stimulus-response pattern or whether such emotional states as anger and fear must be or can be interposed. Similarly, there is some disagreement as to whether additional cues, releasers, or other triggering stimuli must be present for aggression actually to occur. Second, what constitutes a frustration is not a completely objective matter; it often depends upon cognition and interpretation by the individual.[67] Third, some writers distinguish between primary and secondary frustrations and between active and passive frustrations. It is held that the various types of frustrations lead to different kinds of aggressive reactions.[68] Fourth, no clear differentiation is made between frustrations stemming from interference with routinized or frequently repeated goal-oriented behaviors and frustrations arising from interference with novel or "one shot" goal-directed actions. Fifth, although it may be relatively easy to see the operation of the frustration-aggression syndrome in children, it is considerably more ambiguous in adults. Sixth, when aggressive behavior does occur, "it may be deflected from its original goal, disguised, displaced, delayed, or otherwise altered."[69]

This, to say the least, makes for uncertainty as to the connection between a specific frustration and a specific art of aggression, particularly since we are not sure whether frustration "wears off" over time, even if it is not "worked off" in some way besides aggression. One sometimes gains the impression that the frustration-aggression theorists, like the Ptolemaic astronomers of old, are trying to "save the appearance" through the introduction of "epicycles" and that, no matter what kind of behavior is observed, it is interpreted in such a way as to allow the theory to remain intact. The frustration-aggression theory is supported by a convincing body of experimental evidence, and it also appeals to the common sense of most people who know from introspective experience that they have at times felt aggressive urges after being frustrated. There can be little doubt of its utility when it is applied to certain limited and simpler aspects of individual and small group behavior. But it is perhaps more than the theory can bear to use it for the purpose of extrapolating from relatively simple stimulus-response experiments to an explanation of the more subtle and complex modes of human action, especially those which are politically organized at the nation-state level.

FROM INDIVIDUAL TO SOCIETAL AGGRESSION

How do we pass from aggression in the individual to aggression in society? In view of Herbert C. Kelman's warning cited near the beginning of the previous chapter, such a transition should not be taken for granted. Yet the Dollard group transferred the lessons of individual frustration-aggression to the much broader level of collective social behavior without expressing any doubt as to the validity of the transfer and without offering any substantiating evidence or arguments that the transfer can in fact be made. Dollard himself had applied the frustration-aggression principle to an analysis of the black reactions to the frustrations imposed by the white group in a Southern community and thus "was able to reveal the psychological effects of the social structure upon the organization of personality and behavior."[70] The Dollard study carried the suggestion that even the Marxist theory of the class struggle depends implicitly upon the frustration-aggression principle.[71]

A number of difficulties are involved in shifting the analysis of frustration from the plane of the individual to that of the society. Such a shift gives rise to a major "level of observation" problem. Although it may be quite easy to see the frustration-aggression hypothesis validated in experiments with individuals (e.g., withdrawing bottles from babies or interfering with the completion of relatively simple goal-oriented behavior patterns), it is more difficult to verify the hypothesis at the level of large-group behavior. First, the time factor is quite different. The most clear-cut experimental evidence from the study of individuals would seem to indicate fairly rapid time sequences from the onset of frustration to the manifestation of aggressive responses—minutes or hours in most cases, and perhaps days or weeks in some, although it is hard to achieve certitude in these latter cases in view of the fact that the length of time it takes a frustration to "wear off" (if it does) is not known. We have already seen that a series of minor frustrations migh lead to "pentup" aggressiveness, but whether aggression accumulates and retains strength until it is discharged has long been a matter of controversy. Presumably each minor frustration results from a distinct stimulus in the stimulus-response pattern. It seems reasonable to conclude, however, that the longer the time interval between the interference with the goal-directed action and the commission of an aggressive act, the less certain is the connection between the frustration and the aggression, because several other steps may have intervened in the meantime—inhibitions, displacements, substitute responses, and other outlets or adjustments.

At some point, a long series of minor frustrations may shade off toward a continually frustrating condition or set of conditions, every conscious adversion to which constitutes an additional stimulus. But no matter how the time factor for individual behavior is explained, it would seem that social psychological phenomena usually develop at a slower time rate. Frustrating situations are perceived more slowly; the perceptions are less uniform and the interpretations more diverse; the stretched out time provides greater opportunity for individuals to adjust; the variety of responses is broader for large groups than for individuals; responses to frustrating situations are likely to vary according to the cultural values of different groups within the social structure; and, perhaps most importantly, a whole complex of external sociological (rather than internal psychological) factors contributes toward determining the response to frustration. Hence it may be possible to verify the frustration-aggression hypothesis in the behavior of smaller, unstructured groups (e.g., such anomic outbursts as the rioting of an unorganized mob), but it would seem much more difficult, and perhaps impossible, to apply the theory in any precise way to the behavior of larger, more highly institutionalized social entities.[72] Finally, it should be pointed out that most exponents of the frustration-aggression explanation are careful to exclude "learned aggression" from the scope of their theory. This is important to remember in any consideration of organized conflict (such as war, revolution, and guerrilla insurgency) in which training for aggressive conduct plays a significant role. The organized warfare that is characteristic of human societies has no counterpart among animals, and requires a high degree of social learning, as we shall see below.

SOCIALIZATION, DISPLACEMENT, AND PROJECTION

The frustration-aggression school has attempted to move from the individual to the social level more by logical inference than by experimentation. The principal conceptual mechanisms by which the transfer is made are "the socialization of aggression," "displacement," and "projection"—all closely related notions. It is important to understand how these mechanisms are supposed to operate, for they are crucial in the effort to apply the frustration-aggression explanation of conflict to social communities.

Psychologists hold that the process of acquiring social habits invariably gives rise to frustrations of one sort or another, inasmuch as every forced modification of spontaneous behavior from childhood to adulthood, it can be argued, interferes with goal-responses. This holds true for feeding habits, the suppression of crying, limitation of movement, cleanliness and toilet training, table and speech manners, sex behavior, sex typing, age grading, social behavior, the disciplines of schooling, restrictions on adolescents, and the various adjustments required in adulthood, such as marital, professional, or occupational.[73] Most of these examples, of course, are drawn from middle-class American family life. Frustration-aggression patterns are culture-bound; both the factors which make for frustration in human beings and the directions in which aggressive impulses are turned—or the "targets of aggression"—will depend largely upon the values of the specific cultural systems. Every society imposes some sort of social controls upon the spontaneous behavior of individuals. Thus according to the hypothesis, every social system produces in its members frustrations that eventually lead to fear, hatred, and violent aggression. Every culture must develop for itself its own solution to the problem of socially managing the aggressive impulses of its members.[74] The "socialization of aggression" takes place in all human societies, attenuating hostile action among members of the "in-group" by directing aggressive impulses against "out-groups."[75]

A child who is frustrated by the decision of a parent may seek release by substituting a different object of aggression, such as a toy, a piece of furniture, a sibling, another child in the neighborhood, a teacher, a pet, or a neighbor's property. It is deemed preferable that the substitute object be similar, if possible, to the original cause of the frustration. But very often similar targets (such as other adult authority figures) will also be invulnerable because aggression against them will likewise lead to punishment. As one finds safer targets, they frequently bear less resemblance to the original objects. The repression of hostile impulses from the level of consciousness can help in the displacement process by allowing the individual to forget the identity of the original source of the frustration.[76] Repression can lead to projection, which involves an attribution to, and an exaggeration in, others of unfavorable qualities and malicious motives that one is reluctant to recognize in oneself. Individuals seek to reduce their guilt feelings by projecting their intolerable thoughts and feelings to others. Once they have fastened upon their target, perceptual distortion sets in; everything in the target's behavior confirms and justifies their suspicions.[77]

It is quite common for psychologists and social psychologists to cite the frustration-aggression-displacement syndrome as the explanation of hostile attitudes toward "scapegoat" groups within a society and toward foreign nations.[78] But it is not clear how the leap is made from individual psychiatric theory to the analysis of attitudes and behavior at the level of large sociological entities. One might readily agree that a system of rewards and punishments within a family structure will serve to deter overt aggression, which the growing child will then displace.[79] It can also be conceded that there may be significant differences between the personality effects of democratic and authoritarian child-rearing patterns, and that such factors as the relations between fathers and sons, unsatisfied sexual desires, and the success-anxiety that a specific social culture breeds might contribute to the formation of an "authoritarian personality"[80] who harbors hostile suspicions toward selected groups within one's own society and toward selected foreign nations. The psychologists call attention to the fact that the growing child assimilates the attitudes and prejudices of adults, especially parents, and thus the notion of "the enemy," whether internal or external, is perpetuated through transmission from one generation to another. When a critical yet undefined proportion of people within a society becomes sufficiently frustrated or anxious or authoritarian, the society allegedly opts for conflict in an unconscious quest for self-release.

The mechanism by which individual psychic attitudes and complexes of a quasi-pathological character are translated into the concrete political decisions of leaders building up toward the actual outbreak of organized conflict has not yet been adequately defined and described, much less experimentally tested, in a manner intelligible to political scientists. Undoubtedly the frustrations of human beings form an important part of the total matrix out of which social conflict arises. The presence of widespread frustration would seem to lend a conflict potential to any social situation. It might even be said to constitute such a highly "useful" prerequisite as to be almost a necessary condition, at least for certain forms of collective aggression.[81] To admit this is not to deny that the hypothesis contains serious difficulties. We still do not know, for example, what exactly is the relationship between childhood frustration experiences (with their accompanying effects upon personality) and adult sociopolitical attitudes. Nor is there any way to determine whether childhood experiences or contemporary adult frustrations are more important as influences upon behavior. But the frustration-aggression-displacement syndrome alone would not appear to supply both the necessary and the sufficient conditions. Frustration might supply the potential for conflict, but a trigger mechanism is required, and the potential must somehow be organized and given specific direction.

One of the most glaring deficiencies in the frustration-aggression-displacement theory is its failure to explain adequately why particular groups are selected as targets of displaced aggression, especially when alternate targets are available.[82] At various times it has been suggested that targets are selected because they are "safe," because they are highly "visible," because they are "different and strange," because they have been traditionally mistrusted and disliked, or because they are most feared. Yet the target that is singled out for the displacement of aggression is also supposed to have some degree of association with the original frustrator. At the level of international relations, the selection of conflict targets has much more to do with macrocosmic factors—political, economic, ideological, and sociocultural—than with the inner psychic frustrations of individuals, although the latter might play some part if the policies pursued by one state should have a demonstrably adverse effect upon the personal, private interests of another state's citizens.

SOCIAL LEARNING THEORY

Social learning theorists such as Albert Bandura are skeptical of both the biological instinct theories of aggression and of those psychological theories that postulate a frustration-aggression drive. Bandura denies that aggressive energy is cumulatively damned up within the organism to be discharged without any external stimulus and instead places emphasis on the environmental elicitors of aggression. He admits that the human being has a few inborn habits, but he sees that as less significant than the vast human potential for learning. His approach can be summed up in the following passage:

> The social learning theory of human aggression adopts the position that man is endowed with neurophysiological mechanisms that enable him to behave aggressively, but the activation of these mechanisms depends upon appropriate stimulation and is subject to critical control. Therefore, the specific forms that aggressive behavior takes, the frequency with which it is expressed, the situations in which it is displayed, and the specific targets selected for attack are largely determined by social experience.[83]

Bandura cites anthropological evidence that in some cultures aggression is not the typical response to frustration. He contends that the definition of frustration has become so broad as to lose meaning—because it may include not only interfering with the achievement of desired goals, but also personal insults, subjection to pain, deprivation of rewards, and experience of failure. He sees frustration as only one—and not necessarily the most important—factor affecting the expression of aggression. He agrees that the threat of punishment can exert a regulatory (or deterrent) function with regard to aggressive behavior, but he argues that the relation between punishment on the one hand and aggressive behavior and the displacement process on the other hand is more complex than originally believed.[84]

Convinced of the great complexity of human responsiveness in various situations, Bandura sets forth a sophisticated and somewhat intricate theory of aggressive behavior based not on inner impulses or drives, but on social learning, social contexts and roles, modeling and reinforcement, and the learned ability to assess the rewarding and punishing consequences of any given action:

> Most of the intricate responses people display are learned, either deliberately or inadvertently, through the influence of example. . . . Man's capacity to learn by observation enables him to acquire complex patterns of behavior by watching the performance of exemplary models. . . . In social learning theory, human functioning relies on three regulatory systems. They include antecedent inducements, response feedback influences, and cognitive processes that guide and regulate action. Human aggression is a learned conduct that, like other forms of social behavior, is under stimulus, reinforcement, and cognitive control.[85]

LEARNED AGGRESSION AND MILITARY TRAINING

Those who have pondered the causes of war seem at times unable to make up their minds whether the frequency and ferocity of wars in history are due to the fact that men like to fight, or whether most men actually hate to go to war, but perform their soldierly duties out of a sense of obligation to serve their country or to make a sacrifice for preserving ideals and loved ones, or simply because they are coerced by conscription or peer pressures, conditioned to fight in military training, and frightened at the prospect of death if they do not kill first. Within the pages of a single work one can find the somewhat contradictory following passages:

> Men are thus naturally inclined to do battle. If we simply noted the ease with which men go to war, on slight or nonexistent pretexts . . . it would seem natural to conclude that there is some inner surge which blinds

man's reason and hurls him off the precipice of self-annihilation. There seems no doubt but that men love war with a profound passion, while at the same time they fill their books with sentimental nostalgia about love of man. . . .

If there is such a thing as the civilian's natural repugnance at the unaccustomed sight of the gore of warfare, experience, with the help of psychologists, has shown that such resistance to killing is rooted in one's whole psychic history, and is part of a long environmental conditioning process. . . . Even where this resistance can be overcome . . . it is still the case that hatred of the enemy is difficult to inculcate.[86]

Bandura has shown that the conversion of socialized individuals into effective military combatants requires a carefully conceived and executed training program. People who have been brought up to abhor killing as immoral and criminal must be made to accept killing in war as justified. Only in this way can they escape the self-condemning consequences of taking human life in battle.[87] The soldier is taught that he is fighting for family and friends, for country and civilization; for a cherished way of life and moral values, and perhaps for other high ideals, for example, the defense of religion, or democracy, or freedom, or lasting peace.[88] Recruits to military service must be completely reoriented from familiar civilian ways. They are issued new, distinctive clothing and are indoctrinated with new beliefs and modes of behaving. Many behavioral patterns are regulated in accordance with a military code of discipline under which automatic compliance with orders is expected. Soldiers are given an intensive, practical training in the techniques of warfare designed to inculcate a host of survival and combat skills, familiarize them with equipment and tactics, reduce the fear of battle, and enhance fighting unit solidarity, morale, and coordination.

But despite the fact that many social scientists assert rather glibly that human beings "kill enthusiastically" for abstract ideas and theories, those who have made a careful systematic study of the biological and psychological impulses to aggression do not argue that the typical soldier, in waging war, is working out any sort of aggressive instinct or frustration-aggression-displacement syndrome. If politically organized communities really thought that human beings are as innately aggressive as some intellectuals disdainfully take them to be (perhaps thereby passing judgment on themselves rather than on humanity), societies in all probability would long ago have felt some need at the end of a war to devote a significant effort to the retraining of exsoldiers to peacetime life—at least comparable to the kind of training required to inculcate a warlike spirit. But even though a small minority of veterans may be prone to violent behavior as a result of wartime experiences, most veterans seem to encounter little difficulty making the transition to civilian pursuits.

LEARNING THEORY AND INTERNATIONAL CONFLICT

Hadley Cantril's psychopolitical research, "transactional psychology," emphasizes that people do not react directly in a simple mechanistic way to a situation, but rather that their reaction is grounded upon assumptions formed by past experiences: "The way we look at things and the attitudes and opinions we form are founded on assumptions we have learned from our experience in life.... Once assumptions are formed and prove more or less effective, they serve both to focus attention and screen out what is apparently irrelevant and, as reinforcing agents, to intensify other aspects of the environment which seem to have a direct bearing on our purposes."[89]

This theory has important implications for the effective formulation of policy. It emphasizes "the importance of understanding the state of mind of people with whom the Government must deal, at home or abroad, in order to devise the right expression of policy at the right time or to decide the right moment to act." Understanding people's assumptions or states of mind involves knowing "their feelings, the whole complex of their hopes and aspirations, their frustrations and fears ... traditions and customs."[90]

In 1947 Hadley Cantril organized a research program for UNESCO that enlisted the services of social scientists in the study of "Tensions Affecting International Understanding." In response to a resolution of the UNESCO General Assembly, which called for "an inquiry into the influences which predispose toward international understanding on the one hand and aggressive nationalism on the other," a small group of experts from different disciplines and different nations conferred and agreed to a common statement, published in *Tensions That Cause Wars*. A second resolution called for "inquiries into the conceptions which people of one nation entertain of their own and of other nations." Surveys were taken of the attitudes of people in Australia, Britain, France, Germany, Italy, Netherlands, Norway, Mexico, and the United States toward people in other nations. The analysis, which appeared in *How Nations See Each Other*, suggested that "the stereotypes people have of people in other nations are largely results and not causes of the current relationship of their countries: people in one nation are hostile to people in other nations not because they have unfavorable stereotypes; rather they have these unfavorable stereotypes because they think other people are interfering with their own or their nation's goals."[91]

HAROLD LASSWELL

Although considerable emphasis has been placed upon the quantitative study of international relations in the past decade, Harold Lasswell was among the first to suggest that international political phenomena could be so studied. With more adequate knowledge about trends, it would be possible to make predictions that could be altered by "preventive politics." Thus Lasswell was concerned "with the organization of social knowledge to illuminate the margin of manipulable choice in the pattern of future events."[92] According to Lasswell, the utility of his theory lay in its potential for discovering the psychological and social roots of those human insecurities that cause wars and finding substitutes for violence as the means to gain security. In other words, Lasswell sought to develop a "policy science" for the study of international relations.

Lasswell also contended that a single theoretical framework could be devised to accommodate and unify the study of all political processes, whether domestic, comparative, or international. He called for the development of a framework sufficiently broad to accommodate future changes in the world political process.[93]

In every society the pattern of distribution of values—safety, income, and deference—resembles a pyramid. In fact, Lasswell defined politics as the "study of the changing value hierarchy, the pyramids of safety, income, and deference," or the study of "who gets what, when, and how."[94] World politics in the study of the "shape and composition of the value patterns of mankind as a whole." For this reason, Lasswell called for comparative studies of world elites and their values. The elite of the society receives most of its values and attempts to retain its position of ascendancy "by manipulating symbols, controlling supplies, and applying violence."[95] However, mass insecurities and discontent, especially heightened by shifts in the division of labor, in the distribution of the instrumentalities of violence, or in changes in symbols of identification, give rise to class struggles for a redistribution of values.

"Wars and revolutions are avenues of discharge for collective insecurities and stand in competition with every alternative means of dissipating mass tension."[96] An elite with vested interests might prefer a foreign war, rather than domestic social changes, for relieving its insecurities. (This subject is discussed more fully in the following chapter.) As long as the present world political structure existed, violence would persist. Lasswell argues that since elites can be sustained not only by violence, but also by manipulating symbols, what is needed for a stable world order is a world myth or a "universal body of symbols and practices sustaining an elite which propagates itself by peaceful methods. . . ."[97]

AGGRESSION DIVERSION AND REDUCTION

Social psychologists often point out that the expression of aggression within a society may be either covert or overt. Physical aggression may be eschewed in favor of verbal aggression, that is, murder, suicide, and other forms of violence may be rather rare, while the culture sanctions malicious gossip, slander, and the use of sorcery as means of retaliating against those one dislikes. Elton B. McNeil writes:

> Starting with the premise that an average quantity of aggression is the inheritance of each individual, it becomes clear that a dependable relationship exists between the freedom for its overt expression and the degree to which covert forms of it will make their appearance. The quantity of aggression given in the beginning seems fixed and unalterable, and if it finds no overt channel for expression, it becomes covert. . . .[98]

The passage just quoted suggests that societies may develop culturally acceptable ways of either reducing or working off aggressive impulses. In the search for social aggression-inhibitors or aggression-reducers one might logically look to such areas of life as religion, politics, business, sports, and education. In each one of these dimensions we find ourselves faced with ambiguities which prevent us from drawing definite conclusions. Religions that preach a doctrine of love and renunciation of self may significantly lessen the aggressiveness of those adherents who take the doctrine seriously, who apply it not selectively but universally, and who are sufficiently disciplined to follow it in practice. Yet throughout history religious differences themselves have often contributed to the occurrence and the ferocity of war. In the realm of politics, one might argue that, in comparison to authoritarian or totalitarian regimes, democratic states should be less aggressive because they provide a variety of outlets through which political frustrations can be released—freedom of assembly, association, and press, and the opportunity to participate in the political process by running for office, election campaigning, voting, lobbying for a law, or organizing a protest. There is something to this "safety valve" theory of democratic government, but the democratic milieu also permits aggressive individuals and parties to play upon xenophobic attitudes and propagate nationalistic policies, whereas in more tightly controlled societies the function of promoting nationalism is much closer to being a government monopoly. In free market economies, business enterprise undoubtedly siphons off a considerable amount of creative aggressivity. But, although most business people prefer the conditions of peace and order for making their rational profit calculus, some may support trade, or investment, and other economic policies that increase international tensions. A minority, as we saw in Chapter 6, might even expect to gain from war.

Behavioral and other scientists interested in controlling aggression have wondered whether a society might diminish its "fund" of pentup aggressive energy by diverting it into harmless channels such as organized athletic contests. There is no clear consensus on the subject. Konrad Lorenz regards all human sport as a form of ritualized fighting. Even though it contains an aggressive motivation absent in most animal play, it helps to keep people healthy and its main function consists in the cathartic discharge of aggression. Thus it provides a release for that dangerous form of collective militant enthusiasm which underlies aggressive nationalism.[99] Hebb and Thompson suggest that sports may be a useful means of creating and working off an optimum amount of frustration and thus of contributing to social stability.[100] Frank calls attendance at such spectator sports as prizefights and professional football games a vicarious discharge of aggression. He admits, however, that body-contact sports often involve the infliction of pain and may arouse anger and hostility, but notes that the game itself requires the development of self-discipline to control the expression of anger.[101] (Ardent fans may feel less inhibited, and may carry on in a manner which makes it harder for the players to control their tempers. But some aggressive energy must be consumed by spectators who cheer, whistle, applaud, jump up and down, boo the umpires, storm the playing field, tear shirts from the backs of their heroes, pull down the goalposts, and wear out their automobile horns in victory parades.) Lorenz, Frank, and others have perceived much good in the Olympics as promotive of international cooperation and good sportsmanship,[102] although it cannot be denied that on occasion the Olympic Games have been converted into an arena of international hostility (e.g., 1936 in Nuremberg), violent conflict (1972 in Munich), and intricate diplomatic maneuvering to express political opposition to the host country's aggression (Moscow in 1980).

Within recent years, writers have expressed concern that under some circumstances sports may get out of hand, possibly exacerbating both the aggressive impulses of individual players and spectators, and international tension, ill will, and hostility.[103] If there is such a thing as a "fund" of pentup aggressive energy (a hypothesis never proven), competitive sports probably represent on balance a healthy safety valve, because most sports contests are conducted peaceably and the losers, if they are "good sports," do not harbor lasting grudges. International sports competition, if approached purely as sports, in a spirit of fair play, can contribute to the strengthening of international good will and amity, but sports contests, like religion and trade, are neutral from a political standpoint, and do not necessarily lead to peace, especially if governments, ideological movements, political organizations, or ethnic partisans attempt to exploit them for their own ends which have little to do with sports.[104] In the final analysis, we cannot be certain whether sports attenuate or stimulate aggression within individuals and among nations.

The area to which a great many psychologists and social learning theorists attach their hopes for reducing human aggressiveness and fostering international standing is education, in both a broader and a stricter sense. Changes in regard to education have been urged at two different levels. The first pertains to basic modifications in the method of rearing children, aimed at reducing the level of frustration, violence modeling, and aggression within a society. Some theorists who associate warlike cultures with asceticism, celibacy, and strict codes of sexual behavior advocate greater sexual permissiveness.[105] In medieval Europe, however, the celibate priestly class was forbidden to take part in warfare, and the knights who did fight were usually far from celibate. Some psychologists trace the problem to the readiness of parents to mete out physical punishment to children; they urge parents to be more tolerant of children's desires to "express themselves."[106] Still others argue that it is unhealthy to bottle up feelings of rage and anger, and that the "ventilation" of aggression can have a therapeutic effect, despite warnings to the contrary by experimental psychologists.[107] Others yet have called for eliminating violence in the mass media in order to decrease the incidence of violent behavior by imitation.[108] The foregoing proposed remedies involve considerable cultural or social changes which may not be acceptable or easy to achieve. It is a case of saying that if human beings behaved differently from the way they do, they would be less aggressive. But there is no way of knowing, of course, whether these changes—assuming that they could be achieved—would really decrease the propensity toward international war.

The second proposed change pertains to the realm of formal educational efforts, calculated to attenuate international hostility and conflict by promoting understanding among societies. Theorists have long taken it for granted that courses in schools which increase the students' knowledge about foreign cultures and countries, as well as international teacher, student, and cultural exchange programs which facilitate personal contacts and learning experiences across political boundaries, are bound to contribute to the growth of international good will and the strengthening of international peace.[109] But Kenneth N. Waltz has questioned whether misunderstandings among peoples of diverse cultural backgrounds have anything to do with the occurrence of most wars. "Conversely," he asks, "does understanding always promote peace, or do nations sometimes remain at peace precisely because they do not understand each other well?"[110] Thus we cannot assume that increased communication leads inevitably to improved understanding, or that understanding necessarily makes for cooperation rather than conflict. Indeed no political scientist has been more trenchant than Waltz in criticizing behavioral scientists for proposing to bring about world peace through the adoption of radical changes in the behavior patterns of governments that simply are not feasible from a political standpoint.

IMAGE THEORY

In their analysis of international conflict, psychologists frequently relate the phenomena of "displacement" and "projection" to the concept of "national images." These images reflect a process of selective perception (and hence some perceptual distortion) caused by the traditional historic view of other nations as transmitted through the educational system, folklore, the news media, and other channels of socialization. There is nothing mysterious about an *image*. The term, according to Kelman, merely refers to "the organized representation of an object in an individual's cognitive system . . . the individual's conception of what the object is like."[111] Intergroup tensions and the decisions that lead to intergroup or international conflict are often traced to individual states of mind, which are politically manipulable and where distorted perceptions may be more significant than accurate ones.

Kenneth Boulding (who is an economist rather than a psychologist by profession) has pointed out that the behavior of complex political organizations is determined by decisions which involve "the selection of a preferred position in a contemplated field of choice," and which is in turn the function of the decision-maker's *image*. The image is a product of messages received in the past—not a simple accumulation of messages but "a highly structured piece of information-capital." Every nation is a complex of the images of the persons who think about it; hence the image is not one but many. Furthermore, there are in the nation the images of a relatively small group of powerful people who make the important decisions and the images of the ordinary people (the masses) who are affected by the decisions but only indirectly take part in making them—more so in democratic systems, less in dictatorial or totalitarian systems. Boulding then makes this important observation:

> In the formation of the national images, however, it must be emphasized that impressions of nationality are formed mostly in childhood and usually in the family group. It would be quite fallacious to think of the images as being cleverly imposed on the mass by the powerful. If anything, the reverse is the case, the image is essentially a mass image, or what might be called a "folk image," transmitted through the family and the intimate face-to-face group, both in the case of the powerful and in the case of ordinary persons. Especially in the case of the old, long-established nations, the powerful share the mass image rather than impose it. . . . This is much less true in new nations which are striving to achieve nationality, where the family culture frequently does not include strong elements of national allegiance but rather stresses allegiance to religious ideals or to the family as such.[112]

"Mirror Images"

Within recent years, considerable attention has been devoted to the subject of "mirror images." This interest has been perhaps a national outgrowth of the efforts of social psychologists to understand within the framework of their own discipline the Cold War between the United States and the Soviet Union. The notion of mirror images is based on the assumption that the peoples of two countries involved in a prolonged hostile confrontation develop fixed, distorted attitudes that are really quite similar. Each people sees itself as virtuous, restrained, and peace-loving, and views the adversary nation as deceptive, imperialistic, and warlike. Arthur Gladstone describes it in this way:

> Each side believes the other to be bent on aggression and conquest, to be capable of great brutality and evil-doing, to be something less than human and therefore hardly deserving respect or consideration, to be insincere and untrustworthy, etc. To hold this conception of the enemy becomes the moral duty of every citizen, and those who question it are denounced. Each side prepares actively for the anticipated combat, striving to amass the greater military power for the destruction of the enemy. . . . The approaching war is seen as due entirely to the hostile intentions of the enemy.[113]

According to the social psychologists, the perception of the enemy, even though it may be erroneous, can help to shape reality and bring on the self-fulfilling prophecy: When suspicions run high, a "defensive" move by one side may look "provocative" to the other, evoking from the latter a further "defensive" reaction which serves only to confirm the suspicions of the former.[114]

The concept of the mirror image seems to have been elaborated by American social psychologists almost exclusively for the purpose of explaining certain aspects of Soviet-American relations as the Cold War was starting to thaw and perhaps of contrasting Khrushchev's behavior with that of Stalin in such a way as to make the former look "peaceful" and the latter "aggressive." Urie Bronfenbrenner, for example, in a well-known exposition of the idea, argued that both American and Russian citizens believe essentially the same things about each other's societies: *They* are the aggressors; *their* government exploits and deludes the people; the mass of *their* people are not really sympathetic to the regime; *they* cannot be trusted; and *their* policy verges on madness.[115] Even within the restricted context of Soviet-American relations, the concept of the mirror image has given rise to some serious difficulties. One of the difficulties associated with the notion of the mirror image is that it readily gives rise to pseudocorollaries in the minds of untrained observers—corollaries which are not necessarily implicit in the concept itself but which emerge by a process of insinuation: (1) The social and political values of the two sides are scarcely distinguishable from each other. (2) Neither party can properly be cast in the role of aggressor or defender. (3) Both sides are equally right, equally wrong, and equally responsible for pursuing policies that produce international tensions. (4) The strategic behavior of the two sides springs from thought processes that are essentially similar. (5) The reduction of image distortion can be accomplished with equal ease on both sides. In fairness to the advocates of the mirror image theory, it should be pointed out that they often made some effort to dissociate themselves from the illogical inferences which can be drawn therefrom. Ralph K. White, for example, warned:

> The proposition that 'there is probably some truth on both sides' should be distinguished from the quite different proposition that 'there is probably an equal amount of truth on both sides'. . . . [It is] entirely possible to attribute too much validity to the other's viewpoint, leaning over backward to avoid ethnocentrism. . . .[116]

Urie Bronfenbrenner called attention to an important asymmetry:

> It proved far easier to get an American to change his picture of the Soviet Union than the reverse. Although showing some capacity for change, Soviet citizens were more likely than Americans to cling to their stereotypes and to defend them by denial and displacement . . . I am persuaded that a comparative study of modes of adaptation in American and Soviet society would reveal a stronger predilection in the latter for black-and-white thinking, moral self-righteousness, mistrust, displacing of blame to others, perceptual distortion, and denial of reality.[117]

The concept of the mirror image in international relations was at the height of its popularity in the early 1960s, and was logically related to a number of suggestions put forth at that time for reducing the hostility of the Cold War as well as the risks of hot war between the superpowers through unilateral initiative by one side designed to reduce international tensions and evoke reciprocal gestures of cooperation from the other side. The basic idea, of course, was that the process of relating tensions, no less than the process of exacerbating them, is a reaction process, and that if one side can bring itself to break the vicious circle and take the initiative by making friendly gestures and concessions, the behavior of the other will sooner or later change for the better.[118] But although this often works in interpersonal relations, it has more limited applicability in international relations, in which modifying policy directions is much more difficult to execute and easier to misinterpret as a clever ploy than as a genuine transformation of goals and intentions.

In addition to frustration-aggression and social learning theories, there are several other psychological theories of conflict with which the student of international relations should be familiar. These theories often serve to complement and in some cases to modify the theories treated in the foregoing sections. They include the studies of Allport, Klineberg, and others on such phenomena as bias, prejudice, and stereotypes, and the part played by educational and mass communications systems in the shaping of intergroup attitudes.[119] The student should be conversant with the phenomenon that Frenkel-Brunswik calls the "intolerance of ambiguity," or the tendency of human beings to reduce frustrating or anxiety-producing uncertainties and contradictions in the world as perceived by reducing social reality to nice, neat, dichotomous categories— black and white, good and bad, friend and foe.[120] Adorno and his colleagues attempted to correlate a high degree of nationalistic feeling with an "authoritarian personality" that is characterized by neuroticism—an exaggerated fear of weakness, unquestioning submissiveness to authority, a conservative idea of a masculine-feminine dichotomy, and a preference for autocratic, punitive child-rearing methods.[121]

Many writers have sought to probe the murky area of the influence which the personality of national leaders may have upon their foreign policy decisions. Michael P. Sullivan, after reviewing a fair sample of the voluminous literature on the subject, reaches the judicious conclusion that the personality characteristics or attributes of political leaders must undoubtedly have some effect some of the time upon foreign policy decisions, but we are still far from sure as to what types of behavior can be accounted for by personality factors.[122] Also significant for understanding certain aspects of national and international politics is Erich Fromm's thesis concerning the desire of the modern human being to escape the burdens of freedom. Feeling alone and powerless in the face of gigantic entities and social forces that individuals cannot control, they are, according to Fromm, tempted masochistically to dissolve themselves in the omnipotent state, to identify entirely with the state, and to seek their satisfaction vicariously in the fortunes of the larger collectivity. Themselves ready to submit to power within their nation, they want their nation to assert itself at the expense of the weak beyond its borders.[123] These psychoanalytic interpretations of political behavior cannot be examined here in detail; however, merely citing them in this summary fashion should make it obvious to the reader that if either national leadership groups or large segments of their publics should lapse into pronounced forms of the neuroticism which these theories describe, it could have a profound impact upon the international behavior of states.

Festinger and Cognitive Dissonance

One of the psychological theories which warrants particular mention is the theory of cognitive dissonance and consistency advanced by Leon Festinger.[124] Stated in its simplest form, the theory refers to the normal tendency of the individual to reduce inconsistencies which may arise in his knowledge concerning his values, his environment and his behavior. Inconsistency might be reduced by modifying any one of the three. The problem of one's attitude toward smoking provides an apt illustration. Nonsmokers experience no great difficulty when they learn that, according to contemporary scientific research, the smoking of cigarettes is considered a serious hazard to health and to life. Inveterate smokers, however, suffer cognitive dissonance when this is called to their attention. They have always considered personal health to be an important human good. If they are married and have children, they may feel a moral obligation to act prudently to prolong their lives. A wife or husband might plead with the spouse to stop smoking, and she or he may be pained by the thought of causing displeasure. Smokers can attempt to reduce the inconsistencies in their knowledge by pursuing various courses.

First, they could stop smoking, but this may be difficult. They enjoy the pleasure of smoking and they might be convinced that it relaxes them and enhances their ability to concentrate creatively at work. As for the issue of personal health, they might try to persuade themselves that one should not be unduly concerned about longevity of life and sacrifice all sorts of present pleasures for the sake of a future benefit which might just as easily be snatched away as the result of a car accident, a disease unrelated to smoking or a nuclear war. If they perceive the deprivations of a fatherless or motherless family largely in economic terms, they may soothe their conscience by buying more life insurance. Should it be a wife's or husband's critical attitude that is producing the dissonance, she or he may marshal arguments to change the other's opinion, perhaps by deprecating the validity of the hypothesis that correlates cigarettes with health hazards. To reinforce one's own convictions, a person might increasingly seek the company of smokers as well as information calculated to show the advantages of smoking. In rare cases, the individual may even obtain a research grant to prove a less perturbing hypothesis concerning cigarettes or to find a way to reduce the harmfulness of smoking. In each of the foregoing examples, individuals strive to reduce their inner dissonance by changing their behavior, their values, or their environment. Usually, of course, restructuring of one's knowledge is an easier task than changing behavior or altering external reality.

Does this normal tendency away from cognitive dissonance and toward cognitive consistency have significant implications for the study of conflict at the level of international relations? Although the phenomenon seems readily verifiable through the introspection of personal experience, it is not yet demonstrable that it plays a significant part in interstate conflict, and perhaps it will never become so demonstrable in an empirical sense. We might speculate on how it could become operable. If this psychological mechanism does have significance at the level of international politics, it may be within the minds of key decision-makers.

Suppose, for example, that the leaders of a particular nation were convinced on ideological grounds that their country could not achieve permanent security until the adversary who represented the antithesis of their national value system had been destroyed or disarmed as a result of a victorious war. But with the growth of nuclear weapon stockpiles, the same leadership group realizes that direct hostilities between the two powers might very well prove mutually suicidal. Most of the leaders, therefore, in an effort to reduce cognitive dissonance begin to restructure their knowledge patterns concerning the world situation. Some abandon their earlier insistence upon the destruction of the enemy nation and derive satisfaction from the notion that henceforth their national security will be guaranteed by "the balance of terror" or a "favorable correlation of forces." Others deprecate the antithetical character of the two national value systems and express the hope of eventual "convergence." Still others seek different avenues to reduce dissonance: Some hope to disarm the foe by psychopolitical rather than military means; some try to persuade themselves that strategic superiority can be achieved, after which a bold first nuclear strike will bring a quick and tolerably cheap victory; some may perceive in the emergence of a third power a common threat which the two traditional enemies might now collaborate to contain. Several other situations likely to produce cognitive dissonance among foreign policy decision-makers could be cited, for example, the desire to control inflation without reducing trade or increasing unemployment, or the desire of OPEC countries to raise the price of oil without ruining the Western market economies on which they depend, or the effort to use nuclear energy as an alternative to oil without abetting the proliferation of national nuclear weapons capabilities and polluting the human environment with waste materials from reactors.

The theory of cognitive dissonance, which is perhaps related to the "intolerance of ambiguity" discussed earlier, might also cast light on the phenomenon of internal revolution within a society. It is often suggested that when human beings perceive an intolerably wide gap between their social ideals and the operating reality of the existing political system, they become alienated from the latter and seek to reduce their inner dissonance by gravitating toward revolutionary organization for the purpose of restructuring the external environment according to their ideal vision. In revolutionary situations, of course, many individuals will hover precariously on the borderline between continuing to grant the system minimal or passive support and withdrawing from the system to oppose it actively by violence. This is partly a matter of weighing prospective rewards and punishments, and thus falls under the heading of what psychologists call "approach-avoidance" conflicts within the individual, where the antagonistic tendencies are both sufficiently strong to produce ambivalent or neurotic behavior.[125]

We might suggest the following hypothesis concerning the relationship between cognitive dissonance theory on the one hand and the theories of the causes of international war and internal revolutionary conflict on the other: Modern technological developments, particularly in respect to nuclear missile weaponry and to the mass media of communications as a factor in social conflict, produce in the minds of both individuals and social aggregates a form of cognitive dissonance which seems likely to attenuate pressures for direct international military hostilities (at least between nuclear powers and their immediate allies) while increasing the probability of intrasocietal conflict and violence, both in nuclear and nonnuclear weapon countries. There are several different elements in confluence here: the impact of advanced weapons technology and of communications patterns upon the crucial inverse relationship, long hypothesized by social scientists but never conclusively demonstrated, between intrasocietal and extrasocietal violence.

PSYCHOLOGICAL FACTORS IN THE NUCLEAR AGE

More than a third of a century has passed since Alamogordo, Hiroshima, and Nagasaki. Psychologists, strategists, and others have often pondered the impact of the existence of nuclear weapons on the human psyche. Those who believe in the validity of nuclear deterrence (which will be treated at length in Chapter 9) argue that the growth of nuclear weapons stockpiles has made the governments of the leading powers more cautious than ever before in the conduct of their foreign policies. Some would contend that the accumulation of nuclear weapons has compelled political decision-makers to face up squarely to the problem of war for the first time in history and to substitute the deterrence system for the war system. Others hold more pessimistically that the proliferation of nuclear weapons has brought humanity to the precipice of self-extinction; that the superpowers are foolish to base their security upon the morbid and allegedly contradictory premises of "mutual overkill;" that continued competition in the development of nuclear weapons technology arouses fear and neurosis in many quarters and aggravates international tensions; and that the danger is supposedly heightened by a tendency—due to such psychological factors as defensive avoidance, apathy, and habituation—to seek escape from anxiety either by unconscious denial of the threat or by an effort to blot its implications from consciousness by rationalizing them away: "They will never be used."[126]

One and the same psychological factor—fear—is often cited as both increasing and decreasing the danger of war. The issue is by no means simple. Some fears may be rational (i.e., in the sense that they lead to rational calculations and decisions) and some may be irrational if they block rational judgment. Fears may operate with very different effects upon publics, concerned individuals and groups, and policy-making elites. In West Germany, for example, publication of results of NATO military exercises, in which using tactical nuclear weapons to repel a Soviet attack is simulated, usually arouses popular concern and produces a spate of critical press comment for a short time; however, this leads to no drastic change in the policy of a government which believes in the effectiveness of NATO's nuclear deterrent strategy and can perceive no practical alternative to it up to the present time. Japan, the only country ever to feel the physical impact of nuclear weapons in wartime, has long manifested a significant (though fluctuating) psychopolitical aversion to things nuclear. Whenever an American submarine thought to be carrying nuclear missiles or equipment puts in at a Japanese port, a protest demonstration can be expected.[127] Yet the Japanese government, although recognizing the sensitivity of public opinion on this score, supports United States defense policy in the Pacific, because Japan's national security depends on this policy, and the alternatives to that dependence are politically unattractive.

This does not mean that popular fears have no effect upon the policy of governments. Threat appeals that focused upon the dangers of radioactive fallout were undoubtedly exaggerated by the opponents of nuclear testing; nevertheless they were effective in motivating segments of the American public to object to nuclear weapons tests in the atmosphere and in eliciting the support of Administration officials and members of Congress for the Nuclear Test Ban Treaty of 1963.[128] The main point to be made is that psychological factors are bound to affect in different ways the political attitudes of publics (or segments thereof) and of governmental decision-makers. It is inevitable that people who live in the vicinity of the projected construction of a nuclear power plant will worry more about the local safety factor than will national administrators who are under pressure to develop new sources of energy and who are convinced that the safety and environmental problems of nuclear power stations are in the long run more manageable than the problems of returning to coal or drastically cutting energy supplies.

Fear of and respect for nuclear power in all forms are healthy phenomena which should be neither denied nor discouraged. But only if the fear is kept rational will it remain politically efficacious so that the power of the atom can be used for beneficial rather than destructive purposes. The theory of nuclear deterrence as propounded by contemporary strategic analysts presupposes a high degree of "common sense" on the part of national political decision-makers. At this point, psychologists warn that in the lives and decisions of individuals, irrational, unconscious factors frequently prevail over rational, conscious factors. Sociologists who have been influenced by Max Weber rejoin by pointing to the inherently stabilizing rationality which is built into the political-administrative bureaucratic structures of modern states, in which the emotional preferences of individuals are subordinated to and neutralized by a complex network of institutionalized procedures that inhibit or screen out rash and erratic decisional behavior.[129] The scientific, technological, and military personnel who plan, manage, and staff the nuclear deterrent capability may be obliged to worry about the worst case in which deterrence fails, in other words, to "think about the unthinkable" for the purpose of keeping it that way. But this takes place within the larger context of international political decision-making that rests upon the assumption of "rationality" based on some proportionate relationship between long-range value goals and immediate instrumental policies, between ends and means, between the objectives pursued and the costs to be paid.

However, the value attached to goals may differ drastically between and among national governments. The willingness, or unwillingness, to accept damage in a nuclear exchange may be proportional to the importance attached to the objectives held by one state with respect to an adversary. If this is the case, the conception of rationality held by one power may differ substantially from that held by an opponent, and thus the devastation that one would be prepared to accept may be different from the other. The subject of deterrence will be treated in Chapter 9, and the problems of decision-making in time of crisis will be examined in Chapter 11.

CONCLUSION: MICROCOSMIC THEORIES IN PERSPECTIVE

All the theories discussed in this chapter—biological-instinctual, frustration-aggression, social learning, and other theories of aggression—have been modified over time, and the general directions of these modifications in an era of interdisciplinary research and theoretical integration have been toward convergence.[130] The various theories have been presented here in their clear, pristine form for the purpose of helping the student to understand the sources from which contemporary theories are evolving. The student is strongly encouraged to go back to the original insights, to trace them through subsequent modifications, and to formulate their own syntheses based upon their own reflection, analysis, and insights.

In summary, it is undeniable that biological and psychological mechanisms within the individual which pertain to aggressive behavior are somehow related to intersocietal warfare, although the relationship is indirect rather than direct, and may be rather remote at some times and more proximate at other times. Innate aggressive urges or drives may feed or reinforce belligerent political attitudes and give them an emotional basis. In the case of some individuals, highly developed inner aggressiveness may make it easier to train them for fighting and killing in war. Aggressive impulses frequently indulged rather than controlled might contribute to a short temper in a political leader, and dispose the leader to resort readily to force in order to solve a problem which might be managed adequately through negotiation. Conversely, personality factors can also make another leader vacillate and procrastinate in a state of Hamletian indecision until the situation evolves to a point at which either war becomes inevitable or peace prevails by forfeit when everyone loses interest in the crisis. But despite these and several other linkages which could be drawn, it would be inaccurate to conclude that innate biological and psychological drives are the "cause" of wars or peace. They probably constitute one of the important *necessary* conditions for the emergence of aggressive discontents among individual leaders, elite groups, and masses that make the recurrence of war a possibility throughout human history. Of themselves, however, they do not constitute a *sufficient* condition of war. To use an apt analogy, they undoubtedly comprise some of the essential chemical ingredients that go into the ammunition powder. But they are not the whole weapon. They are probably not even the trigger. Most assuredly they are neither the finger on the trigger nor the mind that orders the finger to pull the trigger. Fortunately, there is no compelling reason to think that humanity is being pushed inexorably toward nuclear cataclysm by an unconscious death wish or by some other innate biological/psychological urge to aggression.

Notes

1. Kenneth N. Waltz, *Man, the State and War: A Theoretical Analysis* (New York: Columbia University Press, 1959), Chapter II.
2. Ibid., chapter IV.
3. Ibid., chapter VI. See also "War and the Expectation of War," chap. 7 in Vernon Van Dyke, *International Politics,* 2nd ed. (New York: Appleton, 1966); Gordon W. Allport, "The Role of Expectancy," in Hadley Cantril, ed., *Tensions That Cause War* (Urbana, Ill.: University of Illinois Press, 1951); and Werner Levi, "On the Causes of War and the Conditions of Peace," *Journal of Conflict Resolution,* IV (December 1960), 411–420. Levi notes that war should be traced not to any specific factor but to a constellation of factors. Most attempts to understand the causes of war, he wrote, involve a "search for all possible elements present in the situation to explain the origins of war," but they reflect a failure "to try to discover whether there are missing elements whose presence would lead to the avoidance of the use of violence." Ibid., p. 418. This is a provocative thought—that the nonexistence of one thing might be the "cause" of something else.
4. Kenneth N. Waltz, ibid., pp. 18–20.
5. The word *anomic* here refers to a condition of normless violence flaring up rather unexpectedly.
6. Werner Levi, op. cit., p. 415. Here the reader should review the caution expressed by Herbert C. Kelman in the passage quoted in Chapter 5. See also the following statement by Kelman; "Any attempt to conceptualize the causes of war and the

conditions for peace that starts from individual psychology rather than from an analysis of the relations between nation-states is of questionable relevance." "International Relations: Psychological Aspects," *International Encyclopedia of the Social Sciences* (New York: Macmillan, 1968), vol. 8, p. 76.

7. The founder of sociobiology is Edward O. Wilson, a professor of science and curator of entomology at Harvard University, who outlined the field in *Sociobiology: The New Synthesis* (Cambridge, Mass.: Harvard University Press, 1975). Since 1975, several works have appeared either attacking or defending the field or presenting the debate. These include: D. P. Barash, *Sociobiology and Behavior* (New York: Elsevier, 1977); Arthur L. Caplan, ed., *Sociobiology Debate* (New York: Harper & Row, 1978); Michael S. Gregory et al., eds., *Sociobiology and Human Nature: An Interdisciplinary Critique and Defense* (San Francisco: Jossey-Bass, 1978); and George W. Barlow and James Silverberg, eds., *Sociobiology: Beyond Nature-Nurture* (Boulder, Colo.: Westview, 1979). See also Charles Frankel, "Sociobiology & Its Critics," *Commentary,* 68 (July 1979), 39–47.

8. Peter A. Corning, "The Biological Bases of Behavior and Some Implications for Political Science," *World Politics,* XXIII (April 1971), 339–340. See also Thomas Landon Thorson, *Biopolitics* (New York: Holt, Rinehart and Winston, 1970); and the essays by Albert Somit, David Easton, Roger D. Masters, and John Wahlke, in Albert Somit, ed., *Biology and Politics* (Paris: Mouton, 1976). Corning points out that "there is now considerable evidence that many specific behaviors have a biological basis . . . : the nuclear family (including pair-bonding and parent-sibling affectional bonds), antipathy to strangers, self-motivated learning activities and exploratory behavior, at least some forms of territoriality, fear, ethical or authority-accepting capacities, play, the proclivity for forming peer groups, aggressiveness, individual competitiveness, and the tendency to form fairly stable hierarchies." Ibid., p. 342.

9. Abraham H. Maslow, *Motivation and Personality* (New York: Harper & Row, 1954), pp. 80–98. Maslow argues that basic physical and safety needs demand satisfaction before the higher psychological needs emerge.

10. Robert C. North has shown that the shortages or scarcities which give rise to political conflict are due not only to objective physical causes (such as entropy) but also to psychological perceptions and anticipations of demand in excess of supply. "Toward a Framework for the Analysis of Scarcity and Conflict," *International Studies Quarterly,* 21 (December 1977), 569–591; See also David Novick et al., *A World of Scarcities: Critical Issues in Public Policy* (New York: Halsted, 1976).

11. See William Etkin, *Social Behavior from Fish to Man* (Chicago: University of Chicago Press, 1967), p. 33; George Gaylord Simpson, *The Meaning of Evolution* (New Haven: Yale University Press, 1967), p. 222; Theodosius Dobzhansky, *Mankind Evolving* (New Haven: Yale University Press, 1962), p. 134.

12. Albert Bandura, *Aggression: A Social Learning Analysis* (Englewood Cliffs, N.J.: Prentice-Hall, 1973), p. 3.

13. Ibid., p. 5. Corning, following the approach of the Committee on Violence of the Stanford University School of Medicine, defines aggressiveness as encompassing the entire spectrum of assertive and attacking behaviors found in humans and other animal species. "It includes overt and covert attacks, self-directed attacks, displacement attacks, dominance behavior, defamatory acts, and the motivational and emotional components of any determined attempt to accomplish a task." Op. cit., p. 345. Rollo May notes that, besides being physical, aggression may also be psychological, intellectual, spiritual, or economic. It may employ as its weapons words, artistic symbols, gestures, arguments *ad hominem,* insults, or even prolonged silence calculated to hurt or punish. *Power and Innocence: A Search for the Sources of Violence* (New York: Norton, 1972), pp. 148–152.

14. William McDougall, *An Introduction to Social Psychology* (Boston: Luce, 1926), especially pp. 30–45. See also his *Outline of Psychology* (New York: Scribner's, 1923), pp. 140–141.

15. Sigmund Freud, *A General Introduction to Psychoanalysis*, trans. G. S. Hall (New York: Boni and Liveright, 1920), pp. 170–174.

16. See Urpo Harva, "War and Human Nature," in Robert Ginsberg, ed., op. cit., p. 49. "Aggression and necrophilia are the two deep sources from which war derives its motive energies." Ibid.

17. Sigmund Freud, *Beyond the Pleasure Principle* (London: International Psychoanalytical Press, 1922); (New York: Bantam, 1959), p. 198. See also Albert Bandura, op. cit., pp. 12–14.

18. "Why War?", in a letter from Sigmund Freud to Albert Einstein, written in 1932. Text in Robert A. Goldwin et al., *Readings in World Politics* (New York: Oxford University Press, 1959). After describing the "death instinct," Freud wrote: "The upshot of these observations . . . is that there is no likelihood of our being able to suppress humanity's aggressive tendencies. . . . The Bolshevists, too, aspire to do away with human aggressiveness by ensuring the satisfaction of material needs and enforcing equality between man and man. To me this hope seems vain." But then, paradoxically, he added that "complete suppression of a man's aggressive tendencies is not an issue; what we may try is to divert it into a channel other than that of warfare." Ibid., p. 29. This last statement seems to parallel William James's quest for a "moral equivalent of war." See also Freud's *Civilization and Its Discontents* (New York: Cape and Smith, 1930).

19. Leonard Berkowitz, *Aggression: A Social-Psychological Analysis* (New York: McGraw-Hill, 1962), p. 8; Rollo May, op cit., p. 155.

20. Leonard Berkowitz, op.cit., p. 9.

21. Ibid., p. 10. D. O. Hebb has shown that there is an important relationship between excitation and the human being's mental development. Noting that a mere repetition of responses may weaken rather than strengthen them, he says that prolonged routinized learning has a negative, monotonous effect which often leads to a disturbance or reduction of motivation or loss of interest. Hebb argues that human behavior is dominated not by what is thoroughly familiar and arouses a "well-organized phase sequence," but rather by the "thought process that is not fully organized." He insists upon "the continued need of some degree of novelty, to maintain a wakefulness of choice." He adds that "some degree of novelty, combined with what is predominantly familiar, is stimulating and exciting over a wide range of activities." He also refers to the human "preoccupation with what is new but not too new, with the mildly frustrating or the mildly fear-provoking." As examples he cites the case of children seeking controllably frightening situations, the addiction of adults to dangerous sports (such as mountain climbing and sky diving), or to "ghost stories," and the fascination of problem-solving challenges, even when they involve frustration. He concludes that conflict need not be regarded as "unpleasant and grossly disruptive of human behavior; on the contrary, some degree of conflict is stimulating and necessary to the maintenance of normal responsiveness to the environment." *The Organization of Behavior: A Neuropsychological Theory* (New York: Wiley, 1949), pp. 224–234. Human beings actively seek an optimum level of frustration. Cf. D. O. Hebb and W. R. Thompson, "The Social Significance of Animal Studies," in Gardiner Lindzey, ed., *Handbook of Social Psychology* (Reading, Mass.: Addison-Wesley, 1954). Reprinted in Leon Bramson and George W. Goethals, eds. *War: Studies from Psychology, Psychology, Anthropology* (New York: Free Press, 1968), p. 53.

22. Contemporary psychoanalytic writers have adhered to the aggressive instinct theory. A few, such as Karl Menninger, retain the notion of death instinct. Others,

such as Hartmann, Kris, and Lowenstein, continue to postulate an aggressive instinct, but do not trace it to the death wish. Still others, including Fenichel, have shifted back toward the frustration explanation of aggression. See Berkowitz, op. cit., pp. 11–12.

23. See McNeil's chapter, "The Nature of Aggression," in Elton B. McNeil, ed., *The Nature of Human Conflict* (Englewood Cliffs, N.J.: Prentice-Hall), 1965, p. 15. Peter A. Corning has warned that it "would be fallacious to make an unqualified identification between any given human behavior and apparently similar behavior in lower animals." Op. cit., p. 331.

24. Students of animal behavior-physiology are producing some interesting insights into the problem of aggression, but they would be the first to admit difficulties in interpreting their data and to caution against the hasty application of their findings to the more mysterious realm of human affairs. A useful summary of findings on animal aggression can be found in ibid., pp. 15–27.

25. John Paul Scott, *Animal Behavior* (Garden City, L.I.: Doubleday [Anchor Books], 1963), pp. 121–122. One should note that if human aggressiveness is to be reduced or inhibited, it will have to be by way of learning, since the avenues of electrical, hormonal, chemical, and surgical interventions into the human body are of necessity and, fortunately, quite limited.

26. Leonard Berkowitz, op. cit., p. 15.

27. John Paul Scott, *Aggression* (Chicago: University of Chicago Press, 1958), p. 62.

28. John Paul Scott, *Animal Behavior,* op. cit., pp. 153–155.

29. Konrad Lorenz, *On Aggression,* trans. Marjorie Kerr Wilson (New York: Bantam, 1967), p. x.

30. Ibid., p. 28. "In other words, the threshold value of fight-eliciting stimuli is at its lowest where the animal feels safest, that is, where its readiness to fight is least diminished by its readiness to escape. As the distance from this 'headquarters' increases, the readiness to fight decreases proportionally as the surroundings become stranger and more intimidating to the animal." Ibid., p. 32.

31. Ibid., p. 167.

32. Robert Ardrey, *The Territorial Imperative* (New York: Atheneum, 1966), p. 103; see also pp. 4–7, 110–117, as well as his book *African Genesis* (New York: Dell, 1967), p. 174. For severe criticisms of Ardrey's work on territoriality as unscientific, see the essays by R. L. Holloway, P. H. Klopfer, Geoffrey Gorer, and J. H. Crook in A. F. M. Ashley Montagu, ed., *Man and Aggression,* 2nd ed. (New York: Oxford University Press, 1973).

33. Konrad Lorenz, op. cit., pp. 161–163.

34. Ibid., p. 164. Rollo May writes: "Lovemaking and fighting are very similar neurophysically in human beings." Op. cit., p. 151. See also Anthony Storr, *Human Aggression* (New York: Atheneum, 1968), p. 16.

35. Konrad Lorenz, *On Aggression,* op. cit., pp. 54–65, 69–81, and 99–110. He gives the familiar example of the ceremonial inciting by the female duck who will charge menacingly toward an "enemy couple" until, frightened by her own boldness, suddenly hurries back to her own protective drake to refurbish her courage before the next hostile foray. Thus without actually joining battle she delivers her warning message.

36. Ibid., p. 127. See also pp. 72–74, 122–132, and 232–233. For a further elaboration of Lorenz's views concerning the implications of biological findings for a knowledge of human social behavior, see "A Talk With Konrad Lorenz," *The New York Times Magazine,* (July 5, 1970), 4–5, 27–30. Lorenz's widely cited example of the wolf who submissively exposes his jugular vein to the adversary was later dismissed as having been based on faulty observation. R. Schenkel, "Submission: Its Features and Frustrations in the Wolf and Dog," *American Zoologist,* 7 (1967), 319–329.

Most biologists, however, still subscribe to the concept of aggression-inhibiting mechanisms.

37. Lorenz, op cit., p. 233. See also Jerome D. Frank, *Sanity and Survival: Psychological Aspects of War and Peace* (New York: Random House [Vintage Books], 1968), pp. 42–45 in his chap. 3, "Why Men Kill—Biological Roots." R. L. Holloway, Jr., suggests that the averting of eyes, cringing and tears may serve an inhibiting or appeasing function in humans, even though they are quite weak, in "Human Aggression: The Need for a Species-Specific Framework," *Natural History*, LXXVI (December 1, 1967), 41.

38. John P. Scott, in reviewing the Lorenz book, criticized it for suggesting that destructive aggressive behavior arises from a spontaneous outburst of internal energy. "Actually," Scott reiterates, "there is no evidence that there is any physiological mechanism in any mammal which produces stimulation to fight in the absence of external stimulation. Rather there is much evidence indicating that mechanisms exist which are easily excited by external stimulation and which function to prolong and magnify the effect of this stimulation," in "Fighting," *Science*, CLIV (November 4, 1966), 636–637.

39. Brian C. R. Bertram, "The Social System of Lions," *Scientific American*, 232 (May 1975), 65. See also H. Kruuk, "The Urge to Kill," *New Scientist*, 54, No. 802 (1972), 735–737.

40. Konrad Lorenz, op. cit., chap. 12.

41. The access of modern human beings to push-button remote-control weapons shields them from emotionally experiencing close up the consequences of their destructive, warlike acts. Ibid., p. 234.

42. Desmond Morris, *The Naked Ape* (New York: Dell, 1969).

43. Alec Nisbett, *Konrad Lorenz: A Biography* (New York: Harcourt Brace Jovanovich, 1976), pp. 171–172.

44. Erich Fromm, "The Erich Fromm Theory of Aggression," *The New York Times Magazine* (February 27, 1972), 74, and "Man Would as Soon Flee as Fight," *Psychology Today*, 7 (August 1973), 35–45. A similar criticism may be found in Ralph L. Halloway, Jr., "Human Aggression: The Need for a Species-Specific Framework," in Morton Fried et al., eds., op. cit., pp. 30–31. "The real problem facing men is not to better understand lower animals, but to implement drastic social changes throughout the world; . . . . This problem is a political one, not a biological or a psychological one. Ibid., p. 31.

45. See B. F. Skinner, *Beyond Freedom and Dignity* (New York: Knopf, 1971), in chap. 1, "A Technology of Behavior"; Meredith W. Watts, "B. F. Skinner and the Technological Control of Social Behavior," *American Political Science Review*, LXIX (March 1975), chapter 1, "A Technology of Behavior."

46. Alec Nisbett, op. cit., pp. 131–135, 162–164, and 181–183; M. F. Ashley Montagu, ed., op. cit., *Man and Aggression*, p. 9; Albert Bandura, op. cit., pp. 16–31. See also T. C. Schneirla, "Instinct and Aggression," in Montagu, ed., op. cit., p. 61.

47. These criticisms are documented in Stephen D. Nelson, "Nature/Nurture Revisited I: A Review of the Biological Bases of Conflict," *Journal of Conflict Resolution*, 18 (June 1974), especially pp. 296–302. Donald Owen has cast serious doubt on the validity of the aggressive XYY stereotype. "The 47, XYY Male: A Review," *Psychological Bulletin*, 78, cited in Stephen D. Nelson, op. cit., p. 32.

48. See the references to the research of Gerald E. McClearn, I. Michael Lerner, Mary A. Telfer, and others in Peter Corning, op. cit., p. 350, and to the findings of Drs. John R. Lion, George Bash-Y-Rita, and Frank R. Irvin, ibid.

49. George M. Carstairs, "Overcrowding and Human Aggression," in Hugh Davis Graham and Ted Robert Gurr, eds., *Violence in America*, Report to the National Commission on the Causes and Prevention of Violence, June 1969 (New York:

New American Library, 1969), pp. 730–742. Cf. also Jonathan Freedman, *Crowding and Behavior* (San Francisco: Freeman, 1975); Susan Seagart, *Crowding in Real Environments* (Beverly Hills, Calif.: 1976); and Larry Severy, ed., *Crowding: Theoretical and Research Implications* (New York: Humanities Science Press, 1979).

50. Thomas C. Wiegele, "Decision-Making in an International Crisis: Some Biological Factors," *International Studies Quarterly*, 17 (September 1973), 295–335.

51. See, for example, George Pettee, "Revolution—Typology and Process," in Carl J. Friedrich, ed., *Revolution* (New York: Atherton, 1966), p. 19. Pettee likens the prerevolutionary situation to one of frustration or cramp. Robert C. Williamson writes: "Internecine warfare has been the end result of social, political, and economic frustration as well as of personal anomie" in "Toward a Theory of Political Violence: The Case of Rural Colombia," *Western Political Quarterly*, XVIII (March 1965), 36.

52. Robert L. Heilbroner, describing the problems of economic development in the emerging nations, writes: "Above all, the necessity to hold down the level of consumption—to force savings—in order to free resources for the capital-building process will make for a rising level of frustration, even under the sternest discipline. This frustration will almost surely have to be channeled into directions other than that of economic expectations. . . . In a word, economic development has within it the potential, not alone of a revolutionary situation, but of heightened international friction." *The Great Ascent* (New York: Harper & Row, 1963), pp. 158–159. For a fuller discussion of the revolutionary potential of economic deprivation and development in the light of the frustration-aggression hypothesis, see Chapter 8 of this textbook, particularly the section on revolution.

53. John Dollard, Leonard W. Doob, Neal E. Miller, et al., *Frustration and Aggression* (New Haven: Yale University Press, 1939), p. 1. For another basic work in the field, see Norman R. F. Maier, *Frustration: The Study of Behavior Without a Goal* (New York: McGraw-Hill, 1949).

54. John Dollard et al., op. cit., p. 7.

55. Ross Stagner, "The Psychology of Human Conflict," in Elton B. McNeil, ed., *The Nature of Human Conflict*, p. 53.

56. Abraham H. Maslow, "Deprivation, Threat and Frustration," *Psychological Review*, XLVIII, No. 6 (1941); reprinted in J. K. Zawodny, *Man and International Relations* (San Francisco: Chandler, 1966), 2 vols., I: *Conflict*, pp. 17–19. Maslow writes: "It is only when a goal object represents love, prestige, respect, or achievement that being deprived of it will have the bad effects ordinarily attributed to frustration in general." Ibid., pp. 17–18.

57. Ross Stagner, op. cit., p. 28. Minor frustrations and the residual instigations from them can become cumulative and lead to a stronger aggressive response than would ordinarily be expected from the frustrating situation which immediately triggers the response. Ibid., p. 31.

58. Ibid., pp. 32–38.

59. Norman R. F. Maier, from his study of the role of punishment in the learning process, was led to postulate a relationship between frustration and fixation. See "Frustration Theory: Restatement and Extension," *Psychological Review*, LXIII, No. 6 (1956), 370–388, in J. K. Zawodny, ed., op. cit., pp. 20–29.

60. John Dollard et al., op. cit., pp. 39–47; Otto Klineberg, *Tensions Affecting International Understanding* (New York: Social Science Research Council, 1950), especially chap. 5, "Influences Making for Aggression," p. 196. Bernard Berelson and Gary A. Steiner also have noted that prolonged or intense frustration sometimes produces flight from the goal rather than a further struggle toward the goal. They suggest that when survival is not at stake, and occasionally even when it is, people

may give up and abandon the situation, physically or psychologically. *Human Behavior: An Inventory of Scientific Findings* (New York: Harcourt Brace Jovanovich, 1964), p. 270. This phenomenon would seem to correspond to what the biologists describe as the "fight or flight" reactions of animals in states of anxiety. See Harley C. Shands, "Some Social and Biological Aspects of Anxiety," *Journal of Nervous and Mental Disease,* CXXV, No. 3 (1957); reprinted in J. K. Zawodny, op. cit., especially pp. 9 and 15.

61. Ibid., p. 48

62. According to a later reformulation of the concept of catharsis, aggressive action was thought to have three possible separable effects: reducing, increasing, or producing no observable change in the level of aggressive response. S. Feshbach, "Aggression," in P. H. Mussen, ed., *Carmichael's Manual of Child Psychology* (New York: Wiley, 1970), pp. 159–259. Cited in Bandura, op. cit., p. 37.

63. Elton B., McNeil, "Psychology and Aggression," *Journal of Conflict Resolution,* III (September 1959), 204. McNeil here is following N. E. Miller, "The Frustration-Aggression Hypothesis," *Psychological Review,* XLVIII (July 1941), 338.

64. Leonard Berkowitz, op. cit., p. 29.

65. Ibid., p. 30. Elton B. McNeil observes that "the contention that aggressive behavior always presupposes the existence of frustration has met with little resistance or criticism." Op. cit., p. 204.

66. Albert Bandura, op. cit., p. 167.

67. For an elaboration of these first two points, see Leonard Berkowitz, op. cit., pp. 32–48.

68. Sanford Rosenzweig, "An Outline of Frustration Theory," J. McV. Hunt, ed., *Personality and the Behavior Disorders* (New York: Ronald, 1944), pp. 381–382. Elton B. McNeil, following Rosenzweig, says: "The privation of being born into poverty poses a series of frustrations for the individual; but his reaction to them differs considerably from his responses to being deprived of wealth, once he has possessed it." "Psychology and Aggression," op. cit., p. 203.

69. Elton B. McNeil, ibid., p. 204.

70. John Dollard et al., op. cit., p. 2.

71. The Yale group notes that "when Marxists have described the dynamic human interrelationships involved in the class struggle and in the preservation and destruction of the state, they have introduced unwittingly a psychological system involving the assumption that aggression is a response to frustration." Ibid., p. 23. The frustrating agents, of course, are the bourgeoisie, and the aggressive response by the frustrated proletariat is the organization of a class which finally carries out a revolution. But most sociologists, including Marxist ones, would not use the term *frustration* except metaphorically and in a social context, not in the same sense in which psychologists use it.

72. Sociologists distinguish between the behavior of small groups and that of large groups. Herbert Blumer has called attention also to the differences between "collective behavior" (even by fairly large groups) in "undefined or unstructured situations" and organized social behavior which follows culturally prescribed norms. "Collective Behavior," in J. B. Gitter, ed., *Review of Sociology: Analysis of a Decade* (New York: Wiley, 1957), p. 130. In the elementary forms of collective behavior, the individuals in the group stimulate each other and contribute toward the circular development of a sense of unrest and excitement. Frustration might play a role here, although sociologists generally do not refer to it; even if they did, they would probably subordinate it to the stimulation-reinforcement which occurs. Blumer shows that elementary collective behavior can gradually develop into a more complex social movement as it "acquires organization and form, a body of customs and traditions, established leadership, an enduring division of labor, social

rules, and social values—in short, a culture, a social organization, and a new scheme of life." Ibid., p. 199. Neil J. Smelser, while modifying some of Blumer's ideas, agrees with the distinction described above: "Collective behavior . . . is not institutionalized behavior. According to the degree to which it becomes institutionalized, it loses its distinctive character." *Theory of Collective Behavior* (New York: The Free Press 1963), p. 8. It is interesting to note that Smelser, in his chapter on "The Hostile Outburst," makes no mention of the frustration-aggression hypothesis in his efforts to explain aggression in society. Ibid., pp. 222–269. He does, however, make a brief footnote reference of it elsewhere; see p. 107.

73. John Dollard et al., op. cit., pp. 55–76. E. F. M. Durbin and John Bowlby contended that the conflict within the child arising out of the fear of punishment is an important source of aggressiveness in the adult, because aggression can be controlled but not destroyed. "The boy, instead of striking his father whom he fears, strikes a smaller boy whom he does not fear. . . . And in the same way revolutionaries who hate ordered government, nationalists who hate foreign policies, individuals who hate bankers, Jews, or their political opponents, may be exhibiting characteristics that have been formed by the suppression of simple aggression in their childhood education." (New York: Columbia University Press, 1939), excerpted in J. K. Zawodny, op. cit., p. 97. For another study of the effect of child-rearing practices upon the cultural and personality patterns of adult populations, see John W. M. Whiting and Irwin L. Child, *Child Training and Personality* (New Haven: Yale University Press, 1953).

74. "Which mode or modes of control are selected depends to a great extent on the culture in which the individual participates. Among the Sioux, for example, an infant's tantrums were a matter of pride to his parents, and he was hurt and frustrated as a child to encourage his rage. Rages were later controlled by venting them against extratribal enemies in forays which promised social rewards. Among the Alorese, on the other hand, aggression is suppressed at an early age and later finds expression in intratribal stealing." Martin Gold, "Suicide, Homicide and the Socialization of Aggression," in Bartlett H. Stoodley, ed., *Society and Self: A Reader in Social Psychology* (New York: The Free Press, 1962), pp. 281–282.

75. Robert R. Sears, Eleanor Maccoby, and Harry Levin, "The Socialization of Aggression," in Eleanor E. Maccoby, Theodore M. Newcomb, and Eugene L. Hartley, eds., *Readings in Social Psychology* (New York: Holt, Rinehart and Winston, 1958), pp. 350–352. Robert A. LeVine writes: "The linkage between socialization of the child and customary social behavior is most conspicuous in the case of the aggressive motive." "Socialization, Social Structure, and Inter-Societal Images," in Herbert C. Kelman, ed., op. cit., p. 46.

76. Elton B. McNeil, "Psychology and Aggression," op. cit., p. 212. Albert Bandura notes that the fear of punishment produces an inhibiting or deterrent effect and causes the displacement of aggression from similar to dissimilar targets. *Aggression*, op. cit., pp. 34–35.

77. Ibid., p. 213; Ross Stagner, op. cit., pp. 55–56.

78. Ibid., p. 54; and Ralph K. White, "Images in the Context of International Conflict," in Herbert C. Kelman, ed., op. cit., especially pp. 267–268.

79. Frieda L. Bornston and J. C. Coleman, "The Relationship Between Certain Parents' Attitudes Toward Child Rearing and the Direction of Aggression of Their Young Adult Offspring," *Journal of Clinical Psychology*, XII (1956), 41–44.

80. Cf. Note 121.

81. Albert Bandura, *Aggression*, op. cit., p. 170.

82. Leonard Berkowitz, op. cit., pp. 139, 149, and 193–264; cf. also his "The Concept of Aggressive Drive," in Leonard Berkowitz, ed., *Advances in Experimental Social Psychology* (New York: Academic Press, 1965), vol. II, p. 312.

83. Albert Bandura, op cit., pp. 29–30.
84. Ibid., pp. 32–36.
85. Ibid., p. 44. According to Jerome D. Frank, children can learn aggression as a result of punishment (either the infliction of pain or the withdrawal of affection), the imitation of aggressive behavior by parents or others, and exposure to violence in the mass media. *Sanity and Survival*, pp. 68–74. For a bibliography of the extensive experimental research by Bandura and his colleagues on the imitation of aggressive models, see Bandura, op. cit., pp. 327–329.
86. Donald A. Wells, *The War Myth*, pp. 174–175. Within two pages that follow, Wells first suggests that "war is not so natural or so psychologically grounded in human nature as we have been led to believe," but then arrives at what appears to be an opposite conclusion: "The emptiness of the reasons men verbalize for war suggests that war really does not rest on any rationale. . . . After all, if people didn't like to fight, there are no good reasons why they should do so much of it." Ibid., pp. 176–177.
87. Albert Bandura, op. cit., p. 99.
88. Raymond Aron has noted that, as modern warfare technology has grown more frightful, industrially advanced societies have sought to inspire their citizens to sustain the hardships and sacrifices of war by articulating ever more grandiose statements of war aims. *A Century of Total War* (Boston: Beacon, 1955), p. 26.
89. Hadley Cantril, *The Human Dimension: Experiences in Policy Resarch* (New Brunswick, N.J.: Rutgers University Press, 1967), p. 16.
90. Ibid., p. 156.
91. Ibid., pp. 127–128. See also Hadley Cantril, ed., *Tensions That Cause Wars* (Urbana: University of Illinois Press, 1950, p. 7; Hadley Cantril and William Buchanan, *How Nations See Each Other* (Urbana: University of Illinois Press, 1953).
92. William T. R. Fox, "Harold D. Lasswell and the Study of World Politics," in Arnold A. Rogow, ed., *Politics, Personality, and Social Science in the Twentieth Century* (Chicago: University of Chicago Press, 1969), pp. 376–377.
93. Harold D. Lasswell's writings on the politics of biotechnology, astropolitics, and thinking machine-actors are found in "The Political Science of Science," *American Political Science Review*, I (December 1956), 961–979; *The Future of Political Science* (New York: Atherton, 1962), "Men in Space," *Annals of the New York Academy of Sciences* No. 72 (1958), pp. 180–194.
94. Harold D. Lasswell, *World Politics and Personality Insecurity* (New York: McGraw-Hill, 1935), pp. 207 and 3.
95. Ibid., p. 3.
96. Ibid., p. 25.
97. Ibid., p. 237. For the results of a study of foreign ministers as a small but strategically important segment of the world elite, made up of persons who exhibit a set of background similarities, who share some common values regarding world order and professional diplomatic conduct, and who interact with each other enough to develop some friendships as a basis for elite cohesion, see George Modelski, "The World's Foreign Ministers: A Political Elite," *Journal of Conflict Resolution*, XIV (June 1970), 135–175.
98. Elton B. McNeil, "The Nature of Aggression," Elton B. McNeil, ed., op. cit., p. 35.
99. Konrad Lorenz, op. cit., pp. 271–272.
100. D. O. Hebb and W. R. Thompson, op. cit., p. 53.
101. Jerome D. Frank, op. cit., pp. 75, 87–88.
102. Konrad Lorenz, p. 272; Frank, pp. 88, 241.
103. See Parton Keese, "Violence in Sports: What It Could Mean," *The New York Times* (January 26, 1975); Lowell Miller, "World Cup—Or World War?", *The New York Times Magazine* (May 21, 1978).

104. For an interesting discussion of the implications of international athletic contests for diplomatic recognition, political protest, propaganda, and state prestige, as well as interstate cooperation and conflict, see Andrew Strenk, "The Thrill of Victory and the Agony of Defeat: Sport and International Politics," *Orbis*, 22 (Summer 1978), 453–469.

105. Elbert Russell, "Human Aggression," Paper presented at Canadian Peace Research Institute Summer School, Grindstone Island, Ontario, July 18, 1973; James W. Prescott, "Body Pleasure and the Origins of Violence," *The Bulletin of the Atomic Scientists*, XXXI (November 1975), 10–20.

106. Ibid.; Jerome D. Frank, op. cit., pp. 68–69, 283. Bandura, however, while agreeing that punishment may have unfavorable consequences if it is excessive, ill-timed, erratic, or administered in a spirit of vengeance without providing constructive direction, nevertheless argues that punishment can, under certain conditions, effectively modify undesirable behavior. Op. cit., pp. 298, 304–308.

107. See Leonard Berkowitz, "The Case for Bottling Up Rage," *Psychology Today* (July 1973), 24–31.

108. Jerome D. Frank, op. cit., pp. 72–74, 283–284; Bandura, op. cit., pp. 266–286. Bandura dismisses the disclaimers that, since behavior is determined by multiple factors, it is unfair to place blame on the mass media and that aggressive modeling affects only people who are already disturbed or predisposed to aggression. He argues that in the face of abundant experimental evidence for observational learning, continued equivocation on the aggressive modeling impact of television upon both children and adults cannot be justified. Ibid., pp. 266–271.

109. See, for example, Jerome D. Frank, op. cit., pp. 238–245; Ithiel DeSola Pool, "Effects of Cross-National Contact on National and International Images," in Herbert C. Kelman, ed., op. cit., pp. 106–129: J. Watson and R. Lippitt, "Cross-Cultural Experience as a Source of Attitude Change," *Journal of Conflict Resolution*, 2 (March 1958).

110. Kenneth N. Waltz, *Man, the State and War: A Theoretical Analysis* (New York: Columbia University Press, 1959), p. 48.

111. Herbert C. Kelman in Kelman, ed., op. cit., p. 24.

112. Kenneth E. Boulding, "National Images and International Systems," *Journal of Conflict Resolution*, III (June 1959), 120–131. This and the previous quotations are on pp. 121–122. See also his book, *The Image: Knowledge in Life and Society* (Ann Arbor: University of Michigan Press, 1956); Ole R. Holsti, "The Belief System and National Images," *Journal of Conflict Resolution*, 16 (September 1962) and "Cognitive Dynamics and Images of the Enemy," *Journal of International Affairs*, 21 (1967); and Robert Jervis, *The Logic of Images in International Relations* (Princeton: Princeton University Press, 1970).

113. Arthur Gladstone, "The Conception of the Enemy," *Journal of Conflict Resolution*, III (June 1959), 132.

114. Ross Stagner, op. cit., p. 46.

115. "The Mirror Image in Soviet-American Relations: A Social Psychologist's Report," *Journal of Social Issues*, XVII, No. 3, 46–48. See also William Eckhardt and Ralph K. White, "A Test of the Mirror Image Hypothesis: Kennedy and Khrushchev, *Journal of Conflict Resolution*, XI (September 1967), 325–332; Charles E. Osgood, "Analysis of the Cold War Mentality," *Journal of Social Issues*, XVII, No. 3 (1961), 12–19.

116. Ralph K. White, op. cit., p. 240.

117. "Allowing for Soviet Perceptions," in Roger Fisher, ed., *International Conflict and Behavoral Science*, The Craigville Papers (New York: Basic Books, 1964), p. 172.

118. See, for example, the discussion of "Graduated and Reciprocated Initiative in Tension-Reduction," (GRIT) in Charles E. Osgood, *An Alternative to War or Sur-*

render (Urbana, I.: University of Illinois Press,, 1962), and his "Questioning Some Unquestioned Assumptions about National Defense," *Journal of Arms Control*, 1 (January 1963), 2–13. Cf. also Arthur I. Waskow, *The Limits of Defense* (Garden City, L.I.: Doubleday, 1962), chap. IV.

119. Gordon W. Allport. *The Nature of Prejudice* (Reading, Mass.: Addison-Wesley, 1954); and Otto Klineberg, *The Human Dimension in International Relations* (New York: Holt, Rinehart and Winston, 1964).

120. Else Frenkel-Brunswik, "Intolerance of Ambiguity as an Emotional and Perceptual Personality Variable," *Journal of Personality*, XVIII (September 1949), 108–143; and "Social Tensions and the Inhibition of Thought," *Social Problems*, II (October 1954), 75–81.

121. T. W. Adorno, Else Frenkel-Brunswik, Daniel J. Levinson and R. N. Sanford, *The Authoritarian Personality* (New York: Harper & Row., 1950).

122. Michael P. Sullivan, *International Relations: Theories and Evidence* (Englewood Cliffs, N.J.: Prentice-Hall, 1976), pp. 26–40. See also Alexander L. George, "Assessing Presidential Character," *World Politics*, XXVI (January 1974).

123. Erich Fromm, *Escape from Freedom* (New York: Holt, Rinehart and Winston, 1941), pp. 21–22, 141–142, and 164–168.

124. Leon Festinger, *A Theory of Cognitive Dissonance* (Stanford: Stanford University Press, 1957); and *Conflict, Decision and Dissonance* (Stanford: Stanford University Press, 1964).

125. Judson S. Brown, "Principles of Intrapersonal Conflict," *Journal of Conflict Resolution*, I (June 1957), 137–138. For a different perspective of how psychological factors in the personal background of a political leader may affect his decision to "go revolutionary," see E. Victor Wolfenstein, *Violence or Non-Violence: A Psychoanalytic Exploration of the Choice of Means in Social Change* (Monograph Series, Center for International Studies, Princeton University, 1965).

126. Jerome D. Frank, op. cit., pp. 26–33.

127. See John E. Endicott, *Japan's Nuclear Option* (New York: Praeger, 1975), chap. 2, "The Domestic Political Environment."

128. See Irving L. Janis and M. Brewster Smith, "Effects of Education and Persuasion on National and International Images," in Herbert C. Kelman, ed., *International Behavior: A Social-Psychological Analysis* (New York: Holt, Rinehart and Winston, 1966), p. 227; and Harold Karen Jacobson and Eric Stein, *Diplomats, Scientists and Politicians* (Ann Arbor: University of Michigan Press, 1966), pp. 127, 346–347, 382, and 387.

129. See H. H. Gerth and C. Wright Mills, trans. and eds., *From Max Weber: Essays in Sociology* (New York: Oxford University Press, 1946), pp. 196–203.

130. Peter Corning, op. cit., pp. 345–349.

Chapter 8
Macrocosmic Theories of Violent Conflict: Revolution and War

It is now necessary to leave microanalysis of individual behavior and turn to those who theorize about war at the macrolevel—the level of societies and nation-states. This chapter will be devoted to the insights into large-scale social structural violence which can be obtained from the work of anthropologists, sociologists, political scientists, and international relations specialists. Whereas the microanalysts—especially biologists and psychologists—look within the individual member of the species for unconscious, aggressive drives and tend to be somewhat skeptical of consciously articulated motives for social and international conflict, macroanalysts in general are more inclined to take seriously statements of conscious, verbalizable motives and reasons why people resort to violence within and between societies. They regard these as particularly important for explaining why specific conflicts break out between specific parties at specific times. They ascribe a certain validity to the dictum of Thucydides: If you want to know why men are fighting a war, ask them and they will tell you.

Macrotheorists do not disparage the stated reasons as mere rationalizations of deep, dark, unconscious forces driving toward aggression.

They recognize that such forces undoubtedly exist—not only within individuals but within sociopolitical structures as well, and they regard the latter as more determining. But as *social* scientists they recognize that the distinctiveness of the human species is that it is rational and symbolic, that it is given to the formation of sentiment or value structures, and that values, beliefs, words, ideas, and ideologies come to form a central part of human social and political life. Although they recognize that emotional and instinctive forces play a vital part in all societies, they are also convinced that at the level of social and political activity it is the conscious, symbolic, rational part of the human that organizes and gives direction to irrational biological and psychological needs and impulses.

Social scientists—especially most sociologists and anthropologists—who adopt a macro approach to human phenomena tend to regard conflict as a normal concomitant of group existence, not as the disruptive or dysfunctional or even pathological condition which most psychologists see it to be. Those sociologists who follow Talcott Parsons in emphasizing social adjustment, "common-value orientation," and system maintenance are an exception. More interested in social order than social change, in social statics than dynamics, the Parsonians consider conflict as a disease with disruptive and dysfunctional consequences. However, most European sociologists from Karl Marx to Georg Simmel and Ralf Dahrendorf and most American sociologists in the pre-Parsonian era (e.g., Robert E. Park, John W. Burgess, William Graham Sumner, Charles H. Cooley, E. A. Ross, and Albion W. Small) and some in recent decades (e.g., Jessie Bernard and Lewis A. Coser) have viewed conflict as serving positive social purposes.[1] In other words, they are disposed to regard conflict, perhaps even in its violent forms, as a useful means of resolving disputes within society and between societies. Many social scientists, of course, hold no brief for or against conflict in general. Political scientists, economists, and game theorists, along with most rational political leaders and diplomats, usually prefer to evaluate specific conflicts on the basis of probable or actual outcomes, that is, by weighing the gains of conflict in terms of values at stake versus the risks and cost of the conflict.

For "conflict-as-functional" theorists, conflict not only integrates, but it helps to establish group identity, clarifies group boundaries, and contributes to group cohesion. Nearly every sociologist and social anthropologist postulates some degree of "in-group" hostility for the "out-group." When there are many out-groups, the political scientist can cast light upon why a particular one may be singled out at a particular time as the target of hostility. Historians of nationalism often describe the importance of the external bête noire in the formative period of a nation's consciousness. But beyond this well-known phenomenon, some social theorists contend that even within groups discord and opposition help to hold the groups together by providing inner relief and making the un-bearable bearable.[2] Thus many thinkers in modern times accept conflict as something which is "structured into existence by the very fact of group identifications,"[3] and even "the central explanatory category for the analysis of social change or 'progress.' "[4]

INSIDE VERSUS OUTSIDE DIMENSIONS OF CONFLICT

Many social theorists in different historical periods have taken it for granted that a significant relationship exists between conflict *within* so-cieties and conflict *between* societies. This gives rise to one of the most durable hypotheses in social conflict theory. The relationship can be for-mulated in two ways: (1) internal conflict varies inversely with external conflict; and (2) domestic social cohesion correlates positively with in-volvement in foreign wars. Political rulers in all ages, faced with growing troubles and turmoil at home, have been tempted to provoke foreign mil-itary adventures as a diversionary tactic. Machiavelli recognized this as a fact and recommended it as a strategem.

William Graham Sumner advanced the theory that groups seek in-ternal unity for strength in competition with external enemies; that the sentiments of peace and cooperation inside the group are complemen-tary to sentiments of hostility toward outside groups; that societies which experienced frequent and fierce wars developed stronger governments and legal systems and the whole societal system became more firmly in-tegrated.[5] William James, too, saw war as "the gory nurse that trained societies to cohesiveness" in ancient times.[6]

More recently, it has been suggested that uncertainty over tenure of power among ruling elites may make war more probable by bringing ag-gressive military and political personalities to the fore.[7] Clyde Kluck-hohn writes: "If a nation's intragroup aggressions become so serious that there is danger of disruption, war, by displacing aggression against an-other group, is an adjustive response from the point of view of preserving national cohesion."[8] Robert F. Murphy, who studied the Mundurucú tribe of Brazil, notes that warfare once served that group as a "safety valve institution." Intrasocietal aggressiveness, especially among the males, was siphoned off by directing considerable hostility toward the outside world, all of which was regarded as inimical, and thus served the integration of the society. The contemporary Mundurucú, who do not make war, have undergone community fission.[9] Studies of the Teton In-dians lend support to the hypothesis in an obverse form. Prior to 1850, Teton tribesmen frequently murdered each other in quarrels over the distribution of tribal property. For three decades after the threat of the white man appeared, internal homicide decreased as aggression was directed against the external foe. The homicide rate rose again after the

Tetons made peace with the white man.[10] Simmel noted the reciprocity between social-political centralization and the aggressive impulse to war. War promotes inner cohesiveness, yet internal political centralization increases the probability that external release of tensions will be sought through war. According to Simmel, "war with the outside is sometimes the last chance for a state ridden with inner antagonisms to overcome these antagonisms, or else to break up indefinitely."[11]

Geoffrey Blainey, on the contrary, rejects what he calls the "scapegoat theory" of war despite its undoubted "universal glow" in the eyes of political scientists, historians and anthropologists. Although admitting that more than half of all international wars from 1823 to 1937 studied by him were immediately preceded by serious disturbances in one of the fighting nations, he concluded that scapegoat theorists rely on dubious assumptions, for example, that war can be blamed on one side, that strife-torn nations are more likely to initiate war, and that every mild disturbance poses a threat of disintegration in the absence of war. If scapegoat theorists read the evidence of political history more carefully, he observed, they would cease to overlook two important facts: (1) The troubled nation can more easily suppress internal discontent if it does not become involved in international war; and (2) an external foe, seeing turmoil within a country as a sign of weakness, is more likely to try to exploit the situation by initiating war.[12]

The empirical evidence for the reciprocal relationship between internal and external conflict is not as conclusive as some advocates of the theory suggest. Since the mid-1960s, efforts to prove or disprove the correlation through the application of quantitative analysis methods have led to ambiguous and controversial results. Rudolph J. Rummel, for example, after running correlations, factor analysis, and multiple regression on internal conflict data and external conflict data for 77 nations over a period of three years (1955–1957), concluded (as we noted in Chapter 1 in our more extensive treatment of his writings) that foreign conflict behavior is generally unrelated to domestic conflict behavior.[13] In a subsequent replication of the Rummel study, Raymond Tanter similarly found little positive relationship between foreign and domestic conflict behavior.[14] Later still, in a study of the United States domestic scene during the Vietnam War, Tanter suggested a positive correlation between a foreign war which continues without apparent success and the incidence of domestic turmoil.[15]

Both Rummel and Tanter in their studies took "domestic conflict behavior" to include such phenomena as assassinations, strikes, guerrilla warfare, government crises, purges, riots, revolutions, antigovernment demonstrations, and lethal domestic violence. Under the heading of "foreign conflict behavior" they examine antiforeign demonstrations, diplomatic protests, severance of diplomatic relations, the expulsion or recall of diplomats, threats, military hostilities short of warfare, wars, troop movements, mobilizations, and total war casualties.

Jonathan Wilkenfeld subsequently noted that the findings of Rummel and Tanter contravened the "widely held notion that a nation experiencing internal disorders will tend to engage in external conflict behavior in order to divert the attention of the population from internal problems."[16] Wilkenfeld, using political variables analyzed by Gregg and Banks,[17] rearranged the nations of the world into three political-type groups (personalist, centrist, and polyarchic). He concluded that there is a relationship between domestic and foreign conflict behavior if one takes into account the type of political regime, and for these to co-occur or for the occurrence of one to be followed in time by the occurrence of the other.[18] Thus Wilkenfeld did not show the general findings of Rummel and Tanter to be wrong, but he did show that the lack of relationship between domestic and foreign conflict should be qualified by type of political system.

We do not interpret the traditional theory to mean either that external conflict *always* militates in favor of greater social cohesion or that in the prolonged absence of external conflict internal disintegration *will necessarily* occur. Yet the mind of the social theorist is recurringly intrigued by the appearance of evidence which generally seems to validate the connection. It has become the common stock of international relations writers during the past two decades to take note of a correlation between periodic thaws in the United States-Soviet relations and a loosening of their respective alliances. From 1948 to the late 1950s, the alliances were tightly knit and contacts across alliance boundaries were held to a minimum. During the 1960s, the cohesiveness of alliances underwent partial dilution.[19] In the East, the Sino-Soviet split put an end to the "monolithic unity" formerly ascribed to the Communist world. In the West, France withdrew from the NATO integrated military command. In the early 1970s, there was a great deal of discussion about the transition from a bipolar to a multipolar world. (See Chapter 4.) The intensification of détente diplomacy in Europe led to a series of negotiated agreements ratifying the postwar territorial status quo in that region. But the détente symbolized by the "spirit of Helsinki" and by the Final Act issuing from the Conference on Security and Cooperation in Europe was accompanied by increased problems of maintaining internal social control, especially on the Communist side of the dividing line as a result of a rise in dissident behavior within Eastern Europe and the Soviet Union.

Well-integrated communities, of course, are held together by more than fear, hostility, and external conflict. Shared beliefs and values, as well as the expectation of mutual benefits from living together as a community, can be important integrating factors as we shall see in Chapter 10. What the theory asserts is that external conflict can be *one* important

integrating factor, but not the only one. It might be particularly significant when other factors are beginning to weaken. But if the process of
internal consensus-disintegration has progressed too far, involvement in a
foreign conflict, instead of reversing that process, might actually hasten
it.

It seems probable that any effort to correlate statistically internal
and external conflict behavior will be inconclusive if it ignores such crucial questions as the degree of consensus that exists over the values of the
political system and the societal beliefs about what is at stake in the conflict. Ruling elites cannot always be certain what effect their decision to
undertake a foreign war will produce. The Russian Tsarist government
experienced domestic political discontent and demands for change in the
system during the Crimean and Japanese Wars, and a fatal revolutionary
upheaval during World War I, while in World War II a more modern
and totally organized Communist government was able to mobilize a
relatively high degree of national patriotic unity for the war effort on
behalf of "Mother Russia." The defeat of the Egyptian Army by Israel in
1948 helped to pave the way for the overthrow of King Farouk's government four years later; but the even more disastrous defeat of Egypt's
forces in 1967 did not jeopardize the leadership position of the highly
popular Nasser.

In World War II, the American people were almost unanimous in
supporting the war against Nazi and Japanese tyranny, and the press
gave little, if any, coverage to those who criticized or resisted. In sharp
contrast, the Vietnam War found the American people divided over the
nature of the conflict (e.g., whether it was an "international" or a "civil"
war), the purpose of the United States involvement (whether it was to
carry out a treaty commitment, to contain Soviet and/or Chinese Communism, to preserve Vietnamese national independence, to promote
democratic government, to establish a balance of power in Asia, or any,
all, or none of these objectives), and the degree to which developments in
Southeast Asia could seriously jeopardize the United States national interest. For policy reasons related to arms control and détente, and also
because of the difficulties the military forces of an industrially advanced
democracy encounter in combating insurgency, the U.S. Government,
instead of prosecuting the war in the all-out style of World War II, either
imposed or accepted limits upon the conduct of its own military operations. The role played by the intellectuals, students, organized opposition
groups, the media, and many politicians opened a gap between the government and substantial segments of the public, who were increasingly
confused and frustrated by a war effort that was costly and yet seemed
purposeless and futile. The relation between internal and external conflicts can be evaluated only within a total political context which varies
greatly from case to case. Although empirical studies in this area so far

leave much to be desired, it would seem that the theory of an inverse linkage between intrasocietal and extrasocietal conflict will continue to warrant careful analytical refinement and research by students of international relations.

LESSONS FROM THE PRIMITIVES

A study of primitive societies is not of direct relevance for understanding contemporary international relations. Modern technological advanced civilizations are not lineal descendants of primitive cultures. Ever since the age of discovery and exploration four centuries ago, Western philosophers and social theorists have been fascinated by primitive ways of social organization and life, and have sought to gain from them insights into the problems of civilization, including war. In earlier times, when there were abundant cases of pristine primitive societies, unaffected by contact with the West, there were practically no trained scientific observers, and many superficial or erroneous conclusions were drawn. (Hobbes, Locke, and Rousseau, e.g., all apparently thought that the Indians of North America lived in a "state of nature," without government.) In the nineteenth century, as the science of cultural anthropology developed, the "purity" or authenticity of most primitive cultures had been diluted by the importation of Western religious and social beliefs, ideas, and practices. Considerable care must be exercised, therefore, in the interpretation of primitive institutions and customs. Because primitive societies are relatively uncomplicated and are easy-to-see examples of self-contained social groups, often in interaction with other comparable groups, it is useful to study them for whatever general, rather than specific, lessons can be drawn concerning social structure and behavior.

Anthropologists have not achieved any greater consensus among themselves than have scholars in any of the other social sciences. But after studying many specific societies, they are impressed by the variety in what they see. They avoid striving for a single generalization, for example, that primitives are basically warlike or that they are basically peaceful. Some primitives are extremely belligerent and always spoiling for a fight. Others are almost exclusively peaceful. Clyde Kluckhohn writes:

> Organized offensive warfare was unknown in aboriginal Australia. Certain areas of the New World seem to have been completely free from war in the pre-European period. . . . What is absolutely certain at present is that different types of social order carry with them varying degrees of propensity for war. The continuum ranges from groups like the Pueblo Indians who for many centuries have almost never engaged in offensive warfare to groups like some Plains Indians who made fighting their highest virtue.[20]

Where the word for war as a form of socially organized aggression or fighting is not even a part of some primitive languages—for example, of the Eskimoes and the Andaman Islanders—we must hesitate to attribute this to the "inherently peaceful character" of the people, especially since they are in no proximate contact with well-defined societies. For technologically undeveloped societies, war, like violent crime, is usually a function of physical proximity. Prior to the era of the airplane and the missile, only maritime countries possessed the capabilities to mount offensive warfare at a distance.[21] In fact, even in recent decades most international wars have been waged between those communities that usually have the strongest reasons for fighting, that is, territorially adjacent states.

It would seem that the experience of most primitive societies is similar to that of many modern civilized states: They know alternating periods of war and peace, except that primitive wars (or raids) are more frequent and of shorter duration. Nearly all primitive societies seek to minimize *internal* violence by developing systems of law calculated to prevent the application of the *lex talionis*, which permits vindictive retaliation by individual victims of crime, from escalating out of control.[22] But most of them are willing from time to time to resort to external violent behavior for purposes which they consider important. Andrew P. Vayda has pointed out that war among primitives serves as a regulating variable for the achievement of several different functions: (1) to remove inequalities in the possession of, or access to, certain economic goods and resources (land, camels, horses, water, hunting grounds, etc.) through redistribution; (2) to regulate such demographic variables as population size, sex ratios, and age distribution (as a result of war casualties, obtaining new sources of food, and taking women and others captive); (3) to regulate relations with other groups (i.e., to deter certain types of undesirable behavior in the future by avenging and punishing offenses or wrongs committed; and (4) to regulate psychological variables (anxiety, tension, and hostility) which are adverse to in-group cohesion by directing them outward.[23] Some anthropologists stress singular explanatory variables such as the desire to revenge insults[24] or the determination to protect the tribal reputation against charges of weakness and cowardice that may invite attack.[25]

However, Vayda's analytic scheme is more useful because it is more comprehensive. His own hypothesis synthesizes psychological, demographic, economic, and social variables, in which the regulation of each one depends upon the regulation of another. Vayda wisely refrains from insisting that all of his hypotheses about primitive war could be applied to warfare between civilized states. Moreover, he admits that more extensive data are needed to validate the hypotheses, and that some of the data needed are difficult to obtain.[26]

Finally, it is worth noting that primitive societies do not become involved in conflict over differing patterns of socioeconomic organization (e.g., private or communal property systems), probably because such societies do not develop elaborate "sentiment structures" or ideologies over such things. In some cases, the ferocity of conflict between neighboring primitives is attenuated by common religious beliefs, by endogamy (the practice of seeking wives from other tribes, thereby establishing blood ties), by imposing certain limits on warfare, by the conclusion of peace treaties and the exchange of hostages, and occasionally even by substituting "cold war" (the shouting of epithets and insults) for physical combat. But Vayda concedes that such intercommunity ties as intermarriage, commerce, and beliefs in common descent do not constitute a guarantee against the outbreak of hostilities.[27]

OTHER INSIGHTS FROM THEORISTS OF SOCIETY

Anthropologists and sociologists have formulated a great many hypotheses and partial theories relating to social conflict. It is not possible to examine all of them. Most of them have been suggested only in passing, without ever being subjected to any thorough, systematic development and rigorous testing. All that can be done here is to present in summary form a sample of better known hypotheses and theories, some of which are the stock-in-trade of so many writers that they cannot properly be attributed to any one.

1. Organized and collective fighting is distinct from individual, sporadic, and spontaneous acts of violence. The latter are antecedents of homicide and civil disorder, but not of war.[28]

2. It is worth reiterating that for anthropologists and sociologists, large-scale conflict and war arise more out of social structures and conditions than they do out of biological urges or psychological states. Warfare, said Margaret Mead, is a cultural invention, not a biological necessity.[29] William Graham Sumner argued that war originates from a struggle between groups, not individuals.[30] Bronislaw Malinowski held that war is not primeval or biologically determined and makes its appearance late in human evolution. "Human beings never fight on an extensive scale under the direct influence of an aggressive impulse," Malinowski declared,[31] thereby severing the connection between psychological pugnacity and culturally determined fighting. Most cases of violent action are seen as the result of purely conventional, traditional, and ideological imperatives. "All types of fighting are complex cultural responses due not to any direct dictates of an impulse, but to collective forms of sentiment and value."[32]

3. Discussion of international conflict in the abstract lacks cogency. Social scientists cannot analyze the behavior of nations without refer-

ence to the intervening variable of culture, warn Margaret Mead and Rhoda Metraux, who cite as an example the impossibility of understanding conflict in Lebanon while ignoring the role of religious communities.[33] If Soviet behavior is to be at all intelligible and predictable, they say, one must understand the Russian preoccupation with the full use of strength, insistence on testing the limits, and willingness to be guided by them. "For example, in a situation in which Englishmen, Americans, and Russians are involved as participants, it is useful to know that the English regard compromise as a positive outcome, that Americans regard compromise negatively, and that Russians define behavior which, in English and American eyes, would be regarded as compromise, as a necessary and quite admirable strategic retreat after having put forth all available strength."[34]

4. The basic attitudes and values of societies are deeply embedded in an intricate system of cultural institutions and processes. Hence they cannot be easily or quickly changed. Clyde Kluckhohn has offered this advice to reformers:

> Make haste slowly is usually a good motto for those who wish to institute or direct social change. Because of the enormous tenacity of nonlogical habits, the hasty attempt to alter intensifies resistance or even produces reaction.[35]

5. The larger and older the cultural entity, the more difficult it is to change. Anthropologists generally counsel us to have a healthy respect for enduring cultural differences, to avoid trying to project our own cultural perspectives and biases to other peoples, and not to expect any sudden, fundamental transformation in the behavior pattern of nations.

6. Whereas many social psychologists and political scientists in recent decades, in their desire to minimize the misleading and potentially dangerous consequences of "stereotyped" thinking in an era of mass communications, have become skeptical concerning the concept of "national character," anthropologists are more inclined to attribute a certain validity to it, provided that it is handled with appropriate care.[36]

7. Anthropologists and sociologists are for the most part suspicious of "psychopolitics" or "psychohistory"—the efforts to explain the decisions made while in power by such leaders as Wilson, Hitler, Stalin, de Gaulle, or Mao in terms of childhood experiences or psychological peculiarities. They do not, of course, deny that key individuals might play an important political role in the making of crucial conflict decisions, but they are disposed to explain those decisions in terms of social rather than psychological factors.

8. Ethnocentrism, the overevaluation of one's own group in comparison with other groups, is virtually a universal phenomenon.[37] American intellectuals, educators, and journalists are probably quicker than

those of other nations to look upon the patriotism of the common person as a dangerous display of chauvinism.

9. The relative persistence of culture patterns does not mean that nations are incapable of undergoing significant behavioral changes over time. The popular mood of the American people was quite different in the later stages of the Vietnam War from what it had been during the Spanish-American War. Many writers have called attention to the striking alteration in the political outlook and behavior of Germany and Japan, and the substitution of democratic constitutional systems for dictatorial-militarist regimes, following defeat in World War II. These extreme cases might prompt us to formulate a "trauma" theory of rapid, fundamental social change. More gradual and more complex was the change in the world view, and the conception of her role, that Britain underwent as a result of the profound political-economic-technological-strategic shifts set in motion by the two World Wars. Of still a different genre, and perhaps harder to explain, was the transition of Sweden from one of Europe's most warlike states in the early eighteenth century to one of the world's leading exponents of neutralism, pacifism, and disarmament in the twentieth. Perhaps in the final analysis it was the size of population relative to the other European powers, combined with a particular geographical position, rather than a cultural transformation, which tempered Swedish belligerence.

10. Conflict and war may become more likely as a result of changes in the culture and social structure. (See the section below on "Socioeconomic Modernization and Conflict.") Conversely, war itself, as well as internal revolution, may be an agent of cultural change and bring about significant alterations in social structure.[38]

11. All through history, from the time Archimedes went to a mountain top near the sea and used a glass to focus the rays of the sun on the sails of an enemy ship down to our own days of nuclear warheads and laser beams, war and technological change have been closely related. Preparations for war and waging war itself bring science, technology, industry, and medicine into cooperation with governments for purposes of military research and development which may have "spinoff" applications in nonmilitary dimensions. Scholars have shown how inventions from the canning of food and the sewing machine through many chemicals, down to jet engines, radar, nuclear energy, rockets, electronic communications, and blood plasma received their initial impetus from the military needs of the state.[39]

12. Some anthropological hypotheses may appear to be contradictory, but actually are not. We are told, for example, that both differences and similarities of peoples may lead to bitter conflicts. Substantial differences of an ethnic, linguistic, religious, racial, cultural, or ideological character are easily perceived and thus can give rise to animosity and a

sense of threat, especially when the different groups are physically close to each other. Differences which have been politically muted or controlled for a long time within a single nation may flare up and generate pressures for separatism or autonomy (e.g., Quebec in Canada, the Scots in the United Kingdom, and the Walloons and the Flemish in Belgium). On the other hand, it has often been noted that the closer the parties are together in belief systems, the more intense a conflict between them is likely to be.[40] Thus conflict is particularly intense when a group that was previously united undergoes schism and both groups henceforth claim to be the authentic heirs of the tradition. Examples include Catholic and Protestant Christians, Sunni and Shi'i Muslims, and Stalinists and Trotskyites as well as Khrushchevists and Maoists among the Communists. In such cases, the ferocity of the opposition subsides with the passage of time, and toleration, ecumenical relations, rapprochement, and even reunification may become possible. But instances of complete reunification are extremely rare.

13. Conflict may be studied by reference to the pattern of communications between conflict parties and the language employed in the conflict. As the conflict is developing, communication between the parties declines and intraparty communication (and cohesion) intensifies. Maximum conflict intensity coincides with minimal communication between the parties, as well as with intragroup propaganda of maximum hostility against the enemy. Changes in patterns of communication and propaganda usually signal a change in conflict intensity and a movement toward conflict resolution.

14. Every conflict has its own unique structure, arising out of the nature of the parties, the issues at stake, the circumstances in which the conflict is waged, and the particular dynamic according to which it develops. In analyzing any specific conflict, a knowledge of the particular features of that conflict is just as important as, if not more important than, generalized knowledge of conflict processes.

SOCIOECONOMIC GAPS AND
WORLD REVOLUTIONARY CONFLICT

When the first edition of this book was in preparation in the late 1960s, American social scientists, largely under the impact of the Vietnam War, were preoccupied with the phenomenon of "revolution," especially guerrilla insurgency in the Third World. The advent of nuclear weapons technology appeared to have greatly reduced the likelihood of direct military hostilities between the possessors of such capabilities; the development of alliance systems had also helped to immunize the formal allies of the principal nuclear powers against the threat of overt military attack. Thus the international strategic-political situation in the 1950s and

1960s seemed to militate in favor of a shift in the nature and often in the locus of politically significant conflict. At the same time, the conditions which social scientists usually cite as the source of human conflict potential—that is, socioeconomic discrepancies, the aggressive impulses resulting from frustration, cognitive dissonance caused by measuring the actual against the ideal, withdrawal and alienation from existing social structures, and so forth—were apparently becoming more rather than less common on a world scale. Almost everywhere, thanks to communications technology, the gap between expected (or desired) need fulfillment and actual need fulfillment was (and still is) widening among large numbers of people. It may be that such a gap constitutes the most important single necessary (but not sufficient) condition for the occurrence of internal social conflict on a large scale. Although studies of revolutionary insurgency seemed less policy-urgent in the 1970s, it remains important for the student of international relations to understand the essential characteristics of revolution as a fundamental and recurring form of social conflict.

Especially in the Third World (Asia, Africa, and Latin America), the process of social, economic, and political development is seldom able to provide increasing satisfactions at a pace commensurate with the expanding aspirations of peoples. But even the most advanced countries, including the United States, have problems associated with a so-called technetronic or postindustrial phase in their development, as noted in Chapter 2. It seems that the development process always produces nonsymmetrical effects with respect to the benefits which are bestowed upon peoples. The mass media of technical communications facilitate the drawing of invidious comparisons not only between the "have" and the "have-not" nations, but also within national societies between privileged and disadvantaged groups. In most highly developed—and most rapidly developing—countries, segments of the privileged groups revolt against the conditions of "affluence," become alienated from the institutions which produced the affluence, and cast their lot with the disadvantaged to bring down The Establishment. Both in less developed and in highly developed societies, the breakdown of traditional mechanisms and agencies of social integration plays a crucial role in the growth of revolutionary conflict potential.

Revolution is an old concept in social theory. Classical political theorists were intensely interested in the problems of cyclical change, efforts to overthrow the government by violence, and the moral-political justifications of revolution. They usually attributed revolutionary feelings within a state to a discrepancy between people's desires and their perceived situation—a discrepancy which gives rise to profound political disagreement over the bases on which society ought to be organized. Contemporary theorists distinguish between genuine political revolution

and other phenomena which have often been called by the same name—
for example, the coup d'etat (including "palace revolutions" by rival rel-
atives of a monarch, executive coups or the illegal prolongation of a
leader's term of office, military coups, and other relatively sudden sei-
zures of power by small groups of high status individuals); various forms
of peasant, urban, religious, and other revolts; and the political breaking
away known as *secession* (whether regional, colonial, ethnic, or religious). None of these need have the remotest connection with revolutionary change, says Mark N. Hagopian, who defines revolution as "an
acute, prolonged crisis in one or more of the traditional systems of strati-
fication (class, status, power) of a political community, which involves a
purposive, elite-directed attempt to abolish or to reconstruct one or
more of said systems by means of an intensification of political power and
recourse to violence."[41]

Before the French Revolution, rebellion in Europe against the ruler
usually implied no more than a personnel change in government—hardly
an attack upon the established political order. Hannah Arendt has
pointed out that modern revolutions are of a strikingly different genre,
for they aim at a spirit of freedom and of liberation from an old order of
things. Marked by a "pathos of novelty," revolution involves "the notion
that the course of history suddenly begins anew, that an entirely new
story, a story never known or told before, is about to unfold."[42]

Without suggesting that ideology is the cause or motive of revolution, we can say that modern revolution is normally characterized by a
set of emotion-laden utopian ideas—an expectation that the society is
marching toward a profound transformation of values and structures, as
well as of personal behavior. The revolutionary pictures a vastly improved pattern of human relationships in a future realization, then im-
parts his or her vision to the masses, hopefully to motivate them to revolutionary action. The revolutionary describes a more perfect social
situation—more freedom; more equality; more consciousness of community; more peace, justice, and human dignity; more of the transcenden-
tals which appeal to human beings everywhere. Unlike the utopians of
old, who posited their idyllic states in unreachable geographical places
("nowhere"), the modern revolutionaries locate their utopia in the future: Its eventual achievement is not only possible but inevitable.[43] The
revolutionary credo strengthens the motives for enduring the hardships
of the struggle. The vision of a life free from every form of oppression
justifies the suffering, terror, and chaos which revolution brings. It does
not matter that the present generation of people must endure pain for
the sake of the cause, for without the revolution injustice will continue
indefinitely, piling misery upon misery forever, but as a result of the revolution the human race, or a part of it, will be lifted up to a higher and
nobler plane of existence. The present deprived masses suffer heroically

so that the future fulfilled masses may be happy. Such has always been the ideological rationalization of revolutionaries.

James H. Meisel has presented a profound philosophical account of the role played by discontented intellectuals in historic revolutions. He suggests that the human mind is engaged in an endless quest for the triumph of reason in society, and this quest meets with both success and failure. Nearly every sudden intellectual leap forward seems to end up producing its own form of tyranny, liberating not the intellectuals but the barbarians, or the organization types and totalitarian bureaucrats. Throughout history, the intellectuals provide the breeding ground of revolution. Revolution begins when Mind proclaims some kind of new dispensation of freedom. But eventually mind becomes an enemy of Mind. Every revolution dies in overorganization, or terror, or oppression, or the restoration of the old order, or sheer boredom, or final alienation from technical culture.[44]

According to pre-World War II theories, revolutions occur when the gap between distributed political power and distributed social power within a society becomes intolerable. Certain social classes which are experiencing some of the benefits of progress desire to develop more rapidly than the system will permit, and hence they feel cramped. Discontent spreads over the sharing of economic outputs, social prestige, or political power. Traditional values are openly questioned, and a new social myth challenges the old one. The intellectuals become alienated from the system. Gradually they move from mere criticism to a withdrawal of political loyalty. The governing elites begin to lose confidence in themselves, in their beliefs, and in their ability to command and to solve society's problems. The old elites become too rigid to absorb the emerging elites into their ranks, and this accelerates the polarization. Propagandists assume the intelligentsia's sophisticated criticisms of established institutions, translating them into slogans for mass consumption. The intellectuals join forces with the new and disaffected elites, and the demand for radical reforms increases.

Moderate political elements prove too weak to strike viable compromises between those who agitate for rapid change and those who oppose all change. The breaking point is reached when the instruments of social control, especially the army and the police, collapse or shift their allegiance to the discontented elements, or when the incumbent government proves inept in using those instruments of social control. Such was the classic explanation of revolution advanced by Crane Brinton in 1938, of which it could be said three decades later that not much theoretical progress had been made beyond it.[45]

During the past decade, social scientists have realized that the older theories of political revolution no longer apply toward understanding conflict in the Third World, where most of the guerrilla insurgencies that have occurred since World War II have arisen out of a very different social environment from the historic revolutions of the West. Nevertheless, it would seem that the earlier and the later revolutions ought to have sufficient elements in common to permit at least a certain continuity in the development of conflict theory, with appropriate adjustments to take account of vastly different social circumstances and new social science knowledge.

Contemporary social scientists and policymakers generally look upon the high conflict potential of Asia, Africa, and Latin America as a function of widespread frustration traceable to economic deprivation. Professor Ted Robert Gurr of Princeton University argued that "the necessary precondition for violent civil conflict is deprivation, defined as actors' perceptions of discrepancy between their value expectations and their environment's apparent value capabilities."[46] The disparity between aspirations and fulfillment can be conceived of either as mere economic deprivation or as a combination of various types of deprivation, including economic, psychological, social, and political. Perhaps the least sophisticated theory is that which makes poverty itself the prime frustrating agent. Efforts have often been made to correlate high conflict potential with absolutely low economic variables and with economic stagnation. According to this hypothesis, one can predict the highest incidence of violence in the most poverty-striken countries measured in terms of per capita income. Such a hypothesis, however, contains several problems. Serious violence does indeed occur in many of the countries in the "very poor" category, but it occurs no more frequently in poorer countries than in more affluent Third World ones. The categories of "very poor," "poor," and "middle income" are too imprecise to permit the drawing of firm conclusions. Taken as aggregates, these three groupings of countries may differ from each other in several significant ways besides level of income, and thus other factors besides the degree of poverty undoubtedly contribute to the incidence of conflict.

Admittedly, generalization in the social sciences always involves a certain amount of oversimplification of complex phenomena, but there is probably too much oversimplification here. Violence proneness within a society declines only as a result of social development in many dimensions, of which the economic is but one, and not necessarily always the centrally causative one. Furthermore, although conditions of poverty are frequently linked to criminal behavior and anomic conflict, it has often been pointed out that the most impoverished societies are usually not considered fertile breeding grounds for revolution.

> As Zawadzki and Lazarsfeld have indicated, preoccupation with physical survival, even in industrial areas, is a force strongly militating against the establishment of the community-sense and consensus on joint political action which are necessary to induce a revolutionary state of mind. Far from

making people into revolutionaries, enduring poverty makes for concern with one's solitary self or solitary family at best and resignation or mute despair at worst.[47]

At any given time, one may be able to name several very poor countries in which a revolutionary upheaval is less likely to occur than in a relatively advanced economic system. Economic factors undoubtedly play an important part in many revolutions, but they must be analyzed in relation to other important political, strategic, cultural, and social psychological factors which are not reducible to pure economics. If people subscribe to an absolute economic explanation of revolution, they will be likely to adopt a limited approach to the development of policies for coping with revolutionary situations, and they will be unable to account for revolutions like the one in Iran.

SOCIOECONOMIC MODERNIZATION AND CONFLICT

A more interesting theory, somewhat better borne out by existing data, postulates conflict as a function not of poverty but of social development and change. James N. Rosenau contends that "the more rapid the rate of social change becomes, the greater the likelihood of intrasocietal violence."[48] Arnold Feldman has pointed out that "change contributes to revolutionary potential rather than eradicating dissatisfactions."[49] Many analysts now agree that social frustration and revolutionary potential are not as pronounced in the most backward areas as they are in areas economically and socially "on the move," although it should be pointed out that there are few regions left in the world which are not undergoing "modernization" to some degree. Modernization may be imposed artificially from without, for example, by foreign investors, or it may grow organically from within as a result of a shift of attitude from a fatalistic acceptance of things as they are to an active desire for change. "When the Middle Eastern peasant," writes Manfred Halpern, "realizes for the first time that the structure of life can be concretely improved, and that he is being denied the opportunity to improve his own lot, then the seeds of revolution will have been planted."[50] As Crane Brinton noted in 1938, revolutionists are more likely to be children of hope than of despair.[51]

This should not be taken to mean, however, that the social psychological states of the revolutionary leaders, of active revolutionary followers, and of the masses to whom the revolutionary appeals are addressed are necessarily all the same. In the interaction of these elements, there may be a dialectical relationship between the social psychology of despair and the revolutionary politics of hope. When people of "rising expectations" experience gradual progress at a sufficient rate to be able to perceive an improvement differential in their situation from year to year, they are not a likely target for the appeals of the revolutionary propagandist. But certain groups within the population may become frustrated as a result of nonsymmetrical change. Different sectors of the society, as they perceive the distribution of the benefits of development, are likely to be moving forward at different rates; some may perceive no motion or a loss of relative position.[52] This phenomenon occurs constantly in all developing societies, including the most advanced. The spread of technical communications facilitates the process whereby some groups become keenly aware of discrepancies and draw comparisons between their own position and that of others (within the community, the nation, and the world). Few groups in any country (even the most advanced) experience real improvements commensurate with their mounting aspirations.

The groups that have benefited most visibly from the modernization process in nonsocialist states are quickly identified by disadvantaged groups as satisfied status quo elements standing in the way of genuine social progress. Domestic status quo groups naturally tend to affiliate with the defenders of the international status quo—the capitalist states, while the discontented ally themselves with the international forces opposed to the status quo—at present the Marxist governments. Third World political-economic elites who do business with the West are eventually branded by Marxist-supported "have-nots" as mignons of the capitalists, enemies of the people and perpetrators of the most heinous crimes, regardless of what they may have tried to do to develop their countries.

James C. Davies has called attention to the fact that the gap between what people want and what they get may be tolerable or intolerable. Unfortunately, we cannot determine in advance the point at which the gap becomes so intolerable that revolution occurs, because this depends upon many other cultural, political, and psychological variables in addition to factors which are economically measurable. The perception of the gap may depend largely upon the way in which the revolutionary organization can utilize the communications nets to dramatize the discrepancies. Davies also suggests that the danger of revolutionary conflict becomes more acute when a society that is on the long-term path toward development suddenly experiences a downturn in the economic process.[53] Although Davies' study pertained to economic trends within whole national societies, his "J-curve" theory might well be even more useful if applied to more than economics and to less than nations, that is, if it were applied to the way in which subnational groups perceive themselves as suffering a reversal of their total position within the social systems as a result of developmental change.

Political Instability and Frustration

Ivo K. and Rosalind L. Feierabend have identified political instability with aggressive behavior, which they attribute to unrelieved social frustration. In situations of systemic frustration, they contend, political stability may still be predicted if certain conditions are met, namely, that the society is a nonparticipant one; or that constructive solutions to frustrations are available; or that the government is sufficiently coercive to prevent overt acts of hostility against itself; or that the aggressive impulse can be displaced against minority groups or other nations; or that individual acts of aggression are sufficiently abundant to furnish an outlet. But in the absence of these conditions, aggressive behavior can be expected to result from systemic frustration. In the more extreme cases, political instability is likely to take the form of riots, strikes, mass arrests, assassination of political figures, executions, terrorism and sabotage, guerrilla warfare, civil war, coup d'etat, and other forms of revolt.[54] Referring to the "essentially frustrating nature of the modernization process," the Feierabends offer the following generalization:

> Furthermore, it may be postulated that the peak discrepancy between systemic goals and their satisfaction, and hence the maximum frustration, should come somewhere in the middle of the transitional phase between traditional society and the achievement of modernity. It is at this middle stage that awareness of modernity and exposure to modern patterns should be complete, that is, at a theoretical ceiling, whereas achievement levels would still be lagging far behind. Prior to this theoretical middle stage, exposure can no longer increase, since it already amounts to complete awareness, but achievement will continue to progress, thus carrying the nation eventually into the stage of modernity. Thus, in contrast to transitional societies, it may be postulated that traditional and modern societies will be less frustrated and therefore will tend to be more stable than transitional societies.[55]

One can take issue with certain aspects of the above formulation. It contains, for example, the uncritical assumption that there can be such a thing as "complete exposure" to or awareness of modernization, and it overlooks the fact that since increasingly rapid and profound social change is a permanent feature of the modernization process, there will always be, in every society, relatively traditional, transitional, and modernized sectors—not a comforting prospect for industrially advanced countries. Nevertheless, it is useful to ask how the various subprocesses of modernization may be related to the occurrence of frustration and conflict. It is impossible in international relations theory to examine in detail the various aspects of development that contribute to an environment conducive to conflict, but the student should keep these in mind. As population is being drawn from rural to urban areas, traditional religious values and cultural patterns begin to break down among the intellectuals, professional classes, technically skilled groups, and sectors of the urban masses. Technology is imported; transport and communication nets grow; literacy rates rise; social mobility is enhanced. Family and other social ties that formerly bound individuals together disintegrate. New socioeconomic classes of a functional nature begin to emerge, but they are weaker than the structures they replace when it comes to giving the individual a sense of belonging to a community.

This is what the German sociologist Ferdinand Tonnies referred to in the late nineteenth century as the movement from *Gemeinschaft* (community) to *Gesellschaft* (association). The contrast was perhaps overdrawn, but it is not without some validity.[56] Partially uprooted individuals move more rapidly and receive more varied impressions of the world from the communications media. They are forced to make profound adjustments, but probably can find no satisfactory set of norms to guide them. Both fascinated and frightened by the changes they see, they become psychologically troubled. Edward Shils has shown that the intellectuals in underdeveloped countries have an ambivalent attitude toward things foreign and Western: They appreciate foreign culture but have a sense of inferiority with respect to their own.[57] Moreover, as intellectuals abandon traditional religious and cultural values, acting differently from the way they were taught in their youth, they may develop feelings of guilt from which they may try to escape by projecting hostility against the external agents of social change—the Western imperialist system. Assertive nationalism becomes a means of restoring self-respect.

Incumbent governments in the developing countries, lacking experience in economic planning, find it difficult to impress the unsophisticated masses with the need to accept present deprivations in order to promote long-range economic expansion. Development demands patience in many dimensions: the acquisition of technical skills; improvements in the educational system; the modification of social incentives; the emergence of managerial capabilities; the willingness of traditional elites to admit the new functional elites to a fair share of the system's benefits; responsible fiscal policies; administrative reforms; and so forth. All these imperatives are frustrating to the impatient. Even gradual progress is frustrating to those whose appetites have been whetted to insist upon rapid and far-sweeping changes—instant progress. Meanwhile, population growth places added pressures upon developing systems, cutting into annual GNP growth rates and compounding the demands placed upon inexperienced planners in countries often faced with deteriorating terms of international trade.[58]

Sociologists and anthropologists consider the likelihood of internal social conflict to be on the increase when the integrating mechanisms of a society break down. As immemorial religious-cultural traditions give way to secularization, emergent nationalism as expressed by a charismatic leader might prove powerful enough to preserve domestic solidarity, especially if there is an external bête noire against which aggressive feelings can be directed. So long as national integration remains high, enemy groups do not become salient to each other within the society. But in the absence of an integrating principle, the changes wrought by development would seem to increase the potential for group conflict within nations. As new groups emerge, they forge their own consciousness of group interests and values; they establish their self-identity by directing hostility outward. At this point the configuration of the communications process takes on considerable importance. Since hostility may be aimed outward in many different directions and randomly distributes itself among so many targets as to become dissipated without the occurrence of serious politicized violence in a conflict with a single enemy, it is the function of political organization to channel the aggressive hostility inherent in discontented groups into one coherent direction. An incumbent government might attempt to divert it against a neighbor adversary. (In some regions of the world, such as Latin America, it is difficult to do this, because of the cultural similarity of most members of the regional state system, and therefore it must be aimed at the culturally different imperialist power in the Northern Hemisphere.) A revolutionary organization will attempt to channel it against the incumbent government. In either case, considerable strategic manipulation of social communications is presupposed. Neither external wars nor internal revolutions are typically spontaneous or accidental happenings; both require a high degree of organization and planning.

A society which in one phase of its history may be highly integrated and disposed toward intense external conflict might at another time undergo domestic disintegration and experience serious internal disorders. However, it must be admitted that when social scientists attempt to determine whether a particular community is integrating or disintegrating they encounter difficult ambiguities. One observer, relying on such indicators as the growth of communications, the expansion of the national school system, and the increasing provision of welfare services, might conclude that a given society is becoming more integrated. (See Chapter 10 for an examination of theories of integration.) Another observer, focusing upon such indicators as crime rates, the decline of traditional institutional influences, and the occurrence of riots and demonstrations, might be led to the conclusion that the given society is disintegrating. Even the same data can be interpreted in opposite ways, depending upon the social philosophy of the analyst. In all social transitions, one can discern aspects of integration and disintegration unfolding side by side. If social scientists are divided in their opinions about these things, we are perhaps no worse off than the physicists who cannot agree whether the universe is building up or breaking down.

It is no doubt obvious from what has already been said that revolution is a form of collective action which lends itself to different modes of explanation. Charles Tilly, a Marxian sociologist-historian, has analyzed the phenomenon according to the theoretical systems of Karl Marx, Emile Durkheim, John Stuart Mill and Max Weber.[59] Marx, as we saw in Chapter 6, treated all social conflict in terms of class structures and interests arising out of the pattern of relations determined by the organization of production. Emile Durkheim saw collective action (i.e., the mobilization of large numbers of people for the waging of social conflict) as a response to the interactive processes of integration and disintegration within a whole society. Industrialization leads to differentiation, which in turn leads to a breakdown in shared beliefs. Anomie results from excessive social differentiation and individual disorientation. As the gap widens before the pace of structural change and the institutionalization of social control, pressures increase toward collective action to restore shared beliefs.[60] For the Utilitarian John Stuart Mill, collective action was founded on the calculated pursuit of individual interest. Mill, like James Madison, suspected the self-seeking character of all "sinister" class interests, and hoped that no one class and no combination likely to combine would ever be able to gain control of the government. Mill and his disciples emphasized the rational pursuit of interests within an equilibrium framework, and deprecated crowd action as impulsive and irrational.

Lastly, Max Weber, the political sociologist of religion, leadership, and bureaucracy, traced the structure and action of the social group to a commitment to a particular belief system—a collective definition of the world and of the members themselves. It is the belief system that justifies the power of authorities, and this holds true for traditional, charismatic, and rational-legal systems. Both charisma and rational bureaucracy can bring about revolutionary social change—charisma by transforming the inner life and bureaucratic rationalization by transforming the external environment. Tilly prefers the Marxian explanation, but he leaves open the possibility that Durkheim and Weber may also have been correct.[61]

Societal Breakdown: The Crucial Questions

When scientists ask too general a question, they often obtain an answer of very limited utility. Instead of trying to generalize about such large issues as integration or disintegration of a whole society, it may be more useful to select a small number of major social configurations and to examine them within a specific community. The political scientist, for example, would want to know such things as: (1) the degree to which various strata or groups within the population are being recruited into or are withdrawing from participation in the political system; (2) the ability of the political system to respond flexibly to the various demands made upon it and to produce outputs likely to inhibit the growth of pressures for revolutionary change; and (3) the extent and effectiveness of social and political control, as well as the acceptability of the methods whereby such control is maintained.

Specifically, the political scientist would be interested in securing data concerning the following characteristics: (1) the extent to which people in various social groups feel themselves more loyal to than critical of the system; (2) the extent to which they participate in elections, pay taxes, perform military service, and contribute other expressions of support for the military system; (3) whether the intellectuals who are being educated within the system are also being satisfactorily absorbed by it, or whether they are being excluded and alienated from it; (4) whether the system contains built-in "safety-valves" for the orderly release of social energies (e.g., economic competition, channels for criticism and the expression of new ideas, outlets for religious and humanitarian motivations, and sports rivalry); (5) what kind of relatively stable and cohesive social groups exist (church, army, trade unions, farmers' organizations, professional associations, political parties, etc.) and the direction they are taking within the system; (6) the pattern in which symbolic honors, political power, and economic benefits are distributed among various groups within the system; and (7) the proportionate allocation by various groups of fear-hostility attitudes inside and outside the nation.

This last factor, of course, is of particular interest to the student of international relations, because it bears upon the question of whether the conflict potential in a particular country is for international war or internal revolution. At this point we come back to the venerable hypothesis of political analysts, discussed at the beginning of this chapter and never conclusively proved, that a government can head off impending domestic strife by fomenting a popular foreign war. Whether this can be accomplished may depend upon the presence of readily perceptible and historically significant group differences—ethnic-linguistic, religious, or tribal. If such differences are more pronounced across national borders than within the nation, the government will be in a better position to solidify the nation by going to war. However, if such differences are more pronounced intranationally, they may very well constitute an important factor in the potential for domestic conflict. In this case, going to war with a neighbor is likely to exacerbate the internal conflict if group affiliations extend across the boundaries of two warring nations. Whether or not there is international war, serious ethnic and religious differences within a country caught up in a revolutionary situation are likely to be exploited both by the incumbent government and by the revolutionary organization. The Iranian-Iraqi dispute of 1980 was marked by nationalist tension (Iranian versus Arab), religious tensions (Shi'ite versus Sunni), and the hostility of Islamic fundamentalism toward the modernizing secularism of American and Soviet imperialism.

The economic, psychological, sociological, and political conditions mentioned above provide the matrix out of which revolutionary conflict arises, but they cannot be set forth definitively as the cause of conflict. They are, as it were, the necessary but not the sufficient conditions. Within a society there may be fairly high levels of frustration, alienation, cognitive dissonance, sense of threat, and other attitudes of mind conducive to conflict. There may be nonsymmetrical rates of change. There may be in proximity highly visible groups which have a history of animosity toward each other. Communications between some groups may break down and reach a virtual vanishing point. Yet politically structured conflict will not occur until deliberate decisions to invoke political violence have been taken, and these decisions will normally not be taken until after there has developed a conflict organization capable of managing violence and of supplying political direction to existing resentments and aggressive impulses. The link between the social psychological state and the development of the conflict organization seems to be in the first instance the personalities of a small number of revolutionary leaders, combined with their life experiences in the environment which shaped them.

The Making of a Revolutionary

As Lawrence Stone has noted, we still do not know what makes a person go revolutionary.[62] What identifiable elements in one's personality (such as need for achievement, sense of moral indignation and social mission, propensity for risk-taking, and desire for power) and in one's personal background (childhood, relations with parents, socialization, education, religion, travel, reading, previous military training, and contacts with other conflict organizers) impel the revolutionary to undertake an attempt to overthrow the system by force instead of working from within to reform it? It would be surprising if the leaders of a revolution were motivated by the same psychic forces as are the masses, that is, that they are attracted to insurgency because they have suffered the deprivations of economic poverty. Revolutions are usually led by "elites," and it is an essential attribute of elites that they are moved by more subtle personality factors than those predictable of the masses. Elites and masses differ significantly in their reactions to frustration and in the sources of their frustration.[63] Revolutionary leaders seldom come from the poorest classes. More typically, they derive from middle-class families that have not known economic hardship. Their deprivations are more likely to be psychological rather than economic. What they want frequently are intangible rewards—prestige, a share in political power, fame as part of a charismatic movement struggling for justice, even the stimulation of excitement and danger. In the case of some revolutionary terrorists, the presence of psychopathological elements cannot be discounted.[64]

Once a study of revolutionary conflict gets beyond the difficult problem of trying to develop not only an explanatory theory of the general causes of revolution but also a predictive theory of revolutionary occurrences of a sizable scale—a task in which social science shades into strategic intelligence—there are many other questions about the revolutionary process worthy of study.

POLITICAL OBJECTIVES
What are the avowed political purposes for which the conflict is waged? Modern revolutions have been fought to expel a colonial power and achieve national independence; to change the political system without radically altering the social systems; to terminate an intolerable minority status by achieving either local autonomy or territorial secession from the system; to determine the succession after the expected departure of a colonial regime; to bring pressure to bear from one political system upon another. An insurgency ostensibly begun for one objective may undergo either a *de facto* or an avowed change of purpose during the course of the conflict. Avowed objectives while the revolution is in course are usually a matter of propaganda designed to gain political support. Some objectives of the revolutionary program are usually left unspoken. However, a comparison of avowed objectives with actual outcomes can be an interesting exercise.

DURATION OF REVOLUTIONARY CONFLICT
Mention was made above of the relatively sudden coup d'etat carried out by a small group of high-status individuals to effect a personnel change in the top echelon of government. The coup itself is a conflict phenomenon worthy of investigation,[65] but it is not a genuine revolution. The total revolutionary process is of fairly long duration—usually a matter of several years. Mao Tse-tung insisted upon deliberate protraction and the avoidance of eschatological adventurism as essential elements in the strategy of revolutionary warfare.[66] The history of Third World insurgencies since World War II indicates that guerrilla conflicts which were terminated in substantially less than three years were usually not successful; duration of from three to nine years was marked by about a half-and-half chance of success; conflicts which were prolonged beyond ten years show a perceptible decline in the prospects for revolutionary success, but an increase in the probability of compromise settlement. The

Vietnam War, which lasted nearly 30 years, was a notable exception to the pattern, ending in complete success for the revolutionary forces in the longest lasting and most internationalized of all revolutionary wars.

THE TERRAIN OF REVOLUTIONARY INSURGENCY

The impression has long been common that revolutionary insurgency is a predominantly rural phenomenon, but this notion can be misleading. Social scientists question the stereotyped generalization of the "peasant revolution." Rural peasants are more tradition-bound and apathetic toward the political process than are urban dwellers. The dissatisfied peasant is more likely to migrate to the city than to revolt. Moreover, peasant insurrections, when they occur, are often led by revolutionaries from an urban background. In any event, as the sharp dichotomy between rural and urban cultures dissolves under the impact of modern communications, earlier ideas of the "peasant revolution" may lose some of their relevance.[67]

Revolutionary insurgency as a social-psychological process with important previolent stages seems likely to begin in urban centers where social mobility is high, where traditional norms are weakest and anomie is greatest, where ideas circulate more rapidly, and where certain psychological states such as frustration and dissonance may be more pronounced. But as an externalized strategic process, we often find that the violent stages of guerrilla insurgency begin in rural areas geographically remote from the political capital of the country.

Several considerations help to determine the location of revolutionary conflict. Insurgents are disposed to establish bases in regions with a record of previous revolutionary activity or sentiment.[68] They want access to major political targets, as well as economic self-sufficiency. They are anxious to secure a base in zones of weak political control, not easily accessible to and penetrable by government forces. Hence they are attracted to provinces not served efficiently by road, rail, and air transport and to terrain which, although lending cover to small guerrilla bands, proves hostile to the movement of larger and more cumbersome conventional military forces—mountains, jungles, forests, river deltas, swamplands, and deserts. Not only physical geography but political geography as well enters the picture. Whenever possible, insurgents usually find it advantageous to establish headquarters, training camps, and supply routes close to or across the borders of friendly or neutral countries. The guerrillas may then seek legal sanctuary or political haven when subjected to hot pursuit, thus compelling incumbent government forces to incur international censure if they carry their punitive action to the area of retreat. Moreover, borderlands are frequently zones of ethnic heterogeneity and diversity of political loyalties—factors which revolutionists may find helpful. Quite naturally, logistical considerations always loom large. Sources and routes of foreign supply are extremely important factors in the political geography of guerrilla revolution.

THE INTERNATIONALIZATION OF INTERNAL WAR

In nearly every historic age, the existence of revolutionary conditions within states has led to intervention by strong foreign powers.[69] Weaker revolutionary forces seek to augment their chances of success by inviting outside aid, usually from "revolutionary" or dissatisfied powers. During the period of United States nuclear superiority, the two principal powers committed to a reversal of the international status quo strongly supported "national liberation warfare" (as the Soviet Union called it) or "people's war" (as the Chinese called it). These modes of "indirect" conflict were relatively safe methods of carrying on the international revolutionary movement, compared to the more dangerous methods of direct confrontation with what was then unquestionably a nuclear-superior West. Naturally, if one superpower intervenes in a Third World internal war, the other usually feels some temptation, pressure, or tendency to do likewise in support of the opposite side. In the 1960s, the United States, the Soviet Union, and China intervened at various times in Third World insurgencies, particularly in Asia. In the 1970s, Asia and Africa were arenas of competition among the three major military powers. It was not at all uncommon to find, in such areas as Angola, Rhodesia—Zimbabwe and Eritrea, two or three competing revolutionary organizations, each with a different ethnic or religious base, as well as incumbent regimes— all supported by different outside major powers, or pairs of them.

In the contemporary world, virtually every conflict which occurs within the ken of news-gathering agencies becomes an item in the environment of international relations. A revolution may produce a spillover effect in a neighboring country. There may be spontaneous or organized demonstrations in distant foreign countries to support one side or to protest against the other. The world communications net plays a crucial role in the internationalization of conflict. Revolutionaries must strive to acquire by slow degrees some semblance of an international personality as an object of potential foreign support in the forms of money, arms, diplomatic backing, organized political sympathy, and other kinds of assistance. Conflicts are drawn into the vortex of world politics when they become items in the decisionmaking processes of foreign governments, international organizations (such as the United Nations), regional alliances (such as NATO, SEATO, or OAS), associations of political parties (such as Communists and Socialists), churches, ethnic organizations, individuals. The possible forms of outside intervention and aid are myriad and defy inventory.

It is extremely difficult to determine the relative weight to be assigned in a given revolutionary conflict to external and internal factors as determinants of the outcomes.[70] Obviously, certain internal factors may be of crucial significance, such as the morale, training, leadership, and strategic-tactical doctrines of revolutionary and governmental forces, their ability to utilize communications media and otherwise influence the attitudes of the people, and the ability of the existing system to respond to the revolutionary challenge with a variety of self-strengthening policies. In some cases, however, external factors may prove overriding. Without implying that any one form of external aid (such as military assistance) is necessarily decisive in insuring the success or failure of a revolutionary insurgency, we can say that what appears at the start to be an indigenous conflict may become the focal point of international intervention, overt or clandestine, to such an extent that the conflict can no longer be regarded as an internal one. "If outside manpower, motives, money, and other resources appear to constitute the main capabilities committed to the struggle on both sides," writes Karl W. Deutsch, "then we are inclined to speak of 'war by proxy'—an international conflict between two foreign powers, fought out on the soil of a third country; disguised as conflict over an internal issue of that country; and using some or all of that country's manpower, resources, and territory as means for achieving preponderantly foreign goals and foreign strategies."[71] In this case, local parties to the conflict lose the power of initiative and control to a complex international process of strategic planning, diplomatic bargaining and negotiation, and political-military decision-making—a process in which the local parties within the conflict-ridden nation may play only a subordinate client role. Once the international political prestige of two great powers becomes engaged, their rivalry may very well overshadow in importance the social-psychological attitudes of the inhabitants of the country on whose soil the conflict is being waged, at least in respect to the magnitude and duration of the revolutionary conflict.

POLITICAL SCIENCE AND THE CAUSES OF WAR

It is now time to turn to what is generally regarded as the principal problem of international relations in the contemporary world—war. Among political scientists, some no doubt can be found who are partial to their own single-factor explanations of war, but most are likely to be wary of theories which trace wars to one overriding cause—whether inner biological-psychological urges, or the profit motives of capitalist imperialists, or arms races, or alliances. Recalling the fate of earlier predictions that the replacement of monarchies by republics would lead to a more peaceful world, they are careful about postulating a precise connection between the form of government and the propensity to go to war. The authors of this text are inclined to agree with Kenneth N. Waltz when he says that democratic states are more peaceful than nondemocratic ones,[72] simply because pacifist sentiment can more readily be translated into an effective political force in democratic states. Nevertheless it is undeniable that democracies can occasionally be swept by war fever.

Political scientists are not for the most part easily impressed by the proposals of those who, diagnosing a single cause of war, prescribe a single panacea for it—universal socialism, free trade, universal brotherhood of good will, a radical new approach to education, world government, complete disarmament, or maximum military preparedness or standing firm at all times as well must be woven into a multidimensional framework, and some may be more important than others as a means of reducing the likelihood of specific wars.[73]

Quincy Wright, in his pioneering and comprehensive survey of the subject, stressed the multiple causality of war and warned against simplistic approaches to the problem. "A war, in reality, results from a total situation involving ultimately almost everything that has happened to the human race up to the time the war begins."[74] In his monumental study, which cannot adequately be summarized here, Wright put forth a four-factor model of the origins of war, corresponding to the levels of technology, law, social-political organization, and cultural values. Karl W. Deutsch, in his preface to a reissue of Wright's classic work, wrote of these levels:

> Whenever there is a major change at any level—culture and values, political and social institutions, laws, or technology—the old adjustment and control mechanisms become strained and may break down. Any major psychological and cultural, or major social and political, or legal, or technological change in the world thus increases the risk of war, unless it is balanced by compensatory political, legal, cultural, and psychological adjustments.[75]

Clyde Eagleton, professor of international law at New York University, wrote:

> War is a means for achieving an end, a weapon which can be used for good or for bad purposes. Some of these purposes for which war has been used have been accepted by humanity as worthwhile ends; indeed, war performs functions which are essential in any human society. It has been used to settle disputes, to uphold rights, to remedy wrongs; and these are surely functions which must be served. . . . One may say, without exaggeration, that no more stupid, brutal, wasteful, or unfair method could ever have been imagined for such purposes, but this does not alter the situation.[76]

Social collectivities have gone to war throughout history for a variety of reasons—territory, dominion, security, wealth, prestige, the triumph of an idea, reunifying an ethnic-cultural system, and preserving a set of values. There have been personal wars, feudal wars, dynastic wars, religious wars, nationalistic wars, ideological wars, colonial wars, civil wars within states or empires, wars to build empires, wars of secession, revolutionary wars, class wars, wars of national liberation, wars between alliances, proxy wars, limited wars, and total wars. The motives for which political communities go to war change over time. Four hundred years ago, Europe was torn by a series of ferocious wars over religious issues. Most Europeans would regard such a *casus belli* as unthinkable today. (But the mixing of political and religious issues still occasionally appears, as in the Ulster conflict and the civil war in Lebanon.)

Political scientists generally insist, therefore, that we cannot understand the causes of war exclusively in terms of biological, psychological, or other behavioral factors, but must always return to the level of political analysis to find out why a particular government regards certain foreign governments as allies and others as adversaries. It is out of a matrix of political communications—involving politicians and diplomats, the public, the press, the military, socioeconomic elites, special interest groups in the foreign policymaking process—that governments define their goals, interests, policies, and strategies, weighing the likely consequences of acting or not acting in specific situations, as well as the prospects of success or failure in invoking force. When a government takes a decision for war, it may be for a great variety of conscious reasons, singly or in combination—to preserve its "prestige;" to establish hegemony within a larger area; to support an ally and thus safeguard an alliance against erosion; to maintain an "equilibrium" in a particular region; to fill a "power vacuum"; to protect an economic interest abroad; to dissuade future aggression; to gain control of territory deemed vital to national security; to consolidate the domestic position of a ruling elite or political party; or to enhance internal cohesion and head off domestic strife by deflecting conflict passions abroad. Many other political motives for war could be cited. But these examples will suffice to focus our attention upon an important conclusion: The findings of the behavioral scientists can serve as valuable illuminators to our understanding of the causes of war, provided that we place them in perspective as partial explanatory factors within the larger international political context in which those who wield the power of decision opt either to go to war or to refrain from it.[77]

Violent encounters between organized political communities may have myriad origins. The ground, sea, or air forces of two adversary societies might suddenly and spontaneously find themselves involved in hostile skirmishes without an authoritative political decision having been made by either government, or one government might order a unit of its armed forces to contrive a military confrontation with a unit of the adversary's forces merely to gauge the psychopolitical reaction without intending war. In an era of advanced military technology, many analysts have worried about the possibility of "accidental war," as if nuclear war might be triggered automatically by an incident of technical malfunction. Political scientists and other macrotheorists call attention to the fact that, so far as historical evidence goes, the initiation of war is a matter of conscious, deliberate choice, not of decisionless outbreak.[78] An accident involving one or more nuclear weapons might very well create conditions of overwhelming stress for political decision-makers who suffer from inadequate information, severe time constraints, physical and psychological exhaustion, or sheer political inexperience. (The problems of decision-making in crisis are treated in Chapter 11.) Nevertheless, between accident and war, a political decision must supervene.

A persistent cause of war has been the readiness of societies to resort to force in order to reduce a perceived threat to their security or to their political, religious, ideological, economic, or sociocultural value systems. Undoubtedly, there have been times when the threat perceived was real and proximate, just as there were times when the threat was so remote as to be virtually imaginary. At recurring periods in history, one or more societies have acted more "belligerently," "aggressively," or "imperialistically" than others, whether with or without what would appear to an "objective" observer to be a good or at least understandable cause. When this happens, other societies become apprehensive and they seek to improve their security by engaging in some form of power balancing— especially by increasing their military preparations or by entering an alliance, or both.

The perception of threat therefore becomes a matter of importance to political scientists. For one state to perceive another as a threat, it must see the latter as having both the *capability* and the *intent* to block goal attainment or to jeopardize national security.[79] J. David Singer, for whom national security rather than abstract ideology constitutes *the* categorical imperative in United States and Soviet foreign policy, suggests that two powers which find themselves in a relationship of rivalry or hostility will each be inclined to "interpret each other's military capability as evidence of military intent," and he reduces threat-perception to the quasi-mathematical formula of Estimated Capability × Estimated Intent.[80] Singer hastens to note that the Soviet Union is much more concerned over the British nuclear capability than is the United States. (He might have further distinguished by pointing out that there were times, especially during the era of de Gaulle, when United States government officials were considerably more hostile to the French nuclear deterrent than to the British, even though France was an ally; and that the British, while never fearing a United States nuclear attack against themselves, worried at times about United States nuclear decision-making processes.)

Raymond L. Garthoff has warned against several fallacies in any effort to estimate and impute intentions.[81] Among common examples of fallacious reasoning he cites the following: (1) Since overestimating the enemy's intentions merely costs dollars, whereas underestimating can cost lives, when in doubt it is best to assume the worst. (2) Because it is impossible to read intentions accurately, it is safer to estimate measurable military capabilities and assume an intention to maximize those capabilities. (3) Assume that the adversary's strategic perceptions and ways of thinking are either the same as your own or necessarily always different. (Garthoff advises that both pitfalls should be avoided.) (4) Assume that the leaders of the adversary nation either never mean what they say or always mean what they say. Both assumptions are unfounded. Estimating intentions, he concludes, is difficult enough without allowing such fallacies as the foregoing to enter into the process. Garthoff's discussion of this problem was in the context of the burgeoning debate over whether the Soviet Union is seeking strategic military superiority over the United States, that is, the capability to wage, win, and survive a nuclear war.[82]

Those who see the Soviet Union as striving to achieve a nuclear-war-winning capability do not necessarily contend that the Soviets wish to plan a deliberate "bolt from the blue" first strike against the United States at a time of their own choosing, when their military advantage appears to be at a maximally favorable point. Richard Pipes, Paul Nitze, Colin Gray and others realize that the Soviet leaders, aware of the destructiveness and unpredictability of nuclear war, are anxious to deter it if at all possible, especially since they believe that the forces of history are running inexorably in their favor and against the West. But the Soviet method of making deterrence succeed is markedly different from the American method. Whereas the United States strategic doctrine, which was developed by civilian strategists, calls for each side to place restraints upon its ability to destroy the strategic, and especially the retaliatory, capability of the other, Soviet strategic doctrine, apparently developed by military leaders, does not presuppose such restraint, but requires instead a maximum capability to blunt the nuclear striking power of the adversary if war should break out. Moreover, Pipes insists, if the Soviets should perceive nuclear war to be imminent and unavoidable, they are determined to launch a preemptive strike instead of waiting to absorb a first nuclear blow before retaliating—as official United States doctrine prescribes.[83] (Theories of deterrence are discussed in greater detail in Chapter 9.)

ARMS, ARMS RACES, AND WAR

This brings us to the question of whether armaments themselves constitute a cause of war, or whether they can be a cause of peace through deterrence. The question has been posed recurringly in modern times, and obviously it has not been answered to the satisfaction of all intelligent persons, for it continues to be asked. Many analysts have been of the opinion that arms do not cause wars, but rather are symptoms and consequences of suspicions, hostility and conflicts between societies. Frederick L. Schuman, noting that pacifists have long believed that arms lead to war and disarmament to peace, wrote: "In reality, the reverse is more nearly true: war machines are reduced only when peace seems probable, the expectation of conflict leads to competition in armaments, and armaments spring from war and from the anticipation of war."[84] Hans J. Morgenthau delivered this terse dictum: "Men do not fight because they have arms. They have arms because they deem it necessary to fight."[85]

Perhaps the question needs to be refined. "The contention that arms are the fruits rather than the seeds of war," according to Charles P. Schleicher, "was probably nearer the truth in a simpler age than at present."[86] Given the propensity of modern communications media toward sensationalism, it is difficult to deny that present-day competition in weapons technology—with abundant reports about nuclear-tipped multiple warheads in ICBMs and SLBMs, neutron bombs (or enhanced radiation weapons), Backfire Bombers, air-, sea- and ground-launched cruise missiles (ALCMs, SLCMs, and GLCMs), laser and charged-particle beams, satellite killers, and other developments in lethality—is bound to heighten international fears and tensions, both at the popular level and among the elites who must worry about stable deterrence and adequate defense. One who constantly reads or hears about the growing vulnerability of land-based ICBMs and other developments which are supposed to be dangerously destabilizing cannot cavalierly dismiss the contention that uncontrolled armaments competition between rival powers may create a climate conducive to war.

RICHARDSON'S REACTION PROCESSES

One of the best known efforts to mathematicize arms races is the reaction process model developed by the English pacifist physicist-mathematician Lewis Fry Richardson, whose ideas were posthumously given currency among American political scientists after 1957.[87] Using linear differential equations, Richardson sought to analyze the armaments acquisition policies of two rival parties within the framework of a mutual stimulus-response or action-reaction model.[88] He reduced the rate of change in the military budgets of rival states to the following equations:

$$dx/dt = ky - ax + g$$
$$dy/dt = lx - by + h$$

where x = the armaments of Country A; t = time; y = the armaments of Country B; k is a positive constant standing for A's perception of the menace; a is a positive constant representing "the fatigue and expenses of keeping up defenses;" g is a constant standing for A's grievances against B; and y, l, b, and h have corresponding values for Country B.[89]

Dina A. Zinnes has pointed out that Richardson's focus here is not, strictly speaking, a search for the cause of war, since he does not specifically consider wars in his models, but merely seeks to describe processes which precede and may produce some even if not all modern wars.[90] What Richardson puts forth is a purely theoretical model of the way two rival states interact in the military expenditures dimension. Country A is stimulated by B's arms accumulation, and what A does by way of reaction serves as a further stimulus to B, but each country is constrained by its own total amount of arms and the effects of an increase of armaments upon its own economy. Like all purely theoretical models, it is a highly simplified one in which the only two variables are the arms of the two sides. It omits from its scope such variables as the unique geostrategic requirements of each party, the military preparedness or vulnerability of allied countries, and whether the rivals are pursuing initiative-aggressive or reactive-defensive policies. According to Richardson, the interactive process can be either stable or unstable.[91] The following represents an "intuitive" verbal analysis of the contrast between stable and unstable arms competition. Nations, like individuals, usually behave toward others as others behave toward them. If both nations are xenophobic and mutually hostile, the reaction coefficient will be greater than one. Let us assume that each feels secure only with a 10 percent margin of superiority over the other. The accumulation of 100 units of arms on one side (A) will stimulate the other (B) to accumulate 110; this will provoke A to aim at 121, and in turn B will insist upon 133, and so on, in an indefinite escalation characteristic of an unstable system in which the acquisition lines move away from the equilibrium point. Conversely, as two parties attenuate their hostility and turn toward increased friendliness and cooperation, their reaction coefficient will be less than one, they will deescalate their rates of military expenditure, and their arms acquisition lines will converge toward a balance of power.[92]

Zinnes, who manifests considerable admiration for the pioneering research of Richardson, concedes that his basic model "is exceedingly naïve in its assumptions, and perhaps also extremely narrow in its substantive concern."[93] She justifies devoting a great amount of attention to it on the grounds that it stimulated the efforts of many others to develop extensions, modifications and refinements of mathematical arms race models and to apply Richardson's interaction processes to other fields.[94]

Richardson's basic model, it should be stressed, is more a purely theoretical construct than a hypothesis which can be empirically tested in the complex laboratory of history. The model has been criticized by Martin Patchen[95] on the grounds that it cannot explain more than a small portion of international behavior. Some of Richardson's modifications of his basic model fit the data for the military expenditures of France/Russia and Germany/Austria in the period 1909 to 1914. His equations are less neatly applicable to the period prior to World War II, when the reluctance of the Western democratic states to modernize their military establishments encouraged the antistatus quo dictatorships to increase their armament rate and to become more aggressive in their foreign policies, rather than constraining them.

The Richardson model is no less "tautological" than conventional wisdom has often been thought to be, and it possesses no more predictive power. What it tells us is that if two rivals are involved in an unbridled and constantly escalating arms race, then they are interacting in this one dimension in a tension-increasing manner, and this may indicate that they will end up at war sooner or later unless they alter their course, since arms acquisition policies usually reflect other basic disagreements. His equations cannot enable us to predict when the tensions become so great that the breaking point is reached.[96] Even the data from the period prior to World War I do not prove that the arms race caused that war, but only that it was one of the several factors which contributed to its onset.[97] To say this is not in any way, of course, to deny the important part that an arms race can play in generating a political climate of uncertainty, suspicion, anxiety, and fear in which the complex decisions for war are taken.

No simplified mathematical model can take into account the great variety of factors which affect the course of international relations and which modify action-reaction processes,[98] perhaps leading one party to change more rapidly than the other, or one to misinterpret what the other is doing and to react in a manner not in accordance with the model. This, of course, is a shortcoming not only of the Richardson model, but of all single-factor explanations. In the final analysis, the empirical data on arms races remain sketchy and ambiguous. Arms races are not easy to define. It is difficult to say how many there have been in this century. (Richardson was interested only in three—before 1914, before 1939, and after 1945.) Nor can we always measure arms races merely by reference to levels of military spending, even after correcting for economic fluctuations to obtain "constant" currency units over a period of time. A technological breakthrough might enable a country to enhance its overall military capabilities at lower costs.[99] Conversely, it is quite conceivable, in a period of steady inflation and constantly rising human power (in comparison with weapons) costs, that a nation's overall military capabilities would deteriorate despite modestly rising budgets.

Political, ideological, and strategic conditions of international relations make it necessary for many states to spend a large portion of their resources on military security—resources which under more favorable conditions could be at least partially diverted to human welfare programs. We cannot but recognize that the existence of armaments is a necessary condition of warfare, because in their total absence war could not be waged. But to say that arms are a cause of war in this sense is, as Zeigler observes, about as helpful as the conclusion that "combustible materials cause fire" would be in a fire marshal's investigation.[100] We cannot regard the existence of arms as a sufficient condition of war, and we deem it impossible to prove scientifically that an "arms race" has ever been the primary cause of an international war in the modern era, rather than the effect of other leading causes. We acknowledge that there could be *some* theoretical validity in the action-reaction hypothesis concerning arms competition, for example, in explaining the Arab and Israeli arms acquisition policies over the course of three decades (1948–1978), but even in that case both the competition and the decisions for war were interwoven with other crucial factors. We are more skeptical about the applicability of the action-reaction model to the particular historical case to which most writers currently attempt to apply it, that is, the United States-Soviet competition in nuclear weapons and delivery vehicles.

In a more recent study Albert Wohlstetter concluded that the action-reaction pattern does not provide a convincing explanation of the United States-Soviet arms competition. He denied that the United States overestimated the number of ICBMs the USSR would deploy. He found that over a nine-year period (1962–1971), fewer than 20 percent of the U.S. Defense Secretary's predictions of Soviet weapons deployment behavior proved to be overestimates, whereas more than 80 percent underestimated what they would actually do. Instead of overreacting to the Soviet military build-up, Wohlstetter maintains, the United States underreacted, reducing constant dollar expenditures on strategic weapons by two-thirds from the early 1960s to the early 1970s. Wohlstetter concludes that at least up to the mid-1970s there had not really been an "arms race" between the superpowers.[101]

In an era of sophisticated and constantly changing military technology, not every addition of a new generation of advanced weapons to a nation's deterrent forces is conducive to war. Superpower governments engage in a great deal of internal debate before deciding to deploy a new weapons system, and they are normally anxious to determine not only the effects which the deployment will have upon their military power position but also its implications for international strategic stability or instability. Take, for example, the decade-long debate which took place in the United States during the 1960s about antiballistic-missile (ABM) defense. Military strategists, arms control analysts, and policymakers argued for several years over such questions as these: Is ABM technically feasible? Would it cost more than it would be worth? Would it enhance or jeopardize strategic equilibrium? Should the United States deploy a "thin ABM defense" against China and the possibility of accidental launch or a "thick defense" against the Soviet Union? Toward the latter part of the decade the Johnson Administration began to move toward a "thin defense" posture, and the Nixon Administration later modified this and converted it into a bargaining counter for the SALT I negotiations with the USSR. By the mid-1970s, the United States had abandoned even the modest ABM deployment permitted under the SALT I agreements, although there was evidence that the fixed land-based missile component of United States strategic forces was becoming vulnerable to a Soviet preemptive attack and that at least a portion of such systems could be protected by ballistic missile defense technologies either presently available or within the realm of feasibility. One can hardly characterize the evolution of United States ABM policy from 1960 to 1975 as participation in a frantic arms race.

Pacifists and antimilitarists often condemn all efforts to distinguish between "stabilizing" and "destabilizing" weapons deployments as meaningless rationalizations for the continuation of an arms race. Yet military strategists insist upon drawing such distinctions. Western strategists, for example, have long regarded the vulnerability of missile systems as erosive of stability. (See Chapter 9 for a fuller treatment of this.) They have become concerned, therefore, about Soviet heavy missile deployments in the 1970s which have increased the vulnerability of United States land-based ICBMs and they have called for compensating actions by the United States.[102] The Soviet Union, of course, proceeding from the perspective of a different strategic doctrine, looks upon the growth of its missile power as enhancing its own deterrent capability and consequently as a stabilizing development. We might suggest that in this case it is not the "mirror image" that is dangerous but a "reverse mirror image" that makes it very difficult for the two superpowers to agree on what types of actions stabilize or destabilize.

In the final analysis, strategic stability involves political judgment, not abstract mathematical analysis. The mathematician may look at the arms budgets of two states over a period of time and conclude that they are locked in an unstable arms race. The political scientist feels compelled to introduce other considerations. Analysts who look only at the expenditures of the two superpowers may conclude that "the USA-USSR confrontation is one that lacks both stability and equilibrium and is leading toward continued increments in arms. . . ." But when the superpowers are evaluated not only against each other but as leaders of alliances whose other members spend less than they probably would if they were "on their own" for security, then "the armaments race is both stable and equilibrium-seeking" and "becomes one of control and moderation."[103] This conclusion is cited not as necessarily definitive, but as illustrative of how the broadening of one's political-strategic perspective can lead to a shift in interpreting simplified quantitative data. Whether the arms rivalry of the two superpowers will remain as controllable in the next decade as it has thus far been must await the judgment of future historians.

POWER AS DISTANCE: EQUALITY AND INEQUALITY

Singer and Small in their earlier studies on the incidence of international war (as we shall see) attached greater importance to the number of actors and alliances in the system, and to the degree of polarization within it, than to relative levels of power (or power as *distance* between two actors) and to the dynamism of shifts in power relationships. But from the standpoint of theory it is intriguing to ask which is more conducive to war—equality or inequality of power—and whether the probability of war increases or decreases as equality is approached. At first glance, one might deem it logical to assume that as two rival states move toward equality they should be able to deal with each other more fairly and even-handedly. Certainly one of the most commonly stated assumptions underlying United States-Soviet relations during the decade of the SALT negotiations has been that strategic parity is a prerequisite of stable mutual deterrence and of progress in arms limitation. The question, however, must be probed more carefully.

A. F. K. Organski was among the first to call attention to the danger that the probability of war may increase during a period of power transition.[104] Perceptible inequality of power makes it foolish for the weaker side to initiate a war while the stronger side need not be apprehensive. This is borne out by the experience of India and Pakistan following the Bangladesh War of 1971. Prior to that conflict, the two subcontinent neighbors lived in an almost constant fear of and readiness for war for a quarter century. After Pakistan's population, territory, and resources were substantially reduced and India tested a nuclear explosive device, Pakistan's resentment ran high, but little could be done to alter the situation, and both the probability and fear of an Indo-Pakistani War in the proximate future declined markedly.[105]

One of Organski's principal objections to the classical "balance of power" theory (which had some validity in an earlier period) is that it presupposes a relatively stable distribution of power among units and an ability of prudent statesmen to act in time to compensate for disturbances in the balance, for example, by entering an alliance. In the twentieth century, industrial technology permits the occurrence of rapid shifts of power which perhaps cannot be prevented. Balances are unstable because they are not durable. As power parity is approached, two rivals may become increasingly nervous about the balance and sensitive to fluctuations within it, thereby increasing the danger of war. As the challenger overtakes the erstwhile leader, its more rapid growth rate may breed an excess of self-confidence and tempt it to seek complete victory. This is what happened to Germany vis-à-vis the United States prior to World War II.[106] The converse danger is that the dominant power, viewing apprehensively the expanding capabilities of its rival, may go to war to eliminate the latter while it can.

Such causal processes cannot operate quite so simply in an era of mutual nuclear deterrence. But international relations theorists continue to pay serious attention to the problem of "power as distance" and to the question of whether the approach to power equality leads toward or away from war. Inis L. Claude has succinctly expressed the ambiguity of the situation: "If an equilibrium means that either side may lose, it also means that either side may win."[107] Michael P. Sullivan has suggested that the relationship between approaching equality may be curvilinear:

> The more equal two countries are, the greater the probability of conflict, *except* that at some point the opposite process, as suggested by Claude, begins to operate: high equality stifles aggressive tendencies because of the fifty-fifty chance of losing. . . . Gross inequality would have either low probability of conflict or low conflict; the greater the equality, however, the greater the chance of conflict and, if conflict does break out, the greater the chance of high levels of conflict. When two powers are exactly equal, however, the probability of conflict drops off and if conflict does occur, it will be low level.[108]

The foregoing constitutes an ingenious and thought-provoking effort to reconcile contradictory hypotheses, but it is not without difficulties. In our view, the process of taking a decision for war cannot be reduced to a probability based upon a mere quantitative comparison of power between rivals. Much may depend upon the attitude and outlook of the two states, the nature of their political systems, the hostility or friendship which marks their relationship, the extent to which their vital interests clash, the degree to which the dominant power accepts and accommodates its policies to the expanding power of the challenger, and so forth.[109] A timid preponderant power might lose its competitive spirit, whereas the challenger, though gaining, is still substantially weaker in terms of military power but stronger in ideology, morale, and self-confidence. Accommodation by the satisfied power may either appease the dissatisfied power, making it more patient and cooperative, or it may serve only to whet its appetite and make it more aggressive. We cannot

therefore predict the point at which the opposite process begins to operate, nor can two powers know when they are exactly equal. If two
powers which perceive themselves to be exactly equal should become
involved in conflict, it is likely either to be low level, and of short duration, or to escalate quickly to a high level of intensity.

NATIONAL GROWTH AND INTERNATIONAL VIOLENCE

Nazli Choucri and Robert C. North have contended that the processes of
national growth themselves are likely to lead to expansion, competition,
rivalry, conflict, and violence.[110] Selecting World War I as a test case,
they analyzed long-range trends over the period 1870 to 1914. They applied econometric techniques over time and across six major powers
(Britain, France, Germany, Italy, Russia, and Austria-Hungary) to a variety of aggregate data—demographic, economic, political, and military—as well as interactions among those countries. Choucri and North
focused their attention not upon such discrete events as the assassination
of the Archduke or the Russian decision to mobilize, nor on the personality of key leaders, but rather on the dynamics of population and technological growth, changes in trade and military expenditures, the conflict
of national interests, and patterns of colonial activity, alliance formation,
and violence behavior. These are the variables, say Choucri and North,
which produce changes in the international system conducive to crisis
and war. In their view, the probability of war is not significantly lowered
by good will alone, by deterrence strategy, or by détente and partial
arms limitations.[111]

Choucri and North devote a great deal of effort to explaining their
methodology, apologizing for the lack of statistical significance in many
of the correlations, and pointing out the deficiencies of data in the book
which they call "a progress report on the initial phases of our research."[112] Here we are more interested in the explanatory theory on the
basis of which they proceed, which can be summarized as follows. As
noted in Chapter 2, North and Choucri hypothesize that a growing population experiences an increasing demand for basic resources. As technology becomes more advanced, the greater will be the kinds and quantity of resources required by the society. If demands are not met, the
development of new capabilities will be sought, and if these cannot be
attained within the nation's boundaries, lateral pressures will be created
to attain them beyond. Lateral pressure may be expressed through commercial activities, the building of navies and merchant fleets, the dispatch of troops into foreign territory, the acquisition of colonial territory
or foreign markets, the establishment of military bases abroad, and in
other ways. A country is not absolutely determined to obtain satisfaction
of its needs beyond its territory. It might be content with less and mind

its own business. But most modern industrialized countries manifest strong lateral pressures in some form.[113]

The expansion of one country's lateral pressure may be acquiesced in or resisted by other countries. All lateral pressure contains a potential for international conflict. As interests grow, it is usually assumed that they require protection. This means military expenditures and an increased sense of competition or rivalry. One colonial power is likely to feel threatened each time another acquires new territory. Alliances are formed both to enhance national capabilities and to moderate conflicts of interest among some parties, even though this may arouse the suspicion of others, prompt the formation of a countervailing coalition, and contribute to an exacerbation of international conflict, as the "process of antagonizing" tends to become mutual.[114] "An increase in the political, economic, or military strength and effectiveness of one nation will tend to generate new demands in the rival nation and a disposition among its leaders to increase appropriate capabilities."[115] The study partially validates the Richardson reaction-process hypothesis, but also modifies it in certain important respects because the data show that "arms increases are sometimes better explained by domestic growth factors than by international competition."[116]

Choucri and North draw together in an interesting way historical and/or statistical data which, far from oversimplifying, illustrate the complexity and subtlety of such phenomena as the colonial rivalry of the powers, the Anglo-German naval race, the failure of diplomatic negotiating efforts to control armaments competition, military expenditures, the formation and interaction of alliances, the propensity of the powers to engage in foreign violence behavior, and the peripheral crises and wars which were the prelude to World War I. It is not possible to comment on all their findings. On the subject of alliance formation, they describe in historically realistic terms the very real dilemmas faced by Britain at the turn of the century, when she was uncertain whether to tilt toward the Triple Alliance (Germany, Austria-Hungary, and Italy) or toward the Franco-Russian Alliance. Britain, after all, had long sought to contain Russia, whom she regarded as the greatest *immediate* threat to her colonial empire and potentially the greatest *future* threat to her control of the seas. But Germany's alarmingly rapid rate of growth posed a more urgent threat to British naval supremacy. Without being too explicit, Choucri and North suggest that this is what finally motivated Britain to compose her serious differences with France and Russia. Britain's crucial choice, of course, can finally be explained most convincingly by traditional political analysis, abetted by the application of statistical methods to data which were in one way or another present in the perceptions of British policymakers at the time. Although the Choucri and North study dealt with pre-World War I competition, its general conclusions have some applicability to an era of increasing awareness of resource scarcity in which the West has become apprehensive over Soviet bloc activity in the Persian Gulf area and Africa.

The most important finding to emerge from the study is that domestic growth (measured by population density and per capita national income) is a strong determinant of national expansion, and that these are linked to military expenditures, alliances, and international violence. Such a finding, in the view of Choucri and North, has ominous implications for the conventional wisdom concerning the gap between the strong, rich nations and the poor, weak nations. "For a long time there was a widely shared assumption that by narrowing this gap through technological and economic growth, the probability of conflict and war would be lessened. This assumption now seems dubious."[117] In the end, they raise somber questions about the ability of populous societies, equipped with highly destructive military technology, to live together on a planet which now offers little room for further lateral expansion and increasingly limited opportunities for growth. If uninhibited growth and aggressive competition might lead to international violence on a massive scale, Choucri and North ask, might not the severe curtailment of growth lead just as surely to disaster?[118]

It should be obvious from the foregoing that the authors do not deem it feasible to identify in any neat manner *the* political causes of war. Historically, nations have expected wars to recur, and they have institutionalized their expectations in the form of military establishments. War in the contemporary world may be said to be a function of many things: the nature of the international system of sovereign states; the effectiveness of diplomatic-legal-organizational mechanisms for settling disputes; the clash of nationalisms and political or socioeconomic ideologies; the sentiments of pacifism and militarism in various strata of society, and the impact of various groups' attitudes and opinions upon foreign policy decision-making processes; the nature of military technology and the fears to which it gives rise among masses and elites; the pattern of international alignments and polarization; the stability or instability of the strategic balance; the quality of diplomatic communications and political rhetoric; the tendency of states to intervene in each other's affairs, usually for outcomes other than war; the concern of rival powers for preserving or enhancing prestige; the occurrence of disturbances which may so threaten the national interests of powers as to cause a crisis; the success or failure of decision-makers in managing the crisis without war; the impact of the personalities of key leaders; and so on. Not all of these factors have been treated at length in this chapter. Several are dealt with elsewhere—in the chapters on Systems, Deterrence and Arms Control, Integration and Decision-Making.

NONSTATE ACTORS AND CONFLICT

The increased interest in the role of nonstate actors has led to efforts to study their patterns of political behavior. One such effort, by Richard W. Mansbach, Yale H. Ferguson, and Donald E. Lampert, using events data, compares the conflictual and cooperative behavior of state and nonstate actors between 1948 and 1972 in three regions: the Middle East, Latin America, and Western Europe. Several broad generalizations emerged from this analysis.[119] Between 1948 and 1958 more than half of the events were cooperative and less than a third conflictual in nature; that is to say, conflict between the Soviet Union and the West, in numbers of events, was exceeded by heightened levels of cooperation in the non-communist world. In a second period, 1958 to 1967, the conflictual events were greater in number than the cooperative events, largely as a result of the diminution of bipolarity, whose effect was to increase conflict at the regional and local levels, and especially within alliance systems. In a third period, between 1967 and 1972, there was a moderate growth in cooperative events and a larger decrease in conflictual events.

The authors conclude that, in the third period, nation-states were largely responsible for the decrease in conflict, whereas intergovernmental organizations played a somewhat lesser, but still significant, role. Among their principal findings, moreover, is that "the more conflictual the behavior, the less the state-centric model can explain."[120] Thus their conclusion is that, among the actors examined in a dyadic relationship (events related to conflict or cooperation between pairs of units), intrastate nongovernmental units were more prone to violence than nation-states. Nonstate actors not only constitute a growing percentage of the dyadic groupings, but also account for a greater proportion of conflict than state actors in the global system.

TERMINATION OF WAR

Up to now, we have been primarily concerned with why and how wars begin. Once states are at war, it is important that some thought be given to controlling, limiting, deescalating, and terminating the conflict. "Limited war" has been a much debated issue in the nuclear age. Particularly controversial has been the question of whether nuclear war itself can be limited or it must inevitably escalate to the level of "all-out" mutual destruction. These questions will be discussed in Chapter 9 in connection with the strategy of deterrence. Here our immediate concern is with the winding down and ending of war.

One of the most obvious reasons why wars come to an end is that one side clearly defeats the other. If the struggle is protracted, however, and there is no decisive victory for either party, governments find themselves under pressure to respond to the growing exhaustion of their people. The war fever which characterizes the period immediately prior to and following the outbreak of war begins to subside as the enemy proves stronger than anticipated and as battle casualties mount; war fever is replaced by war weariness and a growing desire for a negotiated peace.[121]

According to Lewis A. Coser, the final decision to end a conflict usually rests more with the loser than with the winner. Magnanimity on the part of the potential victor helps to make it easier for the vanquished to submit, but until the latter is willing to acknowledge defeat at least to self, the struggle goes on. Sometimes the vanquished do not realize that they have been defeated, especially when unambiguous symbolic clues (such as the capture of a capital city) are not present and the contestants have no agreed norms for assessing their respective power positions in the struggle. In such cases, termination can be a very complex process. The leadership of the losing side may be willing to enter into peace negotiations but not acknowledge defeat, and it will try to manage the symbols in order to conceal the extent of the defeat.[122]

William T. R. Fox has lamented that international relations theorists have focused more on how to deter war than on how to control, limit, deescalate, and terminate war once it has started.[123] Fox attributed this to the fear among scholars that they might appear to confer legitimacy upon "limited wars," thus increasing the probability of their reoccurring, to a lack of interest among military strategies in the problem of the rational political control of wartime violence and to the traditional American approach to war, which under the presumed conditions of the nuclear age led to large-scale, protracted limited war in Korea and Vietnam. Fox described the internal and external structure of the Vietnam stalemate. Internally, American opinion was polarized and the government was paralyzed:

> One need not summon up the image of an anthropomorphic, monster superpower on the edge of a nervous breakdown for the analogy of approach-avoidance to have relevance. In an atmosphere of polarized immoderation—with one group calling for early termination by victory, whatever the escalation necessary, however great the cost, and however evil the byproduct in domestic and world political consequences; and a second group calling for early termination, whatever the sacrifice of war aims necessary, however humiliating the frustration and failure, and however disastrous the events which follow abandonment of the struggle—resolute pursuit of some middle way may command wholly insufficient domestic political support; it matters not how rational the in-between, moderate policy may appear in cost-benefit terms. Paradoxically, the more urgent the demands for termination by groups with diametrically opposed programs for termination, the less may be the chance

of a policy commanding sufficient domestic support which would in fact end the war.[124]

Externally, the meshing of strategies by the two parties made for stalemate. The superpower was anxious to wind down the fighting both for domestic and international political reasons, whereas the small-power belligerent was determined to outwait the opponent. It takes two to make peace, unless one side is willing to accept the ignominy of unconditional surrender or withdrawal. Since North Vietnam had the resources to continue the struggle, and believed that the longer the war dragged on, the better the peace terms it could extract, it adopted a policy of "no peace just yet."[125] Fox concludes that it is not easy to combine the objectives of minimizing costs, optimizing gains, and achieving early termination:

> It thus appears in the case of limited war that for the turn toward negotiated peace to lead to peace, enough force must still be applied to keep the military situation stable. Political control over the use of that force must be carefully exercised, however, to insure that the force not be used in ways which destroy the credibility of the peace overture.
>
> Least-cost, highest-run, earliest-termination strategies call for a continuing calculus. On any reasonable estimate, sacrifices still to be endured must not appear disproportionate to gains still to be realized. This triple objective also calls for an open negotiating stance. Only the least possible may be required of the opponent if one is determined to attract him to the bargaining table.[126]

THE DECISION TO ESCALATE

A special word is in order about the problem of escalation and the difficulty of controlling it. The term *escalation* did not appear in military literature much before 1960. The concept, however, was undoubtedly understood. Most of the wars of which we have historical knowledge were waged with some restraint. Even though World War II was a "total war," the contestants held back from using gas weapons, perhaps out of humanitarian considerations but, probably more importantly, because of the fear of retaliation.

Richard Smoke has written a definitive work in which he sums up and analyzes the earlier writing on escalation, and presents seven case studies of prenuclear-age wars in which efforts to control the action-reaction cycle succeeded or failed.[127] Smoke does not regard the escalation process as a very large number of small, graduated, almost imperceptible-steps—which could be plotted as a homogeneous, continuous curve. Following Thomas C. Schelling, he treats escalation as a step, resulting from a calculated decision, that crosses a salient threshold objectively noticeable to all parties concerned, and that thus expands or contracts the general pattern of perceived limits of conflict. Not every increment of military force amounts to escalation. The concept of saliency is crucial (e.g., extending hostilities beyond a national boundary that had marked a limit in earlier stages of the conflict, or crossing the dividing line between conventional and nuclear weapons). The act of escalation represents an effort or a tacit proposal to set new ground rules. The decision-maker who escalates hopes that the new limits will stick, but an element of uncertainty is involved, since the escalation might spark an open-ended action-reaction cycle.[128]

Both the effort to establish stable limits to a conflict and the carrying out of controlled escalations are bargaining processes. Whether or not the escalation can be kept under control depends not only upon its immediate military consequences, but also upon the framework of the conflict. "One of the ways in which escalation gets out of control—one that is not always apparent—is a seemingly careful step that activates some nation's previously latent motive or interest."[129] Asymmetries in capabilities, motivations, and interests may produce a similar effect.[130] The failure of decision-makers in one country to assess how the world looks to adversary decision-makers can lead to serious conceptual failures and the loss of escalation control.[131] In his conclusions, Smoke deals at length with the interplay between objective political-military factors and the subjective perceptions of decision-makers—perceptions of present and future reality.

> The main significance of an escalation lies in its effect on the expectations of policymakers in all the nations concerned. Escalations quickly shift the policymakers' field of expectation about the course and outcome of the war, and this will generally be more significant in subsequent decision-making than the action's direct, physical results.[132]

Smoke describes the complex problem of cognitive consistency which decision-makers encounter in trying to control escalation dynamics. Human beings in difficult and threatening situations try harder to preserve their own cognitive consistency when confronted with new information, and this makes them reluctant to modify their constructs of reality. In an environment of rising stakes and surprises, both of which may contribute to stress and anxiety, decision-makers feel pressures from three directions: (1) self-reinforcement (the need to prove that their earlier perceptions, assessments, and decisions were correct); (2) cross-reinforcement (resulting from the hostile action-reaction cycle); and (3) the tendency to simplify reality (that stems from deepening feelings of anxiety and threat, as well as from fatigue and the stress of information overload).

> As escalation continues, decision-makers' subjective universes of perceptions and images become steadily narrower. The range of expectations

tightens; fewer and fewer possibilities seem plausible. Policymakers begin to feel that the future is closing in on them. . . . The subjective future closes in faster than one anticipates it should because it is closing in for psychological, not just objective reasons.[133]

But in the final analysis, escalation can be controlled, and was in fact controlled in three of the seven cases Smoke studied. He deems it important, however, that an initial image of stable limits be established at the very beginning of the war, which is always a dramatic and dangerous event. If stability in the initial limits can lower the uncertainty, subsequent escalations, even major ones, are possible, and can be perceived as modifications of the basic pattern of a conflict under control.[134]

THE CORRELATES OF WAR

The age-old quest for an understanding of the "causes" of war has culminated in modern times in the collection of a vast amount of quantitative data on war and the myriad factors to which war may be related. Notable among the pioneering efforts in this field were the works of Pitirim A. Sorokin,[135] Quincy Wright,[136] and Lewis F. Richardson.[137] Since the early 1960s, J. David Singer and Melvin Small have built upon the earlier studies just mentioned by conducting continuous research in their Correlates of War Project.[138] Up to now, statistical techniques have produced no startling results, and few conclusive ones, useful for the development of a coherent theory of war. A survey of the findings thus far, however, is not without interest.

Initially and ultimately, Singer and Small were concerned with the "causes" of war. But they realized that the raw data available to scholars on the phenomenon of war left much to be desired. They began, therefore, by compiling an inventory of information on the frequency, magnitude, severity, and intensity of international wars in the period from the end of the Napoleonic Wars (1816) onward. It was expected that other research efforts would be able to take their data as a point of departure.

Singer and Small gathered data for international conflicts (i.e., wars between independent states recognized as members of the state system in which the total number of battle-connected deaths surpassed 1000). They also examined international conflicts between system members on the one hand and independent or colonial entities on the other hand that did not qualify for system membership at the time, and for which system-member battle deaths averaged 1000 per year. Civil wars were excluded. A total of 93 wars were identified—50 of them between system members and 44 between system members and extrasystemic entities (with one conflict cutting across both categories). They found that international war appears to be neither waxing nor waning, but that extrasystemic wars have naturally declined in frequency toward the zero point as colonial empires have been liquidated and nearly all political units have been incorporated into the state system.

Both Richardson in his analysis of deadly quarrels and Singer and Small found that as magnitude (measured in numbers of deaths) increases, frequency decreases. (This is what a traditionalist relying on conventional wisdom would expect.) But whereas Richardson had reached the conclusion that large wars are becoming more frequent than small wars in recent times, his findings were not supported by the results of the Correlates of War Project. Not surprisingly, according to Singer and Small, most of the wars in the period studied were fought by major powers—with England, France, Turkey, and Russia being the most war prone in both the interstate and extrasystemic categories. This does not necessarily mean that those countries were basically more aggressive than others, but only that "the top-ranked nations were compelled to fight often and at length either to maintain their position or to achieve it."[139] As for won-lost records, most of the major powers (with the exception of Turkey) have performed rather well. (Presumably that is why they are major powers; they are expected to win when pitted against lesser powers, as they are most of the time.) It has long been assumed that states initiate war when they expect to be victorious. Singer and Small found that the initiators did in fact prove victorious in about two-thirds of all the wars reviewed for major powers. John G. Stoessinger, however, after examining 11 major wars in the twentieth century, concluded that no nation that began the war emerged a winner.[140]

Theorists of war have often wondered whether in the life of societies war is inevitable in periodic cycles, such as a century (Arnold Toynbee) or the time needed for a new generation to forget the suffering and costs of the previous war (Lewis F. Richardson). In an early publication of partial project findings, Singer and Small wrote:

> Although cycles are not apparent when we examine the amount of war beginning in each year or time period, a discernible periodicity emerges when we focus on measures of the amount of war under way. That is, discrete wars do not necessarily come and go with regularity but with some level of interstate violence almost always present; there are distinct and periodic fluctuations in the amount of that violence.[141]

The notion that war occurs in every generation was usually thought to apply to a single society, where "forgetting the last war" might make some sense (even though policymakers and other elites are not very likely to forget). But the periodic occurrence of war levels throughout the entire international system would not seem to be explicable in terms of generational forgetting. If there is a real periodicity (and thus far the statistical evidence is not very convincing), theorists cannot yet offer any reasonable explanation. Perhaps it is related to worldwide economic cycles, of which a suggestion can be found in the thinking of Gaston Bouthoul and Jacques Ellul.[142] But then the fluctuation in the incidence of international war might just as easily be attributed to pendulum swings in the quality of education which statesmen and diplomats receive, or even to sunspot activity!

Singer and Small have also attempted to correlate the "amount of war in the international system" with the number of alliances in the system in order to determine whether alliance aggregation is a reliable predictor to war. They began with a theoretical model that might be characterized as the diplomatic equivalent of Adam Smith's "invisible hand"—a mechanism whereby the freedom of all nations to interact with each other as national interests dictate would redound to the stability and advantage of the whole international community. It would appear logical, then, that alliances, by reducing the interaction opportunities and freedom of choice of states, would increase polarization and the chances of war within the system. Under this line of reasoning, a highly polarized system should produce a high incidence of war. This is essentially the hypothesis tested by Singer and Small in a series of bivariate correlations between several alliance indicators and the magnitude, severity, and frequency of war, allowing time lags of one year, three years, and five years from the formation of the alliance to the onset of war. Over the whole period surveyed, from 1815 to 1945, they found no significant correlation. But when they divided the period into two parts—nineteenth and twentieth centuries—they found two contrary patterns. For the nineteenth century, the correlation between gross alliance aggregation and the frequency, magnitude, and severity of war was strongly negative. For the twentieth century, the same correlation was even more strongly positive—up to the end of World War II.[143]

Singer and Small, however, were unable on the basis of their data to explain why alliances appeared to be more successful in deterring war or limiting its magnitude in the nineteenth century than in the early decades of the twentieth century. Traditionalists had long realized, of course, that there was a considerable difference between international relations in the nineteenth century "Concert of Powers" and international relations in the "Century of Total War." Singer and Small can only suggest that the structural variable which they utilized—alliance aggregation—may be responsive to other properties of the international system, and that its predictive power may be a function of its interaction with these other variables.[144] Undoubtedly, a study of the two principal alliance systems in the nuclear age (after that part of the twentieth century dealt with by Singer and Small) would show a reversion to a very strong negative correlation between alliance aggregation and war—

much more significantly than in the nineteenth century if only the territorial area explicitly covered by the two major alliances be taken into account.[145]

THE CAUSES AND CONTROL OF WAR

It is clear from the foregoing that there is no single explanation of what causes wars. Prescinding from the microcosmic theories examined in the previous chapter (which are relevant to many dimensions of macrobehavior—for example, the motives of leaders, the formation of national attitudes and public opinion, the displacement of hostility to foreign targets, and the behavior of governmental decision-making units in time of crisis), macrocosmic theorists have traced the origins of war in general or specific modern wars to a great variety of factors. These include (1) nationalist rivalry, aggravated perhaps by ethnic-linguistic, religious, or ideological differences, combined with historical memories of hostility and conflict; (2) capitalist imperialism; (3) the existence or absence of alliances; (4) the dynamics of military technology and of arms races driven by the interests of military-industrial complexes; (5) the balance of power policy; (6) conflicts over territory deemed crucial to the security of two or more states; (7) the domestic insecurity of ruling elites, leading to an effort to solidify their own position and restore internal unity by diverting domestic discontents to foreign targets; (8) intervention in an internal conflict by rival foreign powers; (9) ethnocentrism and the communications warp, with the mass media stirring chauvinistic and xenophobic attitudes inside countries while inadequate communication between countries leads to misunderstanding of goals, intentions, and policies, such that defensive moves appear to be aggressive threats; (10) the absence of effective international peacekeeping machinery, resulting in the condition known as "international anarchy"; (11) the dialectic of international crisis; and (12) the inability of people to devise what William James called the "moral equivalent of war" or to escape from the tendency—as Gordon Allport put it—to institutionalize the expectation of war. The list could be extended, but it is already sufficiently impressive. Perhaps the most startling fact of all is that cases can be found to lend plausibility to every one of the aforementioned "causes."

The pluralism of causes is reflected, as one would expect, in the plurality of remedies suggested for resolving international conflicts and eliminating war. Efforts have been put forth in every age, and have been greatly intensified in the nuclear age, to find nonviolent ways of conflict resolution. Our discussion of the problem of war would not be complete without reference to these efforts.

Historically, the members of the international system have not been involved in constant warfare. Even though states have usually retained a disposition to resort to force if necessary to protect their interests, and even though war could almost always be found being waged somewhere within the system, most states have lived at peace most of the time— many of them for prolonged periods. Conflicts of interest were forever arising, but states have traditionally had at their disposal, especially since the middle of the last century, a wide spectrum of instruments for settling disputes peaceably.

These means included diplomatic negotiation, resort to "good offices," mediation or conciliation by third parties, arbitration according to agreed rules, adjudication under recognized rules of international law, the application of diplomatic or economic sanctions (such as recall of an envoy, severance of diplomatic relations, or trade embargo), and the show or threat of force (e.g., a display of naval power) designed to make its actual use unnecessary. But war always remained the *ultima ratio* of foreign policy. As William D. Coplin has observed, all of the instruments of leverage available to governments for international bargaining purposes along the continuum from negotiation to war depended in the final analysis upon the relative distribution of war-waging capabilities among states.[146] Moreover, international law itself confirmed the acceptability and legality of war as a normal tool with which a state could vindicate a violation of its rights after peaceful remedies had been exhausted to no avail. This assumption concerning the legal permissibility of a state to initiate offensive warfare under certain circumstances began to be questioned only in this century as efforts were made to prohibit the nondefensive use of force by states through adopting new legal norms or to deter such use of force through the collective action of states in international organizations.[147]

Both international law and international organization have played an integrating function within the global system, and have proven their utility in the peaceful settlement of disputes when the states involved, especially more powerful states, have favored such settlement. International law is generally regarded as "true law," but it is acknowledged to be weak law because it is often vague in content, because it lacks authoritative bodies for lawmaking and law enforcement, and because actors regard themselves as bound only by those rules to which they have given their consent and only in cases which they have agreed to submit for adjudication. States normally prefer to conform to international legal norms because they find it in their interest to do so and to maintain their reputation as law-abiding members of international society; but when their vital interests are at stake, they are usually reluctant to accept a judicial judgment unless compelled to do so by political, economic, or military *force majeure.*[148]

Aside from the traditional reluctance of sovereign states to accept international law as binding upon them (except when they perceive it to be in their interest to do so), note should be taken of two additional and serious difficulties which continue to plague international law in the closing quarter of the century. Largely a product of Western culture and the Western state system, international law in both its form and content has been roundly criticized, and at least partially rejected, by Marxists who view it as the legal instrument of capitalist imperialism and by non-Western excolonial peoples who regard it as part of a culturally alien and economically oppressive system from which they seek liberation. Elites in both types of societies place heavy emphasis upon such concepts as self-determination, nonintervention, resistance to all "infringements upon sovereignty," the invalidity of "unequal treaties" imposed during the period of colonial imperialism, and the right to expropriate foreign investments without satisfactory compensation under the traditional "international standard." Yet most Communist and many non-Western states, while remaining opposed or extremely cool to the cultural, philosophical, and economic assumptions of traditional Western international law, manage to tolerate and accommodate themselves to selected aspects of that law which meet their needs, even though they may remain determined gradually to replace its "Western" and "capitalist" elements with "non-Western" and "socialist" values.[149]

As to the degree of international legal consensus which now exists, extremist views are to be avoided. Oscar J. Lissitzyn has given a fair assessment:

> The absolute dichotomy between the presence and absence of worldwide agreement on values is false. In the world community, as in national societies, there is a broad spectrum of values and of degrees of consensus on them. A large measure of agreement on values does, of course, strengthen the cohesiveness of a community and the efficacy of its legal order. But it is not a question of all or nothing.
>
> A black-and-white contrast between a world in which common ideological values prevail and in which peace rests securely on one hand, and a world in which lawlessness and naked force rule, on the other, is out of place here. These are but nonexistent extremes of a continuum in which, as history suggests, international law will play varying roles in different periods. . . .[150]

It is too pessimistic to say that there can be no substantial development of international law before the world achieves a homogenization of cultural, ethical, and political values. If that is ever to be achieved, it may lie in the distant future. During the past few decades, some modest progress has been made in the development, by negotiated convention, of international law in specific areas—the law of diplomatic relations, of the seas, of outer space, of treaties, and so forth. Many of the issues over which cultural and ideological disagreements prevail pertain to the divergence of interests between industrialized and less developed countries, or between Marxist and market economy systems. The inability of the global system to arrive at a consensus over questions of violent conflict (such as the definition of aggression or the best way to deal with terrorism) reflects the cultural and ideological divisions of the world, as well as sharply divergent attitudes over the utility of violence as a method of settling conflicts. But as technological developments make interstate military violence increasingly costly and dangerous, both economically and politically, it is possible that states might strive to rise above cultural and ideological differences for the purpose of controlling and limiting socially destructive violence at the interstate level.

The United Nations has made a significant contribution to international universalist integration in many functional dimensions—intellectual, economic, social, cultural, legal-diplomatic, and political. On occasion it has succeeded, through timely debate, mediation, conciliation, or coordinating international military intervention, in contributing toward the localization, containment, postponement, termination, or resolution of some international conflicts under conditions conducive to the successes of "preventive diplomacy."[151] United Nations police forces consisting entirely of units assembled from middle and smaller powers have played a useful role at times in a number of conflicts.[152] But the United Nations has not been able to make any decisive contribution toward the management or resolution of conflicts involving the vital interests of the great powers.[153] Conflicts of this type require action, negotiation, and adjustment by the principal parties. Furthermore, the most significant international agreements between the Soviet Union and China on the one hand and the principal Western states on the other hand have been reached through bilateral negotiations, not within the context of UN diplomacy.

Recent decades have witnessed a rapid expansion of the fields of "conflict resolution" and "peace research." Some theorists look upon these as relatively new areas of interdisciplinary investigation in universities, private institutes, and governmental agencies. But we should keep in mind that several of the older branches of international law and international peacekeeping organizations certainly qualify as "peace research." Many theorists of deterrence and arms control would claim to be engaged in peace research no less than theorists of general disarmament and world federalism. The terms *conflict resolution* and *peace research* have come to encompass studies in functional integration, international economic development, the formation of national attitudes, cross-cultural understanding, the language of conflict, the social structure of conflict, distinctions between various forms of violence (physical and psychological, personal and structural, manifest and latent, etc.), the uses of game theory and simulation, theories of arms races and the causation of war, the psychology of leaders, the study of images and perceptions, the behavior of decision-makers under conditions of crisis, and so on.[154]

Conflict resolution theorists stress the importance of scientifically analyzing the structure, the parties, and the issues in conflict.[155] Accurate analysis itself, they believe, can contribute toward a resolution of conflict. Conflict can be conceptualized in terms of social organization and structure, patterns of interaction (e.g., escalation and deescalation), modes of violence employed, the values of the parties in conflict (both the values declared and the values actually pursued), changes in the hierarchy of values in the midst of conflict, the tendency for the range of threatened values to become more specific or more diffuse, the degree of incompatibility of goals, the genesis of conflict, the perceptions of symmetric and asymmetric perceptions among the conflict parties, symmetries as to power potential and loyalties, and the way in which the conflict is terminated.[156] Roger Fisher several years ago suggested that conflict might best be handled by "fractionating" it, that is, separating conflict issues into their smallest components and dealing with them one at a time to reduce the risks of war.[157]

John W. Burton has advanced the view that conflict should be looked upon as essentially subjective, in contrast to the older view that it is objective—a view, he says, which is based on an assumption deeply ingrained in political thought that there is a fixed amount of satisfaction to be shared in a given situation and that what A gains B must lose.[158] The difference between the zero sum game and the nonzero sum game is a subject which has evoked a considerable literature in international relations, strategy, and bargaining. (See Chapter 12.) Burton argues that a conflict which at first sight appears to be waged over "objective" differences of interest can be transformed into one with a positive outcome for the combative parties once they "reperceive" each other and discover opportunities for peaceful functional cooperation from which they will both benefit. Those who would mediate in a conflict must help the parties to change their goals as the risks and costs of trying to attain their original goals through conflict are seen to rise.[159] Since political conflicts usually have different parties at different levels of organization, agreements reached at government levels will not necessarily solve conflicts at localized levels of organization. Burton is convinced that the mediator, instead of presenting his or her own plan to resolve the conflict, should draw the solution from the parties themselves. Moreover, he says, parties to a dispute should not be expected to compromise, because compromise settlements often leave the underlying conflict issues unresolved and both parties basically discontented. Conflict resolution, says Burton, should be a problem-solving rather than a bargaining exercise.[160]

In conclusion, all theories which look to the entire elimination of war from human affairs presuppose profound changes in the behavior of large collectivities. All proposed changes are based, either implicitly or explicitly, on assumptions with regard to the causes of war. Inasmuch as social scientists cannot agree on the causes of war, it is not surprising that there is no consensus conserving the foundations on which humanity can build genuine peace.

The governments of the world will undoubtedly continue, in the future as in the past, to seek some values (such as stability and peaceful resolution of conflict) whose benefits can be shared by many states, and some values (such as an improvement in relative influence or power) whose benefits can accrue to only a limited number of states. Evan Luard has referred to the former values as additive and to the latter as subtractive. States will, he notes, continue to mix cooperative with competitive behavior, alternating between concessions and coercion. Luard hopes that over time there might be a slow increase of concessive rather than coercive attitudes in the international system, owing to the increase in knowledge and awareness brought about by the development of communications. "Awareness brings . . . both greater realism concerning the difficulties and costs of coercive action, and greater recognition of the rights and desires of other states." "In general," he concludes, "governments will be more affected by these developments than their populations . . . and more conscious than they are of the value of concessive rather than coercive policies."[161] Several analysts would argue with this, but not with the underlying assumption that it is governments, not the people and not other institutions and groups, that take the crucial decisions for war and peace.

Notes

1. See Georg Simmel, *Conflict,* trans. Kurt H. Wolff, in *Conflict and the Web of Group-Affiliations* (New York: The Free Press, 1964); Lewis A. Coser, *The Functions of Social Conflict* (New York: The Free Press, 1964), pp. 15–38; Jessie Bernard, "Parties and Issues in Conflict," *Journal of Conflict Resolution,* I (March 1957); and Ralf Dahrendorf, trans. Anatol Rapoport, "Toward a Theory of Social Conflict," ibid, II (June 1958). Dahrendorf, a German sociologist, argues that when certain social-structural arrangements are given, conflict is bound to arise. He traces the responsibility for the shift of emphasis within the field of sociology from social conflict to social stability to Talcott Parsons and his structural-functional approach to the study of society. (For a discussion of the work of Parsons and structural-functionalism, see Chapter 4.) This approach contains the following implicit postulates: (1) Every society is a relatively persisting configuration of elements. (2) Every society is a well-integrated configuration of elements. (3) Every element in a society contributes to its functioning. (4) Every society rests on the consensus of its members. Dahrendorf thinks that this social equilibrium conception of society is not compatible with the serious study of conflict. The foregoing postulates not only fail to explain change and conflict, but they exclude these phenomena altogether. When confronted with instances of conflict, the "structural-functional" school treats them as abnormal, deviant, pathological. In contrast to

the "structural-functional" theory, Dahrendorf offers four different postulates: (1) Every society is subjected at every moment to change; change is ubiquitous. (2) Every society experiences at every moment social conflict; conflict is ubiquitous. (3) Every element in a society contributes to its change. (4) Every society rests on constraint of some of its members by others. Dahrendorf's postulates are not presented to replace the Parsonian view, but rather to complement it. The two organic models together, he suggests, would exhaust social reality, and a synthesis of the two would supply us with a complete theory of society in both its enduring and its changing aspects. Dahrendorf, op. cit., especially pp. 173–175. See also Irving Louis Horowitz, "Consensus, Conflict and Cooperation: A Sociological Inventory," *Special Forces*, XLI (December 1962), 177–188. Horowitz insists that conflict as well as consensus must be treated within the framework of social structure, not as a deviation from it.

2. Georg Simmel, op. cit., pp. 16–20.

3. R. L. Holloway, Jr., op. cit., p. 42. Holloway is a physical anthropologist who specializes in the evolution of the brain and human behavior.

4. Lewis A. Coser, op. cit., p. 8. Western theorists as far apart in their fundamental premises as Saint Augustine and Karl Marx regarded conflict as the motor of social change. See Robert A. Nisbet, *Social Change and History: Aspects of the Western Theory of Development* (New York: Oxford University Press, 1969), pp. 76–90.

5. William Graham Sumner, *War and Other Essays* (New Haven: Yale University Press, 1911), excerpted in Bramson and Goethals, eds., *War: Studies from Psychology, Sociology, Anthropology*, Rev. ed., (New York: Basic Books, 1968), pp. 210–212.

6. William James, "The Moral Equivalent of War," in ibid., p. 23.

7. Richard N. Rosecrance, *Action and Reaction in World Politics* (Boston: Little, Brown, 1963), pp. 255, 304–305.

8. Clyde Kluckhohn, *Mirror for Man: A Survey of Human Behavior and Social Attitudes* (Greenwich, Conn.: Fawcett World Library, 1960), p. 173. See also Stephen Withey and Daniel Katz, "The Social Psychology of Human Conflict," in Elton B. McNeil, ed., *The Nature of Human Conflict* (Englewood Cliffs, N.J.: Prentice-Hall, 1965), p. 81; and Nicholas S. Timasheff, *War and Revolution* (New York: Sheed and Ward, 1965), chap. 5.

9. Robert F. Murphy, "Intergroup Hostility and Social Cohesion," reprinted from *American Anthropologist*, LIX, No. 6 (1957), 1018–1035, in Zawodny, ed., op. cit., pp. 602–603. R. F. Maher has reached a similar conclusion from his study of tribes in New Guinea. See Robert A. LeVine, "Socialization, Social Structure and Intersocietal Images," Kelman, ed., op. cit., p. 47.

10. Elton B. McNeil, "The Nature of Aggression," in McNeil, ed., op. cit., p. 37.

11. Georg Simmel, op. cit., p. 93. See also pp. 88–89. M. Mulder and A. Stemerding have shown that a group faced with a threat becomes cohesive and highly tolerant of strong leadership. "Threat, Attraction to Group, and Need for Strong Leadership," *Human Relations*, XVI (1963), 317–334.

12. Geoffrey Blainey, *The Causes of War* (New York: The Free Press, 1973), pp. 71–86.

13. Rudolph J. Rummel, "Dimensions of Conflict Behavior Within and Between Nations," *General Systems Yearbook*, VIII (1963), 24. See also by the same author, "Testing Some Possible Predictors of Conflict Behavior Within and Between Nations," *Peace Research Society, Papers 1, Chicago Conference, 1963*.

14. Raymond Tanter, "Dimensions of Conflict Behavior Within and Between Nations, 1958–1960," *Journal of Conflict Resolution*, X (March 1966), 65–73.

15. Raymond Tanter, "International War and Domestic Turmoil: Some Contempo-

rary Evidence," in *Violence in America: Historical and Comparative Perspectives,*
A Report to the National Commission on the Causes and Prevention of Violence,
June 1969, prepared under the direction of Hugh Davis Graham and Ted Robert
Gurr (New York: New American Library, 1969). See also Ted Robert Gurr, *Why
Men Rebel* (Princeton: Princeton University Press, 1970).

16. Jonathan Wilkenfeld, "Domestic and Foreign Conflict Behavior of Nations," in
William D. Coplin and Charles W. Kegley, Jr., eds., *Analyzing International Relations: A Multimethod Introduction* (New York: Praeger, 1975), pp. 96–112,
quoted on p. 96.

17. Philip M. Gregg and Arthur S. Banks, "Dimensions of Political System: Factor
Analysis of *A Cross-Polity Survey,*" *American Political Science Review,* LIX (September 1965), 602–614.

18. Jonathan Wilkenfeld, op. cit., pp. 97–99, 106–107.

19. See Herbert S. Dinerstein, "The Transformation of Alliance Systems," *American
Political Science Review,* LIX (September 1965), 589–601. Emile Benoit says that
membership in a common defense alliance against an agreed potential aggressor is
a powerful integrating factor, and "the reduced fear of such external aggression
seems to have been a major factor in slowing down the European Economic Community . . . not only weakening the international alliance, but encouraging conflicts, internal dissidence, and secessionist movements within individual countries." "Kenneth Boulding as Socio-Political Theorist," *Journal of Conflict
Resolution,* XXI (September 1977), 557.

20. Clyde Kluckhohn, op. cit., p. 48. According to Alexander Lesser, the concept of
war does not appear among Andaman Islanders, aboriginal Australians, Mission
Indians, Arunta, Western Shishoni, Semang, and Todas. "War and the State," in
Morton Fried and others, *War: The Anthropology of Armed Conflict and Aggression* (Garden City, N.Y.: Natural History Press, 1968), p. 94. In contrast, the Yanomamo who live along the Orinoco River in Venezuela and Brazil believe that
humans are inherently fierce and warlike. Their entire culture is geared to the development of belligerence—threats, shouting, duels, wifebeating, a strong preference for male children, and encouraging the young to strike their elders. Napoleon
A. Chagnon, "Yanomamo Social Organization and Warfare," ibid., pp. 109–159,
especially pp. 124–133.

21. Lewis F. Richardson showed that between 1820 and 1945, the number of foreign
wars with more than 7000 war dead correlated with the number of bordering
neighbors for 33 countries studied. *Statistics of Deadly Quarrels* (Pittsburgh, Pa.:
Boxwood Press, 1960), p. 176.

22. See Robert Redfield, "Primitive Law," in Paul Bohannan, ed., *Law and Warfare:
Studies in the Anthropology of Conflict,* American Museum Sourcebooks in Anthropology (Garden City, N.Y.: Natural History Press, 1967), pp. 3–24.

23. Andrew P. Vayda, "Hypotheses About Functions of War," in Murphy et al, eds.,
op. cit., pp 85–89. According to J. P. Johansen, the Maoris of New Zealand sometimes resolved intragroup tensions by having a member of the tribe commit an act
of violence against another tribe, thereby provoking a retaliation which would
reestablish group unity. Cited by Andrew P. Vayda, "Maori Warfare," in Paul Bohannan, op. cit., p. 380.

24. See, for example, Kaj Birket-Smith, *Primitive Man and His Ways* (New York: New
American Library, 1963), pp. 67 and 195.

25. Anthony F. C. Wallace has observed that for the Iroquois the symbolically arousing stimulus that preceded mobilization for war was a report that a kinsman had
been slain and a survivor was calling for revenge. "Psychological Preparations for
War," in Murphy et al., pp. 175–176.

26. Andrew P. Vayda, op. cit., pp. 89–91.
27. Andrew P. Vayda, "Primitive Warfare," in D. Sills, ed., *International Encyclopaedia of the Social Sciences*, XVI, p. 468.
28. Bronislaw Malinowski, "An Anthropological Analysis of War," in Bramson and Goethals, eds., op. cit., p. 247.
29. Margaret Mead, "Warfare Is Only an Invention, Not a Biological Necessity," in Bramson and Goethals, eds., ibid., pp. 269–274.
30. William Graham Sumner, "War," reprinted from *War and Other Essays* (1911) in Bramson and Goethals, eds., ibid., p. 209.
31. Bronislaw Malinowski, op. cit., pp. 255 and 260.
32. Ibid., p. 260. David Bidney has criticized Malinowski for a too rigid adherence to the view that war played no significant part in the beginnings of mankind. *Theoretical Anthropology* (New York: Schocken, 1967), pp. 231–232.
33. Margaret Mead and Rhoda Metraux, "The Anthropology of Human Conflict," in McNeil, ed., *The Nature of Human Conflict*, op. cit., p. 122.
34. Ibid., p. 128.
35. Clyde Kluckhohn, op. cit., p. 213.
36. Not all social psychologists and political scientists have dismissed the notion of national character. See Alex Inkeles, "National Character and Modern Political Systems," in Francis L. Hsu, ed., *Psychological Anthropology: Approaches to Culture and Personality* (Homewood, Ill.: Dorsey, 1961), pp. 171–202. "National character refers to relatively enduring personality characteristics and patterns that are modal among the adult members of a society." Ibid., p. 172. He admits the many methodological and conceptual problems involved, but argues that it is possible to distinguish those national characters which are democratic from those which are authoritarian, dictatorial, or totalitarian and to measure the differences with scientific validity by reference to such factors as values about the self, attitudes toward leaders and authority, and orientation toward outsiders, especially those outsiders whose values differ. See also Kenneth W. Terhune, "From National Character to National Behavior: A Reformulation," *Journal of Conflict Resolution*, XIV (June 1970), 202–263.
37. Otto Klineberg, op. cit., p. 95; Frank, op. cit., p. 104.
38. David Bidney, op. cit., pp. 361–362.
39. See Lewis Mumford, *Technics and Civilization* (New York: Harcourt Brace Jovanovich, 1934); John U. Nef. *War and Human Progress: An Essay in the Rise of Industrial Civilization* (New York: Norton, 1968).
40. Georg Simmel, op. cit., pp. 43–48; Coser, op. cit., pp. 67–72.
41. Mark N. Hagopian, *The Phenomenon of Revolution* (New York: Dodd, Mead, 1974), p. 1. See chap. 1, "What Revolution Is Not." Other works worth consulting include: Chalmers Johnson, *Revolutionary Change* (Boston: Little, Brown, 1966); Carl Leiden and Karl M. Schmitt, *The Politics of Violence: Revolution in the Modern World* (Englewood Cliffs: N.J.: Prentice-Hall, 1968); Peter Calvert, *Revolution* (New York: Praeger, 1970); Jacques Ellul, *Autopsy of Revolution* (New York: Knopf, 1971); James C. Davies, ed., *Why Men Revolt and Why?* (New York: The Free Press, 1971); John Dunn, *Modern Revolutions—An Introduction to the Analysis of a Political Phenomenon* (Cambridge: Cambridge University Press, 1972); Thomas H. Greene, *Comparative Revolutionary Movements* (Englewood Cliffs: N.J.: Prentice-Hall, 1974); A. S. Cohan, *Theories of Revolution* (London: Nelson, 1975); David Wilkinson, *Revolutionary Civil War* (Palo Alto, Calif: Page-Ficklin, 1975); Mostafa Rejai, *The Comparative Study of Revolutionary Strategy* (New York: McKay, 1977); Anthony Burton, *Revolutionary Violence: The Theories* (New York: Crane, Russak, 1978).
42. Hannah Arendt, *On Revolution* (New York: Viking, 1965), p. 21. See also Robert

Blakey and Clifford Paynton, *Revolution and the Revolutionary Ideal* (Cambridge, Mass.: Schenkman, 1976).

43. Frank E. Manuel, "Toward a Psychological History of Utopias," *Daedalus*, XCIV (Spring 1965), especially pp. 303–309; Karl Mannheim, trans. Louis Wirth and Edward A. Shils, *Ideology and Utopia: An Introduction to the Sociology of Knowledge* (New York: Harcourt Brace Jovanovich [Harvest Books], 1964).

44. James H. Meisel, *Counterrevolution: How Revolutions Die* (New York: Atherton, 1966), pp. 3–16, 209–220. Peter A. R. Calvert warns against the assumption that there is an intrinsic correction between revolution and significant social change. "Revolution: The Politics of Violence," *Political Studies*, V (February 1967), 3.

45. See Crane Brinton, *Anatomy of Revolution* (New York: Norton, 1938). The praise came from James C. Davies, "The Circumstances and Causes of Revolution: A Review," *Journal of Conflict Resolution*, XI (June 1967), 248. For other pre-World War II theories of revolution, see Lyford P. Edwards, *The Natural History of Revolution* (Chicago: University of Chicago Press, 1927); and George Pettee, *The Process of Revolution* (New York: Harper & Row, 1938).

46. Ted Robert Gurr, "Psychological Factors in Civil Violence," *World Politics*, XX (January 1968), 252–253. He identified the frustration-aggression mechanism as "the primary source of the human capacity for violence," in *Why Men Rebel* (Princeton: Princeton University Press, 1970), p. 36, and noted that revolutions occur when discontents have been politicized. Ibid., p. 12.

47. James C. Davies, "Toward a Theory of Revolution," *American Sociological Review*, XXVII (February 1962), 7. The study to which Davies refers is B. Zawadzki and P. F. Lazarsfeld, "The Psychological Consequences of Unemployment," *Journal of Social Psychology*, VI (May 1935), 224–251. See also Ancel Keys et al., *The Biology of Human Starvation* (Minneapolis: University of Minnesota Press, 1950). Robert C. Stauffer, following Ancel Keys, James C. Davies, and others, notes that recurring and prolonged semistarvation produces attitudinal changes in the direction of irritability and apathy. Irritability often leads to increased individual aggressiveness and anomic violence, while apathy leads to modes of withdrawal and passivity which undermine the basis of political community but which preclude concerted revolutionary action against the political system because of the necessity of channeling human energy to the task of sheer survival. "The Biopolitics of Underdevelopment," *Comparative Political Studies*, 2 (October 1969), 364–365. Mark Hagopian has made a similar point in contrasting Marx's "misery theory" of revolution with de Tocqueville's "prosperity theory." *The Phenomenon of Revolution* (New York: Dodd, Mead, 1974), p. 171.

48. James N. Rosenau, ed., *International Aspects of Civil Strife* (Princeton: Princeton University Press, 1964), editor's Introduction, p. 5.

49. Arnold Feldman, "Violence and Volatility: The Likelihood of Revolution," in Harry Eckstein, ed., *Internal War: Problems and Approaches* (New York: The Free Press, 1964), p. 119.

50. Manfred Halpern, *The Politics of Social Change in the Middle East and North Africa* (Princeton: Princeton University Press, 1963), p. 93; See also P. J. Vatikiotis, ed., *Revolution in the Middle East and Other Case Studies* (Totowa, N.J.: Rowman and Littlefield, 1972); and Gerard Chaliand, *Revolution in the Third World* (New York: Viking, 1977).

51. Crane Brinton, *Anatomy of Revolution*, op. cit., p. 115. On this point see also Vernon Van Dyke, *International Politics*, 2nd ed. (New York: Appleton, 1966), p. 327.

52. Mancur Olson, Jr., has shown how rapid economic growth loosens the class and caste ties that bind people to the social order, and how a country's economic growth can significantly increase the number of people who perceive, often cor-

rectly, that their standard of living is declining, even though per capita income figures may be rising. "Rapid Growth as a Destabilizing Force," *The Journal of Economic History,* 23 (December 1963), 529–552. He concludes that "rapid economic growth, far from being the source of domestic tranquility it is sometimes supposed to be, is rather a disruptive and destabilizing force that leads to political instability." Ibid., p. 552.

53. James C. Davies, "Toward a Theory of Revolution," p. 6.

54. Ivo K. and Rosalind L. Feierabend, "Aggressive Behaviors Within Polities, 1948–1962: A Cross-National Study," *Journal of Conflict Resolution,* X (September 1966), 250–256. For a critical analysis of efforts to explain collective violence mainly by reference to "relative deprivation" (in the works of James Davies, Ted Robert Gurr and I. K. and R. L. Feierabend, see David Snyder, "Collective Violence: A Research Agenda and Some Strategic Considerations," *Journal of Conflict Resolution,* Vol. 22 (September 1978), esp. pp. 501–504.

55. Ibid., p. 257.

56. Ferdinand Tonnies, *Community and Society—Gemeinschaft und Gesellschaft,* Charles P. Loomis, trans. and ed. (East Lansing: Michigan State University Press, 1957).

57. Edward A. Shils, "The Intellectuals in the Political Development of the New States," *World Politics,* XII (April 1960), 329–368. See also Robert Waelder, "Protest and Revolution Against Western Societies," in Morton A. Kaplan, ed., *The Revolution in World Politics* (New York: Wiley, 1962).

58. Only the more important works can be cited here: Daniel Lerner, *The Passing of Traditional Society* (New York: The Free Press, 1958); Gabriel A. Almond and James S. Coleman, eds., *The Politics Of Developing Areas* (Princeton: Princeton University Press, 1960); David E. Apter, *The Politics of Modernization* (Chicago: University of Chicago Press, 1965); Lucian W. Pye, *Aspects of Political Development* (Boston: Little, Brown, 1966); Samuel P. Huntington, *Political Order in Changing Societies* (New Haven: Yale University Press, 1968); Jason L. Finkle and Richard W. Gable, *Political Development and Social Change* (New York: Wiley, 1968); Robert Gamer, *The Developing Nations: A Comparative Perspective* (Boston: Allyn & Bacon, 1976); Edward L. Morse, *Modernization and the Transformation of International Relations* (New York: The Free Press, 1976).

59. Charles Tilly, *From Mobilization to Revolution* (Reading, Mass.: Addison-Wesley, 1978), chap. 2.

60. Tilly notes that most theories of collective behavior in this century have embodied the Durkheimian argument in one version or another. As examples, Tilly cites Chalmers Johnson, *Revolutionary Change,* and Samuel P. Huntington, *Political Order in Changing Societies* (see Notes 41 and 58).

61. Ibid., p. 50. Tilly provides a comprehensive bibliography of American and European literature on social conflict, revolution, collective action, and related subjects, pp. 307–336.

62. Lawrence Stone, "Theories of Revolution," *World Politics,* XVIII (January 1966), 168. See also Bruce Mazlish, *The Revolutionary Ascetic: Evolution of a Political Type* (New York: Basic Books, 1976).

63. Even individuals differ in their reaction. Frustration tolerance varies, and different people are frustrated by different things. Gardner Lindzey, "Frustration Tolerance, Frustration Susceptibility and Overt Disturbance," reprinted in Zawodny, op. eit., vol. I, pp. 30–34. It is known, too, that a relationship exists between class background and modes of expressing aggressiveness: poorer, less educated classes are more prone to commit physical aggression; better educated middle classes, to psychological aggression. Martin Gold, "Suicide, Homicide and the Socialization

of Aggression," in Bartlett H. Stoodley, ed., *Society and Self: A Reader in Social Psychology* (New York: Free Press, 1962), pp. 278–293.

64. In Andre Malraux's great novel about the Chinese Revolution, published in 1933, we are given a picture of the revolutionary terrorist Ch'en who conceives of himself as a sacrificial priest before he kills his victims, who despises those who do not kill, who contemplates assassination with ecstasy, and who makes terror the whole meaning of life. *Man's Fate*, trans. Haakon M. Chevalier (New York: Random House [Vintage Books], 1967), pp. 10, 64, 163, and 233. "There was a world of murder, and it held him with a kind of warmth." Ibid., p. 10. For an analysis of Malraux's novel, consult Irving Howe, *Politics and the Novel* (New York: Fawcett, 1967), pp. 209–221. For an expansive discussion of *Man's Fate* as well as of Malraux's ideological posture as novelist, revolutionary, and minister, see Davis Wilkinson, "Malraux, Revolutionist and Minister," Walter Laqueur and George L. Mosse, eds., *The Left-Wing Intellectuals Between the Wars, 1919–1939* (New York: Harper & Row [Torchbooks], 1967). For an analysis of violence as a search for significance and of the "secret love of violence" as something to be enjoyed ecstatically by the rebel, see Rollo May, op. cit., chaps. 8, 9, and 10.

65. See William G. Andrews and Uri Ra'anan, eds., *The Politics of the Coup d'Etat* (Princeton: Van Nostrand, 1969).

66. Mao Tse-tung, "On Protracted War", in *Selected Works of Mao Tse-tung* (London: Lawrence and Wishart, 1954), vol. II, pp. 188, 201–202.

67. See A. F. K. Organski, *The Stages of Political Development* (New York: Knopf, 1965), especially pp. 132–133; Karl W. Deutsch, "Social Mobilization and Political Development," *American Political Science Review*, IV (September 1961); Gil Carl Alroy, *The Involvement of Peasants in Internal Wars* (Princeton: Center of International Studies, Princeton University), 1966.

68. Robert W. McColl, "A Political Geography of Revolution: China, Vietnam and Thailand," *Journal of Conflict Resolution*, I (June 1967), 153–167.

69. "That every internal war creates a demand for foreign intervention," writes George Modelski, is "implicit in the logic of the situation." "The International Relations of Internal War," in James N. Rosenau, ed., *International Aspects of Civil Strife* (Princeton: Princeton University Press, 1964), p. 20. See Richard Little, *Intervention: External Involvement in Civil Wars* (Totowa, N.J.: Rowman and Littlefield, 1975).

70. See Karl W. Deutsch, "External Involvement in Internal War," in Harry Eckstein, ed., *Internal War*, pp. 100–110.

71. Ibid., p. 102.

72. Kenneth N. Waltz, *Man, the State and War* (New York: Columbia University Press, 1959), p. 101. Michael Haas has pointed out that governments which expand their functions without overcommitting themselves to any one such as defense and which engage in structural innovation are less likely to become involved in military operations. *International Conflict* (Indianapolis, Ind.: Bobbs-Merrill, 1974), p. 479. Democratic states are more likely to score high on functional differentiation and structural innovation.

73. Dean G. Pruitt and Richard C. Snyder, eds., *Theory and Research on the Causes of War* (Englewood Cliffs, N.J.: Prentice-Hall, 1969), pp. 4–5.

74. Quincy Wright, *A Study of War* vol. I (Chicago: University of Chicago Press, 1942), p. 17. See also vol. II, p. 739, where he says that war "has politico-technological, juroideological, socioreligions and psychoeconomic causes."

75. Karl W. Deutsch, "Quincy Wright's Contribution to the Study of War: A Preface to the Second Edition," *Journal of Conflict Resolution*, XIV (December 1970), 474–475.

76. Clyde Eagleton, *International Government*, rev. ed. (New York: Ronald, 1948), p. 393. See Quincy Wright on "The Political Utility of War," in *A Study of War*, vol. II, op. cit., pp. 853–860.

77. For a thoughtful and critical analysis of the contributions which behavioral scientists had made prior to 1959 toward the control of interstate violence, see Kenneth N. Waltz, op. cit., pp. 42–79. Waltz anticipated the conclusion reached here, namely, that the behaviorists must take into greater account the political framework of war-peace issues. See also L. L. Farrar, Jr., ed., *War: A Historical, Political and Social Study* (Santa Barbara, Calif.: ABC-Clio, 1978); Geoffrey Blainey, *op. cit.*; and Manus I. Midlarsky, *On War: Political Violence in the International System* (New York: The Free Press, 1975).

78. See Theodore Abel, "The Elements of Decision in the Pattern of War," *American Sociological Review*, VI (December 1941), 853–859.

79. "Motives and Perceptions Underlying Entry into War," Introduction to part two in Pruitt and Snyder, eds., op. cit., pp. 22–26.

80. J. David Singer, "Threat Perception and National Decision-Makers," in Pruitt and Snyder, op. cit., pp. 39–42.

81. Raymond L. Garthoff, "On Estimating and Imputing Intentions," *International Security*, 2 (Winter 1978), 22–32.

82. See Richard Pipes, "Why the Soviet Union Thinks It Could Fight and Win a Nuclear War," *Commentary*, 64 (July 1977), 21–34; Paul H. Nitze, "Deterring Our Deterrent," *Foreign Policy*, No. 25 (Winter 1976–1977), 195–210; "Soviet Strength and Fears," Report by the Center for the Study of Democratic Institutions in *World Issues* (October-November 1977), 22–30. Bernard Brodie, "The Development of Nuclear Strategy, *International Security*, 2 (Spring 1978), 65–83; and Stanley Sienkiewicz, "SALT and Soviet Nuclear Doctrine," 84–100.

83. Richard Pipes, op. cit., pp. 30–31.

84. Frederick L. Schuman, *International Politics*, 5th ed. (New York: McGraw-Hill, 1953), p. 230.

85. Hans J. Morgenthau, *Politics Among Nations: The Struggle for Power and Peace*, 4th ed. (New York: Knopf, 1967), p. 392.

86. Charles P. Schleicher, *International Relations: Cooperation and Conflict* (Englewood Cliffs, N.J.: Prentice-Hall, 1965), p. 413.

87. In 1957, Anatol Rapoport wrote a special monograph issue of *The Journal of Conflict Resolution* devoted exclusively to the work of Richardson.

88. Lewis A. Richardson's principal work on the mathematics of arms races is *Arms and Insecurity: A Mathematical Study of the Causes and Origins of War* (Pittsburgh, Pa.: Boxwood Press, 1960). In another work, *Statistics of Deadly Quarrels*, cit. *supra*, he classified deadly quarrels between states on the basis of the number of persons killed, and examined the frequency of wars between dyads of states, the length of wars and peace intervals, the pattern of war repetitions, the probability that allies and enemies group themselves similarly in subsequent wars, and the correlation between the incidence of wars and such factors as geographical proximity, population, religion and language.

89. Lewis A. Richardson, *Arms and Insecurity*, op. cit., pp. 13–15.

90. Dina A. Zinnes, *Contemporary Research in International Relations* (New York: The Free Press, 1976), p. 332. She adds that "while it is probably fair to say that an underlying assumption of the arms race models is that they provide a possible explanation for processes that appear to result in some wars, it must be admitted that Richardson does not formally link defense expenditure and the outbreak of war in any of the arms race models which he constructs." Ibid., p. 332. This is an extremely important point to keep in mind, inasmuch as so many writers who have not studied Richardson as carefully as Zinnes has, or perhaps have not even read

him, invariably cite his research as demonstrating scientifically and conclusively that arms races lead to wars.

91. The student trained in mathematics will find a complete exposition and analysis of Richardson's basic model in Zinnes, op. cit., pp. 333–369.

92. See Dina A. Zinnes, op. cit., pp. 339–354 and Kenneth Boulding, *Conflict and Defense* (New York: Harper & Row., 1962). pp. 19–40.

93. Dina A. Zinnes, op. cit., p. 369.

94. Dina A. Zinnes devotes chap. 15 to the work of Quincy Wright, Kenneth Boulding, Dean Pruitt, and several others. For the description of an effort to apply the Richardson model to arms negotiations, see P. Terrence Hopmann and Theresa C. Smith, "An Application of a Richardson Process Model: Soviet-American Interactions in the Test Ban Negotiations, 1962–1963," *Journal of Conflict Resolution*, XXI (December 1977), 701–726.

95. Martin Patchen, "Models of Cooperation and Conflict: A Critical Review," *Journal of Conflict Resolution*, XIV (September 1970), 389–408. Charles W. Ostrom, Jr., after empirically testing two models of the U.S. defense expenditure decision-making process, could not distinguish the arms race model from the organizational process model (see Chapter 11, Decision-Making Theories) so far as accuracy of forecasts was concerned. "Evaluating Alternative Foreign Policy Decision-Making Models," ibid., XXI (June 1977), 235–266.

96. John V. Gillespie, Dina A. Zinnes, and others have noted that Richardson's model contains no decision calculus. "The equations are merely a description of what people would do if they did not stop to think," "An Optimal Control Model of Arms Race," *American Political Science Review*, LXXI (March 1977), 226–244, quoted on p. 226.

97. See Note 45 in Chapter 6. Michael D. Wallace has adduced evidence to indicate that disputes preceded by arms races usually do in fact escalate to war (23 out of 28 times) while disputes not preceded by arms races hardly ever escalate to war (3 out of 71 times). "Arms Races and Escalation," *Journal of Conflict Resolution*, Vol. 23 (March 1979), 3–16.

98. When an effort is made to introduce additional variables, such as minimum acceptable arms levels and acceptable ratios of arms levels for rival states, the mathematics becomes much more complex. See William R. Caspary, "Richardson's Model of Arms Races: Description, Critique and an Alternative Model," *International Studies Quarterly*, XI (March 1967), 63–88.

99. David W. Zeigler, citing Samuel P. Huntington, writes: "In the 1860s the British replaced their wooden ships with ironclad ships in response to French innovation, yet they spent less on their navy in these years than they had in preceding ones." *War, Peace and International Politics* (Boston: Little, Brown, 1977), p. 217. In recent years, the U.S. cruise missile, deliverable by older strategic bombers, has emerged as a highly accurate and effective weapon, much cheaper and less vulnerable than a new fixed ICBM would be.

100. David W. Zeigler, op. cit., p. 217.

101. Albert Wohlstetter, "Is There a Strategic Arms Race?", *Foreign Policy*, No. 15 (Summer 1974), 3–20; and "Rivals, But No 'Race'," ibid., No. 16 (Fall 1974), 48–81. Another analyst, after studying U.S. and Soviet arms expenditures over the period 1948–1970, suggested that U.S. military budget increases could be explained in substantial measure by *changes* in U.S. military technology, while the expansion of productive capabilities at a more stable level of military technology was salient in the case of the Soviet Union. W. Ladd Hollist, "An Analysis of Arms Processes in the United States and the Soviet Union," *International Studies Quarterly*, 21 (September 1977), 503–528. Earl R. Brubaker has shown that decisions to accumulate weapons depend partly on anticipations about the military-technolog-

ical character of future war and the problem of residual stocks after the initial expenditure of weapons and subsequent strikes. "Economic Models of Arms Races," *Journal of Conflict Resolution*, XVII (June 1973), 187–205.

102. See, for example, Paul H. Nitze, "Deterring our Deterrent," *Foreign Policy*, No. 25 (Winter 1976–1977), 195–210; and Richard Burt, "Arms Control and Soviet Strategic Forces," *The Washington Review of Strategic and International Studies*, I (January 1978), 19–31.

103. Gillespie, Zinnes, et al., op. cit., 244.

104. A. F. K. Organski, *World Politics* (New York: Knopf, 1958), chap. 12; (2nd ed., 1968), chap. 14.

105. See G. S. Barghava, *India's Security in the 1980s* (London: International Institute of Strategic Studies; Adelphi Paper No. 125, Summer 1976), pp. 5–6. Erich Weede has found that overwhelming or ten-to-one preponderance is favorable to the prevention of war. "Overwhelming Preponderance as a Pacifying Condition Among Contiguous Asian Dyads, 1950–1969," *Journal of Conflict Resolution*, XX (September 1976), 395–411.

106. A. F. K. Organski, op. cit., 1958, pp. 319–320; 1968, pp. 357–359. The hypothesis that lethal international violence between pairs of contiguous states is more probable if the two states are equally powerful was substantiated in an empirical study of a recent five-year period. See David Garnham, "Power Parity and Lethal International Violence, 1969–1973," *Journal of Conflict Resolution*, XX (September 1976), 379–391.

107. Inis L. Claude, *Power and International Relations*, p. 56.

108. Michael P. Sullivan, *International Relations: Theories and Evidence* (Englewood Cliffs, N.J.: Prentice-Hall, 1976), pp. 166–167.

109. John W. Burton has argued that Japan resorted to a policy of force in the 1930s because other powers "were not prepared to make the adjustments necessary to allow Japan to develop" through access to international markets. *Peace Theory: Preconditions of Disarmament* (New York: Knopf, 1962), p. 9.

110. Nazli Choucri and Robert C. North, *Nations in Conflict: National Growth and International Violence* (San Francisco, Calif.: Freeman, 1975).

111. Ibid., p. 2.

112. Ibid., p. 278.

113. Ibid., pp. 15–17.

114. Ibid., pp. 17–22.

115. Ibid., p. 22.

116. Ibid. The authors also found that increases in the military budget of one country might be due to a rival's expansion in a nonmilitary area. See chap. 13, "Military Expenditures."

117. Ibid., p. 284.

118. Ibid., pp. 285–286. The authors point out that actions taken in one part of a system to relieve distress may produce unexpected consequences in another part, and that policies aiming at desirable short-term outcomes may often involve a high long-term price.

119. Richard W. Mansbach, Yale H. Ferguson, and Donald E. Lampert, *The Web of World Politics: NonState Actors in the Global System* (Englewood Cliffs, N.J.: Prentice-Hall, 1976). See especially chap. 11.

120. Ibid., p. 278.

121. Lewis F. Richardson had called attention to the "pacifism, war-fever, war-weariness, pacifism" cycle. He used a model similar to that employed to explain the spread and decline of epidemic diseases. "War Moods," part I, *Psychometrika*, 13 (September 1948), 147–174; part II, ibid. (December 1948), 197–232. See also Joel T. Campbell and Leila S. Cain, "Public Opinion and the Outbreak of War," *Jour-*

nal of Conflict Resolution, IX (September 1965), 318–329; Geoffrey Blainey, op. cit., Chap. 1; and Note 141 below.

122. Lewis A. Coser, "The Termination of Conflict," *The Journal of Conflict Resolution,* V (December 1961), 347–353.

123. William T. R. Fox, "The Causes of Peace and the Conditions of War," in *The Annals (How Wars End),* 392 (November 1970), 2–3.

124. Ibid., p. 8.

125. Ibid., p. 9.

126. Ibid., p. 11.

127. Richard Smoke, *War: Controlling Escalation* (Cambridge, Mass.: Harvard University Press, 1977).

128. Ibid., pp. 30–35, 241–245. Smoke concedes that saliency may be blurred by breaking up the escalatory step into many small increments, but he points out that we usually know when a saliency is being blurred.

129. Ibid., p. 235.

130. Ibid., p. 251.

131. Ibid., pp. 252–253.

132. Ibid., p. 273. In the final analysis, Smoke says, for purposes of controlling escalation it is more important to pay attention to other's expectations than to their objectives. See also Fred C. Iklé, "When the Fighting Has to Stop," *World Politics,* XIX (July 1967), 692–707.

133. Ibid., pp. 294–295.

134. Ibid., pp. 296–297.

135. Pitirim A. Sorokin, *Social and Cultural Dynamics* (New York: American Book, 1937).

136. Quincy Wright, *A Study of War* (Chicago: University of Chicago Press, 1942), 2 vols.

137. Lewis F. Richardson, *Statistics of Deadly Quarrels,* op. cit.

138. J. David Singer and Melvin Small, *The Wages of War, 1816–1965: A Statistical Handbook* (New York: Wiley, 1972).

139. Ibid., p. 287.

140. John G. Stoessinger, *Why Nations Go to War* (New York: St. Martin's, 1974), p. 219. Stoessinger agrees that initiators were usually winners in the nineteenth century. For an account of the misguided faith of many initiators of wars who believed that quick victory would be theirs. See Geoffrey Blainey, op. cit., Chap. 3, "Dreams and Delusions of a Coming War."

141. Melvin Small and J. David Singer, "Patterns in International Warfare," in *The Annals (Collective Violence),* No. 391 (September 1970), 147–149. In this article, the authors mentioned tentatively the possibility of a 20-year cycle. They also cited the work of Frank H. Denton and Warren Phillips, who had derived from the data of Wright, Sorokin, and Richardson a cycle of war every 30 years since 1680. "Some Patterns in the History of Violence," *Journal of Conflict Resolution,* XII (June 1968), 182–195. Singer and Small finally fixed the cycle at between 20 and 40 years, which would seem to be a somewhat irregular cycle. The century cycles of Arnold Toynbee and the generational cycles of Lewis F. Richardson are discussed in Geoffrey Blainey, *op. cit.,* pp. 5–9.

142. Gaston Bouthoul said that war breaks out when there is a "plethora of young men surpassing the indispensable tasks of the economy." Jacques Ellul, citing this statement, writes: "It is the multiplication of men who are excluded from working which provokes war." *The Technological Society* (New York: Random House [Vintage Books], 1964), p. 137. This, of course, is not the same as the Marxist-Leninist explanation of war as the result of imperialism.

143. J. David Singer and Melvin Small, "Alliance Aggregation and the Onset of War, 1815–1945," in J. David Singer, ed., *Quantitative International Politics*, pp. 247–286. Reprinted in J. David Singer, ed., *The Correlation of War: I Research Origins and Rationale* (New York: The Free Press, 1979), pp. 225–264.

144. Ibid., p. 285 (p. 262 in the 1979 reprint). Michael D. Wallace subsequently discovered that both alliance polarization and the switching of nations from one alliance to another show only a weak linear relationship to war. He also concluded, rather interestingly, that moderate polarization is less likely to lead to violent conflict than either extremely high or extremely low polarization. "Alliance Polarization, Cross-Cutting and International War, 1815–1964," *Journal of Conflict Resolution*, XVII (December 1973), 573–604.

145. Virtually all 22 member states of NATO and the Warsaw Pact had participated in both world wars in this century. But during the last three decades or more, none of them has been involved in a war with a member of the opposite alliance. Each alliance system has had some internal conflicts—the Greek-Turkish conflict over Cyprus, the Soviet suppression of the Hungarian uprising, and the Warsaw Pact invasion of Czechoslovakia. It should be noted, however, that several members of NATO sent forces to fight in Korea for Atlantic Alliance reasons.

146. William D. Coplin, *The Functions of International Law* (Chicago: Rand-McNally, 1966), chap. 1.

147. For treatment of the changing status of the concept of war under international law in the twentieth century, see Hans Kelsen, *Principles of International Law*, 2nd ed., revised and edited by Robert W. Tucker (New York: Holt, Rinehart and Winston, 1966), pp. 22–101. See also Julius Stone, *Legal Controls of International Conflict* (New York: Holt, Rinehart and Winston, 1959); Louis Henkin, *How Nations Behave: Law and Foreign Policy* (London: Pall Mall, 1968); Richard A. Falk, *Legal Order in a Violent World* (Princeton: Princeton University Press, 1968); Karl W. Deutsch and Stanley Hoffman, eds., *The Relevance of International Law* (Garden City, N.Y.: Doubleday, 1971). More recently, Bruce Bueno de Mesquita has taken issue with those who base the relationship between polarity and war upon decision-maker response to uncertainty. He has found that the occurrence and duration of wars in this century are closely linked to increases in the tightness of the international system. "Systemic Polarization and the Occurrence and Duration of War," *Journal of Conflict Resolution*, Vol 22 (June 1978), 241–267.

148. See Morton A. Kaplan and Nicholas de B. Katzenbach, *The Political Foundations of International Law* (New York: Wiley, 1961), especially pp. 341–342; Stanley Hoffman, "International Systems and International Law," in Klaus Knorr and Sidney Verba, eds., *The International System* (Princeton: Princeton University Press, 1961), pp. 205–237; Georg Schwarzenberger, *International Law and Order* (London: Stevens, 1971); James P. Piscatori, "The Contribution of International Law to International Relations," *International Affairs*, 217–231.

149. For fuller discussion of Marxist and non-Western attitudes toward international law see Edward McWhinney, "Soviet and Western International Law and the Cold War in the Era of Bipolarity," reprinted from *The Canadian Yearbook of International Law*, vol. 1 (1963), in Richard A. Falk and Saul H. Mendlovitz, eds., *The Strategy of World Order;* vol. 2, *International Law* (New York: World Law Fund, 1966); and Richard A. Falk, "Revolutionary Nations and the Quality of International Legal Order," in Morton A. Kaplan, ed., *The Revolution in World Politics* (New York: Wiley, 1962).

150. Oscar J. Lissitzyn, "International Law in a Divided World," *International Conciliation*, No. 542 (March 1963) p. 68.

151. See Joel Laurus, ed., *From Collective Security to Collective Diplomacy* (New York: Wiley, 1965).

152. These include the Congo, West New Guinea, Jordan, Cyprus, Kashmir, the Lebanese-Syrian border, and the Arab-Israeli conflict.

153. These include Berlin, Czechoslovakia, Hungary, Algeria, the Cuban Missile Crisis, Nigeria, Vietnam, Tibet, Bangaladesh, and the Middle East Wars of 1967 and 1973.

154. Kenneth E. Boulding, "Accomplishments and Prospects of the Peace Research Movement," *Arms Control and Disarmament, 1986*, vol. I (London: Pergamon, 1968), pp. 43–58; Johan Galtung, "Violence, Peace and Peace Research," *Journal of Peace Research*, vol. VI, No. 3 (1969), 167–191; Joan Bondurant, *Conquest of Violence: The Gandhian Philosophy of Conflict* (Berkeley, Calif.: University of California Press, 1967); Erik Erikson, *Gandhi's Truth: On the Origins of Militant Nonviolence* (New York: Norton, 1969); Elise Boulding, *Peace Research in Transition: A Symposium*, Clinton F. Fink and Elise Boulding, eds., *Journal of Conflict Resolution*, XVI (December 1972); Morton Deutsch, *The Resolution of Conflict: Constructive and Destructive Processes* (New Haven: Yale University Press, 1973); Lewis Lipsitz and Herbert M. Kritzer, "Unconventional Approaches to Conflict Resolution," *Journal of Conflict Resolution*, 19 (December 1975), 713–733.

155. Cf. Jesse Bernard, "Parties and Issues in Conflict," *Journal of Conflict Resolution*, I (June 1957), 111–121.

156. "Peace Research and the Concepts of Conflict: Summary and Criticism: Introduction by the Editors," Bengt Hoglund and Jorgen William Ulrich, eds., *Conflict Control and Conflict Resolution*, Interdisciplinary Studies from the Scandanavian Summer University, Vol. I (Copenhagen: Munksgaard; New York: Humanities Press, 1975), pp. 13–35.

157. Roger Fisher, "Fractionating Conflict," Chapter 5 of the work he edited, *International Conflict and Behavioral Science* (New York: Basic Books, 1964), p. 103. Fisher was aware that, if there is not much risk of war, a country may be interested not only in peaceful settlement but also in winning a dispute, in which case it may find the coupling of issues more advantageous. Ibid., pp. 103–104.

158. John W. Burton, "Resolution of Conflict," *International Studies Quarterly*, 16 (March 1972), pp. 9–10.

159. Ibid., pp. 10–11.

160. Ibid., p. 20.

Chapter 9
Macrocosmic Theories of Conflict:
Nuclear Deterrence and Arms Control

THE NATURE OF DETERRENCE

No single concept has dominated international strategic theory during the past two decades so much as that of nuclear deterrence. Two analysts of the subject have furnished this definition: "In its most general form, deterrence is simply the persuasion of one's opponent that the costs and/or risks of a given course of action he might take outweigh its benefits."[1] Thus broadly understood, the concept of deterrence is a very old one. One can find examples in the writings of Thucydides and Machiavelli, even though they never used the term. The balance of power system which prevailed in Europe for a century after the Napoleonic Wars was essentially a technique for the management of power in which statesmen usually sought to make war unprofitable. Deterrence was implicit in such "signaling" or warning communications as the dispatch of naval forces, the exchange of military observers, or the conclusion of alliances, but it came to mean more in the nuclear age, when it took on the character of an explicit threat of heavily damaging retaliation.[2]

The term *deterrence* did not appear in the literature of international relations or strategic theory prior to World War II, although it had been common since the latter part of the nineteenth century for legal theorists to justify punishment as a means of deterring others from criminal behavior. But since the development of nuclear weapons, wrote Bernard Brodie, "the term has acquired not only special emphasis but also a distinctive connotation."[3] Whereas in the past, a nation's military forces were expected to prepare for whatever kind of war current technology made possible, and to wage such a war for the purpose of winning it, in the nuclear age the outbreak of a war fought with nuclear weapons came to be viewed as the greatest of all catastrophes, and henceforth the adequacy of a great power's military establishment was measured by its ability to deter a general nuclear war.[4] This was to be accomplished by discouraging any potential aggressor (assuming his decision-making rationality) from thinking that the gains to be achieved by deliberately resorting to nuclear war could ever outweigh the costs of embarking upon such a course. Thus the concept of nuclear deterrence rests ultimately upon the assumption that governmental policymaking bureaucracies tend toward rational rather than irrational behavior, and normally perform the kind of cost-to-gains ratio analysis of which economic theorists have long been fond. Besides rationality, however, fear is also involved, and fear may be regarded as rational under some circumstances and irrational under others.

During the period when the United States enjoyed a monopoly of atomic weapons (1945–1949), there was no systematic strategic theory of deterrence. The U.S. policy of containment as a response to the threat of Soviet expansion did not involve any specific military doctrine for supporting the policy. True, the idea was gradually taking shape in many quarters that the very existence of atomic weapons had radically altered the character of warfare and would hopefully preclude henceforth the waging of all-out war. But the Soviets did not yet possess such weapons. Still recuperating from heavy losses in World War II, the Soviet Union hardly appeared ready to become embroiled in all-out war with the world's only nuclear power, the United States. The concept of deterrence, still only vaguely understood at the time, did not seem relevant to such localized crises as Greece, Iran, Berlin, and Czechoslovakia. It was under the impact of certain developments and perceptions in the early 1950s that Western analysts began to sharpen and refine their theories of nuclear deterrence. These developments and perceptions include the experience of "limited war" in Korea (which proved highly frustrating to a large portion of the American people); the knowledge that two powers did or would soon possess substantial arsenals of nuclear weapons (both atomic and thermonuclear); and an apprehensiveness that the Western countries, having carried out rapid military demobilization after the war, were inferior to the Communist bloc in conventional forces and probably would find it politically and economically difficult to match the Communist states at that level for a global application of the containment policy over the long haul.[5]

Since the early 1950s the theoretical debate over deterrence has focused on such questions as the following: Exactly what is a nuclear deterrent capability supposed to deter? Can the possession and threatened use of nuclear weapons be expected to deter anything beyond a deliberately planned nuclear attack—if that? Should it also be expected to deter conventional war? If so, what kinds and between what parties? Can a nuclear power, beyond discouraging an attack upon itself, extend deterrence to protect third parties (especially formal allies) against various military threats to their security? How much power is "enough" for deterrence? What are the political and military requirements of credible deterrence? How are these conditions affected by ongoing military-technological innovation? Can a nuclear deterrent effective in one era be rendered obsolete by technological breakthroughs in another? Can a nuclear deterrent force be used not only to prevent another state from carrying out a certain type of action, but also as a "compellent," that is, to force a government to do something it otherwise would not do? Can a nuclear power credibly threaten a nonnuclear state? What types of actions or threats can a nuclear capability not credibly deter? It is questions such as these that have preoccupied theorists of nuclear deterrence.

The debate over nuclear deterrence began in earnest after U.S. Secretary of State John Foster Dulles in January 1954 enunciated the doctrine known as "massive retaliation" under which the United States, instead of feeling constrained to fight an indefinite number of costly and protracted limited wars of the Korean type, without resorting to nuclear weapons, would henceforth reserve the freedom to respond to foreign aggression by retaliating instantly "by means and at places of our choosing."[6] Before analyzing the Dulles policy, it is necessary to account briefly for the origins of the American doctrine of deterrence in the early 1950s.

The Air Force had argued for strategic nuclear forces vastly superior to those of the USSR, such that the United States could "prevail" in a strategic exchange. But President Eisenhower, concerned about the economics of deterrence over the "long haul," was convinced that superiority and a counterforce capability* would be too expensive to pursue, and would undermine the idea that nuclear weapons could be relied upon as an economically efficient substitute for large conventional forces. Eisenhower therefore settled for the concept of strategic "sufficiency," which presupposed the maintenance of large, yet not unlimited, strategic forces—a posture midway between strategic superiority and minimum

---

* For definitions of *counterforce* and *countervalue* strategies, see p. 374.

deterrence. "This strategy," wrote Jerome H. Kahan, "did not merely reflect a doctrinal choice but represented a bureaucratic compromise between those who argued that America had too much strategic power and those who argued that it had too little."[7] Even with such a policy, the United States enjoyed *de facto* strategic superiority over the USSR for many years.

Within a relatively short time, the credibility of this doctrine as an effective bulwark against Communist expansion—except in the case of large-scale attack against Western Europe—was being questioned by several critics. The doctrine of "massive retaliation" implied that the United States would reply to a future Communist attack on such in-between areas as Asia, as well as on NATO territory, with nuclear strikes by the Strategic Air Command against the Soviet Union and/or China. William W. Kaufmann raised objections against such an operational policy. Although conceding that the United States possessed the capacity for carrying out long-range strikes, he questioned whether the policy met the fundamental requirements of effective deterrence when considering the problem of making intentions credible. Kaufmann gave his reasons:

> They [the Communist leaders] would see that we have the capability to implement our threat, but they would also observe that, with their own nuclear capability on the rise, our decision to use the weapons of mass destruction would necessarily come only after an agonizing appraisal of costs and risks, as well as of advantages. . . . Korea and Indochina are important symbols of our reluctance, not only to intervene in the peripheral areas, but also to expand the conflicts in which we have become engaged. . . . Finally, the state of domestic and allied opinion provides them with ample reason to believe that the doctrine would be, if not a case of outright bluff, at the very most a proposal that would still have to undergo searching and prolonged debate before becoming accepted policy.[8]

Paul Nitze, who had served earlier as Director of the Policy Planning Staff in the Department of State, criticized the Dulles pronouncement by distinguishing between a purely "declaratory policy" designed for a psychological or a political purpose and an "active policy" that lends itself realistically to implementation. Nitze contended that the Dulles doctrine contained too wide a gap between what was declared and what could be done.[9] In the mid-1950s, Western strategic analysts sought to tone down the doctrine of "massive retaliation" and reduce the gap between rhetoric and reality by speaking of "graduated deterrence." The term was not a particularly apt one, insofar as it implies that deterrence itself can be graduated. One can argue that aggression either is or is not deterred, but that the application of military force can be graduated once aggression has occurred. The exponents of graduated deterrence suggested that the Western deterrent would be more credible if the West's inferior conventional posture were to be compensated by a doctrine calling not for "massive retaliation" but for the minimum amount of nuclear force needed to discourage, repel, or defeat aggression—entailing the use of "tactical nuclear weapons" in the local theater of conflict rather than the use of "strategic nuclear weapons" against the Communist Heartland.[10] At this point, of course, the deterrence debate opened into two closely related questions which have ever since been subjects of heated controversy among strategic theorists. (1) Can nuclear war be limited? (2) Is it possible to draw such a clear theoretical distinction between "strategic" and "tactical" nuclear weapons that one could reasonably expect it to hold up in actual combat? On these issues more will be said below.

TECHNOLOGICAL INNOVATION AND DETERRENCE

The *credibility* of deterrence constituted one problem—a continuing one, largely of a political and psychological nature. A second problem, related to but theoretically and practically distinct from the first, arose out of the fact that modern weapons technology undergoes constant dynamic change. This is the technical problem of the degree of *vulnerability* or *invulnerability* of nuclear weapons. The concept of deterrence refers primarily to the holding of nuclear weapons capabilities for the purpose of confronting a potential nuclear aggressor with the threat of having to receive an "unacceptable level of damage" in a retaliatory blow even after having carried out a surprise first strike against the deterrer. (No precise quantitative tag, of course, can be placed upon the notion of "unacceptable level of retaliatory damage." A nation cannot satisfactorily define this for itself, much less for an adversary who subscribes to a very different set of values. In both democratic and dictatorial systems, such an estimate, if attempted, is likely to vary over time according to the changing attitudes of leaders and policymaking elites.) In the late 1950s, especially after the USSR launched *Sputnik*, voices were raised in warning against assuming the survivability of nuclear forces, strategic stability, and the automaticity of deterrence. In 1959, one year after the top-secret "Gaither Report" had focused the attention of U.S. government officials upon the problem, Albert Wohlstetter pointed out publicly that impending technological developments would render strategic weapons more vulnerable to surprise attack and that deterrence could be maintained only as a result of difficult defense choices pertaining to the dispersal, mobility, and protection of missile systems.[11]

Analysts argued that if a nation maintained a force of strategic bombers and missiles that were unprotected, these would be "provocative" and would invite attack because it could not be argued that they were intended to serve a purely defensive second-strike role. Since they would not survive to carry out a second strike, they would appear to have a first-strike mission and would give rise to apprehensiveness on the part of an adversary. If both sides retained unprotected (or "unhardened") strategic forces, the international situation would be characterized by a condition of "trigger-happy" nervousness which would make mutual deterrence unstable. Deterrence would become more stable if both sides moved toward secure, invulnerable, second-strike capabilities. By the mid-1960s, there was a widespread assumption among strategic analysts that the superpowers either had achieved or were moving toward such stable mutual deterrence as a result of dispersing and protecting land-based ICBMs and sea-based SLBMs, although Soviet strategists appeared much less interested than their American counterparts in a "second-strike" strategy, and the USSR did not achieve a significant degree of invulnerability of missile forces until the early 1970s.[12] (More fundamental differences in United States and Soviet strategic thought were treated in Chapter 8 and will be referred to again below.)

However, stable mutual deterrence is not something to be achieved once and for all. Weapons technology continues to advance. New developments in the fields of ballistic missile defense (BMD), multiple independently targeted reentry vehicles (MIRVs), and several other significant areas of advanced military technology have prompted writers to express concern over the possibility that the international strategic situation, viewed in objective mathematical terms, would again become unstable. Antiballistic missiles, if deployed to protect a nation's population centers, might arouse an adversary's fears that the nation was enhancing its first-strike option by preparing to blunt the retaliatory blow; MIRVs were looked upon by some as means of increasing the number, penetrability, and accuracy of warheads, and thus of threatening to eliminate a large part of a land-based ICBM force on which the ability to carry out assured destruction in retaliation depended heavily. Some analysts discerned an action-reaction relationship in superpower armaments competition: If one side insisted on deploying BMD to protect its strategic missiles, the other allegedly would probably develop MIRVs in order to compensate with augmented offensive power, and might actually overcompensate, thus prompting the first party both to speed up its BMD efforts and also eventually to develop MIRVs.[13]

The arguments of strategic theorists did not always reflect the complexity of the international environment and the superpowers' domestic environments. The United States enjoyed a wide margin of economic-technological superiority over the Soviet Union, but operated under a much more complex set of political-economic constraints and pressures in defense programming than did the Soviet Union.[14] Nor were the strategic theorists always consistent. Some of them opposed BMD on the grounds that it was technically and militarily of low effectiveness against incoming missiles, and at the same time criticized it because it would be highly destabilizing. Some argued that if the Soviets insisted on deploying their own antimissile missiles, it would be much cheaper and more effective for the United States to upgrade its offensive capabilities by deploying MIRVs; they later argued against MIRVs because they were destabilizing, would set the arms race into an upward spiral, and would not substantially improve the security of the United States or the effectiveness of the deterrent, since they would supposedly provoke the Soviet Union into a compensatory effort. There is always a spectrum of possible interpretations for every military-technological development. What some look upon as desirably stabilizing, others are bound to regard as disastrously destabilizing.[15] Judgment in this area is usually influenced more by political preference than by scientific analysis.

The strategic literature of the past two decades has abounded with esoteric technical and military terms and acronyms. Writers have distinguished between *preventive war*—premeditated to be carried out at a time of the attacker's own choosing—and *preemptive war*—resorted to by a government under the pressure of a conviction that the outbreak of nuclear war is imminent and that it must strike first rather than forfeit to the adversary the undoubted advantages of executing a disarming blow. They have also distinguished between a *countervalue* strategy (under which the adversary's population centers are targeted) and a *counterforce* strategy (which aims at destroying the adversary's strategic weapons sites and other military capabilities). A distinction, too, has often been drawn between the strategy of deterrence, which may implicity involve the threat of all-out use of nuclear weapons (or "spasm response") and the damage-limiting strategy of actually using nuclear weapons with restraint in military operations once deterrence has failed and war has broken out.[16] Whereas earlier deterrence theory was focused on assured retaliatory destruction, deterrence theorists in recent years have shown greater interest in such concepts as selective targeting and limited nuclear options, thereby provoking a debate over whether a shift to the latter type of strategic doctrine increases or decreases the possibility that nuclear weapons might actually be used someday. We shall return to this subject later in the chapter.

The student of international relations theory should be familiar with these basic concepts of nuclear strategy, and also with the various factors which enter into the calculus of deterrence and defense capabilities—multiple warheads, hardening, dispersal and mobility, warning times, effectiveness of surveillance, C^3 systems (command, control, and communication), reliability and guidance-system accuracy of missiles, the performance characteristics of different offensive and defensive types of weapons, and so forth—on which the data can be expected to change along with technology. Facts are important for the development of theory, but a framework for theoretical analysis should not be expressed in such a way that it becomes obsolete whenever new empirical data appear.

DETERRENCE AND THE BALANCE OF POWER

The concept of mutual deterrence is, in a sense, the classical notion of "balance of power" in modern guise. Many writers, including Bernard Brodie, Hedley Bull, Henry A. Kissinger, Robert Bowie, Robert Osgood, Donald G. Brennan, Thomas C. Schelling, and Herman Kahn have treated "mutual deterrence," "stable deterrence," "balanced deterrence," and "stable arms balance" in terms remarkably reminiscent of earlier treatises on the balance of power, and they reflect a keen awareness of the same difficulties which plagued the older theory. It has often been said that the balance of power does not provide a good theoretical basis for foreign policy decision-making because it is uncertain (since there are no reliable criteria for measuring comparative power) and because it is unreal (since nations, feeling uncertain, are not content to aim at achieving a balance, but seek instead a margin of superiority or a unilaterally "favorable balance of power"). Thus contemporary statesmen and their advisors have difficulty in determining whether "stable mutual deterrence" describes that which is or prescribes that which should be pursued, whether it is an objective situation best achieved automatically by the continued efforts of both sides to attain superiority in military technology or whether it is a policy requiring a cooperative conscious quest for a balanced parity by rival governments.

It has never been entirely clear whether the balance of power represents an inexorable application of the laws of nature or a norm which people can freely choose or reject; and whether it represents a mechanistic explanation of what is actually happening, something to be wrought by the workings of an "invisible hand" or something to be sought through voluntary, intelligent coordination. (For a discussion of classical theories of balance of power, see Chapter 1.) In the final analysis, a stable military equilibrium is probably the product of the interaction of technological trends and policy choices, in combination with a variety of other conscious and unconscious elements.

PSYCHOLOGICAL AND POLITICAL FACTORS
IN DETERRENCE

It has long been recognized that deterrence is as much a psychological-political concept as a military concept. It depends not only upon the objective military-technological situation, but also upon the perception and the evaluation that go on in the mind of the potential aggressor. Henry Kissinger wrote:

From the point of view of deterrence a seeming weakness will have the same consequences as an actual one. A gesture intended as a bluff but taken seriously is more useful as a deterrent than a bona fide threat interpreted as bluff. Deterrence requires a combination of power, the will to use it, and the assessment of these by the potential aggressor. Moreover, deterrence is a product of those factors and not a sum. If any one of them is zero, deterrence fails.[17]

A deterrent capability to be effective cannot be kept secret. A certain amount of knowledge about it must be communicated to the adversary. If one side deploys additional weapons or modernizes its weapons arsenal in total secrecy, then it has not really upgraded the effectiveness of its deterrent force. (For a discussion of strategic communication, see the section on Thomas C. Schelling in Chapter 12.) At any given time, of course, governmental policymakers may feel comfortable with their estimates of the existing military situation. All governments carry on intelligence-gathering activities and expect others to do likewise. But different departments and agencies of a government may disagree among themselves concerning intelligence estimates. Individuals may fear inadequate data, contradictions in the data, deliberate deception or distortion of data, and interpretations of the data which are deemed unduly optimistic or pessimistic. Although deterrence requires that some knowledge be communicated to the other side, transmitting too much intelligence might weaken the deterrent if it were to facilitate the planning of an attack. Uncertainties increase as military technology becomes more complex. But the question arises as to whether an increase in uncertainty in the calculus of possible nuclear exchange effects, resulting from the deployment of new weapons systems, is more likely to strengthen or to weaken the condition of mutual deterrence.

Robert E. Osgood has aptly described the part played by uncertainty in the delicate and fragile calculus of deterrence—a calculus which involves a process of "mutual mind reading" in an effort to second guess an opponent with respect to intentions, values assigned to an objective, estimated costs and effectiveness of certain actions, and the probability of specific interactive responses. He notes that up to a point the element of uncertainty in nuclear deterrence, taken together with the frightful implications of miscalculation, may contribute to caution and restraint, and thus to international stability. But he warns against an excessive reliance upon uncertainty:

> It leads to a kind of strategic monism that relies too heavily upon the undeviating self-restraint and low risk-taking propensities of statesmen. It ignores the provocative effect of the fearful uncertainties themselves. It overlooks the tendency of any apparently stable military balance, even one based on great uncertainties and risks, to breed unwarranted confi-

dence in the regularity and predictability of that balance, which in turn diminishes the restraints upon military action.[18]

More recently, Stanley Sienkiewicz has named uncertainty as the central problem in contemporary strategic analysis. A nuclear aggressor planning an attack does not know whether the potential victim will launch vulnerable retaliatory forces as soon as it is clear that an attack is underway. Nor can the aggressor predict how the enemy's command and control systems will function, and how well the retaliatory forces will operate. Sienkiewicz concludes that "the greater the operational uncertainty associated with the forces of both sides—particularly with those that have first-strike capabilities—the greater the crisis stability of the strategic nuclear balance."[19]

Raymond Aron has argued that "there is no deterrent in a general or abstract sense; it is a case of knowing *who* can deter *whom, from what, in what circumstances, by what means.*"[20] Thus, according to the University of Sorbonne sociologist, deterrence must always be analyzed in specific, concrete terms. What deters one government might not deter another. What succeeds in one geographical-cultural context might fail in another. For this reason Aron questioned the value of a certain type of "strategic fiction" which describes dozens of conflict situations or scenarios reduced to simplified schemes that lack historical reality. Such writing, in Aron's view, might make statesmen "overestimate the technical aspect of the diplomatic or military problems, and underestimate the importance of the psychological, moral, and political data" which are unique in each situation.[21] Ole R. Holsti, in a similar vein, points out that although the assumptions of deterrence are valid in most times and circumstances, nevertheless deterrence does presuppose rational and predictable decision processes, and therefore he warns that no system of deterrence

> . . . is likely to prove effective against a nation led by a trigger-happy paranoid, or by someone seeking personal or national self-destruction or martyrdom, or by decision makers willing to play a form of international Russian roulette, or by leaders whose information about and communication with an adversary are so incomplete that their decision-making processes are dominated by guesswork, or by those who regard the loss of most of their nation's population and resources as a reasonable cost for the achievement of foreign-policy goals.[22]

Successful deterrence involves a nonevent. It is difficult enough in the realm of human affairs to demonstrate why something did happen; it is impossible to prove conclusively why something did not happen. Can we be certain, for example, that the Cuban Missile Crisis did not lead to war because nuclear deterrence was successful in that case? Or is that all that is meant by deterrence, namely, that the thing feared (nuclear war) did not occur under circumstances where it appeared to be a distinct possibility? Was either superpower strongly motivated to go to war at the time, only to be held back by an assessment of the consequences, or were both superpowers determined throughout the series of events comprising that crisis to do their utmost to achieve their objectives without resorting to actual warfare? (The Cuban Missile Crisis is treated in detail in Chapter 11, "Decision-Making Theories.") Questions such as these can probably never be answered with finality. The strategic theory of deterrence is not quite the same as mathematics, which proceeds by an intrinsic logical necessity of its own. The analysis of deterrence always involves debatable factors of human judgment, such as political common sense based on experience (which some might call "intuition" or a "hunch"), the interplay of individual and bureaucratic rationality, and "second guessing" as well as risk-taking. In an effort to clarify what is meant by the concept, Patrick M. Morgan has drawn a useful distinction between *general* deterrence and *immediate* deterrence. General deterrence implies a policy stance of regulating an adversary relationship and balancing power over what may be a long period of time through maintainance of a satisfactory level of forces. Most of the time adversaries do not regard war as imminent or proximate. Immediate (or pure) deterrence, in contrast, implies a specific situation in which one side is seriously considering mounting an attack, whereas the other side is preparing a threat of retaliation in order to prevent it, and both sides realize what is going on.[23]

THE LEVELS OF DETERRENCE

George and Smoke have called attention to the fact that deterrence theory and practice have developed at three different levels: strategic war, limited war, and "sublimited" conflict at the lower end of the spectrum of violence. Since the mid-1950s, the deterrence of strategic war has received the greatest amount of attention in the literature and has become a separate and fairly precise discipline in itself, replete with its own specialized concepts, technical vocabulary, and methodologies—game and economic utility theories, systems analysis, and computerized war-gaming. The core concept, of course, on the basis of which the requirements of strategic deterrence are calculated, is the maintenance of an Assured Destruction capability for retaliation after a surprise attack.[24] Virtually all analysts agree that what the policy of strategic nuclear deterrence is designed primarily to deter is strategic, all-out, or large-scale nuclear war, and *perhaps* all nuclear war, however limited (although this latter point is controversial). Because strategic deterrence theory has been so much more highly developed, and so coherent and logically crisp, theorists have tended to employ strategic deterrence as a paradigm case for analyzing deterrence at lower levels.

What other types of undesirable actions or behaviors can be deterred? Does the existence of a strategic deterrent force sufficient to discourage a surprise nuclear attack automatically deter a limited conventional attack? It probably cannot do this by itself, but it is generally assumed that one nuclear superpower cannot realistically expect to inflict upon another nuclear superpower a defeat in a conventional limited war without running the grave risk that the conflict would escalate to the nuclear level. Thus strategic deterrence combined with the normal behavioral characteristics of great powers and the fear of uncontrollable escalation produces a definite inhibiting effect against the outbreak of conventional war directly embroiling the military forces of nuclear great powers. More difficult is the question—to be explored more fully— whether strategic nuclear deterrence can, in combination with other nuclear and conventional defense capabilities, be extended for the purpose of protecting formal allies or other friendly client states against the danger of either nuclear or conventional attack. John H. Herz has argued that the very same nuclear developments which have rendered modern industrial states so vulnerable to the threat of physical annihilation have also rendered the use of conventional military force "unavailable" in the direct relations between major nuclear powers and their allies.[25] Nevertheless policymakers in Western Europe and the United States have continued to worry about the requirements of credible deterrence in the NATO area, as we shall see presently.

As George and Smoke have noted, deterrence at the level of limited war and "sublimited"* conflict is much more complex than at the strategic level. Whether we consider the objectives of the players or the means at their disposal, the number of variables involved is greater. Each side is likely to be unsure of its own motivation and that of the other side to achieve various objectives. Deterrence of lower level conflict is not as readily modeled as "assured destruction." The selection of the means to be employed must be subordinated to the imperatives of escalational control and the political objectives of the conflict, as well as the placation of allies, neutrals, and domestic opinion. At lower conflict levels, deterrence is a context-dependent problem, George and Smoke conclude. "It is dependent not upon comparatively few technical variables, known with high confidence on both sides, but upon a multiple of variables, many of them partially subjective, that fluctuate over time and are highly dependent upon the context of the situation."[26]

---

* The term *sublimited conflict* was introduced in the 1960s to refer to a broad spectrum of conflict below the level of conventional war. It included insurgency, infiltration, demonstration of force, naval blockades, and similar modes of applying pressure.

Bruce M. Russett made an empirical study of 17 cases over the 1935 to 1961 period in an effort to determine under what circumstances "extended deterrence" has been successful in preventing attack upon third parties. His cases therefore stretched over both the prenuclear and the nuclear era. He examined instances in which a major power attacker had overtly threatened a "pawn" with military force and a defender had given some commitment in time to prevent the threatened attack. Admittedly, his study excluded what may be regarded as the most successful instances of deterrence—those in which the potential attackers are dissuaded even from making any overt threat against the pawn. Russett found that the enjoyment of strategic and local military superiority by the defender did not guarantee successful deterrence. More important for the credibility of deterrence was a demonstration of the economic, political, and military interdependence of defender and pawn.[27] Later, Russett and other international scholars came to the conclusion that there are serious limitations in using statistical-correlative methods in the analysis of decision-making variables in deterrence cases, because these variables are often subtle and complex, and may not be perceived by decision-makers at the time of choice in the same way as they are seen by scholars who review them later.[28]

Before leaving this general discussion of deterrence below the level of strategic nuclear conflict, we wish to make a few obvious points concerning behaviors against which a policy of nuclear deterrence cannot be expected to have effect. It should be obvious that nuclear deterrence is not relevant to conventional wars between states that lack nuclear weapons themselves or are not firmly allied to a nuclear-weapon power with a binding commitment. Nor will nuclear weapons be likely under most conceivable circumstances to deter revolution, civil war, and guerrilla insurgencies (which Communists call "wars of liberation"). The Soviet leadership has often publicly declared its willingness to support this last category of conflict. The threat of nuclear retaliation, of course, cannot possibly be brought to bear against organized international terrorism, and cannot even be realistically hurled against the government of a small nonnuclear weapon state that carries out an act of physical provocation against an aircraft or naval vessel belonging to a nuclear-weapon power. In other words, in the nuclear age weakness can become a source of bargaining strength and strength can lead to paralysis. The possession of nuclear weapons superiority cannot be employed to compel a government to take some positive action simply because the threat of nuclear weapons use for noncompliance would lack credibility. Compellance—the use of a nuclear threat to force a party to do something against its will—is more complex, more difficult to achieve, and more dangerous than deterrence.[29] The ability of the United States to force the Soviet Union to withdraw its missiles from Cuba in 1962 (see Chapter 11) may have been due to the assumption of United States strategic superiority which at that time made it plausible for the United States to consider using its local conventional superiority while continuing to deter strategic nuclear war. If that were the case, it was not the nuclear deterrent alone that persuaded the Soviet Union to pull back.

Finally, since deterrence presupposes rational decision-making, even though it proves perfectly successful in discouraging a deliberate choice for nuclear war, it has no direct relevance to the possibility of unintended acts of destructiveness, whether nuclear or conventional, resulting from technical accident, human psychic failure, misinterpretation of warning signals, the seizure and use of nuclear weapons by unauthorized persons or terrorist groups, and similar causes not flowing from the choice of governmental decision-makers. The dangers of cataclysmic destruction which are inherent in the possession of strategic deterrent forces, however, motivate responsible governments to take precautions against the occurrence of unintentional events which might escalate beyond the bounds of controllability.

NUCLEAR DETERRENCE AND FLEXIBLE RESPONSE IN EUROPE

Much of Western strategic literature during the past two decades has been concerned with the problem of credibly extending the U.S. nuclear deterrent to protect against Soviet aggression those countries of Europe allied with the United States in the North Atlantic Treaty and its integrated military organization, NATO. The members of NATO had felt compelled to rely upon United States nuclear power almost from the beginning of the alliance because of what was presumed to be a serious Soviet-Western conventional force imbalance. But generally speaking, the Western Europeans were long unwilling to bring their conventional force contributions up to the levels urged by the United States, preferring instead to rely upon deterrence. In fact, the principal reason why many Europeans were disturbed by the Kennedy Administration's desire to deemphasize "massive nuclear retaliation" and to move toward a strategy of "flexible response" and "multiple options" was that they feared that the Soviet Union might interpret this as a prelude to the withdrawal of the United States' nuclear guarantee. Western Europeans were apprehensive lest the Soviets begin to think that the Americans were so determined to avoid nuclear war in Europe that they would denuclearize the region. In the view of many European strategists, this would have been a serious mistake because it would have so altered the environment that a Soviet conventional attack, hitherto "unthinkable," might become "thinkable."

American policymakers exhorted the European allies to depend less upon immutable deterrence and to begin contemplating the realities of defense planning. But most Europeans vastly preferred to deter an unimaginable horror rather than fight an imaginable war.

There is something to be said for the positions of both the United States and the allied governments of Western Europe during the early 1960s. The advent of nuclear-tipped missiles had greatly transformed the international military situation, and it took time to adjust to the new realities. American and Soviet policymakers were well aware of certain Western military vulnerabilities in Europe, particularly in Berlin. Ideally, it would be nice to have both a high deterrent posture and a high degree of defense readiness in case deterrence fails. Indeed, the latter capability makes the failure of deterrence less likely, because it increases the cost an aggressor must be prepared to pay, aside from nuclear retaliation upon his own territory. But since military budgets are never unlimited, tradeoffs have to be made between deterrence and defense. In the transatlantic debate, the Europeans placed greater emphasis on the nuclear threat, and the Americans, on having a war-fighting capability the day after deterrence failed, if it should fail. American strategists were asking how many million American lives an American president would be willing to risk by ordering an armored column armed with tactical nuclear weapons to open up a closed corridor to Berlin, knowing that this might lead to the launching of Soviet ICBMs against American cities. The air was filled in those days with talk about a "conventional pause," "dual-capability forces," and "tactical" or "limited" nuclear war. In trying to separate nuclear from conventional forces and responses by time, geography, and command and control systems, the United States was pursuing what many American policymakers at the time considered to be the prudent and the responsible way of reducing the chances of nuclear war and increasing the options between the extreme alternatives of holocaust and surrender.

The Western Europeans were quite understandably of two minds on the subject. At times their principal fear was that if a genuine crisis came, the United States would be unwilling to defend them with nuclear weapons; at other times their fear was that it *would* be willing to do so. Their ambivalent attitude was not as contradictory as it seemed. But more precisely, what they probably wanted was this: In advance of and in the midst of a crisis, they wanted the Soviet leaders to be convinced that a minimal nuclear reply (or what the British called a "nuclear shot across the bow") would quickly bring all parties sufficiently to their senses to terminate the war with little or no nuclear destruction. In other words, the Europeans preferred maximum reliance upon deterrence so that there would be no war at all. They were reluctant to contemplate the possibility of tactical or limited nuclear war in the event of attack. Some American policymakers undoubtedly regarded the European attitude as illogical, unrealistic, or ostrichlike in its avoidance of thinking through the potential consequences of relying upon a nuclear strategy. But in the minds of many Europeans, the Americans were being too logical and too mathematical, and not sufficiently psychologically and politically intelligent in European terms. The strategy of deterrence had worked, the Europeans argued. By taking a remote hypothesis of how deterrence might break down, and making that the basis of a new strategic doctrine which was to be substituted for the older one, the United States in the European view would increase the probability that some kind of military conflict would occur, and once a conflict involving Soviet and American forces had been joined, there would be strong pressures for escalation to the nuclear level. Thus the American desire to reduce the likelihood of nuclear conflict had produced a new strategic doctrine which, in the eyes of many European strategists, might well have just the opposite effect by weakening the deterrent.

Strategic theorists have never been able to demonstrate satisfactorily either that nuclear war in Europe could be limited or that it is bound to escalate uncontrollably to general or strategic nuclear war. Soviet writers have been more unequivocal than American analysts in denying that nuclear war could ever be limited, and they have rejected the United States efforts to distinguish between the strategic and the tactical use of nuclear weapons. Some Western theorists have argued that in order to minimize the risk of escalation to all-out nuclear war NATO should reduce its reliance on tactical nuclear weapons (or even withdraw them altogether from Europe) and strengthen its capability for fighting a conventional defensive war if an attack should occur. Such theorists are convinced that a clear "firebreak" should be maintained between conventional and nuclear hostilities, because the distinction between "tactical nuclear war" and "strategic" or "central nuclear war" will be extremely ambiguous and difficult to maintain under conditions of actual combat. Most NATO strategic planners, on the other hand, have long been convinced that the Western alliance, because of the economic obstacles to achieving deterrence principally with conventional forces, is compelled to rely upon a nuclear strategy in Europe. Despite considerable discussion of "flexible response" in the early 1960s, United States defense planners did not really reduce their dependence upon a nuclear strategy for NATO as much as the public rhetoric seemed to indicate. Moreover, although NATO was not able to shift officially from the doctrine of "massive retaliation" to one of "flexible response" until after the 1966 withdrawal of France from the alliance's integrated military command, the action of France, combined with the implications of Soviet military redeployments in Central Europe as a result of the 1968 invasion of Czechoslovakia, as well as of the growing imbalance of NATO and Warsaw Pact forces in the 1970s, appeared to increase the probability that any attack upon Western Europe would provoke an early nuclear response.

Closely related to the issue of waging limited nuclear war in Europe was the development in 1974 of the "Schlesinger Doctrine" (named after then U.S. Secretary of Defense James R. Schlesinger) which involved a modification of the "Assured Destruction" concept (i.e., the threat to destroy in retaliation about a quarter of the enemy's population and from half to three-quarters of its industrial capacity) through introducing more flexible options for targeting enemy military forces and the more discriminate and controlled use of strategic nuclear weapons. As in the case of the debate over the wisdom or imprudence of deploying thousands of United States tactical nuclear warheads in Europe, so theorists disagreed among themselves whether the Schlesinger Doctrine would strengthen the deterrent to nuclear war or make such war more likely to occur. But many European analysts who feared the possibility of a nuclear war confined to Central Europe, leaving the territory of the superpowers untouched, favored the Schlesinger Doctrine because they thought that it would increase the potential costs and risks of an attack by the Soviet Union upon NATO.[30] Many Europeans remained convinced that a forward battle strategy involving the threat of an early nuclear response was better than an apparent intention to fall back rather than go nuclear. They did not think that Europe could survive another liberation.

For several years, knowledgeable European observers have expressed mounting concern over changes in the United States-Soviet global strategic balance and in the theater balance between NATO and Warsaw Pact forces. It has long been assumed that United States tactical nuclear weapons in NATO could compensate for the Pact's three-to-one margin of superiority in the quantity of armor available to it. Since the mid-1970s, however, the Soviet Union has acquired a formidable array of theater nuclear capabilities, including delivery systems of considerably longer range than those at the disposal of NATO forces. Throughout the past decade, often characterized as an era of "strategic parity," European analysts have worried about the possibility that European defense might gradually be "decoupled" from the United States nuclear deterrent, producing a situation (or a process already well under way in the eyes of some) that would enable the Soviet Union, by projecting a shadow of unmatchable military power westward, to "Finlandize" the entire Western European region, and to bring about its eventual political and economic orientation toward Moscow. Apart from the question of the central strategic balance, Western Europeans have been particularly apprehensive over the fact that the superpowers have always excluded Theater Nuclear Forces (TNF) from their Strategic Arms Limitation Talks (SALT—a process treated below).

Fearing the eventual "decoupling" effect of parity at the strategic level, some Europeans have considered the possibility that the Western European allies of the United States, particularly those that are members of the European Community, might develop a deterrent force of their own. From time to time it has been suggested that Western Europe possesses sufficient economic and technological capabilities to develop and sustain a sea-based nuclear deterrent, founded probably upon the coordination, if not the merger, of the modest nuclear forces already owned by Britain and France. It is generally recognized, however, that the political, psychological, and stretegic problems of European deterrence are more difficult to overcome than the economic and technological ones, even though the latter are by no means negligible. If the Anglo-French forces were to become the nucleus of a European Community deterrent, West Germany would certainly wish to play a significant role in its management; this would not only pose serious political dilemmas for Britain, France, and West Germany's other partners, but might well provoke the Soviet Union's wrath much more than does the United States military presence in Europe. Because of geopolitical differences between Western Europe and Soviet Russia, especially in regard to the population-to-space ratio, the credibility of a European deterrent might be lower than that of an American one. Thus Europeans who are motivated toward closer defense cooperation against a possible reduction of the United States defense commitment have not been optimistic about Europe's ability to play an equilibrist role. Western strategic theorists (apart from the French) have advocated the development of European deterrence on the assumption that it must remain linked to the more formidable United States deterrent.[31]

Some French theorists, emphasizing the enormous destructive potential of a single thermonuclear weapon, have argued that a nation need not possess a nuclear force as powerful as that of the United States in order to pursue successfully a policy of deterrence (or "dissuasion") even against the Soviet Union. Pierre Gallois, a retired French Air Force General, became famous in the early 1960s for advancing the thesis that deterrence is a matter of proportion. Great Britain and France do not constitute decisive obstacles to the world hegemonial ambitions of an aggressive power. In order to seize those countries, an aggressive Soviet Union would not run the risks that it might be willing to contemplate for the purpose of removing the threat of its principal rival, the United States. The United States must possess an absolute deterrent, but lesser powers should be able to deter attack with proportionately smaller nuclear forces. Gallois advocated a finite countercity *force de dissuasion*. If France could be certain of her ability to penetrate Soviet defenses and strike 50 targets in the USSR, the Soviet leaders would conclude that the value of overrunning France would not be worth the risk. A national deterrent in the hands of a threatened European nation, Gallois argued, would be more credible than a United States promise or a deterrent force controlled by a group of European governments. But if the smaller power uses nuclear weapons against a superpower, it must be prepared to commit suicide, and if it commits itself to an automatic response, the strategy of dissuasion will work.[32] Up to the present time, most defense officials in Western Europe have perceived no practical alternative to relying on the United States deterrent.

The decade of the 1980s seems likely to witness, within the Western Alliance, an intensifying debate over the adequacy of deterrence in Europe, as misgivings over the shifting balance in strategic and theater nuclear forces become more pronounced. Few European analysts doubt that the Soviet Union would prefer, if at all possible, to achieve its regional objectives without war. Few also doubt that the ability of the USSR to project the shadow of its power over Western Europe will continue to improve in the absence of Western efforts to redress the military imbalance. Balance can be restored either through arms control negotiations to limit Eurostrategic weapons (a subject discussed later in this chapter), through the deployment of new NATO theater nuclear weapons (TNF), such as ground-launched cruise missiles (GLCMs) and medium-range ballistic missiles (MRBMs), to replace the existing Alliance short-range systems which may serve to deter a NATO nuclear response more effectively than they deter a Soviet attack, or through a combination of weapons modernization and arms control diplomacy. Europeans are now debating about the kinds of weapons to be deployed, where they should be located, issues of cost, control, and credibility, and how the planned or actual deployments ought to be linked to East-West force reduction negotiations. At a time when the views of European and American policymakers over Middle Eastern policies appear to be diverging, the burgeoning debate is bound to bring on a new wave of theorizing about the requirements of extended deterrence and whether the deployment of a NATO missile force will make transatlantic ties more or less cohesive.[33]

DETERRENCE AND RATIONALITY

The theory of nuclear deterrence, ever since it became prominent in thinking about international politics, has always presupposed a high degree of rationality on the part of national decision-making structures— especially in the United States, the Soviet Union, and Britain, but less so in France (under de Gaulle) and Communist China. (Paradoxically, France and China as inferior nuclear powers had good reasons throughout the 1960s to be extremely cautious, and their governments were probably more rational than they were generally credited with being by policymakers in Moscow and within the Anglo-American alliance who resented and feared the independent courses of action charted by the French and the Chinese.)

Rationality is a transcendental notion which cannot be precisely defined. Some people may think of "rational" policy choices in moral or ethical terms. Some may contrast the term to behavior of a reckless nature. Others may contend that any nonviolent resolution of a conflict situation constitutes a "rational" course, whereas the option for a violent solution is "irrational." We use "rationality" to refer to some proportionate relationship between ends and means or between goals and policies. It implies, therefore, a certain amount of economic (gains versus cost) analysis. According to this notion, we must try to estimate the value that policymakers assign to a particular objective, before adopting a course of action that might lead to initiating nuclear war and exposing themselves to nuclear retaliation.[34]

The question arises as to whether rationality prescribes the same mode of strategic thinking for the United States and the Soviet Union, and whether the two superpowers adopt essentially similar approaches to deterrence. Until recently many American strategic analysts (for the most part civilians influenced by economic bargaining theory) were inclined to answer in the affirmative. Soviet strategic writers (who are usually military thinkers) had for a long time given answers which the more optimistic American strategists preferred to ignore, while hoping that Soviet planners could gradually be persuaded to accept American theories of deterrence and arms control.

Soviet strategists have always been skeptical of those American theories. They have not shown much interest in "strategic parity" as a goal to be negotiated, nor have they accepted the concepts of "mutual assured destruction" and the second-strike strategy. Soviet theorists have made it clear that they are not content with a strategic doctrine that calls for retaliation after absorbing a first strike. Indeed, in their view such a doctrine is not a rational one. The Soviet Union has good reason to wish to deter general nuclear war. But its political and military leaders insist that the best way to do this is to structure military forces not for passive but for active deterrence. As Richard Pipes, John Erickson, and others have shown from a study of Soviet sources, this involves an effort to achieve a war-winning capability and a readiness to preempt if nuclear war should ever appear to be imminent.[35] According to Leon Gouré, it also requires a much greater interest on the part of Soviet strategic planners in problems of civil defense and postattack recovery than has been shown during the past two decades by their American counterparts.[36]

But the question is whether the effort to deter, if carried too far, might generate irrational fears which will in times of crisis decision-making weaken the assumptions of rationality on which deterrence is based. Some theorists have suspected that the threat of punishment, instead of controlling or inhibiting individual behavior in desired directions, may sometimes have the effect of producing a more intransigent opposition. Thomas W. Milburn has written:

> However much pain (or punishment) might appear to be the logical opposite of satisfaction (or reward) its behavioral consequences are simply not opposite. Rewards may change the direction of an organism's effort and motives; punishments (or threat of them), while they may tend to suppress behavior, serve little to change underlying motives. Punishments are less than ideal means for influencing behavioral change, especially when used alone, because they increase anxiety and hostility in those upon whom they are used.[37]

CRITIQUE OF DETERRENCE THEORY

The concept of deterrence, as we have seen before, belongs no less to the realm of psychology and politics than to military strategy, because it involves an effort to influence the behavior of others through dissuasion. Charles E. Osgood has called into question one of the fundamental assumptions on which deterrence theory rests—namely, that of rational decision-making in the nuclear age. He noted that as emotional stress increases beyond an optimum level, nonrational mechanisms become more prevalent in human thinking. "Faced with an overwhelming threat over which he feels he has no control, the human individual typically denies the reality of danger rather than keeping it in mind and trying to cope with it."[38]

Robert Jervis has provided a trenchant critique of the utility and limitations of deterrence theory. He concedes that it possesses formidable intellectual virtues. It deals with the central questions of international politics and does so in a parsimonious manner. It employs the Game of Chicken analogy (see Chapter 12) to examine the way adversaries in confrontation analyze the matrix of costs and payoffs for retreating or standing firm in a crisis. In fact, the theory is most helpful in the understanding of crises and their outcomes. But it is less helpful in understanding the outcomes of long-range disputes. By stressing punishments rather than rewards, it tells us nothing about how to change another's behavior, or how to transform hostile relations into peaceful ones by defusing tensions. Moreover, deterrence theorists overestimate the rationality of decision-makers operating under high stress; they usually overlook the possibility of miscalculation in those cases, which may indeed be rare, when both sides decide to stand firm; and they underestimate the problems which decision-makers may encounter when they try to integrate large amounts of information in a crisis. Grounded in the experience, culture, and values of the West, the theory fails to account for the possibility that other cultures might produce very different types of analysis. The scholars who have developed the theory have relied too much on deduction, says Jervis, and have conducted an insufficient search for supporting empirical evidence. Finally, the theory contains a central tension—the threat to engage in a senseless act of total destruction.[39]

This brings us full circle to the seemingly contradictory concept mentioned by several strategic writers—"the rationality of the irrational."[40] Fortunately for the world, the two superpowers have not proved quite as reckless, during the past two decades, in hurling threats of nuclear attack as one might be led to expect from reading the more pessimistic psychological literature. Thus far deterrence has worked because the United States and the Soviet Union have managed to devise rules governing strategic interaction which minimize the risks of direct embroilment. Whether they can continue indefinitely to do this despite profound differences in strategic doctrine remains to be seen.

DETERRENCE, DISARMAMENT, AND ARMS CONTROL

It may well be that the political leaders of the existing nuclear weapon states have been overly optimistic about their ability to remain in rational control of their foreign policy choices and defense responses, and thereby to avoid nuclear holocaust. Military theoreticians and planners continue to worry, as they are expected to do, about the "worst possible case" in which deterrence breaks down. But up to now the world's political leaders have acted as if they expect deterrence to continue to work, and as if they assume that there are no rational political objectives which would justify resorting to all-out nuclear war. As we have indicated previously, there are several ways in which deterrence might break down and unintended nuclear war might begin, irrespective of the basic assumption of rationality on the part of decision-makers in the nuclear weapon states.

Since the dawn of the atomic era, many voices have urgently warned that humanity faces "a choice between the quick and the dead," and that the advent of nuclear weapons technology has created an imperative requirement for a fundamental transformation of the international system. But in the fourth decade after that challenge first appeared, no substantial changes of the kind which many deem essential have yet occurred. The world has undergone no radical restructuring. The nation-state remains the basic unit of political organization and seems, if anything, to have been strengthened rather than weakened by scientific-technological developments.[41]

GENERAL AND COMPLETE DISARMAMENT

The most radical proposals for modifications in the thinking and behavior of governments have been those which look to general and complete disarmament (GCD). General disarmament presupposes a willingness on the part of nations to relinquish their primary prerogative of providing for their own defense and of entrusting their security to a new worldwide political organization. Thus GCD, if ever carried out, would mark such a profound alteration in the nature of the international system as to warrant the conclusion that the nation-state, as known historically for more than three centuries, had ceased to exist. The Soviet Union and the United States tabled proposals for GCD in the United Nations—the former in 1959 and the latter in 1961.[42] In the early 1960s, several books, monographs, articles, and reports on the subject of GCD were produced by individual scholars, research institutes, and government agencies.[43]

Several of the most ardent proponents of GCD took the position that unless the nations of the world achieved complete nuclear disarmament, their inevitable fate sooner or later would be general nuclear war. Writers in this vein did not place much faith in the continued effectiveness of deterrence for an indefinitely long period. Some conceded the usefulness of deterrence insofar as it provided time for progress toward disarmament to be made; but even they were inclined to think that the more numerous nuclear weapons became and the longer they remained at the disposal of national governments, the greater would be the mathematical possibility of their actual use in war. Advocates of general and complete disarmament, however, were not able to agree among themselves on whether the "nuclear genie could be put back in the bottle," that is, whether it was possible to contemplate the complete elimination of nuclear weapons from the face of the earth, or whether it would be necessary to create an internationalized monopoly of nuclear military force sufficiently powerful to deter any would-be national violators of a nuclear disarmament agreement. Thus some were so repelled by the idea of nuclear deterrence that they preferred what may be the most difficult of all solutions—the total abolition of nuclear weapons. Others reluctantly accepted the necessity of international deterrence even though they rejected the concept of national deterrence.

It took only a few years of analysis and negotiation to demonstrate that a wide and deep chasm separated the political-diplomatic rhetoric of disarmament from the political, strategic, and military-technological realities of the international situation. Although there was no compelling reason to think that any of the nuclear weapon states wanted nuclear war, but ample cause to think that they would all prefer to avoid it because of its unpredictably costly consequences, nevertheless no nuclear power has acted consistently as if it regards total nuclear disarmament as the optimum means of guaranteeing its security. All have apparently attached a higher priority to policy objectives other than general disarmament. The same advanced weapons technology which has made disarmament appear to many as a more desirable goal now than ever before in history has also made that goal more difficult than ever to attain. Up to the present time, the political, technical, and strategic obstacles to general disarmament have seemed well nigh insuperable to governments, if not to all scholars.

Many analysts would add economic factors to the list of obstacles, thus reflecting a suspicion that the disarmament impasse is traceable to a fear of profit loss for the "military-industrial complex" or to such recessive effects as widespread unemployment. Undoubtedly, general disarmament would give rise to serious economic consequences. But if governments manage to reach agreement on substantial arms reductions, these would have to be phased over several years, thereby providing ample opportunity for policymakers to make the transition without uncontrollable disturbances through using antideflationary policies to bolster aggregate demand. Such policies as timely tax cuts, changes in interest rates and other investment incentives, and shifts to nonmilitary forms of spending in the public sector could help to insure a fairly stable period of adjustment. It is in the most advanced economic systems that pentup demands to reallocate resources away from defense expenditures are greatest—for education, health, medical and welfare programs, urban renewal, transportation, advanced scientific research, environmental control, weather and ocean technology, alleviating world hunger and malnutrition, international development assistance, space exploration, and various other purposes. Most of the principal studies of this subject in the early 1960s pointed to the conclusion that the economic consequences of large-scale armaments reductions would be manageable with intelligent planning.[44] Richard J. Barnet has criticized the view that reconversion to a disarmed world would involve no serious economic problems, charging that such a view is based more on wish than analysis.[45] Neo-Marxists, as we have seen, contend that sinister capitalist interests underlie the arms race and the disarmament impasse.[46]

Technical Problems of GCD

The principal technical obstacles to general disarmament arise from the difficulty of trying to control a constantly changing modern weapons technology through the devices of negotiated diplomatic agreements (the language of which may become obsolete almost as soon as they are written) and verification organizations (which may prove socially intrusive and politically obnoxious). Among states essentially friendly to each other, elaborate control systems are not necessary to furnish a sense of security. However, where levels of suspicion and hostility are high more stringent controls are required. Optimistic analysts argue that when nations enter into carefully prepared arms limitation agreements, it is because they perceive an interest in observing its provisions and this can be relied upon to compensate for deficiencies in the control system. Moreover, say the optimists, as disarmament proceeds and the level of confidence rises, tensions will subside and the need for high-reliability systems will diminish. More skeptical analysts insist that governments demand safeguards because they recognize the possibility that adversaries might cheat and that their efforts to deceive might prove highly ingenious and costly; thus they contend that although limited risks and margins of error may be tolerable in the earlier stages when total arms levels are high, the overall reliability of the control system should increase as disarmament proceeds, because verification becomes more important at lower levels.

The two superpowers disagreed whether inspection should be confined, as the Soviets demanded, to "declared facilities" (i.e., to those arms and forces actually being dismantled in the presence of the disarmament organization) or whether it must be extended, as the United States insisted, to make sure that whatever arms and forces remain do not exceed agreed levels. In an effort to bridge the two positions—bound to be different between an open and a closed society—various analysts suggested as a logical necessity the concept of "progressive verification" under which the amount of inspection during any stage would be proportionate to the amount of disarmament being undertaken and to the degree of risk involved. One variant of this concept envisaged a zonal inspection scheme in which each power divides its territory into a prescribed number of zones of relatively equivalent military worth and then invites the other power to select the zonal sequence in which it would simultaneously carry out complete disarmament with complete inspection.[47] Another variant, called "graduated access inspection," provided for initial disarmament in categories which might be inspected tolerably well with a minimum of politically obnoxious intrusion into sensitive areas of Soviet secrecy and social control.[48]

Disarmament specialists have suggested many different forms of inspection to check on the disarming process and on the continuing state of disarmament that is supposed to follow. Among these have been the supervision of actual weapons destruction by international teams; permanent aerial and satellite reconnaissance to detect the construction of new production plants or deployment sites; the stationing of observers at land, sea, and air transport centers to watch for suspicious movements of goods and personnel; placing resident inspectors at plants formerly engaged in weapons manufacture; spot checks of other plants against the possibility of conversion; strict accounting of critical materials and skilled labor; registration and random surveillance of all scientists; and increasingly close monitoring of governmental budgets and expenditures as disarmament proceeds.[49]

The experts on inspection for GCD readily considered that ways could be devised to evade every single technique. But they argued that the reliability of any verification system would increase as multiple techniques were crossed with each other to achieve greater effectiveness. Leonard S. Rodberg argued that the inspection system itself could become "a means of deterrence, intended to create a risk of detection and make evasion unattractive," but that this would depend "on the supplemental measures each party takes to increase the credibility of its intention to respond effectively if violations are discovered."[50] Fred Charles Iklé noted that potential violators would not be deterred by the mere risk of discovery or by fear of adverse world opinion reactions, but only by an expectation that the gains of violation would be outweighed by the losses. Iklé focused on the following problems that a democratic government would be likely to face in responding to a detected evasion: arguments over the evidence and seriousness of the evasion; the interactive responses of rival political parties and leaders, as well as of government agencies; the reluctance to jeopardize international cooperation by scrapping the disarmament agreement; and the difficulty of convincing the public and the legislative body that the nation should embark upon retaliatory rearmament.[51]

Some analysts proposed radically novel methods of control to resolve the problem of clandestine stockpiles[52] that might be sequestered successfully because of the margin of error inherent in any system that estimates the volume of past production of fissionable materials and they would be undetectable by any known scientific methods. Instead of concentrating on the search for *physical* evidence that a violation had occurred, and on improved "hardware" for discovering such evidence, some scientists tried to shift emphasis to a search for nonphysical evidence, principally in the form of human knowledge. This could be either (1) volunteered knowledge (obtained through "inspection by the people"), which implies that individuals can be motivated by a system of rewards and punishments or by such psychological factors as fear, jealousy, ambition, and devotion to peace to inform against their own government officials, political rivals, or fellow citizens who engage in prohibited activities; or (2) detected knowledge, which involves using modern techniques for discovering truth upon personnel who were most likely to possess information about efforts at evasion.[53] It did not seem likely, however, that governments were ready to enter upon such sweeping disarmament agreements as would presuppose drastic revisions of human political attitudes (e.g., citizen loyalty) or require key officials to be subjected at periodic or random intervals to polygraph tests, hypnotic depth interviews, or "truth serum" injections.

Strategic and Political Obstacles to GCD

Theoreticians pointed to two principal strategic problems in connection with comprehensive disarmament: (1) how to make sure that neither superpower would be placed at an unfair disadvantage during or as a result of the disarming process; and (2) whether disarmament would lead to a dangerously unstable strategic situation compared to the condition of mutual nuclear deterrence. As to the first problem, the geostrategic requirements of each nation are unique because of geographical factors, patterns of population distribution, interests to be protected, and so forth. Each nation's weapons systems are a function of its technological capabilities and preferred military doctrines. Because of these asymmetries, it is always difficult to reach agreement on where the dismantling of arms ought to begin in the first stage. Each superpower suspects that the other, in proposing first steps, is seeking to improve its own relative position. The history of disarmament conferences and negotiations bears out the suspicion. Objectively, it is not easy to conceive of specific arms reductions which satisfy the equity expectations of both sides, especially when the numbers, types, and qualitative characteristics (e.g., yield, range, reliability, concealment, protection, and accuracy) of weapons vary so widely—as they do. It is possible, of course, that a mutually satisfactory agreement for phased arms reduction could be negotiated after a lengthy period of intensive bargaining. Mutual satisfaction, if it can be achieved, is the ultimate political test of equitability.

The second problem is the more crucial one. Several leading analysts have wondered how far the levels of strategic arms can be reduced before the condition of mutual deterrence is corroded to the point of breaking down. In contrast to those scientists who worry about the upper segment of the deterrence spectrum, these analysts focus on "overkill" and insist that the size of nuclear arsenals must be drastically cut to reduce the magnitude of the global catastrophe in case nuclear war occurs. Arms control writers who relied on the notion of deterrence expressed misgivings about proposals for "minimum deterrence" and warned that it could prove tragically unwise to reduce nuclear forces too much, because this might revive incentives to seek the advantage of surprise attack.[54] These writers believed that changes at low levels of forces could be more destablizing than changes at high levels.

Even if all nuclear weapons in the arsenals of nations could be abolished, the danger of nuclear war would not be eliminated. Hedley Bull noted that nations will always possess the technical capacity to "reestablish what has been disestablished, to remember or to reinvent what has been laid aside."[55] In a disarmed world, wrote Schelling and Halperin, in "the absence of some effective policing force, primitive war is still possible, rearmament is possible, and primitive wars that last long enough may convert themselves by rapid mobilization into very modern warfare."[56] The founding editor of *The Bulletin of the Atomic Scientists* warned that war might break out more easily between disarmed powers than between armed nations and that such a war, once initiated, would inevitably become nuclear.[57] It was obvious even to many among the most concerned scientists that once the nuclear genie has escaped it could not be put back permanently into the bottle—that there would henceforth be no perfectly safe road for nations and humanity to follow.

In the final analysis, the most significant stumbling blocks to complete disarmament were probably political. The Soviet Union had a deep-rooted political aversion to (and cultural-psychological phobia of) free-access inspection, while the United States was politically unable to consider seriously a disarmament agreement with a superpower that insisted upon remaining a closed society. Apparently unbridgeable differences persisted in the positions adopted by the two countries toward building those international peacekeeping institutions that would be necessary to safeguard the security and political rights of nations in a disarmed world.[58] Two nuclear weapon states—France and China—took no part in international disarmament negotiations. Soviet leaders, conscious of a widening rift between Moscow and Peking and of China's determination to become a nuclear power, were not motivated to make concessions for the sake of a disarmament agreement with a capitalist adversary then presumed to possess nuclear superiority. Neither superpower was in the least bit anxious to exchange the dangers of a familiar balance of power for the less known dangers of a radically transformed international system. In the early 1960s, interest shifted from GCD to arms control, although the governments of the superpowers continued to pay lip service to the goal of GCD in preamble statements to limited arms control treaties. Although the Soviet Union still supported the idea of convening a World Disarmament Conference in the early 1970s, China and the United States were opposed. All three powers assumed an attitude of indifference toward the United Nations General Assembly's Special Session on Disarmament in 1978, the outcome of which was not particularly hopeful in the view of those who advocate substantial or complete disarmament.[59]

THE MEANING OF ARMS CONTROL

Arms control policies usually aim at some kind of restraint or regulation in the qualitative design, quantitative production, method of deployment, protection, control, transfer, and planned, threatened, or actual use of military forces and weapons. Such policies may imply collaboration between adversary states—formal agreements, tacit understandings, informal cooperation, or unilateral decisions taken with the expectation of reciprocal action. They may also embrace unilateral decisions deemed worth taking even if the adversary does not respond, simply because they enhance stability of the deterrent, controllability, and security against unintended war. Central to the thinking of most arms control proponents is reducing risks and dangers, but specific arms control proposals may have other purposes in the minds of their supporters—to promote détente, to effect budget cuts, to permit a shift of resources to nondefense programs, to preserve "arms control momentum," and so on.[60]

Arms control, to summarize, is an extremely broad and permissive term. It may encompass such diverse (and sometimes contradictory) concepts as the following:

> Invulnerable second-strike capability
> Disengagement
> Demilitarized or nuclear-free zones
> Two-key systems and electronic permissive action links
> City-avoidance strategy
> Freeze on the production or deployment of specified weapons
> No first-use pledge
> Improvement of command, control, and communications facilities
> Limits on testing of weapons systems
> Efforts to retard the proliferation of nuclear weapons to nations not already possessing them

During the nuclear age, the superpowers have entered into a number of multilateral arms control treaties and bilateral arms control agreements.[61] It is not the function of a text on international relations theories to describe the provisions of such diplomatically negotiated instruments. Each one of these generated a certain amount of theoretical analysis—some more extensive and intensive than others. We shall limit our attention here to the two arms control areas that gave rise to the most elaborate efforts at theorizing: (1) preventing the proliferation of nuclear weapons and (2) strategic arms limitation talks (SALT).

PREVENTING OR CONTROLLING
NUCLEAR WEAPONS PROLIFERATION

Nuclear scientists had never doubted that the knowledge of fission bomb technology would sooner or later be globally dispersed. From the late 1950s onward, arms control analysts paid close attention to the prospects for and problems of nuclear weapons proliferation among the members of the international system. As soon as projections appeared for a dozen or more countries to acquire technological capabilities to produce nuclear weapons, a debate began whether an increase in the number of nuclear club members would have a stabilizing effect by compelling governments to act more responsibly and cautiously or whether it would raise the mathematical probability of the occurrence of nuclear war, while at the same time compounding the difficulties of achieving any negotiated international agreement on the limitation of nuclear armaments.[62]

The issue of nuclear weapons proliferation first arose acutely within the Atlantic Alliance when strategic writers began asking whether the United States pledge to defend Europe with nuclear weapons was credible, and when nationalists such as Charles de Gaulle wondered aloud whether a self-respecting state can rely upon an outside power for its defense. After having aided the British nuclear weapons program, the United States Government refrained from giving France similar assistance, while the Soviet Union began to disengage itself from the Chinese weapons effort. Arms control writers sought to persuade aspirants to nuclear power status that the arguments, cited earlier, on behalf of national deterrents by such writers as Pierre Gallois were not valid. Smaller powers, it was said, would not be able to enhance their security very much by going nuclear. The acquisition of nuclear bombs would not be sufficient. Sophisticated delivery, command, and control systems would also be necessary. New national deterrents, unable to match the power and variety of weapons available to the leading powers, would prove much less credible than the American deterrent. Moreover, they would be costly, provocative, and dangerously accident prone; they would become obsolete quickly and would also render young nuclear powers vulnerable to preemptive attack during the early stages of development.[63] There was also a widespread recognition that the proliferation of national nuclear deterrent forces in the West might seriously divide and weaken the Atlantic Alliance.

The smaller powers were admonished that they should not "remain oblivious to the opportunities for moral leadership that their abstinence from nuclear weapons affords."[64] But despite such appeals to altruism and despite the practical arguments that could be leveled against new national nuclear deterrent forces, arms control analysts realized that in the final analysis the drive for national prestige and sense of independence that the possession of nuclear weapons was thought to bestow might prove irresistible to some countries. Perhaps the two superpowers regarded it as almost inevitable that the five states that enjoyed a privileged veto power in the United Nations would have sufficient determination eventually to acquire nuclear forces—as all had begun to do by the mid-1960s. After France and China entered the ranks of the nuclear weapon powers, the question became one of whether the arguments concerning the wastefulness and military nonutility of nuclear forces would serve to dissuade additional countries, especially in the developing world, from trying to "join the club."

The global diffusion of nuclear reactor technology for peaceful power purposes greatly compounded the difficulty of halting the further spread of nuclear weapons. Despite a growing uneasiness over the dangers of environmental pollution from nuclear activities, the mere fact that nuclear energy was becoming economically competitive was enough to insure that it would become more common as a source of power throughout the world. Unfortunately, "atoms for peace" could not be easily separated from "atoms for war." The dissemination of reactor technology was bound to render it easier for several countries to divert fissionable materials to weapons production if they were determined to do so.[65]

From the mid-1960s onward, the United States, as well as several other members of the United Nations, assigned a high priority to obtaining international adherence to a Non-Proliferation Treaty designed to inhibit the spread of nuclear weapons to countries not already possessing them. It was clear to most arms control analysts that the two superpowers could not absolutely prevent proliferation, but could only discourage it by pursuing policies that would affect the incentives and disincentives of "threshold countries" to go nuclear. The negotiation of the treaty gave rise to several diplomatic problems. The European allies of the United States feared that in the future its provisions might be interpreted in such a way as to hinder the operations of the European Atomic Energy Community and the European unity movement. West Germany and Japan feared that it might facilitate industrial espionage and limit their freedom to develop an export business in civilian reactor technology. India called the treaty "an effort by the armed to disarm the unarmed." Several states criticized a treaty which imposed virtually all of its burdens upon the nonnuclear weapon states instead of providing an acceptable balance of mutual responsibilities and obligations. The treaty, charged the critics, infringed upon the sovereign prerogatives of the nonweapon states by requiring them to submit to international inspection while not placing the nuclear facilities of the superpowers under any restrictions. Such a treaty, aimed only at "horizontal proliferation" (to additional states), not "vertical proliferation" (by the existing nuclear weapon powers), would limit the choice of nations on vital matters of defense without offering any security compensations. There was also discontent over the fact that the Non-Proliferation Treaty would prohibit "peaceful purpose" nuclear explosions by nonweapon states.[66]

With the passage of time, the arguments in favor of acquiring nuclear weapons seemed to grow more compelling—even for a country like India with its pacifist, antinuclear tradition. *Militarily*, said proponents, nuclear weapons alone can deter a nuclear-armed foe; and a smaller power does not need intercontinental missiles if it is mainly concerned about a neighbor rather than a distant superpower. Economically, although nuclear weapons programs undoubtedly divert scarce talent and resources from development projects, costs are manageable for a country that has already laid the basis for a civilian reactor program; and nuclear deterrence would eventually permit savings through reducing the size of conventional armed forces. Politically, nuclear weapons provide an ultimate guarantee against a deal by the superpowers at the country's expense. They also furnish a ticket to disarmament conferences and summit meetings where decisions important to the country's interests may be taken.[67] To the argument that a poor country like India should not waste scarce resources on unnecessary weapons programs, the Indian reply was that since the superpowers refused to put an end to their own arms race and to divert a portion of the sums to be saved thereby into peaceful development assistance for the Third World, they should not criticize weaker and more exposed states for refusing to close off the nuclear weapons option.[68] It was obvious that many Indians were concerned over the types of conventional and nuclear military threats which China might pose to their country in the future, and also over the possibility that when a confrontation came, neither the Soviet Union nor the United States might be willing to render deterrence assistance.[69]

Within seven years of the Non-Proliferation Treaty's entering into force in 1970, more than 100 states had signed it, and of these at least four-fifths had ratified it. But several important potential nuclear weapon states, especially in Asia, Africa and Latin America, had either not signed or not ratified the Non-Proliferation Treaty by the time the five-year review conference was held in May 1975.[70] The international oil-energy crisis which was associated with the Middle East War of 1973 greatly compounded the foreign exchange problems of several oil-importing countries in the Third World and made them more interested than ever in nuclear energy as a source of electric power. The 1974 explosion by India of a nuclear device for "peaceful purpose" aroused apprehensions that the "international nonproliferation regime" was about to crumble. Arms control specialists, with eyes on what was then widely interpreted as a United States tendency to scale down foreign defense commitments, particularly in Asia, speculated on the patterns of incentives and disincentives likely to influence the decision either to go or not to go militarily nuclear in such countries as Japan, Taiwan, South Korea, India, Pakistan, Iran, and Turkey.[71] Leaders of at least three states—Pakistan, Libya, and Turkey—announced intentions to go nuclear, but in their nuclear technological capabilities those countries were far from being the most advanced in the Third World.

Some arms control theorists wondered whether there would be, in the wake of the Indian explosion, an opening of the floodgates to new nuclear weapon powers. Might there be a chain reaction effect, with a dozen or more aspirants entering the "club"? It is possible to distinguish between proliferation by defensive reaction (the result of a compulsion to achieve equilibrium between historic adversaries) and proliferation by emulation (resulting from a calculation by one or more states that the acquisition of nuclear weapon status by other states had bestowed benefits beyond improved security). But most arms control analysts recognized that the problem of proliferation cannot be reduced to a simple matter of a chain reaction. Every governmental decision to acquire a nuclear weapons capability or to develop a credible option to move quickly in that direction—which may be more valuable than the capability itself—must be taken in the context of a complex set of political, economic, and strategic-military variables unique to the specific country in relation to the international system. According to Lincoln P. Bloomfield, the fact that India had become a nuclear-capable power did not of itself change the world. "But what could change it would be a snowballing, fatalistic belief that becomes a self-fulfilling prophecy unless it is countered by a different belief that is equally potent."[72]

In the latter 1970s, it was generally recognized that states grown wealthy with petrodollars would probably be able to buy an advanced nuclear-technological base from nuclear powers eager for overseas markets; and that the number and capacity of nuclear power plants throughout the world would increase exponentially between now and the year 2000. The existing safeguards system of the International Atomic Energy Agency (IAEA) and of bilateral agreements between nuclear suppliers and nuclear importers is admittedly deficient. Arms control theorists realized that it would become technologically easier for several governments to acquire nuclear military capabilities, expecially if they should manage to obtain independent control over the nuclear fuel cycle of their reactors. The United States therefore sought to obtain agreements among the supplier nations to tighten controls on the export of nuclear materials, particularly by requiring importing countries to agree to place all their nuclear facilities under IAEA controls before becoming eligible recipients and by prohibiting the transfer of reprocessing plants to states that did not already own them, except perhaps under regional supervision. The Carter Administration also tried to slow down the international drift toward a "plutonium economy" through a unilateral decision to halt developing plutonium as a fuel in power reactors while expanding its supply of the easier-to-control enriched uranium for export overseas. At the same time it has attempted to persuade other industrially advanced countries to deemphasize fast breeder reactors which produce more plutonium than needed to fuel the reactors. United States' efforts along these lines, however, encountered opposition from Third World countries that resented what appeared to them to be dis-

criminatory treatment and infringement of their sovereignty. Allies of
the United States were unwilling to accept self-denying restraints that
would have placed them at a competitive disadvantage in comparison
with the United States nuclear export industry.[73]

Most arms control theorists seemed agreed that the problem of nuclear proliferation was likely to worsen with the passage of time. Although some states might conclude that the acquisition of nuclear weapons would decrease rather than increase their security, others might well
find the political and military incentives stronger than the disincentives.
It was generally thought that as the number of reactors and "threshold
states" in the world increased, the greater would become the danger that
the storage, transit, use, and disposal of nuclear materials would harm
the human environment. It was also feared that, as the effectiveness of
governmental control systems was diluted, nonstate groups (e.g., rival
political factions, revolutionary insurgents, and terrorist organizations)
would be able to circumvent state safeguards and seize weapons or materials with which to make weapons, and that the mathematical possibility
of nuclear weapons being used for blackmail or actually fired in anger
would rise. Furthermore, as the magnitude of the problem grew, the
prospects became dimmer that an international regime would be capable of coping effectively with the problem.

In the mid-1970s, analysts began to worry seriously about the possibility that terrorist groups might gain possession of nuclear materials and
weapons, either by stealing an assembled weapon from a nuclear weapon
state, by purchasing or receiving a weapon from such a state, or by constructing their own nuclear weapon from materials bought or stolen from
the nuclear power industry.[74] The United States long ago put into effect
a variety of administrative, technical, and military protection safeguards
to make sure that nuclear weapons would not fall under the control of
any personnel except those authorized to use them. It is presumed that
other well-established nuclear weapon states (NWS) have taken similar
precautions, and that safeguard systems have been upgraded since the
danger of seizure by terrorists has become salient.

Most analysts seem to be agreed that further proliferation to states
not now possessing nuclear weapons is likely to lead in the long run to
the decay of global political order and the rise of global anarchy.[75] Analysts of the Stockholm International Peace Research Institute have expressed fear that such proliferation is bound to contribute to destabilizing effects in the international system because it will give rise to a
domino effect (encouraging other states to go nuclear); increase the risk
of accidental or unauthorized use; raise the chance that local, smaller
wars may eventually become nuclear; increase over time the probability
of major nuclear war as well as catalytic war (instigated by non-nuclear-
weapon states in order to draw nuclear-weapon powers into an ex-

change); erode the existing "firebreak" against the use of nuclear weapons; provoke or justify a continued arms race among major nuclear-weapon states; render future arms limitation negotiations all the more difficult; and lead to the eventual acquisition of nuclear weapons by "crazy states," "crazy elites" or "crazy terrorists."[76] In summary, most intelligent theorists are of the opinion that a world of many rather than a small number of nuclear-weapon states is likely to be a more dangerous world in which to live.

STRATEGIC ARMS LIMITATION TALKS (SALT)

After several years of diplomatic sparring by the superpowers, the era of the SALT began in late 1969. The process has continued intermittently throughout the decade of the 1970s. SALT is predicated on the assumption that the process of arming must be halted with a verifiable freeze on deployment before the process of reducing armaments can begin. International relations theorists cited several different motivations the superpowers may have had for undertaking to negotiate the distribution of strategic military power between themselves:

1. The Sino-Soviet dispute which broke into the open in the early 1960s led the United States, the Soviet Union, and the People's Republic of China to reassess their strategic relationships with each other in the midst of the Vietnam War. Each of the three found itself in a new triangular balance of power. The United States was tempted to use its diplomatic opening toward China to put pressure on the USSR; China undoubtedly hoped to use the "third player" for deterring Soviet aggression; and the Soviets, tending as always to be suspicious, feared a Sino-American coalition and sought to head it off by intensifying détente with the United States.

2. The conditions of mutual nuclear deterrence and incipient multipolarity have not by any means rendered problems of national security obsolete, but rather had made them much more subtle and complicated as new political, social, economic, and technological forces have come into play. In an era of rapidly changing weapons technology, strategic stability has become more difficult to maintain, and the superpowers may have thought that the processes of formal communication and bargaining would help to maintain it.

3. The Vietnam War induced a domestic reaction within the United States that led to a growing disillusionment with American foreign defense commitments and a demand for a reordering of national priorities to nondefense programs; these trends were reinforced by the assumption that the adversary character of the superpower relationship was becoming more limited in a period of détente.

4. Some analysts, citing the technological uncertainties of the future, feared that the condition known as "stable mutual deterrence" would be undermined by a dangerous interactive process in which one side, overreacting, might create a temporary imbalance which would tempt it to behave imprudently in time of crisis.

5. Others, with an eye on economics, argued that it would be futile for the two superpowers to keep on investing competitively in costly new weapons systems that would be likely to produce not meaningful military superiority but only a mutually canceling effect upon the strategic equation.

6. Even though popular pressures to reallocate resources to nondefense purposes cannot be articulated in Moscow as effectively as in Washington, many Western observers thought that Soviet planners felt constrained to increase investment in agriculture and the consumer industries, and to narrow the "technology gap" which exists between the USSR and the West in a number of areas.

7. The superpowers were under some political pressure from the "nuclear threshold states" to make progress toward the control of "vertical" as well as "horizontal" proliferation. Arms control theorists assumed that the already rickety NPT regime would collapse if the strategic arsenals of the leading powers expanded without limit.

8. Finally, each side found worrisome the specific weapons deployment intentions of the other. The Soviet Union did not want to see the United States lay the foundation for what might become a nationwide ballistic missile defense system. The United States, concerned over the rapid rate at which the Soviets were deploying heavy missiles, wondered whether Moscow could be induced to level off at strategic parity or would try to achieve a strategic superiority which, regardless of whether it could ever be employed to carry out a first strike, might be quite useful as a political instrument.[77]

The SALT I accords signed in Moscow in May 1972 were professedly designed to stabilize the international equilibrium by codifying approximate strategic parity.[78] The accords consisted of an ABM Treaty of unlimited duration, subject to review at five-year intervals; and an Interim Agreement on Strategic Offensive Weapons, with accompanying Protocol, of five years duration. Under the ABM Treaty, the two superpowers renounced the option of deploying a nationwide ballistic missile defense system based on existing technology and agreed to limit themselves to deploying ABM around no more than the national capital and one missile site. The treaty, however, did not prohibit research and development in new missile defense technologies, nor did it prohibit the deployment of new and more effective ABMs as replacements for existing ones already authorized. But, although it prohibits the deployment of all antimissile technologies, whether actual or potential, except as provided for in the agreement, the ABM accord stipulated that if a new principle of defense should emerge (such as one based upon lasers), further discussions would be necessary in order to work out specific limitations upon its deployment.

The Interim Agreement was addressed to the fixing of ceilings on strategic offensive weapons. Rough parity was arrived at by political intuition, rather than by the computation of strict mathematical equality of the superpowers' missile arsenals. The Soviets were assigned a 40 percent margin of superiority in the number of land-based ICBMs and about a one-third margin in the number of ocean-based SLBMs. The agreement was widely criticized in the United States for conceding to the Soviets a substantial advantage in missile payload, but ratification was justified by the Nixon Administration on the grounds that the United States possessed several compensating advantages (such as overseas air and submarine bases, the total number of warheads deployed, the number of long-range bombers, and qualitative superiority in a variety of important technological dimensions) that warranted the assumption of overall strategic parity, and that if there were any danger of the balance tilting because of Soviet deployment rates, such danger might be greater in the absence of an agreement. Critics argued that the larger quantitative base allocated to the Soviet Union would mean eventual strategic superiority for the Soviets once they had narrowed the qualitative technological gap. The SALT I agreements were also faulted by some analysts because by renouncing population defense and apparently codifying the "cities hostage" strategy of mutual assured destruction, they involved abandoning one of the major objectives of arms control—minimizing collateral damage as much as possible in case the nuclear deterrent should fail. Still others complained that the SALT I Accords were fraudulent, since they did not seriously inhibit the two superpowers from doing in the realm of strategic weaponry anything that they were strongly motivated to do.[79]

The U.S. Senate, in ratifying the Interim Agreement, demanded the achievement of more ostensible mathematical parity in SALT II. The next few years witnessed a diplomatic quest for a "conceptual breakthrough" in the arms negotiations. But it proved extremely difficult for the two superpowers—each with distinctive goals, negotiating styles, strategic philosophies, geostrategic requirements, military doctrines, technological capabilities, and specific weapons preferences—to define "parity" or "essential equivalence" to their mutual satisfaction. While negotiating with each other, both governments were obliged to manage the internal bureaucratic bargaining process that goes on among military services and other organized factions. The two delegations argued long and hard over such issues as how to define "heavy" missiles, how to count "MIRVed" missiles, how to control future qualitative improvements, and how compliance with agreements should be verified. Even as detailed points at issue seemed to be tentatively resolved, the appearance of progress toward agreement would sometimes be rendered obsolete by rapidly changing developments in advanced weapons technology. The problems of SALT negotiations were complicated further by the fact that the "central strategic balance" of the superpowers and the regional balance of the two alliance systems in Europe were linked by weapons systems of intermediate range. The Western European allies of the United States manifested sensitivity lest NATO's leading power make concessions in SALT that would adversely affect their local security, and became increasingly concerned over what they called "gray area" weapons systems—medium and intermediate range nuclear weapons in the European theater which were not being addressed either in SALT or in the negotiations between NATO and the Warsaw Pact on the mutual reduction of forces in Europe.[80]

Many advocates of arms control were of the opinion that SALT II, instead of permitting deployments at higher levels than those allowed in SALT I, should aim at substantial armaments reductions. Several were worried about the destabilizing implications of land-based fixed ICBMs becoming more vulnerable to a surprise first strike; and they wondered whether this would lead to new offensive deployments, or a "launch on warning" policy,[81] or a revival of interest in ballistic missile defense, or a general erosion of the assumptions on which mutual-deterrence-with-arms control had rested for a quarter of a century.

The two superpowers negotiated for nearly seven years to obtain a SALT II agreement. During all that time the controversy over what constituted "strategic parity" or "essential equivalence" continued unabated. The public debate and the diplomatic negotiations were complicated by the emergence of new technological possibilities either not foreseen or not provided for in SALT I—the Soviet bomber known in the West as Backfire, United States and Soviet cruise missiles (capable of being launched from the ground, from submarines, or from aircraft), mobile land-based intercontinental missiles, improvements in missile propulsion, reentry, and warhead guidance, control and terminal accuracy, satellite destroyer capabilities, and a new concept of ballistic missile defense based on discoveries in high-energy physics.

In the later stages of the SALT II negotiations, American strategic analysts expressed considerable concern over the degree to which the Soviet strategic build-up would render vulnerable the United States land-based missile system, as well as the United States bomber force on which the greater proportion of American strategic "throw-weight" depended."[82] American analysts took for granted that Soviet antisubmarine-warfare capabilities did not yet pose a substantial threat to the West's sea-based deterrent. Nevertheless they were not comfortable with the thought that one leg of the United States deterrent triad (the land-based ICBMs) had already become highly vulnerable (as a result of Soviet heavy missile deployments and SALT I constraints on antimissile defense), while the second leg depended upon an aging strategic bomber force that would be armed with a newly developed cruise missile pitted against a growing Soviet air defense system unconstrained by any SALT agreement. There were disagreements over which limitations would be treated in a shorter-term Protocol rather than in the SALT Treaty, over the precise characteristics of the new weapons to be tested and deployed during the lifetime of the treaty, and over the ability of the parties to verify by national detection means the restraints on quantitative deployments and qualitative improvements that SALT II would contain.[83]

The technical problems of negotiating a SALT II agreement were complicated by several political-strategic problems confronting the superpowers. The Soviet Union resented certain trends in United States foreign policy: a heightened emphasis on human rights, perceived by the Soviet leaders as a threat to the maintenance of their imperial control; a United States initiative in the diplomacy of Middle East peacemaking that apparently excluded the Soviet Union from the process; and the fostering of friendlier ties between the United States and its industrialized allies on the one hand and the People's Republic of China on the other (a dangerous prelude, in the Soviet view, to the economic and military build-up of China). United States policymakers were concerned about the implications of the Soviet Union's continued accumulation of intercontinental and shorter-range nuclear missiles, armor, naval, and other military capabilities, as well as the effort of the USSR to extend its influence to distant regions of the globe on which the West depended, especially Africa. In negotiating SALT, the United States also had to take into account the apprehensions of its NATO allies that their own security interests might be bargained away for the sake of superpower agreement, thereby creating the conditions for the future "Finlandization" (i.e., Soviet-dictated "neutralization") of Western Europe. Within the United States itself, the SALT process became enmeshed with a changing American mood concerning foreign and defense policy, and also with a complex post-Watergate, postimperial struggle for political power between the Executive and the Congress. Ratification of the SALT II Agreement was delayed because of Senate misgivings over the changing strategic balance, the apprehensions of NATO allies over the meaning of certain provisions, the presence of Soviet combat forces in Cuba, national frustration over the hostage crisis in Teheran, and the Soviet invasion of Afghanistan. No one could confidently predict whether the ratification process would ever be completed.[84]

Many advocates of arms control were convinced that SALT II, instead of permitting deployments of weapons at higher levels than those permitted in SALT I, should aim at substantial armaments reductions—

an objective postponed until SALT III. Some analysts went so far as to conclude pessimistically that the assumptions on which mutual-deterrence-with-arms-control had rested for a quarter of a century were eroding, that arms control policy had failed, and that the formal negotiations of arms control agreements between the two superpowers, originally intended to bring the arms race under control, might now be producing the effect of stimulating armaments competition in some technological areas to compensate for the acceptance of restrictions in others.[85]

As the decade of the 1980s began, the two superpowers appeared to be moving away from détente and into a new cold war period. None of the arms control agreements concluded since 1959 had been repudiated. Nevertheless there was a noticeable decline in enthusiasm not only for SALT II but for other areas of arms limitation in which negotiations had been carried on in recent years—chemical weapons, a comprehensive nuclear test ban, naval capabilities in the Indian Ocean, mutual and balance force reductions in Europe (MBFR), antisatellite destroyers, and the transfer of conventional arms.[86] It was not clear whether the Soviet invasion of Afghanistan would have only a temporary damping effect upon superpower arms negotiations (as the 1968 Warsaw Pact invasion of Czechoslovakia had had) or whether the larger pattern of recent Soviet expansionism in Southeast Asia, the Middle East, Africa, and Cuba would move the superpowers into an era of seeking to achieve mutual stable deterrence without formal arms control negotiations.

Strategic analysts were expressing increasing dissatisfaction with the "traditional" approaches to arms control which had been pursued during the previous two decades. They asked whether diplomatically negotiated instruments designed to place quantitative limits on armaments could be of more than ephemeral relevance in an era of dynamic and rapid qualitative developments in weapons technology.[87] But, regardless of whether governments decided to produce and deploy emerging military-technological systems at the expense of arms control, or renounce them in the interests of arms control, or modify their conceptions of and approaches to arms control to permit both deployments and negotiations to continue, it appeared in 1980 that deterrence in some form and arms control in some form would remain linked at the theoretical level. The debate will continue to rage over such notions as strategic sufficiency and essential equivalence; improvements in missile accuracy and hard-target kill capability (the K factor); counterforce versus countervalue strategies; the doctrine of Mutual Assured Destruction versus the doctrine of Limited Nuclear Options; damage-limiting strategies which might weaken the "cities hostage" effect; and whether a purely retaliatory strategy serves any rational military-political purpose, or only the impulse to revenge.[88] The debate itself will demonstrate that the concept of "stable mutual deterrence," which is the nuclear age version of the much older balance of power theory of which it is the direct descendant, will continue—like its venerable ancestor—to survive several premature interments.

Notes

1. Alexander L. George and Richard Smoke, *Deterrence in American Foreign Policy: Theory and Practice* (New York: Columbia University Press, 1974), p. 11.
2. Ibid., pp. 14–16; and Patrick M. Morgan, *Deterrence: A Conceptual Analysis* (Beverly Hills, Calif.: Sage, 1977), chap. 1. See also George Quester, *Deterrence Before Hiroshima* (New York: Wiley, 1966).
3. Bernard Brodie, "The Anatomy of Deterrence," *World Politics*, XI (January 1959), 174. Morgan, in the work cited, gives several definitions of the term. See also Johannes Andenaes, *Punishment and Deterrence* (Ann Arbor: University of Michigan Press, 1974).
4. Henry A. Kissinger, *The Necessity for Choice* (Garden City, N.Y.: Doubleday, 1962), pp. 11–12. Thomas C. Schelling has noted that a nation today wants from its military forces not so much "victory" as bargaining power. *Arms and Influence* (New Haven: Yale University Press, 1966), p. 31. The same point is made by Morton Halperin, *Defense Strategies for the Seventies*, 2nd ed. (Boston: Little, Brown, 1977), p. 10.
5. Alexander L. George and Richard Smoke, op. cit., pp. 23–27. For a recent examination of the theory of limited war, see Robert E. Osgood, *Limited War Revisited* (Boulder, Colo.: Westview, 1979).
6. *The New York Times*, January 13, 1954, p. 2.
7. Jerome H. Kahan, *Security in the Nuclear Age: Developing U.S. Strategic Arms Policy* (Washington: The Brookings Institution, 1975), p. 34; see also pp. 28–33. For an account of the Gaither Report, the vulnerability issue, and the alleged "missile gap" of 1960, see pp. 35–47.
8. William W. Kaufmann, "The Requirements of Deterrence," in *Military Policy and National Security*, W. W. Kaufmann, ed. (Princeton: Princeton University Press, 1956), pp. 23–24.
9. Paul Nitze, "Atoms, Strategy and Policy," *Foreign Affairs*, XXXIV (January 1956), 188–198.
10. Cf. Sir Anthony Buzzard and others, "The H-Bomb: Massive Retaliation or Graduated Deterrence?", A symposium in *International Affairs*, XXXII (April 1956); Arnold Wolfers, "Could a War in Europe be Limited?," *Yale Review*, XLV (Winter 1956).
11. Albert Wohlstetter, "The Delicate Balance of Terror," *Foreign Affairs*, XXXVIII (January 1959), 211–234. Several writers noted that the aircraft, in comparison with the missile, had the advantage of "recallability," whereas missiles once launched were irrevocable. See, for example, Bernard Brodie, *Strategy in the Missile Age*, (Princeton: Princeton University Press, 1959), p. 287; and Henry A. Kissinger, op. cit., p. 228. Kissinger cited the irrevocability of a launched missile as a reason why it "must be designed to ride out an attack."
12. Thomas C. Schelling and Morton H. Halperin, *Strategy and Arms Control* (New York: Twentieth Century Fund, 1961), pp. 50–54; Morton H. Halperin, *Contemporary Military Strategy* (Boston: Little, Brown, 1967), pp. 19–20; Jerome H. Kahan, op. cit., p. 271.
13. For a representative sampling of the literature, see Carl Kaysen, "Keeping the Strategic Balance," *Foreign Affairs*, XLVI (July 1968), 665–675; Harold Brown, "Security through Limitations," and Donald G. Brennan, "The Case for Missile De-

fense," *Foreign Affairs*, XLVII (April 1969), 422–432 and 443–448, respectively; and "Missiles and Anti-Missiles: Six Views," *Bulletin of the Atomic Scientists*, XXV (June 1969), 20–28; William R. Kintner, ed., *Safeguard: Why the AMB Makes Sense* (New York: Hawthorne, 1969); Abram Chayes and Jerome B. Weisner, eds., *ABM: An Evaluation of the Decision to Deploy an Anti-Ballistic Missile System* (New York: Harper & Row, 1969).

14. See Charles J. Hitch and Roland N. McKean, *The Economics of Defense in the Nuclear Age* (Cambridge, Mass.: Harvard University Press, 1960); Samuel P. Huntington, *The Common Defense: Strategic Programs in National Politics* (New York: Columbia University Press, 1961), especially chaps. 6–12, 14, 16, and 18.

15. One writer has accused the advocates of both ballistic missile defense and MIRVs of exaggerating the strategic significance of those weapons systems and of underestimating the extent to which deterrence stability can remain undisturbed in the face of technological "system shocks." See Benjamin S. Lambeth, "Deterrence in the MIRV Era," *World Politics*, XXIV (January 1972), 224. For a less optimistic view of the emerging technological threat to strategic stability, see Bernard Brodie, *War and Politics* (New York: Macmillan, 1973), pp. 386–392. John D. Steinbruner has argued that in the American debate over the potential vulnerability of land-based ICBMs too little attention has been given to the critical problem dimension of preserving the stability of command, control and communications structures. "National Security and the Concept of Strategic Stability," *Journal of Conflict Resolution*, Vol. 22 (September 1978), 411–428.

16. On this last distinction, see Raymond Aron, *The Great Debate: Theories of Nuclear Strategy*, trans. Ernest Pawel (Garden City: Doubleday, 1965), pp. 32–33. Richard Rosecrance also draws a distinction between the threat of devastating damage posed before aggression occurs and the response actually made after hostilities break out. *International Relations: Peace or War?* (New York: McGraw Hill, 1973), p. 284.

17. Henry A. Kissinger, op. cit., p. 12.

18. Robert E. Osgood, "Stabilizing the Military Environment," in Dale J. Hekhuis, Charles F. McClintock, and Arthur L. Burns, eds., *International Stability* (New York: Wiley, 1964), p. 87. For other views on uncertainty, see A. R. Hibbs, "ABM and the Algebra of Uncertainty," *Bulletin of the Atomic Scientists*, XXIV (March 1968), 31–33; D. G. Brennan, "Uncertainty Is Not the Issue," Ibid., 33–34; Freeman Dyson, "A Case for Missile Defense," ibid., XXV (April 1969), 31–33; John D. Steinbruner, op. cit.

19. Stanley Sienkiewicz, "Observations on the Impact of Uncertainty in Strategic Analysis," *World Politics*, XXXII (October 1979), 98–99.

20. Raymond Aron, "The Evolution of Modern Strategic Thought," in *Problems of Modern Strategy: Part One*, Adelphi Papers No. 54 (London: Institute for Strategic Studies, February 1969), p. 9.

21. Ibid.

22. Ole R. Holsti, *Crisis, Escalation, War* (Montreal: McGill-Queens University Press, 1972), pp. 8–9.

23. Patrick M. Morgan, op. cit., pp. 28–43.

24. Alexander L. George and Richard Smoke, op. cit., pp. 38–41.

25. John H. Herz, "The Territorial State Revisited: Reflections on the Future of the Nation-States," in James N. Rosenau, ed., *International Politics and Foreign Policy* (1969) pp. 80–81.

26. Alexander L. George and Richard Smoke, op. cit., p. 54.

27. Bruce M. Russett, "The Calculus of Deterrence," *Journal of Conflict Resolution*, VII (March 1963), 97–109. See also Franklin B. Weinstein, "The Concept of a

Commitment in International Relations," *Journal of Conflict Resolutions*, XIII (March 1969), 39–56.

28. See Bruce M. Russett, "Pearl Harbor: Deterrence Theory and Decision Theory," *Journal of Peace Research*, 4, No. 2 (1967), 80–106; and Peter de Leon, James Mac-Queen, and Richard Rosecrance, "Situational Analysis in International Politics," unpublished manuscript, UCLA Political Science Department, 1967, summarized in *Behavioral Science*, 14, No. 1 (January 1968), 51.

29. See Patrick M. Morgan, op. cit., p. 31. Morgan cites Thomas C. Schelling, *Arms and Influence* (New Haven: Yale University Press, 1966), pp. 69–91, and the concluding chapter of Alexander George et al., *The Limits of Coercive Diplomacy* (Boston: Little, Brown, 1971).

30. The theoretical strategic issues summarized in this section have generated a vast literature, samples of which follow: Thomas C. Schelling, "Nuclear Strategy in Europe," *World Politics* XIV (April 1962), 421–432, and *Arms and Influence*, op. cit., pp. 105–116; Michael Brower, "Nuclear Strategy of the Kennedy Administration," *Bulletin of the Atomic Scientists*, XVIII (October 1962), 33–41; Alastair Buchan and Philip Windsor, *Arms and Stability in Europe* (New York: Praeger, 1963); Timothy W. Stanley, *NATO in Transition* (New York: Praeger, 1965), chaps. 3–5; James L. Richardson, *Germany and the Atlantic Alliance* (Cambridge, Mass.: Harvard University Press, 1966), chaps. 7–10; General Andre Beaufre, *NATO and Europe*, trans. from French by Joseph Green (New York: Random House [Vintage Books], 1966), especially chap. 4, "Evolution of NATO Strategy"; Timothy W. Stanley, "A Strategic Doctrine for NATO in the 1970s," *Orbis*, XIII (Spring 1969), 87–99; Michael May, "Some Advantages of a Counterforce Deterrence," *Orbis*, XIV (Summer 1970), 271–283; Bruce M. Russett, "A Countercombatant Deterrent?", in S. C. Sarkesian, ed., *The Military-Industrial Complex* (Beverly Hills, Calif.: Sage, 1972), pp. 241–242; Fred Charles Iklé, "Can Nuclear Deterrence Last Out the Century?", *Foreign Affairs*, LI (January 1973), 267–285; Barry Carter, "Nuclear Strategy and Nuclear Weapons," *Scientific American* CCXXX (May 1974), 20–31; Ted Greenwood and Michael L. Nacht, "The New Nuclear Debate: Sense or Nonsense?", *Foreign Affairs*, LII (July 1974), 761–780; Laurence Martin, "Changes in American Strategic Doctrine—An Initial Interpretation," *Survival*, XVI (July/August 1974); Michael J. Brenner, "Tactical Nuclear Strategy and European Defense: A Critical Reappraisal," *International Affairs* (London) LI (January 1975), 23–42; Jerome H. Kahan, op. cit., pp. 245–250; Lynn E. Davis, *Limited Nuclear Options: Deterrence and the New American Doctrine*, Adelphi Papers No. 121 (London: International Institute for Strategic Studies [IISS], Winter 1975/1976); Richard Burt, *New Weapons Technologies*, Adelphi Papers No. 126 (London: IISS, Summer 1976); *Tactical Nuclear Weapons: European Perspectives*, Stockholm International Peace Research Institute (London: Taylor and Francis, 1978).

31. See Ian Smart, *Future Conditional: The Prospect for Anglo-French Nuclear Cooperation*, Adelphi Papers No. 78 (London: IISS, August 1968); François Duchêne, "A New European Defense Community," *Foreign Affairs*, L (October 1971), 69–82; Alastair Buchan, "A World Restored?", *Foreign Affairs*, L (July 1972), 644–659; Paul C. Davis, "A European Nuclear Force: Utility and Prospects," *Orbis*, XVII (Spring 1973), 110–131; Andrew J. Pierre "Can Europe's Security Be 'Decoupled' from America?", *Foreign Affairs*, LI (July 1973), 761–777; Geoffrey Kemp, *Nuclear Forces for Medium Powers: Parts I and II*, Adelphi Papers No. 106 and 107 (London: IISS, Autumn 1974); Johann J. Holst and Uwe Nerlich, *Beyond Nuclear Weapons* (New York: Crane, Russak, 1977); Joseph I. Coffey, *Arms Control and European Security* (New York: Praeger, 1977).

32. Pierre Gallois, *The Balance of Terror: Strategy for the Nuclear Age* (Boston: Houghton Mifflin; 1961), pp. 119–122, 136–142, and 195–201.

33. The authors of this textbook are affiliated with the Institute for Foreign Policy Analysis in Cambridge, Massachusetts, which has published several reports on changes in the global strategic balance and changes in the European theater nuclear balance. These include the following Special Reports: Jacqueline K. Davis, Patrick J. Friel, and Robert L. Pfaltzgraff, Jr., *Salt II and U.S.–Soviet Strategic Forces*, June 1979; Leon Gouré, William G. Hyland and Colin S. Gray, *The Emerging Strategic Environment: Implications for Ballistic Missile Defense*, December 1979; William Schneider, Jr., Donald G. Brennan, William A. Davis, Jr., and Hans Rühle, *U.S. Strategic Nuclear Policy and Ballistic Missile Defense*, April 1980; J. I. Coffey, Lord Chalfont et al., *The Future of U.S. Land-Based Strategic Forces*, September 1980. The shifting balance has also been treated in the following Conference Reports: *NATO and Its Future: A German-American Roundtable*, 1978; *Second German-American Roundtable on NATO: The Theater Nuclear Balance*, 1978; *Third German-American Roundtable on NATO: Mutual and Balanced Force Reductions in Europe*, 1979. The implications of the changing balance for Europe and NATO are elaborated in Walter F. Hahn and Robert L. Pfaltzgraff, eds., *Atlantic Community in Crisis: A Redefinition of the Atlantic Relationship* (New York: Pergamon, 1979). On negotiating limits for Eurostrategic weapons, see Note 80 below.

34. To say that this or that course of action is "rational" or "irrational" presupposes a prior judgment or assumption concerning objectives or goals, and in the final analysis these are based upon values which lie beyond "rational" evaluation. See Hoffman, *The State of War*, op. cit., pp. 12–13; and William A. Scott, "Rationality and Nonrationality of International Attitudes," *Journal of Conflict Resolution* (March 1958), 8–16. On the "rationality" and "credibility" of nuclear deterrence, see Brodie, op. cit.; Maxwell, op. cit., p. 3; J. David Singer, *Deterrence, Arms Control and Disarmament*, (Columbus, O.: Ohio State University Press, 1962) chaps, 2 and 3; Kaplan, "The Calculus of Nuclear Deterrence," *World Politics*, XI (October 1958).

35. Richard Pipes, "Why the Soviet Union Thinks It Could Fight and Win a Nuclear War," *Commentary*, 64 (July 1977), 21–34; John Erickson, "The Chimera of Mutual Deterrence," *Strategic* Review, VI (Spring 1978); Stanley Sienkiewicz, "SALT and Soviet Nuclear Doctrine," *International Security*, 2 (Spring 1978); Fritz W. Ermarth, "Contrasts in American and Soviet Strategic Thought," ibid., 3 (Fall 1978); Colin S. Gray, "Nuclear Strategy: A Case for a Theory of Victory," *International Security*, 4 (Summer 1979), 54–87.

36. Leon Gouré, *War Survival in Soviet Strategy: USSR Civil Defense*, Monographs in International Affairs (Miami: Center for Advanced International Studies, University of Miami, 1976).

37. Thomas W. Milburn, "What Constitutes Effective Deterrence?", *Journal of Conflict Resolution*, III (June 1959), 139–140. See also his "The Concept of Deterrence: Some Logical and Psychological Considerations," *Journal of Social Issues*, XVII, no. 3 (1961), 3–11.

38. Charles E. Osgood, "Questioning Some Unquestioned Assumptions about National Defense," *Journal of Arms Control*, I (January 1963), 3. For experimental evidence of the phenomenon which psychologists call "defensive avoidance," see I. L. Janis and R. F. Terivilliger, "An Experimental Study of Psychological Resistance to Fear Arousing Communications," *Journal of Abnormal and Social Psychology*, LXV (1962), 402–410.

39. Robert Jervis, "Deterrence Theory Revisited," Review Article, *World Politics*, XXXI (April 1979), 289–324.

40. Herman Kahn, *On Thermonuclear War* (Princeton: Princeton University Press, 1960), pp. 291–295; Thomas C. Schelling, *Arms and Influence*, op. cit., pp. 37–38; Maxwell, op. cit., pp. 2–10. The debate over the question of the relationship between the value-optimizing strategy which should logically be adopted and the way

in which players will actually behave in a crisis situation—more a matter of psychological than logical reaction—remains at the center of the debate over the validity of the strategy of nuclear deterrence. John D. Steinbruner has rejected the rational-analytic model, arguing that in a tradeoff relationship, values are pursued separately, not integrated, no attempt is made to optimize values, and decisions are arrived at by the nonrational rules of cognitive operations which tend to suppress the awareness of a conflict between values. "Beyond Rational Deterrence: The Struggle for New Conceptions," *World Politics,* XXVIII (January 1976). See also Jack L. Snyder, "Rationality at the Brink: The Role of Cognitive Processes in Failures of Deterrence," ibid., XXX (April 1978).

41. See Mason Willrich, *Global Politics of Nuclear Energy* (New York: Praeger, 1971), especially chaps. 1 and 11.

42. See Premier Khrushchev's Address to the General Assembly and related documents, *Documents on Disarmament 1945–1959* (Washington: USGPO, 1960), vol. II, pp. 1452–1474 and 1506–1516; and President Kennedy's Address to the General Assembly and accompanying declaration, *Documents on Disarmament, 1961* (Washington: USGPO, 1962), pp. 465–482.

43. See, for example, Grenville Clark and Louis B. Sohn, *World Peace Through World Law* (Cambridge, Mass.: Harvard University Press, 1958); Philip Noel-Baker, *The Arms Race: A Program for World Disarmament* (New York: Oceana, 1960); Seymour Melman, ed., *Disarmament: Its Politics and Economics* (Boston: American Academy of Arts and Sciences, 1962); Arthur Lawson, *A Warless World* (New York: McGraw-Hill, 1962); F. A. Long, "Immediate Steps Toward General and Complete Disarmament," *Disarmament and Arms Control,* 2 (Winter 1963/1964), 1–9; Michael Wright, *Disarm and Verify* (New York: Praeger, 1964); Evan Luard, ed., *First Steps to Disarmament* (New York: Basic Books, 1965).

44. See Gerard Piel, "The Economics of Disarmament," *Bulletin of the Atomic Scientists,* XVI (April 1960), 117–122, 126; *Economic Impacts of Disarmament,* U.S. Arms Control and Disarmament Agency (Washington: USGPO, 1962); *Economic and Social Consequences of Disarmament,* Report of a Study by the United Nations Economic and Social Council (New York: United Nations, 1962); Emile Benoit and Kenneth Boulding, eds., *Disarmament and the Economy* (New York: Harper & Row, 1963); *Report of the Committee on the Economic Impact of Defense and Disarmament, submitted to President Johnson July 30, 1965* (Washington: USGPO, 1965); Emile Benoit, ed., *Disarmament and World Economic Interdependence* (New York: Columbia University Press, 1967); "United States Report to Secretary-General Thant on the Economic and Social Consequences of Disarmament, March 26, 1968," in *Documents on Disarmament, 1968* (Washington: USGPO, 1969), pp. 196–203.

45. Richard J. Barnet, *The Roots of War* (Baltimore: Penguin, 1972), p. 167.

46. See pp. 234–235.

47. See Louis B. Sohn, "Zonal Disarmament and Inspection: Variations on a Theme," *Bulletin of the Atomic Scientists* XVIII (September 1962); and Clark C. Abt, "Progressive Zonal Inspection of Disarmament," *Disarmament and Arms Control,* II (Winter 1963/1964).

48. See Leonard S. Rodberg, "Graduated Assess Inspection," *Journal of Arms Control,* I (April 1963); and Lincoln P. Bloomfield, "The Politics of Administering Disarmament," *Disarmament and Arms Control,* I (Autumn 1963).

49. A voluminous and imaginative literature on inspection for GCD was produced. See, for example, Seymour Melman, ed., *Inspection for Disarmament* (New York: Columbia University Press, 1958); Bernard T. Feld, "Inspection Techniques for Arms Control," in Donald G. Brennan, ed., *Arms Control, Disarmament and National Security* (New York: Braziller, 1961); Report of the Woods Hole Summary Study,

1962, *Verification and Response in Disarmament Agreements* (Washington: Institute for Defense Analyses, 1962); Karl W. Deutsch, "Communications, Arms Inspection and National Security," in Quincy Wright et al., eds., *Preventing World War III: Some Proposals* (New York: Simon & Schuster, 1962); James E. Dougherty, *Arms Control and Disarmament: The Critical Issues* (Washington: Georgetown University Center for Strategic Studies, 1966), chaps. 6 and 7, and the chapters by Philip Windsor, Walter Levison, Michael Howard, and Wayland Young in Evan Luard, ed., op. cit.

50. Leonard S. Rodberg, "The Rationale of Inspection," in Seymour Melman, ed., *Disarmament: Its Politics and Economics,* p. 75.

51. Fred Charles Iklé, "After Detection—What?", *Foreign Affairs,* XXXIX (January 1961), 208–220.

52. Seymour Melman, "How Can Inspection Be Made to Work?" *Bulletin of the Atomic Scientists,* XIV (September 1958). See also Jerome B. Wiesner, "Inspection for Disarmament," in Louis Henkin, ed., *Arms Control: Issues for the Public* (Englewood Cliffs, N.J.: Prentice-Hall, 1961), p. 126.

53. See Jay Orear, "New Approaches to Inspection," *Bulletin of the Atomic Scientists,* XVII (March 1961); Lewis C. Bohn, "Non-physical Techniques of Disarmament Inspection," Seymour Melman, "Inspection by the People," and Ralph W. Gerard, "Truth Detection," in Quincy Wright et al., eds., op. cit.; and Elton B. McNeil, "Psychological Inspection," *Journal of Arms Control,* I (April 1963).

54. Cf. Henry A. Kissinger, "Arms Control, Inspection and Surprise Attack," *Foreign Affairs,* XXXVIII (July 1960), 559–561; Hedley Bull, *The Control of the Arms Race* (New York: Praeger, 1961), pp. 168–169; Glenn H. Snyder, *Deterrence and Defense* (Princeton: Princeton University Press, 1961), pp. 97–103; and Thomas C. Schelling, *The Strategy of Conflict* (New York: Oxford University Press, 1963), pp. 235–236.

55. Hedley Bull, op. cit., p. 34.

56. Thomas C. Schelling and Morton H. Halperin, op. cit., p. 60.

57. Eugene Rabinowitch, "Defenders and Avengers," *Bulletin of the Atomic Scientists,* XVI (November 1960), p. 359.

58. See Lincoln P. Bloomfield, *International Military Forces: The Question of Peacekeeping in an Armed and Disarming World* (Boston: Little, Brown, 1964) and "Arms Control and World Government," *World Politics,* XIV (July 1962); J. I. Coffey, "The Soviet View of a Disarmed World," *Journal of Conflict Resolution,* VIII (March 1964); Arthur Waskow, "Alternative Models of a Disarmed World," *Disarmament and Arms Control,* II (Winter 1963/1964). For a statement of the view that the U.S. Outline Plan for Complete Disarmament was not in the national interest of the United States, see Arnold Wolfers, "Disarmament, Peacekeeping and the National Interest," in Robert E. Osgood, ed., *The United States in a Disarmed World* (Baltimore: Johns Hopkins Press, 1965).

59. See Louis B. Sohn, "Disarmament at the Crossroads," *International Security,* 2 (Spring 1978); "Special Session in Retrospect," editorial, *Bulletin of Atomic Scientists,* 34 (October 1978).

60. See James E. Dougherty, *How to Think About Arms Control and Disarmament* (New York: Crane, Russak, 1973), pp. 29–36.

61. The multilateral treaties included: the Antarctica Treaty of 1959; the Partial Nuclear Test Ban Treaty of 1963; the Outer Space Treaty of 1967; the Treaty of Tlatetolco of 1967; the Nuclear Non-Proliferation Treaty of 1968; the Seabed Treaty of 1971; and the Biological Weapons Convention of 1972. The U.S.-Soviet bilateral agreements included: the "Hot Line" Agreement of 1963 (updated in 1971); the Agreement to Reduce the Risk of Accidental Outbreak of Nuclear War of 1971; the Agreement of 1972 to prevent naval incidents; the Antiballistic Missile Limita-

tion Agreement of 1972; the Interim Agreement on Strategic Offensive Weapons of 1972; the Nixon-Brezhnev Agreement of 1973 on the Prevention of Nuclear War; the 1974 Threshold Test Ban Agreement; the 1974 Vladivostok Agreement on Guidelines for SALT II; the 1976 Treaty on Underground Nuclear Explosions for Peaceful Purposes; the 1977 Convention to Prohibit Military or Other Hostile Use of Environmental Modification Techniques; and the SALT II Agreements of 1979. Texts of all of these agreements except the last named one (discussed subsequently in the text and the notes) can be found in *Arms Control and Disarmament Agreements* (Washington: USGPO, 1977).

62. See *The Nth Country Problem and Arms Control*, A Statement by a Special Project Committee of the N.P.A. (Washington: National Planning Association, 1960); Fred Charles Iklé, "Nth Countries and Disarmament," *Bulletin of the Atomic Scientists*, XVI (December 1960), 391–394; Albert Wohlstetter, "Nuclear Sharing: NATO and the N-Plus-1 Country," *Foreign Affairs*, XXXIX (April 1961), 355–387; Leonard Beaton and John Maddox, *The Spread of Nuclear Weapons* (New York: Praeger, 1962), pp. 168–181; Alastair Buchan, ed., *A World of Nuclear Powers* (Englewood Cliffs, N.J.: Prentice-Hall, 1966). Bertrand Goldschmidt, "A Historical Survey of Nonproliferation Policies," *International Security*, Vol. 2 (Summer 1977), 69–87.

63. See Raymond Aron, Klaus Knorr, and Alastair Buchan, "The Future of Western Deterrent Power," *Bulletin of the Atomic Scientists*, XVI (September 1960), 266–282; Paul M. Doty, "The Role of the Smaller Powers," in Donald G. Brennan, ed., op. cit., pp. 304–314; and R. N. Rosecrance, ed., *The Dispersion of Nuclear Weapons* (New York: Columbia University Press, 1964).

64. Paul M. Doty, op. cit., p. 314.

65. See Sheldon Novick, *The Careless Atom* (Boston: Houghton Mifflin, 1969); Richard Curtis and Elizabeth Hogan, *The Perils of the Peaceful Atom* (Garden City, N.Y.: Doubleday, 1969).

66. See James E. Dougherty, "The Treaty and the Non-nuclear States," *Orbis*, XI (Summer 1967), 360–377; V. C. Trivedi, "Vertical versus Horizontal Proliferation: An Indian View," in James E. Dougherty and J. F. Lehman, Jr., eds., *Arms Control for the Late Sixties* (Princeton: Van Nostrand, 1967), pp. 195–203; Elizabeth Young, *The Control of Proliferation: The 1968 Treaty in Hindsight and Forecast*, Adelphi Papers No. 56 (London: Institute for Strategic Studies, 1969).

67. Sisir Gupta, "The Indian Dilemma," in Alastair Buchan, ed., *A World of Nuclear Powers*, op. cit., pp. 55–67; Shelton L. Williams, *The U.S., India and the Bomb* (Baltimore: Johns Hopkins Press, 1969); George H. Quester, "India Contemplates the Bomb," *Bulletin of the Atomic Scientists*, XXVI (January 1970), 13–16, 48.

68. K. Subrahmanyam, "India: Keeping the Option Open," in Robert M. Lawrence and Joel Laurus, eds., *Nuclear Proliferation: Phase II* (Lawrence, Kan.: University Press of Kansas, 1974), pp. 129–130.

69. Ibid., p. 118.

70. Abstainers in 1975 included India, Indonesia, Pakistan, Israel, Egypt, Turkey, Argentina, Brazil, Chile and Venezuela. See *Preventing Nuclear Weapons Proliferation—An Approach to The Non-Proliferation Treaty Review Conference* (Stockholm: SIPRI, n.d.); Anne W. Marks, ed., *NPT: Paradoxes and Problems* (Washington: Arms Control Association and Carnegie Endowment for International Press, 1975); and William Epstein, "Nuclear Proliferation in the Third World," *Journal of International Affairs*, XXIX, No. 2 (1975), 185–202.

71. See Asok Kapur, "India and the Atom," *Bulletin of the Atomic Scientists*, XXX (September 1974), 27–30; George H. Quester, "Can Proliferation Now Be Stopped?" *Foreign Affairs*, LIII (October 1974), 77–97; Masataka Kosaka, "Japanese Nuclear Option," in Geoffrey Kemp, Robert L. Pfaltzgraff, Jr., and Uri Ra'anan, eds., *The*

Superpowers in a Multinuclear World (Lexington, Mass.: D.C. Heath, 1974), 91–105; John Maddox, *Prospects for Nuclear Proliferation* Adlephi Paper No. 113 (London: 11SS, Spring 1975); William Epstein "The Proliferation of Nuclear Weapons," *Scientific American*, 232 (April 1975), 18–33; John E. Endicott, *Japan's Nuclear Option* (New York: Praeger, 1975); James E. Dougherty, "Nuclear Proliferation in Asia," *Orbis*, XIX (Fall 1975), 925–957; Frank T.J. Bray and Michael L. Moodie, "Nuclear Politics in India," *Survival*, XX (May/June 1977), 111–116; Special Report on Nonproliferation Policies and the NPT (including Jack N. Barkenbus, "Whither the Treaty?"; Pugwash Council, "The Second Review Conference;" and Kathleen Bailey, "When and Why Weapons?") in *Bulletin of the Atomic Scientists*, 36 (April 1980), 36–45.

72. Lincoln P. Bloomfield, "Nuclear Spread and World Order," *Foreign Affairs*, LIII (July 1975), 743.

73. SIPRI, *Safeguards Against Nuclear Proliferation* (Stockholm: Almquist and Wiksell, 1975), p. 56; Frederick Williams and others, "The Nuclear Non-Proliferation Act of 1978: Reactions from Germany, India, and Japan," *International Security*, 3 (Fall 1978), 44–66.

74. David Krieger, "Terrorists and Nuclear Technology,," *Bulletin of Atomic Scientists*, XXI (June 1975), 28; Bruce G. Glair and Garry D. Brewer, "The Terrorist Threat in World Nuclear Programs," *Journal of Conflict Resolution*, XXI (September 1977), 379–403.

75. R. Robert Sandoval, "Consider the Porcupine: Another View of Nuclear Proliferation," *Bulletin of the Atomic Scientists*, 32 (May 1976), p. 97. See also Steven J. Rosen, "Nuclearization and Stability in the Middle East," in Onkar Marwah and Ann Schulz, eds., *Nuclear Proliferation and the Near-Nuclear Countries* (Cambridge, Mass.: Ballinger, 1975) p. 157.

76. *Postures for Non-Proliferation*, Stockholm International Peace Research Institute (London: Taylor and Francis, 1979), pp. 5–7.

77. The background, motivations, and rationales for the SALT I negotiations are discussed in William R. Kintner and Robert L. Pfaltzgraff, Jr., eds., *SALT: Implications for Arms Control* (Pittsburgh, Pa.: University of Pittsburgh Press, 1973); James E. Dougherty, "Soviet-Western Arms Negotiations: SALT and MBFR," *Royal United Services Institute and Brassey's Defence Yearbook 1974* (London: William Clowes, 1974); and Jerome H. Kahan, *Security in the Nuclear Age*, op. cit., chaps, 2, 3, and 5. See also Robert L. Pfaltzgraff, Jr., ed., *Contending Approaches to Arms Control* (Lexington, Mass.: D.C. Heath, 1974).

78. For texts of these accords, see *Arms Control and Disarmament Agreements: Texts and History of Negotiations* (Washington, D.C.: U.S. Arms Control and Disarmament Agency, 1975), pp. 131–149. John Newhouse furnished a detailed account of the SALT I negotiations in *Cold Dawn* (New York: Holt, Rinehart and Winston, 1973).

79. The principal critic of the ABM Treaty on the grounds that it left civilian populations exposed to attack while the Interim Agreement committed the American Government to the strategic doctrine of Mutual Assured Destruction was the late Donald G. Brennan. See his "Strategic Forum: The SALT Agreements," *Survival*, 14 (September/October 1972), 216–219. Representative arguments that SALT I did not really restrain superpower arms programs include Bernard T. Feld, "Looking to SALT II," *Bulletin of the Atomic Scientists*, 38 (June 1972), 2–3; and George W. Rathjens, "The SALT Agreements: An Appraisal," ibid., 38 (November 1972), 8–10.

80. Lothar Ruehl, "The 'Grey Area' Problem," in Christoph Bertram, ed., *The Future of Arms Control: Part I—Beyond SALT II*, Adelphi Papers No. 141 (London: IISS,

1978), pp. 25–34; Robert Metzger and Paul Doty, "Arms Control Enters the Gray Area," *International Security*, 3 (Winter 1978), 17–52; Gregory F. Treverton, "Nuclear Weapons and the 'Gray Area,'" *Foreign Affairs*, 57 (Summer 1979), 1075–1089.

81. Richard L. Garwin, "Launch Under Attack to Redress Minuteman Vulnerability?" *International Security*, 4 (Winter 1979/1980), 117–139.

82. Colin S. Gray, *The Future of Land-Based Missile Forces*, Adelphi Papers No. 140 (London: IISS, 1977) and "The Strategic Forces Triad: End of the Road?" *Foreign Affairs*, 56 (July 1978), 771–789.

83. Robert Perry, "Verifying SALT in the 1980s," in Christoph Bertram, ed., op. cit., 15–24; Carnes Lord, "Verification and the Future of Arms Control," *Strategic Review*, VI (Spring 1978), 24–32; Lee Aspin, "The Verification of the SALT II Agreement," *Scientific American*, 240 (February 1979). The special problems associated with the proposed mobile missile (MX) are treated in Stephen M. Meyer, "Verification and the ICBM Shell Game," *International Security*, 4 (Fall 1979), 40–68.

84. For additional perspectives on SALT II, see James E. Dougherty, "SALT: An Introduction to the Substance and Politics of the Negotiations," in Paul H. Nitze et al., *The Fateful Ends and Shades of SALT* (New York: Crane, Russak, 1979), pp. 1–36; Strobe Talbott, *Endgame: The Inside Story of SALT II* (New York: Harper & Row, 1979); Thomas W. Wolfe, *The SALT Experience* (Cambridge, Mass.: Ballinger, 1979); and *Salt II and American Security*, A Conference Report (Cambridge, Mass.: Institute for Foreign Policy Analysis, 1979). The full text of the accords signed in Vienna on June 18, 1979 may be found in *SALT II Agreement*, Department of State Publication 8986 (Washington, D.C.: U.S. Government Printing Office, July 1979).

85. Richard J. Barnet, *The Giants: Russia and America* (New York: Simon & Schuster, 1978); Bernard T. Feld, "The Charade of Piecemeal Arms Limitation," *Bulletin of the Atomic Scientists*, 31 (January 1975), 8–16; Paul M. Doty et al., "The Race to Control Nuclear Arms," *Foreign Affairs*, 55 (October 1976), 119–132; Alexander R. Vershbow, "The Cruise Missile: The End of Arms Control?" ibid., 133–146.

86. The status of these negotiations is discussed in *Arms Control 1978* (Washington, D.C.: U.S. Arms Control and Disarmament Agency, 1979), pp. 20–47. See also *Armaments and Disarmament in the Nuclear Age: A Handbook*, Stockholm International Peace Research Institute (Cambridge, Mass.: MIT Press, 1976), chaps. 3, 5, and 8; *Chemical Weapons: Destruction and Conversion* Stockholm International Peace Research Institute (London: Taylor and Francis, 1980); Donald G. Brennan, "A Comprehensive Test Ban: Everybody or Nobody," *International Security*, 1 (Summer 1976), 92–117; Donald R. Westervelt, "Candor, Compromise and the Comprehensive Test Ban," *Strategic Review*, V (Fall 1977), 33–44; Walter F. Hahn and Alvin J. Cottrell, *Naval Race or Arms Control in the Indian Ocean?* (New York: National Strategy Information Center, 1978); Richard Haas, "Naval Arms Limitation in the Indian Ocean," *Survival*, XX (March/April 1978), 50–57; Stephen L. Canby, "Mutual Force Reductions: A Military Perspective," *International Security*, 2 (Winter 1978), 122–135; Ann Hessing Cahn et al., *Controlling Future Arms Trade* (New York: McGraw-Hill, 1977); Andrew J. Pierre, *Arms Transfers and American Foreign Policy* (New York: New York University Press, 1979); and Stephanie G. Neuman and Robert E. Harkavy, *Arms Transfers in the Modern World* (New York: Praeger, 1979).

87. Christoph Bertram, *The Future of Arms Control: Part II—Arms Control and Technological Change*, Adelphi Papers No. 146 (London: IISS, 1978).

88. Donald M. Snow, "Current Nuclear Deterrence Thinking: An Overview and Review," *International Studies Quarterly*, 23 (September 1979), 445–486. Concerning the vindictiveness of the MAD strategy, see Philip Green, *Deadly Logic: The Theory of Nuclear Deterrence* (Columbus: Ohio State University Press, 1966), p. 237.

Chapter 10
Theories of International Integration, Regionalism, and Alliance Cohesion

CONSENSUS, FORCE, AND POLITICAL COMMUNITY

Central to the study of politics is the identification and analysis of forces that contribute to the formation and integration of political communities. Like the study of conflict, another major focal point in the study of politics, political integration cuts across the traditional fields into which political science is organized, and is as relevant to the student of politics at the local and metropolitan level as it is to comparative international politics.[1]

Two questions are fundamental both to the study of integration and of politics itself: (1) why subjects or citizens give deference and devotion to the political unit within which they live (or why they do not); (2) how procedural and substantive consensus is achieved and sustained within political systems. It is possible to outline essentially two theories of political integration. First, political systems gain and retain cohesiveness because of widely shared values among their members and general agreement about the framework of the system. Such systems are based on procedural consensus, or general agreement about the political framework and the legal processes by which issues are resolved, and substantive consensus or general agreement about the solutions to problems the political system is called upon to solve. The greater the procedural and substantive consensus, the greater the integration of the political system. As used here, the term *consensus* is similar to legitimacy, as discussed in Chapter 3 with respect to Europe's classical balance of power and, specifically, Henry A. Kissinger's theory of international relations.

Second, as an alternative theory, it has been argued that political systems become or remain cohesive because of the presence, or threat, of force. Writers such as Hobbes and in contemporary sociology, Dahrendorf, have argued for a recognition of the importance of coercive power in the integration of political communities.[2] In the study of international relations, proponents of world government have often seen in the monopolization of power at the international level the key to the reduction of violence, and so-called political realists such as Niebuhr and Morgenthau, as noted in Chapter 3, have argued that world government is not possible without the development of far greater consensus at the global level than has existed in the twentieth century.[3]

FUNCTIONALISM AND THE INTEGRATIVE PROCESS

Contemporary students of political integration owe a considerable intellectual debt to the concept of functionalism which, as Johan K. De Vree has suggested, has provided an alternative to the more traditional legal conceptions of the state and of sovereignty and has posed questions of fundamental importance concerning the future political organization of mankind.[4] In the study of political science functionalism has assumed several meanings. Eclectic functionalists, widespread in political science, ask what functions a political party, an international organization, or an office holder performs. Depending on the analyst, functionalism may provide only a list of activities in which X is engaged, or it may answer questions regarding X's contributions to the performance of certain purposes or activities.[5]

Although structural-functional analysis, as suggested in Chapter 4, occupies an important place in the study of political science, it differs fundamentally from functionalism as used by David Mitrany, whose writings have greatly influenced contemporary integration theorists. Mitrany wrote during the years between the two World Wars, as well as in the generation following World War II. He suggested that the growing complexity of governmental systems had increased greatly the essentially technical, nonpolitical tasks facing governments. Such tasks not only created a demand for highly trained specialists at the national level, but also contributed to essentially technical problems at the international level, whose solution lies in collaboration among technicians, rather than political elites. The growth in importance of technical issues in the twentieth century is said to have made necessary the creation of frameworks for international cooperation. Such functional organizations could be expected to expand both in their numbers and in scope as the technical problems confronting mankind grew both in immensity and magnitude.

Organizations for functional collaboration might eventually supersede, or make superfluous, the political institutions of the past. In functionalist writings, the dominant changes in the world of the twentieth century included economic development, the increasing role of national governments in economic matters and the consequent need for technical, or functional, collaboration across national frontiers, and the challenges to democratic political institutions as a result of the growing complexity of the tasks facing them. For the functionalist, what is technical, or functional, is deemed to be political. To move from a political to a technical framework is to limit drastically, or even to eliminate, the potential for conflict. Hence the functionalist emphasis on the progressive restriction of the role of political actors in favor of the technician.

Functionalism is based upon the hypothesis that national loyalties can be diffused and redirected into a framework for international cooperation in place of national competition and war. Carried to its ultimate conclusion, functionalism contains a form of Fabian socialism on an international scale, for it posits the growing importance of welfare demands upon the state. Because the state is inadequate for solving many problems because of the interdependent nature of the modern world, the obvious answer is said to lie in international organizations, and perhaps eventually in more tightly knit management and resolution of technical issues at the regional or global levels. As Charles Pentland has written "In particular, functionalism draws on the organic, socio-economic reformist ethos represented by British Fabianism and on ideas about the reconstruction of international society found in the writings of continental thinkers such as St. Simon. But the major source of functionalist thought has been in the experience of men who created, worked in, or observed the numerous international organizations that began to emerge in the late nineteenth century."[6]

In Mitrany's theory there is a doctrine of "ramification," whereby the development of collaboration in one technical field leads to collaboration in other technical fields. Functional collaboration in one sector results from a felt need, and generates a felt need for functional collaboration in another sector. The effort to create a common market, for example, gives rise to pressure for further collaboration on pricing, investment, transport, insurance, tax, wage, social security, banking, and monetary policies. Mitrany assumed that functional activity could reorient international activity and contribute to world peace. Eventually such collaboration would encroach upon, and even absorb, the political sector. In particular, "economic unification would build up the foundation for political agreement, even if it did not make it superfluous."[7] His basic strategy was to shift attention to supposedly noncontroversial technical problems.[8] Hence functionalism contrasts sharply with realist theory, which places emphasis upon competition and conflict as a principal, if not the dominant, feature of international politics (see Chapter 3). In contrast, functionalism, as Paul Taylor and A. J. Groom suggest, "begins by questioning the assumption that the state is irreducible and that the interests of governments prevail, and proceeds to the active consideration of schemes for cooperation; it is peace-oriented and seeks to avoid a win-lose stalemate framework."[9]

As a result of both World Wars, Mitrany saw the nation-state to be lacking in its ability either to preserve peace or to improve the social and economic well-being of its inhabitants. Conflict and war spring from the division of the world into separate and competing national units. As an alternative to conflict, Mitrany suggested the gradual creation of a transnational web of economic and social organizations and the remolding of attitudes and allegiances to make the masses of people more amenable to international integration. "Functionalism," he wrote, "was reconcilable with democratic political theory." Indeed, he suggested, functionalism is based "squarely" upon the most characteristic idea of modern democratic-liberal philosophy, that which leaves the individual free to enter into a variety of relationships—religious, political, and professional, social and cultural—each of which may take the individual in different directions and dimensions and into different groupings, some of them of international range. Each of us is in fact a "bundle" of functional loyalties; so that to build a world community upon that liberal conception is merely to extend and consolidate it also between national societies and groups.[10]

Traditional forms of representative government, in themselves, are deemed to be inadequate in light of functionalist theory, which posits that problems, increasingly technical in nature, must be resolved. Herein lies one of the dilemmas of functionalism: Can representative governments, based upon popularly elected officials, cope effectively with a range of problems that lie beyond the competence of political leaders? Mitrany saw one possible solution in the formation of specialist assemblies linking bureaucratic institutions and the public. Thus functionalism is linked to the conceptualization of global politics based upon growing levels of interdependence among actors whose interests and activities are not coincidental with state frontiers. The growth in functionalism has increased the permeability of the nation-state and the difficulties inherent in regulating activities that cross state frontiers. In short, functionalism is related inextricably to the growth of nonstate actors with transnational relationships that, by definition, lie often outside the traditional purview of the nation state. Hence the need for a conceptualization of global politics that extends beyond the international system based largely or exclusively on the nation-state.[11]

Integration as a Process and Condition

Thus Mitrany, like others considered in this chapter, was concerned with the process by which political communities become integrated. Although more recent students of integration have drawn upon Mitrany's work, they have developed their own definitions of integration. Ernst Haas defines integration as a process "whereby political actors in several distinct national settings are persuaded to shift their loyalties, expectations, and political activities toward a new center, whose institutions possess or demand jurisdiction over the preexisting national states."[12] In a later work, Haas conceives of integration as "referring *exclusively* to a process that links a given concrete international system with a dimly discernible future concrete system. If the present international scene is conceived of as a series of interacting and mingling national environments, and in terms of their participation in international organizations, then integration would describe the process of increasing and interaction and the mingling so as to obscure the boundaries between the system of international organizations and the environment provided by their national-state members."[13]

Referring to integration as a condition, Amitai Etzioni asserts that the possession by a political community of effective control over the use of the means of violence represents one criterion by which its level of integration is measured. Such a community has a center of decision-making that allocates resources and rewards and forms the dominant focus of political identification for the large majority of politically aware citizens.[14] In Etzioni's scheme, political unification is the process whereby political integration as a condition is achieved. Unification increases or strengthens the bonds among the units which form a system.[15] Making use of Haas's definition, Leon N. Lindberg, in his work on the European Community, defines integration as "(1) the processes whereby nations forego the desire and ability to conduct foreign and key domestic policies independently of each other, seeking instead to make *joint decisions* or to *delegate* the decision-making process to new central organs; and (2) the process whereby political actors in several distinct settings are persuaded to shift their expectations and political activities to a new center."[16]

Subsequently, Lindberg viewed political integration as part of a broader process of international integration in which "larger groupings emerge or are created among nations without the use of violence," and in which there is "joint participation in regularized, ongoing decision-making," as a result, or as part of "the evolution over time of a collective decision-making system among nations."[17]

According to Charles Pentland, "International political integration is frequently identified with the circumvention, reduction, or abolition of the sovereign power of modern nation-states."[18] Donald J. Puchala proposes a definition of integration as a "set of processes that produce and sustain a Concordance System at the international level," that is, "an international system wherein actors find it possible consistently to harmonize their interests, compromise their differences, and reap mutual rewards from their interactions."[19] Karl W. Deutsch refers to political integration as a process that may lead to a condition in which a group of people has "attained within a territory a sense of community and of institutions and practices strong enough to assure, for a long time, dependable expectations of peaceful change among its population."[20] Deutsch suggests that "integration is a matter of fact, not of time."[21] He also maintains that political integration can be compared to power, for we recall that power can be thought of as a relationship in which at least one actor is made to act differently from the way that actor would act otherwise (i.e., if this power were absent).[22] In another analysis, Philip E. Jacob suggests that political integration has "generally implied a relationship of *community* among people within the same political entity. That is, they are held together by mutual ties of one kind or another which give the group a feeling of identity and self-awareness."[23]

According to other writers, especially those in the 1970s, it is essential to focus upon the structural and institutional dimensions of integration, which is of central importance to the study of politics. Thus, Johan K. DeVree suggests that integration can be defined as the "process of the formation and development of institutions through which certain values are authoritatively allocated for a certain group of political actors or units."[24] In short, integration at the international level is conceptualized as the institutionalization of the political process among two or more states. According to James A. Caporaso and Alan L. Pelowski, integration consists of the development of "new structures and functions at a new system level which is more comprehensive (either geographically or functionally) than previously."[25] Integration consists of the emergence of new structures that may overlay, but not necessarily replace, older ones. These reflect a growing sense of interrelatedness between, or among, political or economic structures. The process by which integration occurs can be measured by using indicators of the growth of decisional capabilities within a specific unit such as the European Community.

Conditions for Integration

After criticizing contemporary theories for allegedly confusing conditions promoting integration and consequences resulting from integration, Johan Galtung defines integration as "the process whereby two or more actors form a new actor. When the process is completed, the actors are said to be integrated. Conversely, disintegration is the process whereby one actor splits into two or more actors. When the process is completed, the actor is said to be disintegrated."[26] Galtung sketches several models designed to establish conditions for integration.

First, integration may be viewed as value-integration. In this category, Galtung sets forth two models. An egalitarian model provides for the integration of values in the sense that actors have "coinciding interests." A second model, the hierarchical model, includes the integration of values which are arranged so that dilemmas and conflicts can be resolved by choosing the value highest in the hierarchy.

In a second category of conditions, Galtung conceptualizes integration as actor-integration. Here he sets forth a model in which integration consists of increasing similarity among actors in rank, demographic composition, and economic and political structure. Similarity is viewed as homology; that is, each member of an actor may find an "opposite number" in the other actor. In this category, there is a second model, the interdependence model. Integration is a process by which cultural, political, and economic interdependence between actors is increased. Actors become linked to such an extent that what harms one actor injures the other.

A third category provides for integration as exchanges between parts and whole. Here Galtung sets forth two models. In the loyalty model, integration develops and endures so long as the unit is supported by its component parts. Support forms an input such as acts of allegiance or the allocation of resources from the parts to the whole. In the allocation model, the existence of the integrated unit depends upon its ability to offer outputs to its parts. Such outputs include a nation providing a sense of identity to individuals, ensuring protection from enemies, or furnishing economic gains such as markets and high living standards.

In itself, none of these conditions is necessary and sufficient for integration. Integration is a process in which great importance is attached both to the constituent actors and their environment. According to Galtung, "Only when the new actor is so firmly integrated that the images formed by self and others coincide is the integration process completed."[27] Although all three types of integration can be present at the same time, Galtung suggests that in the contemporary world, organizations and associations tend to increase more rapidly than territories. If organizations create webs of interdependence and associations produce new points of identification that transcend the territorial nation-state, the problem facing mankind is said to be the development of an alternative to existing forms of territorial integration.

Writers on integration have several features in common. All are concerned with the process by which loyalty is shifted from one center to another. They share an interest in communications within units to be integrated. According to Deutsch and Etzioni, peoples learn to consider themselves members of a community as a result of human communications patterns. In general, integration theorists hold that persons adopt integrative behavior because of expectations of joint rewards or penalties. Initially, such expectations are developed among elite groups both in the governmental and private sectors. Successful integration depends upon a people's ability to "internalize" the integrative process, that is, for member elites, rather than external elites, to assume direction of an integrative process. Moreover, Deutsch, Etzioni, and Haas have utilized systems theory in developing integration models. Each emphasizes the effect of integration in one sector upon the ability of participating units to achieve integration in other sectors. Finally, it is broadly assumed that integration is a multidimensional phenomenon.

TRANSACTIONS AND COMMUNICATIONS: IMPLICATIONS FOR SECURITY COMMUNITIES

To a greater extent than other writers on integration, Karl Deutsch uses both communications and systems theory, drawing upon the mathematician Norbert Wiener's writings on cybernetics and on Talcott Parsons' work on general systems discussed in Chapter 4. Deutsch quotes with approval the following passage from Wiener:

> The existence of social science is based on the ability to treat a social group as an organization and not as an agglomeration. Communication is the cement that makes organizations. Communication alone enables a group to think together, to see together and to act together. All sociology requires the understanding of communication.[28]

Communications among people can produce either friendship or hostility depending upon the extent to which the memories of communications are associated with more or less favorable emotions. Nevertheless, in Deutsch's scheme political systems endure as a result of their ability to abstract and code incoming information into appropriate symbols, to store coded symbols, to disassociate certain important information from the rest, to recall stored information when needed, and to recombine stored information entered as an input into the system. The building of political units depends upon the flow of communications within the unit as well as between the unit and the outside world.

Deutsch is concerned with the relationship between communications and the integration of political communities.[29] Countries are "clusters of population, united by grids of communication flows and transport systems, and separated by thinly settled or nearly empty territories."[30] Peoples are groups of persons joined together by an ability to communicate on many kinds of topics; they have complementary habits of communication. Generally, boundaries are areas in which the density of population and communications decline sharply. Peoples become integrated as they become interdependent. "Wherever there is immediate interdependence, not for just one or two specialized goods or services but for a very wide range of different goods and services, you may suspect that you are dealing with a country."[31] Interdependence among nations is far lower than interdependence within nations. In fact, in some respects, as in the case of foreign trade, most countries are less interdependent today than they were in the nineteenth century. Trade, as a percentage of GNP, has declined.[32]

Deutsch's major substantive contribution to integration theory is found in his work on the conditions for political community in the North Atlantic area. Drawing upon historical data, Deutsch and his collaborators examined ten cases of integration and disintegration at the national level.[33] Since Deutsch's cases, in contrast to Etzioni's, are examples of the building of political communities at the national level, the implicit assumption of his work is that generalizations derived from these comparative studies are relevant to understanding integration at the international level, that there are similarities, or isomorphism, between the process of community building both at the national level and beyond the nation-state. Research and analysis undertaken in this work yielded several important conclusions about the conditions for the formulation of security communities. Deutsch and his associates set forth two kinds of security communities: *amalgamated,* in which previously independent political units have formed a single unit with a common government; and *pluralistic,* in which separate governments retain legal independence. The United States is used as an example of an amalgamated security community, and the United States-Canada or France-Germany since World War II may be called pluralistic security communities.[34]

For the formation of an amalgamated security community, several conditions were found to be necessary: (1) mutual compatibility of major values; (2) a distinctive way of life; (3) expectations of joint rewards timed so as to come before the imposition of burdens from amalgamation; (4) a marked increase in political and administrative capabilities of at least some participating units; (5) superior economic growth on the part of some participating units and the development of so-called core areas around which are grouped comparatively weaker areas; (6) unbroken links of social communication, both geographically between territories and between different social strata; (7) a broadening of the political elite; (8) mobility of persons, at least among the politically relevant strata; and (9) a multiplicity of communications and transactions.[35]

Pluralistic Security Communities

For the formation of pluralistic security communities three conditions were found essential: (1) compatibility of values among decision-makers; (2) mutual predictability of behavior among decision-makers of units to be integrated;[36] and (3) mutual responsiveness. Governments must be able to respond quickly, without resort to violence, to the actions and communications of other governments. In a pluralistic security community, the member units forego war as a means toward settling disputes.

In their study of political community and the North Atlantic area, Deutsch and his collaborators examined cases such as the Austro-Hungarian Empire, the Anglo-Irish Union, and the union between Norway and Sweden, in which political communities disintegrated. Several tentative conclusions emerged about conditions conducive to disintegration: (1) extended military commitments; (2) an increase in political participation on the part of a previously passive group; (3) the growth of ethnic or linguistic differentiation; (4) prolonged economic decline or stagnation; (5) relative closure of political elites; (6) excessive delay in social, economic, or political reforms; and (7) failure of a formerly privileged group to adjust to its loss of dominance.

In Deutsch's conception the integrative process is not unilinear in nature. The essential background conditions do not come into existence simultaneously, nor are they established in any special sequence. "Rather it appears to us from our cases that they may be assembled in almost any sequence, so long as all of them come into being and take effect."[37]

On the basis of findings concerning the building and disintegration of national units, Deutsch and his associates suggested that the North Atlantic area, "although it is far from integrated, seems already to have moved a long way toward becoming so."[38] Several countries have achieved "pluralistic integration": the United States and Canada; the United Kingdom and Ireland. An essential condition for integration in the North Atlantic area is the development among countries of a greater volume of transactions and communications, especially those associated with rewards and expectations of gain. Deutsch and his collaborators suggested the need to develop new functional organizations within the North Atlantic area and to "make NATO more than a military alliance" by developing the "economic and social potentialities of this unique organization."[39]

Other scholars have adapted parts of Deutsch's conceptualization to the study of integration. For example, Roger Cobb and Charles Elder undertook an empirical analysis of 1176 pairings of 49 states in a global sample together with 210 pairings of 15 states in the North Atlantic area. For the measurement and comparison of what they termed *internation relationships* they gathered data on a large number of integrative indicators, including trade, mail, telephone calls, tourism, and student exchange. Such indicators were examined for the 14 North Atlantic countries over the 1952 to 1964 period and for 49 countries from the global sample for 1955.[40] Among their findings were the following: A more positive correlation existed among exchanges of communications and goods, such as trade, mail, and telegraph messages, than among exchanges of people, including tourism and student exchange, but more at the North Atlantic level than on a regional basis; states that are geographically proximate in the global sample showed greater "mutual" relevance than did those in the North Atlantic sample; the greater the homogeneity of states in their social-economic development, the greater their interactions in the global system; and the more similar two states in the global sample are in their bureaucratic capabilities, the higher the levels of their relative interaction.[41] The authors concluded that the most important societal predictors of mutual relevance were associated with "a general development syndrome in the international system," a finding that they viewed as "generally consistent with the functionalist theory of international relations."[42] This finding emerges from other integration studies, including those of Joseph S. Nye, who holds that the effect of technology is to diminish the importance of distance and to enhance the importance of functional-type organizations having a regional core such as the Organization for Economic Cooperation and Development (OECD). The common denominator of such organizations "would be less geographic proximity or imagery than a mutual high level of development."[43]

ETZIONI AND THE STAGES OF POLITICAL UNIFICATION

While Deutsch and his collaborators have completed historical cases of the integration and disintegration of nation-states, Amitai Etzioni has examined four contemporary efforts to form political units at a level beyond the nation-state. Any study of political unification may pose four major questions:

> Under what conditions is it initiated? What forces direct its development? What path does it take? And what is the state of the system affected by the process once it is terminated?[44]

Etzioni's objective in asking such questions was to trace the evolution of a unification process from inception to maturity. One of his principal efforts was the development of a four-stage model of integration: (1) the preunification states; (2) the unification process based on the integrating power manifested in this stage; (3) the unification process, that is, the study of those sectors that became integrated; and (4) the termination state. The propositions contained in his model were juxtaposed with such entities as the West Indies Federation (1958–1962), the Nordic associational web (1953–1964), the United Arab Republic (UAR) (1958–1961), and the European Economic Community (EEC) (1958–1964).

Etzioni advanced the proposition that unions with fewer elite units are more likely to succeed than unions with many elite units, since the greater the number of elite units, the more formidable are likely to be the problems which must be resolved.[45] Egalitarian unions, like unions with few elite units, are more likely to succeed than nonegalitarian unions. The UAR disintegrated despite the fact that it had fewer elite units than the EEC. However, the UAR did not have an effective elite unit, since Egypt possessed neither the assets nor the will to preserve the union. Both the initiative to form the union and to dissolve it came from Syria, rather than from Egypt. Compared to UAR, the EEC was

> comparatively egalitarian in utilitarian matters and elitist in political issues. The new element the EEC introduces is that of the system-elite. We need to augment our propositions by stating that the most effective unions are expected to be ruled by system-elites rather than by member-elites. A system-elite combines the decisiveness found in member-elites with the ability to generate commitment found in egalitarian unions; the decisiveness is gained from the existence of one superior center of decision-making, while commitments are generated because the system-elite represents all the members of the union as well as the union as a collectivity.[46]

The Nordic Union, which survived, was an egalitarian union. In the case of the West Indies Federation, which failed, the external elite, Britain, was unable to develop an internal elite unit in support of the Federation. In the EEC, Etzioni noted the development of a system elite and suggested that "the most effective unions are expected to be ruled by system-elites rather than by member-elites."[47]

In comparing the four cases chosen for examination, Etzioni concluded that the EEC was most advanced in the level and scope of its integration, while the failure of other unification efforts was attributed largely to their deficiencies in utilitarian and identitive assets and capabilities.[48] He hypothesized: "The more utilitarian power the elites initiating and guiding unification command or the more the union-system builds up, the more successful unification will be." This hypothesis was tentatively confirmed. In the EEC the utilitarian power of the union increased, and this in turn advanced the identitive power of the system-unit, and prepared the way for further commitment. In the West Indies, in contrast, the union did not command utilitarian power, and the distribution of power was such that it led to opposition to the union of its two largest members, Trinidad and Jamaica. Therefore, he suggests: "It is hardly surprising that the more utilitarian and identitive power supporting a particular unification effort, the farther it advances, and vice versa."[49] Etzioni, however, did not ignore coercive power as a factor in the unification process. The lack of coercive power, he concluded, hastened the disintegration of the West Indies Federation and the use of such force might have extended the life of the UAR.

Like Deutsch, Etzioni emphasizes communications in the development of unions. In the case of the West Indies Federation and the UAR, communications were distorted, and there was inadequate responsiveness among the units to be unified. In contrast, the EEC had channels for more rapid and effective communication, responsiveness, and representation. He concluded that adequate representation is a prerequisite for adequate responsiveness and that extensive vertical communication and representation, together with responsiveness at intermediate levels, enhance the prospects for unification.

In this study Etzioni was concerned with the dynamics of unification. He suggested that efforts to unify underdeveloped countries are less likely to succeed than efforts to unify industrially advanced peoples because of widespread illiteracy among peoples whose outlook is parochial. Such peoples lack the organizational and political skills needed to cope with problems of regional unification. Both cases in which unification failed, the West Indies and the UAR, consisted of underdeveloped units. Put differently, Etzioni, like Deutsch and Haas, gives a prominent place in his scheme to politically aware elites as moving forces in a unification process.

In yet another proposition, Etzioni views the rewarding of as many units and subunits as possible as important to ultimate success. Widespread rewards contribute to widespread support by creating vested interests in the union and making it possible to withstand the inevitable strains of adjustment. In the West Indies and UAR cases, the adjustment was attempted before widespread rewards were evident to participating units. In the Nordic Union, there was no reallocation and no new integration, while the EEC "quite systematically delayed reallocation until the integrating power was built up."

In a later examination of unifying forces at the international level, Etzioni viewed the world as a "small set of subglobal systems."

> These postmodern subglobal systems differ from earlier, especially colonial, empires in several ways: (a) Their power mix is relatively more balanced; they rely less on direct coercive control (though this is still used frequently as compared to its use in the intranational systems of the superpowers themselves): (b) Utilitarian exchanges seem relatively less exploitive (though there is some "colonial" residue), in that relatively more

genuine technical and economic aid is given, more indigenous development—including some industrialization—is allowed, more of the benefits of production remain in the countries, and a considerable increase in autonomous local administration is tolerated. (c) Relatively higher stress is put on normative control, in the forms of various extended elite-controlled educational and propaganda facilities, a rhetoric of equality, and a facade of multilateralism and formal equality of representation in the General Assembly of the United Nations and various regional bodies. (d) There is also an increase in the upward communication from the non-elite countries to the elite, more "downward" knowledge of the non-elite countries on the part of the elite, and even some increase in responsiveness.[50]

Etzioni views unification on a global scale as a dialectical process that includes essentially three stages. In the first stage, so-called subcommunities containing heterogeneous and conflicting units are formed. Only after the unification of subcommunities has been completed are the member units prepared to build a political community. In the second stage, the subcommunities furnish the "middle tier" for a "multitier consensus formation structure."[51] In the third stage, a community comes into existence linking and, to a large degree, superseding the subcommunities. Thus, because Etzioni sees regional units as crucial to unification at the global level, he has focused his empirically based work on the model building and the comparative analysis of contemporary unification efforts, successful and unsuccessful, in widely separated regions of the world.

NEOFUNCTIONALISM

Neofunctionalism represents the intellectual descendant of functionalism. Neofunctionalism, at least in its early form, has been contrasted with functionalism by the emphasis that neofunctionalists place on supranational institutions, compared with the importance attached by functionalists to the formation of less tightly knit communities. However, the principal difference lies in the elaboration, modification, and testing of hypotheses about integration found in the works of neofunctionalists, including Ernst Haas, Philippe Schmitter, Leon Lindberg, Joseph Nye, Robert Keohane, and Lawrence Scheineman. Many, but by no means all, of the writings of neofunctionalists focus on the formation and evolution of the European Community. As Charles Pentland has suggested, referring to the neofunctionalist literature of the 1960s, "neofunctionalism embodied a desire toward middle range theory, which enabled it to come forth rather early with a convincing and useful—if not always verified—analysis of the European situation."[52]

In contrast to the more comparative focus of Deutsch and Etzioni, the work of Haas deals with specific cases, which Haas analyzes with the use of an elaborate theoretical framework. In his work on the European

Coal and Steel Community, Haas postulates that the decision to proceed with integration, or to oppose it, depends upon the expectations of gain or loss held by major groups within the unit to be integrated. "Rather than relying upon a scheme of integration which posits 'altruistic' motives as the conditioners of conduct, it seems more reasonable to focus on the interests and values defended by them as far too complex to be described in such simple terms as 'the desire for Franco-German peace' or the 'will to a United Europe.' "[53] Haas assumes that integration proceeds as a result of the work of relevant elites in the governmental and private sectors, who support integration for essentially pragmatic rather than altruistic reasons. Elites having expectations of gain from activity within a supranational organizational framework are likely to seek out similarly minded elites across national frontiers.

Haas attempts to refine functionalist theory about integration. Criticizing Mitrany for having taken insufficient account of the "power" element, Haas postulates that power is not separable from welfare. Since few people make the pursuit of power an objective, power may be defined as "merely a convenient term for describing violence-laden means used for the realization of welfare aims."[54] But Haas advances the proposition that "functionally specific international programs, if organizationally separated from diffuse orientations, maximize both welfare and integration." Such programs give rise to organizations whose "powers and competences gradually grow in line with the expansion of the conscious task, or in proportion to the development of unintended consequences arising from earlier task conceptions."

Moreover, as a result of a learning process, power-oriented governmental activities can evolve toward welfare-oriented action. As actors realize that their interests are best served by a commitment to a larger organization, learning contributes to integration. Conceptions of self-interest and welfare are redefined. Haas advances the corollary: "Integrative lessons learned in one functional context will be applied in others, thus eventually supplanting international politics."[55]

Crucial to integration is the "gradual politicization of the actors' purposes which were initially considered 'technical' or 'noncontroversial.' "[56] The actors become politicized, Haas asserts, because, in response to initial technical purposes, they "agree to consider the spectrum of means considered appropriate to attain them." Thus, in contrast to Mitrany, Haas does not hold that technical cooperation bypasses politics, but he does suggest that the requirements of mechanical functionalism lead to new forms of political action.

To the functionalist proposition that a welfare-orientation is achieved most readily by leaving the work of international integration to experts or voluntary groups, Haas offers two qualifications: (1) that voluntary groups from a regional setting, such as Western Europe, are more likely to achieve integration than an organization with representatives from all over the world; and (2) that experts responsible to no one at the national level may find that their recommendations are ignored. Therefore, he suggests that expert managers of functionally specific national bureaucracies joined together to meet a specific need are likely to be the most effective carriers of integration. Haas rephrases the functionalist proposition to read: "International integration is advanced most rapidly by a dedication to welfare, through measures elaborated by experts aware of the political implications of their task and representative of homogeneous and symmetrical social aggregates, public or private."[57]

Again with qualification, Haas accepts the functionalist proposition that political loyalties are the result of satisfaction with the performance of important functions by a governmental agency. Since it is possible for peoples to be loyal to several agencies simultaneously, there may be a gradual transfer of loyalty to international organizations performing important tasks. Haas accepts this proposition with the caveat that it is not likely to hold if the integrative process is influenced by nations with ascriptive status patterns, or traditional or charismatic leadership.[58]

"Spill-over" and the Integrative Process

Central to Haas's work is the concept of *spill-over*,[59] or what Mitrany called the doctrine of ramification. In his examination of the European Coal and Steel Community (ECSC), Haas found that among European elites directly concerned with coal and steel, there were relatively few persons who were initially strong supporters of the ECSC. Only after the ECSC had been in operation for several years did the bulk of leaders in trade unions and political parties—both Socialist and Christian Democrat—become proponents of the Community. Moreover such groups, as a result of gains which they experienced from the ECSC, placed themselves in the vanguard of other efforts for European integration, including the Common Market. Thus there was a marked tendency for persons who had experienced gains from supranational institutions in one sector to favor integration in other sectors. Moreover, Haas suggests that decisions made in organizations at the international level may be integrative. "Earlier decisions spill-over into new functional contexts, involve more and more people, call for more and more interbureaucratic contact and consultations, meeting the new problems which grow out of the earlier compromises."[60] Thus there was an "expansive logic" which contributed to "spill-over" from one sector to another. The process is one whereby the nations "upgrade" their common interests.

In his work on the International Labor Organization, Haas developed a model which brings together the functional analysis of general systems theory and refines the "spill-over" concept found both in his

earlier work and in Mitrany's writings in the form of the doctrine of ramification. Haas is concerned with the extent to which an international
organization can transcend national boundaries and thus transform the
international system. Governmental policies, the product of the interaction of national actors and their environment, constitute inputs into
the international system. The organizations and accepted body of law
form the structure of the international system. The structures receive
inputs and convert them from tasks into actions. Collective decisions are
the outputs of the international system. Such outputs may change the international environment in such a way as either to produce integrative or
disintegrative tendencies within the international system. If the weak
structures of the international system are inadequate to the tasks given
them, their outputs enter an international environment in which national
actors are predisposed either to strengthen or to weaken institutions for
collaborative action at the international level. In either eventuality, the
purposes (defined as consciously willed action patterns) of the actors are
likely to produce new functions (defined as the results of actions that may
bring unintended consequences). Purposes and functions may transform
the international system by (1) producing a form of learning that enhances the original purposes of the actors and thus leads to integration;
and (2) resulting in a learning experience that contributes to a reevalua-
tion of purposes and thus leads to disintegration.[61]

In collaboration with Philippe Schmitter, Haas has set forth three
sets of variables "which seem to intervene more or less consistently between the act of economic union and the possible end product we label
political union."[62] The first set, the *background variables*, includes the
size of member-units, the extent of social pluralism within the units, elite
complementarity, and transaction rates among units. The second set
consists of *variables* at the moment of economic union, such as the
powers delegated to the union and the level of shared governmental
purposes. The third set is termed *process variables.* Included are decisionmaking style, rates of transactions after integration, and the ability of
governments to adapt in response to crisis. According to Haas and
Schmitter, the higher the scores for each variable, the more likely it is
that economic union will spill-over into political integration.[63] Moreover, economic issues in a democratic, pluralistic, industrial setting are
most likely to spill-over into political integration. Thus Haas has focused
much of his investigation upon the international region which most fully
meets these criteria, namely, Western Europe, although he has sought to
find "functional equivalents" in Latin America for phenomena isolated
in a European context.

In this work Haas concluded again that the growth of "legitimate
and authoritative international tasks" was related to a "high degree of
functional specificity: The task must relate to directly experienced needs

and demands of important national elites." Some functionally specific
issues, such as human rights, Haas found, are more likely to lead to spill-
over than others, such as trade union issues. "An over concentration on
trade union issues would seriously delay the growth of a genuine functional law of human rights because once trade union demands have been
established and ratified, there is little left to spill-over from mundane
contract negotiation to civil liberties. Integration in the field of human
rights requires an enlargement of the functionally specific realm to comprehend more and varied aspects of freedom. . . ."[64] In yet another way
Haas acknowledged that there is no automaticity about spill-over. Instead, spill-over will occur only if "actors, on the basis of their interest-
inspired perception, desire to adapt integrative lessons learned in one
context to a new situation."[65] The integration experience of Western Europe in the 1960s led Haas to modify further the spill-over concept. Similarly, Philippe Schmitter has suggested that the spill-over concept must
be modified, refined, and qualified in a typology of strategic options
available to actors. These include: besides spill-over, *spill-around*, that is,
an increase in scope of functions performed by an integrative organization but not a corresponding growth in authority; a *build-up*, or increase
in decisional autonomy and authority of an integrative organization,
without entry into new issue areas; *retrenchment*, or increases in the level
of joint arbitration while reducing the authority of an integrative organization; and *spill-back*, a retreat both in scope of functions and authority
of an integrative organization to a status quo-ante situation. Schmitter
hypothesizes that "successive spill-overs or package deals" encompassing
new issues, as well as less conspicuous forms of "spill-around," may provide the basis for major studies toward political integration.[66]

Political Leadership: Implications for Sector Integration

Examining the European integration movement in the 1960s, Haas concluded that there was some "spill-over." The progress of the Common
Market in achieving such objectives as a common external tariff, uniform
rules of competition, a freer market for foreign labor, and a Community
agricultural policy have "come close to voiding the power of the national
state in all realms other than defense, education, and foreign policy."[67]
Although major decisions are made by the EEC Council of Ministers,
which represents the member governments, the agreements reached
have usually resulted in "increased powers for the Commission to make
possible the implementation of what was decided."

Despite these developments, Haas concluded that the "phenomenon of de Gaulle" was missing from his earlier integration framework.
Events of the 1960s showed that "pragmatic interest politics concerned
with economic welfare has its own built-in limits." This earlier work, it

will be recalled, emphasized the development of expectations of gain among elites in the units to be integrated. The integrative experience of Western Europe after 1957 led Haas to conclude that interest based upon pragmatic considerations, for example, expectations of economic gain, is "ephemeral," because it is not "reinforced with deep ideological or philosophical commitment." A political process which is "built and projected from pragmatic interests, therefore, is bound to be a frail process, susceptible to reversal." If it proves possible to satisfy pragmatically based expectations with modest advances in integration, support for dramatic integrative steps will be lacking. Herein, Haas admits, lies one of the important limitations of pragmatically based expectations of gain.

In addition, Haas contends that a shared political commitment between major elites and governmental leaders is needed if integration is to move forward smoothly.

> This is precisely the condition that, in a pluralistic setting, cannot be expected to occur very often. Otherwise, integration can go forward gradually and haltingly if both leaders and major elites share an incremental commitment to modest aims and pragmatic steps. The difficulty arises when the consensus between statesmen and major nongovernmental elites is more elusive and temporary incremental commitment to economic aims among the leaders will not lead to smooth integration if the major elites are committed to dramatic political steps. More commonly, a political commitment to integration by the statesman will rest on very shaky ground if the interests of the major elites are economic. They rest on an even weaker basis if the statesman's commitment is to national grandeur and the elites' to economic gradualism, as in the case of contemporary France.[68]

Haas contends that "the functional logic which leads from national frustration to economic unity, and eventually to political unification, presupposes that national consciousness is weak and that the national situation is perceived as gloomy. To be sure, the situation may improve. If integration has gone very far by then, no harm is done to the union; but in Europe it had not gone far enough before the national situation improved once more, before self-confidence rose, thus making the political healing power of unions once more questionable."[69] In such a situation the strong political leader becomes crucial, for he can either press forward the integration process or offer rewards at the national level which satisfy pragmatically inspired proponents of integration and thus weaken the integration movement.

By the mid-1970s, Haas had developed even greater reservations about the logic of incrementalism and "spill-over," especially in the European Community context. For example, he saw no imminent prospect for a common monetary policy as a result of the formation of a customs union and agricultural policy for the European Community. Although the issues confronting national governments have grown more complex and numerous, the likelihood that political elites will choose supranational solutions has not grown apace. Instead, Haas proposed a concept termed *fragmented issue linkage* that is said to occur "when older objectives are questioned, when new objectives clamor for satisfaction, and when the rationality accepted as adequate in the past ceases to be a legitimate guide to future action."[70]

Central to the integrative logic of functionalism, as we have seen, is the development of issues in which scientists and technicians play vitally important roles. It is appropriate, therefore, to examine the attitudes of scientific personnel in international organizations in order to ascertain their belief patterns with respect to the relationship between specialized knowledge and collective action for attaining economic, political, and social objectives, and to assess the extent to which international science and technology programs have increased in scope in relating specialized knowledge to growing economic, political, and social objectives. As Haas puts it, "If we could say that a given idea, a certain discovery, or an identifiable network of specialists triggered the development of a political consensus, which in turn legitimated a new international program, we could make a definite observation about the impact of science on collective problem solving."[71]

The evidence presently available fails to yield findings of a positive nature. Haas and his associates interviewed 146 scientists in a large number of international organizations concerned with such fields as environmental protection, industrial development, and agriculture. They included the European Communities, the Organization for Economic Cooperation and Development, the World Bank, the World Health Organization, the Food and Agriculture Organization, the United Nations Environment Program, the Global Environmental Monitoring System, to mention just a few. But there was little evidence of any widespread faith among those interviewed in the development of strengthened international institutions or the efficacy of comprehensive global, or regional, scientific-technical planning for the application of rational policies. Haas concluded that despite the growth of multilateral institutions and forums for deliberating scientific issues—and the ever-increasing importance of scientific knowledge in the late twentieth century—the power of international organizations to bring about change, or to compel members to alter their policies, remains as weak as ever.[72] The international conferences convened under the auspices of the United Nations during the past decade have typically ended by recognizing the complexity of the problems discussed and calling for regional initiatives and national policies suitable to particular circumstances.

In short, the existence of problems whose resolution is difficult, and perhaps impossible, on a strictly national basis, does not lead necessarily to the formation of an increasing web of international collaboration in an international organization. Such issue areas are not always grouped together incrementally in an international setting. National actors may, and often do, seek to strengthen national capabilities for dealing with such issues. Alternatively, they may attempt to find solutions in groupings other than those of a regional nature. According to Haas, the number of issues for which national solutions are not appropriate has grown greatly. But instead of "policy integration," there now exists "policy interdependence," which Haas defines as a "condition—both physical and perceptual—under which governments are so sensitive and vulnerable to what their partners may or may not do that unilateral action becomes unwise or dangerous to their survival."[73] In this context, integration refers to "institutionalized procedures devised by governments for coping with the condition of interdependence." Thus integration and interdependence were closely related in the literature of the late 1970s, with the important caveat, noted by Haas and others, including Robert Keohane, Joseph Nye, and Alex Inkeles, that policy interdependence does not necessarily lead to policy integration.[74]

The emergence of a large number of issues—foreign trade, investment, energy, outer space, technology transfer and technological collaboration, the environment, the oceans, the international monetary system, and food—have led to "fragmented issue linkage" or what Joseph Nye and Lawrence B. Krause have termed *collective economic security,* that is, the acceptance by governments of "international surveillance of their domestic and foreign economic policies, of criticism of the effects of their policies on the economic security of other countries, and of various forms of international presence in the operation of markets."[75] In such a world, groupings of nations are formed to deal with one or more issues, but global institutions are not necessarily strengthened. Because regional solutions are not adequate, in themselves, issues are dealt with often on a broader basis, with results that "cannot legitimately be attributed to the spill-over mechanism but to imperatives of an external nature not captured in regional integration theories."[76] According to Haas, a reversal in the integrative process may occur because of changes in the nature of actors as to the desirability of regional integration or because of a recognition that problems to which regional integration was considered to be a solution are not in fact purely, or even largely, regional in scope.[77]

Although earlier neofunctional theory placed principal emphasis on internal units and their characteristics, there has been growing recognition, especially in the 1970s, of the need to incorporate external causes—what Haas has termed *externalization.* Such factors are said to promote regional integration if they make necessary, as in the case of the European Community, a common negotiating position with respect to nonmembers. External factors may have a reverse effect if they pose for regional integrative institutions pressing problems of a global nature for which solutions beyond the regional unit are imperative. Philippe Schmitter suggests that paradoxically, regional integration has the effect of encouraging "policy externalization" by the new regional institutions as a result of penetration of the unit by private interests and public authorities.[78]

In summary, although Haas has developed an integration framework that embodies features of systems theory and functionalism, he has sought to point up some of the major limitations as well as the potential utility of functionalism in explaining integration at the international level. Therefore, in addition to his own work in the study of international organizations and integration, Haas has provided a critique and elaboration of functionalism.

Other scholars have viewed integration as a multidimensional phenomenon. Hence the first task is to develop a concept, or concepts, of integration that encompasses its major dimensions or to deal conceptually with each of the various components of integration in such fashion as to explicate the linkages among them. According to Philippe C. Schmitter, "Understanding and explanation in this field of inquiry are, as in other fields such as political development, best served not by the dominance of a single accepted grand model, or paradigm, but by the simultaneous presence of antithetic and conflictive ones, which, while they may converge in certain aspects, diverge in many others."[79] As Barry B. Hughes and John E. Schwarz have written: "If, as appears to be the case, integration consists of several dimensions or components, another set of questions is raised. Is there a relationship among the different dimensions of integration, and, if there is, what is it?"[80]

Hughes and Schwarz examine these dimensions of integration: (1) political amalgamation, or the development of central institutions in an integrative scheme including two or more states; (2) intergovernmental cooperation, encompassing the diplomatic arenas other than central integrative institutions; and (3) mass community, or the extent to which there is widespread affinity among peoples in an integrative framework.

Each of these components lends itself to the following various techniques for measurement: for political amalgamation, the extent to which institutions exist that are capable of making binding decisions on behalf of its members; for intergovernmental cooperation, the use of events—interaction data (see Chapter 4 for a discussion of this approach) including state visits, diplomatic messages, and other executive actions between states; and for mass community, data drawn from public opinion surveys. Utilizing such an analysis for the European Community between 1954 and 1965, Hughes and Schwarz concluded that "changes in intergovernmental cooperation at the diplomatic level proceded major instances of Community institutional change (both positive and negative) and these two in turn preceded changes in good feelings among the Community populations."[81]

JOSEPH NYE AND NEOFUNCTIONALISM

Building upon the work of Haas, and of Mitrany before him, several scholars have made an effort to refine neofunctionalist theories of integration. Among such scholars is Joseph Nye, whose contribution lies in developing a neofunctionalist model based upon "process mechanisms" and "integrative potential." Nye seeks to set forth a theoretical framework based upon a neofunctionalist approach that, to a greater extent than that of Haas or Mitrany, is not "Eurocentric." Thus Nye bases his conceptualization upon an analysis of the conditions for integration drawn specifically from European *and* non-Western experiences and modifies greatly the notions of "automatic politicization" and "spillover."[82]

Nye suggests that neofunctionalist literature contains seven "process mechanisms," around which he reconceptualizes and reformulates neofunctionalist theory.

1. *Functionalist Linkage of Tasks, or the Concept of Spill-Over*

Nye holds that this mechanism has been applied, wrongly in his opinion, to include "any sign of increased cooperation," arising, for example, from linkages, or relationships, among problems because of their inherent technical characteristics, or because of actual efforts by integrationist elites to cultivate spill-over. Nye hypothesizes that "imbalances created by the functional interdependence or inherent linkages of tasks can be a force pressing political actors to redefine their common tasks."[83] However, such redefinition of tasks does not necessarily lead to an "upgrading of common tasks. The experience can also be negative."[84] Thus, if the linkage of tasks can cause spill-over, it can also produce spill-back. (Nye's observation on this point may be applicable to the European Economic Community, where elites and interest groups benefited in the earlier stages of integration, but with economic growth they later became more reluctant to take additional integrative steps when growth rates dropped off. When growth rates declined as a result of the energy crisis, national protectionist sentiment flared up and governments hesitated to upgrade common interests if they feared adverse effects upon employment, inflation, payments, and monetary problems.)

2. *Rising Transactions*

As noted elsewhere in this chapter, integration is hypothesized to be accompanied by an increase in transactions, including trade, capital movement, communications, and exchange of people and ideas. Political actors in a scheme for regional integration, faced with heavy demands upon common institutions resulting from an increasing volume of transactions, may choose to deal with them on a strictly national basis, or they may decide to strengthen the common institutions. According to Nye, "Rising transactions need not lead to a significant widening of the scope (range of tasks) of integration, but to an intensifying of the central institutional capacity to handle a particular task."[85]

3. Deliberate Linkages and Coalition Formation

Here, Nye focuses once again upon spill-over, or what he terms *accentuated spill-over*, in which "problems are deliberately linked together into package deals, not because of technological necessity, but because of political and ideological projections and political feasibilities."[86] Drawing heavily upon the experience of the European Community, Nye points to the efforts of politicians, international bureaucrats, and interest groups to create coalitions based upon linked issues. Although such efforts may promote integration, they may have a negative effect if, for example, the political fortunes of a group supporting integration, on an issue identified with integration, decline. The extent to which integration can be broadened in appeal is a function of the extent to which the coalition in favor of integration enjoys widespread public support.

4. Elite Socialization

Nye cites numerous examples of the growth of support for integration arising from elites who have participated actively in an integrative scheme. The extent to which national bureaucrats become participants in regional integration will determine the level of their socialization— deemed to be important because national bureaucrats are said to be wary of integration because of the possible loss of national control. However, if other "process mechanisms" considered by Nye are negative, the socialization of elites, especially bureaucratic groups, in favor of regional integration may serve to isolate them from the mainstream of attitudes and of policy in their home countries.

5. Regional Group Formation

Regional integration is said to stimulate the creation, both formally and informally, of nongovernmental groups or transnational associations. Viewed in the context of both the European Community and other settings, such as Central America and Africa, Nye asserts, such associations remain weak. Only the more general interests are aggregated by such groups at the regional level, whereas the more specific interests remain within the purview of national-level interest groups.[87]

6. Ideological-Identitive Appeal

The establishment of a sense of identity represents a powerful force in support of regional integration. According to Nye, "The stronger the sense of permanence and the greater the identitive appeal, the less willing are opposition groups to attack an integration scheme frontally."[88] Under such conditions, members are more likely than otherwise to tolerate short-term losses, and businesses are more likely to invest in the expectation that they will benefit, on a continuing basis, from the presence of a large market. However, the existence of regional integrative institutions may satisfy a "weak popular sense of regional identity."[89] The growth of ideological-identitive appeal within some groups may serve only to increase the opposition of insecure nationalist leaders and private sector groups, especially if the perceived gains from integration at the regional level are uncertain.

7. Involvement of External Actors in the Process

To a greater extent than earlier neofunctionalist theory, Nye posits the importance of external actors and posits their active involvement in his neofunctionalist model as a part of the process mechanism. He notes the importance of outside governments and international organizations, as well as nongovernmental actors, as catalysts in regional integration schemes.

Central to Nye's neofunctionalist model is what he terms *integrative potential,* that is, the integrative conditions stimulated by the "process mechanism." Here, he sets forth four conditions that are said to influence both the nature of the original commitment and the subsequent evolution of an integrative scheme.

1. Symmetry or Economic Equality of Units

It matters not so much whether there exist "core areas" for integration or whether the prospective participants are relatively equal in size. Instead, a relationship is said to exist among trade, integration, and level of development, measured by per capita income. Such compatibility appears to be important for regional integration. The size of potential participants, measured in total GNP, seems to be of relatively greater importance in integrative schemes among less developed states. Nye hypothesizes: "It almost looks as if the lower the per capita income of the area, the greater the homogeneity in size of economy must be."[90]

2. Elite Value Complementarity

Nye acknowledges that the extent to which elite groups within integrating entities think alike is of considerable importance. In fact, he suggests that the higher the level of elite complementarity, the more likely the prospects for sustained impetus toward regional integration. However, he holds also that elites that have worked together effectively on a transnational basis may subsequently embrace divergent policies that are not conducive to integration.

3. Existence of Pluralism

Functionally specific groups are said to enhance the likelihood of integration. Here, Nye points to a major difference between the West

European experience and that of the Third World, where such groups are relatively absent. According to Nye, "The greater the pluralism in all member states, the better the conditions for an integrative response to the feedback from the process mechanisms."[91]

4. *Capacity of Member States to Adapt and Respond*

This factor is said to depend vitally upon the level of mutual responsiveness within the political units to be integrated into a larger regional entity. The higher the level of domestic stability and the greater the capacity of key decision-makers to respond to demands within their respective political units, the more likely they are to be able to participate effectively in a larger integrative unit.

Next, Nye sets forth three perceptual conditions that are affected by the integrative process. They include: (1) the perceived equity of distribution of benefits—with the hypothesis that "the higher the perceived equitable distribution in all countries, the better the conditions for further integration";[92] (2) perceived external cogency, that is, the perceptions of decision-makers concerning their external problems, including dependence upon exports, threats from larger powers, and the loss of status in a changing international system; and (3) low (or exportable) visible costs, or the extent to which integration can be made to be perceived as relatively cost-free especially in its initial phases—a concept, as Nye points out, that is central to neofunctionalist theory and strategy.

Finally, four conditions are likely to characterize the integration process over time: (1) politicization, or the means by which problems are resolved and competing interests are reconciled or the extent to which the resultant benefits are sufficiently widespread to insure broadening and deepening support; (2) redistribution with the crucial issue being the phasing of the changes in status, power, and economic benefits among groups within the integrating unit. Central to the integrative process is the extent to which redistribution, benefiting some regions more than others, is compensated by growth to the benefit of the unit as a whole; (3) redistribution of alternatives or the extent to which, as the integrative process proceeds, decision-makers face pressures to increase the level and the scope of integration and conclude that the alternatives to integration are less satisfactory; and (4) externalization, or the extent to which members of an integrating unit find it necessary to develop a common position on issues in order to deal with nonmembers, as has happened with the European Community in its various sets of negotiations with outside parties, including the United States. Nye hypothesizes that "the further integration proceeds, the more likely third parties will be to react to it, either in support or with hostility."[93]

A neofunctionalist model, such as that developed by Nye, provides a framework for comparing integrative processes in more developed and less developed regions of the world; and for assessing the extent to which microregional, or functionally specific, economic organizations hold potential for further development toward federations. More likely, neofunctionalist model-building can provide, and has provided, more explicit theoretical propositions essential to understanding the limits, as well as the potential, of this segment of theory both in explaining integration and providing a strategy for advancing an integrative process.

Analyzing the roles, respectively, of macroregional political organizations, such as the Organization of American States (OAS), the Organization of African Unity (OAU), and the Arab League, the microlevel economic organizations, including the European Economic Community (EEC), the Central American Common Market (CACM), and the East African Community (EAC), Nye drew several tentative conclusions with respect to neofunctionalism. Microregional economic organizations are unlikely to develop into new units that encroach greatly upon, or supersede, the existing nation-states. However, microregional economic and macroregional political organizations have contributed to the development of "islands of peace" in the world and "their costs for world peace in terms of conflict creation have been less than their modest benefit to the world in conflict diversion."[94] Given the limited results of the regional organizations studied, the growth of multinational enterprises may be a more important trend in international organization.

Although the impact of technology upon existing political units is such as to reduce the autonomy of the nation-state, only a portion of its national powers are redistributed at the regional level. In summary, microregional economic organizations have strengthened functional links that in turn have improved relationships among members. Macroregional political organizations have played a constructive role in controlling interstate conflict among members, although such organizations were unsuccessful in cases of primarily internal conflict—a serious limitation, Nye admits, in light of the importance of such conflict in the late twentieth century.[95] Indeed, the point can be, and has been, made that in many countries of the world the more immediate challenge to nationalist sentiment in recent decades comes not from universal or regional integration, but from centrifugal subnational forces in favor of local autonomy, secession, expulsion of an unwanted group from the national domain, and on the substitution of the domination of one ethnic, linguistic, or religious group for that of another.

LEON LINDBERG AND NEOFUNCTIONALISM

Elsewhere in this chapter we have noted the importance attached by many, if not most, students of integration to the need for theory based upon a recognition of integration as a multidimensional phenomenon.

The neofunctionalist theorist of the 1970s drew upon systems theory and decision theory for the study of integration—for the analysis of what Leon Lindberg identifies as the "multiple properties of collective decision-making systems."[96] Thus Lindberg views integration as an "interactive multidimensional process" that must be identified, compared, measured, and analyzed. The integrative process contains properties that "bear a systematic relationship to each other at any given point in time and . . . over time as well."[97] The level of collective decision-making—of integration—at any specific time is the product of the past decisions of the system, a system within which decisions are made. Decision-making systems are activated by demands made upon them and responses by appropriate arbitrators. "How such demands are processed into decisions will be determined by the level of *resources* available to collective decision-makers, by the way in which leaders make use of them, and by the *propensity of national bargainers to consume* these resources for the maximization of collective as against individual interests. Finally, the *consequences* that collective decisions may have for the constituent systems can be described in terms of the degree to which the decisions *penetrate* the system, the degree to which the decisions are *complied with*, and the *distributive consequences* of the decisions."[98]

Lindberg sets forth what he terms the variable properties that are said to describe the extent to which a group of nations engages in collective decision-making. They are (1) functional scope of collective decision-making, or the extent to which it embraces a large number or just a few issue areas; (2) the stage in decision-making at which collective processes are involved—at only the beginning or at a whole range of decisional stages, including the choice of options and their implementation; (3) the importance of collective decision-making in determining public allocations on important or only marginal issue areas; (4) the extent to which demands—large in number or few in number—are articulated into the collective arena for action; (5) the degree to which collective decision-makers have available resources that are adequate to their needs; (6) the continuity and strength of leadership at the level of the collectivity; (7) the extent to which the bargaining modalities of the system help maximize the individual interests of nations or enhance those of the collectivity; (8) the effect of collective decisions on the behavior of individuals—whether large or only small numbers of people are affected; (9) the degree to which collective decisions meet with compliance or with apathy or outright opposition; and (10) the distributive consequences of collective decisions—whether they are important or very marginal for constituent systems and for actors within them.

Lindberg maintains that the greater the score or ranking on these properties, the higher the level of political integration and, conversely, if all or most scores are declining, there can be observed a process of disintegration. But, as Lindberg acknowledges, the first difficulty inherent in such conceptualization arises when some scores are high and others are low; and when two or more collective decision-making systems differ widely in their scores on these properties—which is more integrated? This difficulty arises because of the complexity of integration. But it also relates to the problem of giving precise operational meaning to each of the properties, a task that Lindberg sees as crucially important to theory-building. The need exists, in each of these properties, for indicators that are objective and reliable, that permit repeated measurement by different researchers, and that are functionally equivalent to permit cross-system research.

Certain concepts set forth in Lindberg's paradigm were studied in an analysis of the European Community by Leon N. Lindberg and Stuart A. Scheingold. For example, a tabulation of the number of issue areas subject to joint decision-making within the EEC in selected periods between 1950 and 1970 yielded evidence of a substantial increase—from no issue areas in 1950 to 7 in 1957 to 17 in 1968.[99] Ordinal rankings were assigned to issue areas depending upon the "locus of decision-making" in the European Community at different times in the 1950 to 1970 period. Indicators of institutional capacity and structural growth were developed: the size of administrative staff, the quantity of organizational subunits, the numbers of meetings held, and proposals made by the collective unit and acted upon. Trade data were utilized to assess economic interest perceptions, and attitudinal data were analyzed to determine levels of expectations of future gains; belief in legitimacy of collective decision-making; conceptions of a common interest; and a sense of mutual political identification. In the European Community, Lindberg and Scheingold concluded, there existed " 'a permissive consensus' among the general public and elite groups as far as the legitimacy of the Community and its institutions was concerned. This extended to a very wide range of economic and social functions and to a strong, independent role for the supranational Commission."[100]

DELINEATING INTERNATIONAL REGIONS: A QUANTITATIVE ANALYSIS

In an effort to develop empirical evidence about factors which aid or hinder the process of integration, Bruce M. Russett has posed the following questions:

(1) How many groups (regions) are necessary for an adequate summary description of the similarities and differences among types of national political and social systems? (2) What countries are to be found in each group? (3) How do these groups compare with the groupings we call regions, now in use by social scientists? (4) What are the discriminating

variables for distinguishing groups in general, and in distinguishing between specific groups? (5) What is the relevance of our groupings to
theories of comparative and international politics?[101]

In a quest for tentative answers to such questions, Russett focused attention on regions of social and cultural homogeneity, on regions of states
which share similar political attitudes or external behavior as identified
by the voting patterns of governments in the United Nations, on regions
of political interdependence where countries are joined together by a
network of supranational or intergovernmental political institutions, on
regions of economic interdependence as identified by intraregional trade
as a proportion of a nation's national income, and on regions of geographical proximity. Such analysis may make possible the identification
of those areas of the world where the potential for further integration is
great as well as areas with little prospect for further integration.

Russett used factor analysis to delineate regional groupings. He factor analyzed 54 social and cultural variables on 82 countries. Included
were such variables as GNP per capita, primary and secondary school
pupils as a percentage of population, percentage of adult literacy, foreign mail per capita, infant mortality rate, different religious groups as a
percentage of population, and rates of population increase. Using factor
analysis, Russett reduced the 54 separate variables to four dimensions or
factors. In other words, he produced four clusters from the 54 separate
variables: (1) economic development; (2) communism; (3) Catholic culture; and (4) intensive agriculture. For example, the first factor, economic development was so labeled because many variables loaded heavily on it, that is, were highly correlated with it. These included per capita
GNP, newspapers and radios per capita, life expectancy, pupils in primary and secondary schools, and hospital beds and physicians per capita.
After following a similar procedure to derive the other three factors,
countries were grouped according to the extent to which they resembled
each other among a variety of variables. Those countries that loaded
most heavily on each factor were grouped and were given regional
names. Thus a grouping called "Afro-Asia" loaded heavily on the first
factor, *economic development*. Countries in this region resembled each
other in levels of economic development.

A grouping called "Western Community" loaded heavily on a factor which included such variables as governmental expenditure and reve-
nue, total voting turnout, and rate in increase of GNP per capita. The
"Western Community" consisted of Atlantic nations, as well as New
Zealand, Argentina, Japan, Israel, and Trinidad and Tobago. A grouping
called "Latin America" but which included the Philippines, as well as
another grouping termed "semideveloped Latins," loaded heavily on the
factor called *Catholic culture*. In this factor were such variables as Chris-

tians as a percentage of population, votes for socialist parties, speakers of the dominant language, and land inequality. A grouping designated "Eastern Europe" loaded heavily on the factor called *intensive agriculture*. This factor included such variables as overall population density and population density as related to farming land. For each of the regions delineated, it is possible to provide the mean and standard deviation for each set of factor scores. The smaller the standard deviation, the greater the homogeneity of the regional grouping for that factor. Thus the Afro-Asian group has the following profile: very underdeveloped, moderately noncommunist, non-Catholic in culture, and population densities and agricultural patterns that vary widely. The "Western Community" grouping contains states that vary greatly in the intensive agriculture and Catholic culture factors, but have generally low scores on the communism factor and a high level of economic development. In the "Eastern European" grouping communism is the "most sharply discriminating dimension," with moderate levels of economic development and a low level of Catholic culture.[102]

In other analyses, Russett discovered that in United Nations' voting, most of the groups voting together are not defined solely by geographical location, for example, the Brazzaville group included, in fact, non-African underdeveloped states which tend to be pro-Western on cold war issues. However, factor analysis revealed a strong correlation between membership in an international organization and the geographical location of a state. Proximity may contribute to common interest in the solution of problems that cannot be solved at the national level. He found that both membership in international organizations and in voting patterns were stable.

Russett considers trading patterns as but one indicator of political integration. Indeed, countries which are interdependent economically, as in the case of a metropolitan power and its colony, may be highly differentiated on the sociocultural dimension. He contends that only "under conditions of relatively equal impact in the two countries concerned" can one consider trade to induce mutual responsiveness. Most important is the degree of *interdependence*, not simply dependence. The measure of trade must be tied not to an index of relative acceptance, but rather to the ratio of trade between the two countries to the national income or GNP.

A factor analysis of trade among states reveals that although geography exercises a powerful influence on trade, the role of proximity can be exaggerated. Nearly half the countries examined are joined to one or more clusters not identified primarily with their geographic neighbors. Both political orientation and culture have major effects on commercial choice. Nor is trade simply the product of a division of labor between industrial and primary-producing nations. Many of the world's trade groupings are composed overwhelmingly of either developed or under-developed nations.

In discussing integration, Russett does not limit his definition of integration to the presence or absence of violence. He has suggested that states should be considered more integrated the higher the ratio of capabilities to burdens in their relationship. Responsiveness is the behavioral consequence of that ratio, and in turn the responsiveness of states to one another can be defined as the probability that the requests or demands of one will be met favorably. He concluded that a reexamination of theories of international conflict and of international integration must begin with the understanding that war has not necessarily been eliminated within the groupings delineated by the variables examined in this study. Russett suggests that his clusters alone do not reveal where integration has been or will be achieved. They tell us only that for countries within a grouping the prospects for integration are greater than between a typical country within the group and one outside of it. Physical space or geography may be less crucial than social space or sociocultural considerations to the integration of political communities.

ALLIANCE COHESION

Both at the international and domestic levels, groups are formed to enable their members to achieve a shared objective. Since such groups are disbanded when the objective for which they were created has been attained. they are far less enduring than the political communities whose formation and structure are of concern to writers whose work has been discussed earlier in this chapter. Alliances are designed to facilitate the attainment of policy goals by, as Robert L. Rothstein has suggested, "introducing into the situation a specific commitment to pursue them; to a certain extent, it legitimizes that pursuit by inscribing it in a treaty; and it increases the probability that the goals will be pursued because the alliance creates a new status which makes it more difficult for the parties to renege on each other, not only because they would be dishonoring their commitment, and earning a reputation for perfidy, but also because their new status usually creates a response in the external world, such as a countervailing alliance, which would tend to strengthen the bonds in the original alliance, it may also stabilize a situation by forcing enemy decision-makers to throw another weight into the opposing scales."[103]

According to Robert E. Osgood, an alliance is "a latent war community, based on general cooperation that goes beyond formal provisions and that the signatories must continually estimate in order to preserve mutual confidence in each other's fidelity to specified obligations."[104] Thus alliances have usually been formed in international contexts in which conflict, or the threat of conflict, is present.[105] Because of the historic importance of alliances in the international system, and the widespread use of coalitions by political groups intent upon attaining elective office, such collaborative efforts have been the object of scholarly investigation especially by the political realists examined in Chapter 3,[106] but also by writers concerned more specifically with the dynamics and the operation of alliances.

Two scholars in particular, George F. Liska and William R. Riker, have developed theories of alliance behavior. In their theoretical frameworks, Liska and Riker are similar in several respects. First, they agree that alliances or coalitions disband once they have achieved their objective, because they are formed essentially "against, and only derivatively for, someone or something."[107] Although a "sense of community" may reinforce alliances or coalitions, it seldom brings them into existence. In forming alliances to achieve some desired objective, decision-makers weigh the costs and rewards of alignment. A decision to join an alliance is based upon perception of rewards in excess of costs. Each country considers the marginal utility from alliance membership, as contrasted with unilateral action. Ultimately, the cohesiveness of an alliance "rests on the relationship between internal and external pressures, bearing on the ratio of gains to liabilities for individual allies."[108] Once costs exceed rewards, the decision to realign is taken. According to Liska, nations join alliances for security, stability, and status. In Liska's theory a primary prerequisite for alliance cohesion is the development of an "alliance ideology." The function of alliance ideology is to provide a rationalization for alliance. In performing this function, ideology "feeds on selective memory of the past and outlines a program for the future."[109] Periodic consultation, especially between a leading member and its allies, both on procedural and substantive issues, contributes to the development and preservation of alliance ideology and thus alliance cohesion.

After victory, first, the size of the alliance or coalition must be reduced if additional gains are to accrue to the remaining participants. Second, alliances or coalitions are crucial to attaining a balance of power. In Riker's framework, the formation of one coalition contributes to the formation of an opposing coalition. When one coalition is on the verge of victory, neutral actors often join the weaker of the coalitions to prevent the stronger from attaining hegemony. If neutral members do not align themselves with the weaker side, some members of the leading coalition must shift to the weaker of the two coalitions if the system is to regain equilibrium. Equilibrium is the likely result of the existence of two "quasipermanent blocking coalitions," or the presence of such coalitions that "play the role of balancer if a temporary winning coalition sets the stakes too high."[110] In establishing his own rules for equilibrium Riker draws upon those set by Kaplan in his balance of power system. [111] Moreover, in relating alliances or coalitions to balance of power, Liska and Riker incorporate into their theories ideas found in realist international relations theory.

The Optimum Size of Alliances

Liska and Riker suggest that alliance builders, if they act "economically," do not form alliances haphazardly with all available allies. Instead, Liska considers the "marginal utility of the last unit of commitment to a particular ally and the last unit of cost in implementing commitments."[112] Riker stresses the "size principle," according to which participants create coalitions adequate to union and no larger than necessary to achieve their commonly shared objective. If actors have perfect information, they will create a coalition of exactly the minimum size needed to win. Without complete information, members of a winning coalition create a larger coalition than necessary to achieve their objectives; the less complete the information, the larger the coalition. This fact, which Riker observes both at national and international levels, contributes to the short lifespan of alliances or coalitions.

Liska and Riker address themselves to the question of rewards from joining an alliance or coalition. According to Liska, the gains and liabilities associated with alignment can be grouped into pairs. For example, the pair peculiar to security is protection and provocation—"the first to be derived from a particular alliance and the second producing counteraction and counteralliance." Burdens and gains, as well as potential for status enhancement and possible losses in capacity for independent action, must be balanced. Liska contends that "in order to assess a particular alignment all these factors must be compared with hypothetical gains and liabilities of other alignments, with nonalignment, or at least with a different implementation of an unavoidable alliance."[113] In Riker's theory, actors join alliances or coalitions for several reasons: the threat of reprisal if they refuse to align themselves; to receive payments of one kind or another; to obtain promises about policy or about subsequent decisions; or to gain emotional satisfaction.

As noted elsewhere (see Chapter 3), there has been increased interest in the past generation in studying the behavior of small powers in the international system. Alliances usually encompass small powers as well as great powers. Such states join alliances because they must rely fundamentally—and to an extent greater than large states—upon other states. Great powers seek alignment with small states both for the political and military gains afforded, and also in order to restrain the latter from certain actions.[114] But smaller powers, Robert Rothstein notes, may prefer to align themselves with a less powerful state or with a combination of lesser states, rather than with a great power. But small power alliances are said to provide ineffective instruments if a state's goal is to increase its military strength. Their principal potential value lies in maintaining a local or regional status quo, or resolving grievances among small powers without outside great power intervention. Provided small powers can maintain agreement among themselves, they can make it difficult for a great power to intervene in their region.[115]

Alliance Cohesion and Disintegration

In the building of theory about alliance behavior, Liska employs historical data, whereas Riker uses game theory and a mathematical model of coalitions that he then applies to historical data at both the international and American national levels. Both theories give an important place to instability as characteristic of alliance systems. According to Liska, a common factor leading to the disintegration of alliance systems is the conclusion of a separate peace by an ally in war. To induce a member of an opposing alliance to make a separate peace is a major strategic concern of political actors. For both dealignment and realignment, "The basic techniques are coercion, enticement, or combination of the two, unless force alone suffices to compel a separate peace which is tantamount to unconditional surrender. To force defection by means short of the enemy's destruction, pressure has to be applied at the militarily or psychologically weakest part of the adversary alliance."[116] There is, in Riker's scheme, moreover, a "disequilibrium principle" which derives from his "size principle." In groupings where the size principle is operative, participants tend to remove from the coalition those actors deemed unessential for attaining the goals of the coalition. This factor contributes to the instability of coalitions.

Despite the existence of many important differences, one or the other theories of alliance behavior have certain features in common with theories of integration. Riker emphasizes the importance of communications among actors in the formation of coalitions of optimal size. The absence of adequate communications contributes to the formation of coalitions larger than needed to achieve their initial objective. Riker's size principle has its counterpart in the proposition, advanced by Mancur Olson, that the likelihood of achieving an optimum number of partners diminishes as the size of the coalition grows.[117] The larger the coalition, the smaller the percentage of group benefits that will be available to any single partner, and hence the less attractive will be the reward for collective action. But it could be plausibly argued that the group benefits increase as the membership of the coalition grows. Stated differently, the collective good is maximized as the size of coalition is expanded. As in Haas's earlier formulations, pragmatic interests play a major role in leading nations to align themselves. The fact that such interests do not endure contributes to the disintegration of alliances, as well as the ephemeral nature of some of the support for integration noted elsewhere in this chapter.

The roles and claims of alliance members change with alterations in their respective national capabilities. An increase in the strength of the core power is likely to contribute to alliance cohesion. Like the French strategist Pierre Gallois,[118] Liska contends that nuclear weapons have increased the vulnerability of core powers to attack and thus contributed to the decline in alliance cohesion. In addition, Liska has addressed himself to the concept of equilibrium in an international context.[119] The international system is said to rest upon a tendency toward "reequilibrium" after periods of upheaval or rapid change. According to Liska, the system functions effectively when two kinds of interaction processes are present: mechanized checks and balances associated with the balance of power and longer-term transformation inherent in the rise and decline of states relative to each other and the expansion or contraction of the system.[120] He holds that a major power can either make a quest for equilibrium the principal objective of its foreign policy or it can seek expansion in empire.[121] In either case, equilibrium or equilibrating tendencies are present. Drawing upon "the idea of the economic firm in equilibrium," Liska examines equilibrium in international organizations as illustrative of the more general application of this concept to international politics. Liska specifies several conditions for "structural equilibrium" in international organizations:

> A composite organization is in structural equilibrium if there is an overall correspondence between the margins of restraints it imposes on members and their willingness to tolerate them; if the ratios between the influence exercised by individual members and their actual power are not too unequal; and if the respective powers of the different organs correspond to the composition of their membership. . . . More important than structure is the commitment of states participating in an international organization—in our case mainly that for mutual assistance against threats to security. What matters is that the actual readiness and obligation result in pressure on the commitment toward its reduction, decentralization, or evasion, which tends to be cumulative. And, lastly, an international organization is in equilibrium with respect to its functional scope when the functions and jurisdiction which it actually exercises correspond to the extent of the needs relevant to its purpose. Depending on the adequacy of the area covered by the organization, its geographic scope can be analyzed in analogous terms.[122]

Basic to structural equilibrium is the inclusion in the organization of powerful states which can affect its purpose.

In Liska's theory, equilibrium in the international system has similar features. Like domestic politics, international politics consists essentially of efforts to "control the oscillations of a dynamic balance." According to Liska, "A workable organization on national, regional, or global scale requires that institutional, military-political, and socioeconomic factors and pressures for and against stability be deliberately equilibrated." Therefore, international organization is part of a "dynamic interplay of institutional, military-political, and socioeconomic factors and pressures, constituting a multiple equilibrium." (For a discussion of equilibrium in the context of international systems, and especially the balance of power, see Chapter 3.) According to Liska, moreover, alliances perform a regulatory function in the balancing process in the international system "insofar as each actual or prospective alliance-member strives, as a minimum, for parity with fellow allies in the advantages to follow from his individual contribution to, and value for, the collective effort."[123] But alliances also are subject to what Liska terms "complementary equilibriating tendencies," that is, the likelihood that strains will increase among members of an alliance that appears to be winning, while the opposing coalition that seems to be losing will gain in cohesiveness.[124] Thus Liska hypothesizes that the quest by allies to achieve a balance favorable to them is likely to be adversely affected by compensatory efforts by an opposing alliance and by conflicts within alliances themselves.

INTEGRATION THEORY: PROBLEMS OF CONCEPTUALIZATION AND DEFINITION

Although the theorists examined in this chapter have suggested a series of indicators for assessing the level of integration, the theory is not sufficiently advanced that there exists either a commonly accepted definition of integration or general agreement on the relevant indicators of integration.[125] Some writers, as we have seen, emphasize transaction flows such as trade, travel, mail, telephone, radio, and other forms of technical communication as indicators of integration. In examining transaction flows, or communications, Haas has suggested that the question remains whether a rise in transactions precedes, reinforces, results from, or causes integration. According to Haas, the question of *when* these conditions are expected is vital when we try to devise a rigorous theoretical framework to explain the causes of integration. Especially in the case of indicators based on social communication we must know whether the transactions measured among the elites to be integrated preceded the integrative process or whether they are a result of events which characterize the region after integration has occurred for several years. In the latter case, we have merely defined an existing community in terms of communications theory, but we have not explored the necessary steps for arriving there.[126]

Indicators of Integration

In the mid-1960s Deutsch, using transaction flows as one of his indicators to assess the level of European integration, concluded that "European integration has slowed since the mid-1950s and it has stopped or reached a plateau since 1957–1958." In part, he based this conclusion on the fact that since then there had been no increases in transaction flows "beyond what one would expect from mere random probability and increase in prosperity in the countries concerned."[127] In support of his conclusion Deutsch marshaled other evidence, including elite interviews and content analysis of selected key newspapers in France and Germany. Thus, in addition to transaction flows, statistical analysis of opinions expressed by elites and attention accorded in the press are said to form indicators of integration.

Other scholars employing in some cases different indicators, and in other instances similar ones, have reached conclusions about the status of European integration diametrically opposed to those of Deutsch. For example, if integration is defined as Leon Lindberg conceives it, namely, as "the process whereby nations forego the desire and ability to conduct foreign and key domestic policies independently of each other, seeking instead to make joint decisions or to delegate the decision-making process to a new central organ," it is possible to conclude, as Lindberg does, that Western Europe, during the five-year period after the formation of the EEC in 1958, experienced substantial progress toward integration.[128]

Another study, using different attitudinal data, concluded that European integration, far from having halted after 1958, may have moved, in some respects, into full gear only since then.[129] In a self-administered questionnaire in 1964 to 1965, incorporating questions from previous adult surveys, Ronald Inglehart found that a majority of youths in a sample drawn from schools considered to be representative of important social and economic groups in Britain, France, the Netherlands, and Germany were overwhelmingly favorable to European unification. Although there was substantial opposition among adults, especially in France, the younger generation strongly supported further steps toward European integration.[130] Inglehart's assumption attributed the differing attitudes among age groups to the fact that the adults in the sample received their basic political orientation during nationalist periods and that these attitudes were not easily changed. The youths in the sample received their political orientation when nationalism was less in favor. Postulating the stability of attitudes acquired during their formative years, it is possible to project that the generation from which the sample data were drawn will manifest a relatively "European" outlook as adults.

Using other indicators, Carl J. Friedrich concluded that Western Europe had become more integrated since 1957, the year of the signing of the Rome Treaty creating the Common Market.[131] Criticizing Deutsch's contention, and his indicators, that integration had slowed, Friedrich examined the development of sentiment and contacts at the European level in business, agriculture, the trade union movement, and the academic community. In each of these areas he found a marked increase in contacts across frontiers and support among such groups for European integration. Moreover, Friedrich criticized Deutsch and his associates both for their choice of indicators and for their use of statistical data in supporting their conclusions[132]—in short, for giving excessive emphasis to *quantitative* means based on aggregate data and for allegedly having overlooked *qualitative* indicators of integration.

In their examination of economic and political integration in Europe, James A. Caporaso and Alan Pelowski found that the EEC was rapidly integrating in the 1960s even though there was "as yet limited responsiveness" among its various subsystems.[133] Exports from the Federal Republic of Germany to other European Community members, one of the indicators chosen for examination, had tripled since 1958, and there had been an even greater increase in the number of political decisions and regulations at the Community level, another indicator of integration in this study. Moreover, there was a growth in predictability of behavior among members of the EEC, an indicator utilized not only by Caporaso and Pelowski, but also in Deutsch's work of the late 1950s on integration in the North Atlantic area.

Other writers have suggested additional indicators of integration. Claude Ake, for example, proposed quantitative measures, including: (1) the legitimacy score or the extent to which citizens give loyalty to the state and see it as the embodiment of their interest; (2) the extraconstitutional behavioral score or the frequency distribution of the preference of political actors between constitutional and extraconstitutional behavior; (3) the political violence score or the extent to which actors resort to violence to attain objectives; (4) the secessionist demand score; (5) the alignment pattern score or the extent to which major groups competing for power draw their support from more than one geographical area and ethnic, religious, social, and economic groups; (6) the bureaucratic ethos score or the extent to which the members of a political system are prepared to give their loyalty to their political unit and its office holders in spite of personal feelings about them; and (7) the authority score or the degree to which the people accept their political unit as legitimate and are prepared to accept its rule without coercion.[134]

International Systemic Factors and Integration

Integration theorists have been criticized for having given insufficient emphasis to factors in the international environment which affect the integration process. Hoffmann, for example, argues that the apparent failure of spill-over in Western Europe may be attributed at least in part to two variables, namely, the diversity of the national units and the allegedly bipolar international system of the post-World War II period. While the Benelux countries were prepared to rely almost exclusively upon the United States for defense, France sought to accelerate tendencies in the international system toward multipolarity. France's ambivalence toward European integration reflected the attitude that "integration is good if it leads to an entity that will emancipate Europe from any bipolar system, bad if it does not and merely chains France to German national desiderata,"[135] or subordinates France to the United States. In European integration Germany, in the aftermath of World War II, found a framework to regain a place of respectability in the family of Western nations as well as an outlet for national energies. Britain's outlook toward European integration was strongly influenced by British global perspectives of foreign policy. In short, Hoffmann contends, relations among Western European nations have been "subordinated to their divergences about the outside world"; the "regional subsystem becomes a stake in the rivalry of its members about the system as a whole."[136] Beyond Hoffmann's analysis, it is possible to adduce additional examples of variables from the international environment that appear to influence the integration in a region such as Western Europe.

In fact, it has been postulated that the lower the regional autonomy of a regional subsystem such as the European Community, the greater the importance of "exogenous factors." The integrative experiences of Western Europe, and especially those of Latin America and East Africa, "reflect a dynamic interaction between an internal regional dialectic, analyzed by present theory, and changing international environmental pressures relatively unexplored in current neofunctionalist literature."[137]

Research on integration has been criticized not only on the basis of the variables and indicators chosen for examination, but also for the lack of an appropriate theoretical framework. In particular, such criticism has been directed toward research, such as that undertaken by Russett, which relies heavily upon factor analysis in the development of inductive theory.[138] In the absence of a deductive theoretical framework, Young argues, empirical investigation is not likely to provide an adequate basis for predictive theory to take account of intervening variables or offer an adequate explanation of relationships among variables. Such a discussion reflects the disagreement among scholars about the nature of theory noted in Chapter 1. Moreover, the lack of a shared definition of integration inhibits research. According to Donald J. Puchala, who himself proposed a definition, as noted earlier in this chapter: "More than fifteen years of defining, redefining, modeling, and theorizing have failed to generate satisfactory conceptualizations of exactly what it is we are talking about when we refer to 'international integration' and exactly what it is we are trying to learn when we study this phenomenon."[139]

In a concluding chapter to a volume containing essays by several scholars on regional integration, representative of the literature of the early 1970s, Stuart Scheingold pointed to the paucity of information based upon a form of cost-benefit analysis—the losses and gains to groups within societies—although several authors have attached great importance to expectations of joint reward as a catalyst to integration. According to Scheingold, additional research should be conducted to assess the ways in which integrative processes impinge upon national policies in such areas as agriculture, antitrust, medium-term planning, and general commercial policy, as well as upon world politics. Such questions, it is suggested, are more broadly relevant to comparative politics and to international politics. Therefore they would attract interest, as well as potential intellectual contributions, from a larger segment of the academic community. In short, Scheingold saw the need for approaches that were essentially inductive and for the collection of data on a more extensive basis as necessary prerequisites for further theorizing about integration.[140]

Limitations of Functionalism and Neofunctionalism

Functionalism itself has been the object of several kinds of criticisms and modifications, especially in the latter case by neofunctionalists surveyed in this chapter. Among the criticisms of functionalism are the following: (1) that it is difficult, if not impossible, to separate the economic and social tasks from the political; (2) that governments have shown themselves unwilling to hand over to international authority tasks which encroach upon the political; (3) that certain economic and social tasks do not "ramify" or "spill-over" into the political sector; and (4) that the road to political integration lies through political "acts of will," rather than functional integration in economic and social sectors. Research conducted thus far has not produced agreement among students of integration about spill-over or about the catalysts that initiate and sustain the integrative process. There is no widely accepted deductive model about integration in which definitions and conditions for integration as well as processual steps and transformation rules are set forth. To a considerable extent, the disagreement about functionalism may be reduced to a debate between the proponents and opponents, respectively, of the coercion and consensus theories of community discussed earlier in this chapter. But the critique of neofunctionalism by Haas himself is based upon the notion that they are obsolete because they do not address "the most pressing and important problems on the global agenda of policy and research." Haas states that neofunctionalism was inspired by a "sense of orderly process and by the assumption that states manage to cope collectively according to the rationality of disjointed incrementalism.[141] Neofunctionalism is not considered to be wrong, but instead to be inadequate in light of the "turbulent field" of international relations with its numerous global issues in the late twentieth century.

In another critique of functionalism, Charles Pentland concluded that, at least in light of the Western European experience since World War II, there is little evidence to suggest that technology and economic growth, in a shrinking world, will produce integration through functional cooperation. "The relation between functional need and structural adaptation, central to the theory, is 'necessary' only in the sense of being an ideal or norm, not in the sense of predetermining the direction of change."[142] Moreover, political influences and pressures have proven to be of major importance in effecting the integrative process in Western Europe. There has been little or nothing that is "nonpolitical" in nature in the integration experience of Western Europe since World War II, although the institutions of the European Community, adequate for the formation of a customs union, may not be relevant to the fundamental problem of Western European integration—the formation of a political federation.

Nor is a neofunctionalist integration model necessarily adequate for the study of Third World integrative systems. In contrast to industrialized actors, Third World states are likely to have fewer goals that can be satisfied by integration. For example, expectations of economic gains from rising levels of trade, facilitated by the lowering or removal of tariff barriers, have furnished a major motivation for the formation of customs unions, especially in Western Europe. However, the structure of trade and production in much of the Third World, based historically upon the supply of agricultural products and raw materials to advanced industrialized states, has hindered the prospects, at least in the short run, for economic complementarity of a level sufficient to promote integration within the Third World by the formation of customs unions or Common Markets comparable to the European Community.[143] Even in areas such as Latin America and the Arab world, where the sharing of a common language and common cultural values would appear to be conducive to integration, the fact that national economies are oriented outward toward the industrialized areas of the world rather than toward each other poses a serious obstacle to regional integration. Therefore, integration modes adequate to Third World conditions differ substantially from those having relevance for industrialized states, and models examined in this chapter contribute to an explanation for the lack of integration in the Third World.

THE DEVELOPMENT OF INTEGRATION THEORY

What is needed is a model which incorporates propositions from neo-functionalist literature as well as writings which give greater importance to the role of coercion and the impact of the international environment upon integration. Current integration models may be faulted for their relative neglect of the role of conflict as an integrating force. Students of postwar Europe agree, in general, that the experience of World War II was important, if not crucial, as a catalyst in the postwar European integration movement. Yet the phenomenon of conflict—perhaps like the "phenomenon of de Gaulle" in Haas's critique of *his* own earlier works—is missing from models of integration, even when they are applied to the post World War II European experience. Except perhaps as a result of normative biases of students of integration, it is difficult to understand the reason for this oversight, since both traditional and contemporary writers in the field of conflict have examined in considerable depth the integrative role of conflict. Moreover, the integrative impetus of post World War II Europe was based largely upon disillusionment with the nation-state as a result of the Second World War. Thus, even in the European context, conflict may have played an integrative role that is given less prominent consideration than it deserves in the integration literature on Europe.

Several writers have suggested that integration is a multidimentional concept. According to Joseph Nye conceptual distinctions should be made among categories of catalysts, the external environment in which integration takes place, and the types of discontinuities in the integrative process.[144] There is need for integration to be broken down into economic, political, and legal components, which in turn might be divided into subtypes, each of which could be measured. "Rather than allowing us to talk about integration in general and confusing terms, this disaggregation will tend to force us to make more qualified, and more readily falsified, generalizations with the *ceteris paribus* clauses filled in, so to speak, and thus pave the way for more meaningful comparative analysis than that provided by the general schemes used so far."[145] Especially in the 1970s, there were efforts, as we have noted, to study integration as a multidimensional phenomenon. Integration theory has been subjected to extensive quantitative analysis. Nevertheless, major conceptual problems, as well as disagreement about definitions, variables, and indicators, remain, despite the contributions of scholars, especially during the past generation, to theoretical knowledge about integration at the international level.

Notes

1. For an analysis which cuts across traditional fields, see Philip E. Jacob and James V. Toscano, eds., The Integration of Political Communities (Philadelphia: Lippincott, 1964).

2. Thomas Hobbes, *Leviathan* (Oxford: Basil H. Blackwell, 1967), pp. 109, 174. Ralf Dahrendorf, *Class and Class Conflict in Industrial Society* (Stanford: Stanford University Press, 1959), p. 157, and *Essays in the Theory of Society* (Stanford: Stanford University Press, 1968), pp. 147–150. See Chapter 5 for an examination of other writers, traditional and contemporary, who have posited the existence of relationships between conflict and the integration of political and social units.

3. Reinhold Niebuhr, "The Illusion of World Government," *Bulletin of the Atomic Scientists*, V (October 1949), 289–292. Hans J. Morgenthau, *Politics Among Nations* (New York: A. Knopf, 1978), pp. 499–507. For an examination of literature on world government, see Inis L. Claude, Jr., *Power and International Relations* (New York: Random House, 1962), pp. 205–285.

4. Johan K. De Vree, *Political Integration: The Formation of Theory and Its Problems* (The Hague-Paris: Mouton, 1972), p. 45.

5. William Flanigan and Edwin Fogelman, "Functional Analysis," in James C. Charlesworth, ed., *Contemporary Political Analysis* (New York: The Free Press, 1967), p. 73.

6. Charles Pentland, "Functionalism and Theories of International Political Integration," in A. J. R. Groom and Paul Taylor, eds., *Theory and Practice in International Relations: Functionalism* (New York: Crane, Russak, 1975), p. 16.

7. David Mitrany, *A Working Peace System* (Chicago: Quadrangle Books, 1966), p. 97.

8. David Mitrany, "The Functional Approach to World Organization," *International Affairs*, XXIV (July 1948), p. 359.

9. A. J. R. Groom and Paul Taylor, "Functionalism and International Relations," in Groom and Taylor, eds., *Theory and Practice in International Relations: Functionalism* (New York: Crane, Russak, 1975), p. 2.

10. David Mitrany, "International Cooperation in Action," *International Associations*, Brussels (September 1959). Quoted in David Mitrany, "The Prospect of Integration: Federal or Functional?", in A. J. R. Groom and Paul Taylor, eds., op. cit., p. 67.

11. See, for example, Richard W. Marshack, Yale H. Ferguson, and Donald E. Lampert, *The Web of Global Politics: Nonstate Actors in the Global System* (Englewood Cliffs, N.J.: Prentice-Hall, 1976); Flo Burton, *Systems, States, Diplomacy and Rules* (New York: Cambridge University Press, 1968); Robert C. Angell *Peace on the March* (New York: Van Nostrand, 1969).

12. Ernst B. Haas, *The Uniting of Europe* (Stanford: Stanford University Press, 1958), p. 16.

13. Ernst B. Haas, *Beyond the Nation-State* (Stanford: Stanford University Press, 1964), p. 29. (Italics in original.)

14. Amitai Etzioni, *Political Unification* (New York: Holt, Rinehart and Winston, 1965), p. 4. "A political community is a community that possesses three kinds of integration: (a) it has an effective control over the use of the means of violence (though it may 'delegate' some of this monopoly to member-units); (b) it has a center of decision-making that is able to effect significantly the allocation of resources and rewards throughout the community; and (c) it is the dominant focus of political identification for the large majority of politically aware citizens." Ibid., p. 329.

15. Ibid., p. 332.

16. Leon N. Lindberg, *The Political Dynamics of European Economic Integration* (Stanford: Stanford University Press, 1963), p. 6.

17. Leon N. Lindberg, "Political Integration as a Multidimensional Phenomenon Requiring Multivariate Measurement," in Leon N. Lindberg and Stuart A. Scheingold, eds., *Regional Integration: Theory and Research* (Cambridge, Mass.: Harvard University Press, 1971), pp. 45–46.

18. Charles Pentland, *International Theory and European Integration* (London: Faber and Faber, 1973), p. 29.

19. Donald J. Puchala "Of Blind Men, Elephants and International Integration," *Journal of Common Market Studies*, X, No. 3 (March 1972), 277.

20. Karl W. Deutsch et al., *Political Community and the North Atlantic Area* (Princeton: Princeton University Press, 1957), p. 5.

21. Ibid., p. 6.

22. Karl W. Deutsch, *The Analysis of International Relations*, 2nd ed. (Englewood Cliffs, N.J.: Prentice-Hall, 1978), pp. 198–199.

23. Philip E. Jacob and Henry Teune, "The Integrative Process: Guidelines for Analysis of the Bases of Political Community," in Jacob and Toscano, eds., op. cit., p. 4.

24. Johan K. de Vree, *Political Integration: The Formation of Theory and Its Problems* (Paris: Mouton, 1972), p. 11.

25. James A. Caporaso and Alan L. Pelowski, "Economic and Political Integration in Europe: A Time-Series Quasi-Experimental Analysis," *American Political Science Review*, 65, No. 2 (June 1975), 421–422.

26. Johan Galtung, "A Structural Theory of Integration," *Journal of Peace Research*, 5, No. 4 (1968), 377.

27. Ibid., p. 378.

28. Quoted in Karl W. Deutsch, *The Nerves of Government* (New York: The Free Press, 1964), p. 77. See Norbert Wiener, *Cybernetics* (Cambridge, Mass.: M.I.T. Press, 1965).

29. In his work on nationalism, Deutsch wrote: "The community which permits a common history to be experienced as common is a community of complementary habits and facilities of communication. It requires, so to speak, equipment for a job. This job consists in the storage, recall, transmission, recombination, and reapplication of relatively wide ranges of information, and the "equipment" consists in such learned memories, symbols, habits, operating preferences, and facilities as will in fact be sufficiently complementary to permit the performance of these functions. *A larger group of persons linked by such complementary habits and facilities of communication* we may call a people." *Nationalism and Social Communication* (Cambridge, Mass.: M.I.T. Press, 1953), p. 96. (Italics in original.)

30. Karl W. Deutsch, "The Impact of Communications upon International Relations Theory," in Abdul Said, ed., *Theory of International Relations: The Crisis of Relevance* (Englewood Cliffs, N.J.: Prentice-Hall, 1968), p. 75.

31. Ibid., p. 76.

32. Ibid., pp. 84–90.

33. They included the formation of the United States, its breakup in the Civil War, and the reunion which followed—the union of Scotland and England, the disintegration of the Anglo-Irish Union, German unification, Italian unification, the Hapsburg Empire, the union of Norway and Sweden, and the Swiss Confederation. Two other cases, the union of Wales and England and the formation of England itself in the Middle Ages, were studied "less intensively."

34. Here the reader may wish to refer to Chapter 1, where the point is made concerning John H. Herz's theory to the effect that in the nuclear age the ability of the territorial state to provide its citizens with a sense of security has been put in doubt. However, Deutsch's idea of a security community is that members of such a

community do not hold an expectation of war with each other, not that they are necessarily more secure against external attack inside than outside such a community.

35. Deutsch et al., *Political Community and the North Atlantic Area*, op. cit., p. 58.
36. This idea is similar to Parsons social system in which persons develop expectations about each other's behavior. See Chapter 4, pp. 140–143.
37. Ibid., p. 70.
38. Ibid., p. 199.
39. Ibid., p. 203.
40. Roger W. Cobb and Charles Elder, *International Community: A Regional and Global Study* (New York: Holt, Rinehart and Winston, 1970), pp. vi, 6.
41. Ibid., pp. 134–136.
42. Ibid., p. 136.
43. J. S. Nye: *Peace in Parts: Integration and Conflict in Regional Organization* (Boston: Little, Brown, 1971), p. 198: See also Edward L. Morse, "The Politics of Interdependence," *International Organization*, 23 (Spring 1969).
44. Amitai Etzioni, *Political Unification*, op. cit., p. 14.
45. Amitai Etzioni hypothesizes: "In particular, unions having one elite will be more successful than those having two, those with two more than those with three." Ibid., p. 69.
46. Ibid., pp. 296–297.
47. Ibid., p. 296.
48. In Etzioni's scheme, utilitarian assets include technical and administrative capabilities, manpower, and economic possessions. The term *identitive assets* refers to "the characteristics of a unit or units that might be used to build up an identitive power. These identitive potentials are usually values or symbols, built up by educational or religious institutions, national rituals, and other mechanisms." Ibid., pp. 38–39.
49. Ibid., p. 306.
50. Amitai Etzioni, *The Active Society: A Theory of Societal and Political Processes* (New York: The Free Press, 1968), pp. 585–586.
51. Ibid., p. 599.
52. Charles Pentland, "Functionalism and Theories of International Political Integration," in A. J. R. Groom and Paul Taylor, eds., op. cit., p. 18.
53. Ernest B. Haas, *The Uniting of Europe*, op. cit., p. 13. For an analysis of expectations of British official and nonofficial elite groups from European integration, see Robert L. Pfaltzgraff, Jr., *Britain Faces Europe, 1957–1967* (Philadelphia: University of Pennsylvania Press, 1969).
54. Ernst B. Haas, *Beyond the Nation-State*, op. cit., p. 47.
55. Ibid., p. 48.
56. Ernst B. Haas and Philippe Schmitter, "Economics and Differential Patterns of Political Integration: Projections about Unity in Latin America," *International Organization*, XVIII (Autumn 1964), 707. Reprinted in *International Political Communities* (New York: Doubleday, 1966), p. 262.
57. Ernst B. Haas, *The Uniting of Europe*, op. cit., p. 49.
58. Ibid., p. 50.
59. Haas refers to "spill-over" as "the expansive logic of sector integration," and suggests: If actors, on the basis of their interest-inspired perceptions, *desire* to adapt integrative lessons learned in one context to a new situation, the lesson will be generalized." *Beyond the Nation-State* (Stanford: Stanford University Press, 1964), p. 48.
60. Ernst B. Haas, "International Integration: The European and the Universal Process," *International Organization*, XV (Autumn 1961), 372.

61. Ernst B. Haas, *Beyond the Nation-State*, op. cit., p. 81. According to Haas, "The major and perhaps the sole justification for using systems theory in the discussion of international politics is its ability to link the will of governments with the shape of the world to come. It is policy that produces the 'system,' though the system then goes on to constrain future policy or dictate its limits." Ernst B. Haas, *The Web of Interdependence: The United States and International Organizations* (Englewood Cliffs, N.J.: Prentice-Hall, 1970), p. 106, and *Tangle of Hopes: American Commitments and World Order* (Englewood Cliffs, N.J.: Prentice-Hall, 1969), pp. 10–12.

62. Ernst B. Haas and Philippe C. Schmitter, op. cit., p. 366.

63. Ibid., p. 274.

64. Ernst B. Haas, *Beyond the Nation-State*, op. cit., p. 409.

65. Ibid., p. 48.

66. Philippe C. Schmitter "A Revised Theory of Regional Integration," *International Organization*, 24, No. 4 (1970), p. 846.

67. Ernst B. Haas, "The 'Uniting of Europe' and the Uniting of Latin America," *Journal of Common Market Studies*, V (June 1967), 324.

68. Ibid., p. 329. But the opposite may be argued, namely that pragmatically based integration in the so-called technical areas is the most enduring, not the most ephemeral, form of integration. The most technical functions, such as telecommunications and postal service, were the first to achieve integration without "spill-over" into other fields. See James A. Caporoso, *Functionalism, Spill-Over, and International Integration*. Doctoral Dissertation in Political Science, University of Pennsylvania, 1968.

69. Ernst B. Haas, op. cit., 331. A study by Karl Deutsch and others led similarly to the conclusion that de Gaulle, although he did not reverse the integrative process in the European Community, did bring it to a halt. *France, Germany and the Western Alliance* (New York: Scribner's, 1967), p. 223.

70. Ernst B. Haas, "Turbulent Fields and the Theory of Regional Integration" *International Organization*, 30, No. 2 (1976), 184.

71. Ernst B. Haas, Mary Pat Williams, and Don Babai, *Scientists and World Order: The Uses of Technical Knowledge in International Organizations* (Berkeley: University of California Press, 1977), p. 9.

72. Ibid., pp. 7, 352–355.

73. Ibid., p. 210.

74. Ibid., p. 210. See also Robert S. Keohane and Joseph S. Nye, "Interdependence and Integration," in Fred Greenstein and Nelson Polsby, eds., *Handbook of Political Science*, vol. 8 (Reading, Mass.: Addison-Wesley, 1975); Alex Inkeles, "The Emerging Social Structure of the World," *World Politics* (July 1975).

75. Lawrence B. Krause and Joseph S. Nye, "Reflections on the Economics and Politics of International Economic Organizations," *International Organization*, 27, No. 1 (Winter 1975), 331.

76. Ernst B. Haas, "Turbulent Fields and the Theory of Regional Integration," op. cit., p. 178.

77. Ernst B. Haas, *The Obsolescence of Regional Integration Theory*, Research Series, No. 25, Institute of International Studies, University of California, Berkeley, 1975, pp. 8–9.

78. Philippe C. Schmitter, *Autonomy or Dependence as Regional Integration Outcomes: Central America*, Research Series, No. 17, Institute of International Studies, University of California, Berkeley, 1972, pp. 9–10.

79. Philippe C. Schmitter, "A Revised Theory of Regional Integration," *International Organization*, 24, No. 4 (1970), 868.

80. Barry B. Hughes and John E. Schwarz, "Dimensions of Political Integration and

the Experience of the European Community," *International Studies Quarterly*, 16, No. 3. See also Leon N. Lindberg, "Political Integration as a Multidimensional Phenomenon Requiring Multivariate Measurement," *International Organization*, 24 (Autumn 1970), 649–732; Donald S. Puchala, "Integration and Disintegration in Franco-German Relations, 1954–1965," *International Organization*, 24, (Spring 1970), 183–208. Joseph S. Nye, "Comparative Regional Integration: Concept and Measurement," *International Organization*, 22 (Autumn 1968), 855–880.

81. Barry Hughes and John Schwarz, op. cit., p. 290.
82. J. S. Nye, *Peace in Parts: Integration and Conflict in Regional Organization* (Boston: Little, Brown, 1971), pp. 56–58.
83. Ibid., p. 65.
84. Ibid., p. 66.
85. Ibid., p. 67.
86. Ibid., p. 68.
87. Ibid., pp. 71–72
88. Ibid., p. 73.
89. Ibid.
90. Ibid., p. 80.
91. Ibid., p. 82.
92. Ibid., p. 74.
93. Ibid., p. 93.
94. Ibid., p. 182.
95. Ibid., pp. 172, 198–199; and Donald Rothchild. "Ethnicity and Conflict Resolution," *World Politics*, XXII (July 1970), 597–616.
96. Leon N. Lindberg, "Political Integration as a Multidimensional Phenomenon Requiring Multivariate Measurement," in Leon N. Lindberg and Stuart A. Scheingold, eds., "Regional Integration: Theory and Research," Special Issue *International Organization*, CCIV, No. 4 (Autumn 1970), 651.
97. Ibid., p. 652.
98. Ibid., p. 653
99. Leon N. Lindberg and Stuart A. Scheingold, *Europe's Would-Be Policy: Patterns of Change in the European Community* (Englewood Cliffs, N.J.: Prentice-Hall, 1970), p. 74.
100. Lindberg and Scheingold, ibid., p. 121.
101. Bruce M. Russett, *International Regions and the International System: A Study in Political Ecology* (Chicago: Rand McNally, 1967), pp. 7–8.
102. Ibid., pp. 30–34.
103. Robert L. Rothstein, *Alliances and Small Powers* (New York: Columbia University Press, 1968), p. 55.
104. Robert E. Osgood, *Alliances and American Foreign Policy* (Baltimore: Johns Hopkins Press, 1968), p. 19.
105. See Francis A. Beer, ed., *Alliances: Latent War Communities in the Contemporary World* (New York: Holt, Rinehart and Winston, 1970), especially pp. 3–9, 13–67.
106. See, for example, Hans J. Morgenthau, "Alliances in Theory and Practice," in Arnold Wolfers, ed., *Alliance Policy in the Cold War* (Baltimore: Johns Hopkins Press, 1959).
107. George F. Liska, *Nations in Alliance: The Limits of Interdependence* (Baltimore: Johns Hopkins Press, 1962), p. 12. William H. Riker, *The Theory of Political Coalitions* (New Haven: Yale University Press, 1962), pp. 32–76. See also Bruce M. Russett, "Components of an Operational Theory of International Alliance Formation," *Journal of Conflict Resolution*, XII (September 1968), 285–301. For a selection of essays from the literature on alliances, see Julian R. Friedman, Christopher Bladen, and Steven Rosen, eds., *Alliance in International Politics* (Boston:

Allyn & Bacon, 1970); Francis A. Beer, ed., *Alliances: Latent War Communities in the Contemporary World* (New York: Holt, Rinehart and Winston, 1970).

108. Liska, op. cit., p. 175.

109. Ibid., p. 61.

110. William Riker, op. cit., p. 188. For another application of Riker's framework, see Martin Southwold, "Riker's Theory and the Analysis of Coalitions in Precolonial Africa," Sven Groennings, E. W. Kelley, and Michael Leiserson, eds., *The Study of Coalition Behavior: Theoretical Perspectives and Cases from Four Continents* (New York: Holt, Rinehart and Winston, 1970), pp. 336–350. For an effort to relate Riker's framework to balance of power literature, see Dina A. Zinnes, "Coalition Theories and the Balance of Power," in the same volume, pp. 351–368.

111. For an examination of Kaplan's rules for the balance of power systems, see Chapter 4.

112. George F. Liska, *Nations in Alliance*, op. cit., p. 27. See also George F. Liska, *Quest for Equilibrium: America and the Balance of Power on Land and Sea* (Baltimore: Johns Hopkins Press, 1977), p. 6.

113. Ibid., p. 30.

114. Robert L. Rothstein, op. cit., p. 50

115. Robert L. Rothstein, ibid., pp. 173–176.

116. Ibid., p. 43.

117. Mancur Olson, Jr., *The Logic of Collective Action* (Cambridge, Mass.: Harvard University Press, 1965), p. 48.

118. Pierre Gallois, *The Balance of Terror* (Boston: Houghton Mifflin, 1961), chap. 1.

119. George F. Liska, *International Equilibrium: A Theoretical Essay on the Politics and Organization of Security* (Cambridge, Mass.: Harvard University Press, 1957). Liska uses the concept of equilibrium in two ways: as a "theoretical norm or point of reference" and as "denoting an actual tendency toward changing states of temporary equilibrium in political institutions," p. 13.

120. George F. Liska, *Quest for Equilibrium: America and the Balance of Power on Land and Sea*, op. cit., pp. 3–4.

121. Ibid., pp. 202–203.

122. Ibid., pp. 13–14.

123. Ibid., p. 6.

124. Ibid., p. 6.

125. See, for example, Joseph S. Nye, Jr., "Comparative Regional Integration: Concept and Measurement," *International Organization*, XXII (Autumn 1968), 857. For a collection of contemporary writings on integration at the international level, see, by the same author, *International Regionalism: Readings* (Boston: Little, Brown, 1968).

126. Ernst B. Haas, "The Challenge of Regionalism," *International Organization*, XII (Autumn 1958), 445.

127. Karl W. Deutsch, *France, Germany and the Western Alliance* (New York: Scribner's, 1967), pp. 218–220. Deutsch bases his findings on the Relative Acceptance Index, which purports to separate "the actual results of preferential behavior and structural integration from the mere effects of the size and prosperity of the country."

128. According to Lindberg, "Significant national powers have been thrust into a new institutional setting in which powerful pressures are exerted for Community solutions, that is, solutions which approximate the up-grading-of-common interests type. Our case studies have revealed that important and divergent national interests have been consistently accommodated in order to achieve a decision." Moreover, since the founding of the EEC, there has been a shift in political activities and expectations—another part of Lindberg's definition of integration: "This has

been most striking at the level of high policy-makers and civil servants, for the EEC policy-making process, by its very nature, engages an ever-expanding circle of national officials." Leon N. Lindberg, *The Political Dynamics of European Economic Integration* (Stanford: Stanford University Press, 1963), pp. 6, 286–288. See also Leon N. Lindberg and Stuart A. Scheingold, *Europe's Would Be Polity: Patterns of Change in the European Community* (Englewood Cliffs, N.J.: Prentice-Hall, 1970), pp. 24–100.

129. Ronald Inglehart, "An End to European Integration," *American Political Science Review*, LXI (March 1967), 91. For a study of continuity and change in foreign policy attitudes, see Neal E. Cutler, "Generational Succession as a Source of Foreign Policy Attitudes: A Cohort Analysis of American Opinion, 1946–1966," *Journal of Peace Research*, VII (970), 33–47; by the same author, but not related specifically to foreign policy, "Generation, Maturation, and Party Affiliation: A Cohort Analysis," *Public Opinion Quarterly*, XXXIII (Winter 1969–1970), 583–588.

130. Ronald Inglehart, op. cit., p. 92.

131. Carl J. Friedrich, *Europe: An Emergent Nation?* (New York: Harper & Row, 1969), especially pp. 196–215.

132. Ibid., pp. 35–46.

133. James A. Caporaso and Alan L. Pelowski, "Economic and Political Integration in Europe: A Time-Series Quasi-Experimental Analysis" *American Political Science Review*, 65, No. 2 (June 1971), 432–433.

134. Claude Ake, *A Theory of Political Integration* (Homewood, Ill.: Dorsey, 1967), pp. 8–11.

135. Stanley Hoffmann, *Gulliver's Troubles, or the Setting of American Foreign Policy* (New York: McGraw-Hill, 1968), p. 401. At various times European and American analysts have speculated on the feasibility of a European nuclear deterrent. See, for example, Henry A. Kissinger, *The Necessity for Choice* (Garden City, N.Y.: Doubleday, 1962), pp. 129–131; Robert Strausz-Hupé, James E. Dougherty, and William R. Kintner, *Building the Atlantic World* (New York: Harper & Row, 1962), chap. 5. For an analysis of European elite attitudes toward a European nuclear force, see Deutsch, *Arms Control and the Atlantic Alliance*, op. cit., pp. 34, 99, and 136.

136. Stanley Hoffmann, "The Fate of the Nation-State," *Daedalus*, VC (Summer 1966), 865.

137. Roger D. Hansen, "Regional Integration: Reflections on a Decade of Theoretical Efforts," *World Politics*, XXI (January 1969), 270. For another review and critique of the Haas-Schmitter work, see J. S. Nye, Jr., "Patterns and Catalysts in Regional Integration," *International Organization*, XIX (Autumn 1965), 870–884.

138. Oran R. Young, "Professor Russett: Industrious Tailor to a Naked Emperor," *World Politics*, XXI (April 1969), 486–511. For Russett's reply, see "The Young Science of International Politics," *World Politics*, XXII (October 1969), 87–94.

139. Donald J. Puchala "Of Blind Men, Elephants and International Integration," *Journal of Common Market Studies*, X, No. 3 (March 1972), 267.

140. Stuart A. Scheingold. "Consequences of Regional Integration," in Leon N. Lindberg and Stuart A. Scheingold, eds., *Regional Integration: Theory and Research* (Cambridge, Mass.: Harvard University Press, 1971), pp. 395–398.

141. Ernst B. Haas, *The Obsolescence of Regional Integration Theory*, Research Series, No. 25, Institute of International Studies, University of California, Berkeley, 1975, p. 17.

142. Charles Pentland, *International Theory and European Integration* (London: Faber and Faber, 1973), p. 98.

143. Lynn Krieger Mytelka, "The Salience of Gains in Third-World Integrative Sys-

tems," *World Politics,* 25, No. 2, 237–243. See also David Morawetz, "Harmonization of Economic Policies in Customs Unions: The Andean Group," *Journal of Common Market Studies.* XI, No. 4. "It is extremely unlikely that the Andean Group is an optimum, or even close to an optimum currency area." This stems from labor immobility within and between countries; artificially low foreign trade percentages because of import-substitution policies; heavy vulnerability of the balance of payments to external forces; and significant differences in inflation rates among member states.

144. J. S. Nye, "Patterns and Catalysts in Regional Integration" *International Organization,* XIX, No. 4 (Autumn 1965); reprinted in Joseph S. Nye, *International Regionalism: Readings* (Boston: Little, Brown, 1968), pp. 333–349.

145. Joseph S. Nye, Jr., "Comparative Regional Integration: Concept and Measurement," op. cit., p. 858.

Chapter 11
Decision-Making Theories

DECISION-MAKING ANALYSIS: ITS NATURE AND ORIGINS

Since World War II interest has increased in *decisions* as a central element in the political process and as a focal point for study by social scientists. Thus the literature of decision-making has encompassed (1) the study of how decisions supposedly are actually made; and (2) techniques and criteria for the taking of decisions by policymakers and executives so as to achieve prescribed goals. Decisions are, in David Easton's terminology, the "outputs" of the political system, by which values are authoritatively allocated within a society. The concept of decision-making had long been implicit in some of the older approaches to diplomatic history and the study of political institutions. But the process of decision-making first became the subject of systematic investigation in other fields outside of political science. Psychologists were interested in the motives underlying an individual's decisions and why some individuals had greater difficulty than others in making decisions. Economists focused on the decisions of consumers, producers, investigators, and others whose choices affected the economy. Business administration theorists sought to increase the efficiency of executive decision-making. In government and especially in defense planning in the 1960s, techniques known generally as "cost effectiveness" were utilized in the decision-making process, including the acquisition of new weapons systems. Decision-making was a focal point for political scientists interested in analyzing the decisional behavior of voters, legislators, executive officials, politicians, leaders of interest groups, and other actors in the political arena.[1] Thus the study of foreign policy decision-making concentrated on one segment of a more general phenomenon of interest to the social sciences and to policy-makers. In international relations, such conceptualization has often emphasized decision-making under crisis conditions. We shall first examine decision-making theory in general. Because many analysts have concerned themselves with decision-making in crisis situations, the latter part of the chapter will deal with that subject.

Decision-making is simply the act of choosing among available alternatives about which uncertainty exists. In foreign policy perhaps even more than in national politics—because the terrain of the former is usually less familiar—policy alternatives are seldom "given." They must often be gropingly formulated in the context of a total situation in which disagreements will arise over which estimate of the situation is most valid, what alternatives exist, the consequences likely to flow from various choices, and the values that should serve as criteria for ranking the various alternatives from most to least preferred. There are controversies both over the nature of the decision-making process and the appropriate paradigms for its study. Within the last generation, attention has shifted from decision-making as mere abstract choice among possible maximum-utility alternatives to decision-making as an incremental process containing partial choices and compromises among competing organizational interests and bureaucratic pressures.

Approaches to Decision-Making Theory

The decision-making approach to an understanding of international politics is not novel. Twenty-four centuries ago the Greek historian Thucydides, in his *The Peloponnesian War*, examined the factors that led the leaders of city-states to decide the issues of war and peace, as well as alliance and empire with as great precision as they did under the circumstances confronting them. He focused not only on the conscious reasons for statesmen's choices and their perceptions of the systemic environment—both of which are reflected in the speeches which he attributes to them—but also on the deeper psychological forces of fear, honor, and interest that in varying combinations motivated them as individuals and set the prevailing tone of their particular societies. Thus Thucydides was indeed an early student of decision-making.

Many other political writers—classical and modern—have given princes and policymakers substantive advice on the kinds of decisions they should make. All normative international relations theory is illustrative. Much of the extensive literature of comparative foreign policy analysis deals with the kinds of decisions that political leaders actually do make.

Decision-making theory, the focus of this chapter, identifies a large number of relevant variables, and it suggests possible interrelationships among these variables. DM theory (as we refer to it here) marks a significant shift from traditional political analysis in which writers sometimes have been prone to reify or personify nation-states as the basic actors within the international system. DM theory directs attention not to states as metaphysical abstractions or to governments or even to such broadly labeled institutions as "the Executive," but instead seeks to highlight the behavior of the specific human decision-makers who actually shape governmental policy. As Richard Snyder, H. W. Bruck, and Burton Sapin put it:

> It is one of our basic methodological choices to define the state as its official decision-makers—those whose authoritative acts are, to all intents and purposes, the acts of the state. State action is the action taken by those acting in the name of the state.[2]

By narrowing the subject of investigation from a larger collectivity to a smaller unit of persons responsible for decisions, DM theorists hope to make the locus of political analysis more concrete and more precise, and thus more amenable to systematic analysis. Nevertheless, it is assumed that decision-makers act within a total perceived environment that includes their national political system as well as the international system as a whole—an internal environment as well as an external environment.

Perception is assigned a central place in DM theory. When dealing with the "definition of the situation," most DM theorists regard the world as viewed by decision-makers to be more important than objective reality.[3] They thereby accept the distinction drawn by Harold and Margaret Sprout between the "psychomilieu" and the "operational environment" (discussed in Chapter 2). Joseph Frankel, however, argues that DM theory must take the objective environment into account, for even though factors not present in the minds of policymakers cannot influence their choices nevertheless such factors may be important insofar as they set limits to the outcome of their decisions.[4] Similarly, Michael Brecher insists that "the operational environment affects the results or outcomes of decisions directly but influences the choice among policy options, that is, the decisions themselves, only as it is filtered through the images of decision-makers."[5]

THE DECISION SITUATION (OR OCCASION)[6]

Braybrooke and Lindblom suggest that decision-making, although it cannot be fully identified with, nevertheless may be generally equated with, rational problem solving.[7] The question now arises as to how decision-makers define the situation in relation to the problem confronting them. How do they see objects, conditions, other actors, and their intentions? How do they define the goals of their own government? What values strike them as most important, not in the abstract but insofar as they appear to be at stake in this particular situation?

Snyder observes that some situations are more highly structured than others. Some are readily grasped in their meaning, whereas others may be more fluctuating and ambiguous. The urgency of situations, or the pressure to take action, will also vary widely. Whether a problem is considered primarily political, economic, military, social, or cultural will normally have implications for how it is to be handled and by whom. It is difficult, out of the welter of opinions from professional diplomats, scholars, journalists, and others, to arrive at a relatively accurate assessment of the various trends and forces active in a foreign situation (and here foreign policy decision-making is probably more complex than domestic). Analyzing another state's intentions can be even more treacherous. Decision-makers in one state, anticipating a policy initiative by their counterparts in another, may regard their own move to deter or preclude as a purely defensive response, but these measures might seem offensive to their foreign counterparts, as we saw in Chapter 8.

THE DECISIONAL SETTING

The decision situation encompasses the total "external setting" and "internal setting" in which the choice must be made. The external setting includes the state's geopolitical position within the global system and all relevant power relationships. Decision-makers of states that are not superpowers or great powers must usually consider their position within a subordinate regional system as well as dominant bilateral relations. Two crucially important variables in the internal setting are, of course, the state's military and economic capabilities which set limits to what the government can do. The internal setting, however, extends to the whole structure of the political system. Are the decision-makers part of a system in which they are expected to respond to "cues from above" (e.g., a strong leader or a single ideological party) or "cues from below" (such as shifts in public opinion, the demands of organized pressure groups, and the competition of elites)?[8] Is an election pending? What is the role of the press, and from what diplomatic and intelligence sources do the decision-makers obtain their information and evaluations?[9]

Finally, there is the question of the temporal-psychological context in which the need for decision arises. Whether the requirement for reaching a decision comes as a complete surprise or as the result of prior planning; whether the time available for deliberation and choice is adequate for the demands of the situation; and how important are the values at issue thought to be by the decision-makers—these factors have much to do with the quality and intensity of the decisional process, and they may be used to distinguish critical from noncritical decisions. Crisislike decisions can be defined for the moment as those which "arise without prior planning, allow short time for response, and have high value consequences."[10] The concept of crisis will require further elaboration later.

BUREAUCRATIC POLITICS

We have referred to the hypothesized tendency of decision-makers to allow their conceptions of national interest to be colored by their perceptions of what is good for their own bureaucratic unit. Because governmental decisional units operate under budgetary constraints, advocates of various types of foreign policy and defense programs find themselves in competition for the allocation of scarce resources. Foreign policy and defense programs compete not only with domestic programs (education, health, social security, agriculture, transportation, welfare, energy, construction, conservation, crime control, and urban renewal), but with each other—various types of military-technological programs and arms transfers, force deployments, alliance diplomacy, foreign development assistance, information and cultural exchange programs, intelligence activities, support for international organizations, and the strengthening of peaceful change processes. Differing interests within and among the departments and agencies that have a role in foreign policy and national security, as well as differences among the military services, are illustrative of the bureaucratic politics dimension of decision-making.

Morton H. Halperin, in a study of several foreign policy decisions, has shown how "politics within a government influence decisions and actions ostensibly directed outward"[11] and how the way in which officials focus on issues often depends on their bureaucratic position and perspective. Halperin concludes that actions or proposals by one government to influence the behavior of another government are usually based on the simple model of two individuals communicating accurately with each other, when in fact they have probably emerged from a complex bureaucratic process of "pulling and hauling" that is not fully understood by those who must carry out the decision. Furthermore, he says, the response of the foreign government is likely to be the result of a similar bureaucratic process of pulling and hauling.[12] (See the subsequent section, "Allison's Three Models.")

Both within and between governmental units, conflicts arise among individuals, factions, and modes of substantive expertise for influence, prestige, and ultimately dominance. Therefore, information about personality clashes and rivalries may be important in understanding specific decisional outcomes, especially when combined with information about who has access to whom within the power hierarchy. Comparably important may be the distinctive thought patterns institutionalized within a specific department or agency in the form of memoranda, directives, statements of objectives, intelligence estimates, and strategic plans.[13] How seriously the individual decision-maker may regard the fixed policy guidelines inherited from the past in comparison with the dynamic facts and impulses of an unfolding situation may be a function of personality as well as a consequence of the organization's personnel recruitment policies and training programs.

Frances E. Rourke has cited the law of bureaucratic inertia: "Bureaucracies at rest tend to stay at rest, and bureaucracies in motion tend to stay in motion."[14] Recent presidents have been exasperated on occasion at the slowness with which bureaucracies at rest respond to their orders, but Rourke observes that this might save a political leader from the consequences of a rash decision. Conversely, executive agencies that have been stimulated to develop certain capabilities, whether for waging combat, exploring space, negotiating arms control agreements, or selling arms or grain abroad, may feel compelled to prove their usefulness through activity which justifies expanded budgets. Once bureaucracies gain momentum, they are difficult to slow down. Rourke points out that the "irreversibility" of certain types of activity by large organizations contradicts the hypothesis that policymaking in the United States "moves incrementally in one sequential step after another from initial decision to final outcome, thus permitting a discontinuance of effort or the reversal of direction at any point. . . ."[15] He concludes that, while they can shape the views of political leaders and the public on foreign policy issues, and often possess technical capabilities which enable them to influence the flow of events, nevertheless bureaucratic agencies comprise only one part of a democratic political system. Their power ultimately depends upon the willingness of others—for example, Congress and the President—to support them, accept their advice, or legitimize their activities by going along with them.[16]

Alexander L. George of Stanford University has called attention to the fact that the Executive, instead of using centralized management practices to neutralize intrabureaucratic disagreements over policy, can use a "multiple advocacy model"—a mixed system combining elements of centralized management with certain features of pluralistic participatory models to harness diversity of views and interests for the sake of enhancing rational policymaking.[17] One of the dangers of bureaucratic politics against which the Executive wishes to guard is the possibility that organizational subunits might restrict competition with each other and work out compromises among themselves before the policy issues are aired at the highest level, so that the final decision is likely to be based on the preferred option which results from the internal bargaining process. Under these conditions, of course, policy options which might be viable but which are unpopular with the bureaucracy are rendered unavailable as a result of unfavorable presentation or inadequate information. But George warns the Executive against overcentralizing and overbureaucratizing the early "search" and "evaluation" phases of policy analysis prior to "choice." In an overcentralized system, the Executive might receive too narrow a range of "orthodox" options based upon cues transmitted, whether intentional or not, from the top down.

According to George, conflict and bargaining within the bureaucracy might contribute to a better policymaking process if it can be managed and resolved properly. He therefore espouses a multiple advocacy model as "an integral part of a *mixed system* in which centralized coordination and Executive initiative would be required."[18] The Chief Executive encourages competition among bureaucratic units while reserving the power to evaluate, judge, and choose among the various policy options articulated by the advocates. Since the advocates compete with each other only for the Executive's attention, this is a system of perfect competition, highly preferable to the imperfect competition which prevails in the bureaucratic bargaining-and-compromise model.

MOTIVATIONS AND CHARACTERISTICS OF DECISION-MAKERS

Richard C. Snyder has emphasized the importance of motivational analysis as a major determinant of the decision-making process.[19] People constantly attribute motives to the behavior of states, and these are really not separable from the motives of individual decison-makers who speak on behalf of states and rationalize their policy actions. In Snyder's view, motivation is only one component of action. It is not to be equated with causation, which is a broader concept. He assumes a multiplicity of motives of differing strengths, as well as the likelihood of conflict among motives, within organizational units and within the individual decisionmaker. Motives, although they are related to something in the external order, lie hidden in an internal psychic structure. Hence they cannot be observed directly but only inferred indirectly from the symbolic, verbal acts by which diplomats and statesmen are forever explaining the basis of their decisional behavior both to their own constituencies and to their foreign counterparts.

Synder has drawn a useful distinction between two types of motivation—"in order to" motives and "because of" motives.[20] The former are conscious and verbalizable: The decision-makers are taking this particular decision in order to accomplish such and such an objective of the state which they serve. For example, the administration of President Johnson sought a nonproliferation treaty "in order to" promote international stability by restricting the number of states that might independently opt for the initiation of nuclear hostilities. "Because of" motives, on the other hand, are unconscious or semiconscious motives, those which arise out of the previous life experience of the decision-makers, and which predispose or impel them toward certain kinds of policy orientations for private psychological reasons. In the example cited for the conclusion of the Non-Proliferation Treaty, it would be necessary to probe the biographies of those policymakers who most assiduously pressed for negotiating the treaty and search out those elements in the childhood, social background, education, life experience, and previous organizational conditioning of the treaty's most ardent proponents. As we have seen in Chapters 7 and 8, however, most macrotheorists are wary of "psychohistory" as a means of explaining the decisions and actions of political leaders.

Originally, Snyder thought that DM theorists ought to be concerned primarily with the postulated future consequences of an act, rather than with a psychoanalytic inquiry into the decision-maker's personal past.[21] James N. Rosenau paraphrases Snyder's position as follows:

> Snyder contends that usually the behavior of officials can be satisfactorily explained through an exploration of motives derived from their decision-making organization, from their interpretations of the society's goals, and from their reactions to demands of situations in the internal and external settings—and that therefore it is usually not necessary to investigate their "because of" motives.[22]

But later, although he remained justifiably suspicious of indiscriminate borrowings from the field of psychological research by persons trained as political scientists, Snyder showed heightened interest in such personality characteristics of decision-makers as "propensity to assume high risks, tolerance of ambiguity and uncertainty, intelligence, creativity, self-esteem, dominance, submissiveness, need for power, need for achievement and need for affiliation."[23] Most decision-making theorists, like most political historians, would agree that biographical knowledge about policymakers—including their education, religion, critical life experiences, professional training, foreign travel, residence or service, and previous political activities—might help to cast light upon the deepest motives and values of those who make specific decisions. However, little is known about the relationship between the total inner psychic experience of individuals and their overt policy choices in an organizational context. Probably few DM theorists would be willing to go so far as Martin Patchen, who, in commenting upon the delicate task of measuring personal motivations in the U-2 crisis of 1960, offered the following provocative suggestion:

> One approach is to analyze projectively verbal materials—such as informal interviews, speeches, articles, letters, etc. A second, and perhaps more promising, method is to analyze conditions of reward and punishment in a person's past history which are known to contribute to various motives. For example, we might be able to assess the strength of Khrushchev's motivation to avoid war on the basis of our knowledge of his past experience with war. Did he suffer personally in the past wars? Did he lose a son? Did he witness horrible scenes? His motivation for personal success and achievement might be assessed from knowledge of the learning conditions of his own childhood, if such information is available; or if it is not, one could rely on knowledge of the child-raising practices of the Ukrainian peasant society from which he came.[24]

It is one thing to acknowledge that an individual's background is significant, especially in cases where there are unusual behavioral aberrations from what would "normally" be expected on the basis of the analysis of known social roles and processes. But it is quite another thing to draw a definite causal link between the previous psychic event (perhaps years earlier) and the present deviant action. One of the difficulties with this type of psychohistorical explanation is that it can lend itself too easily to the workings of an overactive dramatic imagination as a substitute for rigorous analysis of real evidence.

THE DECISION-MAKING PROCESS

David Easton has defined politics as "the authoritative allocation of values for a society."[25] This, in essence, is what political decision-making is all about. But DM theorists are not in general agreement as to whether the process of political decision-making is fundamentally the same as the process of nonpublic or private decision-making. As political scientists, the authors of this book are strongly inclined to agree with those who postulate important differences among decisions in a family, in a university, in a business corporation, and in a government department.[26] Even though private and public decision-making are both characterized by various mixes of individual and collective processes, nevertheless the frames of reference and the "rules of the game" exhibit rather unique properties.

It was suggested earlier that a decision involves a choice among alternatives. Now the question is how this expression of intent is arrived at.

Is it basically a psychological-intellectual process which goes on in the minds of policymakers, or is it a social bargaining process in which various competing, conflicting, and accommodating forces and pressures in the external environment clash to produce a synthesis as in the Bureaucratic Politics Model? (This model will be described later in the chapter.)

Since economists and students of business administration made significant early inputs to DM theory, the theory as originally developed reflected many of the assumptions of the Enlightenment and Benthamite Utilitarians, with their emphasis upon reason and education in the making of human social choices. It assumed a rational person who is clearly aware of all the available alternatives and who is capable of both calculating their respective outcomes and then freely choosing according to the order of value preferences. Such assumptions have been seriously questioned recently.

According to the classic model of decision-making, policymakers make a calculation in two basic dimensions—utility and probability—and, assuming that they are "rational," they will attempt to maximize expected utility. In other words, after all the available alternatives have been surveyed and the product of weighted values and assessed probabilities has been obtained, decision-makers can choose their optimal course.[27] Snyder points out that "decision-makers may be assumed to act in terms of clear-cut preferences," but that these preferences, instead of being entirely individual, derive from the rules of the organizational system, shared organizational experience over a period of time, and the information available to the decisional unit, as well as from the biographies of individuals.[28] Snyder, however, refrained from subscribing fully to the classic explanatory formula of "maximization of expected utility," which had already been subject to question before he wrote his principal essay on the subject.[29]

Next we must raise the question of whether the theories with which we are dealing in this chapter presuppose the rationality of the DM process, and whether they confine themselves to the rational components of that process. For many decades, the Western intellectual's faith in the essential rationality of human behavior (inherited from the Enlightenment) has steadily disintegrated. Freud virtually completed the erosion process with his discoveries concerning the powerful role played by the unconscious in life. Nevertheless political science and international relations students tend to assume that there are some rational elements in the political process insofar as individuals set forth in explicit fashion their goal priorities and devise categories of means for attaining them. Moreover, if our knowledge of the individual prompts us to postulate irrationality, the demands of social organization require us to grope in the direction of rationality, and to employ the criteria of "rationality" in order to identify and understand "the irrational." The assumption of rational behavior has been deemed to be central to much of international relations theory. Rationality is socially defined.

However, decision-making theory, for example, that developed by the Snyder group, does not necessarily assume the rationality of decision-makers. Rationality is an element to be validated by empirical analysis rather than to be assumed. But Snyder and his associates do not differ substantially from those modern theorists of governmental decision-making who have been influenced by Max Weber's concept of bureaucracy which develops according to a rational plan. There is in the theory an assumption of purposeful behavior and explicit motivation; behavior is seen not as merely random activity. The DM process is said to combine rational elements, value considerations in which the rational may be synthesized with the nonrational, the irrational, or the supranational, and such irrational or nonrational factors as the psychic complexes of the policymakers. J. David Singer, among others, has pointed out that under conditions of stress and anxiety decision-makers may not act according to standards of utility that could be called rational,[30] and Martin Patchen has suggested the need for greater attention to the presence of nonrational and partly conscious factors in the personalities of those who make decisions.[31] After examining both nonrational and rational models of decision-making, Sidney Verba concludes that it may be useful under certain circumstances to assume that governments "make decisions as if they were following the rules of means-end rationality" and choose the alternative that enables them best to attain the ends or promote the values of the decision-makers.[32]

Braybrooke and Lindblom reject as unsatisfactory for most important decisions (i.e., those which affect significant changes in the external social world) the "synoptic conception" of decision-making by which policymakers are presumed to spread out before them all their available alternatives and to measure, against their scale of preferred values, all the probable consequences of the social changes implicit in the various courses of action under consideration. This synoptic schema, in their view, simply does not conform to reality. It presupposes omniscience and a kind of comprehensive analysis which is prohibitively costly and which time pressures normally do not permit. Every solution, they assert, must be limited by several factors, including the individual's problem-solving capacities, the amount of information available, the cost of analysis (in personnel, resources, and time), and the practical inseparability of fact and value.[33]

No one has challenged the classic model of rational decision-making more fundamentally, while yet remaining within a rational framework, than the eminent economist and theorist of administration, Herbert Simon, who postulates a world of "bounded rationality." For the classic concept of *maximizing* or *optimizing* behavior, he substituted the notion of "satisficing" behavior. This presupposes that the policymakers do not really design for themselves a matrix which shows all available alternatives, the value "pros" and "cons" of each, and the probability assessments of expected consequences. Instead, Simon suggests, decision-making units examine alternatives sequentially until they come upon one which meets their minimum standards of acceptability.[34] In other words, people keep rejecting unsatisfactory solutions until they find one which they can agree is sufficiently satisfactory to enable them to act. (It was for this theory that Simon won the 1978 Nobel Prize for Economics.) Braybrooke and Lindblom, who are partial both to Simon's "satisficing" model and to Karl Popper's idea of "piecemeal engineering," suggest that pragmatic experimentalism embodies a strategy of "disjointed incrementalism." Put in its simplest form, this means that policymakers, especially in democratic states, prefer to separate their decision-making problems into small segments which enable them to make "incremental" or "marginal" rather than far-reaching or profound choices.[35]

Another factor which deserves mention in this context is the phenomenon known as *decisional conflict;* this term has been defined by Irving L. Janis as referring to "opposing tendencies within an individual, which interfere with the formulation, acceptance, or execution of a decision."[36] Such conflicts might arise either out of the psychological personality of the individual policymaker or out of the intensity of cross-pressures on the part of competing groups, or out of both. In other words, external pressures for contrary or contradictory policy courses might produce within the individual policymaker symptoms of uncertainty, vacillation and tension, or even issue-avoidance. Moreover, intrapersonal conflict might be a cause of intergroup or international conflict. In acute cases, individual negotiators might reach international agreements which are repudiated by their home governments and suffer such post-decisional conflicts as to induce them to withdraw altogether from subsequent negotiating roles.[37] More will be said later about "uncommitted" and "committed" decision-makers.

The foregoing consideration serves to remind us that decision-making is not only an intellectual process involving the insight, perception, and creative intuition of policymakers, but it is also a matter of social and quasi-mechanical processes.[38] Among political scientists, Arthur F. Bentley and David B. Truman have done much to stress the importance of interest groups in the decisional process, and William F. Riker, in his study of coalitions, suggests that decision-making may depend at least partially upon quasi-mechanical processes in which the actors are unconscious of their decision-making roles.[39] A striking example of group conflict in United States policy in the Middle East is the divergent interests of pro-Israeli elements and the oil industry. Quasi-mechanical processes may be illustrated in the case of individuals who, for motives of personal economic advantage, engage in international economic transactions such as importing, foreign investment, travel or capital flight to overseas banks, which virtually compel governmental policymakers to adopt regulatory decisions (e.g., in a balance-of-payments crisis). Robinson and Majak conclude that decisions can normally be understood best in the light of three types of processes (intellectual, social, and quasi-mechanical), even though all three may not be equally relevant in a given instance.[40]

ALLISON'S THREE MODELS

According to Graham T. Allison, most foreign policy analysts think about and explain governmental behavior in terms of the Rational Actor Model or "Classical" Model, in which policy choices are seen as the more or less purposive acts of unified governments based on logical means of achieving given objectives. The model represents an effort to relate an action to a plausible calculation.[41] Morgenthau's statesman contemplating what the national interest calls for in a certain situation, Schelling's game theorist calculating the requirements of stable mutual deterrence or the points of saliency at which limited wars can be kept limited, Herman Kahn's strategic analyst playing out his scenarios of nuclear war by a mathematical process of gain-to-cost reckoning—all use a form of Rational Actor Model.[42] The analyst who employs the Rational Actor Model, like the classical economist, assumes that a person strives to be consistent, to make optimal choices in narrowly constrained, neatly defined situations, and to rank and maximize values by choosing the most efficient alternative. Rational people discern clearly their objectives, the options available, and the likely consequences of each alternative choice before making their decision.[43]

"Although the Rational Actor Model has proved useful for many purposes," says Allison, "there is powerful evidence that it must be supplemented, if not supplanted, by frames of reference that focus on the governmental machine."[44] Allison offers two such frames of reference: an Organizational Process Model and a Bureaucratic Politics Model. The Organizational Process Model envisages governmental behavior less as a matter of deliberate choice and more as independent outputs of several large organizations, only partly coordinated by government leaders. "Government leaders can substantially disturb, but not substantially control, the behavior of these organizations,"[45] which is determined primarily by standard or routine operating procedures, with seldom more than gradual, incremental deviations except when a major disaster occurs.[46] The Organizational Process Model that Allison prefers is that of Herbert Simon, based on the concept of bounded rather than comprehensive rationality, and characterized by the factoring or splitting up of problems; the parceling out of problem parts to various organizational units; the type of "satisficing behavior" described previously; limiting the search to the first acceptable alternative; and avoidance of uncertainty or risk through developing short-run feedback and corrective procedures.[47] Organizations operate to solve problems of immediate urgency rather than to develop strategies for coping with longer-range issues.[48]

Allison's third model, the Bureaucratic Politics Model, builds on the Governmental Process Model, but instead of assuming control by leaders at the top, the Bureaucratic Politics Model hypothesizes intensive competition among the decision-making units, and foreign policies are the result of bargaining among the components of a bureaucracy. The players are guided by no consistent strategic master plan, but rather by conflicting conceptions of national, bureaucratic, and personal goals. Sometimes one group may triumph over other groups committed to different alternatives. Often, however, different groups pulling in different directions produce a resultant or decisional mix that is distinct from that intended by any individual or group. The outcome depends not on the rational justification for the policy or on routine organizational procedures, but on the relative power and skill of the bargainers.[49]

All theories of the decison-making process encounter conceptual difficulties. Miriam Steiner, after analyzing comparatively the works of Snyder and Allison, concluded that each contains contradictions. Snyder claims to put human plans and purposes at the center of his conceptual framework, but does not follow through consistently. "When in the interests of 'objectivity,' he attempts to outfit himself with a 'hard methodology,' he inadvertently reduces his responsible decision-makers to organizationally programmed automatons. . . ."[50] Allison, on the other hand, insists for the sake of accuracy that events be explained not teleologically in terms of goals and purposes, but scientifically in terms of causal determinants that are subject to investigation. But into his integrated explanation, "he unwittingly introduces goals and purposes as 'the essence of decision.' "[51] Thus neither Snyder nor Allison, in Steiner's view, succeeds in providing an approach that achieves objectives consonant with its own distinctive methodology. Instead, each begins at an opposite pole and moves in the direction of the other. Perhaps this is inevitable.

THE REFINEMENTS OF SNYDER AND DIESING

Glenn H. Snyder and Paul Diesing have tested empirically three theories of decision-making in about 50 cases of crisis:[52] (1) utility maximization (the classical rational theory); (2) bounded rationality (borrowed from Simon's "satisficing" model); and (3) bureaucratic politics. Their Rational Actor Model, like Allison's, is based on the choice of one alternative out of all those available that maximizes expected utility. In the bounded rationality tradition, one assumes that if a choice must be made between two different values (e.g., peace and national security), there is no rational way of calculating how much of one should be sacrificed to obtain a given amount of the other. Decision-makers cannot maximize; they operate under constraints and search for an acceptable course. Snyder and Diesing argue plausibly that maximizing and bounded rationality are not irreconcilable explanations, but may be combined by taking either theory as basic and the other as supplementary. They also make the sensible suggestion that the bureaucratic politics theory supplements rather than competes with the other two theories. "It focuses on the internal political imperatives of maintaining and increasing influence and power rather than on the purely intellectual problems of choosing a strategy to deal with an external opportunity or threat."[53] The problem-solving theories apply best to some cases; the bureaucratic politics theory, to others. The former are most applicable when only one or two people are involved in the decision. When three or more people are involved, as in a committee or a cabinet, the Bureaucratic Politics Model—which Snyder and Diesing see as a process of forming a dominant coalition—applies best.[54]

Snyder and Diesing draw an interesting distinction between "rational" and "irrational" bargainers in a crisis. Rational bargainers do not pretend to know at the very beginning of a crisis what the precise situation is, or what the relative interests, power relations, and main alternatives are. They recognize that their initial judgment may be mistaken, but they are able to correct initial misjudgment and perceive the outlines of the developing bargaining situation in time to deal with it effectively.[55] They make tentative guesses as they go along, and constantly modify their assessments as new information is received.

"Irrational" bargainers, on the other hand, proceed from a rigid belief system. They are certain about the adversary's ultimate aims, bargaining style, preferences, and internal problems. They receive advice (which they seek especially from those whose opinion they value) but make their own decisions. They see themselves as the architects of the one strategy that has a chance of succeeding, and they firmly adhere to that strategy in spite of all difficulties, regardless of new incoming information. If their initial strategy was correct, irrational bargainers can be highly successful; if not, they are unlikely to realize their mistake in time to avert defeat or disaster.[56] Deception is always a problem in bargaining. The rational bargainer is open to being deceived by the opponent; the irrational bargainer, by himself or herself. In solving the information-processing problem, a rigid image of the adversary as totally untrustworthy may be as much a hindrance as a rigid image of the adversary as totally trustworthy.[57]

Social scientists will probably never be able to agree whether the decision-making process originates in the minds of people or whether it is adventitious, that is, arises out of the external social situation, whether individuals on balance affect reality more than they reflect it. Decision-making is an aspect of human culture, which is in turn a product of the organic interaction of human beings and their environment. Within recent years, some theorists groping toward a more satisfying explanation of decision-making have looked toward cybernetics as a possible focal point for analysis.

THE CYBERNETIC THEORY OF DECISION

We have seen that the classical utilitarian theory of decision-making, based upon the assumption of a rational weighing of value-costs and value-outcomes, has come under increasing criticism in recent decades. As an alternative to the traditional "analytic paradigm," John D. Steinbruner has set forth the "cybernetic paradigm" as a foundation for theories and models of decision-making, because the former does not explain all the observed phenomena of decision-making. He doubts that human beings normally try to analyze complex problems by breaking them down into all their logical components (which rational theory requires them to do), or that they have access to all of the information and perform all of the calculations, especially with regard to value tradeoffs (which the classical theory presupposes). Steinbruner, moreover, expresses dissatisfaction with most of the efforts the analytic school has made thus far to apply to collective decisions concepts originally developed to explain decisions by individuals.[58] For example, Steinbruner notes that some glaring failures of deterrence might be attributable to the fact that governments have acted against what would appear to have been compelling analytic logic. He cites as cases in point Japan's attack on the United States at Pearl Harbor and the mobilization of the Egyptian Army before the outbreak of the Six Day War in June 1967.[59]

Steinbruner offers as potentially more fruitful than the analytic paradigm a cybernetic one by which highly successful or adaptive behavior might be explained without resort to elaborate decision-making mechanisms. He begins by describing a few more or less familiar instances of simple cybernetic decisions. When worker bees locate pollen-bearing flowers at a place remote from the hive, they inform other workers of its location by engaging in a dance which contains instructions for navigating according to the angle and direction of the sun in reference to the field. In another example, practiced tennis players are cybernetic decision-makers. Each time they move to meet the ball with their rackets, they select one pattern of psychomotor responses out of thousands of possible patterns, and they do it without making mathematical calculations of the speed and trajectory of the oncoming ball, their precise point of interception, the stroke they will use to hit it, and their target point in the opposite court. Steinbruner draws additional analogies pertaining to cybernetic servomechanisms from the thermostat which keeps temperature within desired bounds, the Watt governor which regulates the speed of an engine, radar homing devices, the cat who changes position near the hearth as the fire grows hotter or dimmer, the retail store manager who adjusts item prices according to volume of sales, and the cook who follows a recipe and keeps tasting when performing a sequence of culinary operations without having a clear, rational concept of the final product.

The cybernetic decision-maker, in other words, deals with situations which we call "simple," but which nevertheless have a complexity of their own, by eliminating variety, ignoring elaborate calculations concerning the environment, and tracking a few simple feedback variables which trigger a behavioral adjustment. Cybernetic decision-makers, believing the decision process to be a simple one, strive to minimize the calculations they must perform, whether they be mathematical or value-related. They monitor a small set of critical variables, and their principal value is to reduce uncertainty by keeping these variables within tolerable ranges. They see no need for a careful calculation of probable outcomes, which they are not likely to make in any case. The sequence of decisional behaviors is related less to an intellectual analysis of the problem at hand than to past experience from which there emerges an almost intuitional approach to problem-solving.[60]

It is relatively easy, of course, to accept the cybernetic paradigm as applied to the tennis player or the cook or the retail store manager, each of whom faces a large number of simple choices on each sequence. The question is whether the validity of the cybernetic paradigm is affected by the much greater complexity of decisions in the foreign policy and the defense fields. Steinbruner is convinced that the cybernetic model is applicable to highly complex decisions, which he defines as decisions affecting two or more values, in which there is a tradeoff relationship between the values, in which there is uncertainty, and in which the decision-making power is dispersed over a number of individual actors and/or organizational units. He concedes that greater complexity entails greater variety, and that "under conditions of complexity the decision-maker must have a more elaborate response repertory if he is to retain adaptive capacity."[61] The problem is solved by increasing the number of decision-makers within a collectivity. Complex problems are not analyzed comprehensively by all the members of the decision-making group. Instead, they are broken down into a large number of limited-dimension problems, each confronted by a separate decision-maker or unit. "This is the natural cybernetic explanation for the rise of mass bureaucracy."[62]

To sum up, Steinbruner relies upon theories of organizational behavior to extend the cybernetic paradigm from individual decision-making in relatively simple situations to collective decision-making designed to cope with a highly complex environment. The higher levels of organizational hierarchy do not perform the integrating calculations called for by the analytic paradigm. Drawing upon the work of Cyert and March, Steinbruner summarizes as follows:

> Top management, in their view, focuses in sequential order on the decision issues raised by separate subunits and does not integrate across subunits in its deliberations. Decisions are made solely within the context of the subunit raising the issue. Complex problems are thus fragmented by organizations into separate components having to do with subunit organization, and the decision process at the highest levels preserves the fragmentation.[63]

Organizational theory alone is not enough, however. Steinbruner combines it with highly intricate modern theories of cognitive processes, including those developed by Noam Chomsky, Ulric Neisser, Leon Festinger, Robert P. Abelson, and others. He calls attention to the consensus among cognitive theorists that "a great deal of information processing is conducted apparently prior to and certainly independently of conscious direction and that in this activity the mind routinely performs logical operations of considerable power."[64] Steinbruner surveys the findings of many studies relating to perception, learning, memory, inference, consistency, belief, and the ways in which the human mind either controls or copes with uncertainty, and concludes that cognitive theory provides an analysis of the effects of uncertainty on the decision process which is fundamentally different from that of the analytic and cybernetic paradigms. Thus he uses cognitive theory to modify the cybernetic paradigm, especially with regard to the subjective resolution of uncertainty, and to introduce into his treatment of political and organizational phenomena the concepts of *grooved thinking* (in which the decision-maker rather simplistically categorizes the problems into a small number of basic types); uncommitted thinking (in which the decision-maker who does not know what to think about the problem oscillates between groups of advisers, and may adopt different belief patterns at different times on the same decision problem); and theoretical thinking (in which the decision-maker is committed to abstract beliefs, usually organized around a single value in patterns which are internally consistent and stable over time, even under conditions of uncertainty).[65]

Steinbruner devotes the major part of his work to applying his modified cybernetic-cognitive paradigm to studying a single complex policy decision issue—that of sharing control of nuclear weapons among members of the Atlantic Alliance in the early 1960s. The United States was caught in a value tradeoff between its general political purposes in Europe (including the credibility of the United States defense guarantee) and the requirements of stable deterrence, to which the proliferation of national nuclear weapons capabilities was seen as a threat. It is not possible to do justice to the ample treatment accorded to the strains in the alliance caused by the two-value problem—the development of nuclear sharing proposals and the rise and demise of the NATO Multilateral Force (MLF).[66] Steinbruner concludes that the ability of the State Department to produce momentum for the deployment of an MLF to which the Secretary of Defense and most United States military leaders and Europeans generally were opposed was a "political anomaly" that might best be understood in terms of the cognitive and cybernetic processes of bureaucratic decision-makers rather than in terms of the analytic paradigm.

The MLF emerges in the study as a neither politically nor militarily sound idea. It resulted from "theoretical thinking" on the part of a group long committed by experience to the single-minded objective of promoting European integration. The group screened out from its perception all information and assessments concerning the vulnerability of the proposed MLF, the possible consequences of deterrence failure, or the possibility that the force might whet rather than satisfy the German desire for a nuclear weapons role. Defense Secretary McNamara and Presidents Kennedy and Johnson are portrayed as essentially uncommitted thinkers who went along with the idea most reluctantly. European policymakers were unhappy over many substantive aspects of the proposal, but they were inclined to defer to initiatives by the alliance leader. According to Steinbruner, "The overall interaction in the alliance between the American commitment and the European response can then be seen as a self-amplifying positive feedback system, as in the often-encountered example of the microphone picking up the signal of its own speakers, thus recycling and reamplifying its own output until some natural limit is reached."[67]

Clearly, Steinbruner does not regard the cybernetic-cognitive paradigm as intrinsically superior to the analytic one. Rather he suggests that the two paradigms operate as substitutes for one another in processing complex problems, and produce different types of decisions. In our effort to understand governmental decision-making under conditions of complexity and uncertainty, the cybernetic-cognitive approach may provide a coherent explanation of behavior which, in an analytic framework, appears to be stupid, absurd, incompetent, or incomprehensible, without in any way implying approval of such an outcome.[68] Interestingly enough, Steinbruner suggests that President Johnson's decision in December 1964 to reverse his advisers and to kill the MLF "can readily be understood by analytic logic."[69] In the end we are left with two competing paradigms, each partially confirmed. Fitting them together in a satisfactory synthesis remains a task for future analysis.

DECISION-MAKING IN CRISIS

Since the mid-1950s, a considerable amount of literature has appeared on specific foreign policy decisions, much of it in the form of case studies of decisions telescoped in time and circumscribed as to the number of decision-makers. These include the decisions which led to the outbreak of World War I, the United States intervention in Korea, British intervention in the Suez, and United States responses to crises in or over Berlin, Quemoy, the Bay of Pigs, and the emplacement of Soviet missiles in Cuba.[70] There have been studies of decisions characterized by longer time frames and larger, more complex groups of actors, including legislative bodies, political parties, and multiple governments. Such decisions, which may be of historic significance and yet not "crisis decisions" in the sense used here, might pertain to such events as the French scuttling of the European Defense Community in 1954, Britain's quest over more than a decade for entry into the European Economic Community, and the United States pursuit of SALT agreements with the Soviet Union, a negotiated peace settlement in the Middle East, or, as in Steinbruner's study, a policy for nuclear sharing in NATO. This type of study is often more difficult than the "crisis" type to cast in the mold of precise decision-making analysis because it involves a harder-to-research cumulative process which takes place in a sprawling bureaucratic labyrinth and a more comprehensive political arena over a longer time period. The three case studies which follow—the United States intervention in Korea, the outbreak of World War I, and the Cuban Missile Crisis—are presented not in chronological order but in ascending order of theoretical complexity of the analyses performed.

The United States Decision to Intervene in Korea

Among the case studies mentioned earlier, one which was consciously designed for the purpose of applying a theoretical DM model was Glenn D. Paige's account of seven days of United States national decision-making in response to the Korean crisis. Paige reflects an awareness of the problem of applying to a single case the Snyder-Bruck-Sapin model, and of trying to verify any hypotheses merely on the basis of the Korean decision. He acknowledges that the single case produces lessons that can lead only to "a relatively low level of abstraction."[71] But he argues that the single-case method can have pedagogical as well as theoretical uses and can lay part of the empirical foundation for the subsequent comparative study of decision-making. Throughout the work, Paige is concerned with establishing an objective methodology. He approaches his task as would an historian who seeks a better understanding of crisis decision-making by reconstructing an actual instance of it. Using the materials on which any student of decision-making must primarily rely—newspaper accounts, official governmental publications, the diaries, memoirs, and other documents of policymakers who were involved in the decision, interviews with key figures, and the comment of other experts—Paige seeks to improve his objectivity by "decontaminating" the narrative, that is, separating his own analytical interpretations and normative judgments from the reconstruction of the historical events.[72]

Paige is essentially faithful to the Snyder-Bruck-Sapin model, with its emphasis upon such concepts as "spheres of competence," "motivation," "communication and information," "feedback," and the "path of action." He places the Korean decision in the context of its internal and external setting and devotes to each a chapter covering the political-historical background from 1945 to 1950. Within the domestic setting are included biographical sketches of three principals: the President (Harry S. Truman), the Secretary of State (Dean Acheson), and the Secretary of Defense (Louis A. Johnson). Paige touches briefly on their learning experiences, their views on such subjects as history and "power," and their conceptions of office, insofar as these might have a bearing upon their decisional behavior. He then discusses the state of relations existing between the Executive policymakers and the Congress, the impending Congressional election of 1950, and some salient features of public opinion at the time.[73] The treatment of the external environment stresses the bipolarity of the world, the postwar development of the "containment policy," national security estimates and requirements, and the policy posture of the United States toward Asia, especially Korea.[74]

Paige then presents nearly 200 pages of meticulously reconstructed narrative—sometimes on an hour-by-hour basis—of the decision-making events which transpired in Washington between Saturday, June 24, and Friday, June 30, 1950. Most relevant to our present purposes are the empirical propositions derived from the case study, which are set forth not so much as valid generalizations in themselves but rather as hypotheses which might be tested in other studies of crisis DM.[75] The Korean decision, Paige concludes, can be viewed either as a unified phenomenon or as a developmental sequence of choices (of which most decision-makers were aware) which contributed "to a stagelike progression toward an analytically defined outcome"—a sequence in which policymakers were apparently affected by "positive reinforcement" in the form of supporting UN action, favorable editorial opinion, and Congressional and international expressions of approval, as well as evidence of a temperate Soviet response.[76] Only a few of Paige's numerous propositions can be cited here:

> Crisis decisions tend to be reached by ad hoc decisional units.
>
> The greater the crisis, the greater the felt need for face-to-face proximity among decision-makers.
>
> The greater the crisis, the more the leader's solicitation of subordinate advice.
>
> The more prolonged the crisis, the greater the sense of adequacy of the information about it.
>
> Costly responses to crisis tend to be followed by decline in the salience of the values associated with them.
>
> The greater the crisis, the greater the efforts of decision-makers to diminish popular anxieties.
>
> The greater the crisis, the more frequent and the more direct the interactions with friendly leaders in the external setting.[77]

Many other conclusions are stated as hypotheses that postulate relationships among the nature of the decision-making group, the perceived threat to values, the role of leadership, the quest for information, the framework of past responses, the shared willingness to make a positive response, the effort to secure international support, and so forth. Some of the propositions are novel and interesting; some might strike the reader as slightly tedious confirmations of what might otherwise be deduced logically; but it should be remembered that the validation of "obvious" truths, based on data, is essential to the scientific method and thus to the development of social science theories.

Perception and Decision-Making: The Outbreak of World War I

The use of content analysis with a stimulus-response model represents a quite different methodological approach to the study of decision-making. In studies of the outbreak of World War I and the Cuban Missile Crisis, Ole R. Holsti, Robert C. North, and Richard A. Brody have attempted to measure the messages exchanged during crisis situations.[78] Such an approach focuses not upon interaction *within,* but rather upon interaction *between* the decisional units.

The model used in these studies relates perceptions to behavior (S-r:s-R). The symbol S is the stimulus or input behavior: It is a physical event or a verbal act. The symbol R represents the response action. Both S and R are nonevaluative and nonaffective; r is the decision-maker's perception of the stimulus (S), and s is the expression of intentions or attitude. Both r and s include factors such as personality, role, organization, and system that affect perceptual variables.

The outbreak of World War I was selected as the initial case because of the large amount of available documentation and because it was a classic example of crisis escalation. The perception units for analysis were abstracted from the historical documents in the following terms: "the perceiving party or actor; the perceived party or actors; the action or attitude; and the target party or actor."[79] Over 5000 such perception units were extracted from the documents authored by selected British, French, Russian, German, and Austro-Hungarian decision-makers.

Initial studies were done based solely upon perceptual data. Using only the frequency of themes for analysis of the relationships between perceptions of threat and perceptions of capability in international crisis, support was found for the hypothesis: "If perceptions of anxiety, fear, threat, or injury are great enough, even the perceptions of one's own inferior capability will fail to deter a nation from going to war."[80] When it became evident that not only the frequency of perceptions is important, but also their intensity, the documents were coded again to measure the intensity of the perceptions of "hostility, friendship, frustration, satisfaction, and desire to change the status quo."[81] The results were then aggregated into 12 time periods. Results showed that "decision-makers of each nation most strongly felt themselves to be victims of injury precisely at that time when its leaders were making policy decisions of the most crucial nature."[82]

Next, the authors of the study undertook correlational analyses between the perception data and various types of "hard" or action data, because they recognized that the value of content analysis depends upon the relationship between the statements and the actual decisions made by statesmen. Thus the authors attempted to find correlations between the results of the content analysis and such actions as mobilization, troop movements, and the breaking of diplomatic relations. Other actions, such as the financial indicators—gold movements and the price of securities, which are sensitive to international tension levels—were examined. "Given fluctuations of financial indicators, correlated with increases and decreases in international tension, these indicators can be used to check the validity of content analysis data. If the latter covary both with the political/military actions of nations participating in the crisis and with fluctuations of financial indicators that respond to the tensions born of these actions, confidence in the content analysis techniques is substantially enhanced."[83]

The next step was to combine the perception and action data to test the basic interaction model (S-r:s-R). Correlating the 1914 perception data with the spiral of military mobilizations, the authors concluded that a rise in hostility preceded acts of mobilization. Stated differently, decision-makers responded "to verbal threats and diplomatic moves, rather than troop movements."[84]

The action data, S and R, included all military events of the 1914 crisis. The action data were coded in terms of both frequency and intensity. It was assumed that a given amount of violence or action (S) will yield an appropriate level of expressed response (r), expressed intent (s), and a response (R) at about the same level of violence as the original stimulus (S). However, when the 1914 crisis data were divided into the two coalitions, a consistent lack of congruence was found in the actions of the two alliances. The difference corresponded to the different levels of involvement of the respective coalitions. This finding raises doubt about the classical theories built on a simple S-R model. The hypothesis that "the correlation between input action (S) and policy response (R) will be better in a situation of low involvement than in one of high involvement"[85] was tested with the 1914 crisis data. The Triple Entente was less involved, having only 40 perceptions of hostility compared to 171 for the Dual Alliance. As the hypothesis suggested, it was found that the degree of congruence between S and R was higher for the less engaged Triple Entente and lower for the highly engaged Dual Alliance. This suggests that perceptions $(s$ and $r)$ may be less crucial in low involvement situations but are important in high involvement situations.

A second hypothesis, concerned not only with congruence or lack of congruence but also with the direction of the differences, was tested: "In a situation of low involvement, policy response (R) will tend to be at a lower level of violence than the input action (S), whereas in a high involvement situation, the policy response (R) will tend to be at a higher level of violence than the input action (S)."[86] It was found that the highly involved Dual Alliance was indeed consistently overreacting to the threats, whereas the less involved Triple Entente underreacted.

Since the action variables, S and R, alone failed to account for the escalation of war, the intervening perceptual variables, r and s, were analyzed. No significant difference was found between the two coalitions in the s-R step. In both low and high involvement cases, the response action (R) was at a higher level of violence than was suggested by their leaders' statements of intent (s). Moreover, in the r-s link, there was again little difference between the Triple Entente and Dual Alliance: In both groupings of nations the level of hostility was perceived to be consistently greater in the other's policy (r) than in their own statements of intent (s).

However, a significant difference appeared in the S-r step which could account for the escalation. In the low involvement situation, r tended to be at a lower level than S, whereas in the high involvement situation, r tended to be higher than S. Decision-makers in the highly involved Dual Alliance consistently overperceived the level of violence of the Triple Entente. The leaders of the less deeply involved Triple Entente underperceived the actions of the Dual Alliance. Moreover, in the latter stages of the crisis, after both alliances had become highly involved, there was less difference between the two coalitions in the way actions (S) were perceived (r) than before. The authors concluded, therefore, that intervening perceptions may perform an accelerating or decelerating function. In this case, the S-r link served a "magnifying" function. "This difference in perceiving the environment (the S-r link) is consistent with the pronounced tendency of the Dual Alliance to respond at a higher level of violence than the Triple Entente."[87]

L. L. Farrar, Jr., adopts a different interpretation of the 1914 crisis. Following Theodore Abel and Bruce M. Russett, he suggests that one should not seek causes but analyze processes, beginning with the background from which the decisions of governments emerge. The final decision for war is not reached on the spur of the moment and is not triggered by the irrational motivations and emotional elements often associated with decision-making under conditions of stress. Rather it is based on a series of rational calculations that may antedate the crisis by several years. The crisis itself may be the result of precrisis decisions involving an assessment over a long period of time concerning several alternative ways of acting under a variety of circumstances. Although leaders may experience stress during the crisis, the crisis is due not to psychological tensions but to decisions previously taken, which are more important than personality characteristics. Farrar presents the 1914 crisis as the logical result of rational policy considerations, given the assumptions underlying the state system. Farrar sums it up as follows:

> Each power did what seemed necessary to remain a power. All perceived a choice among diplomatic victory, diplomatic defeat, and war. All preferred diplomatic victory since it implied the rewards of war without the risks, but one power could win diplomatic victory only if another accepted diplomatic defeat. All rejected diplomatic defeat since it implied the price of military defeat without the possibility of victory as well as defeat. Thus diplomatic victory was impossible because diplomatic defeat was inconceivable, whereas war was conceivable. Consequently when a choice seemed imperative, war became inevitable.[88]

The Cuban Missile Crisis

Using their same interaction model described earlier, Holsti, Brody, and North also investigated the Cuban Missile Crisis of 1962. An example of escalation conflict like the 1914 case, the Cuban Missile Crisis provides an opportunity, therefore, both for comparison and contrast with the earlier study. An effort was made to find "patterns of behavior that distinguish the situation which escalated into general war (as in the 1914 crisis) from those in which the process of escalation is reversed"[89] (as in the Cuban Missile Crisis).

The source materials for the analysis of perceptions (s and r) consisted of 15 American, 10 Soviet, 10 Cuban documents. The documents were content analyzed. Action data (S and R) were coded from a 0 to 10 level of violence or potential violence. Objective financial indicators, which had revealed a striking correlation to the perceptions and expressions of hostility in the 1914 crisis and which were available on a day-to-day basis, were also incorporated into the analysis of the Cuban Missile Crisis.

It was found that the actions of the United States and the Soviet Union correlated closely; each increase or decrease in the level of violence of one party was followed by a similar pattern of action by the other. "The pattern of perceptions was relatively consistent with the course of events surrounding the Cuban crisis. In each case October 25 to 26 was the point at which mutual perceptions appeared to change."[90] Thus at this point the trend reversed from escalation to deescalation.

In the Cuban Missile Crisis, unlike the 1914 crisis, there was found to be "close correspondence between the actions of the other party (S) and perceptions of the adversary's actions (r)." Here both sides accurately perceived the nature of the adversary's actions and acted at an appropriate level. Efforts made by either party "to delay or reverse the escalation were generally perceived as such and responded to in a like manner."[91] Such behavior differed from that of the 1914 crisis in which, at the beginning, the Dual Alliance consistently reacted at a higher level than the Triple Entente and also consistently overperceived the level of violence in actions taken by the Triple Entente. Subsequently, this difference in the S-r link between the two coalitions lessened as both were drawn into escalation and war. From the analysis of the 1914 crisis and the 1962 crisis, Holsti, Brody, and North found indications that "the more intense the interaction between parties, the more important it is to incorporate perceptual data into the analysis."[92]

Graham T. Allison applied each of his three decision-making models (discussed previously) to the Cuban Missile Crisis. He concludes that his three case studies "do not settle the matter of what happened and why," but "do offer evidence about the nature of explanations produced by different analysts."[93] The Rational Actor Model analyst explained the crisis in terms of strategic choices by the two superpowers. The USSR placed missiles in Cuba not merely as a bargaining counter for the withdrawal of U.S. missiles in Turkey, nor to attract a U.S. move against Cuba to cover a Soviet move against Berlin, nor to deter a U.S. attack against Cuba, nor to demonstrate to the world that the USSR could make with impunity a bold Cold War move against an indecisive United States, but rather to bring about quickly and at low cost a rectification of the adverse nuclear missile balance by converting Cuba into an "unsinkable carrier" and doubling the Soviet capability for a first strike against the United

States.[94] The United States decision to respond with a naval blockade was an apt, limited, yet effective, way of exploiting U.S. superiority at both strategic nuclear and local conventional levels to carry out a value-maximizing escalation while minimizing Moscow's humiliation.[95] Most American strategic analysts agreed that Khrushchev, recognizing Soviet military inferiority in the vicinity of Cuba in the face of implicit threats of further action (e.g., an air strike against or invasion of Cuba), had no choice but to withdraw the missiles from the island.[96]

In his Organizational Process Model approach to the Cuban Missile Crisis, Allison stresses the amount of organizational activity and degree of coordination required to move more than 100 shiploads of medium and intermediate range missiles, Beagle Bombers, MiG-21 interceptor aircraft, surface-to-air missiles, cruise missiles and patrol boats, and 22,-000 Soviet soldiers and technical personnel to Cuba.[97] But American experts were puzzled that the Soviets, who could not have expected their missile sites in Cuba to escape detection by U-2s, failed to complete their radar system and SAM network prior to installing the MRBMs, and made no attempt to camouflage the missiles until after the United States publicly disclosed what the Soviets were doing.[98] Some analysts of the "rational model school" sought motives to explain the apparent inconsistencies of Soviet behavior. Allison suggests that the anomalies might best be explained simply by assuming that large organizations "do what they know how to do." SAM sites and missile sites were constructed in Cuba just as they had been in the Soviet Union, without either camouflage or hardening.[99] Other construction and phasing anomalies can be similarly explained by the characteristic problems that typically beset large organizations—lack of a strategic overview, poor coordination, delays in communication and implementation of directives, and cumbersome operating procedures. Allison also speculates plausibly that the actual Soviet decision to place missiles in Cuba may have been pressed upon the Praesidium by the relatively new Strategic Rocket Forces. These Forces, locked into a budgetary rivalry with the Soviet Ground Forces, had been compelled to defer acquisition of ICBMs and they were worried about the strategic nuclear balance after the Kennedy Administration announced in November 1961 that not only was there no "missile gap" but that the United States actually enjoyed strategic nuclear superiority.[100]

On the American side, says Allison, the precise timing of the Cuban Missile Crisis was a function of the organizational routines and standard operating procedures of the U.S. intelligence community, for these factors determined when the crucial information came to the President. Many reports and isolated items of information had to be pieced together and analyzed before U-2 surveillance flights over Cuba were ordered, and then several more days passed while the State Department urged a less risky alternative and the Air Force and CIA carried on a jurisdictional dispute over who should fly the U-2. When a "surgical air strike" was being considered as a possible course of action, there was a vast discrepancy between what that term meant to President Kennedy and his White House advisers (who would have restricted it to the missile sites) and what it meant to the military (who added the missile sites to the existing contingency plan for an air strike against all Cuban storage depots, airports, and artillery batteries opposite the U.S. naval base at Guantanamo). A hastily formulated and probably erroneous military estimate that an air strike could be only 90 percent but not 100 percent effective against the missiles, of which a small number might be launched first, prompted the political leaders to eliminate the air strike option and to concentrate on the naval blockade option.[101]

Allison concedes that it is difficult to analyze Soviet decision-making in the Cuban Missile Crisis in terms of the Bureaucratic Politics Model, but the documentation for applying this model to the United States action is abundant. After the Bay of Pigs fiasco, Kennedy was under heavy pressure from public opinion and from critics in Congress to prevent the Soviet Union from converting Cuba into an offensive base. In September 1962, when reports of the Soviet military build-up began reaching the United States, the President distinguished between defensive and offensive preparations, and gave public assurance that the latter would not be tolerated. Administration figures denied the presence of Soviet offensive missiles, discounted the suspicions of CIA Director John McCone, and elicited from the United States Intelligence Board on September 19 an estimate to the effect that the emplacement of Soviet offensive missiles in Cuba was "highly unlikely." Early in September a U-2 had been shot down over Mainland China. Fear that another U-2 might be lost contributed to a ten-day delay after a decision was taken on October 4 to carry out photograph reconnaissance flights. Confronted with the evidence, the President was angered by Khrushchev's duplicity: "He can't do that to *me!*" Given the political environment, with Congressional elections only three weeks away, Kennedy knew that signs of weakness had to be avoided and firm action taken. Recommendations from his advisers varied from "doing nothing" or "taking a diplomatic approach" to "air strike" or "invasion" before the Soviet missiles became operational. Attorney General Robert Kennedy was responsible for working out a near consensus on a compromise between inaction and potentially unlimited action—the limited response of a naval blockade.[102] Allison calls the blockade decision "part choice and part result—a melange of misconception, miscommunication, misinformation, bargaining, pulling, hauling, and sparring, as well as a mixture of national security interests, objectives, and governmental calculations. . . ."[103]

In the final analysis, however, the blockade alone did not lead to the withdrawal of Soviet missiles from Cuba. That was accomplished only after a conciliatory offer to give a United States assurance against an invasion of Cuba combined with a threat of "overwhelming retaliatory action" unless the President received immediate notice that the missiles would be withdrawn.[104] But whether the ultimatum "caused" the withdrawal, as the Rational Actor Model would argue, or whether the language of threat was a public posturing designed to screen a private deal offered by President Kennedy to Premier Khrushchev—withdrawal of Soviet missiles in Cuba for withdrawal of United States missiles in Turkey (something that Kennedy had ordered before the Cuban Missile Crisis developed and which was actually carried out a few months afterward)—Allison leaves in the realm of unanswered questions.[105] His study "demonstrates each model's tendency to produce different answers to the same question," as well as "differences in the ways the analysts conceive of the problem, shape the puzzle, unpack the primary questions, and pick up pieces of the world in search of an answer."[106]

TOWARD A THEORY OF CRISIS BEHAVIOR

James A. Robinson has asserted that "there is no theory of crisis."[107] Nevertheless, several international relations analysts have devoted many years of effort to acquire a better understanding of crisis behavior and to gain deeper insights into why some crises lead to war while others lend themselves to nonviolent resolution.[108] According to Michael P. Sullivan, crisis is now the most widely researched situational variable of all occasions for decision.[109]

Charles A. McClelland has noted that analysts of international crisis behavior have focused on five "approaches": (1) definition of crisis; (2) classification of types of crisis; (3) the study of ends, goals, and objectives in crises; (4) decision-making under conditions of crisis stress; and (5) crisis management.[110] An earlier widely accepted definition of crisis developed by Robinson and Hermann had postulated three elements: (1) threat to high-priority goals of the DM unit; (2) restricted amount of time available for response; and (3) surprise.[111] A Jerusalem "Crisis Seminar" in 1975 to 1976 concluded that surprise, which is not always present and is not measurable from content analysis, is not an essential ingredient. The Jerusalem Seminar defined a foreign policy crisis as "a breakpoint along the peace-war continuum of a state's relations with any other international actor(s), characterized by the following four necessary and sufficient conditions:

1. A change in its external or internal environment, which generates
2. a threat to basic values, with a simultaneous or subsequent
3. high probability of involvement in military hostilities, and the awareness of
4. a finite time for their response to the external value threat.[112]

The Jerusalem Seminar led to a project in which 469 international crises were identified over the period 1938 to 1975, including 79 crises during World War II. Preliminary data for the 469 crises are being computerized to facilitate comparative research into the frequency of different situations that bring on crisis (sources or trigger mechanisms) and the distribution of crises according to various dimensions: *gravity* (measured by a hierarchy of values-at-stake from the most to the least vital); *complexity* (defined in terms of quantity and uncertainty); *intensity* (measured by the volume and quality of acts during various phases); *duration; communications patterns;* and *outcomes* (war, peaceful resolution, stalemate, continuation of the value threat, etc.).[113]

Glenn H. Synder and Paul Diesing define international crisis as "a sequence of interactions between the governments of two or more sovereign states in severe conflict, short of actual war, but involving the perception of a dangerously high probability of war."[114] The crisis has always been central to international politics—a moment of truth in which several latent elements "such as power configurations, interests, images, and alignments tend to be more sharply clarified, to be activated and focused on a single well-defined issue."[115] In the nuclear age, crises can be looked upon as surrogates for war, rather than merely dangerous episodes that are the prelude to war. "Their systemic function is to resolve without violence, or with only minimal violence, those conflicts that are too severe to be settled by ordinary diplomacy and that in earlier times would have been settled by war."[116] According to Oran R. Young, an international crisis consists of a "set of rapidly unfolding events which raises the impact of destabilizing forces in the general international system or any of its subsystems substantially above normal (i.e., average) levels and increases the likelihood of violence occurring in the system."[117] Young suggests that crises are situations in which rapidly rising demands are made on the control and regulatory mechanisms of the system, which in turn produce responses which have the effect of leading the originators of demands to additional activities; hence there is feedback.

The behavior of states in a crisis is affected by the structure of the system (bipolar or multipolar) and by the nature of military technology. The rivalry of the United States and the Soviet Union was ordained more by structure (their power preponderance over all others) than by ideology. Snyder and Diesing agree with Kenneth N. Waltz's hypothesis that a bipolar system is more likely than a multipolar one to be stable. (See the discussion on bipolarity and multipolarity in Chapter 4.) In the bipolar system, alignments are clear and realignments do not alter the balance of power significantly. In the multipolar system, alignments may be unclear and shifts may be important. Because of their greater ambiguity, multipolar systems are more prone to changes in the perception of interests, to gambling or risk-taking, and to miscalculations that make crises more dangerous. The tension between bargaining among allies and bargaining between adversaries (or between restraining the ally and deterring the opponent) is more difficult to manage in a multipolar system crisis.[118] Détente reduces the likelihood of a crisis erupting. A crisis can break out, however, in which superpowers are drawn into a confrontation by client states, as they were in the 1973 Yom Kippur War.

Nuclear weapons technology has had a considerable effect on international crises by widening enormously the gap between the value of the interests in conflict and the possible cost of war for the holders of such weapons. Nuclear powers strive to protect, and indeed to advance, their interests, but they arc said to be motivated by the "disaster-avoidance" constraint to be more cautious and prudent in crisis management and to raise, as if by tacit consent, the "provocation threshold" of war, thereby increasing the range for maneuvering in crises.[119] The nuclear powers have substituted psychological force in the form of carefully managed risks of war for war itself.[120] Herein lies a linkage between crisis decision-making and deterrence theory which, as noted in Chapter 9, encompasses the threat of escalation, and escalation itself. The power able to demonstrate to its opponent the capacity to punish at a higher level of conflict—or a higher rung on the escalatory ladder—holds the potential for deterring in a crisis situation. Crisis management, it may be inferred, is the ability of one of the parties, by credibly threatening escalation, to deter its adversary from escalation and to produce a crisis deescalation outcome in accord with its interests. This does not mean, however, that a crisis ends only when one adversary party capitulates or backs away. A crisis may also be resolved through a process in which both contestants exercise restraint and seek a face-saving path of mutual retreat or a compromise which transforms the situation without being incompatible with the irreducible interests of either.

CRISIS FORECASTING

In recent years, there has been a growing interest among social scientists and governmental policymakers in crisis forecasting. Crisis forecasting and crisis management are seen as separable but closely related problems.[121] Charles A. McClelland has argued that sensors or orbiting satellites and other modern means of gathering information, as well as computers for large-scale information processing, make possible "a global warning system directed to the detection of every kind of seriously endangering situation," and that a major transformation of the international system, reflected in changing concepts of crisis, strengthen the likelihood that a global warning system will be created.[122]

Both World Wars, says McClelland, began because of a failure of crisis management.[123] But a third prolonged period (1945–1962) of recurring crises from Berlin to Cuba did not lead to war between the principal protagonists, the United States and the Soviet Union. Despite the "tight bipolarity" of the early post-World War II years, there was sufficient flexibility to provide time for "the relaxation of the international system structure into a somewhat less dangerous, but more complex, form."[124] This does not mean that the danger of World War III has permanently passed. The superpowers might move into a new series of crises leading to war, or war might occur without crisis as a prelude. Since the mid-1960s, according to McClelland, the meaning of crisis has become diffused, refracted, and obscure. The problems of military deterrence and defense remain, McClelland concludes, but threats, tensions, dangers, and disturbances of a nonmilitary nature—for example, inflation, energy and raw materials shortages, famine, and the seizure of diplomatic personnel as hostages—can arise to harass governments and fan international conflict, and the global warning system should be designed to bring early indicators of all dangerous situations to the attention of policymakers.[125] It must be stressed, however, that crises are by definition unique events which are—as we saw in the discussion of international forecasting in Chapter 1—extremely difficult to predict by social science methods, even if they might lend themselves to short-term prediction by governmental intelligence agencies.

PSYCHOLOGICAL COMPONENTS OF DECISION-MAKING IN CRISIS

One of the most interesting aspects of crisis decision-making pertains to the element of choice under pressure of time. Even in normal decision-making circumstances when there is ample time to think about the situation, it is difficult for policymakers to process the large volumes of information that inundate them and to consider all available alternatives. We have already reviewed the Holsti-North-Brody study in which perceptions of hostility in both verbal communications and action signals were shown to be important, the more so as the decision-makers became more deeply engaged and involved in the crisis. Holsti has asked whether decision-makers, under the stress of crisis that may require a round-the-clock watch, can be expected to be efficient in identifying major alternative courses of action, estimating the probable costs and gains of each option, discriminating between relevant and irrelevant information, and resisting premature cognitive closure and action.[126] Analysts are not in agreement on whether moderate stress improves human performance[127] or interferes with problem solving.[128] It can be said that all crisis decisions give rise to situations of threat and counterthreat which produce tension within the participants whether in the form of excitement, fear, anxiety, frustration, dissonance, or some other psychic state. A knowledge of how conditions of stress affect the solidarity and problem-solving ability of small groups may cast light on the way leaders behave at crucial decision-making junctures.

Stress is a function of many different variables. In the internal setting, these might include in addition to the pressure of time in which critical decisions have to be made, the necessity of having to attend to several different policy problems simultaneously; the simplicity or complexity of the organization for decision-making; the demands of conflicting interest groups; the existence of public opinion unfavorable to courses of action which the policymakers feel compelled to consider; serious disagreements over the assessment of the situation, the values at stake, and the anticipated consequences of various courses of action; the fear of war and its consequences on the part of the decision-makers; and the clash of personalities within the decisional unit. In the external setting, the variables might include: the total strategic power position of the contesting parties; the strategic doctrines and cultural-psychological attitudes of the adversary; the assessment of the adversary's objectives, intentions, and "staying power"; the efficiency of the international communications system and the intelligence system on which the decision-makers depend for the flow of information; and the attitudes of allies and neutrals, or "world public opinion." Some of these factors will cause greater stress than others, and will be more significant for one individual, or one decisional unit, or one side than the other. In any given international conflict situation, the stress experienced by decision-making groups at any critical juncture will vary qualitatively among the parties according to their perceptions of the total situation and their own reactions to it.

Psychologists have designed experiments to test the effects of stress upon group integration and the problem-solving efficiency of groups. It has been found, as one might expect, that individuals in groups react differently to stress. Herman Kahn has noted that in a crisis a decision-maker "may be able to invent or work out quickly and easily what seems in normal times to be . . . complex or otherwise difficult."[129] We know that for both individuals and groups, increased stress may lead to aggression, withdrawal or escape behavior, regression or various neurotic symptoms. John T. Lanzetta has furnished the following description of his experiments with groups:

> It was found that as stress increased there was a decrease in behaviors associated with friction in the group; a decrease in the number of disagreements, arguments, aggressions, deflations, and other negative social-emotional behaviors, as well as a decrease in self-oriented behaviors. Concom-

itant with this decrease was an increase in behaviors which would tend to result in decreased friction and better integration of the group; an increase in collaborating, mediating, cooperating behaviors.[130]

Lanzetta suggests that the reason for this phenomenon is to be found in the tendency of group members, faced with conditions that produce stress and anxiety, to seek psychological security in the group through cooperative behavior. But the hypothesis of group integration under stress seems to be valid only up to a point. It may be that group members provide mutual reinforcement for each other only while they expect to be able to find a solution to their common problem. Robert L. Hamblin designed an experiment that led him to suggest that group integration during a crisis will begin to decrease if no likely solution appears to be available. Cooperation is likely while it is potentially profitable, but when the members of the group meet one failure after another no matter what they do, they experience a frustration that leads to the displacement of antagonism against one another. In some cases, individuals attempt to resolve the crisis problem for themselves by withdrawing and leaving the other members to work out their own solution if they can—a process tantamount to group disintegration.[131]

Hamblin's findings may prove relevant for understanding the behavior of leadership groups in international conflict when they perceive that the tide is beginning to turn against them, regardless of which strategy or tactics they pursue. But here a caveat is in order. The behavior of national or other political leadership groups is a more complex phenomenon than the behavior of a small ad hoc group playing an experimental game. The stress conditions encountered during the course of a struggle that lasts for weeks or months or even years are much more intricate psychologically than those experienced in a two-hour game. The internal and external settings are infinitely richer in variety, as are the values, perceptions, cross-pressures, information, and political-cultural guidelines which impinge upon the decision-makers. In a larger-scale and more prolonged crisis, the time factor may permit various subtle adjustment mechanisms to come into play which can never operate in a brief experiment.

One cannot deny, however, that there is some relationship between stress and problem-solving efficiency. Dean G. Pruitt, synthesizing the findings of several writers in the field, concludes that the relationship is probably curvilinear, with some stress being necessary to motivate activity, but too much stress causing a reduction in efficiency.[132] Crisis inevitably brings in its wake a foreshortened perspective, a difficulty in thinking ahead and calculating consequences, and a tendency to select for consideration only a narrow range of alternatives—those which occur most readily to the decision-makers.[133] Naturally, if more time were available, a wider spectrum of choices could be evaluated, but the preciousness of time is built into the definition of crisis. Contingency planning can help, but the crisis which comes is invariably somewhat different, at least in its details, from the crisis which was abstractly anticipated in contingency plans.

Holsti lists other effects of stress uncovered as a result of empirical research: increased random behavior; increased rate of error; regression to simpler and more primitive modes of response; problem-solving rigidity; diminished focus of attention; and a reduction in tolerance for ambiguity.[134] He notes that "the common use during crisis of such techniques as ultimata and threats with built-in deadlines is likely to increase the stress under which the recipient must operate" because they heighten the salience of the time element and increase the danger of fixation upon the single, familiar approach regardless of its effectiveness in the present situation.[135] Other analysts have found that diplomatic communications transmitted during international crises that were settled peacefully (Morocco, 1911; Berlin, 1948; Cuba, 1962) were characterized by greater flexibility and sublety of distinctions, as well as by more extensive information search and usage, than were communications during crises that led to war in 1914 and 1950.[136] Finally, in connection with the time variable it should be noted that if in the past international crises were often marked by insufficient information, in recent decades technological conditions, combined with a desire of bureaucrats to generate and transmit vast amounts of information during crises, create the opposite danger of "overloading" the circuits of the decision-making system.

Groups that make the most crucial decisions in national security cases are usually limited in size—perhaps 12 to 20 persons. Irving Janis has analyzed what he calls "groupthink" and has described its characteristics. The members of a small group of decision-makers often share an illusion of invulnerability which may encourage them to take extreme risks. Their self-confidence is mutually reinforcing, such that they may discount warnings or information which runs counter to their own assumptions. They often have a stereotyped and simplified view of the enemy, and an unquestioned belief in their own inherent morality. They are quick to censure and drive out of circulation viewpoints which do not conform to the dominant assessments and judgments of the group, and they take the silence of dissenting or doubtful members to mean that there exists virtual unanimity in the thinking of the group.[137] It should not be taken for granted that "groupthink" is necessarily bad. The dominant element within the group may well be correct in its assessment of the situation and in its views on the proper course to be pursued. Furthermore, the tendency of a group to impose a dominant view upon all its members—which is a natural social phenomenon—may produce more adverse consequences in an ideologically monolithic society than in a democratic one, and also more adverse consequences at lower bureaucratic echelons, where indivduals are less independent and outspoken, than at top levels, where more powerful personalities are usually present to speak their minds.

There is no reason, on the basis of available psychological data, to be unduly optimistic or unduly pessimistic about the ability of decision-making groups to conduct cooperative, rational problem-solving operations under conditions of crisis. This observation may be of small comfort in a nuclear age of international relations when recurring crisis has become a normal and expected feature of the world's political-strategic landscape. The two leading members of the international system have begun to accumulate a certain amount of steadying experience in the restrained management of those crises in which they confront each other directly. The pessimist cites every new crisis as evidence that humanity's luck is running out and that the leaders of the powers cannot be expected to weather another storm like the last one without making fatally absurd moves. The optimist, on the other hand, regards each passing crisis as a gained experience, and thus a contribution, however meager, toward developing a maturing and stabilizing process, or what Raymond Tanter has called a process of "socialization of nations" analogous to the socialization that takes place among individuals who have a capacity for learning.[138] Some comfort might also be derived from the studies of Dina A. Zinnes and colleagues which show that decision-makers do not perceive or behave differently in time of crisis, that they do not see hostility where none exists, and that they do not become paranoid under the stress of a crisis situation.[139] At the very least, we can say that foreign policy decisions occur in a context which normally minimizes the influence of personal and emotional factors and makes it likely that the collective political decision will embody a more practical wisdom than do most everyday personal decisions of individuals.

CONCLUSIONS

The field of decision-making is a broad one, and we do not pretend to be able to cover it all. The decision-making process is a function of many different factors relating to the behavior of individuals and of large organizational structures. The DM role is shaped by both the system and the individual's interpretation of it, and the influence of personality in comparison with social ideology will vary markedly from one system to another. Democratic and totalitarian states make foreign policy in very diverse ways. Most decision-making theories which have been developed in the United States have, quite understandably, focused upon the American political experience—upon the role of public opinion, the state of Executive-Congressional relations, the nature of the bureaucratic competition in the annual battle of the budget in Washington, and so on. There is an inevitable tendency on the part of social scientists, unless they guard against it, to universalize from particulars, and to assume that at least certain aspects of a phenomenon studied in one cultural-political context can be *mutatis mutandis* given a more generalized application. Thus there is a danger that when Americans think about such basic concepts as rationality in decision-making, or bureaucratic competition for scarce resources, or action-reaction processes in prolonged arms "races," or in acute crisis, lessons drawn from an observation of the behavior of American decision-makers can be readily carried over to the behavior of decision-makers in vastly different environments—Moscow, Peking, Tokyo, New Delhi, or Cairo.

We must admit that we do not know a great deal about foreign policy decision-making in non-Western capitals, particularly those far removed from any constitutional democratic experience. Even among the Western democratic states with which American political scientists are generally most familiar—Britain, France, Italy, and the Federal Republic of Germany—considerable differences exist in the organization of governments for the conduct of foreign affairs, as well as in the ways elites typically conceive of their national interests. The difficulties of extrapolating from American experience to foreign decision-making processes become even more pronounced when we are dealing with governments and countries that are politically, ideologically, socioeconomically, and culturally very different from those of the West. Within the past two decades, significant strides have been made in the comparative study of leadership, bureaucracy, value orientations of elites, and decision-making in Communist or Socialist countries.[140] More specifically, the student should become acquainted with the comparative study of foreign policy decision-making in Western societies, Communist societies, and the developing societies of the Third World.[141] The field of comparative foreign policies is distinct from that of international relations theory and specifically from theories of decision-making in the international system, but the former has much to contribute to the latter by way of concrete data and perhaps of insights leading to useful new theoretical approaches.

Notes

1. See Paul Wasserman and Fred S. Silander, *Decision-Making: An Annotated Bibliography* (Ithaca, N.Y.: Graduate School of Business and Public Administration, Cornell University, 1958).
2. "Decision-making as an Approach to the Study of International Politics," in Richard C. Snyder, H. W. Bruck, and Burton Sapin, eds., *Foreign Policy Decision-Making* (New York: The Free Press, 1963), p. 65; see also pp. 85–86.

3. Ibid., p. 65. See also Robert Jervis, *Perception and Misperception in International Politics* (Princeton: Princeton University Press, 1976).

4. Joseph Frankel, *The Making of Foreign Policy: An Analysis of Decision-Making* (New York: Oxford University Press, 1963), p. 4.

5. Michael Brecher, *The Foreign Policy System of Israel: Setting, Images, Process* (New Haven: Yale University Press, 1972), p. 4. For a thorough discussion of objective environment and decision-makers' perception, see Hyam Gold, "Foreign Policy Decision-Making and the Environment: The Claims of Snyder, Brecher and the Sprouts," *International Studies Quarterly*, 22 (December 1978), 569–586.

6. Students of decision-making have suggested several different ways of analyzing the phenomenon. Harold Lasswell, for example, presents seven functional stages: information, recommendation, prescription, invocation, application, appraisal, and termination. *The Decision Process: Seven Categories of Functional Analysis* (College Park: University of Maryland Press, 1956). See also James A. Robinson and R. Roger Majak, "The Theory of Decision-Making," in James C. Charlesworth, ed., *Contemporary Political Analysis* (New York: The Free Press, 1967), pp. 178–181, including bibliographical references; John P. Lovell, *Foreign Policy in Perspective: Strategy, Adaptation, Decision-Making* (New York: Holt, Rinehart and Winston, 1970), especially pp. 205–261. Michael Brecher makes elite image the decisive input of a foreign policy system. Op. cit., p. 11.

7. David Braybrooke and Charles E. Lindblom, *A Strategy of Decision* (New York: The Free Press, 1963), p. 40.

8. Michael Brecher, op. cit., p. 8, and chaps. 2 and 3; Snyder et al., op. cit., p. 86.

9. See, for example, Bernard C. Cohen, *The Press and Foreign Policy* (Princeton: Princeton University Press, 1963); and Roger Hilsman, Jr., *Strategic Intelligence and National Decisions* (New York: The Free Press, 1956).

10. James A. Robinson and Richard C. Snyder, "Decision-Making in International Politics," in Herbert C. Kelman, ed., *International Behavior: A Social-Psychological Analysis* (New York: Holt, Rinehart and Winston, 1965), p. 442.

11. Morton H. Halperin with the assistance of Priscilla Clapp and Arnold Kanter, *Bureaucratic Politics and Foreign Policy* (Washington: The Brookings Institution, 1974).

12. Ibid., p. 312.

13. All decision-makers in established (as distinct from entirely new) systems can draw upon a fund of previous practices, or what David Easton calls a "social memory bank, encapsulated in the traditional modes of operation of the system," *A Systems Analysis of Political Life* (New York: Wiley, 1965), p. 456.

14. Francis Rourke, *Bureaucracy and Foreign Policy* (Baltimore, Md.: Johns Hopkins University Press, 1972), pp. 49–50.

15. Ibid., p. 54.

16. Ibid., pp. 62–65.

17. Alexander L. George, "The Case for Multiple Advocacy in Making Foreign Policy," *American Political Science Review*, LXVI (September 1972), 751–785.

18. Ibid., p. 758. See also chaps. 7 and 8 on advocacy of interest groups and competing elites in Brecher, op. cit.

19. Richard C. Snyder et al., op. cit., pp. 137–171.

20. Ibid., p. 144.

21. "This relieves us of the necessity to connect what the Secretary of State had for breakfast with his conduct at meetings of the National Security Council." Snyder, ibid., p. 161.

22. James Rosenau, "The Premises and Promises of Foreign Policy Decision-Making," in James C. Charlesworth, ed., op. cit., p. 201. But Rosenau goes on to say that in Snyder's analytic scheme "in order to" motives may not always produce satisfactory explanations and that there may be times when the more idiosyncratic "be-

cause of" motives will have to be explored. Nevertheless, he adds, time and energy can normally be saved by studying "in order to" motives first and regarding as a residual category the more deep-rooted psychological factors which need to be taken into account only under unusual circumstances. Ibid.

23. James Robinson and Richard Snyder, op. cit., p. 444.

24. Martin Patchen, "Decision Theory in the Study of National Action," *Journal of Conflict Resolution,* LVII (June 1963), 173. Other writers have focused on a "cognitive process" approach which looks to the belief structures of decision-makers and the implications of these structures for the way international events are understood and policy alternatives are considered. See Michael J. Shapiro and G. Matthew Bonham, "Cognitive Process and Foreign Policy Decision-Making," *Journal of Conflict Resolution,* 17 (June 1973), 147–174.

25. David Easton, *The Political System* (New York: Knopf, 1953), p. 129.

26. Paul Diesing attributes a distinctive rationality to economic, social, technical, legal, and political decisions. *Reason in Society: Five Types of Decisions and Their Social Conditions* (Urbana: University of Illinois Press, 1962). Others, too, including R. C. Wood and William L. C. Wheaton, have cautioned against extrapolating from private to public decision behavior. Cf. Robinson and Majak in Charlesworth, ed., op. cit., pp. 177–178. Anthony Downs, on the other hand, is thought to equate private with public decision-making. Ibid., p. 178. But even he differentiates sharply between individual and organizational decision-making. See *Inside Bureaucracy,* A Rand Corporation Research Study (Boston: Little, Brown, 1967), pp. 178–179.

27. See for example Marshall Dimock. *A Philosophy of Administration* (New York: Harper & Row, 1958), p. 140; J. David Singer, "Inter-Nation Influence: A Formal Model," *American Political Science Review,* LXII (June 1963), 424; Bruce M. Russett, "The Calculus of Deterrence," *Journal of Conflict Resolution,* VII (June 1963), 97–109.

28. Richard Snyder, op. cit., p. 176. Snyder emphasizes that the explanation of DM motivation implies a concept of multiple membership of the individual in a culture and society, in such social groupings as the profession and class, in the total political institutional structure, and in the decisional unit. Ibid., p. 172.

29. Snyder had accepted earlier the notion of "maximization of expected utility." See his "Game Theory and the Analysis of Political Behavior," in *Research Frontiers and Government* (Washington: The Brookings Institution, 1955), pp. 73–74.

30. J. David Singer, "Inter-Nation Influence: A Formal Model," *American Political Science Review,* LVII (June 1963), pp. 428–430.

31. Martin Patchen, op. cit., pp. 165–169.

32. Sidney Verba, "Assumptions of Rationality and Nonrationality in Models of the International System," in James N. Rosenau, ed., *International Politics and Foreign Policy,* rev. ed., (New York: The Free Press, 1969), p. 231.

33. David Braybrooke and Charles Lindblom, op. cit., chap. 4.

34. See Herbert A. Simon, *Administration Behavior* (New York: Macmillan, 1959); "A Behavioral Model of Rational Choice," *Quarterly Journal of Economics,* LXIX (February 1955), 99–118; and "A Behavioral Model of Rational Choice," in Simon, ed., *Models of Man: Social and Rational* (New York: Wiley, 1957), pp. 241–260. See also William D. Coplin, *Introduction to International Politics: A Theoretical Overview* (Chicago: Markham, 1971), pp. 32–37.

35. David Braybrooke and Charles Lindblom, op. cit., pp. 71–79 and chap. 5.

36. Irving L. Janis, "Decisional Conflicts: A Theoretical Analysis," *Journal of Conflict Resolution,* III (March 1959), 7.

37. Ibid., pp. 7–13, where the author contrasts the reactions of two negotiators, Presi-

dent Wilson and Count Bernstorff, to the setback which the Zimmermann telegram represented to their peace efforts.

38. James Robinson and Roger Majak, op. cit., pp. 180–183.

39. Ibid., p. 182. The references are to Arthur F. Bentley, *The Process of Government* (Chicago: University of Chicago Press, 1908); David B. Truman, *The Governmental Process* (Chicago: University of Chicago Press, 1951); and William H. Riker, *The Theory of Political Coalitions* (New Haven: Yale University Press, 1962).

40. Ibid., pp. 182–184.

41. Graham T. Allison, op. cit., pp. 4–5, 10–11.

42. Ibid., pp. 13–18.

43. Ibid., pp. 29–30.

44. Ibid., p. 5.

45. Ibid., p. 67.

46. Ibid., p. 68. For more on this, see the section, "The Cybernetic Theory of Decision."

47. Ibid., pp. 71–72.

48. Ibid., p. 77.

49. Ibid., pp. 144–145. See also Graham T. Allison and Morton H. Halperin, "Bureaucratic Politics: A Paradigm and Some Policy Implications," *World Politics*, XXIV (Spring Supplement 1972), 40–79.

50. Miriam Steiner, "The Elusive Essence of Decision," *International Studies Quarterly*, 21 (June 1977), 419.

51. Ibid.

52. Glenn H. Snyder and Paul Diesing, *Conflict Among Nations: Bargaining, Decision-Making and System Structure in International Crises* (Princeton: Princeton University Press, 1977).

53. Ibid., p. 355.

54. Ibid., pp. 355–356. The authors did not find that attitudes of leading decision-makers are significantly determined by bureaucratic role. "Thus the most distinctive point of the Allison-Halperin 'bureaucratic politics' theory does not survive our analysis." (Note on p. 408.)

55. Ibid., pp. 333–335.

56. Ibid., pp. 337–338.

57. Ibid., pp. 338–339.

58. John D. Steinbruner, *The Cybernetic Theory of Decision: New Dimensions of Political Analysis* (Princeton: Princeton University Press, 1974), chap. 1.

59. Ibid., p. 47.

60. Ibid., pp. 48–67. Steinbruner acknowledges that some of his own criticisms of the analytic paradigm had been anticipated in Herbet Simon's "satisficing" model, but in his view Simon had not gone far enough. Ibid., p. 63.

61. Ibid., p. 68.

62. Ibid., p. 69.

63. Ibid., p. 72. The reference is to Richard M. Cyert and James G. March, *A Behavioral Theory of the Firm* (Englewood Cliffs, N.J.: Prentice-Hall, 1963), chap. 6. It should be noted that Steinbruner incorporates into the cybernetic paradigm the work of Charles Lindblom (especially his "incrementalism") and the Organizational Process Model of Graham Allison (see pp. 77 and 80). He fully agrees with those who hold that organizational routines, once established, are very difficult to alter.

64. John Steinbruner, op. cit., p. 92. Cf. also Robert Jervis, *Perception and Misperception and International Politics*, op. cit., chap. 4.

65. Ibid., chap. 4. According to Snyder and Diesing, Steinbruner's "theoretical

thinker" is equivalent to their "irrational bargainer." *Conflict Among Nations,* op. cit., p. 337.

66. These matters are thoroughly covered in Chapters 6 to 9.

67. Ibid., p. 320.

68. Ibid., p. 70. See also chap. 10, especially p. 329.

69. Ibid., pp. 320–321.

70. See, for example, Ole R. Holsti, "The 1914 Case," *American Political Science Review,* LIX (June 1965), 365–378; Ole R. Holsti, Robert C. North, and Richard A. Brody, "Perception and Action in the 1914 Crisis," in J. David Singer, ed., op. cit. (1968); Glenn D. Paige, *The Korean Decision, June 24–30, 1950* (New York: The Free Press, 1958); Erskine B. Childers, *The Road to Suez* (London: MacGibbon and Kee, 1962); Charles A. McClelland, "Access to Berlin: The Quantity and Variety of Events, 1948–1963," in Singer, ed., op. cit., pp. 159–186, and "Decisional Opportunity and Political Controversy: The Quemoy Case," *Journal of Conflict Resolution,* VI (September 1962), 201–213; Graham T. Allison, *Essence of Decision: Explaining the Cuban Missile Crisis* (Boston: Little, Brown, 1971; and Herbert S. Dinerstein, *The Making of a Missile Crisis* (Baltimore, Md.: Johns Hopkins Press, 1976.)

71. Glenn D. Paige, op. cit., p. 10.

72. Ibid., p. 14. Paige's empirical analysis, normative analysis, and suggested implications for future crisis management are reserved for three chapters at the end.

73. Ibid., pp. 21–49.

74. Ibid., pp. 51–76.

75. Paige notes that a crisis is "thrust upon the decision-makers from outside their organization and from outside the territory and population over which they exercise official control." Ibid., p. 275. For a fuller discussion of the definition of crisis, see the section, "Toward a Theory of Crisis Behavior."

76. Glenn D. Paige, op. cit., pp. 276–279.

77. Ibid., pp. 281, 288, 290, 293, 301, 303, and 312.

78. Ole R. Holsti, Robert C. North, and Richard A. Brody, "Perception and Action in the 1914 Crisis," in J. David Singer, ed., *Quantitative International Politics* (New York: The Free Press, 1968), pp. 123–158. Ole R. Holsti later discussed the limits of validity of relying on financial data as indicators of international tensions and concluded that such data constitute only a partial and indirect check on the validity of content data from other sources such as diplomatic documents. See the section, "Perceptions of Hostility and Financial Indices in a Crisis," in chap. 3 of *Crisis, Escalation, War* (Montreal: McGill-Queens University Press, 1972), pp. 51–70.

79. Ibid., p. 136.

80. Ibid., p. 136.

81. Ibid., p. 137.

82. Ibid.

83. Ibid., p. 138.

84. Ibid., p. 46. The phenomenon described here is similar to the hostility-friendliness continuum and the unstable reaction coefficients studied by Lewis F. Richardson in his research on the arms races of 1908 to 1914 and 1929 to 1939. See *Arms and Insecurity* (Pittsburgh, Pa: Boxwood, 1960), and *Statistics of Deadly Quarrels* (Chicago: Quadrangle Books, 1960).

85. Ole Holsti et al., in Singer, ed., op. cit., p. 152.

86. Ibid.

87. Ibid., p. 157.

88. L. L. Farrar, Jr., "The Limits of Choice: July 1914 Reconsidered," *The Journal of Conflict Resolution,* XVI (March 1972), 1–23; quotes from p. 20.

89. Ole R. Holsti, Richard A. Brody, and Robert C. North, "Measuring Effect and Action in the International Reaction Models: Empirical Materials from the 1962 Cuban Crisis," *Journal of Peace Research,* I (1964), 174.

90. Ibid., p. 177.

91. Ibid.

92. Ibid., p. 158. See also Ole R. Holsti, "Time, Alternatives and Communications: The 1914 and Cuban Missile Crises," in Hermann, ed., op. cit., pp. 58–80.

93. Graham T. Allison, *Essence of Decision,* op. cit., p. 245.

94. Ibid., pp. 40–56. Albert and Roberta Wohlstetter provided the military argument for the "rectifying the nuclear balance" hypothesis in *Controlling the Risks in Cuba,* Adelphi Papers No. 17 (London: Institute for Strategic Studies, April 1965).

95. Graham T. Allison, op. cit., pp. 58–62.

96. Ibid., pp. 62–66.

97. Ibid., pp. 102–106.

98. Ibid., pp. 106–108.

99. Ibid., pp. 109–113.

100. Ibid., pp. 113–117.

101. Ibid., pp. 117–126.

102. Ibid., pp. 187–210.

103. Ibid., p. 210.

104. Ibid., p. 228.

105. See ibid., pp. 229–330, 248–249.

106. Ibid., p. 249.

107. James A. Robinson, "An Appraisal of Concepts and Theories," in the work edited by Hermann (see Note 108), p. 27.

108. In addition to the book by Graham T. Allison on the Cuban Missile Crisis, other important contributions to the subject include Charles F. Hermann, ed., *International Crises: Insights from Behavioral Research* (New York: The Free Press, 1972); Ole R. Holsti, *Crisis, Escalation, War,* op. cit.; and the March 1977 issue of *International Studies Quarterly.* See also Thomas J. Price, "Constraints on Foreign Policy Decision-Making, ibid., 22 (September 1978), 357–376; and Michael Brecher, "State Behavior in International Crisis," *Journal of Conflict Resolution,* 23 (September 1979), 446–480.

109. Michael P. Sullivan, *International Relations: Theories and Evidence* (Englewood Cliffs, N.J.: Prentice-Hall, 1976), p. 82.

110. Charles A. McClelland, "Crisis and Threat in the International Setting: Some Relational Concepts," unpublished memo cited in Michael Brecher, "Toward a Theory of International Crisis Behavior," *International Studies Quarterly,* 21 (March 1977), 39–40.

111. Charles F. Hermann, "International Crisis as a Situational Variable," in James N. Rosenau, ed., op. cit. (1969), p. 414.

112. Michael Brecher, op. cit., pp. 43–44.

113. Ibid., pp. 48–49.

114. Glenn H. Snyder and Paul Diesing, op. cit., p. 7.

115. Ibid., p. 4.

116. Ibid., p. 455. Although crises are dangerous, they are seen to be more functional than dysfunctional.

117. Oran R. Young, *The Intermediaries: Third Parties in International Crises* (Princeton: Princeton University Press), 1967, p. 10.

118. Ibid., pp. 419–445.

119. Ibid., pp. 450–453.

120. Ibid., p. 456.

121. Robert A. Young, "Perspectives on International Crisis," *International Studies Quarterly,* 21 (March 1977), 8.
122. Charles A. McClelland, "The Anticipation of International Crises," op. cit., pp. 15–16.
123. Ibid., p. 17.
124. Ibid., p. 18.
125. Ibid., pp. 24–26.
126. Ole R. Hosti, *Crisis, Escalation, War,* op. cit., p. 10. See also the reference in chap. 7 to Thomas C. Wiegele's work on biological factors in crisis decision-making. Supra, p. 266. See also Wiegele's "The Psychophysiology of Elite Stress in Five International Crises," *International Studies Quarterly,* 22 (December 1978), 467–512.
127. See Kurt Back, "Decisions under Uncertainty," *American Behavioral Scientist,* IV (February 1961), 14–19.
128. See Wilbert S. Ray, "Mild Stress and Problem Solving," *American Journal of Psychology,* LXXVIII (1965), 227–234.
129. Herman Kahn, *On Escalation: Metaphors and Scenarios* (New York: Praeger, 1965), p. 38.
130. John T. Lanzetta, "Group Behavior Under Stress," *Human Relations,* VIII (1955); reprinted in J. David Singer, ed., *Human Behavior and International Politics: Contributions from the Social-Psychological Sciences* (Chicago: Rand McNally, 1965), pp. 216–217.
131. Robert L. Hamblin, "Group Integration During a Crisis," *Human Relations,* XI (1958), in Singer, ed., op. cit., pp. 226–228.
132. Dean G. Pruitt, "Definition of the Situation as a Determinant of International Action," in Kelman, ed., op. cit., p. 395.
133. See ibid., p. 396, where Pruitt refers to the work of M. J. Driver and Charles E. Osgood.
134. Ole R. Holsti, op. cit., p. 13.
135. Ibid., pp. 14–15.
136. Peter Suedfeld and Philip Tetlock, "Integrative Complexity of Communications in International Crises," *Journal of Conflict Resolution,* XXI (March 1977), 169–184.
137. Irving Janis, *Victims of Groupthink* (Boston: Houghton Mifflin, 1972), pp. 197–198.
138. Raymond Tanter, "International System and Foreign Policy Approaches: Implications for Conflict Modeling and Management," *World Politics,* XXIV (April 1972), 14–15.
139. Dina A. Zinnes, Joseph L. Zinnes, and Robert D. McClure, "Hostility in Diplomatic Communication: A Study of the 1914 Crisis," in C. F. Hermann, ed., op. cit., p. 160.
140. See R. Barry Farrell, ed., *Political Leadership in Eastern Europe and the Soviet Union* (Chicago: Aldine, 1970); Alvin Z. Rubinstein, Carl Beck, et al., *Comparative Communist Political Leadership* (New York: David McKay, 1973); Vernon V. Aspaturian, "Moscow's Options in a Changing World," in Gary K. Bertsch and Thomas W. Ganschow, eds., *Comparative Communism* (San Francisco: Freeman, 1976), pp. 369–393.
141. See David Wilkinson, *Comparative Foreign Relations* (Encino, Calif.: Dickenson, 1969); James N. Rosenau, "Foreign Policy as Adaptive Behavior," *Comparative Politics,* II (April 1970), 365–387; Roy C. Macridis, ed., *Foreign Policy in World Politics,* 5th ed., (Englewood Cliffs, N.J.: Prentice-Hall, 1974); James N. Rosenau et al., *World Politics* (New York: The Free Press, 1975).

Chapter 12
Game Theory, Bargaining, and Gaming

GAME THEORY AND THE STUDY OF POLITICAL PHENOMENA

Some people are either shocked or offended or both at the suggestion that such serious phenomena as politics and human conflict should be treated as "games." The analogy seems almost sacrilegious insofar as it implies a conceptual reduction of important human affairs to a sport or recreation. Yet throughout history generals and strategists have engaged in a practice known as "war gaming," which involves an effort to second guess the opponent in advance, and many a party politician and government official has referred to his profession at times as part of "the great game of politics." Johan Huizinga (1872–1945), a distinguished Dutch philosopher-historian, argued that human culture cannot be fully comprehended unless we realize that the human being is a "player," *homo ludens,* and that human beings play games from childhood through old age in all dimensions of life from making love to making war.[1] Today it is assumed that many human behaviors often acquire a gamelike quality. This is true for labor-management bargaining, price competition among large industrial firms, the rivalry of two suitors for a woman's hand in marriage, the strategy of guerrilla insurgency, or the conduct of international arms control negotiations, as well as buying a house or deterring tantrums in a child.[2] Even nuclear deterrence rests on game theory.

Game Theory as Decision-Making

Game theory is a specialized form of decision-making theory and a controversial one at that. Some condemn it as completely useless simply because they do not understand it. Others perhaps claim too much for it, insinuating that it can provide answers to the policymaker's dilemma when it was never intended to do so. The analysis of games will not furnish a normative code of how to behave in any concrete situation. Nor does it give us a complete empirical theory of how people actually do behave in real-life situations. We do not expect from game theory a reliable predictive capability in international politics. Nevertheless, we believe that after its deficiencies have been discounted and its limitations recognized, game theory remains a useful tool in the field of international relations. Managed skillfully, games can serve as analogies or models of actual conflict situations; they can be useful heuristic devices in teaching, research, and policy analysis; they can help us to clarify our thought about available choices, suggest novel possibilities which might not otherwise have occurred to us, and induce us to penetrate beyond a mere verbal description of a problem to a deeper, more generalized level of comprehension.[3] Anatol Rapoport writes:

> Game theory, when it is pursued beyond its elementary paradox-free formulations, teaches us what we must be able to do in order to bring the intellect to bear on a science of human conflict. To analyze a conflict scientifically, we must be able to agree on relative values (to assign utilities). We must learn to be perceptive (evaluate the other's assignment of utilities). Furthermore, in order to engage in a conflict thus formalized, we must be able to communicate (give a credible indication to the other of how we assign utilities to outcomes).[4]

We have been talking about game theory and also about games. Actually these are two different things. *Game theory* is a mathematical tool which enables rational players to discover the optimum strategy which they ought to pursue. *Game playing* permits us to see what strategies players actually do choose in specific situations. Pure game theory, since it involves mathematical certitude, is immune to criticism, although people are entitled to ask whether it has much relevance for international relations. Studies involving the use of games have been criticized frequently on a number of grounds, for example, triviality or unreproducibility of results, misinterpretation of motives underlying the players' choices, invalidity of generalizations drawn from games, and lack of isomorphism (structural similarity) between games and social reality.[5] No one doubts that games are merely skeletal representations of the real world. It is hoped, however, that just as the geneticist's tinker-toy model of the structure of DNA can serve a useful didactic purpose, so games might help the student, the social scientist, and perhaps the policymaker to understand better complex life situations by simplifying them and capturing their essential characteristics.[6]

Intellectual Origins and Definitions

Martin Shubik's definition of game theory as a method of studying decision-making in conflict situations is a good point of departure.[7] "This theory," says Thomas C. Schelling, "is concerned with situations—games of 'strategy,' in contrast to games of skill or games of chance—in which the best course of action for each participant depends on what he expects the other participants to do."[8] Both Shubik and Schelling, along with other game theorists, have built upon the foundation laid in the pioneering work of John von Neumann and Oskar Morgenstern.[9] The latter pair, one a mathematician and the other an economist, analyzed the various strategies that might be pursued by players in relatively simple games and found that mathematical methods enabled one to identify all possible sequences of moves and to select an optimum strategy for playing.[10] They suggested that some of the lessons to be learned from game theory may be applicable to more complex social situations.

Game theory is based upon an abstract form of reasoning, arising from a combination of mathematics and logic. Nearly all game theorists would agree that the theory with which they deal is addressed to what is "rationally correct" behavior in conflict situations in which the participants are trying to "win," rather than to the way individuals actually do behave in conflict situations. Individuals can and often do conduct themselves irrationally and emotionally in conflict situations, but for the sake of theoretical analysis, games theorists assume rational behavior, simply because they find this assumption more profitable for theory-building than the obverse of it. If we were to assume that all human behavior is fundamentally absurd, neurotic, or psychotic, then there could be no theory, either of games or of any other social phenomena. Games theorists, then, subscribe to some such notion as the following: If people in a certain situation wish to "win,"—that is, to accomplish an objective which the other party seeks to deny them—we can sort out the intellectual processes by which they calculate what kind of action is most likely to be advantageous to them, assuming that they believe their opponents also to be rational calculators like themselves, equally interested in "second guessing" and trying to outwit the opponent.[11]

A few rudimentary concepts should be considered. Every game is characterized by the following elements: (1) two or more players who are trying in some sense either (in a zero-sum game) to get the best of each other or (in a non-zero-sum game) to achieve a solution which is best for both; (2) a payoff or a set of payoffs which may mean various things to the players because of discrepancies of their value systems; (3) a set of ground rules or guidelines which must be observed if the game is to be played according to the definition of the game; (4) information conditions which determine the quality and quantity of knowledge which each player has of the environment and of the choices made by the other player(s); (5) the total environment in which the game is played, whether fully perceived by the players or not; and (6) the interaction of competing moves, in which every choice by one may prompt the other(s) to modify subsequent choices.

Zero-Sum Games

The most commonly drawn preliminary distinction in game theory is that between a zero-sum game and a non-zero-sum game, with variations of each. In a zero-sum game between A and B, what A wins, B loses. Chess, checkers, two-person poker, or blackjack—all of these are zero-sum games. Each game ends with one player having a score of plus one and the other minus one, and the value of "one" for the game depends upon the "stakes" or the size of the "pot." Examples of real-life situations which contain aspects of zero-sum games would include an electoral race between two candidates for a Congressional seat, most military tactical situations in which the objective which one side seizes is lost to the other, at least temporarily, such as an "air duel" or a battle over a hill, and the rivalry of two men for a woman's hand in marriage. It should be noted that a three-man race for an elective office is not really a zero-sum game unless we break it down into two different contests between the winner and each loser. We might also observe that in a tactical military situation the ground gained by one side equals the ground lost by the other, but there might have been a considerable discrepancy in the cost to each side when measured in casualties. The same notion holds true for the election campaign and for courting a fair lady: There is a single payoff, but the contending parties may spend widely varying sums in the effort to win. Writers on game theory distinguished the *outcome* of a game (win, lose, or draw) from the *payoff* (the value attached by a player to an outcome). The relationship between payoff and motivation is critically important, but it is difficult to establish.[12]

Two-Person Zero-Sum Games

In most of the literature on the subject, games are schematically represented in a "normalized" form in which no details of the game are given, but in which the strategies for each player and the accompanying payoffs are depicted in a matrix. Moreover, the payoff values are often assigned in a purely arbitrary manner, merely to facilitate the illustration of a point. (The student therefore need not worry too much about how the payoff values were arrived at—at least not yet.) Moreover, the strategies may consist of fairly complex plans and yet be designated simply as Strategy 1 or Strategy 2 or Strategy N for each player. Thus, in mathematical theory, both strategies and payoffs are treated abstractly. In the most helpful form of notation, each matrix contains the payoff which each player receives when he or she chooses one of the two strategies that converge at that point. The student may, however, come across a matrix which shows only the payoffs to one player. The following three simplified 2 by 2 matrices, borrowed or adapted from Shubik, will be sufficient to illustrate our discussion of two-person zero-sum games:

MATRIX I		Strategy for Player 2	
		A	B
Strategy for	A	+4, −4	−3, +3
Player 1	B	−3, +3	+4, −4

MATRIX II		Strategy for Player 2	
		A	B
Strategy for	A	−5, +5	−7, +7
Player 1	B	+8, −8	+1, −1

MATRIX III		Strategy for Player 2	
		A	B
Strategy for	A	−20, −20	+5, −5
Player 1	B	−5, +5	−2, −2

Matrix I refers to a game in which there is no saddlepoint. First it will be noticed that in each matrix the sum of the payoffs is zero.[13] But there is no point at which the strategies of the competing players logically converge. If both players opt for the A strategy, No. 1 wins 4 and the other loses 4. If No. 1 plays the B strategy and No. 2 chooses the A strategy, the former loses 3 and the latter gains 3. If students analyze this payoff matrix for a minute, they will see that the best strategy for each player in a long series of runs is a random strategy, determined by the toss of a coin, for this will eventually produce a balancing out of the wins and losses of 4s and 3s. In other words, the game schematized in Matrix I reduces to a game of chance with which game theory is not directly concerned.

Matrix II refers to a zero-sum game in which there is a saddlepoint. This is the point at which the minimum values in the rows (across) and the maximum values in the columns (up and down) converge at equality, or where the maximum values in the rows and the minimum values in the columns converge. The point of convergence is known as the *minimax value*. It is an axiom of game theory that in a two-person zero-sum game, a rational strategy is based on the minimax principle: Each player should seek to maximize the minimum gain of which he or she can be assured, or to minimize the maximum loss which needs to be sustained. Let us suppose, again following Shubik, that Player 1 is a police force in a country torn by guerrilla insurgency and Player 2 is the guerrilla force. The police in this particular game can choose either to go into the jungle in pursuit of the insurgents (Strategy A) or to avoid the jungle and to protect key areas (Strategy B). The choice of open battle or attritional skirmishes is up to the guerrilla force. The police do better out of the jungle than in it, where they stand to lose in both battles and skirmishes (−5 and −7, respectively). The guerrillas' preferred strategy, whether in or out of the jungle, is to skirmish, for in this way they can maximize their gains (+8) or hold their losses to a minimum (−1). In the simplified game described, two rational players would tend to converge at the saddlepoint of +1, −1; that is, the police would probably choose key areas outside the jungle, whereas the guerrillas would skirmish and eschew open battle, thus holding their losses to −1 instead of −8.[14] This, of course, only describes the tactical encounters between guerrillas and police. For an insight into the strategic outcome of a guerrilla insurgency, something much more complex than a simple 2 by 2 matrix would be required. (In real life, the guerrillas might lose most tactical exchanges and yet win strategically because of psychopolitical factors.)

The minimax strategy is a cautious strategy. Four points are to be remembered in connection with the minimax strategy: (1) It applies only to zero-sum games. (2) It is proof against information leakage. (3) It is useful and normative only against an opponent who is presumed to be playing a rational game. If the adversary is stupid, prone to make blunders, or usually motivated by emotional factors (which might, e.g., incline the person to play his or her "hunches"), then the minimax strategy is not necessarily the optimum one to pursue. (4) The utility of the minimax strategy is validated in a series of plays, not in a one-shot game. (5) It is a rather dull, no-fun strategy, but it may be unavoidable. Shubik offers the following caveat:

> Apart from appreciating the two-person zero-sum game as the definition of a strictly competitive situation, the general political scientist will not gain too much insight from an intense study of this topic. . . . There is also a considerable amount of misinterpretation concerning the role in general game theory of the famous result concerning two-person zero-sum games known as the minimax or saddlepoint theorem. Zero-sum games are of extremely limited interest in the behavioral sciences in general.[15]

The type of game referred to in Matrix III above leads us partially out of two-person zero-sum games (ZSG) toward the non-zero-sum (NZSG) in that it is not exclusively competitive in the sense that what one gains another must lose. The sum of gains and losses need not add up to zero. There is room in this type of game for elements of both conflict and cooperation; on some plays, both parties might win, and at the end of the game both parties might be ahead by varying amounts. In a non-zero-sum game there are often several different payoffs, some of which may be very good or very bad, some marginally good or bad. The payoffs depend upon whether the players cooperate with each other, cut each other's throats, or mix their strategies of conflict and cooperation in varying combinations.

What is interesting about Matrix III is the fact that it refers to a game which might be a ZSG under some circumstances and a NZSG under others, depending upon the outcome. Actually, this matrix depicts the possible payoffs in a game of Chicken, similar to that popularized many years ago in a Hollywood film in which two youths drive toward each other in their fathers' automobiles at 80 miles an hour, each with his left set of wheels on the highway dividing line. If neither one swerves to the right, they will both be killed in the crash—an outcome which is arbitrarily assigned a numerical value of −20 for each. It could just as easily have been −200 or another figure, but in any event this becomes a minus-sum game in which both players lose as heavily as possible. If one stays on the course and the other veers, one gains esteem and the other loses in the eyes of the peer group. The latter is "chicken." This condition is indicated in the two matrices containing a +5 and −5. Thus if either driver swerves and the other holds longer to the course, the game turns out to be zero-sum. If both veer to the right simultaneously, each suffers dishonor in the eyes of the peer group, but since the reputation for being "chicken" is shared between them, so that no invidious comparisons can be drawn, each suffers only a −2. We should hasten to point out that the payoff matrix as shown is partly a function of the distorted value system of the youthful peer group, as perceived by the two drivers. Actually, the peer group chiefly craves the excitement of the game, and regrets the tragic outcome later. Certainly the parents and fiancées of the two youths would assign a larger negative valuation to their deaths and a high positive valuation to an outcome in which both have enough sense to veer off course before it is too late.[16] It ought to be made clear that the game of Chicken, played with human life at stake, is a game that is entered into only by irrational players, one or both of whom may become rational enough during the course of the game to save their lives. The analogy between the game of "Chicken" and the collision course of two nuclear superpowers in a crisis has been drawn many times, and should be obvious, but the latter is vastly more complex than the former.

Non-zero-Sum Games

Two-person non-zero-sum games can be played either "cooperatively" or "noncooperatively." In a "cooperative" game, the players are permitted to communicate with each other directly and to exchange information in advance concerning their intended choices. In a "noncooperative" game, overt communication is not permitted, but the choice of each becomes obvious to the other after the play. There is, however, a slight ambiguity in this terminology. Even if a game is "noncooperative" insofar as the rules prohibit overt or direct communication, it is possible for the players to cooperate tacitly through inferred communication, by which one player interprets the other's intentions from the kinds of choices made in a long series of plays.

THE "PRISONER'S DILEMMA" GAME (PDG)

The best-known example of a two-person NZSG is "Prisoner's Dilemma." Two individuals are taken into police custody and accused of a crime. Since they are interrogated separately, neither knows what the other will tell the district attorney. Each is aware that if both remain silent or deny all allegations, the worst they can expect is a sentence of 60 days in the county jail for vagrancy. If one turns state's evidence and the other remains silent, the former will receive a one-year commuted sentence and the other will be sent to the state penitentiary for ten years. If both confess, both will receive from five to eight years in prison. Their optimum strategy, of course, is a tacit agreement to remain silent, but in the absence of communication, neither can trust the other. Each makes the following assessment of the situation: If I remain silent, I will get either 60 days or ten years, depending upon whether my partner confesses. If I confess, I will receive either a commuted sentence or five years, depending upon whether he confesses. In either case I can assure myself of a lighter sentence by confessing. Since he is undoubtedly making the same sort of calculation, the chances are that he will confess, and hence I would be foolish to remain silent and count upon the slim chance that he would do likewise. Thus each, by choosing what seems to be the safer course, contributes to an outcome highly disadvantageous to both—a sentence of five years instead of 60 days.[17]

Game theorists have devised several variations of Prisoner's Dilemma, one of which will be described and analyzed presently. But at this juncture two points must be reiterated. First, there is an important difference between game theory, which is based on mathematical-logical analysis and which purports to show what kind of strategy a rational player *should* play (when he presumes his opponent rational), and experimental gaming, which is designed to furnish empirical evidence of how individuals *actually do behave* in game situations. Second, there is an important difference between "one-shot" games and games which are played over a series of runs by the same players who, as a result of experience, acquire insight into the strategic thought processes of each other.

In one variation of PDG, pairs of college students played 50 trials of a game in which the payoffs depended upon whether they pursued competitive or cooperative strategies. The subjects were seated on opposite sides of a partition. In front of each one was a panel with a red button and a black button. The experimenter gave the following instructions:

> Each of you will have a chance to make some money in this situation. . . . You see in front of you a red button and a black button. On each trial you will press either the black button or the red button. If you press the black button, two things can happen. If you press the black button and the other person also presses the black button, you get three cents and he gets three cents. If you press the black button and he presses the red button, you get nothing and he gets five cents. Suppose you push the red button. Again, two things can happen. If you push the red button and the other person presses the black button, you get five cents and he gets nothing. If you push the red and the other person also pushes red, you get one cent and the other person gets one cent.[18]

The subjects were not allowed to communicate directly with each other, but since the payoffs were made after each trial, each player knew which button the other had chosen.

The reader will note immediately that in such a game the best way to maximize monetary gains is for the two players to cooperate tacitly and to choose black on every trial. This, however, is not what happened in the experiments at Ohio State University. Only a few pairs sought to maximize monetary returns in this manner. The great majority played competitively; they were out to win more than their opponents even if this meant losing some money. In other words, the dominant strategy was to choose red most of the time, apparently on the assumption that this was the best way to do the opponent in, regardless of whether he or she was a beneficent or a maleficent adversary. It is possible, of course, that people might play more cooperatively as the economic payoffs are increased (say, from cents to dollars), but this becomes a costly method of playing experimental games which few supporters of scholarly research are eager to underwrite.[19] Several experimenters have concluded that cooperation in Prisoner's Dilemma games increases when monetary incentives replace mere winning on points; others have found no difference, and still others have correlated increased monetary rewards with decreased cooperation.[20] It is possible that many people play games for a satisfaction which is not readily reducible to economics. "Winning" is often much more fun than cooperation to optimize financial gains. Whether in this type of situation the competitive desire to win is any less "rational" than the cooperative desire to maximize economic income is a question for the philosophers of games theory to debate.

Games (both Prisoner's Dilemma and Chicken) have also been devised to determine whether sex differences influence the choice for cooperative or competitive behavior. Here, too, as with the question of monetary rewards, the results have been somewhat inconclusive, whether subjects play against programmed opponents (who have been instructed as to their choice) or play against each other (in mixed sex and same sex pairs).[21] The results have been less ambiguous for Prisoner's Dilemma than for Chicken. Three PDG experimenters all found that males opposing males tend to be more cooperative than females opposing females.[22] Another concluded that females are more "rational" (i.e., capable of earning more money) in a "one-shot" game, whereas males earn more in a series, when optimal strategy requires a longer time horizon.[23] Conrath, after research on games of Chicken, finds the explanations of sex role behavior in games thus far inadequate. If differences do exist, the "why" is important. "It is not likely that the biological aspect . . . is the determining factor, but rather the social and educational roles which distinguish the sexes."[24]

Prisoner's Dilemma has become a staple item in the literature of games, a full bibliography of which now runs into scores of articles, book chapters, and other studies. *The Journal of Conflict Resolution, The Journal of Social Psychology, The Journal of Personality and Social Psychology*, and other periodicals have consistently carried articles on the subject for many years. One authority on games has noted that "research in bargaining utilizing the Prisoner's Dilemma paradigm has become less concerned with questions of cooperation, competition, and the bargaining process, and more concerned with studying the Prisoner's Dilemma paradigm itself."[25] But Schlenker and Bonoma defend the preoccupation with the paradigm as being "necessary to understand the limits and dimensions of the laboratory world before useful experiments can be conducted."[26]

N-Person Games

This brings us to N-person non-zero-sum games, involving three or more players, all of whom are assumed to be independent decision-making limits and to possess some method for evaluating the worth of outcomes.[27] As might be expected, much less is known about these than about two-person games, because the number of permutations or interacting strategies increases at an exponential rate with the number of players. Physicists have never found a mathematical solution to the "three body" problem. Hence it is not surprising that no single theory has yet been developed for N-person games. Probably the most fruitful avenue of inquiry to date has been in the area of coalition formation. (For an examination of literature on alliances and coalitions, see Chapter

10.) When several players are in a game, it becomes quite natural for two or more to form a coalition against the others, in which case the others are induced to do likewise in order to insure their survival and maximize their gains. Sometimes the rules of the game may encourage the alignment of coalitions before starting to play; sometimes coalitions are formed, either tacitly or overtly, after the game is in progress. If two coalitions emerge, forcing all players to choose one or the other, the game in effect is reduced to a two-person zero-sum game.[28] It is conceivable, however, that at a particular stage of the game there might be three coalitions, one of which would eventually find itself under pressure to coalesce with one of the other two. The crucial question, it would appear, is to work out to the satisfaction of all the allies "a rational division of the spoils."[29]

If coalitions are formed before the start of the game, all the partners should be considered equal and entitled to an equal share of the payoff. What is much more interesting, of course, is a situation in which the payoff is divided according to the contribution each partner makes to the victory of the coalition, and in which the contribution is in some sense a function of "power" and "weakness." Sometimes there may be "founding members" of the coalitions with others permitted to join later after bargaining for terms which reflect both the power of the coalition leaders and the more desperate straits of the applicants for entry. In addition to the division of the payoff and to the circumstances under which coalitions are formed, other questions worthy of games theorists' attention pertain to the motives which might drive a member of one coalition to defect to another and whether it is possible for a coalition to enforce against its own members any sanction that is stronger and more efficacious than the bond of mutual interest.[30]

INTERNATIONAL RELATIONS AS A "GAME"

It is now time to ask what all this has to do with international relations or, more narrowly, with international politics. First, it should be made clear that international relations—or the operation of the international system—cannot be fully comprehended merely within the analytical framework of a "game." But the patterns and processes of international relations undeniably manifest certain gamelike characteristics. Since game theory and gaming are closely related to decision-making and bargaining, they are bound to have some relevance to the study of international relations—a field in which we commonly speak of making moves on the diplomatic chessboard, bluffing, upping the ante, and trying to second guess or outwit the opponent. The application of analytical techniques derived from game theory can therefore aid in improving our understanding of the subject, provided that this approach is employed with the balanced intellectual perspective of those who regard it as one among several useful tools. Within the past decade or so, some have ascribed too many wonderful problem-solving powers to game theory; others have condemned it outright, especially when applied to such strategic issues as nuclear deterrence, the prevention of local aggression, and the conduct of limited war.[31] The authors of this book prefer to pursue a *via media* between these extreme views.

It does not take much imagination to apply game theory to diplomatic negotiations for a treaty limiting strategic weapons, an agreement to reduce NATO and Warsaw Pact forces in Central Europe, or a convention establishing a regime governing the exploitation of ocean resources. In all these cases the parties seek to maximize gains and minimize losses. They all try to lead from positions of strength while masking their real weaknesses, even while accusing others of trying to take advantage of weakness. Those able to do so build up bargaining chips, perhaps expecting thereby to be able to make subsequent concessions less costly than they might otherwise appear to be. Governmental agencies responsible for developing negotiating strategies engage constantly in a process of calculation: If we offer this, what might we hope to obtain in return? Can we offer something which is not really important to us, but make it look like a major concession to the other side and to the world? What will be the cost to us of further postponement or a failure to reach agreement? These questions are typical of those asked by people who are game players.

Virtually all game theorists agree that international relations can be best conceptualized as an N-person non-zero-sum game, in which a gain by one party is not necessarily at the expense of other parties. An example of this, drawn from international economics, can be seen in the fact that the more advanced industrialized countries of the West, as well as Japan and the Soviet system states, do not suffer a loss in their absolute or relative economic position as the national economies of Asia, Latin America, and Africa develop. Indeed, economic expansion in less developed countries often leads to an intensification of trade, aid, and investment relations with the wealthier countries of the Western system. But note that this example, which is quite clear-cut, comes from the realm of economics. Several writers who have pioneered in the effort to apply game theory to the social sciences (e.g., Oskar Morgenstern, Thomas C. Schelling, Martin Shubik, and J. C. Harsanyi) have had economic training or have done extensive research into problems of economic competition. Competition between economic firms can be either a zero-sum or a nonzero-sum game. Economic analysts see the latter as the preferable, more rational alternative because both firms stand to gain, at least in the shorter run, if the mutual wounds of excessive competition can be avoided. Perhaps it is not too much to say that within the American economy the desirable has gradually become, or is becoming, the actual: The rivalry among the largest corporations in a field is looked upon as a non-zero-sum game. "Most social phenomena," writes Martin Shubik, ". . . are best represented by nonconstant sum games. In other words, the fates and fortunes of the parties involved may easily rise or fall together. There is no pure division into total opposition."[32]

International Relations as a Game
of Conflict and Cooperation

But whether international politics can be as readily reduced as international economics to a non-zero-sum game will probably be for a long time a subject of debate between political scientists and economists. To be sure, there are some political scientists who do not distinguish sharply between politics on the one hand and economics or psychology on the other. But the authors of this book are convinced that "the political" is not perfectly interchangeable with "the economic" or the "psychological." As we pointed out in a previous chapter, there are important differences between political decisions and decisions made by business firms or by individuals.[33] William D. Coplin has also persuasively argued that there is a considerable difference between the bargaining process in domestic society from the process that goes on in the international setting.[34] Hence we caution against efforts to make a hasty and uncritical transfer of the NZSG concept to international politics. In our view, international politics can be best understood within the game theoretical framework as involving a complex and fluctuating mixture of tendencies toward zero-sumness and nonzero-sumness.

Joseph Frankel suggests that French relations with Germany, for example, "developed from a zero-sum game in the early postwar period, when the French wished—and hoped to be able—to keep the Germans down, into a variable-sum game within the (European) Communities in which cooperation changed the competitive character of the game and rapidly increased the payoff for both sides."[35] The English peace theorist, John W. Burton, has proposed a method of resolving such conflicts as that between Greeks and Turks over Cyprus by inducing the parties to view the situation as one not with a fixed-sum outcome that requires a compromise "cutting of the cake," but with outcomes from which both sides can gain through functional cooperation that will produce a larger cake.[36] But there is a circularity in the kind of reasoning that prescribes resolving a conflict by converting it into cooperation.

The shift from the ZSG to the NZSG perspective does not, of course, solve all problems of conflict in international relations or in other dimensions of life. Both Prisoner's Dilemma and Chicken games are mixed-motive nonzero-sum games which human beings do not always play according to the strategies prescribed by rationality. In the former, the player is tempted to choose a noncooperative strategy by suspicion that the other player will not cooperate; in the latter, the players must make a last-moment choice between prestige and survival. Glenn H. Snyder has drawn the following contrast:

> The spirit or leading theme of the prisoner's dilemma is that of the frustration of the mutual desire to cooperate. The spirit of a chicken game is that of a contest in which each party is trying to prevail over the other. In both games, perceptions of the other party's intentions are crucial, and the actors face a problem of establishing the credibility of their stated intentions. But in the prisoner's dilemma, establishing credibility means instilling *trust*, whereas in chicken it involves creating *fear*.[37]

Neither game, when applied to international relations, is likely to lead to optimistic conclusions. Anatol Rapoport has applied the Prisoner's Dilemma model to the problem of international disarmament and found that, although ideally both parties might prefer to benefit economically from disarmament, neither one can be sure of the long-range intentions of the other, and thus both pursue the more prudent course of maintaining a costly balance of armaments.[38] Critical confrontations between the nuclear superpowers—such as the Cuban Missile Crisis—have often been likened to the game of Chicken.[39] Schelling distinguishes between a game of Chicken in which one has been deliberately challenged in a test of nerves and a game into which two parties have been drawn by the course of events. He admits that in the real international world it is hard to know with which kind of crisis one is confronted.[40] In a dangerous international crisis requiring careful management the rules of procedure are not well defined.[41] Those who treat critical confrontations between superpowers as instances of Chicken usually do not want to press the analogy too far. In the Cuba Missile Crisis, Brams observes, "Neither side was eager to take any irreversible steps, such as the teenage driver in a game of Chicken might do by defiantly ripping off his steering wheel in full view of his adversary, thus foreclosing his alternative of swerving."[42]

There can be no doubt that it is highly desirable in the nuclear age to stress the elements of mutual interest and tacit cooperation in the avoidance of general war, in the hope that these will outweigh the elements of divergent interests and conflict. But the understandable desire to attenuate the dangerous excesses of international ideological conflict has perhaps led some analysts to overlook the fundamental difference between the *ought* and the *is*. The conduct of international politics would probably be more restrained if the political leaders of all the major powers were convinced that international politics is a non-zero-sum game in the nuclear age. However, for scholars to assert that it always has been so, and always will be necessarily so, is to propound conclusions which a serious study of history does not substantiate.

It might be more accurate to say that international politics is usually a non-zero-sum game for most "players," because most governments normally tend to observe rational limits in their decision-making processes. But in every age there may be some political-strategic adversaries who view their confrontation with each other as having certain characteristics analogous to those encountered in a two-person zero-sum game. Undoubtedly, much of the zero-sum quality that marks certain bilateral interstate relations in this century is a function of ideological attitudes combined with the dialectics of communications systems and mass politics. In some cases, leaders may feel compelled to pay lip service to the ideological objective of "the annihilation of the enemy" even if they have no serious intention of embarking upon an Armageddon during their tenure of rule. But if individuals and groups in one country speak frequently as if the bilateral relationship is a zero-sum game, their counterparts in the second country will sooner or later do likewise. It will always be important to distinguish the way in which a bilateral conflict is viewed by the governmental policymakers, by various politically conscious social groups, and by individuals. If an ideologically oriented group which perceives the conflict as a zero-sum game should seize control of the government, the conflict may indeed become a zero-sum game.

International Relations: Limitations of Game Theory

Those who would apply the game theoretical framework to the analysis of international politics require a greater precision of language than they have sometimes employed in the past. It is not enough to say merely that we are dealing with a non-zero-sum game. We must carefully define the structure of the game we are discussing: the players, the rules and objectives of the game, the payoffs and the values which the players attach to them, the whole context in which the game is played, and the interaction of the various strategies pursued. A specific game might appear to be a zero-sum game in the eyes of the country's leaders but not in the eyes of the whole people. Take, for example, World War II as it was waged between Germany and the Allied Powers. The strategic objective of "unconditional surrender" enunciated by Roosevelt and Churchill certainly made the war look like a zero-sum game to Hitler's Nazi regime because the latter could not possibly accept such terms and still survive politically, even though the German people could survive "unconditional surrender" and endure as a nation, albeit a divided one. In short, when two parties are striving toward mutually exclusive objectives and one succeeds and the other fails, this is a zero-sum game. If the contest ends in a complex compromise which leaves neither party entirely satisfied, but where both parties are willing to settle for less than their original objectives rather than bear the cost of prolonging the struggle, then this is a nonzero-sum game. Thus the zero-sumness or non-zero-sumness of a subgame in international politics must be defined in terms of the various alternative outcomes and payoffs as these are perceived by the players.

The difference between a ZSG and a NZSG does not, contrary to popular opinion, depend on whether the game is conceptualized in such a way that one side must survive while the other perishes. Extreme Communist ideologues might perceive their conflict with "capitalism" in this way, and so might extreme Arab nationalists describe the solution of the problem of "Israeli-occupied Palestine." But zero-sumness pertains to the exclusive winning or losing of a payoff, not necessarily to the players' survival except in a weird game of tic-tac-toe in which the loser forfeits his or her life, or in a game of Russian Roulette which goes on until one player dies. Fortunately, most zero-sum games are not so absurd, either in the parlor or in the international arena. Take, for example, the conflict between India and Pakistan over Kashmir. Control over this region is the payoff in a zero-sum game; as long as India retains control, Pakistan is deprived of it. But the Pakistanis may continue to hope that someday the situation may be reversed, just as a person who has lost a chess game to the opponent may aspire to win the next round. This raises the interesting question as to when both parties in a specific international conflict recognize that the zero-sum game is over and is not to be replayed. This might require an uncommonly high degree of political rationality. The frequent historic replay of zero-sum games between two states over the control of a disputed territory might eventually arouse political passions to such a point that the stakes are escalated far beyond the original objective of the game to include the physical integrity of the players.

In the final analysis, it is difficult in the extreme—perhaps impossible—for either the human mind or the world's largest computer to grasp the "game" of international politics in its utter complexity. A three-person parlor game in which a very limited number of simple moves and countermoves can be made may be reducible to mathematical analysis. However, the triangular relationship of the United States, the Soviet Union, and the People's Republic of China is comparable not to such a parlor game but to the "three body" problem in Newtonian physics which, as we noted previously, is still insoluble in a precise mathematical formula.[43] Moreover, it is impossible to conceive of a purely triangular relationship in which the interactions of those three powers are insulated from interactions with Western Europe, Eastern Europe, Japan, and other actors on the world scene. Nevertheless, although recognizing the limitations of game theory, we can still find it a useful means for suggesting hypotheses that may illuminate the study of strategic choices faced by foreign policy decision-makers.[44]

SCHELLING'S BARGAINING THEORY

Thomas C. Schelling of Harvard University, although widely regarded as a leading game theorist, is not primarily concerned with the mathematics of games. Like Morgenstern, he began as an economist and soon began to focus his attention upon bargaining.[45] In Schelling's work we find a combination of the social-psychological and the logical-strategic approaches to the subject of human conflict—conflict viewed not exclusively as the opposition of hostile forces, but rather as a more complex and delicate phenomenon in which antagonism and cooperation often subtly interact in the adversary relationship. His theory seeks to make use of game theory, organization and communication theory, and theory of evidence, choice, and collective decision. This strategic theory, according to Schelling,

> takes conflict for granted, but also assumes common interest between the adversaries; it assumes a 'rational' value-maximizing mode of behavior; and it focuses on the fact that each participant's 'best' choice of action depends on what he expects the other to do, and that 'strategic behavior' is concerned with influencing another's choice by working on his expectation of how one's own behavior is related to his.[46]

Schelling, then, is mainly interested in such problems as the conduct of negotiations, the maintenance of credible deterrence, the making of threats and promises, bluffing, doublecrossing, the waging of limited conflict, and the formulation of formal or tacit arms control policies. His writing reflects a conviction that in most international strategic situations the notion of the zero-sum game is simply irrelevant. In his view, the two superpowers cannot rationally suppose themselves engaged in a zero-sum rivalry that could be played out to the bitter end of a full-scale nuclear exchange. The resultant score of such a game would in all probability be not zero but minus two. (If one asks "minus two what?" the answer is, at the very least, "minus two superpowers.") Schelling therefore does not devote much attention to the rational analysis of this ultimate irrationality. Indeed, his "theory of interdependent decisions," as he prefers to call it, is addressed less to the *application* than to the threat of violence as a means of influencing another party's behavior. Going to war might be the height of folly under certain circumstances, but posing a controlled threat or risk of war might prove to be a strategically shrewd move.[47]

Although Schelling is very much interested in what constitutes rational behavior between parties in a conflict situation, he shies away from the notion that rationality can be neatly measured along a quantitative utility scale. This may be possible in respect to human action in the economic order in which a precise monetary standard is available.

But he deems the concept of utility as applied to international political and strategic decision-making much more ambiguous and fluid, and hence less relevant. Thus, instead of looking for the "minimax solution" to conflict situations, Schelling is more interested in what we might not inaptly call "motivational dialectics." He goes so far as to suggest that even though rationality is a desirable commodity, it is not always and under all circumstances desirable to *appear* rational.

> It is not a universal advantage in situations of conflict to be inalienably and manifestly rational in decision and motivation. . . . It is not true, as illustrated in the example of extortion, that in the face of a threat it is invariably an advantage to be rational, particularly if the fact of being rational or irrational cannot be concealed. It is not invariably an advantage, in the face of a threat, to have a communication system in good order, to have complete information, or to be in full command of one's own actions or of one's own assets. . . . The very notion that it may be a strategic advantage to relinquish certain options deliberately, or even to give up all control over one's future actions and make his responses automatic, seems to be a hard one to swallow.[48]

Schelling focuses particularly upon what is sometimes called the "limited adversary" relationship, or what he himself refers to as "the theory of precarious partnership or . . . incomplete antagonism."[49] This implies a situation in which parties to a conflict, despite their strategic opposition to each other, perceive some minimum mutual interest, even if this amounts to no more than the avoidance of reciprocal annihilation. Even when, for one reason or another, parties cannot carry on direct or overt communication with each other, they can nevertheless tacitly coordinate their moves by fixing upon certain salient points of common interest and converging expectation. He illustrates the possibility of tacit communication by citing several examples from nonhostile relationships in which two parties share an interest in finally arriving at the same meeting place.

If a husband and wife become separated in a department store, each might try to figure out where the other is most likely to go with a view to rendezvous. In another situation, two parachutists drop into the same vicinity at some distance from each other. In order to be rescued, they must get together quickly, but they cannot communicate directly concerning their exact location. Each one knows, however, that the other carries a copy of the same map of the area, showing a central salient feature (such as a bridge) which furnishes a focal point for coordinated behavior. In a third example, a number of people in New Haven, Connecticut, were told that they were to meet someone in New York city on a specified date, but they received no instructions as to the exact place or time. Since they could not communicate with the other party, they had to make an intelligent guess. A majority of those queried chose the information booth in Grand Central Station at high noon on the date given.[50]

It might be objected in reference to this last illustration that people taking the train from New Haven to New York always pass through Grand Central. But this need not vitiate the validity of Schelling's theory. Perhaps it only serves to demonstrate that choices based upon mutual expectation of convergent decisions reflect not merely abstract logic but also concrete historical experience—an input which might help to render prediction more reliable. There is no guarantee, of course, that this method of tacit bargaining will work in any particular two-party situation. Schelling modestly claims no more than that a shrewd selection of those convergence points that seem likely in the mind of one party to be relatively unique and unambiguous in the mind of the other party is superior to a system of purely random guesses as to a focal point of agreement.

Bargaining parties are not motivated solely by a desire to agree. Divergent interests skew the quest for convergence. But if agreement is finally reached, it means that forces for agreement proved stronger than forces for severance of negotiations. Moreover, although tacit coordination does not at first glance seem applicable to explicit bargaining in which formal communication is normal, nevertheless it is probably present even under explicit bargaining conditions. As examples, Schelling cites the tendency to "split the difference" in price haggling, and the recurring willingness to follow a conspicuous precedent embodied in an earlier compromise. Although the power to communicate alters a bargaining situation, it does not repeal the relevance of convergent expectations and the role of objective coordinating signals. Granted that in bargaining contests one side often manifests either greater power or a stronger determination to press for a unilaterally favorable settlement, still Schelling notes that the outcome can often be predicted "on some basis of some 'obvious' focus for agreement, some strong suggestion contained in the situation itself, without much regard to the merits of the case. . . ."[51]

Schelling contends that the limitation of conflict is not only theoretically possible but also historically actual. Recent cases in point include the mutual abstention from using gas weaponry in World War II and the various restrictions imposed upon the conduct of the Korean War with respect to geographical boundaries, the political identification of parties involved, the kinds of weapons employed, and the types of military operations permitted. Tacit agreements, he argues, require terms of reference which can be distinguished qualitatively, not just quantitatively. Thus Schelling would wish to preserve a clear firebreak between conventional and nuclear weapons on the battlefield, and would not recommend the deployment of such low-yield tactical nuclear weapons in Europe as to provide a continuum that would blur the distinction and render escalation inevitable. In short, the step levels of conflict limitation must be unambiguous so that they can be clearly perceived under the pressures of time and emotional confusion which crisis generates in any decision-making system.[52]

Schelling also suggests that it may be possible to make arrangements prior to the outbreak of conflict which increase the likelihood that limits could be observed once hostilities are under way. This involves keeping channels of communication open, clarifying in advance the authority and authenticity of messages calculated to reduce the pressures for uncontrollable escalation, and identifying parties who might plausibly act as intermediaries. But he concedes that there are certain exigencies in the strategy of threats, bluffs, and deterrents which may render one or both superpowers in the nuclear age reluctant to enter into such contingency plans as might reduce the fear of unrestrained war. In other words, the strategic condition of mutual nuclear deterrence might be gradually undermined by a growing assumption that one or both adversaries would seek desperately to keep war limited once it had been initiated and to terminate it as soon as possible. But the fact that advance preparations by one side are not reciprocated by the other at the time does not necessarily mean that they are useless. Unilateral prior signaling might later prove advantageous if the message is remembered by the adversary after the onset of the crisis.[53]

Perhaps Schelling's principal contribution to this sector of international relations theory is his stress upon the necessity of avoiding extreme formulations. At one extreme of the spectrum he sees the zero-sum game as the limiting case of pure conflict, not as a point of departure for realistic strategic analysis. At the opposite extreme he places the "pure collaboration" game in which there is no divergent interest because the players always win or lose together. Schelling is primarily interested in the situations which lie in between—that is, in those bargaining or "mixed-motive" games that contain elements of both conflict and mutual dependence, of divergence and convergence of interest, of secrecy and revelation—all in what he calls the "spiral of reciprocal expectations,"[54] which is usually a matter more of psychological than of mathematical calculus.

The major objective in bargaining, Schelling constantly reiterates, is for each party to make commitments, threats, and promises credible to the other party, so that the latter cannot conclude that the former is bluffing. If your adversary thinks that you are leaving yourself an avenue of retreat, he or she will take neither your commitment nor your threat seriously. Hence there may be a strategic advantage in making an overt commitment from which there can be no retreat and in communicating this clearly to the adversary. This can be achieved by staking your reputation on the adherence to the commitment or the execution of the threat, or by making it clear that if the other party commits an act which you wish to deter, you will have no flexibility in respect to punishing the party simply because you have already set up an automatic response which is irreversible. This makes the threat of punishment not merely probable but certain, and the adversary must take this into account before deciding to make a move.[55] It is the rich variety of subtle signaling problems associated with this type of political game that makes Schelling's *The Strategy of Conflict* one of the most interesting and readable works in international relations theory.

SIMULATION IN INTERNATIONAL RELATIONS

Many teachers of international relations courses are old enough to remember the simulation games which appeared on the market prior to World War II, for example, *Monopoly and Politics.* Younger teachers as well as students may have played one or more of the several new games which have been developing during the past decade or so, specifically geared to international political, economic, and military interaction processes—*1914, Blitzkrieg, Diplomacy, Oil War, Sinai,* and *World War III.* The newer games incorporate at least three elements: (1) an effort to achieve historical accuracy in a simplified way; (2) the quantification of units, space, and time; and (3) the element of luck (involving a roll of the dice and reference to a computerized outcomes table). Some of the games people play are "environment poor," and some are "environment rich." The former involve minimal scenarios, and their rules are rather easily comprehended by all players; the latter begin with intricate scenarios, and the rules can be free-wheeling and subtle enough to produce conflicts over their interpretation and even their development as the game proceeds.[56]

Simulation is different from game theory and gaming, although related to them. Whereas game theory seeks the optimum mathematically rational strategy for playing a game (purely as a game, with no reference to the "real world"), simulation theory deals with a "let's pretend" situation. A simulation experiment is a game that has been designed not merely for the sake of "playing the game," but rather for the purpose of demonstrating a valid truth about actual social processes through the unfolding of an artifically constructed yet dynamic model. Thus simulation techniques are essentially laboratory techniques or nonlaboratory contrivances that permit the study of replicated human behavior. Through the use of these techniques the researcher attempts to learn something significant about a complex phenomenon "out there," which he cannot control, by creating "in here" a more simplified version of that phenomenon that he can control and that is in some way analogous or isomorphic. Social scientists have long complained that it is virtually impossible to obtain from the real world certain kinds of data needed to verify their hypotheses. The experimental method of simulation represents an effort to compensate for these data deficiencies.[57]

War Gaming and the Varieties of Simulation

Simulation techniques have found many uses in this century. War games and other exercises in strategic analysis have a long history that perhaps reflects the disposition of people in widely separated cultures to regard war itself as containing a "play element."[58] Every strategic planner has some sort of model or simulation in mind when attempting to forecast the outcome of a contest. The notion of a "scenario" to describe the situation at the start of the game (even though the term "scenario" is a modern importation) was always implicit in military gaming. Formalized political-military gaming with government personnel as participants made its appearance in the period between the two World Wars, and became quite common after 1945 in the work of the RAND Corporation and other institutes.[59] Simulation devices, including moot courts and mock nominating conventions, were familiar fixtures of the American educational scene before World War II.[60] Since the late 1950s, simulation has become a widely accepted teaching tool in international relations at both collegiate and high school levels.

Simulation may assume a variety of forms, depending upon the political knowledge-level and experience of the participants; the total resources available, including personnel, physical facilities, and administrative support; and the purpose intended to be served by the exercise. Simulation experiments in the field of international relations are commonly designed with a view toward one or perhaps a combination of the following objectives: (1) teaching and training students; (2) advancing the policy sciences and clarifying policy alternatives through the interaction of professional practitioners; and (3) promoting theoretical research and analysis through the testing of social science hypotheses. It is important to keep distinct these three functions of "political gaming," at least conceptually.

The Uses and Limitations of Simulation

Many proponents of simulation techniques are convinced that their greatest utility is in teaching. In one rather well-known version, Inter-Nation Simulation, which was developed as an educational device by Harold Guetzkow, participants role play the key domestic and foreign policy decision-makers of five or six, fictitious states. (Fictitious rather than real states are used so that subjects can make their decisions in response to the interactive process of the game, uncomplicated by presuppositions and theories as to how the leaders of actual countries ought to act in various situations.)[61] Players learn about their roles and their country situations by reading background papers. They learn the game both by orienting themselves to its rules and even more by playing it. This, like the great majority of all political games, is characterized by the compression of real time—for example, a few hours of play might be made to represent a month or a year of historical time. National goals may be either given at the outset or defined by the participants as play proceeds. Periodically, each nation is assigned basic resources which can be allocated by the leaders' choices to internal or external purposes. Aside from national goals, action is guided by the presumed desire of the decision-makers to remain in office. They can be replaced if either domestic consumer satisfaction or national security falls below a minimum standard that fluctuates somewhat arbitrarily according to rules that permit differentiating democratic from totalitarian regimes. The game permits both bilateral and multilateral communications—the former through "restricted messages" and the latter through a "world newspaper."[62] Simulation experiments may involve the periodic feeding of game results to a computer for the purpose of speeding up the evaluation of decision-consequences according to a preprogrammed formula, but computerization is not a necessary part of simulation.

SIMULATION AS A TEACHING DEVICE

Advocates of simulation for teaching purposes argue that participation in a game enables a student to become actively involved in an interactive process which emulates selected basic features of international reality. Those educators who evaluate gaming most highly are likely to be those who believe that "doing something" is a superior learning experience to "hearing something." They point out that games stimulate interest and motivation essentially because they are "fun"; they provide an opportunity for students to test their theoretical knowledge gained from reading, lectures, and other sources; they introduce students to the concrete pressures that impinge upon the policymakers, the dilemmas that face them, and the constrictions that limited resources place upon them; they enable students to experience decision-making in a group context; the game furnishes a glimpse into a model world which students can grasp more easily than they can the real international system.[63]

Simulation as a heuristic device, however, is not without its critics. It has been pointed out that a substantial proportion of students can be expected to be uninterested or skeptical; that gaming may arouse interest in the fun of the game without producing a serious attitude toward the study of international relations; that students seldom know enough about either the real political world or the roles they are supposed to play to act "even remotely as real-world politicians do in making their institutions and their political machinery work."[64] In view of these pros and cons, the promises and the problems, each teacher has to decide whether his or her students will approach the game with sufficient maturity and seriousness of purpose to warrant the investment of teaching time which simulation requires.

GAMING AND THE POLICY SCIENCES

In games designed to serve the policy sciences, an effort is usually made to achieve as much "realism" as possible. Professional policymakers generally derive greater profit by representing officials not of fictitious countries but of actual states engaged in the subtleties and complexities of the international interactive process which professionals understand best. Players might be instructed to play either "predicted strategies" (based upon the way specific governments would be expected to behave from historical experience) or "optimal strategies" (based upon what the individual deems best under the circumstances, regardless of existing domestic and other constraints) or a combination of the two approaches. Frequently the element of "nature" or "fate" is introduced into the game by allowing the control group to provide for such unexpected events as technological breakthroughs, the death of key leaders, and the outbreak of civil turbulence. Occasionally the "scenario" will be used to project the opening of the game sufficiently far into the future to prevent the simulation from being overtaken by daily news developments. Participants have found that by participating in a gaming experiment of a critical international problem they have acquired fresh insights into the complexities of situations, into the unexpected turns which events might take, and into the psychological-moral-intellectual pressures and uncertainties which accompany the making of foreign policy decisions.[65] It is impossible, however, from the outcome of a "crisis game" to predict the actual outcome of a real-world political encounter, no matter how many times the game is played with similar results.

GAMING AND THEORY-BUILDING

The third principal use of political gaming is in the area of research and theory-building. Here the primary objective is not to provide a worthwhile personal experience via the gaming process either to students or to policymakers, but rather to test social science hypotheses. The utility of simulation as a tool for confirming or disconfirming theoretical propositions about the international system is a matter of considerable controversy within the field of international relations theorists and among the "simulators" themselves. One might admit that from carefully observing the behavior of a group of experienced policymakers in a realistically simulated crisis (e.g., a future Berlin crisis), one might be able to make some interesting inferences concerning the political values, strategic preconceptions, psychological attitudes, and preferred methods of conflict management which would be likely to characterize those particular policymakers if a real crisis were soon to arise in a closely similar form. But this, after all, would be a highly particularized and concretized kind of prediction, more appropriate to diplomatic intelligence than to social science. The social scientist is much more interested in universally applicable generalizations than in those subtle nuances of unique historical situations which comprise the special intellectual competence of the country or area expert. Policymakers wish to know as much as possible about "this" particular crisis or policy situation so that they can favorably influence its outcome. Social scientists, on the other hand, are not primarily oriented to "this" situation. Their principal concern is with universal generalizations and probabilities. Of what use can simulation be to them in this more comprehensive quest?

The crucial question is: What is the relation between a game and reality? What can we learn about the real political world from empirically observing the results of political gaming? A game, after all, is only an analogical model, which may or may not be partially parallel to the real world in respect to both elements and interactive processes, depending upon the intelligence that has gone into the construction of the model combined with the maturity and seriousness with which the game is played out. Eugene J. Meehan of Brandeis University lays down the following useful guidelines:

> If a model is used as an aid to explanation, then the interaction of elements in the system is prime; if the model is used for prediction, the outcome of dynamic processes in model and empirical world must be similar. . . . Models are always partial and approximate, as are analogies. It follows that there will be properties of observed reality not duplicated in the model, at least potentially, and it is always possible that models have properties that are not duplicated in the empirical world. Furthermore, models and analogies may be useful in creating some expectations with regard to reality (supposing them to have congruence with reality) but may be quite useless and even misleading in other respects.[66]

THE GAME WORLD AND THE REAL WORLD

The first question to be asked is whether the game is "isomorphic" or congruent with reality? Richard E. Dawson has implicitly recognized the need for traditional political knowledge in simulation experiments when he noted that before researchers can validly model a real political system, they have to know a great deal about the workings of that system.[67] It is not enough that a game be "realistic" in flavor. In its substantive details, a game might bear a superficial resemblance to a real-world political situation and yet be quite unlike reality in the playing, that is, in its basic dynamic processual features.

Snyder asks whether participants can ever escape the realization that what they are involved in is only a game and not "the real thing." He then cites evidence to the effect that people can become totally absorbed in the simulation exercise.[68] But the fact remains that total absorption in a game does not necessarily bridge the gap between simulation and reality. We are faced here with such problems as the compression of time and the concomitant pressure of hurried decisions from a sketchy information base; the selection of a small number of nations out of the whole complex international system; the cultural provincialism of nearly all gaming experiments to date—virtually all decision-makers have been Americans; the fact that national decisions are made by a small number of decision-makers, completely abstracted from an institutionalized context; and the realization that the reward-punishment matrix and indeed the whole sociopsychological environment of decision-making in a game are quite different from those in real life.

For guidance in constructing models and evaluating the results of simulated international interaction, students of simulation have turned to the writings of scholars in other fields, both traditional and contemporary, who have theorized about international relations. Similarly, models of international simulation have provided for the observation of the behavior of actor participants in differing environments and in a multiplicity of relationships over time. Although simulation models have necessarily been more parsimonious than the literature of international relations in general, both in variables under investigation and in the description of international relationships, students of simulation have attempted to compare simulation models with models explicit or implicit in international relations literature to compare the *results* of simulation runs with empirically derived descriptions of international behavior, for example, in crisis simulations.[69]

GAMING AND SIMULATION: THE DEVELOPMENT OF INTERNATIONAL RELATIONS

To summarize, it can be said that simulation experiments are regarded as potentially useful heuristic devices by many teachers of international relations, provided that suitable facilities are available and the students are properly motivated to learn from them. But games are time consuming and they require very careful planning and administration. The teacher should not take it for granted that simulation is in all circumstances worthwhile merely because it gets the students "actively involved." Policy-oriented games played by experienced decision-makers can also prove valuable tools for the improved understanding of specific foreign policy problems, insofar as they may cast light upon factors and suggest alternatives which might otherwise be overlooked. But here, too, it must be recognized that the best games take several days or even a few weeks to run, and the time which government officials can devote to such exercises is strictly limited. As for the use of simulation in research and theory-building, some writers are more optimistic than others about the possibility of using political games to validate hypotheses about the real political world. But nearly all the authorities in this area cautiously refrain from asserting that simulation techniques can produce any predictive capability. Most would probably agree that much more needs to be known before simulation can be accepted as a reliable tool for the verification of theory.

Notes

1. See Johan Huizinga, *Homo Ludens: A Study of the Play Element in Culture* (Boston: Beacon, 1955); and James S. Coleman, "Games as Vehicles for Social Theory," *American Behavioral Scientist*, 12 (1969), 2–6.
2. These and other gamelike situations are cited for heuristic purposes by Thomas C. Schelling, whose theories are summarized in a subsequent section of this chapter.
3. See Barry R. Schlenker and Thomas V. Bonoma, "Fun and Games: The Validity of Games for the Study of Conflict," *The Journal of Conflict Resolution*, 22 (March 1978), 9–13, where the authors describe claims that have been put forth on behalf of games. They also cite the arguments that games enable us to study deviations of individual behavior from normative criteria of rationality and to test hypotheses derived from theories of conflict, power, and bargaining.
4. Anatol Rapoport, "The Use and Misuse of Game Theory," *Scientific American*, CCVII (December 1962), 118. See also Martin Shubik, "Game Theory and the Study of Social Behavior: An Introductory Exposition," in Martin Shubik, ed., *Game Theory and Related Approaches to Social Behavior* (New York: Wiley, 1964), pp. 4–5.
5. Barry Schlenker and Thomas Bonoma, op. cit., pp. 13–14.
6. Ibid., pp. 10–11.
7. Ibid., p. 8. See also Martin Shubik, *Games for Society, Business and War: Towards a Theory of Gaming* (New York: Elsevier, 1975), chap. 1, especially p. 14.
8. Thomas C. Schelling, *The Strategy of Conflict* (New York: Oxford University Press [Galaxy Books], 1963), pp. 9–10. A game has also been defined as a structural abstraction of a situation in which the outcomes of two or more persons in interaction are conjoint but uncertain. J. Tedeschi et al., *Conflict, Power and Games* (Chicago: Aldine, 1973), p. 2.
9. John von Neumann and Oskar Morgenstern, *Theory of Games and Economic Behavior* (Princeton: Princeton University Press, 1944, 1953).
10. It should be stressed that this holds for simpler games. It has not yet proved possible, even with computers, to work out the "perfect" strategy for such a game as chess which potentially involves trillions of alternate choices, depending upon the interaction of the two players' choices. See Martin Shubik, ed., *Game Theory and Related Approaches*, op. cit., p. 12.
11. As Anatol Rapoport has asserted quite cogently, a theory is a collection of theorems, and a theorem "is a proposition which is a strict logical consequence of cer-

tain definitions and other propositions." "Various Meanings of 'Theory,'" *American Political Science Review*, LII (December 1958), 973. He notes that Freudian "depth psychology" is "singularly poor in predictive capacity, either deterministic or statistical" (ibid., p. 982), but he does not suggest that the reason for this perhaps resides in the basic irrationality of the subject matter. If one really assumes the irrationality of behavior, a person must at the same time accept its unpredictability, at least for the time being, until the behavior becomes rationally penetrable. In the social universe, observers can ascribe no greater rationality to their own theoretical explanation of a phenomenon than they are willing to attribute to the "decision-makers" who collectively comprise the action-situation or process they are trying to describe and explain. Rapoport does concede, however, that the special merits of game theory derive from its assumption of "perfectly rational players" (ibid., p. 984). This may, of course, also constitute a major weakness if, in contrast to Freudian psychoanalytic theory which emphasizes irrationality, game theory runs to the opposite extreme and places excessive stress upon the mathematically rational factors which enter into human decisional behavior. The notion of "second guessing" may be more psychological than logical-mathematical. Which strategic philosophy do good strategists adopt? Do they play the board, or do they play the opponent? Do they formulate their strategy on the basis of a mathematical computation of available moves, or do they formulate it much as psychological warfare experts would try to size up their adversary? Rapoport, who is a mathematician-psychologist-game theorist at the University of Michigan, concedes that pure game theory is essentially mathematical and hence contains no uncertainties. "Although the drama of games of strategy is strongly linked with the psychological aspects of the conflict, game theory is not concerned with these aspects. Game theory, so to speak, plays the board. It is concerned only with the logical aspects of strategy. It prescribes the same line of play against a master as it does against a beginner." "The Use and Misuse of Game Theory," *Scientific American*, CCVII (December 1962), 110.

12. Martin Shubik, *Games for Society, Business and War*, op. cit., pp. 50 and 56.
13. Details of a simple game may help the student to envisage the game. Let us call it Defenders and Attackers. The latter can strike at either of two towns. The Defenders can fully protect only one. If the Defenders select the right town and meet the Attackers, the latter will be destroyed. If Defenders select one town and Attackers select the other, the town is destroyed. Martin Shubik, "The Uses of Game Theory," in James C. Charlesworth, ed., *Contemporary Political Analysis* (New York: The Free Press, 1967), p. 247.
14. Martin Shubik, "Game Theory and the Study of Social Behavior," op. cit., pp. 15–17.
15. Martin Shubik, "The Uses of Game Theory," in Charlesworth, ed., op. cit., p. 248. See also his *Games for Society, Business and War*, op. cit., pp. 93–97. "Social, political, and economic problems," Shubik notes, "almost always call for a non-zero-sum formulation." Ibid., pp. 97–98.
16. The mathematicization of utilities or value preferences is always a tenuous business. Even in respect to zero-sum games, Thomas C. Schelling notes that the value systems of two individuals are incommensurate. "If two feudal noblemen play a game of cards, one to lose his thumb if he loses and the other to lose his eyesight, the game is 'zero-sum' (as long as neither cares about the other's gain) and there may be no way of comparing what they risk losing. It is precisely *because* their value systems are incommensurable that, if their interests are strictly opposed, we can arbitrarily represent them by scales of value that make the scores of payoffs add up in every cell to zero." "What is Game Theory?" in Charlesworth, ed., op. cit., p. 216. An approach which contrasts with that of Schelling is presented by Morton A. Kaplan in his discussion of the work of Duncan Luce and Howard Raiffa. In an analysis of

some variant games, Kaplan agrees with Luce and Raiffa that in certain games the outcome will be determined by the *psychologies* of the players. "A Note on Game Theory and Bargaining," in Morton A. Kaplan, ed., *New Approaches to International Relations* (New York: St. Martin's, 1968), pp. 507–509.

17. Many descriptions of Prisoner's Dilemma can be found. See A. W. Tucker and P. Wolfe, eds., *Contributions to the Theory of Games,* vol. III, *Annals of Mathematic Studies,* No. 39 (Princeton: Princeton University Press, 1957); R. Duncan Luce and Howard Raiffa, *Games and Decisions* (New York: Wiley, 1957); pp. 94ff; Anatol Rapoport and A. M. Ghammah, *Prisoner's Dilemma* (Ann Arbor: University of Michigan Press, 1965); and Martin Shubik, "The Uses of Game Theory," in Charlesworth, ed., op. cit., pp. 264–268. The problem of "trust" and "suspicion" between players in mixed-motive games has been dealt with by Morton Deutsch, "Trust and Suspicion," *Journal of Conflict Resolution* IV (December 1958), and by Anatol Rapoport, "Formal Games as Probing Tools for Investigating Behavior Motivated by Trust and Suspicion," *Journal of Conflict Resolution,* VII (September 1963), 570–579. Two psychologists at Kent State University conducted gaming experiments on a variation of Prisoner's Dilemma in which they separated "temptation" (i.e., the desire to obtain the largest payoff by being the only defector) from "mistrust" (i.e., the fear that the other would like to be the lone defector), and found that "temptation" is a more likely source of noncooperative behavior than is "mistrust." V. Edwin Bixenstine and Hazel Blundell, "Control of Choices Exerted by Structural Factors in Two-Person, Non-Zero-Sum Games," *Journal of Conflict Resolution,* X (December 1966), especially p. 482.

18. Alvin Scodel, J. Sayer Minas, Philburn Ratoosh, and Milton Lipetz, "Some Descriptive Aspects of Two-Person Non-Zero-Sum Games," *Journal of Conflict Resolution,* III (June 1959), 115. See also p. 118.

19. J. I. Shaw and C. Thorslund, "Varying Patterns of Reward Cooperation: The Effects in a Prisoner's Dilemma Game," *Journal of Conflict Resolution,* 19 (March 1975), 108–122.

20. See Robert Radlow, "An Experimental Study of 'Cooperation' in the Prisoner's Dilemma Game," *Journal of Conflict Resolution,* IX (June 1965); H. H. Kelley et al., "A Comparative Experimental Study of Negotiation Behavior," *Journal of Personality and Social Psychology,* 16 (November 1970), 411–438; P. S. Gallo and J. D. Winchell, "Matrix Indices, Large Rewards and Cooperative Behavior in a Prisoner's Dilemma Game," *Journal of Social Psychology,* 8 (1970), 235–241; S. Oskamp and
C. Kleinke, "Amount of Reward as Variable in the Prisoner's Dilemma Game," *Journal of Personality and Social Psychology,* 16 (September 1970), 133–140.

21. Daniel R. Lutzker, "Sex Role, Cooperation and Competition in a Two-Person, Non-Zero-Sum Game," *Journal of Conflict Resolution,* V (December 1961), 366–368. See also Philip S. Gallo, Jr., and Charles G. McClintock, "Cooperative and Competitive Behavior in Mixed-Motive Games," *Journal of Conflict Resolution,* IX (March 1965), 68–78; and J. T. Tedeschi et al., "Start Effect and Response Bias in the Prisoner's Dilemma Game," *Psychonomic Science,* 11 (1968).

22. David W. Conrath, "Sex Role and 'Cooperation' in the Game of Chicken," *Journal of Conflict Resolution,* XVI (September 1972), 433–443. For additional subtle sex-related differences see William B. Lacy, "Assumptions of Human Nature and Initial Expectations and Behavior as Mediators of Sex Effects in Prisoner's Dilemma Research," *Journal of Conflict Resolution,* 22 (June 1978), 269–281.

23. Ibid., 434.

24. Ibid., 442.

25. C. Nemeth, "A Critical Analysis of Research Utilizing the Prisoner's Dilemma Paradigm for the Study of Bargaining," in Leonard Berkowitz, ed., *Advances in Ex-*

perimental Social Psychology, vol. 6 (New York: Academic, 1972) p. 204. See also Jeffrey Pincus and V. Edwin Bixenstine, "Cooperation in the Decomposed Prisoner's Dilemma Game: A Question of Revealing or Concealing Information," *Journal of Conflict Resolution,* XXI (September 1977), 519–530.

26. Barry Schlenker and Thomas Bonoma, op. cit., pp. 14–15. The December 1975 issue of the *Journal of Conflict Resolution* carried seven articles on the subject.

27. Martin Shubik, *Games for Society, Business and War,* op. cit., p. 32.

28. Anatol Rapoport and C. Orwant, "Experimental Games: A Review," *Behavioral Science,* VII (January 1962), 1–37.

29. Abraham Kaplan, "Mathematics and Social Analysis," *Commentary,* VII (September 1952), 284. The mathematical and psychostrategic intricacies of the three-person game can be appreciated by reading William H. Riker, "Bargaining in a Three-Person Game," *American Political Science Review,* LXI (September 1967), 642–656.

30. For theoretical insights into the formation and dissolution of coalitions, see Chapter 10 and the following works: George F. Liska, *Nations in Alliance: The Limits of Interdependence* (Baltimore, Md.: The Johns Hopkins Press, 1962); William R. Riker, *The Theory of Political Coalitions* (New Haven: Yale University Press, 1962); Julian R. Friedman, Christopher Bladen, and Steven Rosen, *Alliance in International Studies* (Boston: Allyn & Bacon, 1970); Swen Groennings, E. W. Kelley, and Michael Leiserson, eds., *The Study of Coalition Behavior: Theoretical Perspectives and Cases from Four Continents* (New York: Holt, Rinehart and Winston, 1970); and Martin Shubik, *Games for Society, Business and War,* op. cit., pp. 49–51, 149–151, 170, and 259–260.

31. James Newman, for example, has written: "The theory of games can fairly be said to have laid the foundation for a systematic and penetrating mathematical treatment of a vast range of problems in social science. . . . The theory of games is today regarded as the most promising mathematical tool yet devised for the analysis of man's social relations." *The World of Mathematics,* vol. II (New York: Simon & Schuster, 1956), p. 1265. See also Colonel Francis X. Kane, U.S.A.F., "Security Is Too Important to Be Left to Computers," *Fortune,* LXX (April 1964), 146–147. "In order to construct models and manipulate them mathematically, we need masses of data on repeated events. This necessitates the discarding of data on individual events that do not fit into the mass. Such unique events lie principally in the field of decisions that have occurred only once in history—e.g., the Japanese decision to attack Pearl Harbor, the United States decision to defend South Korea, the Soviet decision to put missiles into Communist Cuba. These individual acts cannot be handled by scientific methodology." In England, R. H. S. Crossman, P. M. S. Blackett, Sir Solly Zuckerman, and Bertrand Russell, and in the United States, Stuart Highes, David Reisman, Michael Macoby, Arthur Waskow, and Eugene Rabinowitch have been numbered among the critics of "game theory" strategists. See Albert Wohlstetter, "Sin and Games in America," in Martin Shubik, ed., *Game Theory and Related Approaches,* op. cit., pp. 209–225.

32. Martin Shubik, *Games for Society, Business and War,* op. cit., p. ix.

33. See Chapter 11, p. 476.

34. William D. Coplin, *Introduction to International Politics: A Theoretical Overview* (Chicago: Markham, 1971), pp. 258–269.

35. Joseph Frankel, *Contemporary International Theory and the Behavior of States* (New York: Oxford University Press, 1973), p. 96.

36. John W. Burton, "Resolution of Conflict," *International Studies Quarterly,* 16 (March 1972), 5–30.

37. Glenn H. Snyder, " 'Prisoner's Dilemma' and 'Chicken' Models in International Politics," *International Studies Quarterly,* 15 (March 1971), 84.

38. Anatol Rapoport, *Strategy and Conscience* (New York: Harper & Row, 1964), pp. 48–52.
39. See Steven J. Brams, *Game Theory and Politics* (New York: The Free Press, 1975), pp. 39–47; Thomas C. Schelling, *Arms and Influence* (New Haven: Yale University Press, 1966), pp. 120–123.
40. Ibid., p. 121.
41. Martin Shubik, op. cit., p. 37.
42. Steven J. Brams, op. cit., p. 42.
43. Pierre Maillard, "The Effect of China on Soviet-American Relations," in *Soviet-American Relations and World Order: The Two and the Many*, Adelphi Papers, No. 66 (London: Institute for Strategic Studies, 1970).
44. Steven J. Brams, op. cit., p. 50.
45. Thomas C. Schelling, *National Income Behavior: An Introduction to Algebraic Analysis* (New York: McGraw-Hill, 1951), and "An Essay on Bargaining," *American Economic Review*, XLVI (June 1956), 281–306.
46. Thomas C. Schelling, *The Strategy of Conflict* (New York: Oxford University Press, 1963), p. 15.
47. Ibid., p. 15. Schelling notes that "inmates of mental hospitals often seem to cultivate, deliberately or instinctively, value systems that make them less susceptible to disciplinary threats and more capable of exercising coercion themselves." A self-destructive attitude expressed as a threat ("I'll cut a vein in my arm if you don't let me . . .") can put an "irrational" person in an advantageous position vis-à-vis a "rational" one. Ibid., p. 17.
48. Ibid., pp. 18–19.
49. Ibid., p. 15.
50. For these and analogous examples, see ibid., pp. 53–58.
51. Ibid., p. 68. See also pp. 71–74, where he speaks of the "mutually identifiable resting place," the search for which characterizes both tacit and explicit bargaining. "If one is to make a finite concession that is not to be interpreted as capitulation, he needs an obvious place to stop." Ibid., p. 71.
52. Ibid., pp. 74–77.
53. Ibid., pp. 77–80. For other discussions by Schelling of the problems of limiting conflict, see his "Reciprocal Measures for Arms Stabilization," in Donald G. Brennan, ed., *Arms Control, Disarmament and National Security (New York: Braziller, 1961);* see also Thomas C. Schelling and Morton H. Halperin, *Strategy and Arms Control* (New York: The Twentieth Century Fund, 1961), especially chaps. 2 and 8.
54. Thomas C. Schelling, *The Strategy of Conflict*, op. cit., p. 87.
55. Ibid., pp. 22–46, 119–139. "Hardly anything epitomizes strategic behavior in the mixed motive game so much as the advantage of being able to adopt a mode of behavior that the other party will take for granted." Ibid., p. 160.
56. Martin Shubik, op. cit., pp. 9–17.
57. Richard C. Snyder, "Some Perspectives on the Use of Experimental Techniques in the Study of International Relations," in Harold Guetzkow et al., *Simulation in International Relations: Developments for Research and Teaching* (Englewood Cliffs, N.J.: Prentice-Hall, 1963), pp. 2–5.
58. Johan Huizinga, op. cit., chap. V, "Play and War," pp. 89–104.
59. Herbert Goldhamer and Hans Speier, "Some Observations on Political Gaming," *World Politics*, XII (October 1959); reprinted in James N. Rosenau, ed., *International Politics and Foreign Policy: A Reader in Research and Theory* (New York: The Free Press, 1961), pp. 498–499.
60. Lincoln P. Bloomfield and Norman J. Padelford, "Three Experiments in Political Gaming," *American Political Science Review*, LIII (December 1959), 1105.
61. The notion of relating game decisions to personality factors was given an interest-

ing reverse application in a study designed to investigate the use of an actual historical situation to validate simulation. An effort was made (with somewhat inconclusive results) to select participants for the roles of such figures as Edward Grey, Raymond Poincaré, the Kaiser, and the Tsar by matching personality characteristics as much as possible. See Charles F. Hermann and Margaret G. Hermann, "An Attempt to Simulate the Outbreak of World War I," *American Political Science Review*, LXI (June 1967), especially pp. 404–405.

62. Harold Guetzkow, "A Use of Simulation in the Study of Inter-Nation Relations," in Guetzkow et al., op. cit., pp. 24–38. This is a reprint of his article which appeared in *Behavioral Science*, V (July 1959). For a description of student games which involved a specific international crisis, see Bloomfield and Padelford. op. cit., pp. 1107ff.

63. Chadwick F. Alger, "Use of the Inter-Nation Simulation in Undergraduate Teaching," in Guetzkow et al., op. cit., pp. 152–154.

64. Bernard C. Cohen, "Political Gaming in the Classroom," *Journal of Politics*, XXIV (May 1962), 374. Cohen is quite skeptical in regard to what it is that the students find interesting about the game, as well as their level of political knowledge, their serious desire to emulate real decision-makers, and their willingness even to observe the basic rules of the game, compared with their determination to make sport of their personal acquaintances who are supposed to represent "foreign countries." For evidence that simulation is not superior to the case study as a teaching device, see James A. Robinson et al., "Teaching with Inter-Nation Simulation and Case Studies," *American Political Science Review*, LX (March 1966), 53–65.

65. Herbert Goldhamer and Hans Speier, in Rosenau, ed., op. cit., pp. 499–502. Richard E. Barringer and Barton Whaley report that "the politicial-military game is a most intense and vivid experience, seemingly for even the most sophisticated individuals," that the insights gained depend largely upon the knowledge and experience of the participant and that the game suggests *unanticipated* policy alternatives. "The M.I.T. Political-Military Gaming Experience," *Orbis*, IX (Summer 1965), 444–448.

66. Eugene J. Meehan, *Contemporary Political Thought: A Critical Study* (Homewood, Ill.: Dorsey, 1967), pp. 31–32.

67. Richard E. Dawson, "Simulation in the Social Sciences," in Harold Guetzkow, ed., *Simulation in Social Sciences* (Englewood Cliffs, N.J.: Prentice-Hall, 1962), pp. 13ff.

68. Richard C. Snyder, "Some Perspectives on the Use of Experimental Techniques in the Study of International Relations," op. cit., pp. 12–14.

69. See, for example, William D. Coplin, "Inter-Nation Simulation and Contemporary Theories of International Relations," *American Political Science Review*, IX (September 1966), 562–578; Richard W. Chadwick, "An Empirical Test of Five Assumptions in an Inter-Nation Simulation about National Political Systems," *General Systems*, XII (1967), 177–192; Walter C. Clemens, Jr., "A Propositional Analysis of the International Relations Theory in Temper—A Computer Simulation of Cold War Conflict," in William D. Coplin, ed., *Simulation in the Study of Politics* (Chicago: Markham, 1968), pp. 59–101.

Chapter 13
International Studies:
Beyond the 1970s

E. H. Carr has suggested that "when the human mind begins to exercise itself in some field an initial stage occurs in which the element of wish or purpose is overwhelmingly strong, and the inclination to analyze facts and means weak or nonexistent."[1] Whatever the validity of this statement in the development of other disciplines it describes the growth of international relations, especially in its formative years between the two World Wars.[2] Since the early twentieth century, the study of international relations has passed through three stages which may be characterized as utopian, realist, and behavioral, or stated differently, normative, empirical-normative, and behavioral-quantitative.[3] By the end of the 1960s the study of international relations had entered a fourth phase.[4] If the 1960s was a decade in which broad theoretical constructs were developed by what James N. Rosenau has termed the "first generation I.R. scientists," "those committed to the scientific study of international relations more recently have restricted their efforts by and large to more narrowly defined concepts and research. They have refined and tested theories, or propositions drawn from the broader theoretical frameworks of the preceding period. According to Rosenau, "The first generation analysts tended to be practitioners of a 'revolutionary' science while their successors are inclined to adhere to the practices of a 'normal' science."[5] Elsewhere in a less sanguine analysis, Rosenau has noted that the dearth of funding since the 1960s for large-scale projects has forced scholars to focus upon "secondary analysis, if not in third, fourth, fifth, and sixth passes at the same materials." In somewhat of a self-criticism, he maintains that: "The events of the late 1960s both corresponded with and fostered a realization that our capability, game-theoretic, policymaking, and systemic models were insufficient to the practices of world politics in the 1970s."[6] No existing paradigm in itself seems adequate, he asserts, to the study of international relations in the late twentieth century. Other assessments of the current status of international relations theory and research reflect this perspective: Our understanding of the contemporary international system allegedly has not kept pace with the transformations that are shaping the world of the late twentieth century because "theoretical development in our discipline is presently lagging behind the evolving reality of day-to-day practice in international affairs."[7] Nevertheless, in this fourth phase the quest continues for concepts and methodologies from other disciplines, although with less certainty about the outcome of such efforts than in the preceding phase. Although the emphasis remains on comparative studies at many levels and units of analysis, there has been a renewed interest in efforts to bridge the gap between normative and behavioral-quantitative theories, and between theory and policy.

THE BEHAVIORAL CRITIQUE

If by the 1950s political realism had largely replaced the earlier utopian-normative orientation in the study of international relations and thus the field had moved from its first to its second stage of development, a rising generation of scholars was no more satisfied than its predecessors with prevailing modes of analysis. Over the past three decades, much of the proliferating literature of international relations has reflected dissatisfaction with the state of the field.[8] In the behavioral-quantitative stage of the development of international relations, the following critical themes were present. (1) Earlier approaches had only limited utility in the identification and analysis of important problems, because the research tools available to the practitioner of traditional research were considered to be crude. Even when traditionally oriented scholars had identified the most important problems, they had not stated them in such a way as to enhance the prospects for their systematic and scientific investigation. (2) Traditional theory has been based upon international systems and models of international systems, which differed fundamentally from the contemporary international system. Therefore, it provides inadequate concepts for the building of theory addressed to the existing, or the emerging, world. (3) Because the explanatory and predictive capacity of international relations theories is limited, they cannot be utilized with great confidence, by the scholar or the policymaker, in evaluating the present or predicting the future. Scholars and, to an even greater extent, policymakers therefore revert to pragmatic solutions for specific and immediate problems. (4) The literature of international relations is replete with untested and implicit assumptions about human behavior and international conduct. (5) Many of the most widely used terms of international relations, such as balance of power and collective security, as well as conflict, integration, and power, are employed in virtually incompatible ways by different scholars, and even by the same scholar. Such usage contributes not only to theoretical fuzziness, but also to difficulty in communicating within the discipline.[9] (6) The absence of widely accepted agreement on usage of terminology hinders the development of cumulative literature of international relations. We have noted this problem in several chapters, especially in our discussion of power, decision-making, conflict, and integration. Because even those behaviorally quantitatively oriented scholars have often not addressed themselves to similar concepts, theories, paradigms, and hypotheses and more traditionally oriented scholars have assumed the uniqueness of events, the building of a body of generalizations about international phenomena has progressed only haltingly and—to some—all too slowly. (7) The availability of quantitative methodologies and conceptual frameworks borrowed or adapted from other disciplines provides the tools for major breakthroughs in the building of theory. The advent of the computer and advanced technologies of information storage, retrieval, and analysis are said to enhance the prospects for testing theory and allegedly provide unprecedented opportunities for developing international relations theory. Since the conduct of research in international relations—as in other disciplines—has usually been strongly influenced by younger scholars impatient with the conventional wisdom of their elders, "credibility gaps" and "generation gaps" emerge periodically as they have since the 1950s. Such a gap, by the late 1970s, was based in part upon a division between those who assigned primacy to empirical-analytic theory and the proponents of normative theory, and between those who attached greater or lesser importance to qualitative or quantitative techniques of research and analysis.

Although the assumptions of traditional writers were sometimes not explicitly stated, the "conventional wisdom" of international relations has contained a series of assumptions which scholars, especially since the 1950s, have questioned and sought to subject to more systematic examination. (1) It was once assumed that nations were sovereign in their domestic affairs and that foreign powers could not exert major internal influence upon them. Clearly, such a model does not fit the contemporary international system and perhaps it never provided an adequate conceptualization, because states, however legally sovereign, have always confronted domestic problems resulting from the impact of events originating outside their frontiers. Since the late 1960s, in fact, a burgeoning literature has emerged whose authors have sought to examine "linkages" between national and international systems, and to study "penetrated" political systems whose domestic policies are influenced by developments beyond their boundaries.[10] (2) As noted at the beginning of this chapter, the critique of our understanding of the contemporary international system, related in turn to the inadequacy of models or theories inherited from the past, is based largely on alleged changes—structural, procedural, and substantive—especially of the past generation in the international system.[11] The international system of the late twentieth century, for the first time, is global in nature. It is said to include as a central feature latter-day variants of traditional military and security issues, together with new conflict-laden issues, as noted subsequently. But it also contains a broadening range of problems, some of them associated with economics, or the politics of economics, in a North-South context and in relations between industrialized states. Some issues are transnational in nature, as noted later in this chapter and elsewhere in this text.

The international system of the late twentieth century is said to contain a large number of diverse, divergent, and incompatible forces—nationalism-internationalism; cosmopolitanism-parochialism; power-welfare; economic growth-redistribution; interdependence-dependence; integration-disintegration—all of which increase the complexity of the task confronting both the scholar and the policymaker. (3) Decision-making units, it was assumed, were not subject to major internal strains and conflicts concerning objectives, policies, and the nature of the national interest, and little effort was made to study the decision-making process as such, especially with the use of models other than those positing the rationality of actors, such as bureaucratic and incremental decision-making, both of which gained increasing prominence in the 1970s.

Especially since World War II, however, literature on foreign policy has accorded a prominent position both to the domestic factors which impinge upon foreign relations and, especially since the 1960s, to a variety of decision-making models,[12] including those encompassing bureaucratic factors noted in Chapter 11. (4) the traditional assumption was that only nation-states could be the actors of international politics. The rise of international organizations at the global and regional level, the increasing importance of the multinational corporation and other nonstate actors, including especially since the 1970s terrorists and revolutionary movements and the expansion of transnational contacts and notions of interdependence, have given a new set of dimensions to international relations which has been reflected in the literature, as noted in our earlier chapters. (5) Political behavior in an international context, it was once assumed, differs fundamentally from political behavior within the national unit. Therefore, studies of international political behavior could be separated from the analysis of political behavior within the national unit. The distinction between domestic and international behavior stemmed principally from a model in which decision-making was centralized in the former case and decentralized in the latter instance. Governments within the national units held a monopoly of the coercive capabilities of the units, in contrast to the decentralization of decision-making and coercive capabilities in the international system. Increasingly, scholars have stressed similarities rather than differences between the political process at the national and international levels, although the centralization-decentralization distinctions still appear relevant, in an abstract sense, in delineating international relations and studies of other political phenomena. Especially since the 1950s, scholarly interest in the political systems of less developed areas, in which tribal loyalties often compete with modernizing forces and effective political power remains decentralized, has contributed to a reassessment of older notions about the uniqueness of international political processes as contrasted to those at other levels.

International relations research, as has been noted throughout this book, has been guided by a variety of concepts, theories, models, and paradigms. One student of the history of science, Thomas S. Kuhn, has suggested that in the natural sciences, periods of "scientific revolution" have alternated with eras of "normal science." One set of concepts has furnished the basis for cumulative knowledge. He defines scientific revolutions as "noncumulative developmental episodes in which an older paradigm is replaced in whole or in part by an incompatible new one."[13] According to Arend Lijphart, international relations has followed such a pattern of development.[14] The traditional paradigm, based upon conceptions of state sovereignty and international anarchy, was challenged, as noted previously, even though a large body of theory about international relations had evolved, dating from antiquity and providing a "basis for a coherent tradition of research."[15] The scientific revolution, beginning in the 1950s, was based on a large number of new approaches and methodologies. The critique of the traditional paradigm that the scientific revolution embodied accords with Kuhn's thesis about the nature of inquiry. In its recent phase, then, students of international relations were engaged in a quest for a new "behavioral paradigm" and the decisions among scholars focused more on the nature of the appropriate paradigm, together with the appropriate methodologies for research and to a much lesser extent the scope and substance of international relations.

THE NATURE OF QUANTITATIVE-BEHAVIORAL RESEARCH

The basic trends which characterized international relations in its behavioral-quantitative stage may be summarized as follows: (1) the adaptation of theories, propositions, conceptual frameworks, methodologies, and ideas from other disciplines, including in particular sociology, social psychology, management-administrative science, psychology, anthropology, economics, and mathematics; (2) an attempt to relate phenomena from other disciplines to allegedly similar phenomena at the international level, which takes the essentially two mutually reinforcing forms of the examination of international phenomena by (a) the use of conceptual frameworks, theories, and propositions by which similar phenomena in other disciplines have been examined and (b) the comparative analysis of phenomena such as conflict, integration, bargaining, negotiation, and deterrence in an international context and other fields; (3) a focus upon problems of units of analysis, including attempts to distinguish conceptually and methodologically among such units as the individual decision-maker, the decisional units, the state, international subsystems, and the international system itself; (4) a concern about problems of level of analysis, including an effort to draw clear-cut distinctions between macro-theory or grand theory and the so-called middle ranges of theorizing, and a tendency for scholars to focus explicitly upon one or the other levels of theory; (5) a greater effort to become comparative *within* the study of international relations that has essentially two dimensions: (a) a comparative analysis of phenomena in a contemporary context and (b) a systematic attempt to compare various aspects of international relations in a historic context and to draw comparisons between contemporary and historic international phenomena; (6) a focus upon problems of data collection, an attempt to exploit more skillfully existing data, to develop new resources, and to build archives or data banks equipped with facilities for the storage and retrieval of materials for scholarly use; (7) an increase in the range of methodologies, but a lack of consensus as to those most appropriate for the study of international phenomena; and (8) a more conscious effort to link research to theory-building, including the development of criteria of relevance for research, the statement of problems and their investigation in such a fashion as to make it possible for other scholars to replicate, or duplicate, such research and attempt to develop knowledge that is cumulative. A major contribution of quantitative research, it has been suggested, has been the production of findings that separate "useful conceptions of international relations from those that are inadequate."[16] These are said to include inventories, albeit preliminary, of the "causes and effects of national power, the political characteristics of the international system, national support of supranational-ism and integration, and the dynamics of conflict-cooperation."[17] From this view quantitative research has resulted in the reformulation and testing of propositions from earlier literature.

The problems of scope, methodology, the nature of theory, and the relevance of other disciplines to the study of international relations remain unresolved, even though by the end of the 1970s there appeared to be a recognition of the need for diverse approaches—qualitative and quantitative—to the building of international relations theory. Critics of certain of the trends outlined above have doubted the extent to which events or other political phenomena can be treated as similar. Skepticism remains as to whether the most important problems of international relations can be made operational so that indicators of quantitative nature[18] can be developed. The authors of this book conclude that dogmatism, either "traditional" or "behavioral," does little to enhance the development of international relations. Such dogmatism, as well as the focus upon questions of method and scope, indicates the uncertainty that students of international relations have about the appropriate techniques and focal points for analysis. The issue is not *whether* one methodology or another, one form of theorizing or another, one analytical focal point or another is appropriate. Far from being mutually exclusive, alternative methodologies and research interests—qualitative and quantitative—are potentially mutually reinforcing.[19] It seems obvious that the only appropriate criterion for judging the alternative approaches is the extent to which they fulfill the specific research task set for them.[20]

MAJOR FOCAL POINTS OF CONTEMPORARY RESEARCH

Several major focal points of research over the past generation are indicative of the interests of scholars in the behavioral-quantitative and postbehavioral stages of international relations. In other chapters, we have examined systems theory, as well as conflict, integration, and decision-making theories, all of which have drawn upon other disciplines in their conceptualization and in methodologies.[21] Especially in the 1960s general systems theory, for example, had a major impact upon theorizing efforts of a macrolevel as well as the middle-range theories of decision-making, conflict, and integration, although by the late 1970s, as noted in Chapter 4, there was considerable skepticism about the future utility of systems theory for international studies, even though an alternative macrolevel theoretical framework had not replaced it. It should be pointed out, however, that strategic analysts concerned with "international stability" generally accept the basic assumptions of systems theory. Writings in conflict and integration illustrate the growth of both a comparative and quantitative focus based upon systems theory. The literature of the 1960s and the 1970s manifested an interest in comparing such phenomena in an international context with supposedly similar phenomena in other settings. Writings in these fields, as well as those using systems theory, indicate the growth of interest in broadening both the data base and the focus of concern not only to comparative materials, but also to points of time in the recent and distant past. Studies employing general systems theory and decision-making theory, in particular, reflect the concern with developing more explicitly defined units of analysis.

Theory-building efforts of the past 30 years have produced several macrotheories or grand theories. In political science, Almond's and Easton's formulations illustrate conceptualization at the macrolevel—the political system. In international relations, realist theory and general systems theory represent approximations to macrotheory. Realism was a theorizing effort at the macrolevel because its proponents generally sought to isolate one variable, namely power, in order to explain and predict a broad range of international behavior. In addition to its focus on power as a crucially important variable, realism provided frameworks for the analysis both of international politics and of foreign policy or, stated differently, furnished conceptualization both at the level of the international system (macrotheory) and at the level of the national actor. At the level of the international system, realist writers often used a classical balance of power framework similar to the balance of power model subsequently developed more formally by Morton A. Kaplan and discussed in Chapter 4.

At the national level of analysis, realists concerned themselves with the elements of national power, and for comparative purposes developed a classificatory scheme for analyzing the respective capabilities of nations, although in the case of at least one theorist, Henry A. Kissinger, an effort was made to relate foreign policy behavior to models of status quo and revolutionary political systems, respectively. Thus the proponents of realism were aware, implicitly at least, of what J. David Singer has termed the "level of analysis problem" in international relations;[22] they concerned themselves with analysis both at the international systemic level and at the level of individual states and their foreign policies. However, despite all the efforts to study foreign policy and its "domestic-international linkages," there was little, if any, consensus as to typologies of state actors and their foreign policies. Correlations between domestic violence and the propensity of a state toward violence in its foreign policy behavior were not evident, just as it was not possible to predict definitively foreign policy patterns from levels of economic development or from the domestic political structure. If realism made use of materials and insights from history, geography, strategic studies, economics, and political science, systems theory purported to provide a framework for the utilization of data, concepts, and propositions from an even larger number of disciplines.

Many of the theorizing efforts of the past generation represent "islands" of theory which may (or may not) be linked one day into a grand theory of international relations, although there is no consensus among theorists about the appropriate conceptualization, or the methodologies, for a macrolevel, or grand theory, of international relations. How such linking might take place, whether by enlarging existing "islands," or by developing new "islands" of theory, or by a major breakthrough toward a macrotheory within which middle-range theories could be linked, has been an object of debate among social scientists. The emphasis of the 1970s upon the narrow theory-building efforts in the so-called islands of theory has produced in turn a concern that the larger dimensions of theory at the macrolevel, the linking of the islands in a grand theory, will be neglected. It is an issue which remains unresolved and there is little prospect that it soon will be. Perhaps it need not be resolved, because the development of more adequate theory would result from the efforts of scholars at *both* the macrolevel and the microlevel.

Especially in the 1960s the proponents of quantitative analysis generally assumed that the eventual product of their labors would be the development of a cumulative knowledge, a set of theories, or a grand theory as discussed elsewhere in this chapter. Such theories would be tested to a stage of verification adequate both to set forth a series of generalizations and to provide the basis for other research whose effect in turn would be to extend the frontiers of knowledge and theory. A broadening web of theory would emerge, tested by the research of many scholars and having explanatory and predictive value both for the scholar and the policymaker.

Such expectations, to say the least, have proven premature. Judged by such a criterion, the results of the theory-building efforts of the behavioral-quantitative phase have been slim indeed. The research underway in the present phase shows no assurance of registering more than modest increments in the building of a cumulative theory of international relations. Perhaps for this reason, a broader conception of the nature of the growth of knowledge and cumulative theory gained adherents in the 1970s, especially among those committed to the scientific study of international relations. According to this conception, the reconceptualization of existing theories—the development of a variety of comparative methodologies and data bases, and the constant search for knowledge by research at more than one level of analysis—represents in itself a contribution to cumulative theory. As a proponent of this broader conception, Bruce Russett contends that a greater effort should be made to link and expand various "islands" of theory through detailed incremental research on specific problems. At the same time, however, it is doubtful that a "narrow and exclusive application of the cumulative model would produce marginal returns comparable to those to be expected from maintaining, along with it, a more broad-based attack on international relations theory and substance."[23]

THE POSTBEHAVIORAL STUDY
OF INTERNATIONAL RELATIONS

The prevailing trends in international relations theory in the "postbehavioral" stage reflect the interests of the large and diverse group of scholars of the late twentieth century. These include (1) not only the continuing effort to delineate the nature and scope of international relations, but also an attempt to establish international relations more firmly as an "autonomous" field of study. Even though by the end of the 1970s, many of the problems of scope, definition, and conceptualization remained unresolved, such issues had been superseded by a renewed emphasis upon substantive, in contrast to methodological, debates of the preceding phase; (2) the kinds of theorizing appropriate to the building of theories *with* greater explanatory and predictive capacity *with* perhaps by the 1970s a realization that quantitative *and* qualitative analyses were indispensable to the development of theory; (3) the division of labor between "basic" and "applied" research and the question of the "relevance" of international relations research to the crucial international problems of the late twentieth century; and (4) efforts to develop more precise linkages among various levels of analysis (or "actors") along the continuum from the microcosmic (the individual person) to the macrocosmic (the international system).

In summary, the development of a broad range of methodologies, together with the research and substantive interests of the past generation, has given greater stature to international relations as a field of study or discipline, although other, older disciplines have focused upon problems of central interest to international relations in anthropology, economics, history, political science, psychology, public administration, social psychology, and sociology.[24] International relations is becoming, if it has not already become, a discipline—or an interdiscipline—which incorporates, builds upon, and synthesizes insights from most, if not all, of the social sciences and, where appropriate, from the natural and physical sciences.[25]

EMERGING SUBSTANTIVE INTERESTS

Several substantive interests are likely to be dominant in the theory-building efforts of international relations for at least the next decade. In light of the *raison d'être* of international relations from its early years, together with the large number of conflict-laden issues and the availability of weapons of unprecedented lethality to a growing number of states and nonstate actors, the problems of war and peace will continue to attract principal attention both among scholars and policymakers. In the years ahead, the study of conflict theory will differ from earlier approaches largely by the techniques, methodologies, conceptual frameworks, and data bases employed in theory-building. Sociology, psychology, and perhaps even psychiatry may afford important insights into the motivations for terrorism and, for example, hijacking so prevalent in the early 1970s, and thus provide knowledge about social and political behavior with, of course, important normative policy implications. The utilization of findings from psychology about personality theory and the effects of organizational variables upon social and political behavior could conceivably contribute to a greater understanding of several important problems of international relations, including conflict, integration (or community building), and decision-making. Some of the promising subject areas worthy of further research for theory-building purposes are elaborated upon briefly below.[26]

Conflict

There is a relative dearth of knowledge concerning the relationship between international and intrasocietal aggressive behavior, and those studies, especially quantitative in nature, completed since the early 1970s, have failed to yield definitive insights. Over the past generation, intrasocietal conflict has risen in many states including, as noted elsewhere in this text, the most advanced states. What are the implications of various modes and levels of socioeconomic development for the incidence of tensions, conflict, and violence, as well as for stability or instability, within the units that comprise the international system? This is a question of long-standing interest to those scholars who have studied conflict, and especially revolution, as noted in Chapter 8. Intrasocietal conflict is relevant to international relations research not only because it gives rise to a large number of the nonstate actors in the late twentieth century—groups seeking revolutionary change within existing states and, in some instances, the formation of new political entities—but also because it often leads to interaction by outside intervening powers. What part do the electronic media play in the molding of attitudes with respect to issues of international cooperation and conflict, détente and crisis?

Questions such as these have been the object of research in the past decade, although the analysis, in particular, of the implications of television news for the shaping of public opinion or shaping of foreign policy remains in its infancy. But there has been renewed interest of substantial proportions in geopolitical, or geostrategic, analysis and in studies of the relationship among resources, population, growth, technology, and food, as noted in Chapters 2 and 8. Such interest was the result of the major importance attached to energy and other resource issues in the 1970s, as well as the revival of neo-Malthusian analyses of the impact of resource constraints upon population and conflict.

Integration

The study of integration, of long-standing concern to students of international relations, especially since the work of David Mitrany in the period between the two World Wars, continues to attract the attention of many scholars. The creation of international organizations at the global and regional levels in the generation after World War II not only contributed to the rise in interest in the study of integration, but also provided an important source of data for scholarly investigation. In the 1970s, the growing importance of the multinational corporation, together with an interest among scholars in nonstate actors, added yet another object of study of international relations.[27] The emergence of this entity coincided with the publication of numerous books and article-length studies based in particular on neofunctionalist propositions and analyzing transnational relationships between and among nongovernmental entities in a world hypothesized to be increasingly interdependent. The conceptualization of interdependence, and its relationship to concepts of integration and of power, attracted the interest of scholars in the 1970s. (See Chapters 3 and 10.)

Existing theories of political integration owe a considerable intellectual debt to earlier studies of nationalism as well as cybernetics and systems theory. The study of the normative conditions for political community, characteristic of international relations in its first stage, gave way to specific case studies and comparative analyses of integration, both at the global and regional levels although scholars concerned with the development of empirically based theory have usually had a strong interest in, if not philosophical commitment to, the normative implications of integration. The earlier work, especially of Karl Deutsch, on transactions as indicators of integration led to further such efforts in the 1970s. Such studies, discussed in Chapter 10, examined and in some cases refined relationships among transactions such as exchanges of people and trade flows, communication patterns, and memberships and voting patterns in international organizations.

Efforts were made, moreover, to conceptualize more fully the linkage among institutional growth, intergovernmental cooperation, and elite and mass attitudes, that is, to consider integration as a phenomenon having institutional and attitudinal dimensions. A need remains for greater definitional and conceptual clarity in the integration literature. This is a task to which students of international relations have turned in the past decade. The neofunctionalist refinement of propositions with respect, for example, to spill-over is illustrative of this tendency. The achievement of greater agreement among writers about the nature of integration, its necessary components, and the stages and transformation rules by which it is achieved might contribute to major breakthroughs in knowledge about the building and disintegration of political communities. The need exists to develop a theory, or theories, of integration encompassing interaction between and among official elites (governmental decision-makers), nonofficial elites (important nongovernmental groups and actors), and the mass level. To what extent, if at all, can integration take place, or at least be pressed decisively, by nongovernmental elites? At what level, and at what stage in an integrative process, is support at each of these levels indispensable to success? Moreover, a theory of integration adequate to the needs of the future should probably be based upon conceptualization including a processual model—how and when does the integrative process lead from a condition of separateness to a condition defined as political community and what are the stages and relevant indicators that are present during the integrative process?

Subnational Forces

If the thrust of scholarly literature and thought in the policy community has been the building of political units beyond the nation-state, there is evidence that scholars and policymakers have neglected an especially salient phenomenon of the past generation—the emergence of centrifugal forces within the existing national units. Neither the developed nations nor the developing states have been immune from the rise of linguistic-ethnic nationalism. Even units such as Great Britain, France, and the United States, where the literature of political science, in its conventional wisdom, long ago dismissed forces making for separateness in favor of assumptions about the homogeneity of population and in the case of the United States, the "melting pot," have faced disintegrative forces. Other countries, including, for example, Canada, Cyprus, Belgium, Nigeria, India, Pakistan, the United Kingdom, and Zaire, have been beset with separatist movements which sometimes have resulted in secession and civil war and have raised questions about the political future of existing political units. If the decade following World War II was characterized by a movement toward regional organization as reflected in the literature of international relations, it was followed by a period of dissatisfaction by peoples in many parts of the world, with the political units in which they live.

Although the causes of this ferment are complex, those who have expressed dissatisfaction with the status quo aspire to such goals as to (1) gain a greater voice in the decision-making process of existing units; (2)

achieve in some cases greater decentralization of power; or (3) replace existing units with wholly new structures. The late twentieth century is an era of opposition to the bigness of units which reflect the impersonal forces of bureaucracy and technology—an era that has spawned literature on technology and society and, in particular, the effects of technology in political, social, and economic structures.[28] We face several conflicting forces, some of which, such as technology, give impetus to larger political units; others contribute to the perpetuation of existing political units; and still others enhance the prospects for the fragmentation of present units. The study of such forces, together with the devising of political forms which reconcile the need for bigness with the desire of peoples for freedom from centralized controls, is a task which will confront scholars of international relations and policymakers alike over the remaining years of this century. An understanding of the nature of integration as a result of more adequate conceptualization as noted above could yield insights into the process by which existing units are fragmented, as well as the necessary conditions for integration.

Comparative International Studies and Decision-Making

The effort to examine linkages between foreign policy and domestic policy, as well as to understand the domestic and international determinants of foreign policy, reflects the growth of interest in comparative international studies. In the 1970s increased emphasis was placed on the comparative study of foreign policy, although such interest was by no means new to international relations. The quest for theoretical frameworks for decision-making and notably the conceptualization and research nearly a generation ago of Richard C. Snyder[29] and his associates as well as more recent efforts such as those of Wolfram F. Hanrieder and James N. Rosenau[30] are indicative of such interest. Events data analysis, together with the study of decision-making, especially under crisis conditions, is illustrative of the interest manifested in the 1970s in the comparative study of foreign policy. As in other areas, such as conflict and integration, numerous propositions about decision-making behavior (see Chapter 11) have been generated and tested with uncertain results. The potential linkage between theory and policy in crisis decision-making studies, especially in the 1970s, contributed to a growing interest in crisis indicators that could be made available to official policymakers. A capability for the analysis of intelligence and other relevant data with the use of crisis indicators would have obvious implications both for crisis management and decision-making and for the development of more adequate theories of crisis management, escalation, deescalation, communications, and other phenomena related to patterns of interaction within, and between and among, decision-making units.

Especially since the late 1960s decision-making research has focused on the development of models, together with the conduct of research designed to test hypotheses. As noted in Chapter 11, decision-making under conditions of crisis has continued to attract attention. Large numbers of hypotheses have been tested, some of them with the use of events data based on the analysis of patterns of interaction between opposing decisional units at the international level during periods of crisis.

In a collection of essays reporting on research on international crisis conducted in the late 1960s, including decision-making, Charles Herman listed 311 hypotheses. They include the effects of stress and fatigue and constraints on the time available for the search for alternative courses of action; the nature of the decisional-unit and the level of participation of decision-makers; the volume and quality of messages between and within decisional units, perceptions, and expressions of hostility; crisis escalation and bargaining; and the credibility of threats between adversaries.[31] This has been the development, to a limited extent, of a cumulative knowledge of crisis behavior.

Strategic Theory

Closely related to the comparative study of foreign policy is the need for more adequate conceptualization in the field of strategic studies. Although the study of military strategy and the development of strategic theories have concerned both the scholarly community and the military since World War II, and although the role of power has been the focal point of much of international relations theorizing, existing theories, especially those of deterrence, remain inadequate in several respects. First, the deterrence theory of the nuclear age has been based for the most part upon strategic-nuclear bipolarity. To what extent, it should be asked, is such theory relevant to a world of several nuclear powers? Stated in practical and specific terms, what are the conditions, including the force levels, necessary for the deterrence of more than one potential adversary? In a multinuclear world, does it become necessary for atomic weapons states to acquire the capability to deter several other nuclear powers simultaneously? Alternatively, it has been hypothesized that nuclear multipolarity reduces the risks of nuclear confrontation by making it impossible for any single nuclear power to destroy the retaliatory capability of all or perhaps even several other nuclear powers. Among the questions that should be addressed is whether and to what extent, if at all, nuclear multipolarity will enhance the prospects for stable deterrence,[32] or whether nuclear proliferation, ipso facto, is undesirable.

A second problem inherent in deterrence theory is ambiguity in the meaning of rationality—the assumption of a calculus between potential risk and potential gain. American strategic theory has contained such a calculus derived largely from a projection to adversaries of United States calculations of what would constitute "unacceptable damage" in a nuclear exchange. Are calculations made in America, or in any other state in fact, accurate in a world in which peoples have widely differing value systems, cultures, conceptions of national security, and international objectives? Do such calculations as the bases for rationality err in merely "mirror imaging" Soviet values and goals from American values and goals and thus representing little more than an exercise based upon ethnocentrism? Closely related are basic differences between states, notably the superpowers, as suggested in Chapters 8 and 9 in strategic-military doctrines and conceptions of the adequacy of force levels for attaining their respective objectives.

The sharp contrasts between United States and Soviet strategic-military thought, noted in Chapter 9, point up the need for a field in international relations, or in international security studies, devoted to comparative strategic-military analysis. As Fritz Ermarth has suggested, "Systematic comparative studies of strategic doctrine could serve to clarify what we think and how we ourselves differ on these matters, as well as to organize what we know about Soviet strategic thinking."[33] Comparative research, focused not only on the superpowers but also on other states, might yield insights into such issues as the purposes of strategy and its relationship to force levels and political goals; the decision-making process with respect to strategic-military policy; the perceptions held by political elites of the strategic-military policies of adversaries; the relationship between strategic-military capabilities and other elements of statecraft; and the propensity of states to invoke various forms of military power to achieve political objectives.

Power

Power has always been difficult to conceptualize in international relations as we have noted especially in Chapter 3. The problems of conceptualization have grown as a result of the advent of nuclear weapons and the emergence of issues, such as resource scarcity, that may afford new forms of power—to withhold or not to withhold scarce resources—from those in need of them. Within the past decade we have seen numerous efforts both to conceptualize and to measure power more precisely as a multifaceted phenomenon. The concept of power, of course, is inextricably linked to alternative structures of the international system, for example, bipolar and multipolar. Polarity as a defining characteristic of the international system connotes a hypothesized distribution of power. Hence a necessary prerequisite to an understanding of such international systems lies in the study of power itself. For this reason, the increased emphasis in the 1970s upon international systems characterized allegedly by the diffusion of capabilities to new actors coincided with an effort to understand more fully the nature of power itself. If we may foresee the growth in number of international actors—state and nonstate—in the late twentieth century, together with weapons of unprecedented destructiveness and new conflict issues, it follows that the conceptualization of power in its many dimensions—military, economic, psychological, and ideological—will continue to hold central interest for scholars and policymakers alike.

There has been uncertainty about the political utility of military power in an era when the potential for devastation is unprecedented as a result of the revolutionary changes in weapons technology of the twentieth century. The question of the meaning of disparities between and among states in the conception of power and its political utility arises, especially at the level of strategic-nuclear weapons and the debate over the nature and the meaning of strategic-nuclear superiority. If one state concludes that vast military power is in fact usable either to threaten or actually to coerce an adversary, does that state not gain a considerable, and perhaps even decisive, advantage over its adversary? More reliable knowledge about the relationship between military force and other national capabilities, the development of strategic doctrine, and the propensity of nations to use specific types of power unilaterally or in collaboration with other nations would represent a significant contribution to international relations theory. This problem, of course, is closely related to the question raised above with respect to the implications of differences in values, culture, and national objectives for a state's propensity to use force, and at what level, to attain its objectives.

Comparative and Cross-National Research

Since the mid-1960s the tendency toward a more comparative focus in international relations research has been manifested in a growth of interest in cross-national analyses at the subnational level.[34] Such problems include ecological change and its implications for the social and political order, urban studies and violence, and the political values of elites. The growth of issue areas of common concern to postindustrial, industrial, or industrializing societies is likely to accelerate the tendency toward the comparative study of problems that until recently have not been considered central to the field of international relations, or what as a result of such interests is now called "international studies," or a greater interest in transnational studies—the comparative analysis of phenomena other than governmental entities themselves.[35]

As in the past, students of international relations will be faced with both too much and too little data for the testing of theories. On the one hand, vast amounts of data have always been available to the student of international relations; on the other hand, the development of quantitative research techniques, together with elaborate theoretical frameworks, increases the need for large new amounts of data. Many of the most important kinds of data relevant, for example, to the study of foreign policy decision-making (including health records and psychological profiles of decision-makers)[36] are not easily gathered, and, in fact, may never be available to the scholar. Much of decision-making analysis has emphasized international crises which are, as Thomas C. Wiegele has suggested, "stress-inducing" situations whose effect is to "put pressures upon the foreign policy decision-maker."[37] It follows that, as the author concludes, biological factors such as physical and mental health, fatigue, age, biological rhythms, and the use of various forms of medication should be stressed. In the 1970s there was increasing scholarly interest in the development of conceptual models of stress for political analysis.[38] This in turn points up the need for research on the "intersection between psychological variables" and "decision-making variables."

Advanced storage and retrieval systems now make it possible to desensitize data from governmental sources for the use of the scholarly community. The creation of a national archive consisting of data from governmental sources would contribute greatly to the conduct of research in international relations and the other social sciences. It has been estimated that in the Department of State alone, "original" items and distributed copies of "communications" were of the order of 64 million in one year.[39] Such archives, to the extent that they lessened the need for the collection of new data for certain types of projects, would bring a wider range of research problems within the capabilities of the individual scholar. They would be especially useful in the quantitative analysis of foreign policy by means of events data as discussed especially in Chapter 4, and in the testing of propositions about communications between, and among, decision-making units, for example, in crisis situations considered in Chapter 11.

A QUALITATIVE-QUANTITATIVE SYNTHESIS?

It is not difficult to anticipate greater efforts to develop more refined indicators and to introduce a greater qualitative element into quantitative studies. The quest for a reconciliation between quantitative and qualitative theory-building efforts may have important implications both for teaching and research. One example will suffice. In the post-World War II period, the so-called area program and studies of specific countries, especially the Soviet Union, took hold in political science and international relations programs in American universities at a time of increasing interest in international affairs both in the official and private sectors in the United States. Because of their emphasis on governmental systems as well as on the intellectual and political history, literature, language, and economic problems of specified regions, such programs attracted not only students preparing themselves for academic careers, but also persons in training for governmental and business careers abroad.

The rise of specific country and area studies programs in universities closely followed the growth of interest in a country or an area as the United States became more actively engaged as a global power in the generation after World War II. Hence those scholars interested in specific countries and regions—almost by definition concerned with the uniqueness of political phenomena—parted intellectual company with the behavioral-quantitatively oriented scholar whose interest was the development of techniques and methods for the examination of political phenomena, such as conflict and integration, on a comparative basis cutting across older delineations both geographically and academically.[40]

Data about problems under examination can sometimes be found only in one region. For example, the study of historical political development, integration at the international level, and the behavior of nations in alliance of necessity must be based largely upon the experience of the North Atlantic area, although there have been numerous examples, as noted in Chapter 10, of efforts to study integration in Third World settings. Moreover, much of the study of integration, especially the neofunctionalist research of the early 1970s discussed in Chapter 3, as well as conceptualization of regional subsystems examined in Chapter 4, focused on the regional level corresponding to traditionally defined areas, for example, Latin America, Africa, and the Middle East, in addition to Europe.

Studies of areas, or regions, or states, or even smaller entities have potentially valuable qualitative contributions to make to the quantitative study of political phenomena, for example, both in proposing hypotheses and interpreting the findings of persons engaged in bivariate or multivariate analysis. The area specialist or the scholar specializing in any other aspect of international relations—depending on the focal point of research—may be able to give meaning to both the correlations presented by quantitatively oriented students of politics and a qualitative dimension to the quantitative flows of information and transactions which are contained in literature, such as that related to integration, conflict, or alignment.[41] Area and country specialists can contribute to knowledge of national processes and the uniqueness of certain kinds of phenomena and make us properly wary of sweeping generalizations just as the theorist can provide an understanding of the broader meaning of seemingly discrete phenomena.

THE QUEST FOR RELEVANCE

The focus of research upon empirical-analytical theory, especially in that third phase of the evolution of international relations theory, contributed to a reduction in interest among scholars and policymakers in each other's immediate problems, although much of the funding of social science research in the behavioral sciences has come from the United States Government. To the policymaker charged with the formulation of immediate responses to pressing problems, the methodologically laden writings of international relations scholars sometimes have appeared to provide few, if any, solutions, even though much of the research of the field has been focused upon issues of war and peace that have relevance to the policymaker. The policymaker may find inadequate theories containing only statements of probability with respect to the effects of a change in one variable upon another variable. For their part, many scholars are concerned with basic research and long-range problems, rather than with solutions to the urgent, every day problems of governments. The issues that command the attention of official decision-makers are inevitably those of the moment, rather than those of the distant future, just as a decision-maker's power in a government is measured by his contribution to the resolution of immediate issues, in contrast to those who are relegated to long-range policy planning and are thus effectively isolated from the centers of influence.

As Richard Smoke has suggested, policymakers have little interest, per se, in how often a particular combination of variables has been present in historic context, unless, of course, that combination is present in a current situation of immediate interest.[42] Therefore, it is by no means accidental that the scholar interested in basic research and theory and the policymaker concerned with the immediate have often had interests seemingly irrelevant to each other. Much of international relations research may seem not only unintelligible, but also irrelevant to the immediate concerns of the policymaker, as perhaps indeed it is. Although it is difficult to assess with precision the impact of international relations research upon policymakers, nevertheless the policy community has made extensive use of academic writings. In particular, the development in international relations of a subfield in strategic affairs or national or international security studies, especially deterrence and defense, has furnished a body of literature upon which policymakers have drawn not only insights, but also the theoretical framework and the explicit assumptions upon which United States strategic-nuclear forces have been based. To an unprecedented extent, the development and study of strategy, and more broadly, military affairs, have passed from the professional military to the civilian policy analysts and theorists. Much of the literature of this field of international relations theory is examined in Chapter 9.

The longer-range outcome of basic research, including theory-building and testing, if the proponents of such research have their way, would be to produce a body of knowledge which would explain and perhaps even predict patterns of interaction among political variables. For example, it might eventually be possible to specify with a higher degree of certainty than now exists the conditions essential to political integration within a national or international context, or to state with a greater degree of precision within carefully specified parameters the conditions which give rise to particular forms of international conflict. If the study of international relations theory were to reach this stage of development, we would have achieved an understanding of those international phenomena deemed most important to scholars and we would have developed a body of theories of importance to the policymaker. Although the quest for such an understanding of international phenomena will continue to be pressed, the research conducted thus far holds promise, at best, of only limited success in reaching such a goal.

If it were possible to develop and test theories, for example, about such phenomena as political integration or international conflict, a series of "if-then" propositions relevant to the needs of scholars and policy-makers could be advanced. For example, a greater knowledge of the essential conditions for integration or conflict would make possible an understanding of alternative outcomes of various policy choices, since certain kinds of policy choices could be expected to produce certain kinds of outcomes. A new linkage between international relations theory and policy formulation would have been forged, unless, of course, an understanding of the implications of alternative policy outcomes permitted policymakers to alter the basic variables upon which the theory was based and thus to invalidate the theory itself. Herein may lie one of the fundamental differences between theory-building in the physical and natural sciences and in the social sciences—the capacity in the latter case for the objects of study—human beings—to effect changes in their behavior as a result of knowledge gained from a particular theory of behavior. In this respect political and social phenomena differ fundamentally from elements in a test tube.

POLICYMAKING AND INTERNATIONAL RELATIONS THEORY

The literature of international relations, traditional and contemporary, qualitative and quantitative, contains assumptions and conclusions which may have relevance to the policymaker. Policy decisions are frequently dictated by the underlying assumptions of the policymaker even though these assumptions may be only implicitly stated, or perhaps not even recognized as such. One objective of the study of international relations, we note parenthetically, should be to sensitize the student to the assumptions, or the propositions, contained in his or her theory of international relations, or in those of decision-makers whose policy choices we must study as scholars or evaluate as citizens. Such an understanding is indispensable to one's own analysis of international relations whether we are policymakers or observers of the political process. As Trevor Taylor has suggested, one of the functions of international relations is the development of explicitly stated assumptions and propositions on which to base research and policy, since all analyses of a problem of international relations or foreign policy rest on hypotheses of some kind.[43] For this reason the need exists to engage in a systematic examination of the assumptions that guide policymakers in the formulation of major policies. The statements of policymakers and the memoirs of statesmen can, and should, be analyzed to understand the assumptions that guide policy choices. An attempt should be made to match such assumptions, as well as policies, with assumptions and policies contained in theoretically oriented literature of international relations.

A major systematic effort is needed to make international relations literature, especially the writings of the past generation, more relevant to the policymaker. An inventory and matching of major assumptions, theories, and findings about international phenomena from policy statements and the literature of international relations would enhance the relevance of academic research to the needs of the policymaker. Such an inventory would contribute to a greater understanding of the current status of international relations theory and provide an indication of those areas in which concentrated new efforts are needed. Such a matching exercise could provide insights into the theories, explicit or implicit, which guide policymakers, and would contribute to a better understanding of those theories of international relations which have had the greatest impact upon thought in the policy community.

THEORIZING ABOUT THE FUTURE

Of the highest importance to a study of international relations which purports to be "relevant" is the development of conceptual and methodological tools to anticipate change, for change must be anticipated if it is to be moderated for beneficial purposes. The speed of change as a result of technology has become a major concern of political leaders and publics nearly everywhere. Transformations within the nation-state and in the international system itself make urgent the availability of more systematic and reliable knowledge about the future. In the development of weapons systems and in the designing of policies, whether in foreign affairs or the urban field, an understanding of future technological developments is crucially important.[44] Although such knowledge is needed if governments are to understand the nature of change and to create the means to influence change, the problems of forecasting are formidable indeed.

Although for centuries people have attempted to set forth their conceptions of the future, the need for more systematic forecasts (the development of statements about the future to which is attached a higher or lower probability as in a weather forecast based on, say, a 30 or 60 percent probability of rain or snow) has grown as the lead-time for policy planning, the complexity of issues facing policymakers, and the urgency of problems have increased and as the need has grown to influence to the extent possible the impact of technology upon the political order and transform technology from the "independent" to the "dependent" variable, if such an analogy to international relations theory is appropriate here. The result has been the emergence of the "futurologist," who seeks to "invent the future" by technological forecasting.[45] If technological forecasting could clarify the choices available to nations by reducing uncertainty about the future, it could contribute to innovative efficiency by making it possible to calculate more accurately the lead-time and the resources needed for alternative policy choices. Forecasts about future patterns of interaction among variables, especially resources, have existed at least since the writings of Thomas Malthus in the late eighteenth century. In the 1970s, as noted in Chapters 1, 2, and 8, there was renewed interest in forecasting, especially the development of a series of neo-Malthusian projections into a future allegedly characterized by population pressure, resource scarcity, and technological change.

The urgency of problems facing political systems—advanced and less developed—together with the quest for a more "relevant" field of inquiry is likely to give increasing impetus to the development within international relations of a subfield called "futurology." But straight-line projections will be no less adequate in the future than they were in the past. The question, of course, is which, if any, of the trends that can be discerned in a present context will be operative in a future timeframe. What new forces will intervene to shape the future? If projections based largely upon extrapolating the future from the present are inadequate in themselves, can alternative hypothetical future international systems, or their subsystems, be developed? Such an exercise places a high premium upon creative imagination about the future and upon the generation of hypotheses about variables, and interaction among variables, that may have no place in today's scheme of things. Technologies that cannot be foreseen today may transform the future, just as technologies that were not imaginable a century, or even 50 years ago, have profoundly altered the world of the late twentieth century. Such hypothetical models of international systems have their analogy in deductive theory as discussed in Chapter 1. The projection of trends from the present to the future, in turn, is analogous to inductive theory considered in the same chapter. Hence understanding the forces shaping the emerging world lies in the creative intermingling of inductive and deductive approaches to futurology.

This is not to suggest that theories of international relations will achieve a level of predictability even about existing phenomena sufficient to make possible a high degree of specificity of alternative policy choices. To expect high levels of predictability from international relations theory on a broad range of issue areas, given the many variables which must be considered until and unless more parsimonious and reliable theories are developed, would be to anticipate a level of performance that lies beyond theories in the physical sciences. As Morton Kaplan has suggested:

> Modern theoretical physical science has reared its present lofty edifice by setting itself problems that it has the tools or techniques to solve. When necessary, it has limited ruthlessly the scope of its inquiry. It has not attempted to predict the path a flipped chair will take, the paths of the individual particles of an exploded grenade, or the paths of the individual molecules of gas in a chamber. In the last case, there are laws dealing with the behavior of gases under given conditions of temperature and pressure, but these deal with the aggregate behavior of gases and not the behaviors of individual particles. The physicist does not make predictions with respect to matter in general but only with respect to the aspects of matter that physics deals with; and these, by definition, are the physical aspects of matter.[46]

Nevertheless, theories examined in preceding chapters, to varying degrees, have contained predictive statements that have enhanced, to a greater or lesser extent, our understanding of a period after they were formulated. For example, MacKinder's analysis of the impact of the technology of land mobility upon power relationships in Eurasia, as well as Nicholas Spykman's view of the shape of the post-World War II international system, noted in Chapters 2 and 3, are illustrative of a capacity to make use of certain variables in combination to examine the future with a considerable degree of accuracy. Such variables—implications of geography, resources, and technology for national capabilities—can be utilized in an analysis of the forces shaping the world of the late twentieth century. Perhaps it is less than coincidental that there has been a revival of interest in geopolitical analysis that has coincided with a growth in salience in resource issues and in forecasting the future.

THE ROLE OF NORMATIVE THEORY

In the current stage of its development, international relations has experienced efforts to establish linkages between normative theory, on the one hand, and empirical-analytic theory, on the other. The question of a value-free study of politics is of long-standing interest to students of politics, although it is a matter of debate among scholars as to whether such an objective is either desirable or attainable. One of the leading proponents of quantitatively based scientific theory of the 1960s, Rudolph Rummel, writing in the mid-1970s, concluded that human behavior cannot be understood by reference to cause-effect processes comparable to those of physical objects. Because man is "teleologically guided by his future goals," Rummel maintains, "the future lies in his hands and not in some causative features of his environment such as distance, power, geography, poverty, deprivation, and underdevelopment."[47] Thus Rummel raises fundamentally important questions for the conduct of scientific research about international behavior. Can the human being be studied scientifically, for example, as one would study the interaction of elements in a test tube? If people are guided in their political behavior by some objective, is there an inherent and logical contradition in the idea of a value-free study of politics?

By the end of the decade of the 1960s, there was a growing belief that if political scientists chose to emphasize empirical-analytic theory to the relative neglect of normative theory, they would have removed themselves from a problem area which historically had been of great concern to them. They would have chosen to ignore the task of defining the meaning of "the good life," the designing of political structures, and the establishment of normative standards for mankind in a future fraught with growing problems and dangers of unprecedented dimensions. The urgent issues created by the impact of technology upon political institutions, the changes in the political environment resulting from ideology and technology, and the implications of increasing popular pressures and demands upon existing political structures will continue to lead students of international relations, and politics more generally, to a greater interest in normative theory. Empirical-analytic theories have not provided adequate answers to the question of the kinds of political institutions, practices, and values appropriate to the world of the future, although from the findings of such studies the student of policy and the policymaker alike may gain vitally important insights.

In almost dialectical reaction against the so-called behavioral revolution of the 1960s, the "new revolution" of postbehavioralism of the 1970s, according to David Easton, contained the following arguments:" (1) it is more important to be relevant to contemporary needs than to be methodologically sophisticated; (2) behavioral science conceals an ideology based upon empirical conservatism; (3) behavioral research, by its focus upon abstraction, loses touch with reality; (4) the political scientist has the obligation to make knowledge available for the general benefit of society."[48] The emphasis in this critique was upon questions of values, goals, or preferences—upon the development of policy choices for immediate problems and the generation of objectives, and norms of behavior, for future international systems. As Rosenau has suggested, in the early 1970s, there emerged in international relations studies a "crisis of confidence," together with a loss of faith in the "slow, painstaking methods of science" as scholars sought to make themselves "relevant in ways that but a few years ago we would have found irresponsible and illusory."[49]

In the field of international relations there have always been groups of scholars whose principal interest was the development and analysis of public policy. In its utopian and realist phases, international relations study was strongly focused upon policy. Over the past generation, the efforts of scholars to give the field a more theoretical orientation and to emphasize the methodological basis of inquiry have represented more a supplement to, rather than a replacement of, a concern for policy problems.[50] Indeed, considerable emphasis has been placed on the creation of more rigorous techniques for the analysis of public policy, especially in the form of systems analysis.[51] The goal has been to devise criteria to aid in choosing and evaluating alternative policies or strategies, or mixes of policies or strategies, for the attainment of specified objectives. The effort has been to find "optimal" or preferable solutions among a series of alternatives based upon relative costs and benefits by using such techniques as mathematical models, gaming, and the canvassing of expert opinion. Such cost-benefit studies represented a reaction against policy recommendations based upon unstated assumptions, untested hypotheses, and uncertainty as to the implications of alternative choices and outcomes. The deficiencies of systems analysis in dealing with such irrational forces as charisma and ideology, or the propensity of actors to adopt high-risk or low-risk strategies, and its inadequacies in explicating the value assumptions of analysis—all serve to point up the need for additional work toward a policy science field either within international relations or as a separate discipline or "interdiscipline."[52]

Given the likely increase in pressing political problems, it will be necessary to strike a balance between empirical-analytic theory and normative theory, and between basic and applied research. Normative theory can suggest alternative goals and preferences for political institutions and can also provide propositions for testing; empirical-analytic theory can furnish guidance as to the kinds of political behavior which are essential for attaining desired goals.

In summary, just as the study of international relations has moved from the extreme preoccupation with the normative theory of the 1920s to the empirical-analytic theory of the 1960s, a new generation of scholars seeks to achieve theories of international relations relevant to the manifold problems facing international society, while at the same time attempting to find broadly based explanations and to develop a predictive capacity. In this sense they pursue goals that have been sought by preceding generations of students of international relations theory, based upon a greater synthesis among those concerns that have been of principal importance in each of the stages through which the field has passed since its beginnings in the early years of this century. Thus the search for a theory, or theories, adequate to the needs of an ever-changing international system continues.

Notes

1. E. H. Carr, *The Twenty Years' Crisis, 1919–1939* (New York: Harper & Row [Torchbooks], 1964), p. 4.
2. See Kenneth W. Thompson, *Political Realism and The Crisis of World Politics* (Princeton: Princeton University Press, 1960); William T. R. Fox, *The American Study of International Relations* (Columbia: University of South Carolina Press, 1968), pp. 1–35.
3. This is not to suggest that the concerns of students of international relations during each of these stages have been mutually exclusive. Examples of each can be found at every stage of the development of international relations.
4. For an examination of current trends in political science, see David Easton, "The New Revolution in Political Science," *American Political Science Review*, LXIII (December 1969), 1051–1061. Because the study of international relations has been linked closely to political science, the methodological, conceptual, and substantive trends of political science can be expected, as they have in the recent past, to influence the development of international relations.
5. James N. Rosenau, "The Restless Quest", in James N. Rosenau, ed., *In Search of Global Patterns* (New York: The Free Press, 1976), p. 5.
6. James N. Rosenau, "Assessment in International Studies: Ego Trip or Feedback?", *International Studies Quarterly*, 18, No. 3 (September 1974), p. 344.
7. Donald J. Puchala and Stuart I. Fagen, "International Politics in the 1970s: The Search for a Perspective," *International Organization*, 28, No. 2 (Spring 1974), 247.
8. See Andrew M. Scott, *The Functioning of the International System* (New York: Macmillan, 1967), pp. 2–6.
9. See Inis L. Claude, Jr., *Power and International Relations* (New York: Random House, 1962), pp. 11–39; Ernst B. Haas, "Balance of Power: Prescription or Propaganda," *World Politics*, V (1953), 442–447.
10. See, for example, James N. Rosenau, ed., *Linkage Politics: Essays on the Convergence of National and International Systems* (New York: The Free Press, 1969); "Compatibility, Consensus, and an Emerging Political Science of Adaptation," *American Political Science Review*, LXI (December 1967), 983–988; and Wolfram F. Hanrieder, "Compatibility and Consensus: A Proposal for the Conceptual Linkage of External and Internal Dimensions of Foreign Policy," *American Political Science Review*, LXI (December 1967), 971–982.
11. Donald J. Puchala and Stuart I. Fagen, op. cit. p. 247.
12. See, for example, Gabriel Almond, *The American People and Foreign Policy* (New

York: Harcourt Brace Jovanovich, 1950). For a more recent example, of such literature, see James N. Rosenau, ed., *Domestic Sources of Foreign Policy* (New York: The
Free Press, 1967).

13. T. S. Kuhn, *The Structure of Scientific Revolutions* (Chicago: University of Chicago
Press, 1970), p. 92.

14. Arend Lijphart, "The Structure of the Theoretical Revolution in International Relations," *International Studies Quarterly*, 18, No. 1 (March 1974), 41–73.

15. Ibid., p. 55.

16. John A. Vasquez "Statistical Findings in International Politics," *International Studies Quarterly*, 20, No. 2 (June 1976), 171–218.

17. Ibid., p. 207.

18. For an examination of this debate, see the following: Klaus Knorr and James N. Ro-
senau, "Tradition and Science in the Study of International Politics"; Hedley Bull,
"International Theory: The Case for a Classical Approach"; Morton A. Kaplan,
"The New Great Debate: Traditionalism vs. Science in International Relations"; J.
David Singer, "The Incompleat Theorist: Insight without Evidence"; Marion J.
Levy, Jr., " 'Does It Matter if He's Naked?' Bawled the Child?", in Klaus Knorr and
James N. Rosenau, eds., *Contending Approaches to International Politics* (Princeton:
Princeton University Press, 1969), pp. 3–110.

19. See Johan Galtung, "The Social Sciences: An Essay on Polarization and Integration," in Knorr and Rosenau, eds., op. cit., pp. 243–285.

20. There is, of course, a need for criteria both for the establishment of research
agendas and for the conduct of research itself. Given the differing conceptions of
the nature of theory and the disparate research and methodological interests of students of international relations, prospects for reaching agreement upon such criteria are not great.

21. The word *theory* itself has been used in several ways in the field of international relations, and there is disagreement among scholars about the nature of theory. See
Chapter 1 for a discussion of the various uses of the term *theory.*

22. See J. David Singer, "The Level-of-Analysis Problem in International Relations," in
Klaus Knorr and Sidney Verba, eds., *The International System: Theoretical Essays*
(Princeton: Princeton University Press, 1961), pp. 77–92. See also the treatment by
the authors of this text in Chapter 1, pp. 13–16.

23. Bruce M. Russett, "Apologia pro Vita Sua," in James N. Rosenau, ed., *In Search of
Global Patterns*, op. cit., p. 36.

24. For a useful effort to delineate the boundaries of international relations, see E. Raymond Platig, *International Relations Research: Problems of Evaluation and Advancement* (Santa Barbara, Calif.: Clio Press, for the Carnegie Endowment for International Peace, 1967), especially pp. 26–44.

25. One contemporary student of international relations, Johan Galtung, has suggested:
"One may say that the relationship between international relations and political
science is the same as the relationship between sociology and psychology: It is the
transition from the meticulous study of one unit at the time to the study of the interaction structure between the units that characterize the relations between these
pairs of sciences." Johan Galtung, "Small Group Theory and the Theory of International Relations," in Morton A. Kaplan, ed., *New Approaches to International Relations* (New York: St. Martin's, 1968), p. 271.

26. See Walter Isard, in association with Tony E. Smith, Peter Isard, Tze Hsiung Tung,
and Michael Dacey, *General Theory: Social, Political, Economic, and Regional*
(Cambridge, Mass.: M.I.T Press, 1969).

27. See, for example, H. Ferguson, and Donald E. Lampert, Richard W. Mansback,
Yale, *The Web of World Politics: Nonstate Actors in the Global System* (Englewood
Cliffs, N.J.: Prentice-Hall, 1976).

28. See, for example, Zbigniew Brzezinski, *Between Two Ages: America's Role in a Technetronic Era* (New York: Viking, 1970); Victor Basiuk, *Technology, World Politics, and American Policy* (New York: Columbia University Press, 1977); Hans J. Morgenthau, *Science: Servant or Master?* (New York: American Library, 1972); Eugene B. Skolnikoff, *International Imperatives of Technology: Technological Development and the International Political System* (University of California International Studies, 1972); Hilary Rose and Steven Rose, *Science and Society* (Baltimore: Penguin, 1970); Ira Spiegel-Rosing and Derek de Solla Price, eds., *Science, Technology and Society* (Beverly Hills, Calif.: Sage, 1977).

29. See Richard C. Snyder, H. W. Bruck, and Burton Sapin, eds., *Foreign Policy Decision Making* (New York: The Free Press, 1963).

30. See Wolfram Hanrieder, op. cit., James N. Rosenau, "External Influences on the Internal Behavior of States," in R. Barry Farrell, ed., *Approaches to Comparative and International Politics* (Evanston, Ill.: Northwestern University Press, 1966), pp. 27–92; James N. Rosenau, *Comparative Foreign Policy—Fad, Fantasy, or Field.* Paper prepared for presentation at the Conference Seminar of the Committee on Comparative Politics, University of Michigan, 1967.

31. Charles F. Herman, ed., *International Crises: Insights From Behavioral Research* (New York: The Free Press, 1972), pp. 304–320.

32. See Geoffrey Kemp, Robert L. Pfaltzgraff, Jr., and Uri Ra'anan, *The Superpowers in a Multinuclear World* (Lexington, Mass.: D. C. Heath, 1974); See also Robert L. Pfaltzgraff, Jr., "The Evolution of American Nuclear Thought," in B. Mitchell Simpson, III, ed., *War, Strategy and Maritime Power* (New Brunswick, N.J.: Rutgers University Press, 1977), pp. 280–282.

33. Fritz W. Ermarth "Contrasts in American and Soviet Strategic Thought," *International Security*, 3, No. 2 (Fall 1978), 139.

34. See, for example, Robert T. Holt and John E. Turner, *The Methodology of Comparative Research* (New York: The Free Press, 1970).

35. For an extended analysis of new weapons technologies, other than nuclear weapons, see Geoffrey Kemp, Robert L. Pfaltzgraff, Jr., and Uri Ra'anan, eds., *The Other Arms Race: New Technologies for Non-Nuclear Conflict* (Lexington, Mass.: D. C. Heath, 1975).

36. However, there are two volumes of potential use in a study of decision-making which takes account of the medical histories of key participants. They include Hugh L'Etang, *The Pathology of Leadership* (London: William Heinemann Medical Books, 1969); Lord Moran, *Churchill: Taken from the Diaries of Lord Moran, The Struggle for Survival, 1940–1965* (Boston: Houghton Mifflin, 1966).

37. Thomas C. Wiegele "Decision-Making in an International Crisis: Some Biological Factors," *International Studies Quarterly*, 17, No. 2 (June 1973), 305.

38. See Thomas C. Wiegele, "Models of Stress and Disturbances in Elite Political Behaviors: Psychological Variables and Political Decision-Making," *Psychological and Political Leadership* (Tulane Studies in Political Science); see also, by the same author, "Physiologically Based Content Analysis: An Application in Political Communication, in Brent D. Rupin, ed., *Communication Yearbook 2* (New Brunswick, N.J.: Transaction Books, 1978), pp. 423–436; "Health and Stress during International Crisis: Neglected Input Variables in the Foreign Policy Decision-Making Process," *Journal of Political Science*, III, No. 2 (Spring 1976), 139–144.

39. Willard Fazan, "Federal Information Communities: The Systems Approach." Paper prepared for the annual meeting of the American Political Science Association (September 1966). Quoted in Davis B. Bobrow and Judah L. Schwartz, "Computers and International Relations," in Bobrow and Schwartz, eds., *Computers and the Policy-Making Community: Applications to International Relations* (Englewood Cliffs, N.J.: Prentice-Hall, 1968), p. 9.

40. In addition, area programs have been affected by reduced government funding.

41. For a recent critique of such literature and an attempt to engage in qualitative analysis of transnational interaction and integration in Europe, see Carl J. Friedrich, *Europe: An Emergent Nation?* (Boston: Little, Brown, 1969), pp. 24–25. See also Oran R. Young, *Systems of Political Science* (Englewood Cliffs, N.J.: Prentice-Hall, 1967), pp. 60–62.

42. Richard Smoke, "Theory for and about Policy," in James N. Rosenau, ed., op. cit., p. 191.

43. Trevor Taylor, "Introduction: The Nature of International Relations," in Trevor Taylor, ed., *Approaches and Theory in International Relations* (London and New York: Longmans, 1978), p. 3.

44. As a *New York Times* writer has suggested: "Because of the lead-time in building new strategic systems, the decisions we make today substantially determine our military posture—and thus our security—five years from now. This places a premium on foresight and planning." *The New York Times*, February 19, 1970.

45. There are three general types of technological forecasts: the exploratory, opportunity, and normative. The *exploratory* forecast suggests future technology likely if the current level of support continues. The *opportunity* forecast depicts probable effects of increased effort in one technological "problem area" or another. The *normative* forecast combines desired goals and technological possibilities, using the goals as a guide for the allocation of resources.

Numerous techniques have been used to obtain such forecasts. The most frequently used is still the trend correlation and its variations: trend correlation in several fields and growth analogy. A new technique for obtaining "intuitive" rather than statistical forecasts is the Delphi method, an elaborate polling device for obtaining an expert consensus without a conference or panel discussion. Systems analysis, such as Program Evaluation and Research Technique (PERT), originally developed by the U.S. Navy, has been especially helpful for opportunity forecasting as well as R & D administration. Finally, mathematical modeling and the "feedback" concept are intended to aid normative forecasting in correlating the goals of government and industry with technological capabilities.

The most comprehensive general treatment of technological forecasting is Eric Jantsch, *Technological Forecasting in Perspective* (Paris: OECD Publication, 1967). An explanation of forecasting techniques may be found in Robert V. Ayres, *Technological Forecasting and Long-Range Planning* (New York: McGraw-Hill, 1969). See also James R. Bright, *Technological Forecasting for Industry and Government: Methods and Applications* (Englewood Cliffs, N.J.: Prentice-Hall, 1968). For the more literary and speculative side of the movement, see Bertrand de Jouvenel, *The Art of Conjecture*, trans. N. Lary (New York: Basic Books, 1967); Herman Kahn and A. J. Wiener, *The Year 2000: A Framework for Speculation* (New York: Macmillan, 1967); Dennis Gabor, *Inventing the Future* (New York: Knopf, 1964), and Daniel Bell, ed., *Toward the Year 2000: Work in Progress* (Boston: Houghton Mifflin and the American Academy of Arts and Sciences, 1968); Neville Brown, *The Future Global Challenge: A Predictive Study of World Security, 1977–1990* (New York: Crane, Russak, 1977).

46. Morton A. Kaplan, "Problems of Theory Building and Theory Confirmation in International Politics," in Klaus Knorr and Sidney Verba, eds., *The International System: Theoretical Essays* (Princeton: Princeton University Press, 1961), p. 7.

47. R. J. Rummel, "The Roots of Faith," in James N. Rosenau, ed., *In Search of Global Patterns* op. cit., p. 30.

48. David Easton, "The New Revolution in Political Science," *American Political Science Review*, LXIII (December 1969), 1052. Similarly, Easton was among the first to discern the behavioral revolution in political science. See David Easton, *The Po-*

litical System: An Inquiry into the State of Political Science (New York: Knopf, 1954), especially pp. 37–125; by the same author, *A Framework for Political Analysis* (Englewood Cliffs, N.J.: Prentice-Hall, 1965), pp. 6–9.

49. James N. Rosenau, "Assessment in International Studies: Ego Trip or Feedback?" *International Studies Quarterly*, 18, No. 3 (September 1974), 346.

50. For a collection of essays by scholars concerned with the relationship between social science and public policy in the post-World War II period, see Daniel Lerner and Harold D. Lasswell, eds., *The Policy Sciences* (Stanford: Stanford University Press, 1951), For a more recent discussion, see Norman D. Palmer, ed., *A Design for International Relations Research: Scope, Theory, Methods, and Relevance.* Monograph 10, The American Academy of Political and Social Science (October 1970), especially pp. 154–274.

51. Charles J. Hitch and Ronald N. McKean, *The Economics of Defense in the Nuclear Age* (Cambridge, Mass.: Harvard University Press, 1963); Ronald McKean, *Efficiency in Government through Systems Analysis* (New York: Wiley, 1958); Raymond A. Bauer and Kenneth J. Gergen, eds., *The Study of Policy Formation* (New York: The Free Press, 1968); Harold Lasswell, "Policy Sciences," in *International Encyclopedia of the Social Sciences* (New York: Macmillan and The Free Press, 1968), pp. xii, 181–189.

52. See Yehezkel Dror, *Analytical Approaches and Applied Social Sciences* (Santa Monica, Calif.: The RAND Corporation, November 1969); monograph.

Index of Names

575

Index of Subjects

ABM (Anti-Ballistic Missile System), 337, 373
ABM Treaty, 403–404
Action-reaction process, 333–338
Actors, international, 13–15, 343
Acute international crisis, 152
Aggression
  aggressive behavior in individuals, 186, 253–280; animal behavior studies, 259–266; critique of instinct theories, 258, 264–266; defined, 256; difference between individual aggressiveness and societal aggression of war, 186, 252–254, 269–271, 273–275; diversion and reduction of, 277–280; and education, 280; frustration as origin of, 266–269; hostile, 256; instinct theories of, 256–258; instrumental, 256; learned, 270, 274–275; and religion, 278; ritualization of, 262; socialization of, 271–273; social learning and, 273–276; species-preserving function of, 260–263; and sports, 278–279
Ahimsa, 190
Air power
  de Seversky on, 65–66; Douhet on, 65
Alliances, 161
  and balance of power, 449–450, 452–453; cohesion, 448–450, 451–453; and foreign policy goals, 448; and national capabilities, 452; optimum size, 450–451; and small powers, 450–451
Alternative world futures, 38–40, 41
American foreign policy
  based on national experience,

103–105; and the Cold War, 240–245; containment policy, 65, 107; Cuban Missile Crisis, 492–496; early realism, 103; geographic factors, 97–98, 104, 106–108, 118–119; Kennan on, 103–104, 107–108; Kissinger on, 113–117; legalistic-moralistic tendencies, 95–97, 104–105; Monroe Doctrine, 100; Morgenthau on, 100, 101, 102; Spykman on, 97–98; Strausz-Hupé on, 118–120
American security
  and German-Japanese alliance (World War II), 97; and Japan, 97, 98, 115; and limited nuclear war, 113; and Monroe Doctrine, 100; and People's Republic of China, 114–115; and Russo-German relations, 106, 108; and Soviet Union, 97–98, 102, 106–108, 115, 119; and the United Nations, 106, 110; and Western Europe, 115, 118, 120; and Western Hemisphere, 97, 100, 104; *See also* Deterrence, Nuclear Proliferation, Nuclear war, SALT, and Strategic doctrine and theories
Anarchism, 200–202
Animal behavior studies, 259–264
Area programs
  in international relations, 561; *See also* International relations
Arms control, 395–408
Arms race
  as a cause of war, 333–338; substitute for imperialism, 234–235; *See also* Disarmament, Non-Proliferation Treaty, SALT